BEST DOCUMENTARY OF 2007
New York Film Critics Circle

BEST DOCUMENTARY/NON-FICTION FILM OF 2007
Los Angeles Critics Association

SPECIAL JURY PRIZE, DOCUMENTARY
2007 Sundance Film Festival

No End in Sight is a coolheaded and devastating exposé of the Bush administration's bungling of the Iraq war—a definitive anatomy of disaster ... *No End in Sight* leaves you furious at an administration of armchair warriors, yet it offers the catharsis of cold, hard truth.

—Owen Gleiberman, *Entertainment Weekly*

Mr. Ferguson ... presents familiar material with impressive concision and impact, offering a clear, temperate and devastating account of high-level arrogance and incompetence. ... It's a sober, revelatory, and absolutely vital film.

—A.O. Scott, *The New York Times*

We need to hear the story again and again, for no amount of rage and disbelief can turn what the Bush Administration did into someone else's problem. The occupation is our problem, a dead eagle hanging around our necks ... Modest and attentive and quietly outraged, this collection of interviews, news footage, and narrated history gathers weight and strength and delivers, in chronological order, an overwhelming pattern of folly ... *No End in Sight* is an exposure of the psychopathology of power.

—David Denby, *The New Yorker*

The script of Charles Ferguson's *No End in Sight* would certainly be in the hands of prosecutors in the event of impeachment hearings. The documentary is a furious, if quietly stated, indictment of the president and all his men in re the debacle that our adventure in Iraq has turned into. Ferguson builds a compelling case of bad judgment, error, stubbornness, arrogance, all of it adding up to a mess with no end in sight.

—Stephen Hunter, *The Washington Post*

DISCARDED

WEBSTER COUNTY LIBRARY
P.O. BOX 89
MARSHFIELD, MO 65706

Those who never liked the smell of this war will find urgent, cogent analysis in *No End in Sight*. Those who, for whatever reason, did believe in it will find the same, while experiencing this beautifully argued film as a tipping point.

—Michael Phillips, *The Chicago Tribune*

Prepare to be riveted: *No End in Sight,* Charles Ferguson's first film, is without question the most important movie you are likely to see this year.

—Richard Schickel, *TIME Magazine*

Two very big thumbs up. It is essential viewing for any patriot. I love this film because I love my country.

—Richard Roeper, *Ebert and Roeper*

Remember the scene in *A Clockwork Orange* where Alex has his eyes clamped open and is forced to watch a movie? I imagine a similar experience for the architects of our catastrophe in Iraq. I would like them to see *No End in Sight*.

—Roger Ebert, *Chicago Sun-Times*

This powerhouse of a movie should be required viewing for every member of Congress. The executive branch is likely to avert its eyes.

—*Newsweek*

Everyone in this film is competent. Everyone in this film knew how to do their job, and did their job as ordered. And not just in spite of, but because they did what they were ordered to do, thousands of Americans have died, thousands of Iraqis have died, our laws and allies have fallen by the wayside. ... Our ability to defend ourselves from true terror and the credit it requires to make such claims is lost. ...

Watch this. Get your friends to watch it. Talk about it. Argue about it. And then call someone, anyone who will have to respond: your Congressman, your Senator. It's only the lives of our brothers and sisters at stake. Maybe you're doing something more important right now.

I hope so.

—George Clooney

Forging better policy towards Iraq requires an understanding of the Bush Administration's devastating policy errors and their consequences. With *No End in Sight*, we now have a comprehensive, objective analysis of Iraq's descent.

—Congressman Rahm Emanuel

Please send everyone you know to see it ... The film convicts the Bush administration more clearly, specifically and forcefully than any previous documentary.

—Stuart Klawans, *The Nation*

If any movie can rid Americans of "Iraq war fatigue," it's Charles Ferguson's muscular documentary *No End in Sight*. It provokes potent new feelings of outrage and catalyzes fresh thoughts about the right way to run a government, especially ours.

—Michael Sragow, *Baltimore Sun*

No End in Sight is a biting critique of the Bush administration's handling of the war in Iraq.

—*The Situation Room*, CNN

A masterfully assured piece of filmmaking.

—Peter Rainer, *Christian Science Monitor*

Charles Ferguson's lucid, concise and devastating account of what went wrong in Iraq ... a heartbreaking, soul-searching chronicle of how America snatched defeat from the jaws of victory.

—Carrie Rickey, *Philadelphia Inquirer*

A raft of documentaries have come along since the start of the war, some of them accusatory, some investigative, some empathetic, nearly all of them skeptical. None is better argued or more searing than *No End in Sight*. ... The film is tough-minded and essential—a severely galling reality check.

—Wesley Morris, *Boston Globe*

No End in Sight will leave you floored, agape and enraged anew. ... The cumulative, comprehensive body of interviews and images is just completely damning—exhaustive and exhausting, painful to watch but necessary.

—Christy Lemire, *Associated Press*

No End in Sight, the latest Iraq documentary, is the first to attempt a detailed historical overview and probably the only one with the potential to reach across partisan lines, a true rarity in the sphere of political filmmaking ... a model of concision and clarity. Ferguson is less a polemicist than a historian, and the power of his film has much to do with its calm, stark emphasis on facts that speak for themselves.

—Dennis Lim, *The Los Angeles Times*

No End in Sight is the most coolheaded of the Iraq war documentaries, the most methodical and the least polemical. Yet it's the one that will leave audiences the most shattered, angry and astounded.

—Mike LaSalle, *The San Francisco Chronicle*

Charles Ferguson's *No End in Sight* itemizes the errors, misjudgments and follies that have defined the Bush Administration's invasion of Iraq. In his first doc, Ferguson delivers the calm, meticulous survey of U.S. policy that legions of critics of Michael Moore's *Fahrenheit 9/11* have been waiting for.

—Robert Koehler, *Variety*

The film is a meticulous, thoroughly engrossing lesson in how not to win friends (or wars) and influence people (or potential terrorists) ... *No End in Sight* proves there's nothing more subversive than a somber, lucid recitation of facts.

—David Edelstein, *New York Magazine*

NO END IN SIGHT

NO END IN SIGHT

IRAQ'S DESCENT INTO CHAOS

CHARLES FERGUSON

WEBSTER COUNTY LIBRARY
P.O. BOX 89
MARSHFIELD, MO 65706

PublicAffairs
New York

Copyright © 2008 by Charles Ferguson

Published in the United States by PublicAffairs™,
a member of the Perseus Books Group.

All rights reserved.

Printed in the United States of America.

No part of this book may be reproduced in any manner whatsoever without written
permission except in the case of brief quotations embodied in critical articles and reviews.
For information, address PublicAffairs, 250 West 57th Street, Suite 1321, New York, NY
10107. PublicAffairs books are available at special discounts for bulk purchases in the
U.S. by corporations, institutions, and other organizations. For more information, please
contact the Special Markets Department at the Perseus Books Group, 2300 Chestnut
Street, Suite 200, Philadelphia, PA 19103, call (800) 255-1514, or email
special.markets@perseusbooks.com.

Book design by Jane Raese
Text set in 11.5-point Adobe Garamond

Cataloging-in-Publication Data is available from the Library of Congress

ISBN 978-1-58648-608-2

FIRST EDITION

10 9 8 7 6 5 4 3 2 1

To read the transcripts in their entirety, please visit www.noendinsightthebook.com.

CONTENTS

PREFACE

This book expands upon, and brings up to date, my 2007 documentary *No End in Sight*. While the film is quite comprehensive and, obviously, conveys many things that words cannot, it did impose limits. At an hour and forty minutes, the film contained less than 1 percent of our research and often astounding interviews. More recently, I also wanted to address the debate over the 2007–2008 military surge and the dilemmas of future Iraq policy. Hence this book.

I must say, however, that making the film was one of the most intense, powerful experiences of my life. I initially had the idea to make *No End in Sight,* my first film and I very much hope not my last, in 2004, when I first realized that conditions in Iraq were far worse than generally believed. The sharpest stimulus was a dinner in New York with George Packer, whom I had met when I was a graduate student at the Massachusetts Institute of Technology (MIT). George is not an ideological person and, like me, had initially been sympathetic to the idea of using force to depose Saddam Hussein. Yet over the course of three hours of conversation, it became clear that what he saw in postwar Iraq was very scary.

At the time, George was preparing to write his book, *The Assassins' Gate;* he had just returned from his second or third trip to Iraq and had already done a great deal of research. I had no doubt that he would produce an excellent book, and I knew that other books were on the way. Perhaps, however, there was an opportunity for a movie. This idea was the combined product of my love of film, my background in political science and policy analysis, my having made some money, and events in Iraq.

I have loved film since I was a child; in high school, I watched everything I could, even eight-hour Soviet films of the boy-meets-tank variety.

My interest in studying political power came more gradually. As an undergraduate, I was a dilettante, eventually a mathematics major. For graduate school, I applied to only one political science department—at MIT. In the end, I went there, and studied defense policy, European politics, political philosophy and political economy, economics, economic history, and international relations.

Meeting my Ph.D. thesis adviser, Carl Kaysen, was a turning point. Carl is ridiculously smart, and his life showed it: OSS (Office of Strategic Services) in World War II, tenured professor at Harvard in his thirties, deputy national security adviser for President Kennedy, director of the Institute for Advanced Studies, et cetera, et cetera. He also has a wicked sense of humor, which he used to keep me in line, while giving me enormous freedom. In the late 1980s, I wrote my Ph.D. thesis on the globalization of the information technology sector, particularly the rise of Japanese and Asian competition therein, and its implications for the United States. I got it about half right, and continued at MIT doing postdoctoral research.

In 1992, I left MIT and became a consultant, doing strategic analysis for the top managements of high-technology firms—Motorola, Xerox, Intel, Apple, Texas Instruments. But in late 1993, after a consulting project for Apple that allowed me to contemplate the lamentable state of what was then called the online services industry (the commercial Internet still being in its infancy), I had an idea for a software product. Someone really should do this, I thought. It would be really cool, and they could make a lot of money. And then I thought, Why not me?

In early 1994, I met Randy Forgaard, a brilliant MIT-trained software technologist. Together, we founded Vermeer Technologies (named after my favorite painter, after other names failed their trademark clearances). We developed the first software product that enabled a mere mortal—a normal person, not a software engineer—to develop and manage Web sites. We worked insanely hard, at a time when the Web was growing 20 percent per month. Netscape and Microsoft threatened to compete, yet simultaneously courted us. We sold the company to Microsoft, and at 5 pm EST on January 13, 1996, while getting slightly drunk on an airplane, I became financially secure for life. I couldn't afford private planes or private islands, but I would never again have to do anything I didn't want to do.

The question of what I *did* want to do turned out to be more difficult than I imagined. After Vermeer, I was utterly exhausted, and simply recovering took a couple of years. Then I wrote two more books, which was fun, and started another company, which wasn't (and which consequently failed). In 2003, I decided that I would finally try filmmaking. I began investigating, speaking with people, doing research. I started thinking about what film to make and came up with several ideas.

And then came Iraq. Although generally moderate or even liberal in my political views, I had thought there was a good case for using military force to remove Saddam. He was a quasi-genocidal, possibly psychopathic dictator who had caused three bloody wars, killed over a million people, developed chemical weapons and used them on civilians, and had come perilously close to developing nuclear weapons before the first Gulf War. He was being held in check only by a draconian sanctions regime that was driving Iraq's population into severe poverty and Islamic fundamentalism. His tenure seemed all too secure, and it appeared that he might be succeeded by either or both of his two sons, one of whom was even more ruthless than Saddam, the other of whom was clinically psychotic. Moreover, the United States bore substantial responsibility for these conditions, having supported Saddam militarily in the 1980s in order to weaken Iran, then allowing Saddam to remain in power after the first Gulf War, and finally imposing the sanctions regime.

I also found the record and arguments of many liberals or Democrats somewhat questionable. Only eight Democratic senators had voted in favor of waging the first Persian Gulf War—Al Gore had been one of those eight; John Kerry had not. Yet, because sanctions didn't involve American troops, many liberals apparently had no trouble with the sanctions regime, which killed many more Iraqis than the war had.

While I did not completely oppose the Bush administration's decision to invade Iraq, I was ambivalent because even before the war, I saw many disquieting signals about how, specifically, the administration would proceed. The administration seemed arrogantly intent on alienating the entire world, rejecting international treaties (e.g., the Kyoto Protocol on climate change, the Anti-Ballistic Missile Treaty, the International Criminal Court) and disdaining alliances. Donald Rumsfeld offensively and publicly dismissed the objections of "old Europe," and clearly had no patience for the United Nations, for weapons inspectors, or for criticism from any quarter. A month before the war, Army Chief of Staff Eric Shinseki warned that many more troops would be required, only to have Rumsfeld and Deputy Secretary of Defense Paul Wolfowitz undermine him publicly. And the administration seemed to like and believe Ahmed Chalabi's predictions about Iraq, despite his clearly being a charlatan of the first order.

So I was worried. Yet never even in my wildest nightmares did I imagine that the occupation of Iraq would be conducted with such arrogance, stupidity, and incompetence as it was. Despite all my training and experience, which certainly included lessons in skepticism, I would have laughed if someone had told me before the war, look, it's going to be like this: They won't start any planning for the occupation at all until two months before the war, and then they'll start completely from scratch. They'll exclude the State Department and CIA people who know the most about the country. They won't have telephones or e-mail for months after they arrive in Iraq. Our troops will stand by as nearly every major building in the country is looted, destroyed, and burned. They will spend the first month preparing to install an Iraqi government, restart the administration of the country, and recall the Iraqi Army for use in security and reconstruction. And then, with no consultation or warning, in a one-week period, a newly appointed head of the U.S. occupation will reverse all those decisions, crippling the administration of the country and throwing half a million armed men into the street, destitute. As an insurgency builds, they will deny its existence and refuse to negotiate, even when leaders of the insurgency signal a desire for compromise. They will airlift $12 billion in hundred-dollar bills into the country, with no accounting controls, and three-quarters of it will remain permanently unaccounted for. In a separate program, Congress will appropriate $18 billion for desperately needed reconstruction, but the occupation will be so incompetent that it will spend only a billion of it in the first year. A twenty-two-year-old college graduate will be placed in charge of Baghdad traffic planning; a twenty-four-year-old will run the Baghdad stock exchange. The head of the civilian occupation will dislike the head of the military occupation, and neither will be clearly in charge, so that the two will have severe coordination problems. It will take more than two

years after the invasion to provide adequately armored vehicles to the majority of U.S. forces, resulting in hundreds of avoidable American deaths.
After sovereignty is restored, the first Iraqi defense minister will personally
steal $1 billion, and nobody will notice; then he will be permitted to fly to
London. And so on.

And yet these things, and many more, took place. By 2004, the intelligent, practical people with whom I spoke, and who had spent time in Iraq,
all told me the same frightening things and predicted that conditions
would get far worse before they got better. Even more surprising, however,
was the reaction—or nonreaction—of most of the American media. Coverage by the television networks and many of the nation's largest newspapers remained superficial and uncritical. Some newspapers, magazines, and
individual journalists published excellent, honest work—Jim Fallows at
The Atlantic, George Packer and several journalists at *The New Yorker*,
Mark Danner in *The New York Review of Books*, and among newspapers,
the Knight-Ridder papers and the *Washington Post*. Then, in 2004 and
2005, a dozen good books appeared, primarily by journalists. But the average quality of mass-media journalism was poor, and nobody had made a
film about the big question of how and why all this had occurred. The
closest thing to such a film was a collection of *Frontline* episodes, several of
which did discuss the problems of the Iraqi occupation.

So in mid-2004, I began to explore the possibility of making a documentary about American policy in Iraq. I spoke to a number of well-
placed, experienced friends in the film world and in journalism. Somewhat
to my surprise, they advised me not to do it, for three reasons. First, they
said that this would be a difficult first film to make; I should practice on
something easier. A serious documentary about Iraq would involve a lot of
research, many interviews, and, above all, filming in Iraq, which would
raise a host of security, insurance, and logistical concerns, as well as being
expensive. Second, my friends said, you'll have tough competition and
probably lots of it. This subject is so important and so obvious that there
will be ten films about it, made by experienced documentary filmmakers
and financed by the BBC, CNN, wealthy individuals, and independent
distributors. And third, access will be a problem, because you have no
record as a filmmaker and no organization backing you.

At first I took this advice seriously and decided not to proceed. I had started writing a suspense novel and resumed thinking about other, quite different film ideas. Nearly a year passed. And then one day in early 2005, I realized that it was still true that nobody had made a serious film about American policy in Iraq. Many Iraq documentaries had been released—some of them very good—but they had very specific, personal, individual subjects: following a group of GIs, profiling an Iraqi family. Nobody had tackled the essential, large question. So in mid-2005, I went back to my media and journalistic friends and said, Don't tell me about all the problems I'll face or about all the people who will make this film in the future. Just tell me if anyone is making this film *now*. They replied that, to the best of their knowledge, nobody was. So I decided that I would.

Getting Started

A decade earlier, when I started my software company, I had stumbled upon the essential secret of doing something well—or at least avoiding the worst, when you've never done it before. It's very simple: If you hire good people, your employees will teach you your job. At my software company, my engineers taught me software project management and, sometimes, how to deal with venture capitalists as well. In the case of *No End in Sight*, I learned how to make a film from everybody around me. The hard part was persuading good people to take the chance that I was educable.

My friend Tom Luddy, the director of the Telluride Film Festival, referred me to a number of film professionals, some of whom were very helpful and generous with their time. But in the end, it was a random encounter that proved most valuable. I had seen two documentaries by Alex Gibney that I liked very much: *Enron* and *Lightning in a Bottle*. By bothering Alex enough, I persuaded him to meet with me. We liked each other and eventually agreed on a consulting arrangement whereby Alex would look over my shoulder, comment on my work, and help me hire the people I needed. In the end, Alex proved to be not only extraordinarily helpful, but also quite generous, even when he was making another documentary on a related subject, which placed us, to some degree, in competition. (His film *Taxi to the Dark Side* is about the use of torture by the United States in

Afghanistan, Iraq, and Guantanamo.) Alex opened his Rolodex, commented on my documents, and watched our rough cuts. He helped find me office space and instructed me on budgets, lawyers, film crews, distributors, film deals, and much else. I owe him an enormous debt.

My then personal assistant, Audrey Marrs, who had proved to be enormously gifted and competent, expressed interest in becoming involved in the film's production. But like me, she had no prior experience. Alex told me that I therefore needed to find (a) a full-time producer and (b) a film crew. He referred me to several producers, and in late 2005, I hired Jennie Amias, who worked on the film for our entire production period and for the first two or three months of postproduction (i.e., editing). I told Jennie that part of her job was to train Audrey, who eventually became the film's principal producer. Maryse Alberti, a cinematographer who had filmed *Enron,* referred me to Antonio Rossi, who became our principal cinematographer, and to David Hocs, who handled our audio.

The next problem was content. In mid-2005, few people were willing to speak on the record, much less in front of a camera. George Packer, Anthony Shadid, David Phillips, Larry Diamond, and others were able to write their books because (a) they had been there and (b) they could rely on off-the-record interviews. But would anybody talk to me?

Well, George Packer would, and so would Yaroslav Trofimov, a *Wall Street Journal* reporter who had covered the war since the invasion. They were my first two interviews, three hours each, on the same day in the late summer of 2005. George was extremely generous with his time, his sources, and his insight. Through him, through others, and then increasingly through my own research, I began to locate people willing to talk. Some, of course, hesitated or refused; Ambassador Robin Raphel, for example, had left the State Department, but still depended on government contracts and would not speak on the record. Military officers still on active duty generally would not talk at all, although I had one friend, a highly placed army officer, who talked to me off the record. L. Paul Bremer initially agreed, but then backed out, as did his former press spokesman, Dan Senor. Donald Rumsfeld, Colin Powell, George Tenet, Paul Wolfowitz, Douglas Feith, Lawrence DiRita, Dick Cheney, Condoleezza Rice, Robert Zoellick, Robert Blackwill, Richard Haass, Tommy Franks, and

John Negroponte all refused to speak with me. But as time passed, an increasing number of former government officials, including some who had held high-level jobs during the war and early occupation, were willing to speak. Some were even eager to do so, having watched helplessly as enormous mistakes were made but not widely reported in the media. In late 2005, Lawrence Wilkerson, who had been Colin Powell's chief of staff in the State Department, delivered a fierce speech at the New America Foundation, which signaled a new openness about the war. When I approached him, he agreed to talk to me. To my surprise, Walter Slocombe, who had worked for Bremer and was the architect of Bremer's order disbanding the entire Iraqi military, also agreed to be interviewed, and then even to be reinterviewed after I had discovered major discrepancies in his story. I will never entirely understand why he agreed; I suspect that guilt or shame played a role. Former Deputy Secretary of State Richard Armitage spoke with me for over an hour, the only long interview about Iraq that, to my knowledge, he has ever given. A number of senior military and intelligence officers spoke with me off the record.

In the end, we filmed more than fifty interviews in the United States—more than we needed and indeed more than we could use. (If I were to do it over again, I would conduct many more audio interviews before filming, in order to target filming more precisely. Recording audio is essentially free. Filming costs $3,000 to $7,000 per day, and thus is definitely *not* free.) By early 2006, I felt that we had reached diminishing returns, and it was time for me to go to Iraq. That turned out to be simultaneously easier, and harder, than I imagined.

Getting Ready for Iraq

Because I was an independent filmmaker with no institutional affiliation, everything in Iraq would be more difficult. If you are a reporter working for ABC or CNN or the *New York Times*, your organization arranges housing, equipment, crews, transportation, security, press credentials, insurance, and so forth. If you get kidnapped, they will bring pressure for U.S. forces to pay attention to finding you, they will negotiate for your release, they will print stories about you. If you get shot or blown up, they will fly you out—after they make sure you've been taken to the CASH, the combat hospital maintained by the United States inside the Green Zone. I, conversely, would have no organizational support. When I came to realize just what that meant, I developed great respect for the risks taken by freelance and independent journalists.

Obviously, it would also be desirable to have as much cooperation as possible from the Defense Department. Many months before my proposed trip, I wrote a long letter to the public affairs office of the Pentagon requesting various forms of cooperation and assistance, both in America and in Iraq. For example, the Defense Department had shot more than two hundred hours of high-definition footage of the war and early occupation, less than one hour of which has ever been released. We asked for the footage; they refused. We hired a lawyer; they evaded and delayed. I also sought interviews with senior Pentagon officials and military officers. And for my visit to Iraq, I asked to travel with the U.S. military for a week as an "embedded" reporter, as well as to visit U.S. military facilities and to interview military officers. The Defense Department responded, "Your request is complex," and then in effect said that they would get back to me when they were ready—in, say, twenty or thirty years. I forwarded my letter to a senior military officer I knew, who personally transmitted my request to Larry DiRita's office in the Pentagon. The answer stayed the same. If anything, the tone hardened.

So I really would be going to Iraq on my own. I started looking for people to help me: an interpreter, a private security firm to guard me, and guides and fixers who would know how to secure interviews, reach people, get things done. I spoke to journalists, photojournalists, fixers who lived in Beirut, managers of private military contractors, and documentary filmmakers who had worked in dangerous places. After many meetings and phone calls, I decided to bring two people with me for the whole trip, one of whom I would train in New York in the use of our new high-definition digital camcorders. (Our normal crew didn't want to go, and in any case, I preferred someone who knew Iraq well.) The first person I selected was Nir Rosen, who had covered the war as an independent journalist since 2003 and who spoke good Arabic. We agreed that we would train Nir to use our camcorders and archiving system, which was a complicated process. A very quick study, Nir wound up taking most of our footage in Iraq, in addition to introducing me to many useful people. Although his political views were to the left of mine by a considerable margin, Nir helped me in every way he could. He knew everyone and everything in Iraq and was extremely generous with his knowledge and contacts. He also drove me crazy—more about that later. The other person I decided to bring was Warzer Jaff, a Kurdish journalist and former Kurdish intelligence agent who would be my guide, Kurdish interpreter, and bodyguard.

I interviewed a number of private security contractors and spoke with many people who had used security in Iraq. After the Samarra bombing of February 2006, Iraq had become much more dangerous, and white guys with cameras were not very popular—except as targets. For American journalists, there were two basic security strategies: high profile and low profile. If you travel high profile, you cannot conceal your identity; your security is obvious, but, hopefully, sufficiently strong to deter or repel attackers. This means two or three armored cars, at least a half-dozen men with automatic weapons, body armor, and probably one or more former Special Forces personnel. If you travel low profile, you wear Iraqi clothes, no body armor; you travel in an old (and unarmored) Iraqi car, with at most a few Iraqi guards who carry only concealed pistols. In this way, you are much more likely to blend in and to avoid notice, which reduces the probability of an attack by at least 95 percent. But you are also much more vulnerable if you are attacked or if you just happen to be in the wrong place at the wrong time.

Wherever possible, the smart foreigners travel low profile. Not that it always works. Marla Ruzicka was as smart as they come, traveling in perfect low profile when she drove to the Baghdad airport in April 2005. She was twenty-eight years old, known throughout the American NGO and journalistic communities for her work on Iraqi civilian casualties, for her parties, and for her life force. But on the airport road, she found herself stuck immediately behind an American convoy, which is one of the most dangerous places to be. As often happens, a suicide bomber attacked the convoy. Marla burned to death in her unarmored car. Several of the people I met, including the *Washington Post* people I stayed with in Baghdad, had been friends of hers.

When filming, we would be obvious, anyway, due to our cameras, microphone, and interpreter, and so we would rarely be able to use the preferred low-profile strategy. In Baghdad, I would therefore need access to high-profile security. After interviewing several firms, I accepted Nir's recommendation to use Falcon, a Kurdish firm with American top management, American leaders for PSDs (personal security details), and mostly Kurdish guards. For the most part, this proved to be a good choice, although there were some problems, which I will describe shortly.

We needed a place to stay in Baghdad. A journalist friend, Ed Gargan, put me in touch with his friend John Anderson, a *Washington Post* reporter who was about to start an assignment in Baghdad and who would be there during my visit. John put me in touch with the Baghdad bureau chief, Ellen Knickmeyer (who has since moved to Cairo). I called Ellen in Baghdad, and within five minutes, she had invited me to stay at the *Washington Post* house in Baghdad. I will forever be in her debt. That house, which is outside the Green Zone, is in a heavily guarded compound that also includes several other houses rented by journalists, as well as one of Baghdad's very few still-functioning hotels. Jaff would stay next door at the hotel. Nir decided that he would stay at the Baghdad headquarters of our private military contractor; the contractor had cordoned off an entire neighborhood, which was heavily guarded and, therefore, by Baghdad standards, secure.

Before I left, I wired $1 million to Audrey, in the event of a serious emergency, and asked a close friend, Alex Schuessler, to be in effect my executor, negotiator, and caretaker in the event that something went wrong. I told my mother I would be doing research in Europe.

Being There

Jaff said that he would go to Baghdad ahead of us, through Amman, so that he could buy a weapon, cell phones, and some Iraqi clothes for me, as well as take the pulse of Baghdad, where conditions change frequently and unpredictably. Nir and I would go through Istanbul. We almost didn't make it out of Kennedy Airport. I had taken with me $25,000 in cash, which I did not realize that I needed to declare, even though I was leaving the country, not entering it. They found the money while we were going through security. I explained to the guard—a large, tough, but very kind woman—what I was doing, and she let us through. Whoever she was, I'm eternally grateful. We used every penny of the money.

We had expected to stay in Istanbul two or three days before taking a plane to Baghdad. Unfortunately, the day after we arrived in Istanbul, the Baghdad airport was closed because of a security emergency. It stayed closed for a week while we became involuntary tourists, staying in the luxurious but utterly antiseptic Istanbul Four Seasons. Nir practiced with the cameras; we interviewed an interesting Iraqi American friend of his; I saw Istanbul's beautiful new contemporary art museum, admired the Blue Mosque; and Nir grew frustrated.

Nir, it turns out, is not one to let grass grow beneath him. After a week cooling our heels in Istanbul, he persuaded me that we should fly to Southern Iraq and then drive through Turkish Kurdistan, across the border, and on to Irbil (also spelled Erbil, Arbil), the largest city in Iraqi Kurdistan, where our private security firm was headquartered. We took the flight and did the drive, which was indeed very instructive: Kurdistan is (a) beautiful, (b) harsh, and (c) heavily militarized. I also began to notice that Nir could be a problem. To say that Nir is risk-prone is rather like saying that Joseph Stalin was occasionally unpleasant; it's true, but it doesn't quite cover it. Nir doesn't just like living on the edge; he has never seen an edge that he could resist skating on, on one foot, with both hands tied behind his back.

At this point, the idea as propounded by Nir was still to fly to Baghdad, but from Irbil. Why I believed this would work, given that the Baghdad airport was entirely closed, now eludes me. We spent several interesting days in Irbil, meeting various friends and contacts of Nir's, interviewing some of them, and going to a party for all the former Special Forces security guys. The party was instructive; the difference between the Americans, many of them very testosterone-poisoned, and the Brits, Aussies, and lone New Zealander, remarkably civilized, was palpable. The lobby of our hotel, the Irbil "Sheraton"—not really a Sheraton, but called so by everyone— was straight out of the bar scene in *Star Wars*: greasy businessmen, mercenaries, journalists, U.S. military and intelligence types, fixers, a few Kurdish ex-pats visiting family, the omnipresent Kurdish secret police, the occasional lady of the night—and me.

But the Baghdad airport was still closed. Arguing that we shouldn't wait, Nir persuaded me that we should instead join a Falcon-operated convoy to Baghdad. I agreed. And so we drove overnight in a convoy of four up-armored Chevrolet pickup trucks with turret-mounted machine guns in the back. As we prepared to leave, Nir asked one of the American ex–Special Forces guys if he could have a pistol. No spare pistols, came the reply, but how about an MP-5 machine gun? "Well, I've never used one," says Nir. "Show me how." Approximately thirty seconds of instruction followed, after which Nir took the weapon. He held it between his legs for the duration of our ten-hour trip to Baghdad, sitting next to me. Somehow, this did not make me feel more secure.

More importantly, we had to stop three times en route because improvised explosive devices (IEDs) had either just been found or had just detonated ahead of us. If this incidence is representative, it suggests that road travel in Iraq is, in fact, extremely dangerous. We also found ourselves behind several American military convoys, which slowed us by hours and, of course, made us inviting targets as well. Nobody shot at us. But later, when I told George Packer and others about the trip, the consensus was that it was insane. One fake checkpoint, said George, one serious IED, and that would have been that. I had sensed this myself, and from then on, I got tougher with Nir.

We arrived in Baghdad at about 5 A.M., slept for an hour or two, had breakfast, and were driven to the *Washington Post* house where I would be staying. We discussed my security arrangements, and I discovered that the head of my PSD would be the man who had given Nir the machine gun. Over the next two days, I also discovered that this man was dangerously, foolishly macho, as are many private military contractors in Iraq. At one checkpoint to the Green Zone, he was stopped by an Iraqi soldier who spoke no English. Rather than ask one of the other guards to interpret, he jumped out of the car and began screaming at the Iraqi guard, which was unbelievably stupid for about thirty reasons. First, he was exposing himself; the first time we tried to enter the Green Zone, we were turned away because a guard had been killed there half an hour before. Second, the entrances to the Green Zone are watched by insurgents, who attempt to identify foreigners and their cars for later targeting; he was painting a big, red "X" on our car. Third, he left the car door open, which breached the envelope of the car, making it much less secure in the event of a bombing or shooting. He also drove very aggressively, which called attention to us in Baghdad traffic. After two days, I fired him. His replacement, Dan, was a model of cool, sanity, and intelligence, and a pleasure to be with. As it turned out, Falcon was also an excellent choice for another reason: The Americans who worked for Falcon were still in the U.S. military reserves, which meant that they had Green Zone passes, a very valuable commodity even for Americans. The passes allowed us to bypass Baghdad traffic by cutting through the Green Zone and, if necessary, escape to safety there if something big went wrong.

Baghdad was surreal in a thousand ways. In order to reduce U.S. casualties, the Green Zone perimeter was increasingly guarded not by Americans, but by cannon fodder: a motley collection of Iraqi, Peruvian, and Georgian guards who spoke no English and frequently had no common language among themselves. We went to interviews early and left early, never staying in any one compound more than ninety minutes. There were miles of concrete blast walls everywhere; I made a crude estimate that there were at least $250 million worth of blast walls in Baghdad. The *New York Times* compound was a world apart, with extremely impressive security; the *Times* had simply blocked off the road on one side—one of the largest streets in Baghdad—to improve security further. It was as if a private company in New York City had simply closed off the West Side Highway or FDR Drive.

Usually, our weapons and cell phones were confiscated and we were searched before we entered buildings, yet, during our time in Iraq, it was still possible to stop in a wealthy neighborhood halfway across town for an ice cream or fruit juice. (That's a distant memory now.) The food was generally awful, and I was frequently ill, which surprised me, because I had previously spent a month in Africa without getting sick once.

Private security convoys would routinely halt traffic, drive on the wrong side of the street, and order drivers to move over. We heard gunfire and explosions frequently, and sometimes very close by. A few times, Jaff escorted me on low-profile trips, so that I could walk the streets and talk briefly with people. Once, I was able to attend one of the Friday sermons, at which Muslim religious leaders often make political as well as religious speeches. Among the many intelligent, sensitive people I interviewed, the sense of sadness, loss, and desperation was pervasive. So was the tension and fatigue caused by the need for constant alertness. Nir got himself arrested by the Iraqi police—not a move that enhances life expectancy—when they caught him filming and then found that he was carrying an unregistered gun. He was able to make a cell phone call to our guards, who immediately drove over to recuperate him. Nir took risks, some of which endangered others as well as himself. But he also got some of our best footage, much of it taken covertly, including a sermon delivered by Moqtada al-Sadr. Nir was simultaneously infuriating and indispensable, immature and courageous, foolish and extremely perceptive, a caricature of the crazy but wily war journalist. Jaff was tense in just the right way, permanently watchful but never drawing attention to himself, and he turned out to know everyone, from the guards at the *New York Times* compound to the president's press secretary.

On my last day in Baghdad, Jaff took a risk. He took me, low profile, to lunch at one of the few remaining restaurants on the banks of the Tigris, of which there were formerly hundreds. The restaurants specialized in Mazgouf, the justly famous national dish of Iraq. A fish is sliced open, grilled very slowly two feet from the coals, and then finished briefly underneath the embers. This restaurant was comparatively safe, because it was near the point at which the *New York Times* had blocked off the riverside road. After two weeks of confinement in Baghdad, it was bliss to spend two hours sitting in the sun, eating delicious food. But when Jaff wanted a beer, I discouraged him. I felt bad about denying him his beer, but we were still in Baghdad, and I wanted him alert.

Then we returned to Kurdistan. Nir introduced us to the warlord who controlled most of Kurdish Kirkuk. The man took us around town in his modest convoy of half a dozen vehicles and twenty guards, stopping traffic and blocking roads at will. He took us to visit thousands of Kurdish refugees squatting miserably in a stadium; they were kept there by the Kurdish government as political pawns in the Kurds' drive to exhibit the injustices inflicted on them by Arab Iraqis. We visited Sulaimaniya and then drove back to Irbil, bypassing Mosul for security reasons—a long but exquisitely beautiful trip. Iraqi Kurdistan, quite tightly controlled, with checkpoints everywhere and an extremely efficient secret police organization, felt a world apart from Baghdad. It was safe, comparatively prosperous, moderate, reasonable. In Irbil, a former army base from the Saddam era had been turned into an enormous park, with lawns, paths, artificial lakes, and concerts. I went jogging there, which drew stares but no hostility as long as my interpreter spoke to the guards in advance.

Editing and Releasing the Film

When we returned from Iraq, we were ready to start assembling the film. Documentaries, I learned by experience, are made in the editing room in a way that feature films cannot be. After several false starts, I had found two young editors who proved wonderful. Chad Beck and Cindy Lee had worked together before. Their contrasting styles complemented each other excellently, and they were totally great. Chad had studied philosophy and film at Johns Hopkins; Cindy had studied international relations at Wellesley and in Sweden. First, they watched all 250 hours of our footage and read our several thousand pages of transcripts. Then, I wrote documents while they generated a 5½-hour "assembly" of our best footage. From there, it was a process of refinement, gradual but intense.

We were under serious time pressure. Our lawyer at Sloss Law introduced me to John Sloss, who made it clear that the Sundance Film Festival was the place to be for this documentary, which meant that we had less than five months to produce a cut that would get us in. Jennie Amias said we couldn't do it, but I overrode her and told the editors that we were in for some hard work. They responded stunningly well. But the biggest surprise I encountered was about myself. I discovered that I completely loved making movies. I was with the editors every day, usually for at least six hours, and I was utterly transfixed. The process of editing the film was one of the peak experiences of my life.

We got into Sundance, and won the special jury prize. The film festival was an amazing experience, primarily because I met some wonderful, kind, gifted filmmakers there, especially Jason Kohn, who made *Manda Bala,* a visually breathtaking documentary about crime and corruption in Brazil, and Shimon Dotan, whose *Hot House* examined the condition and surprising importance of Palestinian prisoners in Israeli prisons. When all three of us won prizes, we were quite elated, and we have since become friends. After Sundance, however, there was reality to contend with. Obtaining a distributor was difficult, a process in which I made some mistakes due to inexperience. But in the end, Magnolia bought the film. The New America Foundation and the Center for American Progress helped us with preview screenings, and the film opened at the Film Forum in New York and the E Street Cinema in Washington, D.C., on July 27, 2007. The film received stunningly positive reviews, far beyond my wildest hopes, and grossed $1.4 million, which I regard as both a great success and a serious disappointment. On the one hand, we were the second-highest grossing documentary of 2007, a very difficult year. (Between 2004 and 2007, the documentary share of total U.S. box office revenue declined from 2.5 to 0.8 percent.) At the same time, certain statistical indicators, such as revenue per screen on opening weekend, suggest that the film could or should have grossed substantially more than it did. I was learning on the job. I still am.

Even as I was making the film, I knew that I was doing far more work than the film itself strictly required. But I hoped that the material would be useful, and from very early on, I thought that a book would be a valuable addition to the historical record as well as to current policy debate and our understanding of what has gone so terribly wrong in this war. When Peter Osnos got in touch with me after seeing the film, I was extremely gratified, and I hope that the result justifies his confidence in me. For this book, I conducted another two dozen interviews to bring the material up-to-date, to include a discussion of policy options going forward, and to fill some gaps in our previous research. It was at once fascinating and sad to plunge back into this dark subject.

One of the few frustrations of making the film had been the necessity of leaving out many interesting things. While the film contained 1 percent of our interview material, this book contains perhaps 10 percent. In addition, after the film was released, a number of military and intelligence officers volunteered extremely useful additional information about such matters as prewar planning, how the looting was (not) handled, and the disbanding of the Iraqi military. I also had the interesting experience of interviewing former New York Police Commissioner Bernard Kerik, who had been in charge of the Iraqi police for three months in 2003, about one week before he was indicted.

Producing this book was a powerfully emotional experience, and a difficult one. Most of those I interviewed feel that Iraq has not improved in the year since I finished the film. Indeed, as readers will see, one area of surprising unanimity was the view of both Iraqis and American analysts that "the surge" was a creature of American politics that was not helping Iraq. Although some analysts believe that stability and relative peace might be achievable within, say, five years, many fear the worst. I close this book with several chapters that offer a wide array of expert opinion about the consequences of the war, current U.S. policy, optimal policy going forward (including the potential effects of a U.S. withdrawal), and what this experience has taught us. Although it is too late now for the hundreds of thousands who have been killed or wounded, it is more important than ever to improve American policy in Iraq. For both Americans and Iraqis, I fervently hope that there will, one day, be an end in sight.

New York City
December 2007

To read the transcripts in their entirety, please visit
www.noendinsightthebook.com

PART ONE
PREPARATION AND INVASION

CHAPTER ONE

WAR

Even well before September 11, 2001, some Bush administration officials wanted to invade Iraq to remove Saddam Hussein. One day after the September 11 attacks, senior Pentagon officials including Defense Secretary Donald Rumsfeld and Undersecretary Douglas Feith spoke to senior military officers about Iraq and the need to remove Saddam. Eighteen months later, they got their wish. On March 17, 2003, the U.S. government issued an ultimatum to Saddam Hussein in a speech televised in the United States and worldwide, including to American troops stationed in Kuwait.

> Saddam Hussein and his sons must leave Iraq within forty-eight hours. Their refusal to do so will result in military conflict commenced at a time of our choosing.
> —President George W. Bush, March 17, 2003

By this time, over 150,000 U.S. military personnel were already in Kuwait, preparing for war. Marine Lieutenant Seth Moulton was among them.

SETH MOULTON: I joined the marines because I think … I've always just felt it's a really important job and I didn't feel like I'd be content with myself going through life knowing that other people had fought for my freedom.

… So I finished training in December of 2002. And Iraq was not at all a foregone conclusion at that point. So I went home for Christmas, my first bit of leave in the Marine Corps. And I think I got a call on Christmas Eve from my new battalion XO, out on the West Coast, and [he] said, you know, you have to come out here very quickly.

And so, uh, within the week, I had loaded a U-Haul and, uh, a friend of mine—future roommate who lived in New York—and I drove out to California. And about ten days after we arrived in California, we were on a ship sailing out of San Diego, on the way to Iraq.

CHARLES FERGUSON: Tell us what happened next.

SETH MOULTON: Sure, so ... so I got assigned a platoon. Um, we had forty-five days, or thereabouts, on the ship, sailing to Kuwait, during which time we just did all the training that we could in that environment. And we got to Kuwait at the end of February in 2003.

Moulton spoke highly of the U.S. Marines' combat readiness, particularly their preparations for chemical warfare. His unit also trained in urban warfare tactics.

CHARLES FERGUSON: During that time, were you prepared in any specific way for Iraq? Did you, you know, take Arabic? Did anybody tell you about what Iraq was like; anything of the sort?

SETH MOULTON: Well, we certainly prepared for the war, the initial ... the war, uh, without question. Uh, we understood that, uh, chemical weapons would be a big problem, for example, so we did a lot of extra training for how to deal with chemical weapons. And we, you know, understood that the ... the fighting would probably be pretty brutal, and so we did an awful lot of extra medical training. And we understood that there probably would be a lot of house-to-house fighting in Baghdad, so we did a lot of urban warfare training. ...

CHARLES FERGUSON: How can you train for urban combat on a ship?

SETH MOULTON: Well, you gotta be creative. I mean, you go down to the deck, where they have all the vehicles, and ... and containers stored. And you tape out rooms. And you say, all right, well, this is a house, and this is a hallway. And you practice going in ... um ... going in there. Uh, you practice shooting techniques, by shooting targets off the back of the ship. You know, there are special shooting techniques you use for urban warfare. Uh, so you work on those. You sit down and have classes on tactics. Um, it's a lot of just, uh, dry run-throughs. But it's amazing what you can accomplish when you're creative. And we did a lot of creative training on the ships. But you know, marines have been on ships for a long time, so I mean these things ... these are things that are passed down, and you learn how to train in that environment.

Moulton was less sanguine about preparations for the occupation. His unit did not, for example, train in counterinsurgency tactics, learn Arabic, or study Iraqi culture.

SETH MOULTON: So absolutely, we prepared for Iraq. But not in the way that you prepare for the counterinsurgency that's going on now in Iraq. I mean, we spent very, very little time learning Arabic. We had a little, you know, some ... they're called pointy-talky cards, that have the most basic words and phrases. And we were basically just issued those, but we didn't spend much time, you know, learning them or memorizing them.

We, uh, learned a little bit about the history of Iraq. But not too much. Um, [we were] much more focused on just the tactical aspect of defeating the ... uh, defeating Saddam's forces and ... and taking the country.

So, uh, I remember when I was on the helicopter, on the way into Kuwait from the ship, I took out my Iraq country handbook and started reading about the history of the people, and some of the, um, some of the cultures and stuff. And, you know, and that's about it.

Saddam did not respond to President Bush's ultimatum. And thus, two days later, America was at war.

At this hour, American and coalition forces are in the early stages of military operations to disarm Iraq, to free its people, and to defend the world from grave danger.

—President George W. Bush, March 19, 2003

Seth Moulton's marine company was the first to enter Baghdad.

SETH MOULTON: I was a rifle platoon commander assigned to Alpha Company, First Battalion, Fourth Marines. Part of Regimental Combat Team One, First Marine Division.

And so, uh, we essentially invaded Iraq on the eastern flank, far away,

Seth Moulton (right) on his first tour in Iraq, 2003.

up, uh, Route Seven. And so, when I got to Kuwait, I just continued the infantry training. And we crossed, uh, on Day One; we crossed into Iraq. And ... and fought our way north. My company ended up being the first marine company into Baghdad. And that's where we ended our ... our portion of the major combat action. So we were ... um, we got into Baghdad, and ended up spending about two weeks there.

Yaroslav Trofimov is a Ukrainian-born journalist who covered the Iraq war for the *Wall Street Journal,* after having spent several years on assignment in the Middle East, an experience chronicled in his book *Faith at War.* He speaks Arabic and Hebrew as well as fluent English. He also embodies the war correspondent's ethos. Without permission or support from the military, he simply decided to drive alongside the invading forces as they proceeded from Kuwait through Southern Iraq to Baghdad. In Kuwait, he rented an SUV from Hertz—probably not being entirely truthful about how he intended to use it—and he followed the war all the way to Baghdad, arriving there only a few days after U.S. forces entered the city.

Very soon after the war started, Trofimov saw evidence that not everything would go smoothly. And while Trofimov's assessments of the war and occupation tended to be more pessimistic than those of other Western journalists, I found him generally reliable. When I interviewed him in the late summer of 2005, he predicted intensifying sectarian conflict and said that Iraq was on the verge of civil war. Although this prediction was considered extreme at the time, it proved to be right. Most observers found that Iraqis were initially favorably disposed, or at least not hostile, to the American invasion. Trofimov, however, encountered hostility as soon as he crossed the border.

YAROSLAV TROFIMOV: The Kuwaiti government had declared the … the entire northern half of the emirate a closed military zone. And so, uh, the American and the British troops had been massing there, in force, with thousands of tanks and helicopter gunships just parked on the sides of the roads. And in theory, we journalists, unless we're embedded with actual military units, weren't allowed to go. But of course, in the confusion of the war, nobody was checking anything. So we just, uh, put on our camouflage chemical suits and drove a big SUV truck, following the tank tracks of the British tanks across the berm. And it was really, really easy. There was a big hole in the sand, and a big sign saying, "The Royal Fusiliers welcome you to Iraq." And there we were.

CHARLES FERGUSON: And nobody minded that you were there, driving your SUV in the middle of the war?

YAROSLAV TROFIMOV: Well, uh, once you actually got into Iraq, technically, uh, the … the Allied forces could not expel us back to Kuwait, because they had no legal authority to do so. And so, they strongly advised us to go back. And some people did go back, because we were shot at quite, quite often in the first few days. But I decided to stay. And I didn't go there alone, of course. It was about seven, uh, cars in a convoy—journalists in there. And we packed enough water and food to last us all the way to Baghdad and back. And uh, there were jerricans of fuel that were strapped to the … to the roof of our SUV. So if somebody had actually hit them, we'd go up in a huge fireball. …

CHARLES FERGUSON: … What did you see on the way to Baghdad?

YAROSLAV TROFIMOV: Well, the very, very first thing we saw there, uh, was a road to Qasr, which is the Iraqi port, the biggest port in Iraq, that lies just across the frontier from Kuwait. And since the first minutes of the war, there were [all these] announcements that Qasr has already fallen, and, you know, the troops have advanced far beyond it. [But] when we drove into it, we heard lots of shooting. And ... and there was a car, uh, speeding in our direction, saying, "Just don't go there. There is still war going on there!"

So we stopped by the roadside, and put on our flak jackets and our helmets, and um, [taped] big TV signs on the windows of the cars. And there was a marine, uh, amphibious vehicle parked by the side of the road. So we talked to the marines, trying to figure out what's going on. And they were all very frazzled and ready for war.

And uh, at that point, an Iraqi taxicab—a very old taxicab, packed with people—tried to drive by it, very slowly—this white and orange, sort of thirty-year-old Iraqi cab. And ... and the marines, noticing this ... this car, were so scared, already in the beginning, that they just opened up with fire, and they just ... just strafed the whole front of the car. Uh, they didn't kill the occupants, but they did damage the car. And all of us journalists—some of us with our backs to the marines—didn't know what's going on. So suddenly, there was a scene of pandemonium and panic with everybody diving and ducking under the cars, and looking for cover. So that was our very, very ... This happened literally in the first fifteen minutes of being across, across the berm.

From there, we went into a big highway intersection, with one way going to Baghdad, and one to Basra. And there, sort of on the cloverleaves of that intersection, the British had set up a temporary camp to detain prisoners of war, some of whom surrendered to us. [They had seen] us as ... as being unarmed, and [they] wanted us to escort them to the British because they were afraid they would be shot on sight. And so we parked our cars there and started to talk to our first actual Iraqis, who could ... who could, um, speak out their minds. And very early on, [we] realized that there were no flowers. ... There was no open happiness at ... at being liberated. All those expectations of the cheering crowds did not materialize.

Many combat decisions were made far from the battleground—at the U.S. Army's Central Command (CENTCOM) Headquarters in Qatar, in Kuwait, or in Washington, D.C. When the war began, Marc Garlasco was in the Pentagon. He had worked for the Defense Intelligence Agency for seven years and was the senior analyst for Iraq leadership targeting; his job included trying to kill Saddam Hussein and senior officials of the regime. It was also his idea to create the "deck of cards" distributed to U.S. soldiers, which contained the photographs and names of the fifty-four most wanted senior officials of the regime. Garlasco told me that he had been personally opposed to the war, but that he had decided to remain in his job until it was over. He felt that he knew the targeting issues in Iraq better than anyone else did, and that if a less experienced person took his job, more civilians would be killed. He also felt that for the most part, the U.S. military took great care to avoid civilian casualties during the war and was very successful in doing so.

MARC GARLASCO: Targeting in the war was handled extraordinarily professionally. I think people would be shocked if they knew the utter gymnastics that the U.S. military goes through to minimize collateral damage. …

There was one [strike]. It was across the street from the [al Yarmouk] maternity hospital. And the last thing you want to do is put bombs down near a hospital. And this is about a hundred yards away from the hospital. Big problem.

What happened is some of the Iraqi units had gone in, and … and had basically taken over this … this large fairgrounds area. It's like a convention center, international convention center. So a lot of buildings [were] there. And that required a lot of big bombs. And so we put nine two-thousand-pound weapons into a very small area. And that's, you know, eighteen thousand pounds of high explosives a hundred yards away from a hospital. Don't really want to do it.

But we took incredible precautions, and people did things to make sure that no one was harmed in the hospital. [A] plane came in from the hospital, and dropped the weapon towards the convention center. … What we did to minimize civilian casualties was fly the aircraft at such an angle that it pushed the debris away from the hospital. We had five-millisecond delayed fuses on these penetrators, so that they would go bury into the ground, and basically collapse the buildings in upon themselves. So that you don't have the blast and fragmentation damage going out and killing people.

It was shot at night, so that there's no one on the street. And it did a great job. In fact, no one got killed. The hospital lost a few windows. I went there shortly after the war—went in and spoke to the director about it. And I was just amazed that we could drop eighteen thousand pounds of bombs a hundred yards away, and the worst that happened was they lost some windows.

So you know, I think people would be surprised if they knew everything that goes into these air strikes.

There were, however, some cases in which the military was not careful to avoid civilian casualties or perhaps did not know that it was inflicting them. Shortly after the war, Garlasco resigned from the Defense Intelligence Agency and joined Human Rights Watch. His first assignment was to go to Iraq and conduct a survey of civilian casualties in the war, including the effects of his own targeting decisions. First, he described the principal source of civilian casualties that he discovered.

MARC GARLASCO: [The U.S. Air Force] had learned the lessons in Kosovo and Afghanistan, of what they'd done incorrectly, and had killed an awful lot of civilians. And after spending five, six weeks on the ground in Iraq, we had found almost no air strikes with, uh, cluster bombs in civilian areas. So they ... they really changed their ways.

The problem is, [during the invasion] you've got the army going in, and they have these ... cluster weapons, but in rockets. And so they shoot the rockets ahead of their forces. And another problem is, the Iraqis are fighting from areas, uh, you know, civilian areas. They've got their units right in there, mixed in with ... with schools and mosques and people's homes. And so when the U.S. would fire these weapons on the Iraqis, they're landing basically in very densely populated areas. And each of these rockets contains six hundred and forty-four little bombs. And so initially, when the rockets go out—and they tend to shoot six rockets at once—you're looking at, four, five thousand little bombs dropping in an area the size of a football field. And if you're outside when that happens, you're dead.

And the other problem is, you know, you're looking at upwards of twenty percent of these that don't explode on impact. … And when you're talking four or five thousand, you're talking now about hundreds of these. And the other thing is, the army's ones have these … these little white … um, these white kind of catches on them, made out of … uh, it's a fabric. The army ones, they're very small. And they have these white fabric triggers … to stabilize in the air because it has to hit the ground completely perpendicular to the ground in order to explode correctly, and if it doesn't—if it hits at an angle—it won't explode. And so that's why you have so many. But additionally, because it's got this … this thing, they'll hang in the trees. [And so] you have kids and people go over, and pull on them. And all of a sudden, they're dead, because it blows right at them. And kills them. Or it maims them. And I found a lot of kids, no arms, no legs, or just, just horrific, horrific injuries.

And … and that was the single largest contributor to civilian casualties in the war. There were other things—ground fire, people being shot in crossfire and whatnot, civilians killed in air strikes—but by and large, it was this single weapon that led to a majority of the civilian casualties that we saw on the ground.

CHARLES FERGUSON: Do you have any idea how many there were? Any estimate?

MARC GARLASCO: We do, we do. I've got the … the number. There … the … if you go by bomblets—and I'm sorry, I don't have the number in my head right now; I could, I can get it for you—uh, but it's in the millions.

CHARLES FERGUSON: Of these bombs?

MARC GARLASCO: Of the bomblets, uh, of the little ones. … It's thousands of rockets. And then when, you know, thousands times six hundred and forty-four, you're talking about millions of explosives. And then you multiply that by twenty percent, there's a lot of stuff on the ground that people are picking up. So you've got this, you know: [Explosive] hits the ground; civilians are … are killed or injured. And then postwar, you're looking at the first few weeks, you've got a huge spike in civilian casualties. And a casualty is an injury or a death. You've got a huge spike. And then, as they become educated, it goes down. And as the cleaning teams come in, it … it goes down drastically. But there's one battle, the battle of Hilla. In the battle of Hilla, which is just south of Baghdad, which happened from March 31st to April 4th of 2003, we counted somewhere over five hundred civilian casualties. And it's purely from these cluster weapons.

Garlasco also commented on one other problem: the targeting consequences of inadequate intelligence. He saw some of them in an extremely personal, painful way.

MARC GARLASCO: Now that said, we did a terrible job when it came to the leadership targeting. Now, we had specifically fifty specific attacks against these guys in the deck of cards. And in grand total, we hit all of the targets, and we got no guys in the deck of cards. Zero. We were zero for fifty. And the problem is, in a number of those strikes, we had civilian casualties. Maybe eighteen, twenty casualties, in some, in many of those strikes.

I think that the problem was not in how the targets were planned, because people do an amazing job … of planning strikes to minimize civilian casualties. I think the problem was in the intelligence, and in where you thought the target was. Because we were wrong. We were often wrong at what the target was—there were no leaders there; there was nobody there. It was somebody's home. And then, you know, it … it all goes to hell.

You know, for example, there was one night. We're in the Pentagon. And we have information that Chemical Ali is in Basra. We know specifically where he is. He's in the residential area, just across from the Iraqi intelligence service in Basra.

Chemical Ali is a very bad man. You know, he's responsible for killing thousands of Iraqis with chemical weapons, thousands of Kurds with chemical weapons. And so he's a war criminal, very bad. Killing him, it's the right thing to do.

And so, you know, we work up the plan, very quickly. And, you know, we were thinking, well, you know, the British are only five miles away. Why don't we just roll in, and … and have the Brits, you know, pull him out? But folks figured no, you know, we … we wanna, we want to take him out. Because [he'd] been really tough to this point. You know, we'd been tracking him, and [it] was very difficult to track his movements.

And so I'm watching [on a computer screen], and there's a Predator [unmanned aerial vehicle]. And the Predator is overhead. And you know, everything's basically reverse, white and black—all of the ... the really hot stuff is white, and the black is cold. And I'm looking down at this ... at these buildings. And I can see this guy walking. You can see him walking. And it's almost like this countdown going on; you know the bombs are gonna strike.

And the first one hits. [*makes explosion sound*] And the screen goes white for a second, because of the heat of the bomb. And it missed by three blocks. It went right into an intersection. A five-hundred-pound laser-guided bomb, and I have no idea how the damned thing missed, because those are the most accurate that we've got.

But something like three seconds later, the next weapon goes in. And it drills right into the building. And it hit exactly where it was supposed to. And we just went, Yeah! You know, we gave this cheer. And I'm sitting in there with my group of people. Uh, I had twelve people that I was running at the Pentagon during the war; we had six on, six off.

And we're all standing there, cheering, and going, "Yeah, we got him! We got him!" And you could watch. And as the white heat of the explosion starts to go down, you could see this rag doll body, floating up into the sky, and coming down, and hitting, and bouncing. And we're like, "Okay, okay, okay," covering up the screen. And it was in a ... saved as an MPEG. And then we're taking bets. "Okay, how many times did he bounce? Come on, guys. How many times did he bounce? We've got [two] bounces, three bounces. What are the bets, what are the bets?"

And ... and I know it sounds terrible. But it's kind of like this thing that you need to do, uh, just for yourself, because you know you're ... you're ... that people are dying on the other end. Uh, but it's like when you watch *MASH* or some things with gallows humor, where just for your own psyche, you're trying to throw some comedy into a moment. And ... and it sounds awful. But he was a very bad man.

And we believed that we got him. Heh. And we didn't kill him. And months later, there I am, standing in this crater. Maybe, I don't know, twenty, thirty feet deep. And I'm face-to-face with this seventy-year-old guy, this seventy-year-old Iraqi, who's telling me that his children are dead, and his grandchildren are dead, and his whole family has been wiped out. And that was a really hard moment. ...

And I feel ... I feel incredibly ... I feel incredibly torn about it. You know, on the one hand, I took part in ... in annihilating this guy's family. And while, okay, you know, I didn't fly the mission, and I didn't specifically plan the mission, you know, we were involved. It's a big team, and you're ... you're giving recommendations, and you know, we'd given the thumbs-up on this one. And so there's some level of participation there.

But on the other hand, I knew what we did to make sure that civilians were not killed; I knew how hard we were working. And we were using penetrating weapons, so that they would go under the ground, and explode underground, to contain the bomb blast. And I knew that we flew, the ... the plane flew in a certain angle, so that the debris wouldn't go towards people's homes. And it was shot in the middle of the night, so most people are not out in the streets. So we did a lot of things to minimize the damage. But the problem is, [Chemical Ali] wasn't there. And some families paid the price for it.

And that happened time and again in the leadership strikes, and that was very difficult to stomach.

Overall, however, the war went faster and more smoothly than anticipated. There was no use of chemical weapons, because as it turned out Iraq did not possess any. Saddam did not set fire to Iraq's oil fields. And for several reasons, Iraq's military provided little effective resistance.

In 2003, Paul Hughes was an army colonel who had spent the previous six years in the Pentagon performing strategic analysis for senior Defense Department officials. In early 2003, he was assigned to work on the occupation of Iraq, becoming director of strategic policy for the Organization of Reconstruction and Humanitarian Assistance, which was responsible for the occupation of Iraq through May 2003.

PAUL HUGHES: We weren't expecting a three-week war. I mean, the war plan was actually programmed out ninety to a hundred and twenty days of actual combat. Three weeks—that was a surprise. ...

In part, the invasion went quickly because most of the Iraqi military melted away. In some cases, soldiers simply chose to desert rather than fight. But in many cases, Iraqi military units were obeying instructions from the United States. The U.S. military and the CIA had conducted an extensive covert prewar campaign in which U.S. officials urged Iraqi military leaders to cooperate with the U.S. forces, promising favorable treatment for those who did. Iraqi commanders were told that if they arranged their equipment in a square formation, they would not be attacked unless they opened fire on U.S. forces. Many commanders obeyed and encouraged or allowed their men to go home.

PAUL HUGHES: In the advance to Baghdad, our troops ran into some battle positions that were manned, and there were some terrific fights. I mean, truly terrific, horrible fights. Other places, they'd run into a battle position, and there wouldn't be any Iraqi soldiers. But there wouldn't be any weapons; there wouldn't be any uniforms. They'd just be empty.

So the question you have to ask yourself is, Where did those guys go? Okay, certainly there were deserters. Out of a four-hundred-thousand-man army, yeah, there were deserters. But not a hundred percent of them. Where did they go, and what were their intentions?

On May 1, 2003, President George W. Bush declared an end to major combat operations in Iraq, announcing: "In the battle of Iraq the United States and our Allies have prevailed."

Initial Iraqi Reaction to the War

When American and coalition forces first entered Iraq, the initial reaction of the civilian population was mixed. Many, possibly the majority of Iraqis, were elated. But many were also angry or suspicious. They saw civilian casualties and other "collateral damage"; they recalled America's support for Saddam in the 1980s, its betrayal of the Shiites in 1991, and the effects of the sanctions throughout the 1990s. And they felt wary of America's role in the Middle East, and in particular, its interest in oil.

While the reaction of Iraqis was quite heterogeneous, ranging from hatred to delight, the average or predominant reaction seems to have been a cautious, conditional optimism that the American invasion would be a good thing if the Americans demonstrated that they were sincere—that they weren't there just for oil—and if daily life improved. Most people assumed that life would, in fact, improve, including Yaroslav Trofimov and Iraqi journalist Omar Fekeiki.

OMAR FEKEIKI: Under Saddam Hussein the, uh, the government planned for my future. I wasn't able to leave the country to start my own career in anything. I wasn't able to start journalism here, because the journalism under Saddam wasn't what I wanted to do. I didn't want to be a journalist directed by the government, and just a mouthpiece for the government, so I didn't have a future. I just was waiting for the war to happen, because it was the only ray of hope I, uh, had to look for. When it happened, I was excited that things will move slowly, but, um, towards better circumstances.

Iraqis waving to American convoy.

OMAR FEKEIKI: I've seen people welcoming the coalition trucks. Because we thought everything is planned. Everything is prepared.

YAROSLAV TROFIMOV: We all came into Iraq with this idea that the U.S. government would be competent. We expected the basic ability to deal with the situation. And so did the world. The U.S. is a superpower. So people everywhere in Iraq, in the Arab world, and in Europe thought that the U.S. would be able to restore order fairly quickly and provide basic services.

The most pro-American segment of Iraqi society, and the one group that has remained so, was, predictably, the Kurds, many of whom—particularly those living in

Kurdistan as opposed to Arab Iraq—did not even view themselves as Iraqi. American journalist Chris Allbritton started covering the war in Kurdistan and followed the fighting south.

CHRIS ALLBRITTON: It's like Crawford, Texas, up there. I've never seen a place that's more pro-American, uh, than Iraqi Kurdistan. When I was there in April 2003 … we had a guide by the name of, um, Abdullah. And he knew all the names of the foreign secretaries and foreign ministers at the UN. He knew exactly who Condoleezza Rice was, who Donald Rumsfeld was. He had great things to say about George Bush, Rumsfeld, Condoleezza Rice, Colin Powell. He had very bad things to say about the French. And he often drew his finger across his throat when he was talking about, uh, Dominique [de] Villepin. It was … it was one of the most bizarre kind of geopolitical lessons that I had ever experienced from this kind of mountain guerrilla, who was … dedicated to fighting Saddam, who said he had lost five of his sons, uh, in fighting any number of the groups—the Turks, the Syrians, the Iranians, the … the Iraqis, as he called them. And yet he was, uh, absolutely in favor of this.

Even in Tikrit, Saddam's birthplace, the population was happy that the regime was gone.

CHRIS ALLBRITTON: And then, after that, we just kind of made our way further south, as the fighting allowed. We made our way down to Tikrit [Saddam Hussein's birthplace], where we were some of the early reporters into there. And [we] found the Arab fighters there, possibly for the last time, incredibly welcoming.

The reception in Baghdad, however, was much more mixed.

CHRIS ALLBRITTON: The hostility of the people in Baghdad, um, the Iraqis: They gave us very hostile, very guarded stares, in the cars, as we were passing. There were thousands of cars, and they had all come up from the Gulf, and from Saudi, more so than Baghdad could ever support. The streets were absolutely just chockablock with traffic. Unlike Kurdistan, where they would see a Western face and they would be incredibly welcoming, and even in Tikrit, where once they figured out we weren't Kurdish, they were gracious; in Baghdad, they were hostile. They were, uh, quite suspicious.

But there were also people who were very hopeful, as well. And there was any number of people pleading with me to help because they thought, You're a Westerner, you're an American, you're a reporter. You know things. You know people. They wanted to know about their relatives who had disappeared. They would hand me slips of paper, uh, with names on it, asking me to help find this person. ... [They were] desperate for contact with the outside world. They wanted to use my Thoraya [satellite phone]. And I tri ... I let as many as I could, uh, while the battery lasted. And they wanted to call relatives around the world, to let them know they were okay.

And while there was hostility, as I said, there was also a great deal of hospitality, and a lot of people who were glad to see the Americans there. They were convinced that things were going to be much better.

Um, the Americans—the marines, in this case, 'cause they were the ones who really had taken over the Palestine and [Ferdus] Square area, where the statue came down, and where I was kind of dealing with the Americans—they had set up their command center in the Palestine Hotel. Uh, the marines were much more hostile to the press than to anyone else.

So it was ... it was a confusing, loud, noisy, scary, hopeful place, all kind of wrapped up together. Um, I would see kids with ski caps on that said "FBI" across it. And they would be giving me the big thumbs-up. And then I would have other young men, who were probably Fedayeen in civilian clothes, giving me very hard stares, and ... and, you know, kind of sizing me up, and always kind of looking at the license plate of the car. We kept away from them.

Among the journalists I interviewed, Trofimov tended to express some of the most negative views of Iraqi popular reception to the invasion. Even he, however, found that most Iraqis were open-minded, if skeptical.

YAROSLAV TROFIMOV: Well, the immediate reason why they were angry, at that point, was [they were] being killed. But the ... all of these other arguments—about betrayal in 1991, and about oil, and ... and general resentment of being occupied—have already surfaced. I remember holding a conversation with one man that day, and he said, "Well, thank you for, you know, getting rid of Saddam, but what we want now is to know when America will leave—for America to leave right away." So people were thinking in quite sophisticated ways already then.

Nir Rosen is a rather left-wing American journalist who has been highly critical of U.S. policy in Iraq and in the Middle East generally. His judgments and predictions, however, are often quite insightful, and his factual assessments generally accurate. He arrived in Baghdad only a few days after the regime fell in April 2003, and he spent the next four years covering the war, traveling widely throughout the country. Like Trofimov, Rosen speaks Arabic. He is ethnically half Persian and can pass for an Arab. Even more than Trofimov, Rosen was the quintessential war correspondent, often taking extreme personal risks. I took him with me when I traveled to Iraq in March and April 2006.

When Rosen first arrived in Iraq just after the war, he found considerable suspicion of the Americans, but he also found much goodwill, optimism, and gratitude among Iraqis, the overwhelming majority of whom were delighted to see Saddam Hussein removed from power.

NIR ROSEN: Those early days, um, there still was not the tension that existed. The … the tension [that] was soon to come had not yet started. The Iraqi people were not the enemy yet, as they are now. There was very little security, in terms of force protection, or protecting the hotels where journalists were staying. The atmosphere was far more relaxed. American soldiers were in far better spirits at the time. They were, of course, the liberating victors, and nobody hated them yet.

In the beginning, there was a certain gratitude. You heard mixed voices. Um, in the end of April, there was [Arba'in al Hussein]. It's the second-most-important Shia holiday, where they commemorate the martyrdom of Hussein, grandson of the Prophet. The most important Shia holiday is the actual commemoration of Ashura, which occurred during the American war. The end of the forty-day mourning period, [Arba'in al Hussein], happened within two weeks, three weeks of the war ending. So you had hundreds of thousands, perhaps millions, of Shias descending upon Karbala, free to exercise their religious practices for the first time in perhaps thirty-five years. In fact, you had pilgrims coming from throughout the Shia world.

And you had different voices. You had people saying they wanted to be the fifty-first state. You had people saying they wanted America out right now. You had people saying the same thing, uh, two opposite things. Nobody was really sure what was going on. Nobody had a definite opinion yet. Um, even the main clerics were careful not to condemn the Americans, not to support them. But given that for years, Muslims have been hearing the same thing, whether Sunni or Shia, uh, that America supports Israel; America is the enemy of Islam; America, of course, bombed Iraq for well over a decade, destroyed their country with sanctions. America is also the country that encourages the Shias to rise up against Saddam in the first Gulf War, and then abandoned them. The Shias remembered this. They were quite skeptical.

And nobody believed the Americans had come to liberate the Iraqi people. But at the same time, you heard people saying, quite often, actually, um, as long as the Americans can set up a government, they can have half of our oil. They can take oil profits to justify what they've done.

There was gratitude at … at the time. You also heard people denying that the Americans had liberated Iraq at all. God liberated Iraq; the Americans had nothing to do with it. This was a very common thing to hear.

Shortly after the war, Deputy Defense Secretary Paul Wolfowitz traveled to Iraq and toured the country with a group of journalists—an act that would be utterly unimaginable and impossible today. One of the journalists who traveled with him was Christopher Hitchens, who had been—and to a large extent still is—a proponent of the war and of American policy in Iraq. Hitchens reported finding much optimism and gratitude among Iraqis.

CHARLES FERGUSON: When was the first time you met Paul Wolfowitz?

CHRISTOPHER HITCHENS: The first time I met Paul Wolfowitz would have been in late 2002 or early 2003. … It was at a time when the atmosphere of Washington was being sucked into the argument about regime change in Iraq.

CHARLES FERGUSON: How did it come to pass, and what came to pass?

CHRISTOPHER HITCHENS: I was invited by a group of, uh, East and West Europeans and some Americans to join a group called The Committee for the Liberation of Iraq, which I agreed to do. It came originally through some friends of Vaclav Havel's in Czechoslovakia and their ... friends in Washington, and, uh, with Kanan Makiya, an Iraqi friend of mine that wrote *The Republic of Fear,* the original anatomy of the nature of the Baathist Regime ... and some others. I became a member of this committee for the removal of Saddam Hussein. ... On the same day, I think, that I attended the inaugural dinner of this committee, I got a call ... an invitation to have a discussion with [Mr. Wolfowitz] personally. ... And I've seen him since, perhaps three or four times. One of them importantly, in that I went with him to Iraq with some other journalists on the trip in the summer of 2003, about three or four months after the liberation of Baghdad.

CHARLES FERGUSON: So were you in Baghdad then?

CHRISTOPHER HITCHENS: Sure. I was in Baghdad twice in 2003. ... I've been to Iraq many times, but I went ... early in the ... in the war, the intervention, the liberation. I came from the southern front from Kuwait City to the town of Safwan, the town where in 1991 Norman Schwarzkopf had signed the deal keeping Saddam Hussein in power. I didn't get much further than that at that stage, um, because I wasn't embedded. I'm not the embedment type, perhaps. Anyway, [I] wasn't—neither wanted to be or was asked to be embedded—but now I should do it.

And then I went on a, uh, press trip with Secretary Wolfowitz, Deputy Secretary Wolfowitz in—it must have been July–August 2003. And landing in Baghdad, going to the marshes, to Najaf, to Karbala, to Basra, uh, to a meeting of the original government council and eventually through, by way of Mosul and Kirkuk, to Sulaimaniyah and Irbil, Kurdistan, leaving on what I think was the first direct flight from, um, Kurdistan to the United States.

CHARLES FERGUSON: What were your conversations like then, and what did you think of the situation at that time?

CHRISTOPHER HITCHENS: Well, I actually took the opportunity traveling with him of talking to other people. I mean, if you travel with someone like this, you will see a lot of Iraq in a short time. So I ... I went to see various friends of mine, Iraqi and Kurdish, who I had promised I would have a reunion with when Iraq had been liberated, and I kept that promise, I think, with all of them: with Kanan Makiya in a hotel in Baghdad with his sister; with an exiled Iraqi diplomat who, who'd come back to work in the foreign ministry; with Ahmed Chalabi in his house in Baghdad; with, um, Barham Salih, now Deputy Prime Minister, one of the leaders of the Patriotic Union of Kurdistan in the north; with Mr. Barzani. So that I wasn't part of the baggage train of Mr. Wolfowitz, but ... but traveling with him, it meant I could move fast. And we went to town meetings in several cities and religious—and we were received with huge welcome, um, in the *masjids* [mosques]. We went out on, as you know, the Iranian border, the area of the wetlands in Iraq that had been burned out and drained and devastated by Saddam Hussein.

I might add that I read almost every day, uh, sarcastic remarks to the effect that it was promised that American forces would be greeted with sweets and flowers in Iraq and that they were not. I can simply tell you, I went ... I can't deny the evidence. I ... I saw that happen day in, day out for hours on end, everywhere I went. I have seen American and British soldiers welcomed with extraordinary enthusiasm, generosity from one end of Iraq to another, in unplanned, unscheduled arrivals and events—things that couldn't have been faked by anybody.

In fact, even most American soldiers found the atmosphere in Iraq, including that in Baghdad, to be quite relaxed and welcoming immediately after the war. It was common for Americans to go out to dinner in Baghdad restaurants unescorted and sometimes even unarmed. Colonel James Torgler arrived in late April 2003 on assignment to the civilian occupying authority.

COLONEL JAMES TORGLER: In May of '03, they still liked us. I rarely carried a sidearm. I was just ... I would throw on my flak jacket because there was still occasional rockets and mortars and whatnot, and I would stroll down;

I would walk down to the convention center. It was a pleasant time. It had not gotten terribly hot yet.

As it would turn out, however, the invasion and the few weeks immediately following it constituted a very short honeymoon. As early as June 2003, only two months after the fall of Baghdad, large portions of the Iraqi population had already begun to turn against the Americans, in some cases violently. In part, this was the result of policy choices made early in the occupation; in part, however, it was the result of decisions made even before the war.

CHAPTER TWO

PREWAR PLANNING

As early as December 2001, Defense Secretary Donald Rumsfeld had ordered the U.S. military to begin planning for a possible war with Iraq. One of the first people assigned to this effort was Army Colonel John Agoglia, who would play a major role in the planning of the war and the eventual occupation of Iraq for the U.S. Army's Central Command (CENTCOM), which was and remains in charge of U.S. military activities in Iraq. Colonel Agoglia is currently the director of the U.S. Army Peace Keeping and Stability Operations Institute (PKSOI) at the U.S. Army War College in Carlisle, Pennsylvania. I interviewed him in 2007.

CHARLES FERGUSON: How did you come to be involved in the Iraq war?

JOHN AGOGLIA: Okay. I was the deputy chief of plans in the J-5, which is the Plans Division ... working for a guy named Mike Fitzgerald. And when 9/11 hit, it was the J-5, working with the J-3 planners, that pulled together the planning team that started doing the initial planning for Afghanistan. Based on that, once we did the Afghanistan piece, we then developed a campaign plan for the global war on terror. And based on that, six of us were pulled on into the initial Iraq planning in late November '01, early December '01.

CHARLES FERGUSON: So in December of '01, half a dozen of you were assigned to start planning for a war in Iraq?

JOHN AGOGLIA: We were to start talking about, conceptually, what would it look like if we were to potentially go to war with Iraq, yes.

Troop Levels

For about a year before the invasion of Iraq, an intense debate took place within the U.S. government about the troop levels required for the invasion and occupation of Iraq. (As discussed later, a related debate took place regarding police forces.) On one side were Donald Rumsfeld and Paul Wolfowitz; on the other side were the senior officers of the U.S. military, particularly the army, as well as three senior officials in the State Department (Colin Powell, Deputy Secretary of State Richard Armitage, and Colin Powell's chief of staff, Lawrence Wilkerson). The eventual result was a compromise, yielding a military force level generally regarded as seriously inadequate for the occupation.

Rumsfeld and Wolfowitz initially felt that an invasion and occupation of Iraq could be conducted with less than 100,000 troops. Rumsfeld was also generally impatient with what he viewed as the outmoded and bureaucratic thinking of the military. He felt that modern wars could be fought and won with radically smaller numbers of highly mobile troops using very high technology. In terms of fighting wars against other armies, he was at least partly correct; the capital intensity, technology level, and information systems of the U.S. military are now vastly superior to those of any other army in the world. Occupations, however, are a different matter, and senior military officials were deeply concerned about the need for more troops in postwar Iraq—to maintain order, to prevent rioting and ethnic conflict, to secure critical infrastructure, to search for WMD (weapons of mass destruction) supplies, and to guard weapons. Their experience in the Balkans, Haiti, and Africa, as well as problems specific to Iraq, led them to believe that far higher troop levels were required.

As Colonel Agoglia helped plan the war and occupation, he observed his superior officers in the army trying to resist pressure from Donald Rumsfeld to use smaller force levels. After a compromise on troop levels was reached with Rumsfeld, Agoglia and his superiors still thought that they would be able to obtain additional forces for the occupation once Baghdad was taken.

CHARLES FERGUSON: Did you consider the question of troop levels required for the invasion and occupation?

JOHN AGOGLIA: [*laughs*] Absolutely. … There was tremendous pressure to reduce the number of troops. It was an issue from the very start. It's something we were always pushing back on—trying to expand and increase the number of folks in the plan. The first plan we put together, it was called the Generated Start. And the plan was briefed conceptually on PowerPoint slides … to the president on or around 19 June of '02. The president said, "Okay. This is a viable plan." But the sec-def [Rumsfeld] and his crowd pushed back on General [Tommy] Franks. Said, "Well, you know, we think it's too long. We think you're taking too much time to build up. We think there's significant strategic risk, and you've got too many troops." …

… I'm trying to think of the specific reason why they pushed back. Troop levels was one of them. The other was the speed with which … the regime would collapse. Because this whole time it's going on, we're getting more and more of a picture of things itself in Iraq, and we're starting to see that, from our vantage point, the regime is really … it's a bubble. I mean, it's going to pop. Its forces aren't arrayed to really defend against an external attack. There's indications that we're talking about an external attack, and they're not repositioning the forces. And the forces are positioned to prevent a coup, is how the forces are really positioned, and to deal with some of the nastiness down in the south and to keep the Kurds in check along the Green Line. I mean, that's the positioning of the forces, but not to prevent any sort of attack from the south. They really weren't positioned. So we started seeing that we thought the regime was going to collapse quicker.

… We were nervous about that as planners. And when we talked to General Franks about that, General Franks' point was, "Guys, don't worry about it. When I get to Baghdad and take Baghdad, which is going to collapse very quickly, no one's going to argue with me asking for additional forces." And in the Generated Start—I mean, in the hybrid plan—again, we had the other forces on call, but the Secretary of Defense had us put in there what he called off ramps, i.e., if we were as successful as we thought we were going to be in the initial push to Baghdad, we had the ability to turn back particularly two divisions, those being the 1st Cavalry Division and the 1st Infantry Division, coming out of Europe; the 1st Cav coming out of Fort Hood, Texas. So there were off-ramps for those units, off-ramps for other parts or portions of what's called the tip-fid [for TPFDL, Time-Phased Force and Deployment List]. But from our point as planners, we went and talked to General Franks. He said, "Look, we know we need those forces. There's no doubt in our mind that we need those." And again, he said, "Don't worry about it," you know. "You'll get those forces. No one's going to argue with the commander when we take Baghdad." So we believed that it wasn't going to be an issue.

In the end, the military did not get those additional forces. In late April, Secretary Rumsfeld canceled the deployment of the 1st Cavalry Division and ordered the 3rd Infantry Brigade to return home.

I spoke to Joseph Nye, a Harvard professor who had been assistant secretary of defense for international security policy in the Bill Clinton administration, about the Bush administration's reasoning.

JOSEPH NYE: They thought that, uh, we were going to be greeted as, uh, liberators; that we [the United States] were wildly popular. I remember one of the top officials, uh, a neocon, telling me, [in] the period before 2000, that we could win in Iraq with fifty thousand troops.

Nye would not tell me who that "top official" was. In any case, several others confirmed that during the planning period, senior Pentagon officials initially wanted a stunningly small invasion force. And while there is some question as to how hard General Tommy Franks and the Joint Chiefs of Staff resisted the Pentagon's wishes, there is no question that the eventual force used was both larger than Rumsfeld had initially wanted and far smaller than the military had initially proposed.

In 2002, when the military began planning for the Iraq war in earnest, Colonel Paul Hughes was director of national security policy at the Institute for National Security Studies, a think tank that serves the secretary of defense and the Joint Chiefs of Staff. In late 2002, he was ordered to conduct a study of requirements for postwar Iraq.

PAUL HUGHES: There was a huge argument between General Franks and … and the secretary [Donald Rumsfeld] early on, as it's been related to me, about the size of the force. CENTCOM wanted to have, eh, I think it was close to four hundred thousand soldiers for the invasion. And the secretary said, "You're crazy. You're not gonna get it." And he had, uh, some army colonel who had written a book about how divisions can fight in this modern era using, you know, high technology, and stuff like that. And uh, the secretary talked to this colonel, and the colonel said to him, "You know, you could take Baghdad with sixty thousand soldiers." And so he was told, "Get down to Tampa. Work with Franks' staff and get a realistic number."

And so it eventually came to … a happy medium, you know, a compromise. Well, in war, you don't compromise like that. If you're going to go do a regime change, achieve unconditional surrender, you need overwhelming force. Because you own it all.

George Packer is the journalist who, more than any other single person, was responsible for my decision to make a film about the occupation of Iraq. After serving as a Peace Corps volunteer in Africa, Packer became a writer and then later a journalist for *The New Yorker* magazine. He has been studying and visiting Iraq since 2003. His book *The Assassins' Gate* is one of the best books to have been written about the Iraq war and occupation.

CHARLES FERGUSON: Now, Franks' initial plan called for five hundred thousand troops?

GEORGE PACKER: Well, it actually came from Franks' predecessor at Central Command, um, General Anthony Zinni, who had a war plan that called for five hundred thousand or so troops, based on what the Gulf War had … had taken. …

Rumsfeld cared more about his vision of transforming the American military and winning postmodern wars with a combination of, uh, high-tech firepower, light troop levels, and local indigenous forces than he did about winning Iraq—and not just winning it in three weeks, but winning it over the long haul. He wanted to be out of Iraq, largely, within three to four months of the fall of Baghdad. And so he forced his commander, Tommy Franks, to whittle down his plan over the course of about a year, from maybe half a million to about a hundred and sixty thousand. And by many accounts, it … it would have gone under a hundred thousand if Franks had not resisted to some extent. But Rumsfeld got his way.

Ironically, in the Bush administration, the State Department contained more people with combat experience than the entire senior levels of the Defense Department and the White House staff combined. Richard Armitage, Colin Powell, and Lawrence Wilkerson were all retired career military officers who had seen extensive combat in Vietnam; all three of them expressed concern about the troop levels planned for Iraq.

None of the senior civilians in the Defense Department and the White House had ever seen combat, and only one—Rumsfeld—had served in the military at all. Vice President Dick Cheney had avoided military service during Vietnam through five draft deferments. Rumsfeld was a navy pilot in the 1950s, but had never seen combat. Neither Paul Wolfowitz nor Condoleezza Rice had ever served in the military. Bush had avoided the Vietnam draft by joining the Texas Air National Guard. Incidentally, he also had no foreign policy experience prior to becoming president.

I asked two of the former-military State Department officials about the debate over troop levels. First, Richard Armitage:

CHARLES FERGUSON: Mr. Armitage, do you believe that the United States used enough troops in the occupation of Iraq?

RICHARD ARMITAGE: Clearly, not in the occupation. We had more than enough troops for the victory and not enough for the occupation to secure the peace.

CHARLES FERGUSON: And have you said so to the administration?

RICHARD ARMITAGE: During the run-up to the war, as Tommy Franks' book points out, Secretary Powell and, to the same extent, myself, we argued for more and more troops. And we made some difference. But, ultimately, it didn't seem that we made enough of a difference.

... Some people ... would say that part of the problem was with people like Mr. Powell and myself who ... who had multiple combat tours, and have seen enough blood for one lifetime, and it makes us too cautious. And perhaps the middle ground is probably just about right. To protect equities. But I myself would tell you unabashedly I'm very slow to the use of force, and very vicious and fatal when we use it—that I want to be—and as heavy-handed, if we get to the point where we use force, as possible. And I'm pretty slow to that point, and not ashamed of it.

Next, Lawrence Wilkerson:

LAWRENCE WILKERSON: Um, probably my estimate of the troops that would have been required, uh, is even more excessive than perhaps some of the other estimates. Um, I would have said a half a million, clearly, a half a million troops, a … a good majority of which would have been military police—infantry, infantrylike—and lots of armor.

Several senior military officers were so disturbed about the troop levels planned for the war that they could not keep silent. The most notable of these was Army Chief of Staff Eric Shinseki. On February 25, 2003, only a month before the war, defying Rumsfeld and Wolfowitz, Shinseki testified before the Senate about troop levels required for an occupation of Iraq. He was questioned by Carl Levin, U.S. senator from Michigan and ranking member on the Senate Armed Services Committee.

CARL LEVIN: General Shinseki, could you give us some idea as to the magnitude of the army's force requirement for an occupation of Iraq following a successful completion of the war?

ERIC SHINSEKI: In specific numbers, I would have to rely on combatant commander's exact requirements. But I think—

CARL LEVIN: How about a range?

ERIC SHINSEKI: I would say that what's been mobilized to this point, something on the order of several hundred thousand soldiers, are probably, you know, a figure that would be required. We're talking about post-hostilities control over a piece of geography that's fairly significant with the kinds of ethnic tensions that could lead to other problems. And so, it takes significant ground force presence to maintain [a] safe and secure environment, to ensure that the people are fed, that water is distributed, all the normal responsibilities that go along with administering a situation like this.

Rumsfeld and Wolfowitz reacted immediately, criticizing Shinseki both privately and publicly. Wolfowitz's response was delivered two days later, on February 27, in testimony before the House Budget Committee.

PAUL WOLFOWITZ: That great Yankee catcher and occasional philosopher Yogi Berra once observed that it's dangerous to make predictions, especially about the future. That piece of wise advice certainly applies to predictions about wars and their aftermath. And I am reluctant to try to predict anything about what the cost of a possible conflict in Iraq would be, or what the possible cost of reconstructing and stabilizing that country afterwards might be. But some of the higher-end predictions that we have been hearing recently, such as the notion that it will take several hundred thousand U.S. troops to provide stability in post-Saddam Iraq, are wildly off the mark.

First, it's hard to conceive that it would take more forces to provide stability in post-Saddam Iraq than it would take to conduct the war itself and to secure the surrender of Saddam's security forces and his army. Hard to imagine. Second, in making predictions, one should at least pay attention to past experience. And in the case of Iraq, we have some recent experience to look to. The northern third of Iraq has been liberated from Saddam Hussein's grasp since Operation Provide Comfort, which we undertook just one month after the cease-fire in the Persian Gulf War in 1991.

It was ironic that Wolfowitz invoked Operation Provide Comfort. The operation had been commanded by General Jay Garner, who had just been appointed to manage the occupation of Iraq. When I asked General Garner later about troop levels, he responded that in Operation Provide Comfort, he had twenty-two thousand troops for an operation covering only 3 percent of Iraq, and he never felt that he had more people than he needed.

On the same day that Wolfowitz criticized Shinseki in his congressional testimony, Rumsfeld responded similarly during a press conference.

REPORTER: Mr. Secretary, there's been a lot of effort to pin the administration down on a cost estimate of combat in Iraq and postwar Iraq, and also the number of troops that would be involved. Tuesday, Army Chief of Staff General Shinseki said it would take several thousand—several hundred thousand—troops on the ground to secure Iraq and provide stability. Is he wrong?

DONALD RUMSFELD: He was asked, I believe, in a Senate hearing what the magnitude of the army's force requirement for occupation of Iraq would be following the war. And he responded something like that; that he said he didn't know. And then they said, well, do you have a range? And so then he said, well, several hundred thousand, roughly what it would take to win the war. Something like that, I think.

The fact of the matter is the answer to the question that was posed to him is not knowable. We have no idea how long the war will last. We don't know to what extent there may or may not be weapons of mass destruction used. We don't know—have any idea whether or not there would be ethnic strife. We don't know exactly how long it would take to find weapons of mass destruction and destroy them—those sites.

There are so many variables that it is not knowable. However, I will say this: What is, I think, reasonably certain is the idea that it would take several hundred thousand U.S. forces I think is far from the mark. The reality is that we already have a number of countries that have offered to participate with their forces in stabilization activities, in the event force has to be used. Second, it's not logical to me that it would take as many forces to win the war, following the conflict, as it would to win the war.

So I can assure you that there are so many variables that it's not possible to come out with a point answer to the question. You'd have to first say: If you assume this, this, or this with respect to the variables, how many other forces are going to be participating besides ours? Until someone decides that there has to be a conflict and that the conflict's over, you're not going to know the answer to that question. So it's simply not knowable. And I will say that I do think that any idea that it's several hundred thousand over any sustained period is simply not the case.

The former military officers running the State Department were also concerned that the war in Iraq was being launched so soon after the occupation of Afghanistan. They, and others who declined to speak on the record, told me that the U.S. military was not large enough to handle both missions simultaneously, and that the war in Iraq drained critical resources from the war in Afghanistan. At the time, the Bush administration deemed the Afghanistan operation such a success that Rumsfeld referred to it as a model for planning the war in Iraq. A number of people I interviewed, however, felt strongly that invading Iraq so soon after invading Afghanistan compromised both efforts seriously. One man I interviewed off the record had been an Army Special Forces officer in Afghanistan in 2002 and later became a senior executive of a private security contractor operating in Iraq. He said that beginning in late 2002, critical resources—people, equipment, money—had been shifted from Afghanistan to Iraq, seriously affecting his unit's operations and, in his view, the entire Afghan effort. Richard Armitage and Lawrence Wilkerson were both concerned about this issue.

RICHARD ARMITAGE: It's well documented that I was not opposed to the war. But I had some real questions about the timing of the war because I felt that we needed some more consolidation in Afghanistan before we moved on to Iraq.

No question, I ... I did feel war was justified. I think that subsequent, successive UN Security Council resolutions had made the point. But I was of the opinion that more was better than, than less. That ... that we should wait a little while. Not that we shouldn't do it—don't make that mistake—that we should wait because I thought Afghanistan needed to be consolidated. And because I was on the diplomatic end of things, quote unquote, I thought that we might usefully use the time to get a slightly larger coalition of the willing than we ultimately got. That we had thirty-odd countries.

LAWRENCE WILKERSON: I do have my views. And my views as a military man—as a strategist, and as a military man—my views are that it was badly timed. And it was badly timed because of several factors. First and foremost, we weren't finished in Afghanistan. Second, we were in Afghanistan for the long haul, and we had not done anything in America to prepare America for the long haul. We had done nothing. Nothing.

Planning for Postwar

Rumsfeld and Wolfowitz felt that it would be both possible and desirable to disengage quickly from Iraq after conquering it. In fact, they believed that most American troops could and should be withdrawn by the fall of 2003. In part, this derived from their ideological opposition to "nation-building" of the sort they felt was mistakenly occurring in the Balkans and elsewhere. In part, this view derived from their belief that the Americans would be greeted as liberators in Iraq; that postwar Iraq would be peaceful and easily governed; and that Iraqi exiles sympathetic to the United

States would prove popular in Iraq. In forming these views, the administration relied heavily on these very exiles, particularly Ahmed Chalabi, the president of the Iraqi National Congress. The exiles' predictions dovetailed perfectly with Rumsfeld's preferences for fewer troops and rapid disengagement.

GEORGE PACKER: And so the plan was, essentially, we'll stay for three or four months. We will install a government made up of exiles, and led by Ahmed Chalabi. And then, in August or September of 2003, we will begin a drastic reduction of troops. We'll go down to thirty thousand. That was the plan. That was Rumsfeld's plan as … as executed by Wolfowitz and [Undersecretary of Defense for Policy Douglas] Feith.

And um, it was a ludicrous plan. It was a plan that didn't begin to grapple with how difficult and dangerous and complex these postwar situations are. We learned that in the nineties; we learned it in Somalia, in Bosnia, in Kosovo; we learned it in Afghanistan, under this administration. But Donald Rumsfeld and the officials under him decided that they were not going to be deterred by history, that that was sort of the history of … of failure. That was failure thinking. They were gonna do it a different way. And it was gonna go the way they said it was gonna go. They weren't going to be, um, saddled with the failures of others. They had found a new way to do it: without nation-building; without deep, long commitments; without quagmires. And I think they convinced themselves that they were right, it would go that way.

Several former U.S. officials, including Colonel Paul Hughes, confirmed that the administration planned to remove most troops by August or September 2003.

PAUL HUGHES: They wanted to get rid of Saddam, but they wanted to get the American forces out of there as quickly as possible. Larry Di Rita [a special assistant, later spokesman, for Donald Rumsfeld] addressed us in one forum, and said, by the end of August of 2003, we will have all but twenty-five to thirty thousand troops out of Iraq.

CHARLES FERGUSON: You heard him say that?

PAUL HUGHES: I heard him say that, in a roomful of people. And I turned to my colleagues, and I said, "This guy doesn't know what he's talking about. It's physically impossible. Not only is it physically impossible, but operationally, it doesn't make sense."

But it was not just Rumsfeld who neglected postwar planning. Both observers and participants felt that the U.S. military never took postwar planning for Iraq seriously enough, both because such planning had lower status in the military, and because the administration discouraged it.

LAWRENCE WILKERSON: I have come to believe that ... the military was totally unprepared for what they would have called—did call—Phase IV. The military was prepared, and did expertly the first phases, which led to the ... the fall of the regime in Baghdad. They were utterly unprepared for the aftermath. And I fault—now, having done, uh, a lot of research—I fault two dimensions of our leadership for that. And this is interesting, because it turns out my study of the Vietnam conflict proves pretty much the same thing. Um, H. R. McMaster's book *Dereliction of Duty* substantiates my views on this, that the military—the uniformed military—and the civilians were roughly equally complicit in this. It wasn't just the civilians or just the military.

The military had made a decision—uh, by that, I mean General Tommy Franks and his staff—had made a decision that they were not going to do Phase IV any differently than what Douglas Feith and others perceived Phase IV to be, i.e., a cakewalk: um, Iraqis in the street with flowers; Ahmed Chalabi installed as their leader; and, uh, a brief time when everything would be stood up, and Chalabi would be in charge, and then we're gone. And when I say "brief time," I think they were contemplating ninety to a hundred and twenty days, which in retrospect borders on lunacy. But I do think that's what they were thinking.

So General Franks' concern was to get his military in, and get his military out. And not get them stuck with any kind of occupation duties, or nation-building duties, or whatever. I also think that was Secretary Rumsfeld's view. I think Secretary Rumsfeld wanted 'em in, and out.

James Fallows, national correspondent for *The Atlantic Monthly,* has covered military affairs for over twenty years. He began covering preparations for the Iraq war in 2002.

JAMES FALLOWS: The main cultural force inside the military is what people have sometimes described as a B-team phenomenon, and sometimes as the Phase IV phenomenon. In the lingo of the modern Pentagon, there are four phases of war, and Phase III is the fun part; that's when you're actually blowing things up, and killing people, and dropping bombs, and doing the … uh, what they call the kinetic activity. Phase IV is after that. It's the occupation, it's the peacekeeping, it's the peacemaking. It's, uh, trying to develop [a] society, the nation-building. And while in theory everybody recognizes that's important, at least until recently, and certainly before the Iraq war, it was … it was not a real all-star's job. If you were looking for that next star, if you're going to be one of the Joint Chiefs of Staff, or whatever, you didn't want to be a Phase IV guy. And so the oomph was all on the people planning the combat, and not afterwards. That was one cultural force inside the military.

For the administration as a whole, there were political issues, too. I think, partly, there was an almost partisan sense of contempt for the very idea of the slow, messy work of nation-building. Even to mention this to people like Donald Rumsfeld or Dick Cheney seemed to mean sinking into the can't-do atmosphere of the Clinton years, where things were messy, and they took a long time to do, and you had to deal with the allies. And so it wasn't in keeping with the sort of … um, the confidence that the administration wanted to convey about what the administration, and America, could do on its own.

Uh, another reason inside the administration is that almost by definition, these postwar plans involved a lot of complicating alliances. A lot of the expertise in peacekeeping is possessed by the Europeans, you know, people who were at odds with some of the war effort in general, involved some of the nongovernmental organizations, involved the United Nations. And all these different groups who could be most helpful after the war were sort of most unenthusiastic before the war. So there was also that, that built-in [tension].

Finally there was, I think, a political sense of the administration that it didn't even need to prepare for these things, because a lot of the advisers that it was paying the most attention to—and probably the best known of these is Mr. Chalabi, but others, too—were saying, don't worry. Once you pull the lid off here, once you remove the tyrant, you're going to have a vibrant, uh, well-educated, successful society, and you can sort of step back, and let good things happen. I think people genuinely, in the administration, genuinely believed that.

MARC GARLASCO: The postwar planning, as far as I'm concerned, just never happened. Uh, the things that we concerned ourselves with were "Doc X": document exploitation. You know, we would sit down in meetings and say, "Okay, when the war is over, we're gonna collect thousands upon thousands of documents from various Iraqi intelligence services, or from their WMD programs. And so we're gonna need to have just huge factories of people, and photocopy machines, and scanners, and translators, to go through all of that stuff, and to catalog it, and to see where was the WMD; where did it move, where did they get it." And we were very concerned with document exploitation. But nation-building, or anything like that, security, you know, that was the army's job on the ground. Uh, and they'll figure it out afterwards. ...

You know, we really thought it was Paris in the Second World War, where people are gonna be throwing flowers, and welcoming the U.S. Or at least that's what the, uh, policymakers thought. And that kind of ... you know, came down to us; it ... it rolled down the Hill, and percolated to our level. Where there really was no planning, until, gosh, it must have been around [the] second week of the war, when, uh, the general came in who was the J-2, the general in charge of intelligence. And he said, "Okay, there's gonna be a group of you people now that we're gonna take off the actual war fighting. And you're gonna be working now on planning the postwar. And you know, you don't need everybody now. And [you can] pull people out of some of the cells for areas like air defense or Air Force analysts, where the Iraqi planes aren't flying, so those people really aren't doing anything substantive."

And you know, we kind of spoke with ourselves: They are doing this now? We're planning the postwar now? And I thought ... we had always thought there was somebody somewhere—very smart—thinking this stuff up, whether it was over at the Department of State or somewhere else in the building.

The U.S. Army also made major internal errors in staffing the postwar planning effort. As the war approached, CENTCOM war planners realized that they did not have sufficient personnel for effective postwar planning. They were offered the assistance of an additional unit of experienced planners who had worked together before. But at the last minute, the CENTCOM war planners were given an inexperienced group instead, a change that would have serious consequences. While the change in staffing may have been influenced by political signals from above, it was not directly dictated politically; it was made by an army general. Colonel John Agoglia was deputy chief planner for CENTCOM at the time.

JOHN AGOGLIA: So when we were offered the opportunity for another headquarters coming in and act as a planning staff for postconflict, we're like, you know, "That would be very helpful." So we told General Franks, "Yeah, we'd love to have that." I mean, what he was offered by General Casey was the potential to get what's called a standing joint—the JFCOM, standing joint task force headquarters—which is a group of fifty-eight folks who are battle rostered, who have worked together, and who are capable of coming on as a core of a planning headquarters and start helping that headquarters become a joint headquarters, or could start taking on a planning mission, and then you can build a headquarters around that core. So we were pretty excited. We thought, you know, standing joint task force headquarters: Here's a group of folks, they had just finished doing the Millennium Challenge exercise; they had done some exercises already. So that's what we thought we were getting, and that's what General Franks thought he was getting.

In fact, what we got was fifty-eight folks who had never worked together pulled from across the services, and some shareware from the JFCOM folks, saying, "Hey, by using the shareware with these fifty-eight guys and here's the SOP [standard operating procedure] and the standing joint task force, they can do the planning." And it just made no sense.

We were kind of shocked because we thought we were going to get a standing headquarters that is called a standing joint task force that had worked together as a team, that had its processes in place, understood its processes, understood who could do what, had a hierarchy in place, and had all that laid on out, and were used to operating together as a team.

And in fact, what we got were fifty-eight brand-new guys, another ad hoc organization. And they just couldn't … we just couldn't bring them up to speed. That was just an additional drain on us instead of a help, trying to get them up to speed. And after about four weeks, we just gave up. We just said, "We're just going nowhere." …

CHARLES FERGUSON: Why did that happen? Why didn't you get what you thought you were going to get?

JOHN AGOGLIA: [*laughs*] I heard after the war … General Monte Meigs apparently approached Admiral Giambastiani and asked him, "Why didn't you provide the standing joint task force headquarters?" And he said, "I couldn't give up my ace in the hole in case another contingency came up—something more important came up—so I figured we could use the concept and export the concept to get fifty-eight people, and that would be good enough. But I couldn't give them my actual standing joint task force, because then I'd have no contingency in case something else came up." Now what the hell he was thinking—something else was going to come up—I have no idea. But that was his answer to General Meigs as relayed by General Meigs, so you're getting it secondhand from me. You could probably go to the source and talk to General Meigs and ask him. I don't think he'd hesitate to answer that.

CHARLES FERGUSON: To the best of your knowledge, though, this was not a political thing. It did not come from the White House or from Rumsfeld or anybody like that. It was an internal military thing?

JOHN AGOGLIA: It was internal military, yeah. I mean, again, you know, the myth that the military … we have no warts. We had quite a few, unfortunately. So that was one of them. That was an extremely short-sighted decision, and it had some real impact. And the impact was, hey, here we are thinking that we're going to have this capability to put together a solid post-conflict plan because we know we have the guts; we've got a framework that makes sense; we've got the right questions identified. We haven't gotten the answers; we've got to push harder to get those answers. We're still working the other finalization of the combat portion of the plan; we're still working the additional force flow; we've got a lot of things that we're working.

This would have been a great boon to get those guys on in because they could have continued asking with precision the questions that we probably weren't asking precisely enough and weren't able to follow up on. They could have. But in fact what happened is we got fifty-eight folks, and they were a bigger drain on the system than a help.

Agoglia and others also saw evidence that the military's inadequate planning for Phase IV was in part the result of the Pentagon's rivalry with—and exclusion of— the State Department during the planning process. In late 2007, I interviewed a very senior former military officer who confirmed the substance of Agoglia's comments here.

JOHN AGOGLIA: When we did the first briefing of the plan in June, we went … General Franks went to the sec-def and the president [and] said, "Look, this is the Generated Start plan. Here's what we have." We asked, "Where's the State Department planners? Can we meet with them?" There was silence from the joint staff; silence from OSD [Office of the Secretary of Defense]. We are told to do the second plan, which we called the Running Start plan. We did that in July. We finished it in July. We said, "Okay, got it. Here's some things we want to get—questions, specific policy questions, since we're not seeing the planners. The policy questions we'd like to get answers to are, What are we going to do in terms of de-Baathification? What's our policy guidance? So we're asking this question in June, July of '02: What's going to be the policy guidance for de-Baathification? What's going to be the policy guidance for the currency? Are we going to change the currency out? Is someone thinking about that? Are we going to start planning on doing that now? What's it going to look like? UN oil embargo: What's the policy guidance on how you're going to lift the UN oil embargo? Because once we take over that country, we are in fact occupiers and according to the laws of land warfare and the Geneva Convention, we have responsibility to govern that land. And we also are responsible for any international treaties that are levied against that government unless we repeal them. The UN has an oil embargo; what's our policy for repealing that? How are we going to take that on? What were some other key issues? Those are probably the three big ones: de-Baathification, currency, and oil, okay?

And the oil one was based on the fact that you have a vibrant oil economy and the potential to sell that oil and use that to help pay for part of the rebuilding of postwar Iraq, okay? Now there were folks in Wolfowitz's office [who] said it could pay for the whole thing. We're not economists. We didn't know. But we knew that before you could start selling it, you had to get this oil piece lifted.

So those are three policy questions. Probably some others, but those are the three big ones that pop out of my head. We don't get any answers on those, you know? So we're getting kind of frustrated because we want to sit down and start planning the other piece, the humanitarian disaster. What if there's a humanitarian disaster? How are we going to plan that? What's going to happen? Who are we going to work with to get that taken care of?

CHARLES FERGUSON: Do you have a sense of why there was no answer to these policy questions?

JOHN AGOGLIA: No. That was the great mystery, you know: Why are we not getting any answers, you know? And it's almost like, "Hey, don't worry about it. We're taking care of that. You guys still don't have your act together for the military plan yet, so we're not ready to share it." That's kind of what we thought. We just didn't know.

The most important source of unrealistic optimism about postwar Iraq was Ahmed Chalabi, the Iraqi exile who exerted enormous influence upon the White House and Pentagon.

Ahmed Chalabi is a remarkable combination of intellectual, patriot, and con man. Born into a wealthy Iraqi Shiite family that left Iraq when he was a child, Chalabi was raised in the United Kingdom and the United States. After obtaining his B.S. in mathematics from the Massachusetts Institute of Technology (MIT) and his Ph.D. in mathematics from the University of Chicago, he joined the faculty of the American University in Beirut. In 1977, he founded the Petra Bank in Jordan, which, like many of Chalabi's activities, was both innovative and fraudulent. It eventually failed, causing the government of Jordan to spend $300 million to compensate depositors. An Arthur Andersen audit found that 40 percent of the bank's loans were nonperforming and that 14 percent of the bank's loans had been made to Chalabi's family and friends. Chalabi's brother controlled two financial institutions that failed at the same time, and for the same reasons. Chalabi fled, was convicted in absentia of bank fraud, and returned to London, where he founded the Iraqi National Congress (INC). For several years, the State Department and Central Intelligence Agency (CIA) funded him, but they later dropped him when they found his information unreliable and his financial practices dubious. In 2002, however, Chalabi and the INC found an even better patron in Donald Rumsfeld's Defense Department, which paid the INC over $300,000 per month, believed the often fraudulent intelligence Chalabi provided, and trained a seven-hundred-man private militia for him, which was eventually flown to Iraq after the conquest of Baghdad. At President Bush's January 2003 State of the Union address, Chalabi was seated directly behind Laura Bush. He was already positioned as Iraq's future leader. Many who had actually studied or dealt with Chalabi and the INC, however, had a jaundiced view of him. In Iraq, I met several former members of the anti-Saddam Iraqi resistance who said that in their experience, he was thoroughly dishonest.

Ahmed Chalabi, former leader of the Iraqi National Congress, 2003.

MARC GARLASCO: Yeah, you know, the INC ... uh, when I look back on all the sources that I ever worked, on all the Iraqis—the defectors or the INC folks that came out—you know, it's very clear to me that you can look at the two very separately. You have Iraqi sources who provide really clear, important information, that assists the United States. And then the INC, which is ... you know, at best, I think, uh, they were liars. And at worst, they were provocateurs.

And it became clear, because at one point, you know, things really started to change, where the reporting would come out. And you're calling your friends at CIA, or at NSA [National Security Agency], or wherever. And you pick up the phone and say, "Hey, listen: I just spoke to this guy, you know, in country X, and we're writing the report up. You're gonna see it come out. [It] says some really interesting things. But he's INC." And you always kind of categorize things like that. If it's an INC source, it was always looked at very, very skeptically by the analysts. But that wasn't the case with the policymakers.

While it was known that the Bush administration supported Chalabi, the administration was extraordinarily secretive with its plans for postwar Iraq. Few outsiders were able to discern what, if any, concrete plans existed.

JAMES FALLOWS: It's clear, several years afterwards, that the people I was speaking with before the war, in the summer and fall of 2002, were under a number of constraints when it came to talking about—talking publicly about—what was going to happen after the war. One of those constraints was, it was [in] the administration's clear interest to suppress this talk, both publicly and, to a degree, internally, because the more you talked about all the things you'd have to do, once you were in control of Baghdad and once Saddam Hussein was gone, ... not only did you sort of diminish the case for a quick and easy war with these complications, but also you diminished the idea that you could do it fast, you could do it soon. Because a lot of the argument by the prewar planners was, Take some time to do this right. Get the spare parts there; get the peacekeepers there; see if you can get some Arabic-speaking allies. That the more carefully you prepared, the longer it was likely to take.

And so there was a kind of suppression. And most of the ... again, in retrospect, the military officials I was speaking to at this time had their attention, I guess understandably, diverted to what they call the kinetic stage of the engagement, that is, the actual bombing, the actual tanks rolling, the actual, uh, rounding up of bad guys. And there was a sort of diminution of … of thinking carefully about postwar activity. So, it was easy for me, as a reporter, to find people who had ideas before the war. It was less easy to think that they were really connected to the machinery of how policies were being made.

CHARLES FERGUSON: Was it visible to you that these things were not being prepared for adequately? Or could you not tell?

JAMES FALLOWS: I couldn't really tell. Uh, the Bush administration has been remarkably different, and … and remarkably more successful than past administrations by one measure, which is maintaining secrecy. Usually, administrations simply can't keep many things secret. And that's become less so for this administration as time has gone on. But there certainly was a lot of operational secrecy. So it was easy to find public source discussion, unclassified discussion, of what should happen. It was much harder for me, at that time, to tell how much of this was being, uh, woven into the action plan.

The Prewar Analyses of Postwar Iraq

To a remarkable extent, the difficulties encountered by the United States in postwar Iraq not only were predictable, but were also, in fact, predicted. Most of the issues encountered by the U.S. occupation were examined in detail by a series of studies, some public, others classified, conducted both within the government and by various academic, journalistic, and policy organizations. These analyses included earlier military contingency plans for the invasion of Iraq; the Future of Iraq Project, conducted by the State Department in 2002 in cooperation with several hundred experts and Iraqi exiles; a detailed study of postwar Iraq occupation issues conducted by the Army War College; a heavily researched article written by James Fallows and published in *The Atlantic* in late 2002; an extremely prescient article written by Anthony Cordesman of the Center for Strategic and International Studies and titled "Planning for Peace as a Self-Inflicted Wound"; various analyses performed by portions of the federal government, including the CIA, the National Intelligence Council, and the Departments of Justice and State; and other independent analyses conducted by academics and think-tank experts. Many are discussed and quoted from on the following pages.

To an astonishing extent, these analyses agreed both on what the principal challenges of occupied Iraq would be and on how to handle them. The studies focused on the need to maintain order and security in the face of looting, crime, and civil unrest; the need to restore essential services such as electricity, water supplies, and food distribution; the need to deal carefully and sensitively with the Iraqi government and military; the risks of organized crime, insurgency, and terrorism; and the need for adequate numbers of troops, police, interpreters, and civil affairs personnel.

Remarkably, however, none of these analyses were requested by the administration, and several were suppressed or dismissed by it. In fact, the administration never asked the intelligence community for any analysis of postwar Iraq, either before the war or for more than a year after it. Paul Pillar was the national intelligence officer for the Near East and South Asia between 2000 and 2005. When appointed, he had spent over twenty years working in the CIA on Iraq and on counterterrorism issues.

PAUL PILLAR: Uh, it was clear, certainly from the advent of the current Bush administration, beginning in January of 2001, that Iraq was a major concern, a major focus of attention. We were not asked—or I was not asked by the administration—to produce particular intelligence assessments on the subject, although, uh, clearly there were many indications that it was, uh, a focus of concern.

CHARLES FERGUSON: And so, give us an example of something that was asked of you or said that led you to believe, by mid-2002, that the administration had already decided upon war.

PAUL PILLAR: Well again, it wasn't so much questions asked of me, because the administration never asked for any, uh, estimate or community assessment on Iraq before we went to war.

CHARLES FERGUSON: Okay. So what, if anything, did the administration ask you to do?

PAUL PILLAR: The administration didn't ask me to do anything. By the administration, I mean policymakers. Um, at a different level, the U.S. military, as it was trying to prepare itself for this operation, uh, had a lot of dialogue, especially, not with me personally, but with my colleagues who were more involved with military forms of analysis, to try to prepare them-selves for what became Operation Iraqi Freedom. That's really one of the most salient aspects of this part of the history, I think. ... Prior to this ex-tremely important decision—initiating an offensive war, really, the first time this country has done that in over a century—um, not asking the in-telligence community to provide any kind of community assessment, a strategic-level look at any of several different issues. There was the whole weapons-of-mass-destruction issue, of course, which eventually became the subject of a national intelligence estimate asked for by Congress. Um, but none of the other things that presumably would have been very important ingredients into such a decision—like what would be the aftermath in Iraq, what sort of challenges would we have to deal with once we went in and overthrew Saddam Hussein—nothing was asked about that.

Uh, we tried to be as useful as we could by initiating our own projects. And we produced some community assessments on exactly those sorts of issues: what sort of challenges would we face in Iraq after the old regime was gone, what sort of regional repercussions there would be once there was a change of regime in Iraq. But again, these were never asked for by ... by Bush administration policymakers.

CHARLES FERGUSON: They were initiated by you.

PAUL PILLAR: Yes.

CHARLES FERGUSON: And, by you personally.

PAUL PILLAR: Uh, in the case of the last couple of products I mentioned, by me personally, yes.

CHARLES FERGUSON: And after you produced these documents, these as-sessments, what did you do with them?

PAUL PILLAR: Uh, they were given a broad dissemination, to include all of the senior policymakers, as well as ones not so senior. And in at least some cases, uh, my superiors—those who were participating in the senior-level meetings at the White House—drew attention to the products and ... and tried to distribute them and call attention to them.

CHARLES FERGUSON: And what happened?

PAUL PILLAR: Well, I have very little [to] report with regard to any sort of reaction or response. Um, I got one response to one of these assessments that was basically, "I don't like it. You guys aren't seeing the possibilities here." ...

CHARLES FERGUSON: Where did that come from?

PAUL PILLAR: I can't tell you.

At various times since the first Gulf War, the military had constructed plans or had engaged in war-gaming exercises for another war with Iraq. The most comprehensive of these earlier plans was constructed at the request of General Anthony Zinni, the former head of CENTCOM. Called Desert Crossing, the plan did address various potential problems in a postwar Iraq scenario. According to George Packer, however, it was disregarded by the Bush administration.

GEORGE PACKER: Interestingly, Zinni also had a postwar plan—which very few people know about—called Desert Crossing, which he began to draft after the December '98 bombings of Iraq. That was ... uh, that followed the expulsion of the inspectors by Saddam, the weapons inspectors. That bombing did more damage to both WMD infrastructure, and to the regime itself, than anyone here knew. And Arab leaders privately told Zinni that the regime was hollow and shaky, and that you might end up with an implosion on your hands. Uh, you did more damage than you know.

And Zinni, being an insightful commander, realized that if that happened, it would fall upon the U.S. military to try to fill the vacuum of an imploded Iraqi regime, in case of a ... of a war, of a second war with Iraq. And so he began to work on a postwar plan. And he got the State Department to cooperate, although they were somewhat resistant.

And there's an eternal problem here, in ... in the military and civilian wings of our government collaborating on these complex reconstructions. It's been the case, all through our modern history, and Iraq is, you know, maybe one of the most [poignant] examples.

But anyway, Zinni drafted Desert Crossing. It included plans for securing the borders and how to deal with the Iraqi Army, and the Baath Party, and even the role of women, and election. I mean, it was a comprehensive postwar plan.

So you might ask, What happened to Desert Crossing? Why didn't Desert Crossing simply get transferred to Iraq in 2003? Well, a few weeks before the war in 2003 began, Zinni, who was beginning to sense that the administration was not ready for what … what it was going to find, contacted Central Command. He was retired by that time. But he contacted his old command and said, "You know, you guys might want to, uh, take a look at Desert Crossing. Take it off the shelf and dust it off." And the deputy commander at CENTCOM said, "What's Desert Crossing?" No one there knew about it, because Rumsfeld, several years earlier, had … had said, "This is too negative in its assumptions. Uh, we don't need it." It was seen as part of the failures of the Clinton administration.

Another retired military officer, Colonel Sam Gardiner, also tried to warn the administration of the difficulties it might face after an invasion of Iraq. Gardiner was a retired army colonel whose last active-duty specialty was war games centered on Iraq. In retirement, he was also a consultant to the Joint Chiefs of Staff. When war approached, he took it upon himself to understand what the impact of war on Iraq's infrastructure and public health would be, and to speak to administration officials about these issues.

CHARLES FERGUSON: Tell us how you got interested, concerned, about what would happen during and after the second Gulf war.

SAM GARDINER: Well, it started when I received, from a friend in Sweden, an analysis of what the bombing had done in Belgrade. Uh, the Swedes did a study of how bombing affected the Belgrade electrical system, and the interesting thing was that it showed how a little bit of damage to the electrical system had a big damage to the humanitarian system, in other words, to the things that kept people alive in the city. So I was sort of fascinated by that and wondered if anybody had been doing that kind of thing in preparation for the second Gulf war.

CHARLES FERGUSON: And tell us what you did next, and what happened.

SAM GARDINER: Well, I took that analysis, and, uh, sort of began expanding it, because what you sort of do, it's sort of like a circle: uh, and that is, if you have problems with the electrical system, what happens to the water system; what happens to the medical system; what happens to the health-care system. There's sort of ... there's a circle of events that goes out.

So I did what I call the Net Assessment, which was, on the Net, on the Internet, [and] began looking into the situation in Iraq and how problems with the electrical system would affect the humanitarian situation in the country. So it was a series of moving out from electrical to sort of trying to understand what an attack would do on essentially the people of Iraq.

CHARLES FERGUSON: So tell us what you found.

SAM GARDINER: Well, what ... what became clear—and it was interesting; the evidence was so easily available—what became clear was that we were going to disrupt the humanitarian situation, the human condition, in Iraq, by even a minimum attack, uh, that we were gonna see a whole series of problems unfolding. And what also became clear—and you didn't have to know what was going on inside the offices of government to know that we weren't prepared to do that, uh, that we weren't prepared to deal with the consequences that anybody could have uncovered, had they done analysis on the Net.

CHARLES FERGUSON: What makes you say that?

SAM GARDINER: Well, I put together a presentation which said, you know, here's how fragile the system is; here's what an attack will do. Uh, and then I had some friends who took me around Washington to some relatively important people, and I briefed that. And in almost all cases, uh, it was clear from the way they responded, that the United States had not prepared to do what needed to be done to protect the ... the system that ... the people of Iraq.

CHARLES FERGUSON: Give us some examples of the evidence that you found about what the impact of an attack would be.

SAM GARDINER: Well, the presentation I put together had about sixty slides in it. It was a PowerPoint presentation. So it's kind of complex, but in ways, it's kind of simple. One could find out, for example, that the water plants in Iraq, most of the water plants, which were small, did not have electrical arresters. Now, what that meant was that if there were a power surge, that the electrical system of the water plants would be shorted out. So that if we attacked the electrical system, or if the people who are running the electrical system weren't there, then you'd have this power surge, and the … the fresh-water plants would be burnt out, and then you'd have to go through a major process of fixing that … and they had no backup generators. So you could say, with a fair degree of confidence, uh, that what we're going to find after we attack Baghdad is [that] throughout the country, there's gonna be a water system that is unable to meet the needs of the people of Iraq, because they didn't have some of the basic things that one would expect to find in a water system.

CHARLES FERGUSON: Okay. And what happened when you started telling people about this?

SAM GARDINER: Well, the people that I told that were [in] sort of different categories. Uh, the first thing I did was I took the presentation to the Rand Corporation in … I have a lot of friends at Rand. And these are a group of people who do, actually, the kind of analysis that I had done. Uh, I gave a presentation there. And actually, they were very supportive and found it interesting and suggested that it was important that people in the government see it. So sort of based upon that, I was encouraged that there might be something valuable that I could go around town and show with the briefing. So that was sort of the first step.

Um, I, through the process of contacts, ended up setting up a presentation within the Department of Defense. I briefed the director of plans for the Joint Chiefs of Staff, the general in charge of planning. I ended up briefing the U.S. Agency for International Development, the people who were preparing for the recovery plans for Iraq. Um, I ended up briefing Zalmay Khalilzad, now the ambassador to Iraq, who at that time was on the National Security Council and advising on preparations for the war. So I was … able to get in to see people. And, in a fairly nonrushed environment, was able to go through this large presentation to show the interconnectivity of the systems in Iraq and what was likely to happen after the attack.

CHARLES FERGUSON: And what did they say?

SAM GARDINER: Well, the answer was sort of varied in different things. Uh, [I] actually heard from one of them probably the thing that was most discouraging. Um, and I think I remember the exact sentence now: "Oh, this is kinda hard. You know, the president has already spent an hour on the postwar stuff. ... " "We can't raise anything again," was the implication of that statement; he'd already talked about it. That was frightening.

While it is quite unlikely that President Bush literally spent only one hour on postwar occupation planning, it does appear that he spent very little time on it, and that Gardiner's warnings had little or no effect.

CHARLES FERGUSON: How much difference do you think it would have or could have made, if people had taken the specific things that you've pointed out seriously?

SAM GARDINER: Well, the best way to say this is, if you look at the military history of the United States—the history of American military planning—one of the primary things that stands out is that we have done things well prepared. Yeah, probably the thing that most people know about is the invasion, in Europe in ... in 1944, the Overlord. We had prepared that for years, so that we had everything thought through. This was completely different. We were hurrying to go to it.

I ... I did get a call from somebody who was working on the water systems in the U.S. Agency for International Development and [who] said, "Well, what do we need to do, uh, to make sure that the ... your prediction about the water system going down doesn't happen?" And I was actually able to give them a list of things that ought to be on a ship, awaiting the invasion because you could identify that from the Web. You need to have generators of this quality; you need to have resistors of this quality; uh, you need to be able to replace some of the things in the small water plants. I mean, we could have had that stuff on a ship, waiting. We didn't do any of that until after the invasion had taken place, and we were in Baghdad. Um, there was no reason to have waited to do that, except being in a hurry to fight the war.

CHARLES FERGUSON: How long would it have taken to get prepared, do you think?

SAM GARDINER: Probably six to nine months to get prepared to do that. We would have had to go to the Congress. ... You wouldn't necessarily have had to do [everything to] get all prepared. But you could have been incrementally prepared. You know, every day longer that you prepared to do, uh, what the military now calls stability operations, which is the postwar stuff, we'd have been more ready to do that. Uh, you could have had generators available. And, well, that was an easy step to do. Then you could have had replacement parts for the water system. That was fairly easy to do. We knew what the electrical system was like. We could have had preparations to repair the Iraqi power generation capabilities.

In February 2003, the Strategic Studies Institute of the Army War College produced an extraordinarily detailed and prescient report titled "Reconstructing Iraq: Insights, Challenges, and Missions for Military Forces in a Post-Conflict Scenario." The document was circulated within the government and was also made available to the public.*

The report gave extremely explicit warnings concerning the risk of looting and disorder; the deterioration of Iraq's infrastructure; its ethnic, tribal, and religious tensions; the need to produce tangible benefits to the population; and the risk of insurgency, specifically including terrorism and suicide bombings. The only respect in which the report deviated from the consensus of the prewar analyses was its estimate of required U.S. troop levels—only 100,000. This estimate, however, was accompanied by a generally pessimistic view of the occupation's prospects, in light of the aforementioned warnings. Nor did the report's troop-level estimates foresee the disbanding of Iraq's army, special and paramilitary forces, and intelligence services.

Here is the entire one-page summary of the report:

*At the time of printing, "Reconstructing Iraq: Insights, Challenges, and Missions for Military Forces in a Post-Conflict Scenario" was available at www.strategicstudiesinstitute.army.mil/pdffiles/PUB182.pdf.

CONCLUSIONS

To be successful, an occupation such as that contemplated after any hostilities in Iraq requires much detailed interagency planning, many forces, multiyear military commitment, and a national commitment to nation-building.

Recent American experiences with post-conflict operations have generally featured poor planning, problems with relevant military force structure, and difficulties with a handover from military to civilian responsibility.

To conduct their share of the essential tasks that must be accomplished to reconstruct an Iraqi state, military forces will be severely taxed in military police, civil affairs, engineer, and transportation units, in addition to possible severe security difficulties.

The administration of an Iraqi occupation will be complicated by deep religious, ethnic, and tribal differences which dominate Iraqi society.

U.S. forces may have to manage and adjudicate conflicts among Iraqis that they can barely comprehend.

An exit strategy will require the establishment of political stability, which will be difficult to achieve given Iraq's fragmented population, weak political institutions, and propensity for rule by violence.

The report then surveys Iraq's history and its ethnic, religious, and tribal structures. Midway through the report is a discussion of how to handle the issue of the Iraqi military:

A FORCE FOR UNITY: DEALING WITH THE IRAQI MILITARY

While a struggle for power between civilian and military elites would contribute to Iraqi fragmentation, the military can also serve as a unifying force under certain conditions. ... To tear apart the army in the war's aftermath could lead to the destruction of one of the only forces for unity within the society. Breaking up large elements of the army also raises the possibility that demobilized soldiers could affiliate with ethnic or tribal militias.

... It is conceivable that the Iraqi Army would be willing to work with U.S. or coalition forces in a postwar environment under the proper conditions. U.S. occupation policy may therefore be well-served by attentiveness to the potential willingness and capabilities of the Iraqi military in rebuilding the country.

The next section of the report, "The Potential for Terrorism Against U.S. Occupation Forces," discusses various insurgency and terrorism risks, including suicide bombing:

Major postwar improvements in the quality of daily life of the population may soften such concerns, but they are unlikely to eliminate them.

Although Iraq is one of the most repressive countries in the world, it is not a disarmed society. Unlike a variety of other dictatorships, many Iraqi citizens have access to firearms. ... These weapons can become a problem following the war. ...

Following Saddam's defeat, the United States will further need to seek indigenous forces to aid in law and order functions and to help prepare for a post-occupation Iraq.

The final section of the analytic portion of the report, titled "Winning the Peace in Iraq," contains a foresighted warning:

The possibility of the United States winning the war and losing the peace in Iraq is real and serious. ... The longer the occupation continues, the greater the potential that it will disrupt society rather than rehabilitate it. Thus important and complex goals must be accomplished as quickly as possible. ...

Successfully executing the postwar occupation of Iraq is consequently every bit as important as winning the war. ... Without an overwhelming effort to prepare for occupation, the United States may find itself in a radically different world over the next few years, a world in which the threat of Saddam Hussein seems like a pale shadow of new problems of America's own making.

Journalist James Fallows conducted extensive research on the subject in 2002. He published his results in an *Atlantic Monthly* article titled "The Fifty-First State."

JAMES FALLOWS: Before the war, I spent the spring and summer of 2002 [researching], when it was still theoretically an open question about whether or not the United States would wait for sanctions to take place [and] have their effect, or wait for Saddam Hussein to disarm himself, as the term was then. I began interviewing civilian experts and historians, and active-duty military personnel, about what the U.S. could expect if it went to ... to war in Iraq and after it, uh, unseated Saddam Hussein, as it certainly would, since the U.S. military power was [unmatched then] and, to a degree, now.

And I found a surprisingly easy-to-obtain consensus about what the situation was likely to be in ... in Iraq. Uh, this was based on people who had served long ago in Germany or Japan after World War II, who'd worked more recently in the Balkans, or in Somalia, or in Haiti, or in Panama, or in Grenada, or elsewhere. And they said there was a fairly predictable set of circumstances for postwar scenarios in general and for Iraq in particular.

For postwar scenarios in general, they said, the two main certainties of occupying a country after this kind of decapitation strike: First was the sort of paramount need for public order. You're going to be removing the controlling force that had kept the lid on a society for quite a long time. And very quickly after that, somebody had to be in charge. So the main postwar emergency was going to be providing some sense of order, that people could be safe, that even with the dictator gone, there was some new sheriff in town, was the way many people put it.

The other main certainty, people said, about postwar occupations in general is how very, very quickly a liberating force becomes an occupying force. This is a certain process, as certain as the aging process in human beings, but a million times faster. And so that a clock would start ticking right away. And the U.S. had to ... to plan for the war, with the knowledge of the war's outcome—that very, very quickly, its presence would begin to be ... uh, to be resented, no matter how grateful people were for the removal of a dictator. And so they had to have that ... that certainty in mind.

Then, for the circumstances of Iraq in particular, people said there were a lot of very predictable, um, peculiar circumstances about this country that had to be taken into account. One was the deep-seated regional difference and ethnic difference, which had been there from the time of the Ottoman Empire, when these were three different provinces of the Ottoman Empire. There was the resentment among ethnic groups, or religious groups, because of the way the Sunnis had been so prominent and powerful under Saddam Hussein. There were all the sort of vengeance killings that were likely to occur. There was the question of how the oil would be gotten up and running again, how the oil revenues would be distributed, how the electric power would be gotten going, et cetera.

So, uh, before the war, the main message I had was: Number one, there were a lot of challenges that would be there once the war took place and was over. And number two, these were foreseeable enough that part of preparation for regime change in Iraq would naturally and properly and inescapably be preparing for the day after, for what is called Phase IV, that is, after the actual hostilities.

The November 2002 issue of my magazine, *The Atlantic Monthly,* carried an article by me that we actually rushed to get on our Web site in August, you know, three months early, because it was done then. And the title was "The Fifty-First State." And the argument was, if we went into Iraq, then actually conquering it would be fairly easy, and the complications would happen after that, and we'd be in for ten years or more of real … a real handful there. And this was based on extensive interviews with a lot of people who were veterans in past occupations, laying out a sort of day-by-day and week-by-week timetable of what you could expect: from the need to provide public order during the first couple of days after the invasion, to six months or so after that, having jobs be re-created, reconstituting a security force, et cetera.

And at the time, it got a modest amount of attention. I think it's gotten somewhat more attention, or at least I've heard from more people as time has gone on, basically because that timetable, laid out by nonclassified experts, you know, a year before the war, has basically proven to be correct.

CHARLES FERGUSON: And did you get any reaction from anyone in the administration from that article?

JAMES FALLOWS: Not directly the administration. Through people who I won't exactly refer to as cutouts, but perhaps sort of friends of friends,

friends of mine who also were close to members of the administration. I heard from them, saying this was just unduly pessimistic.

It's significant to remember how ... how much of what we could call the neoconservative mind-set looked on the whole hand-wringing, as they saw it, and defeatism, as they saw it, and little American ... uh, little American-ism, as they saw it, of the Democrats in the Clinton years—that this country can't do anything, and everything is too hard, and if there's one bad weekend in Somalia, we leave. And they thought that that was just a kind of weakness that this venture, through its quickness, its success, its élan, would show that they were able to actually prove that America was capable of big things again.

So the main reaction I had from the administration ahead of time was a sense of, "Oh, you will never learn; there's all this hand-wringing." And the hand-wringing, they said, will be like before the first Gulf War, when people warned that the Iraqi Army would be so great, and it just disappeared. It'll be the same kind of thing now. "You're doing all this fretting. You're ... you're knitting your brow. And it's gonna turn out fine." ...

Actually, I spoke to [Undersecretary of Defense] Douglas Feith. It was quite a bit later than that. It was in, uh, well into 2003; it was after the war had been going, the occupation had been going for several months, and things obviously were not going so ... so well according to plan. So I, uh, went in, to ask him, "Uh, tell me, in retrospect, what turned out the way you expected, and what didn't? You know, what's been a surprise, what's been predictable." And he, in a very sort of affable way, said, "Well, let me just challenge your first premise. We didn't really expect anything. If you came into Donald Rumsfeld's office with the idea that something was expected, he'd say, no, you can't make plans for this kind of thing. You can't predict what's gonna happen. You know, that life is uncertain; you have to kind of live in the moment." And he went on and on to say that if you'd gone in with any kind of set of expectations about Iraq, you would have been booted right out of the office. Now, as a human trait, there's something charming about this kind of spontaneity. But if you're planning to run an entire country, and to transform a part of, uh, of the Middle East, it would be like Dwight Eisenhower, before D-Day, saying, "Hell, who knows what's gonna happen when they go up those ... those cliffs?"

Anthony Cordesman holds the Arleigh Burke Chair for Strategy at the Center for Strategic and International Studies. He is a cold-blooded realist and is not, by any conceivable measure, a leftist. Before the war, he had had long experience with Iraq. Almost alone among the academic and think-tank strategy analysts who wrote about Iraq at the time from outside the government, Cordesman had actually been there many times. In December 2002, shortly after Fallows' article was published, he published his own article warning that U.S. planning for postwar Iraq was dangerously naive and overly optimistic.* I asked him about his experience in Iraq.

ANTHONY CORDESMAN: Well, my first trip to Iraq was in the early 1970s, when I was at the U.S. Embassy in Iran. And we did not have formal relations with Iraq. I went there repeatedly afterwards, during the Iran-Iraq War. The last trip was in the spring of 1990. I visited Southern Iraq briefly in 1991, after the defeat of Saddam's forces. I have been involved in looking at Iraq's military forces, its security forces and political structure, for now more than thirty years.

CHARLES FERGUSON: You wrote an article just before the war. Tell us the title of the article; tell us what you said, why you thought it.

ANTHONY CORDESMAN: Well, I wrote quite a number of articles. I think the one you're probably referring to is "Peace as a Self-Inflicted Wound" [the title was actually "Planning for a Self-Inflicted Wound"]. And basically, the problem that was emerging is that we were going into an Iraq which was militarily weak, where we already knew that with the forces we had, we could relatively quickly defeat its conventional military, but where it was far from clear that we had a plan to provide stability in Iraq after we invaded, [or that] we knew what to do with the political, social, and economic problems that would follow. And I provided a whole list of things which might go wrong if we did not have the capability to deal with them, and some that would go wrong, almost regardless of what we did.

We were, after all, moving into a country with very deep religious and ethnic differences. And these are not something that you can solve, regard-

---

*At the time of printing, Anthony Cordesman, "Planning for a Self-Inflicted Wound: US Policy to Shape a Post-Saddam Iraq," rough draft, December 31, 2002, was available at www.csis.org/media/csis/pubs/iraq_wound.pdf.

less of how you deploy your forces, or how well you try to create political and economic incentives. As we have seen in the Balkans or example after example throughout the world, when you remove a dictatorship suddenly, when reform does not come from within, all of the problems that have [built] up, sometimes over decades and sometimes over centuries, then have to be resolved, and they rarely play out smoothly or easily.

"Planning for a Self-Inflicted Wound" was explicit about the challenges of peace-time planning: "The hardest part of war is often the peace ... it is the quality of planning that is at issue. Unless it sharply improves, it may well become a self-inflicted wound based on a series of 'syndromes' that grow out of ignorance, indifference to Iraq's real needs, and ethnocentricity."

The article goes on to list eighteen syndromes that in Cordesman's view were plaguing the planning. For example, "Iraq cannot be treated as an intellectual playground for political scientists or ideologues."

Syndrome number fourteen was labeled "The Dismantle the Army and Police Force Syndrome":

The Revolutionary Guards [sic; Cordesman apparently meant the Republican Guard], the secret police, and other Saddam loyalists are contemptible, but the idea we disband the entire army and security forces and start over with training and ground up new groups is impractical and dangerous.

Many elements of the regular army are nationalist, not pro-Saddam. We don't want 400,000 nationalists in the streets and hostile. We don't want to leave a weak army in service and an angry army in the streets. ... By all means clean the army up, clean up the officer corps, provide political training etc., but leave the professional and competent elements intact. Leave Iraq with some dignity and coopt the army rather than destroy it.

Leaving the police in place, after the same purging, is even more important. The first priorities are food and security and then jobs and security.

The largest single effort to understand the needs of postwar Iraq was conducted inside the federal government, by the State Department in 2002. The Future of Iraq Project was an enormous effort, with both classified and public components, involving both State Department personnel and hundreds of external consultants, including representatives of many Iraqi exile groups. It produced a multivolume study over two thousand pages long, with individual reports from specialized working groups devoted to questions such as the energy sector, the military, health and social policy, finance, and the political structure of a post-Saddam state.

David Phillips consulted for the State Department and worked on the Future of Iraq Project. He first came into contact with Iraq when he worked for a human rights organization, and was exposed to Saddam's atrocities against the Kurds in the 1980s. He made subsequent trips to Iraq in the early 1990s, right after the Gulf War, when he again had extensive dealings with the Kurds and Northern Iraqis.

DAVID PHILLIPS: I served as a senior adviser at the State Department from 1999 to 2003 and, at the end of that tenure, worked in the State Department's Near Eastern Affairs Bureau and was a part of the Future of Iraq Project, uh, particularly the Democratic Principles Working Group, which was one of the Iraqi bodies that was convened to look at the new Iraq. ...

CHARLES FERGUSON: When you were working on the Future of Iraq Project, did you have direct dealings with, did you speak with, people in DOD [Department of Defense], people in the White House—

DAVID PHILLIPS: Hmm.

CHARLES FERGUSON: ... people in the National Security Council?

DAVID PHILLIPS: I did.

CHARLES FERGUSON: What did you tell them? What did they tell you?

DAVID PHILLIPS: Uh, you know, there was a march to war that, from the summer of 2002 onward, seemed inevitable to me. Uh, the planning for postwar, and the debate about, uh, intelligence and WMD, seemed to be geared around justifying policy conclusions that had already been made.

CHARLES FERGUSON: Did you ever express concerns to them about the inadequacy of postwar planning or the nature of their plans?

DAVID PHILLIPS: Ah, sure, I expressed concerns from the beginning about the importance of, uh, having a dialogue with Iraqis; about giving them ownership of the political transition; about a timetable, which was accelerated and which didn't allow for consensus to emerge.

CHARLES FERGUSON: And what did they say?

DAVID PHILLIPS: Uh, they took on board those concerns. I think that they shared those concerns, but decisions had been made at the top that this was going forward. I think everybody was reconciled to that fact.

CHARLES FERGUSON: Hmm, I see. ... Is there anything that I didn't ask about that you'd like to talk about at all?

DAVID PHILLIPS: Uh, sure, I could talk a little bit more about a few items.

CHARLES FERGUSON: Please.

DAVID PHILLIPS: You know, the Future of Iraq Project prepared a list of sites that, um, should be protected in Iraq. And when there were missile and ... and Air Force attacks on Iraq, prior to the land invasion, uh, those sites were protected, indeed. But the field commanders were never given the list of sites, which contributed, in part, to their inability to secure strategic positions and institutions in the country.

Through the Future of Iraq Project, we talked about de-Baathification and what to do with the Iraqi armed forces. And we shouldn't be under any illusions: Everybody in the group viewed the Baath Party as, uh, a criminal institution and felt that the leadership of the Baath should be held accountable.

Uh, there was disagreement among Iraqis about whether or not the whole party should be banned. But they did agree that individuals should be held accountable and that there should not be guilt through association in criminal procedures going forward.

There was also extensive discussion about what to do with the security situation, uh, right after the decapitation of the regime. And, Iraqis emphasized the ... the likelihood of violence and recrimination. Uh, there was debate about what to do with the Iraqi security services. And here again, we should be very clear that the Mukhabarat [Saddam's secret police] and the Special Republican Guard that were responsible for atrocities ... uh, were viewed by Iraqis as having no place in the new Iraq. But they did recognize that other security structures that were not directly tainted with war crimes or atrocities could be co-opted and turned into partners in security.

CHARLES FERGUSON: Such as?

DAVID PHILLIPS: Such as the Iraqi Army.

And indeed, the public, unclassified version of the report of the Future of Iraq Project was quite explicit about the importance of proper postwar handling of the Iraqi Army and the other military and paramilitary forces of the regime. The report recommended that the Iraqi Army and the Republican Guard, among other organizations, be reorganized, while the Special Republican Guard, the Fedayeen Saddam, and other paramilitary and repressive forces personally loyal to Saddam be disbanded. The report concluded that the army could play a role in reconstruction and in providing security for the population. The report also warned that proper and careful disarmament, demobilization, and reintegration (DDR) procedures were essential, and that many members of the military possessed no other skills. It also warned that an abrupt disbanding of the forces loyal to Saddam could precipitate resentment, crime, and instability and suggested that even these forces should perhaps be retained, though with careful screening. A post-Saddam army of 150,000 to 200,000 men was recommended:

> The present Iraqi regime has managed to militarize a large fraction of the Iraqi population in the past 30 years. Military to many is the only trade or form of life they know and they will lose through demobilization their only marketable skill, social network, and political influence. Therefore, all combatants who are included in the demobilization process must be assured by their leaders and by the new government of their legal rights and that new prospects for work and education will be provided to them by the new system. Constant governmental and institutional attention must be given to the demobilization process with the requirement of a generous capital of resources. ... Short time savings like limited staffing, non-existence of a mandate for human rights activities and the lack of institution building may come at a very high long term price.*

---

*Future of Iraq Project, Defense Policy and Institutions Working Group, Report, p. 36, available at www.thememoryhole.org/state/future_of_iraq/future_defense.pdf.

The concluding section of the report contained a series of remarkably prescient and, in retrospect, poignant recommendations and cautionary remarks, starting with the Iraqi Army:

THE ARMY

We mean by this the decades old Iraqi Military Establishment which is part of the inheritance of the modern Iraqi State since its formation. Iraq saw varied successive political regimes while the army's loyalty, on the whole, was for Iraq as a homeland with few exceptions, which cannot be considered as the rule. This is proved by the representation, to a great extent, of all segments of society, racially or religiously in the army.

Saddam Hussein realized ... that he will not be able to earn the loyalty and trust of the army with its varied character in spite of the many attempts to purify or clean the army from its disloyal elements—as he called them. ...

In any event we think it is necessary to keep the basic structure of the army, which can be easily rehabilitated, more so than the Special Forces, through the following and other means:

It is possible to discharge those who do not want to continue to serve in this establishment, with the condition that proper procedure should be taken to provide work opportunities. ...

Retiring the high ranking officers; helping some of them in obtaining suitable civil service jobs or in the private sector or helping them in managing some small projects.

It is necessary to utilize the services of the low and middle ranked officers, especially those who want to continue to serve in the army, after their rehabilitation according to the new regulations of the army and the defensive strategy.*

Finally, the report concluded with some exceptionally direct warnings about the handling of the "Special Forces," that is, the military and paramilitary forces created by Saddam to be loyal to his regime, such as the Special Republican Guard and the Fedayeen Saddam. It is worth excerpting extensively:

*Future of Iraq Project, Defense Policy and Institutions Working Group, Report, p. 68.

THE MEANS OF DEALING WITH THE SPECIAL FORCES

There are two conflicting methods to deal with these forces in post Saddam Hussein Iraq:

First Method: This calls for its destruction and elimination wherever it existed and referring its surviving element to special courts to decide their fate because they committed crimes against Iraq, its people, and its interests. They're [sic] some who call for the destruction of these forces at the beginning of the change because it is a source of evil in addition [to] being the protective fence of the regime.

Second Method: This method deals with the situation in a more practical manner. It considers the large number of people who work in these forces. Many of whom think that they are serving Iraq in one way or another. Some of them found themselves in these forces because of the absence of opportunities and choices in a political system, which made fighting, and war a profession with privileges, or they implement the policy of the regime similar to what the elements of the army do. ... Thus their destruction or the elimination of their roles completely, from the viewpoint of the proponents of this method, is a continuation of the circle of violence and injustice. ...

But as for the Special Forces, we see that the discharge has political, economical and social effects, which may not be temporary or easy on an Iraq which seeks to regain its health after many illnesses and great sufferings. Especially if the discharge is compulsory, and contrary to the will and desire of these forces, which will feel the weight of the loss of their roles, positions, and privileges. This will prepare the ground for instability and lack of security through direct or indirect confrontation between the forces and those who are in charge of post Saddam period. ... In this sense, the discharged elements will be extremely effective and dangerous, if they move under the sectarian cover. Under this cover they will not hesitate to use their expertise in provocation, preparation and destructive means, which they are good at. ...

On the other hand, the discharge of a large number of these forces into the society will cause an increase in crimes such as murder and theft especially in big cities. The security organizations will have a big role in this situation for they are good and professionals in the art of crime, which they practiced under the law to protect the regime. ...

Some of the elements of these forces will intensify the economic crimes and organize it. They will form mafias practicing extortion and violence in commerce and the national economy. ...

Thus we are not for the discharge of these forces, especially a compulsory discharge. We are talking about more than half a million fighters whose fate and role in the future cannot be ignored positively or negatively. In fact as long as these forces are in defined areas, observed and supervised, their effect will be less harmful, especially if they were disarmed from heavy weapons. ...

The Special Forces contain organizations that are considered part of the Iraqi state inheritance, it was established more than five decades ago, like Public Security and Military Intelligence. These organizations have cumulative expertise that may be beneficial to the post Saddam period.*

The concluding sentence of the report points to the importance of knowledgeable politicians:

Whatever happens, perhaps the matter in the coming stage will depend on the wisdom and political capability of the coming regime and politicians more than anything else.

CHARLES FERGUSON: Okay. So your point being that the work that was done in the Future of Iraq Project anticipated a number of the issues that arose, and made recommendations contrary to the decisions actually taken by the Bush administration and the occupying authorities.

DAVID PHILLIPS: [Yes], the Future of Iraq Project emphasized the importance of a speedy handover to Iraqis. Iraqis emphasized the importance of their own sovereignty and responsibility. And they warned U.S. officials that if the U.S. troops were ever viewed as an occupying force, that there would be a backlash, and resentment, against, uh, U.S. troops on the ground.

CHARLES FERGUSON: And what happened to the work done by your working group and the Future of Iraq Project?

---

*Future of Iraq Project, Defense Policy and Institutions Working Group, Report, pp. 70–72.

DAVID PHILLIPS: On January 21 of 2003, the president assigned to the office of the Secretary of Defense lead responsibility for postwar civilian administration in Iraq. And because the work of the Future of Iraq Project highlighted problems that might have slowed down the, uh, march to war, a decision was taken within Don Rumsfeld's office, uh, to suppress the work of the Future of Iraq Project and essentially ignore it, and take steps to undermine it. ...

CHARLES FERGUSON: What did you recommend? What did you feel?

DAVID PHILLIPS: The importance of handing over sovereignty quickly to Iraqis; of defining early on a role for the international community; of developing a power-sharing arrangement that decentralized authority from Baghdad to the regions and that took into account the primary victims of Saddam's atrocities in the allocation of responsibilities in the new Iraq. ... It was a planning process. And implicitly was consultative, involving a whole broad range of Iraqis. That didn't jive with the Bush administration's plan to give power to Ahmed Chalabi and the Iraqi National Congress, so that they could then do our bidding in Iraq: transform the country into a liberal democracy, a launching point for getting rid of the Baathists in Syria, the mullahs in Iran, creating a safe space for U.S. interests in the broader Middle East.

Another issue bearing upon the security and stability in postwar Iraq was the question of how to handle police functions and the Iraqi police force. In late 2002, this issue became more urgent after Saddam Hussein opened his prisons and released nearly a hundred thousand ordinary criminals, even arming some of them in the process.

   Robert Perito is a former foreign service officer. He served thirty years in the State Department with several of his assignments in postconflict situations. In 1995, Perito joined the Department of Justice, where he managed the Department of Justice's International Police Training Program. I asked him how he came to be involved with Iraq policy matters.

ROBERT PERITO: At the end of my work on my book [*The American Experience with Police in Peace Operations*], I got an opportunity to brief Richard

Perle, who at the time was the head of the Defense Policy Board, about my work on the use of police and constabulary forces in postconflict interventions, particularly in controlling civil disorder—looting, violence—that usually goes with the end of, or with, a foreign intervention into a … into an international conflict.

In February of 2003, right before the U.S. intervention in Iraq, I got an invitation to come and brief the Defense Policy Board. At that time, Richard Perle was the chairman. The Defense Policy Board is an advisory panel that advises Secretary Rumsfeld on defense policy matters.

CHARLES FERGUSON: Tell us what you said.

ROBERT PERITO: This was about just a few weeks before the U.S. actually intervened in Iraq. What I told them was that based on our experiences in previous peace operations and on what had happened in Iraq historically, it was very likely that if the U.S. intervened and captured Baghdad, that we were likely to face massive civil disturbance—widespread looting and a kind of eventuality that our military forces wouldn't be prepared to deal with. I told him [that] I thought we ought to have specially trained forces there to deal with civil unrest and violence perpetrated by civilians rather than by military forces.

CHARLES FERGUSON: Tell us why you came to that conclusion.

ROBERT PERITO: Well, I'm a historian of peace operations, basically. And in every intervention that we had, beginning with Panama—during Operation Just Cause in the early nineties—there have been wide-scale civil unrest, looting, mob violence, rioting, et cetera, that had occurred following the intervention. This occurred in Haiti and in Bosnia and in Kosovo.

And it had taken months if not years to deal with this unrest. So it was only prudent that we be ready to deal with that. At the same time, because of the political realities at the time, we really couldn't expect to count on our allies as we had in previous interventions, or on the United Nations, because, as you remember, there was a split in the Security Council on this issue.

So it looked as if we were going to be up against widespread civil disorder. And it was going to be the U.S. military alone there to deal with it. And the U.S. military just wasn't prepared.

CHARLES FERGUSON: You said that also, Iraq's previous history suggested this would be an issue. Tell us about that.

ROBERT PERITO: Well, if you remember, at the end of the Gulf War, when order broke down in the south of Iraq, there were massive … it was a massive uprising on the part of the Shia against the Saddam government. And this went on until the Saddam government very ruthlessly restored order. And then later on, in a period when the United States was conducting air strikes against any effort by the Saddam government to interfere with our overflights, there was a period of several days when order was … was not in effect, in which there were another massive uprising of … of Shia and other people around the country. So it seemed, based on what had happened in Iraq itself, it was very likely that if order broke down, that the Iraqi police would probably disappear; security services would also disappear. And it would be likely that U.S. forces would be left to deal with widespread civil unrest.

CHARLES FERGUSON: What was their response?

ROBERT PERITO: Well, it was kind of interesting. This is, I have to emphasize that [as] an advisory panel, this is not a policymaking group. And it's a panel of very prestigious people who hold, held, positions in previous governments—several former secretaries of defense, secretaries of state, retired generals.

And the response was a very lengthy discussion. I was supposed to have about fifteen minutes to talk to them. And then at the end, we had about an hour and a half talk in which we went pro and con and up and down and over this issue.

In the end, they agreed to then two things. One, that it was interesting and they had to look at the issue further. But they also agreed that there wasn't enough time and that while this was a good idea, to have specially trained forces to deal with civil unrest, but maybe for the next war. Unfortunately, three years into the conflict, we could still use those forces—today [early 2006].

CHARLES FERGUSON: What did you suggest?

ROBERT PERITO: I suggested that we needed about twenty-five hundred constabulary forces. These are forces like the French gendarmerie or the Italian carabinieri—about four thousand civil police, street cops, and then teams of judicial advisers and corrections officers, so that we would have a capability to rapidly establish, reestablish the rule of law in Iraq from the very beginning. In fact, that capability wasn't present.

As you know, there was widespread looting. The governmental infrastructure was destroyed. Hospitals were destroyed. Universities were burned. The libraries were destroyed. Industrial facilities were ransacked. And it just set the whole process of reconstruction and the restoration and stability back, perhaps fatally.

CHARLES FERGUSON: Did Richard Perle have any response?

ROBERT PERITO: Well, he was very interested in the concept. And he suggested that it need[ed] to be looked at further. But then, I don't know what happened. After that, I never heard. And … and I'm not sure whether the recommendation ever went forth.

CHARLES FERGUSON: Did you ever hear back … hear any further comment?

ROBERT PERITO: No, I never heard anything more.

In 2004, James Fallows revisited the question of the prewar analyses of postwar Iraq. He analyzed the various prewar analyses and compared them to actual U.S. behavior in the invasion and occupation of Iraq.

JAMES FALLOWS: The article that I published early in 2004 was called "Blind into Baghdad." And the question was, How can we explain—not whether we should condemn—but how can we explain the contrast between the very, very effective and successful planning and execution of the actual combat for Iraq (you know, the couple-week campaign to take over Iraq and to evict Saddam Hussein and to establish new power) and the apparent just failure to foresee what was going to happen after that: to be prepared for looting, to be prepared for insurgency, to be prepared for everything else?

And so I went back and I tried to talk with people inside the military, inside the State Department, inside nongovernmental organizations, about what they had been actually doing in the months leading up to the war. This was a kind of bookend to the article I had done previously, called "The Fifty-First State," about what could be foreseen. Now I was asking, What had actually been foreseen; what had they actually planned?

And the great surprise to me was the postwar difficulties were not because nobody was doing any planning. In fact, a lot of people were doing very careful planning, and planning that stood up very, very well. The problem was there was this fatal disconnect between the very accurate and prescient scenarios that people had come up with, even the government, and those actually making the decisions.

Probably the most striking of these was the gap between what the U.S. Army War College, from Carlisle Barracks, PA, had prepared for, and what the actual U.S. Army did. The Army War College had this superb report that was available four or five months before the war, inside the government, saying, Let's think about occupations in general, and see how they go. Let's think about Iraq in particular, and see what its problems are. And from those two things let's, uh, put together an actual plan. They had this very, very detailed plan: how to prevent looting, how to get a police force established, how to get the electricity running, how to prevent the hospitals from being defunct, how to keep doctors protected, how to do all the sorts of things you would need to do.

And anybody looking at that, after the war, would say, Why wasn't this done?

CHAPTER THREE

ORHA

In the year prior to the war, an intense power struggle took place over control of Iraq policy in general and occupation policy in particular. On one side were Vice President Dick Cheney and the Pentagon leadership (Donald Rumsfeld, Paul Wolfowitz, and Douglas Feith); on the other side were the State Department and, to some extent, the CIA.

The Pentagon won. One result of this was that on January 20, 2003, President Bush officially gave the Defense Department control of the Iraqi occupation. At this point, only two months before the war started, no organization for managing postwar Iraq had yet been created. In contrast, the United States began planning the occupation of Germany more than two years before the end of World War II.

GEORGE PACKER: So to me, if you want to date the beginning of the disaster of postwar Iraq, it would be January 20th, 2003, when Bush signed, without, as far as I can tell, any real discussion within the White House or the administration, National Security Presidential Directive Number 24, which gave control of postwar Iraq to the Pentagon, which was out of keeping with precedent, and which set up a unit within the Pentagon called ORHA [the Organization for Reconstruction and Humanitarian Assistance], to be led by retired general Jay Garner. That document essentially made Donald Rumsfeld the ... the main actor on postwar Iraq. And the reason why this was a disaster is because Donald Rumsfeld had no interest in postwar Iraq.

Lawrence Wilkerson, who was Colin Powell's chief of staff at the time, described the shift in control away from the State Department.

LAWRENCE WILKERSON: Now, you didn't ask me why Powell made ... acquiesced in the decision in January, when the president decided that the Defense Department would be the lead. Others have asked me that question. Um, I, as ... as a soldier, I don't have much problem with that decision, because you're looking at an organization that gets four hundred billion dollars and has millions of people, and an organization that has, discounting its foreign service nationals, maybe sixteen or seventeen thousand people and thirty billion dollars. That's the difference between the Defense Department and the State Department. So I have no problem with Powell, uh, acquiescing in the president's decision, even supporting— and he did—the president's decision to make the Defense Department the lead agency on postinvasion Iraq. What I have a problem with is making the Defense Department the lead agency to the exclusion of the State Department.

Only after National Security Presidential Directive Number 24 (NSPD-24) gave control to the Pentagon did Rumsfeld create an organization to manage postwar Iraq: the Organization for Reconstruction and Humanitarian Assistance, called by its acronym, ORHA. Rumsfeld appointed retired Army General Jay Garner to run ORHA. In the first Gulf War, Garner had commanded 22,000 soldiers responsible for humanitarian operations in the Kurdish zone of Northern Iraq. This time he would be running the entire country, though he was told his appointment would be temporary, probably for six months.

JAY GARNER: Well, I got a call from, um ... the Office of Secretary of Defense in late January. I got a call from Doug Feith's office, from Brigadier General [Hagee]. And he said he was calling on the behalf of the secretary of defense, Mr. Rumsfeld. And they would like for me to consider putting together a staff that, should we go to war in Iraq, that staff would go to Iraq and be used in the postwar effort, uh, to handle humanitarian affairs, reconstruction, uh, events, and civilian government, reestablishing civilian government. And that they [would] like for me to consider that; they'd like for me to lead that effort. But the probability was that I would not take the organization to Iraq; that by that time, the president would name a presidential envoy. And the thinking was, the smart thinking was, it would be somebody of name recognition, probably a former governor. Because of the president's background, it would be a former governor.

Army Colonel Paul Hughes was one of ORHA's earliest employees. He had just supervised a study of how to manage postwar Iraq.

PAUL HUGHES: I wound up being assigned to the Office of Reconstruction and Humanitarian Assistance, under Jay Garner, and I was the director of strategic policy for him. ... Uh, and I was assigned to that office on the 24th of January. I was, I think I was, like, the fourth or fifth guy assigned to the office after Jay Garner accepted the position.

Hughes was frustrated by the lack of resources made available to ORHA—and, of course, the lack of time it had to accomplish its goals. Everyone I interviewed about ORHA, in fact, noted that it had not been given nearly enough attention, money, or people.

CHARLES FERGUSON: Did the level of preparation and funding and planning and staffing that was given to ORHA and to the postwar management effort—did it strike you as adequate? Did you think that it had been given enough time, people, money, resources, et cetera?

PAUL HUGHES: We never had enough people. Never had enough people.

CHARLES FERGUSON: I see. Okay. What did you think about the nature, extent, quality of prewar planning for the postwar?

PAUL HUGHES: That's a complicated question, because when we got into it, in late January, uh, the task was very complex, not only in terms of the intellectual thought that had to go into it, but also the ... the coordinating that had to go on among government agencies. And you know, just to throw in, trying to set up offices in the Pentagon. We were given a suite of offices that had been unoccupied for a couple of years, had no computers in it. Uh, you have people showing up daily, asking, "Where do I sit?" They wanted telephones and things like that. So there was a lot of that going on, about, you know, running around, trying to find things to work with. ...

You know, to put it into a historical context: on the 7th of December of 1941, Pearl Harbor was attacked. And on the 8th of December, the United States was at war with three different countries; Japan, Germany, and Italy. And in January of 1942, less than thirty days later, George Marshall, chief of staff of the army, stood up an office to plan for the occupation and governance of all defeated Axis countries: Germany, Italy, and Japan. And that didn't occur until the summer of 1945. We had two and a half to three years to plan all of that. The postwar planning office for Iraq was stood up on the 20th of January, and on the 16th of March, it flies away to war. It had less than sixty days to pull it all together, something that took almost three years to do during World War II. It was chaos.

And I'll tell you that the people who flew with us to Kuwait, I would take with me anywhere. [Well, with] a couple of exceptions, but I'd take all of 'em with me, for the most part, because they were Americans who were willing to take on hard tasks and do tough jobs in impossible situations. ORHA wound up being an office that was given tremendous responsibilities [and] was given very few resources with which to accomplish those responsibilities.

Barbara Bodine was a senior foreign service officer who had worked in the Middle East for twenty years before the 2003 war. She served in the U.S. Embassy in Baghdad during the Iran-Iraq war of the 1980s, and then was in the U.S. Embassy in Kuwait when Saddam Hussein invaded in 1990. After Saddam refused to allow U.S. citizens to be evacuated, she volunteered to stay in Kuwait as a hostage in the U.S. Embassy, living on water and canned food for five months until Saddam agreed to permit the evacuation of all U.S. citizens. She later served as U.S. ambassador to Yemen. In March 2003, she was hired to work for ORHA, which placed her in charge of Baghdad and the central region governorates of Iraq. She stayed through May. She has since retired from the Foreign Service and now teaches at Princeton University.

AP Photo/Hasan Jamali

Barbara Bodine.

Bodine joined ORHA only three weeks before the war began. She was one of the few State Department Middle East experts that the Pentagon allowed into Iraq.

BARBARA BODINE: I wasn't looking to go to Iraq, I can assure you of that. Um, I was at Los Angeles Airport, on my way to a job interview. And I got a phone call on my cell phone from someone at the State Department, telling me that Richard Armitage was looking for me, and wanted me back in Washington right now. And I went to the counter of the Red Carpet Lounge and changed my ticket, and went back to Washington directly. And uh, it was then that I found out that the State Department was looking for a senior officer to go over and be part of the leadership of what was called the Office of Reconstruction and Humanitarian Affairs, the precursor to Jerry Bremer's [L. Paul "Jerry" Bremer] group.

And uh, I went over there, interviewed for a job with Jay Garner, was accepted. And that was on a Thursday. And on a Friday, we sort of finished all of the bureaucratic details. I went back to Santa Barbara, where I was teaching. And by Tuesday, I was back on a plane. And Wednesday, less than a week later, I was at the Pentagon, uh, having been designated the coordinator for reconstruction for Baghdad and the ... the central governorates.

CHARLES FERGUSON: And so this occurred—

BARBARA BODINE: This is the first week in March.

CHARLES FERGUSON: So before the war.

BARBARA BODINE: Before the war, barely.

This pattern was repeated elsewhere. Each cabinet department was ordered to create an advisory team that would travel to Iraq to supervise its corresponding Iraqi ministry. But these ministerial advisory teams were created and staffed hurriedly and incompletely. Walter Slocombe, who was chosen to lead the Department of Defense advisory team, which would be in charge of Iraq's Ministry of Defense and military, was appointed in mid-March, just as the war began. When he finally arrived in Iraq full-time in June, at least half of the positions in his organization were still vacant.

CHARLES FERGUSON: So when did these discussions begin for you?

WALTER SLOCOMBE: Well ... essentially at the same time the fighting started, which was, what, early March, mid-March of 2003.

CHARLES FERGUSON: I see. Okay. When you got that call, or had that first discussion, did it cross your mind to think, you know, isn't it kind of late for them to be thinking about this?

WALTER SLOCOMBE: Yes.

CHARLES FERGUSON: Did you tell them that?

WALTER SLOCOMBE: No. ... The reason I didn't say anything about it was, if I had, there was nothing you could do about it. It was the fact. I was prepared to go out even on ... on that basis. But I didn't ... I didn't think it was a fundamental problem. It was certainly true that more time to prepare would have been useful.

Bodine was surprised by the staffing decisions in Washington.

BARBARA BODINE: Well, I think one of the things that, um, that very much surprised me when I went over to the Pentagon to talk about the job is, I was initially asked to head up the civil administration reform part of the ... of the program, which would be the restructuring of all the ministries and the bureaucracy, that side of it. And when I got to the Pentagon, uh, that job had already been filled by a ... a law partner of Doug Feith. So the job was no longer available.

What I have to admit surprised me a great deal is that when I looked at the staffing patterns. There were three substantive directors—for humanitarian assistance, infrastructure reconstruction, civil administration—and then there were three geographic coordinators—north, south, and central. And I was very surprised that the only job that was still open—and this was the first week in March—was the coordinator for Baghdad and the central governorates. And it struck me then as particularly odd that the core of the country—the capital city and what we now call the Sunni Triangle—as of March 3rd, did not have anybody coordinating any of the plans for that part of Iraq. And uh, that struck me as something a bit odd, to say the least.

CHARLES FERGUSON: And what did you come to think of Mr. Feith's law partner? Did he have any previous background in Mideast affairs, or any of this kind of work?

BARBARA BODINE: No, he really didn't. Um, he had … he did not have any significant—I'm not sure how much—but [he] really had no significant overseas experience; he didn't have a great deal of grounding in Middle East affairs, or Iraqi affairs; and I'm not sure that he really had spent a great deal of time working within the U.S. government bureaucracy. Uh, and his job was to oversee the revitalization and reconstruction of the Iraqi bureaucracy. So the best that I know, he did not have postconflict experience, he did not have Middle East experience, and I don't think he really had a great deal of government bureaucratic experience of his own.

CHARLES FERGUSON: Hmm. So why did Jay Garner appoint him?

BARBARA BODINE: Um, well, I would say that he was probably appointed more by the civilian leadership of DOD. Um, and I think he was … they selected him because he was known to them—both a friend and a political colleague. And I think they just felt very comfortable having the reconstruction of the Iraqi bureaucracy in the hands of somebody that they knew and trusted. And that seemed to be a more important qualification for the job than area or postconflict experience.

Bodine was also shocked by the situation she found at ORHA only two weeks before the war.

BARBARA BODINE: Well, I mean, having then agreed [to] the job and turned my life upside down and gotten back to Washington to do it, my next, I have to say, my next surprise was, having taken on this part of the reconstruction, was to discover that not only did they not have a coordinator for that, but they had no staff. Uh, I had no personnel; I had … I had nothing, from either a senior deputy down to a secretary. And when I asked about either staffing or structure or anything like that, I was told basically to hire whomever I wanted, and whomever I wished to go out and recruit, and to structure my office any way that I so chose. And on one side, it's very nice to have that much, um, authority and flexibility. But it felt much more like there really just wasn't any structure, or any real plan about what we were supposed to do, and how we were supposed to do it. And you … you can't hire people in a vacuum. You have to know what they're going to do—what do you need them to do? Uh, you don't just go out and hire fifteen people that you know and like. They're supposed to fit missions and objectives, and it was completely unstructured. There were no plans. There truly were no plans.

Jay Garner was much more generous, uncritical, and optimistic in his description of the situation than other interviewees. Even he admitted, however, that ORHA did not have adequate time or resources to prepare for its mission.

CHARLES FERGUSON: What did you think about the fact that you were being asked to do this on such short notice, so soon before a war was likely?

JAY GARNER: Well, it came at an absolutely horrible time for me, for a lot of reasons. I mean, business standpoint, personal standpoint, that. But it's … the question in my mind is, How do you say no? I mean, how do you say no to your country? You don't do that.

CHARLES FERGUSON: Um, fair enough. But, I was thinking more in terms of what this implied about the nature and extent of postwar planning …

JAY GARNER: Well, it's a Herculean effort, I mean, to … to wrap your arms around something of that magnitude in that short a period of time, starting from, really, from ground zero. Although, I'll say this … the secretary, uh, Donald Rumsfeld, told me, he said … he said, "Jay, I want you to realize, there has been a lot of planning, but the problem with the planning is all the planning has been done in the … in the vertical stovepipe of each one of the agencies. In the … in the time you have," he said, "what I suggest you do is try to do some horizontal integration of those plans, and see where you are, see what the deltas are, and how do you work on the deltas."

Which is what we did. We got … we got the planning. It took us from the 1st of February through at least the first two weeks of February to get a team together of around a hundred people initially. And then we took all the plans. And we went over to the National War College [National Defense University], Fort McNair. And we spent the 20th and the 21st of February over there, two long days, beginning about seven thirty in the morning, going to about eight o'clock at night. And we vetted all the plans. Tommy Franks sent over a large portion of his staff. We had assistant secretaries from every one of the [inter]agencies. And we went through every plan, and looked at where they are, and ... and tried to determine, uh, what we agreed with; what, where the holes were; and what we needed to do—that type [of] thing. And then, essentially, from that point on, from the last week in February on, we worked on the problems that we had uncovered as part of the review of those plans.

CHARLES FERGUSON: Okay.

JAY GARNER: And I'll tell you, some of the plans, very good. State Department had some very good plans. The Treasury Department had excellent plans. So ... I think Rumsfeld was right; it was ... the problem, the only problem, the main problem with the plans is it was done in that vertical stovepipe of the agency, without the ... much interrelationship to other agenc[ies].

Most of those who witnessed ORHA's efforts—even those sympathetic to Garner's ideas—found ORHA's planning and resources severely inadequate.

LAWRENCE WILKERSON: Um, the plan for the occupation ... Actually, [it] really wasn't envisioned as an occupation; it was envisioned as a little bit of refugee control; uh, perhaps some efforts to stem problems with ... related to the oil fields, particularly fires, as we had experienced, you may recall, in the first Gulf War; and some delivery of some humanitarian assistance, was about all that I saw in the postwar, or postinvasion planning. Which worried a lot of us. Um, it also worried us that there was only [one] meeting, essentially, of Jay Garner's group—the ORHA group, Organization for Reconstruction and Humanitarian Assistance, that originally went into Kuwait, and then into Baghdad, postinvasion—there was only one meeting, at the National Defense University, and it was the, I think, the consensus opinion of the people who went to that meeting with whom I spoke afterwards, um, that hey, this is crazy. That was our first meeting, and we're not given a whole lot of confidence by that first meeting because essentially, we didn't do anything except meet each other. It's clear that there hasn't been any significant planning; it's clear that this is very ad hoc; and it's clear that Jay Garner thinks, essentially, he's going in to do the three things I just enumerated: deliver humanitarian assistance, maybe fight some oil fires, and maybe do a little refugee control.

RICHARD ARMITAGE: I also expressed to General Garner the ... I didn't quite understand ... though I admired his ... his dedication and his courage ... I didn't quite understand, how was he going to be able to bring about what he was tasked to do without having a great number of resources—and that means money—in hand? The general feeling—and it's been testified to by the administration—was that the Iraqis with their oil wealth would be able to basically fund as they go. And it was a big mistake.

The Pentagon Versus the State Department

The most extensive and detailed effort to plan for postwar Iraq was clearly the State Department's Future of Iraq Project. Yet, the Pentagon failed to use it, did not inform Garner about it, and prevented some of those who had supervised it from joining ORHA.

DAVID PHILLIPS: A month after, uh, after Jay Garner was appointed the head of the Office for Reconstruction and Humanitarian Assistance, he convened a dry run on postwar planning, at the National Defense University, on February 21 and 22.

CHARLES FERGUSON: Were you there?

DAVID PHILLIPS: I was not there.

CHARLES FERGUSON: Okay.

DAVID PHILLIPS: That was the first time that General Garner even learned that there was such a thing as the Future of Iraq Project.

CHARLES FERGUSON: I see. And what were you doing during this time, in January and February of 2003?

DAVID PHILLIPS: The center of gravity had shifted to [Special Presidential Envoy for Afghanistan] Zalmay Khalilzad and the White House; my work had been primarily with the State Department. So the period of my extensive involvement in postwar planning was really from August [2002] through January [2003]. The White House kept a very close hold on the assignment of roles for postwar administration. And it was clear that anyone who raised questions about the feasibility of going to war, or who highlighted problems, wasn't welcome in that process. There were a number of State Department officials and other experts on Iraq who, uh, were not allowed to participate. And even the initial deployment of Jay Garner's group excluded many of the civil servants in the U.S. government who had worked on Iraqi issues for many years.

CHARLES FERGUSON: Okay. And in particular, it excluded you, too.

DAVID PHILLIPS: My interest was in giving Iraqis a voice. Uh, my voice wasn't important. I was glad to work with them, and to have the opportunity that I did. But it was clear that the ideas that I had, and that were represented through my work, weren't viewed with favor by the administration.

Wilkerson also noticed the exclusion of qualified people:

LAWRENCE WILKERSON: There was growing concern on the part of everyone at the State Department, including the secretary of state, as we saw this unfold, and as we saw, particularly the manager at the Department of Defense ... of what was happening in Iraq postinvasion—Douglas Feith, the undersecretary for policy, undersecretary of defense for policy—we saw him excluding key people from the State Department, and key aspects of our more thorough, more robust, in my view, plan for postinvasion Iraq. And so I ... I think I can say that the secretary's frustration, along with my own, grew at that time, as we watched this unfold, and as we watched, essentially, our careful planning, our detailed planning, under what was called Project Iraq, um, essentially discarded, and the people who'd been involved in it essentially discarded, so that more loyal, in line with the Republican Party's views and so forth, people could be appointed to key positions in Iraq. And I think this came back to haunt us, because some of those people, uh, were not the best-qualified people to perform in post-invasion Iraq.

Nearly everyone I spoke with agreed that Cheney and Rumsfeld systematically excluded the State Department in general, State Department Middle East experts in particular, and even more specifically those who had worked on the Future of Iraq Project from participating in prewar planning and from joining ORHA. Again, Jay Garner was the most charitable of those with whom I spoke, although even he noted that the director of the Future of Iraq Project, Tom Warrick, was personally banned by Rumsfeld from working in ORHA.

JAY GARNER: I brought Tom Warrick; I met him when we were vetting those plans I talked about in February at the … National Defense University. I met Tom Warrick there. And he told me what he had … what he had done. He'd spent the last year doing that. And I said, you know, "You don't need to be doing that. You need to be on my team." He said, "I'd like to be on your team." I said, "Well, come. Show up Monday morning. You're on the team."

So he did. He came over. He's a very energetic guy. Uh, he wire-brushes people a little bit, which isn't bad. You want a guy like Tom Warrick in … in every organization. But towards the end of the week, the secretary [Rumsfeld] asked me to remove Tom. And he didn't know who Tom Warrick was. I mean, I'm convinced of that. I was in his office, and he kept looking around for a piece of paper. Finally picked [it] up. He said, "You have somebody on [the] team named Warrick?" And I said, "Yeah, I got Tom Warrick, who did the Future of Iraq study." And he said, "Well, I've got to ask you to remove him." And I said, "He's too valuable." He said, "And I've been asked to do this from … from such a level that I have to ask you to … to… uh, comply with what I'm … I'm requesting of you."

So I went back, and told … I couldn't find Tom. And I had to go see Condoleezza Rice that day. So I told, uh, Colonel Tom [Althazar]. I said, "Find him; tell him that he's off the team right now, but I'll get him back on." And so, Tom said, "Why is that?" And I said, "I don't know." He said, "Well, I'll find out why."

So the next morning, he said, "Look, I call[ed] around. Everybody thinks it probably came out of the vice president's office." But everybody knows that Rumsfeld didn't know who they were, so I don't know whether it came out of the vice president's office or not. But it was clear to me that Rumsfeld—that wasn't his decision. He didn't know who they were. He might not even know what the Future of Iraq study was. Probably didn't.

CHARLES FERGUSON: Okay.

JAY GARNER: Now the interesting thing in that is ... that study was done by Iraqis. You know, it was done by expatriates. And many of those ended up on ORHA because ... we brought a lot of expatriates over after we came into Baghdad. We put together a team here, over in Crystal City, in Washington, with, oh, I don't know, sixty or seventy expatriates, many of which had been on the Future of Iraq study. So a lot of those ... a lot of those who contributed to the study ended up in Iraq.

Shortly after the two-day planning meeting at the National Defense University, ORHA presented its first recommendations for management of postwar Iraq to Rumsfeld and then, later the same day, to President Bush and the National Security Council (NSC). Among other things, Garner recommended restructuring the Iraqi military and using it for the reconstruction of Iraq. The recommendation was approved, and Garner began negotiating with two U.S. companies to handle retraining, management, and an orderly disarmament, demobilization, and reintegration (DDR) process for the Iraqi military. He emphasized that simply disbanding the Iraqi military was impractical. Here are exact copies of the briefing documents Garner used for his presentations to Rumsfeld and to the president and the NSC.

SECRET

Talking Paper: Reforming the Iraqi Military 28 Feb 03

- Macroview:
  - ✓ Restructured & reformed Ministry of Defense
    - Civilian defense minister
  - ✓ Reformed and professionalized military
    - No threat to neighbors or region
    - Able to maintain territorial integrity
  - ✓ One full-spectrum intelligence organization

- Imperatives:
  - ✓ Ensure a professional apolitical force based on merit
  - ✓ Reform all military training institutions and curricula
    - Professional Officer and NCO Corps

- Regular Army 300-400k
  - ✓ Cannot be immediately demobilized
  - ✓ Use in reconstruction (engineer, transportation, logistics, etc.)
  - ✓ Skill set matches task
  - ✓ Long process required (2-3 years)

- Recommendation:
  - ✓ Contract now
    - Estimate $15M required for the rest of FY 03
    - Contract vehicles exist for rapid execution

And here is the briefing paper for the president and NSC meeting later that same day:

Talking Paper — NSC Presentation 28 Feb 2003

➤ 21 Jan 2003—Office formed
  ○ Organization chart with NSPD tasks
  ○ Regional groups

➤ Focus: Pull together Interagency plans
  ○ Operationalize the Planning
    ▪ Vision (agency end state)
    ▪ High impact (1st 30 days)
    ▪ Measures of effectiveness (90, 180, 270, 360 days)
    ▪ Issues & showstoppers

➤ Interagency Rehearsal 21-22 Feb @ NDU
  ○ 150-200 Attendees: Interagency, CENTCOM, UK
  ○ Macro-Issues:

- Funding
- Stability Forces
- Post-War use of Iraqi Regular Army
  - ○ Upcoming Rehearsals
    - Food distribution
    - Water
    - Oil

- ➢ US-UK Iraqis
  - ○ Each ministry: 2-4 technocrats
  - ○ Each of 17 provinces & Baghdad: 3-5 representing culture
  - ○ Interpreters: 12-15

- ➢ Current Efforts
  - ○ Internationalize the Effort
    - Engaging NGOs & IOs
    - Diplomatic Corps presentation (25 Feb)
    - UN Visit
    - UK/Australian LNOs … More to follow
  - ○ Deployment
    - Advanced party ~ 10 Mar
    - Main body ~ 20 Mar

ORHA leaves for Kuwait

In mid-March, just before the war began, most of ORHA's staff flew to Kuwait, where they waited until they could enter Iraq after the war.

CHARLES FERGUSON: So when you and your team went to Kuwait, when did you go to Kuwait?

JAY GARNER: Went to Kuwait on the, uh … 16th of March.

CHARLES FERGUSON: When you went to Kuwait, did you think that you were prepared to run Iraq?

JAY GARNER: I don't think we were ever prepared. I mean, it ... you know, to ... uh, a task of that magnitude probably takes years to prepare. But of course, nobody had years. But I thought that we had made good effort of the time that we had. And I thought, at that point in time, we were about as prepared as we could be. ...

Garner and senior ORHA staff waited out the war in Kuwaiti hotels, trying to do research, planning, and further hiring. These tasks were extremely difficult, since there were no readily available libraries, experts, or research facilities.

PAUL HUGHES: On the 16th of March, uh, ORHA ... flew out to Kuwait City, where we were to link up with the Land Forces Command Headquarters and coordinate activities with them. Um, we had a hundred and sixty-seven people that flew with us; a hundred and sixty-seven people that were to essentially become the government of a country of twenty-five million.

BARBARA BODINE: We stayed in Kuwait for about a month, uh, waiting for first the invasion, and ... and then the situation to stabilize enough that we could go in. It was really during that month in Kuwait that something that approximated a plan was drafted. It was maybe about an inch thick. It was called the Unified Military Plan. Um, it is in draft status, even today. I think it's dated ... the last version was dated April 17th, and it was a March draft. And this was supposed to be the entire interagency plan for the reconstruction of Iraq. And it was an inch thick and a month old. And that's what we went in with.

Drew Erdmann, a young Harvard Ph.D. candidate who had volunteered to work in the postwar occupation, was one of those who flew to Kuwait with ORHA. Shortly thereafter, he was placed in charge of policy for Iraq's education system. He told George Packer an extraordinary story.

GEORGE PACKER: Erdmann was among the two hundred or so mostly Americans in Kuwait who were waiting to go into Baghdad after the fall of ... of the city in April of 2003. Um, they were unfocused in their work. They had very little information at their disposal. They had a kind of lack of ... of coherence in the team. They had spotty, and in some cases, very poor leadership.

And so Drew Erdmann, being a resourceful and smart man, together with a few of his colleagues, started coming up with tasks that they could do while they were in Kuwait, waiting to go into Iraq. And one task that Erdmann and a few others set themselves was to draw up a list of sites in Iraq that should be secured and protected by the U.S. military as they took them over. And—

CHARLES FERGUSON: This had not already been done?

GEORGE PACKER: There'd been a lot of talk about, uh, civil disorder, the need for policing. It had all been talked about, but nothing in the way of a serious plan that could be executed quickly on the ground was in place. They didn't ha—

CHARLES FERGUSON: When the United States military went into Iraq, went into Baghdad, it did not already have a list of important places to be protected and secured?

GEORGE PACKER: No, it didn't. And ... and, I think even beyond that, the soldiers had no orders or sense of their commanders' intent to secure those places. They didn't see themselves in that role. Their role was to destroy the Iraqi army and to seize the country. But beyond that, all the things that you have to imagine happening once you've destroyed the enemy's army and toppled its regime had not been thought through, in any serious way, by either the armed forces or the civilian administration in Washington.

So Drew Erdmann is in Kuwait. With this, this assortment of mainly American government officials, waiting to go into Iraq, waiting to become the administration of Iraq, which is an amazing ambition, when you think about it. And he and a few others drew up a list of sites that should be protected. And the first site was the central bank. And the second site was the national museum. And the others were ministries. And the oil ministry was number sixteen.

They sent this list to the ... I think the planning staff of the joint task force that was essentially the invasion force, that was up at the border at Camp [Doha]. And they thought it reached the right people there. But on

April 9th and 10th and 11th, they began to see, on their hotel TV screens, all of these key institutions of Iraq being looted and burned and gutted. And they went up to Camp [Doha], and Erdmann described how he met a British officer at ... at the headquarters, and basically said, "What happened? Didn't you get the list that we sent?" And the officer said something like, "Well, you know, we've been focused on war fighting."

Soon afterward, Barbara Bodine watched the results:

CHARLES FERGUSON: Did you see the looting? Did you watch the looting?

BARBARA BODINE: We watched it on television with everyone else.

CHARLES FERGUSON: So you realized it was going on.

BARBARA BODINE: Oh, absolutely.

CHARLES FERGUSON: And did that alarm you?

BARBARA BODINE: Absolutely. I mean it was ... it was ... I mean, it was the very practical issue, you know: If all the ministries had been looted, where do we go and meet the Iraqis to start working? I mean, if there are no desks, and there are no chairs, there are no typewriters left, where do you have your ministry? But more fundamentally, there was the realization that there was absolute lawlessness and chaos going on in Iraq. And that most of the operating assumptions—[that we were] going to be liberators and not occupiers; that we were going to be out in a couple of months; that this thing really didn't take any planning or staffing because it wasn't going to be broken, so we didn't really have to fix it—all of that was ... was absolutely wrong. And we went into a city and a country that had been destroyed. Some of it by us, and some of it by the Iraqi looters.

... One of the operating assumptions, um, from DOD—Jay Garner and the way that we were structuring ourselves—is that we would go in, and there would be a fully functioning Iraqi bureaucracy. They would all be in their offices, at their desk, pen and paper at the ready. And we would come in and essentially, you know, take them off the pause button. And the Iraqi bureaucracy would continue to function, and they would run Iraq and the city and everything else.

Despite the naïveté that these people would all just be sitting around, waiting for us to show up, there was also the reality, while we were sitting in Kuwait, that the ministries were being looted. There weren't going to be any desks for these people to sit at. There weren't going to be any pens and paper for them to have at the ready.

A looted and destroyed palace from Saddam's regime, 2003.

ORHA Begins Operations

On April 19, ten days after American forces took Baghdad, most of the ORHA personnel in Kuwait, by now numbering about four hundred people, finally left for Baghdad. Almost all drove, but Garner and a few other senior personnel flew by military aircraft and helicopters. Garner flew ahead and began meeting with the Iraqi exiles that ORHA and the Pentagon expected would soon be running Iraq. He began working on three major initiatives: creating an interim Iraqi government, restoring basic services, and recalling the Iraqi Army.

JAY GARNER: When I got to Baghdad, I had to wait two days for my team to get there, 'cause they're road-marching there. So I decided to go up to Northern Iraq and sit down with [Jalal] Talabani and [Massoud] Barzani. So I did. I flew up there the next morning, sat down with them, and we discussed what their plan was, which turns out they weren't going to ... to do that. What they were going to do is bring into Baghdad the leadership that Zal Khalilzad had been working with for the past year, and Zal had been working with Talabani and Barzani from inside Iraq. And then Chalabi, um—

CHARLES FERGUSON: Pachachi, I think.

JAY GARNER: Yeah, Pachachi. Uh, Allawi. And [Ayatollah Muhammad Baqr al-] Hakim, then the leader of SCIRI. And so, they were going to bring all those together … uh, inside Iraq. And I said—of course, Talabani and Barzani and I know each other very well from our time together in '91— and I turned to Talabani, and I said, "Jalal, do you really think you want Hakim in here?" I said, "He's a little bit too Iranian for me." And Talabani put his hand on my leg, and he said, "My friend, it's better to have Hakim inside the tent than outside the tent," which turned out to be great advice.

So I said, "Okay, what we'll do is all of you come to Baghdad. Uh, you set yourselves up in Baghdad. I want you, all of your deputies, to colocate in one place. And then I want your deputies to work directly with my headquarters. And if this works out, what you will [be to] me is a face of leadership for the Iraqi people. I want you to talk to them on the radio every day; I want you to … We'll tell you what we're doing. I want you to make announcements to them, that type of thing. And if this works out, we'll consider making this organization … come up with arrangement to make this organization an interim government until such time as we [can] have elections."

And so they did. Within a week, they were all in Baghdad, and that was … now that's … by that time, it's the first week in May. They came to Baghdad, and set up. Set up a deputies' committee, which reported to my headquarters. And I began giving them things to say on the radio, and things to read out to the Iraqi people.

Garner also began work on restoring essential services in Iraq.

JAY GARNER: I took a, a senior ORHA person, and Dave McKiernan, General Dave McKiernan, took a general officer, and we put them together, and we worked on the ten initiatives. Those were initiatives like fix the fuel crisis; improve the security; bring the ministries to a functioning level; pay civil servants; bring back security forces; maintain health care and avoid epidemics; reestablish the [food] distribution program; buy the cro— … buy the harvest, harvest the crops and buy the crops; appoint town councils in all towns that are a hundred thousand or larger in population—that type of thing. So we started on that as a … as a major effort to begin to rapidly improve things.

Garner wanted to use Iraqi companies for as much of the reconstruction effort as possible—one of many policy decisions that would be reversed after he was replaced by L. Paul Bremer.

JAY GARNER: And our thoughts were, when we first went into … into Baghdad, is what we had to do is every U.S. or British or Western contractor that won a contract, we would force them to do … to spend a certain portion of that contract, up to 40 percent, um, bring in [an] Iraqi company to do the work, and to mentor them to help build a, really, a middle class, which is not really existent throughout the country.

But Garner had trouble getting contracts approved and funds released quickly.

JAY GARNER: We had a hard time getting money. There, it was … Uh, we just had a difficult time getting money released, and I don't know why that is. We had a difficult time from OMB, the Office of Management and Budget. I dealt through the comptroller in the Pentagon, Dov Zakheim, who was very supportive. But he had a hard time, too.

Uh, and [a] big problem we had at that time is contractors. Because what had happened is, you know, we don't have an agency in our government that goes out and rebuilds countries. I mean, we put some people over there to manage what goes on. But the … the heavy lifting is done by contractors. We hire contractors to come in and do that type [of] thing.

What happened in this case is, the contracts that supported reconstruction weren't signed until after the war started. Most of them weren't signed until about mid-April. And … and the largest contracts weren't signed till about the 15th or 16th of May. Now once the contract is signed, then, the contractor goes out and builds his team. Once he gets the team together, the team has to go through the CENTCOM process of being qualified to go into the country and work. And so there's a long lapse time from the time you sign the contract till the time you get the first guy in [the] country. So we really never had contractor teams in there doing reconstruction till … the first ones came in about the 1st of June, but the real … the real effort of contractors really didn't get started in [the] country till probably July, August. So that was a problem.

Most ORHA personnel drove to Baghdad from Kuwait in convoys of unarmored SUVs. There were eight convoys, each with about twenty SUVs. At this time, ORHA had very little communications capability; it was limited to a very few satellite phones—one per convoy—and some of the convoys got lost for substantial periods before finding their way to Baghdad.

Before the war, ORHA had contracted with Raytheon to purchase four mobile communications centers, vehicles that would drive into Iraq with the convoys. In principle, these mobile communications centers could support large numbers of telephone and Internet access lines. But they never worked properly, and as a result, the lack of telephones, e-mail, and Internet access continued for weeks and, in some cases, months into the occupation.

CHARLES FERGUSON: When you arrived and started work ... what was that like?

BARBARA BODINE: Well, it was interesting to ... we ... Going to work, we had no resources. We had no phone list. We had no phones for a while, so I guess having no phone list was not really that important. But we were supposed to put together a meeting in Baghdad, for Jay [Garner]. This was a Monday, was the day that I went in. And on, I think, Thursday, Jay was going to come in, and we were supposed to have a meeting with at least Baghdad notables.

And this was going to be something analogous to the [Nasiriyah] conference. But we were starting from zero, trying to find out who should be invited, where to find them, did they have phones, would they answer the phones, would they come to something that we even invited them to. You know, and we were doing this from, you know, the confines of a ... of a military installation in the middle of ... of ongoing operations. And ... trying to do this with really absolutely nothing. I mean, we had ... we had no information, as well as no resources.

And I have to give a great deal of credit to the State Department political officer who came in with me, named Andy Morrison, who literally sat in the middle of an open lot with a cell, a satellite phone, and managed to put together a conference with about a hundred people in four days.

But we were operating with ... We didn't know who to call; we didn't know where to go. I was responsible, for example, for Baghdad City. It wasn't even clear to us where the mayoralty was, or what the names were of the deputy mayors, or the director generals. Um, we had no information whatsoever—basic, basic information.

If you're going to rebuild the city, you probably ought to know who was managing it before. And we didn't. And that made our lives, you know, virtually impossible.

Jay Garner agreed that the available intelligence on Iraq's economic, bureaucratic, and political condition was poor.

CHARLES FERGUSON: What do you think of the intelligence analysis that you saw, the quality of the intelligence analysis that you saw?

JAY GARNER: The problem I had on intelligence is, like, I couldn't ... I couldn't find out what salaries were. How much does somebody in the Ministry of Health make? What does a sergeant make? What does a major make? That type [of] thing. I was never sure I had the right locations of the buildings that we had to have.

So I always had a queasy feeling about intelligence, and I think for all the right reasons. And I just don't ... and I think our intelligence wasn't that good, because we don't have good human intelligence. This is a problem we ... we've had for a long time, probably still have. ... We had that problem long before this war, and we're going to have that problem long after this war, until we do something about it.

CHARLES FERGUSON: Okay. So you concur that that problem exists?

JAY GARNER: Sure, I do.

While there was not yet any organized insurgency in Iraq, there was a high level of street crime and looting by criminal gangs. There were also isolated acts of targeted violence directed against both Americans and Iraqis. These security problems affected ORHA's ability to function. It was also hard for ORHA to protect itself. The organization had no armored vehicles, most of its employees had no body armor, and there were very few U.S. military personnel available for escort duty.

BARBARA BODINE: We had staff meetings every morning, almost all morning, while we were there. And it became increasingly a theme of the staff meetings, as you were reporting, you know, what you had done the day before, what you were going to do that day, what progress had been made ... The increasing drumbeat behind every briefing, every day, was: But all of this is being, you know, either undone, or thwarted, by the lack of security. And the security problem ... increasingly ate into our ability to do our job, and increasingly became an element of the briefings every morning: that we cannot do our job because of the deteriorating security situation outside the walls. And it ... it was dropping precipitously, you know, while we were there.

JAY GARNER: Number one, there was not enough security there to provide us with enough security every day to move our whole force out to do the work that had to be done, although we moved out probably seventy-five to ninety percent of it every day. Uh, we had to contract for our own security in Baghdad. We had to ... contracted ... had Gurkhas, Gurkhas for our perimeter security. And we had South Africans for personal security, for people like myself and other principals on the ORHA team.

Then the other problem is ... is there was far more requir— ... My observation was that there were far more requirements on the military to secure static things. Like there were, like, static ammunition dumps, uh, buildings that had been looted, that type [of] thing. And the military itself just ran out of troops. They did [not] have enough troops to do everything they had to do ... The force levels weren't high enough at the end of the war. They were more than high ... enough to win the war, but not high enough at the end of the war.

Bodine offered several examples of how the security situation impeded ORHA's progress. Here is one:

BARBARA BODINE: One of the things that we mentioned in an early meeting with these people was that I had hoped to establish some neighborhood advisory councils as a way of being able to sort through what … what ought to be the priorities for the reconstruction, for example. And who would know better what was needed in every neighborhood [than] the neighborhood advisory councils. So [I wanted] to build some grassroots participation, give us some way of connecting with the people in the city. And I said, you know, "… Before I do this, I really need to understand how this city is structured. I don't." And the deputy mayor said, "Well, come back tomorrow morning, and … and these three director generals, who were relatively younger men, will brief you on the structure of the city."

We came back the next morning. These three director generals gave probably the most coherent briefing on the structure and organization of a fifteen-hundred-year-old city that I think anyone could have gotten. Baghdad actually started to make sense when they explained it. And they certainly knew how it was structured. That was interesting and impressive. But [what] was truly impressive is then one of them [Faras] launched into this plan for neighborhood advisory groups throughout the cities that would then build to district advisory groups, that would then build to, and would ultimately become, a … a city advisory group. And he had the … he had the principles, the structure; he understood starting with one or two model neighborhoods, and then expanding it. Um, he had this whole grassroots, bottom-up, democratization thing nailed. It was an absolutely beautiful plan. And it was not one that he had come up with overnight. This is something he had been working on, clearly, for a very, very long time.

And I remember asking him, you know, "Well, where did you go to school?" I mean, you know, obviously somebody who was born and raised in Iraq could not possibly, um, understand this kind of … of grassroots participatory democracy. And he was born and raised in Iraq, was a graduate of Baghdad University, and on one level, should not have understood, been able to conceptualize, or had the courage to propose such a plan. And he did. And I think at that point, I decided that Iraq really did have a chance of making this work. …

… Our job, with Faras, was not to draw, you know, a plan on how to do this, but really, just to give him the … the support and the resources, and hopefully the security bubble, within which he could do it. And that made the whole local advisory council plan an Iraqi plan. It was a Baghdadi plan.

It wasn't American. We probably would have come up with something very similar. But before we could table a proposal, he had it on the table, and it was complete.

CHARLES FERGUSON: And what happened to it?

BARBARA BODINE: He was assassinated. Uh, he was one of the first Iraqi government officials assassinated by, you know, I guess what we now call the insurgency. ... And so in a sense, watching his plan was one of the more encouraging things that happened while I was in Iraq. And hearing about his assassination was one of the most discouraging: that if this ... if he was the sort of person that the insurgency was going after, then Iraq was going to destroy its own future. And it was ... it was horrible.

Recalling the Iraqi Army

Although the U.S. military almost never intervened to stop crime or looting, both ORHA and the military were concerned about the security problem in Iraq. For this reason—as well as others, such as reducing unemployment, assisting reconstruction, and avoiding the perception of a foreign occupation—both ORHA and CENTCOM undertook efforts to recall the Iraqi Army, which had essentially disappeared during the invasion. CENTCOM concentrated on planning, while ORHA, and in particular Colonel Paul Hughes, dealt directly with the Iraqi officers who were coming forward to negotiate with the U.S. authorities.

A recall of the Iraqi Army had been part of ORHA's and CENTCOM's policies since well before the war. After the war, CENTCOM continued to revise and update its plans. Initially, it planned to recall only a relatively small fraction of the Iraqi Army, but the numbers grew rapidly as CENTCOM commanders realized the depth of the security problem in Iraq. By May, CENTCOM plans called for recalling three Iraqi divisions every ninety days, until nine divisions—about 100,000 men—were back in service.

CHARLES FERGUSON: It was your plan to bring back the Iraqi Army.

JAY GARNER: Oh yeah. We had a set of contractors there that we had contracted. We had ... we had ... DOD had let a competitive contract, which had been won by two companies. And they had brought contractor teams into Kuwait, and those teams traveled with us into Baghdad.

CHARLES FERGUSON: To do what?

JAY GARNER: To ... to help us bring back the Iraqi Army, and begin using them the ways we needed to use them, and begin to set up a retraining program for them.

CHARLES FERGUSON: I see. And you thought that was a perfectly feasible thing to do, after, you know, after you'd been in Iraq for a few weeks, and gotten a sense of what the place was like?

JAY GARNER: Yeah, the problem with that is ... is the Iraqi Army didn't surrender in this war, like it did in the first Gulf War. It just evaporated, you know. They took off their uniforms, and just folded themselves back into the civilian population.

Army Colonel James Torgler, who was working for Garner at ORHA, started collaborating with CENTCOM on the army recall effort only days after Baghdad fell.

JAMES TORGLER: If you remember, our information operations campaign, or our IO campaign, said to the Iraqi military: "If you stand aside, if you put down your arms and stand aside, we will go past you and we will, you know, stop fighting. ... "

And Paul [Hughes] felt that we should use whatever [Iraqi] forces that we had to secure the borders. ...

CHARLES FERGUSON: You used Iraqi Army forces?

JAMES TORGLER: We used Iraqi Army forces to basically ... as a trip wire along the Iranian border. We were not so much concerned about Turkey, because ... the Kurds had that under control. Jordan certainly was not going to invade; neither was Kuwait. So truly the threat was from Iran. ...

I said, "Well, I think what we do is we use these guys and have them set up basically a series of posts with, you know, radios and small arms and pickup trucks and everything, and basically they patrol the border and let us know if there are issues and we will take care of the rest." That was Paul's and my idea.

General [John] Abizaid felt that we needed to use them for internal security, walking the streets with American soldiers. Put an Iraqi face on it, which in retrospect might have been a good idea but, you know, the number we were talking was around forty thousand. …

And so … General Abizaid asked for a planner from ORHA to go to Qatar the next day and start working with his people. And since I was the lowest-ranking guy in the room, I won the prize. And so I got on a plane and headed to Qatar and started meeting with his folks and talking about, okay, how do we do this? And at the point, at that time, General Abizaid—

CHARLES FERGUSON: What date? I am sorry.

JAMES TORGLER: He wanted something in place by the end of May, and I remember we had, like, five weeks, so it had to have been the third week of April that we were having this discussion.

Meanwhile, Garner placed Colonel Paul Hughes in charge of ORHA's recall effort.

JAY GARNER: We kept trying to find them, and eventually … they began to reappear. And I had a … an army colonel named Paul Hughes, who was … had a team that was … was, uh, seeking out the Iraqi Army, and he was beginning to find a lot of them. And he had found a lot of them. And we had made overtures to bring them back.

While Paul Hughes made progress contacting Iraqi soldiers, he expressed frustration at the lack of support he received from the Department of Defense. Each cabinet department had created ministerial advisory teams, which would be seconded to ORHA and would serve as advisory and supervisory groups for relevant Iraqi ministries. In early May, nobody from the Department of Defense advisory team had even arrived in Iraq.

CHARLES FERGUSON: Excuse me a second. Are you saying that the Department of Defense didn't designate anybody to monitor the Iraqi Army?

PAUL HUGHES: To monitor the Iraqi Army? Well, when you had a hundred and ninety thousand soldiers over there to monitor the Iraqi Army—

CHARLES FERGUSON: Well, sure—

PAUL HUGHES: But, you mean in terms of … in terms of administrating, uh, administration? In terms of accountability? In terms of dealing with the Ministry of Defense?

CHARLES FERGUSON: Yeah. Where are they? Where's their equipment? Where are their weapons?

PAUL HUGHES: Yeah, see, they did set up a team. But the team stayed in Washington, D.C. The team was headed by Walter Slocombe, former undersecretary of defense for policy under the Clinton administration. Actually, [Slocombe was] one of my old bosses when I was in the Office of the Secretary of Defense back then [in the Clinton Administration]. And he was the fellow I would tell, "You need to come over here. There are people waiting on you."

Every other ministry in the Iraqi government had what we called the ministry advisory team with ORHA. Those were the contributions from other federal departments of the United States government. We had a team from Commerce, a team from Justice, team from State, eventually. And they were working with their counterparts: the Ministry of Trade, the Ministry of Planning, the Ministry of Finance, et cetera. We didn't have anybody for the Ministry of Defense. And so it fell to me.

In the absence of the DOD advisory team, Hughes was left to proceed on his own, sometimes in conjunction with CENTCOM planners.

PAUL HUGHES: This battalion commander from the 101st Airborne came to me, and he said, "Listen, Sir, I've got a group of Iraqi officers. They want to talk to somebody from ORHA." I said, "Okay, set up a meeting." And the next day, he came and got me, and we drove out to the Republican Guard's officers club on the banks of the Tigris River, in north Baghdad. And these eight officers came in. Um, a couple of them ... three of ... I think, three of them were general officers, and the rest were colonels and lieutenant colonels. And they were all wearing civilian clothes.

And so we had a session, where I explained to them what the rules were going to be. And they asked me about how they could get the twenty-dollar payment. Are you familiar with the twenty-dollar payment? In Iraq, every federal government employee was going to be given a twenty-dollar payment by ORHA once we linked up with the ministry and verified employment rosters, and things of that nature. In a country that was socialist like that, a huge amount of the population worked for the government in some capacity. And Saddam had not been paying salaries for four to six months. A salary over there for somebody like you or me would have been five or six dollars a month. For a policeman, it would have barely been a dollar. And we wanted to give these people a twenty-dollar bill so that they could buy food for their family and have a little bit of allegiance to ORHA, that they knew that ORHA was here to help them, and that they wouldn't take off, and do nefarious things. At least that was my goal with the Iraqi military.

These officers had seen their … their peers in other ministries getting this money. Well, they wanted some of it, too. And so they came to this American outpost in Baghdad and said, "We need to talk to somebody about this." Well, the battalion commander didn't know who to talk to. He certainly didn't have the money. And so he came and found me. And so I was there to set up how we were going to keep our hands on these Iraqi soldiers, these officers. Uh, they claimed to represent, at that particular point in time, around twenty-nine thousand Iraqi soldiers.

These officers had all worked in the Ministry of Defense prior to the invasion. And when they knew the war was coming, they all knew they were going to lose. And so they started planning for the aftermath. They removed computers; they removed disks; they removed papers, and surreptitiously took them home—something that would have gotten them killed had Saddam found out about it. So quite obviously, these guys were folks that were vested in the future of Iraq.

They came to us, at great risk to themselves, because they wanted to take care of their soldiers and their junior civilians and such, make sure that these folks get their twenty dollars. And in the aftermath of the collapse of the Saddam regime, they had organized themselves into a group they called the Independent Military Gathering at the Air Force Officers Club in downtown Baghdad. What they wanted from me was a certificate, a letter of authorization, that they could use in case they were raided by American soldiers. Uh, so that they could show them that [they] were doing something legitimate, and working with us.

Well, I had … I was empowered to do that. I had to go talk to Mr. Slo-combe about that. And eventually, I got his permission to give them a letter, but it had to be with the proviso that the letter could be rescinded at any moment. [I] said, "That's fine; that's not a problem. These guys will accept it."

Another interesting thing about this group of officers is that not one of them wanted to rejoin the Iraqi Army, not one. What they wanted to do was take care of their soldiers, and then they wanted to go into the private sector, and live a normal life, as they anticipated Iraq would be able to give them.

So over the course of about four or five meetings, through, uh, late April and into early May, we laid out the arrangements of how the payments would take place. And during this time, I was laying new demands on them, demands that related to intelligence issues. Um, you know, [I] wanted to know where the high-valued Iraqi officials were. You know, the famous deck of fifty-five … [I] wanted to know where those guys were; wanted to know about [Scott Speicher].* Wanted to know about American prisoners of war taken during this current campaign. Wanted to know about WMD. And I had people with me who were absorbing everything these men were saying.

Concurrently, ORHA began negotiating contracts for the DDR program it would use to reconstitute the Iraqi Army, filter out criminals and Saddamists, and retrain those who would be returning to civilian life rather than staying in the military.

PAUL HUGHES: While we were in Kuwait, the issue of DDR came up again. And as my records indicate, on the 18th of April, I had my first discussion, uh, via secure video teleconference, with Walt Slocombe, who had been chosen to be the lead for the ministry advisory team for the new Iraqi Ministry of Defense. In that discussion that I had with him, I had already met with some contractors that had come over to help devise the … this … the

---

*On January 18, 1991, Captain Michael Scott Speicher's aircraft was hit by an Iraqi surface-to-air missile and crashed during the first coalition offensive of the first Iraq War. Although Secretary of Defense Dick Cheney has said Speicher was killed, the pilot is still officially listed missing in action.

DDR plan. We had two companies that were working with us: RONCO, a consulting firm based here in Washington, D.C., and San Francisco; and MPRI, the Military Professional Resources International, which is based in Alexandria.

Uh, RONCO was doing the DDR plan. MPRI would do what we called the works project program. We would have soldiers who would be accountable as Iraqi units. And MPRI would use them to clear rubble or to clean out irrigation systems throughout the agricultural area. Or ... or whatever. You know, just keep them at work; don't let them be alone, doing nothing. And as their turn came, they would be cycled through the DDR program that RONCO was setting up. Initially, we were going to set up three camps.

And the DDR program was quite intricate. It would ... it would take soldiers, and it would vet them; it would register them first, and then vet them; check them for their health; check it out ... their unit history, their individual history. And they'd have to fill out forms and whatnot. And then we would take them through a demilitarization program, where they would learn about, you know, classes on democracy or the rule of law or their future. And there are organizations around the world that do this, and do it very well. You know, we ... we've done—not we, uh, the United Nations has done DDR programs throughout Africa. There was a DDR program done by the NATO allies in Bosnia and Kosovo. I mean, these are not new kinds of operations. There are many experts in the world who know how to do these things. And I had two of the best advising me from RONCO.

And so the issue was, When do we get the okay to begin this? And with the okay, when do we get the money to start doing this? And as I said, this was a prototype project that was estimated to cost, if I remember the figure correctly, it was around ninety thousand dollars. I could be short on that one. But it was going to be expensive for a small prototype to do three thousand soldiers. And then, if it ramped up, it would become even more expensive because you'd have to build more camps. And the most expensive part is the reintegration portion, which consists of basically job training. You take the vetted soldier through the process, and when he gets to reintegration, he's taught a skill.

So on the 18th of April, when I had this first conversation with Walt, and he wanted to know, how would this program work? You know, what was the sequence of events? How many people did we think we would be doing? Et cetera. So I faxed or e-mailed to his staff the briefing slides that RONCO had prepared.

And then, when we got into Kuwait, or into Iraq, the conversation kind of dropped a little bit. I don't recall … I don't have records that suggest that I was calling him every day. But uh, it was towards the end of April when I had another conversation with him, and it was just general DDR, you know, "What are we going to do about these guys?" No decision had been made. And the … the majority of the conversation was about how Walt would deploy with his team to Baghdad.

Hughes commented again on the difficulties caused by the fact that Walter Slo-combe and his DOD advisory team had not come to Iraq.

PAUL HUGHES: Ironically, of all of the ministry advisory teams that were created for ORHA to work with, you'd think that DOD would have had theirs up there first and foremost. In fact, DOD's was the very last one to come to Iraq. We had … we had advisory teams for … from our Department of Commerce, our Department of Treasury, our Department of Interior, Department of Justice; they were all over there, and DOD was the very last one, which I found a little surprising. And I remember telling him one time that he needed to come over as quickly as possible because people were hanging on for his decisions.

On May 10, Hughes left Baghdad for a two-week trip to the United States. He spent several days in Boston to attend his daughter's college graduation, and then he went to Washington, D.C., to finalize the DDR contracts.

But during the first week of May, unbeknownst to either Garner or Hughes, the newly appointed L. Paul Bremer, with Walter Slocombe and a few senior Pentagon officials, were quietly deciding to reverse all of ORHA's most important policies.

CHAPTER FOUR

THE LOOTING

It is difficult to convey what happened in Iraq immediately after the United States deposed Saddam Hussein. While much of the population welcomed Saddam's removal, the resulting security vacuum opened the country to destruction and violence on an enormous scale. Iraq was overtaken by anarchy, crime, vandalism, and chaos. The term *looting* does not begin to adequately describe what happened. A nation that had been subject to a repressive, criminal, corrupt regime for twenty-five years—and which had been reduced to extreme poverty by a decade of sanctions—was suddenly set loose with no order, control, or justice. In addition, six months before the war, Saddam had released all of Iraq's common criminals from prison.

The chaos erupted as soon as the war began. Everyone I spoke with—those who had been through the entire war, both journalists and soldiers—said that whenever a city was taken by the coalition, looting broke out immediately and proceeded unchecked. Insufficient troop levels and pressure from the Pentagon for a short war meant that U.S. forces went straight through cities or even bypassed them without leaving forces behind to maintain order. This also meant that U.S. and British forces had encountered severe looting for over two weeks before U.S. forces entered Baghdad. Yet nothing was done.

Journalist Yaroslav Trofimov followed the leading edge of coalition forces all the way from Kuwait to Baghdad. The first significant town he encountered that was liberated by the coalition forces was Safwan.

YAROSLAV TROFIMOV: When we drove into the city, which was being completely looted at that point, there was this big, huge gas station ...

CHARLES FERGUSON: The city was being looted.

YAROSLAV TROFIMOV: Yeah ... Safwan, that ... that border town that we were in, at the border. Uh, the gas station was already being looted, so everybody converged there, [just] sucking the petrol out of the ... of the tank, of the big storage tank. ...

Looting started immediately. There was no law and order, and looting started immediately. And so, we went through that town. That was still the first day.

Marine Lieutenant Seth Moulton, who fought in the entire war, witnessed the looting firsthand as his unit moved from Kuwait through Iraq and into Baghdad.

SETH MOULTON: I think it was apparent relatively early on that there would be ... some irregular ser— ... forces that we'd essentially bypassed, and not dealt with on the way to Baghdad, that would likely still be a problem. And the looting and everything just indicated a general lack of ... of security, again, very early on, both from our perspective, in terms of what the Americans could ... could expect to do with the number of people we had there, and also from the Iraqi perspective because there obviously weren't any Iraqi police or Iraqi army soldiers running around stopping this.

CHARLES FERGUSON: So did you see looting yourself early on?

SETH MOULTON: Oh, absolutely.

CHARLES FERGUSON: So, tell us what you saw.

SETH MOULTON: We saw looting all the way up, um, to Baghdad. But it was most dramatic when we got into Baghdad itself. And I think on, um, Day 2, I believe it was about Day 2 of my battalion's entrance into the city. We were ... we were [among] the first marines into Baghdad. We would just be clearing sections of the city. So we were still assaulting Baghdad, still, you know, encountering pockets of resistance. And there would just be swarms and swarms of people, um, carting off all manner of things, everything you can imagine.

In December 2007, I was able to conduct a three-hour-long interview, off the record, with a former senior military officer who held broad responsibilities during both the war and occupation. He confirmed that the U.S. military had known that severe looting broke out in every major Iraqi city as soon as it was taken by coalition forces. He noted in particular that when the British took Basra, they reported an immediate outbreak of large-scale looting. Thus, U.S. forces had approximately two weeks' notice that looting was a major problem before entering Baghdad. For reasons that remain somewhat mysterious, this information resulted in no action; nothing was done to forestall or stop the looting of Iraq's capital or other critical locations.

The Looting of Baghdad

When U.S. forces entered Baghdad and the regime fell in the second week of April 2003, massive looting erupted throughout the city, with catastrophic results. Baghdad contained the national government, most of the country's critical economic and technological infrastructure, and the headquarters of Iraq's most important political, military, economic, and cultural institutions, as well as a quarter of the country's total population. Thousands of buildings were looted, gutted, and then burned. The destruction went far beyond what the term looting normally conveys. Many interviewees commented on the extraordinary destructiveness of the looting, and its almost pathological, obsessive thoroughness.

SETH MOULTON: I remember one time we were …we were assaulting a factory next to some sort of an electricity station or substation or a power plant or something. And you see these Iraqis running off with, like, five-foot-long insulators. You know, and I mean it's hard to imagine what on earth anyone would do with this gigantic piece of electrical equipment, let alone someone, you know, who needs to spend his time looting.

I mean, New Orleans was bad, but this was not just people stealing stuff from grocery stores. I mean, this was … this was people, you know, chipping concrete walls into little pieces so they could take the rebar out. I mean, this was people stealing, you know, huge reels of electrical cable that … I mean, what on earth are these people even going to do with it? I mean, it was just … it was really surreal.

… The degree of lawlessness was just … was pretty amazing. And we had no orders whatsoever to stop it. I mean, we were essentially, you know, we … Well of course, at that time, we were still clearing the city; we were still … I mean, the war was still going on. I mean, we were still engaged in com-

Looters in Baghdad, April 2003.

bat. So you know, we were not ... we were told, you know, "Don't devote any of your effort to trying to stop these looters. You know, that's a problem we'll deal with once ... once we've defeated Saddam and his army."

PAUL HUGHES: One of the Special Ops guys told me that during the battle for Baghdad, there was a huge tank fight in the streets outside the ministry between the marines and some special Republican Guard units. That during that battle, literally tens of thousands of Iraqis had descended on this huge compound and were stripping it of everything. One of them saw four Iraqis pushing a rooftop air-conditioning unit down the street, in the middle of the battle, because it was something to take. That was the extent of the looting. It ... it was just phenomenal.

JAY GARNER: The problem I had with the looting was, we were going to bring back twenty of the twenty-three ministries. And of the twenty ministries we were going to bring back, sixteen of those buildings were destroyed as a pro— ... as a function of the looting. And so we didn't have facilities to ... to put the ministerial personnel in. And as you know from being there, there are no excess facilities in Baghdad. ... So that problem compounded itself in several ways. First, the ministerial people had no place to come to work, so they stayed at home. They didn't come back to work. So then, I had to put people out on the street, walking around, asking, "Do you know anybody that's in the Min— ... Do you know people in the Ministry of Health? Do you know the people that were in the Ministry of Interior? Do you know the people in the Ministry of Education?" That type of thing.

So it took us anywhere from a week to ten or fifteen days, in some cases, to bring together a core ministerial team of the Iraqis who had been in that ministry. Then, when you brought them together, they didn't have anywhere to meet, because the building was gone. So we had to move them, like, in the convention center, over in the ORHA building, places like that.

That was further compounded by the fact that what we wanted to immediately do is pay them, get them back on the payroll, get some money in their pockets, make them ... make them want to come back to work. But we didn't have the roster of who they were, because the buildings were gone; the records were gone. Well luckily, you know, each one of the ministries—generally, the little old lady in tennis shoes—showed up with a disk or something with the ... with the people on it. So after we'd been there a couple weeks, we were able to put those together, and we actually began pay ... were able to begin paying ministerial officials on the 24th of May. But the looting—[we] had incredible problems with this that were magnified because of [the] looting.

PAUL HUGHES: I went out to the Ministry of Defense compound—I can't remember exactly when it was, but it was just within a couple of days after I arrived in Baghdad. Some Special Ops guys and I went out there. And the compound was massive. There was no fight there, on the compound— one building had been bombed early in the air campaign—but the place had been looted beyond belief. And the magnitude of the looting defies Western conceptions. Just imagine the room, the suite that we're sitting in, and all that you have is concrete walls. Everything is gone. The wood on the wall, the ... the texture material on the wall, it's all gone. The rug's gone; everything's gone. That's the extent of looting over there.

Gerald Burke was a senior adviser to the Iraqi Ministry of Interior, responsible for the Iraqi police. Here is what he found when he arrived in Baghdad in May 2003.

GERALD BURKE: Every building in the [police] academy, which was probably seventy buildings or so, had been totally looted. Not just furniture and air-conditioning units, but windows, doors. Wiring was stripped from the walls. Metal edging on a step had been taken off the steps for scrap metal. So all the buildings of the academy had to be rebuilt. Every police station in the city was in similar condition. There were eighty-some-odd buildings in the city, police stations in the city, plus seventy at the academy, which was a major undertaking, to get all of those buildings up and running.

Although an enormous amount of damage was done in the first few days after the fall of Baghdad, looting continued for weeks. In some ways, it grew worse, as it transformed from initially unorganized, individual activities into increasingly organized, large-scale theft and destruction.

SETH MOULTON: Our firm base [in Baghdad] was at this cigarette factory. And the cigarette factory consisted of a tall office building and a walled compound immediately around that, which essentially we made into our base. And then just beyond … just on the other side of the walls, right behind where we were staying, were these vast warehouses that were filled with cigarettes. And I mean, we would just … Just in guarding our little base there, you know, you'd see all these just swarms and swarms of people going into these warehouses, and running off with cigarettes. And on Day 2 or 3, you know, someone lit the warehouse on fire, and the whole thing went up in flames. …

BARBARA BODINE: We're not talking about a couple of guys going in and stealing chairs or, you know, basic fixtures, and taking them down to the black market. We're talking people coming in with … with industrial cranes, and walking off with parts of a power plant. I mean, this is serious. This is not your penny-ante, you know, shoplifting. This is broad daylight … walking off with parts of … of power plants and water sewage plants.

Trofimov remarked that, from the start, little was done to stop the looting.

YAROSLAV TROFIMOV: The local food storage depot was in the town. And the … the manager of the depot, which held enough food for weeks, came out, and said, "Look, everybody's looting it and we just came to the American army, asking them to help us to stop the looting because this is the food that we need to survive for the coming month." And the military refused. Actually, he said, the military had encouraged looters to go in and … and, you know, take the stuff, because … Well, lots of military commanders, uh, at the time told me that looting is a good thing. Looting is liberating; looting undermines the, uh, the old regime. And also, some looting is … is seen by many commanders … is seen as necessary, because unless there is some looting before the arrival of the occupying force, then nobody appreciates the occupying force imposing order and law and … and pacifying the country.

Now, that second part never quite happened, unfortunately, in Iraq. … That week, I remember talking to the spokesman for the British military contingent in South Iraq. And I told him, "Look, I have witnessed all these scenes of people just carting off factories; [unintelligible] stripped down to the door frames, and then the wires pulled out of the ground. Schools, hospitals, everything's just completely, completely destroyed. And what are you doing about this? This is … this is going to undermine completely your efforts to … to rebuild Iraq. Why didn't you stop looting?"

And he just straightened his uniform, and said, "Do I look like a police-man? It's not our job."

So that was not seen as a job of the military at the time. And that's … that's a huge mistake that really cost the prestige of the U.S. and the … and the coalition forces.

Chris Allbritton, an American journalist who entered Iraq on the heels of the U.S. in-vasion, said that while the worst looting had already occurred by the time he arrived in Baghdad in late April, it continued at a lower level, still unchecked, for weeks. Many others confirmed this. Like Trofimov, he questioned why the military wasn't doing anything to stop it.

CHRIS ALLBRITTON: I saw lots of burned buildings that did not have bomb damage. Uh, the bomb damage was actually fairly precise. You could tell which buildings had been targeted, and they were generally hit, and the buildings around them were relatively undamaged. The looting was much more widespread. I mean, I saw the devastation at the Iraqi Museum [Iraq Museum]. I saw devastation at some of the … at one of the universities. And the Americans weren't doing anything. They … they would sit at cer-tain intersections, but they wouldn't actually get out of the Humvees, or out of the tanks, and … and really do much.

CHARLES FERGUSON: How come? Did you ask them?

CHRIS ALLBRITTON: Uh, no, we weren't allowed to get up too close to them. I only got up to the Palestine [Hotel], was able to talk to some of the peo-ple, and they said, "It's not our job to do this. We're here to just, you know, secure these areas, and that's it."

In contrast to Allbritton, Jay Garner claimed that the looting had ended by the time his ORHA team reached Baghdad, in late April. He was also reluctant to place blame on the military for failing to control it.

JAY GARNER: The looting was over by the time my team got to Baghdad. We didn't get into Baghdad till ... Uh, the whole team didn't get there till the 24th ... of April, yeah. But I talked to a lot of soldiers about the looting—most of them in the 3rd ID [Infantry Division] and in the Armored Cavalry [Regiment]. And ... and they came up with three different stories for me, all based on each one's experience. First story was, you know, "I'm here on First Avenue, in the fight over there, and on Third Avenue, but I'm not there yet. The ... they're burning the building, the looting's going on. So when I got ... Sir, when I got there, the building's already on fire."

The second was, "I'm there; the looting's going on, but I'm being engaged, I'm being engaged by the enemy. And, and so [I have] to fight the enemy." The problem with looting, to stop looting, [it] almost has to be like riot control. You have to stand up; you have to have a phalanx; you have to have loudspeakers; you have to force people to do things. If you do that, and you're being engaged, you're a target.

And the third one was, "Hey, Sir, I've been fighting for seventeen, eighteen days, and there's some women and kids carrying out chairs and TVs and things. I'm not going to shoot them."

This is one of the very few issues in regard to which Garner's factual claims appear to be inaccurate. Many people told me that looting continued for weeks, and that even months after the fall of Baghdad, organized looting was still occurring.

John Sawers was a British official stationed in Baghdad. On May 11, a month after U.S. troops occupied the city, he wrote a diplomatic cable to his superiors. The cable was reproduced in Michael Gordon and Bernard Trainor's book *Cobra II*. It included the following passage:

No progress is possible until security improves. Crime is widespread (not surprising as Saddam released all the criminals last autumn). Car-jackings are endemic, with the cars driven to Iran for sale. Last week the Ministry of Planning was re-kitted out to resume work; that night it was looted again. The evening air is full of gunfire.

Inadequate troop levels, and the administration's excessive optimism, were clearly contributing factors. On February 27, 2003, less than a month before the invasion, Paul Wolfowitz had expressed skepticism that elevated postwar troop levels would be needed to maintain security in Iraq: "It's hard to conceive that it would take more forces to provide stability in post Saddam Iraq than it would take to conduct the war itself and to secure the surrender of Saddam's security forces and his army. Hard to imagine."*

GEORGE PACKER: "Hard to imagine." Anyone who had any experience in the interventions of the nineties knew that the opposite was true. You need *x* numbers of soldiers per thousand citizens simply to provide a modicum of security. … But Paul Wolfowitz couldn't imagine it.

Some people, particularly military officers, argued that with the number of troops available, it was simply impossible to control the looting, even if the military had been ordered to do so. General Paul Eaton, who was placed in charge of training the new Iraqi Army in May 2003, arrived in Iraq in June. He saw evidence of large-scale, organized looting of Iraqi military equipment.

PAUL EATON: We flew over [parks] of vehicles that had been destroyed, tanks that hadn't been destroyed by military action, but had been destroyed by looting, where anything that could be salvaged [was taken], so all the wiring harnesses were gone. The tank engines had been, uh [un]screwed; the … the tires and engines removed from the trucks. So we … we truly understood that we were at a white sheet of paper, ground zero, to build this thing.

CHARLES FERGUSON: Why was that level of looting permitted?

PAUL EATON: You—

CHARLES FERGUSON: No, forgive me, but if you saw large numbers of vehicles, especially tanks, with their wheels and engines removed. You know, that's not somebody with a shopping cart taking a mattress; that's, you know, a different level of—

---

*Paul Wolfowitz, testimony to U.S. House Budget Committee, February 27, 2003.

PAUL EATON: I ... I can't spe— ... I wasn't on the ground then. What I do know is that you ... you had the 3rd Infantry Division; you had the Marine Division; you had the 101st in motion, still in motion, up to the north. We had failed to get Turkey to allow us to bring the 4th Division into ... into the fight from the north. Uh, so essentially, you had a ... you had a robust corps ... going after a country's armed forces, which in this case worked.

But [that] in no way gave you the troops, the boots on the ground, to assure the security of the country, to pick up the security function from a country that has just failed. The country, the ... the Baath Party, the government, when it stood down, everybody went home. So the worst elements of a society came out. And the ... the results were apparent.

CHARLES FERGUSON: And don't you think, though, that if the military had been told to stop the looting as best it could, that it could have done more than it did?

PAUL EATON: There is no way that the number of soldiers that we had on the ground could have prevented that looting. There is no way. Baghdad is an enormous city. And you essentially had the 3rd Infantry Division trying to control it. Now, there were just ... it ... There was just nowhere near enough soldiers to provide the security coverage of that nation.

Most others, whether military or civilian, believed that if the U.S. military had been ordered to stop the looting, it could have done so. At a minimum, they felt, it could have guarded critical facilities and national institutions. I asked Seth Moulton about how he felt in light of his own experience in Baghdad.

SETH MOULTON: We're a platoon of marines. I mean, we could ... we could certainly stop looting if we ... if that was our assigned task. If we were [sent] to, you know, stop assaulting this house—go stop the looting in this neighborhood—absolutely, we could have gotten it under control. ...

I ... It seems to me like since Baghdad was the focus of the American invasion, and at the end of major combat you had a lot of units in Baghdad, that it seems to me that stopping the looting in Baghdad itself would have been pretty ... pretty reasonable.

The preponderance of the evidence suggests that much, though not all, of the looting could have been prevented if U.S. forces had been ordered to stop it. Most interviewees, particularly those with military backgrounds, believed that inadequate troop levels were an important contributor to the military's inability and reluctance to control the looting, but most agreed that more could have been done. Seth Moulton felt that the failure to control the looting was the combined result of insufficient forces, a focus on eliminating any remaining resistance, and insufficient awareness of how much damage the looting was causing. He said that nobody ever instructed U.S. forces to stop the looting.

SETH MOULTON: After Baghdad fell, we would do security patrols out there. But it was still really trying to root out any last bits of resistance. We were never, that I recall ... During that time, we were not sent out, we were never sent out to stop looting. Now I ... I don't remember exactly how orders may have changed in ... You know, there may have been a point at which we were told to discourage it, or something. But certainly, certainly in the days immediately following the ... the fall of Baghdad, our focus was still on insuring security from a standpoint of any leftover, uh, comb— ... any leftover elements of the resistance.

CHARLES FERGUSON: Okay.

SETH MOULTON: So it was not, it was not to stop looting. ... I mean that was ... that was never our assigned task, to prevent that. I mean, we ... we had other jobs. And we were never told to stop the looting, even [when] it was going on right in front of us there.

CHARLES FERGUSON: Hm. Could you have stopped it?

SETH MOULTON: We absolutely could have stopped it. But it's not like we were just sitting around doing nothing. I mean, we had other missions. So had they decided to use us to stop looting, as opposed to doing these security patrols or something, then we certainly could [have]. But it's ... But I certainly don't want to give you the impression that we were just sitting around Baghdad, doing nothing all day. That was not the case.

CHARLES FERGUSON: Well, let me ask a more specific question and also a more general question. The more specific question is, If you had been told that it was a good idea to stop the looting that you saw, could you personally, and your unit—could you have done more than you did? Could you have had some effect on the environment that, you know, you—

SETH MOULTON: Sure, absolutely. Now, whether we could have stopped the looting in the city at large or anything, I mean that's dependent on how many forces you have and everything. You know, it would ... You could say one platoon of marines might have been able to control a certain neighborhood or a certain small section of the city of Baghdad, and prevented looting for as long as [they] were there. But, whether or not you can, you know, expand that, based on the number of forces we had, and the other missions we had to accomplish, to stop looting throughout Baghdad or throughout Iraq, um, you know, that's [hard to] answer.

CHARLES FERGUSON: Well, that was indeed my more general question. What could have been done about the looting in general? Was this an avoidable problem, a preventable problem, a stoppable problem, or not?

SETH MOULTON: Uh, not with the force, not with the number of people we had. Because, I mean just in ... in the way we got to Baghdad, I mean, we would bypass all these cities. It wasn't like we were leaving American forces there once we fought through there. ... So in our certain area, if we had been told that a priority is to stop the looting, I'm sure that we could have stopped it in that area. But then there are all these other cities and towns, on the entire road back to Kuwait that were, at least for a time, or for certain amounts of time, unoccupied.

Paul Hughes agreed that lack of resources was the most important single contributor to the initial failure to control the looting. Because the military did not have enough troops, military police, or interpreters, the scarce resources could not be spared for controlling looting and other police functions, and the military therefore allowed it to occur.

PAUL HUGHES: We didn't have the force structure. We were still fighting battles. I mean, we still had to go up to Salah ad Din. We hadn't even gone into Al-Anbar yet. We had gotten as far as Fallujah. You know, [we] had a huge firefight in Fallujah. No, there were still fights to fight. There just weren't enough forces. We had traffic control points set up. Traffic control points aren't guys that are out walking the street. When you take a heavy division of the United States Army, you don't have a lot of what we call dismounts, soldiers who walk as infantrymen, on foot. Marine divisions have many, many more dismounts than army divisions do.

And in that kind of urban setting, that's what you've got to do. You've got to get out, and you have got to patrol. You have got to walk, and talk to the people, and see what's going on. Taking a Bradley fighting vehicle down a street, at twenty kilometers an hour, is not a patrol, not in an urban setting, because you're going by things too fast. You don't hear what the people are saying. The fact that we didn't have translators was another problem, but [*claps*] you know, we just didn't have the forces to do it.

Hughes also said, however, that more could have been done. He cited several failures on the part of the military, including this one:

CHARLES FERGUSON: It wouldn't have even been possible to guard, you know, the hundred most important buildings in Baghdad?

PAUL HUGHES: Well, we had, uh, turned in a list to General McKiernan's headquarters of, I think it was thirty-two buildings or sites that we needed to have defended, needed to secure, to make sure they didn't get burned or … or damaged. And it turned out that over at his headquarters, requests for things related to the postwar setting were things that were just not high-priority; they were fighting a war. And one officer told one of our guys, "Eh, yeah, it was in a box over there. We didn't get to it. We had too many other things to worry about."

Barbara Bodine confirmed this story. She also said that military officers had told her that the Pentagon had ordered the military not to interfere with the looting.

BARBARA BODINE: When we found out about the looting of the … of the National Museum [the Iraq Museum], which I think was the … the one that really galvanized a lot of people. And someone on my staff came to me that evening, you know, with word that the National Museum was just being stripped and looted. And we went next door to where the senior military leadership was. And said, you know, we had word that the museum was being looted, and you know, we needed to get troops over there, and protect it. And this was a, you know, a world heritage, not just an Iraqi. And I will say, it was very interesting. The British generals, by and large, understood the importance of protecting the museum, and started to respond almost immediately. And the American generals, by and large, just looked at us with, "What do you expect us to do about that?" And there was a ... there was a very noticeable difference in the response to the news. They were not given the mandate, the mission, or the resources. But I'm not sure that there was ... fundamentally an understanding about how critical to ... to protect those sites were.

We had done a list of twenty sites that we thought needed to be protected. Um, historical, cultural, artistic, religious. And we had provided that. And it really made no difference whatsoever. And in defense of our military, they were not given the troops to do that. And to the extent that they tried to do it, um, the clear impression was that the word came from Washington that that's not your job. You know, that's ... We're not getting involved in that. We're not going to stop the looting; we're not doing police work; that's not what we're here for. And I think—

CHARLES FERGUSON: So there were explicit instructions from Washington to not interfere with the looting.

BARBARA BODINE: Yes. And I think we have to remember that we had a secretary of defense who stood up and said, "Well, this is just messy. This is ... this is part of democracy, you know. A part of democracy is people get to make mistakes and do bad things." So we not only explicitly told our military not to get involved, but we publicly distanced ourselves from any sense of responsibility to ... to maintain law and order in Baghdad.

The images you are seeing on television you are seeing over, and over, and over, and it's the same picture of some person walking out of some building with a vase, and you see it twenty times, and you think, "My goodness, were there that many vases?" [*laughter*] "Is it possible that there were that many vases in the whole country?" ... But in terms of what's going on in that country, it is a fundamental misunderstanding to see those images over, and over, and over again of some boy walking out with a vase and say, "Oh, my goodness, you didn't have a plan." That's nonsense. They know what they're doing, and they're doing a terrific job. And it's untidy. And freedom's untidy. And free people are free to make mistakes and commit crimes and do bad things. They're also free to live their lives and do wonderful things, and that's what's going to happen here.

—Donald Rumsfeld, Department of Defense news briefing, April 11, 2003

In fact, shortly after making his public comments, with looting still under way and general crime increasing sharply, Rumsfeld canceled the deployment of the 1st Cavalry Division and other additional forces that General Tommy Franks had planned to deploy to stabilize Iraq.

JOHN AGOGLIA: [On April 16] we find out there is a VTC [video teleconference] with the secretary of defense talking about the two additional divisions coming in. We have a VTC, and we are asked to write talking points for General Franks. The VTC consists of General Franks, General Abizaid, the CENTCOM staff, the component commanders Keating, McKiernan, Wallace, Buz Mosley from the Air Force. And then from D.C., you have the secretary of defense, Deputy Undersecretary Wolfowitz, and Feith. You have the chairman and the vice chairman.

They go through, "Hey, Tommy, do you still need those additional two divisions? 1st Infantry, 1st Cav?" He [General Tommy Franks] has about ten talking points, which my guys wrote for him. He goes through his talking points as to why he needs those two additional divisions. The other component commander gets to chime in, and he states emphatically that he needs those two additional divisions: "Again, we need them to go out there to the west and north and east." He [Rumsfeld] says, "Okay, guys. You got them. No problem."

About four days later, we're having another VTC. Lo and behold, the topic is, Do you still need those two additional divisions? Now what in God's name changed in those four days, I don't know, but I was asked to write the talking points for it. So I grabbed the set of talking points from the other time, and I just kind of moved them around a little bit. I remember, I was walking down the hall with General Franks, and I handed him the points and said, "I don't know what to tell you. All I did was move them around. I made ten [become] three, three six, one five, five one. I kind of moved them around." He just kind of laughed and said, "Yeah, John, I don't know what the hell we're going to talk about."

We walked in; it's the same cast of characters. Same set of questions. General Franks says, "I need the two divisions. Here's why." Secretary of defense says, "Tommy, you got them." Okay. So that VTC was [April] 17; the other VTC was [April] 20 or 21.

Right after that VTC, myself and the team of folks got on a plane and flew into Baghdad to set up the second interim Iraqi governance meeting that occurred on 28 April in Baghdad. ...Well, we do the interim Iraqi governance meeting in Baghdad, come back from that—I get into Qatar on or about 1 May or 30 April. When I get back to Qatar, I find out that we're not getting the two divisions. The 1st Cav has been turned off; 1st Armored [Division] is coming, but 3rd IB [Infantry Brigade] is going home. So the net gain is zero.

Unchecked by coalition forces, the looting began to mutate into organized crime, some of which was perpetrated by militias. Bodine recalled one particularly blatant carjacking performed by members of Ahmed Chalabi's seven-hundred-man private militia, which had been funded and trained by the U.S. Defense Department and then flown to Iraq on U.S. military aircraft.

BARBARA BODINE: I got there on a Monday. So on a Tuesday, a senior U.S. general and I went to meet with a group of, I don't know, fifteen or twenty Baghdadis to talk about their concerns. And after we listened to kind of the general comments, they then, of course, went straight to, you know, "What are you doing in order to maintain law and order, to protect us?" And, as if almost to drive the point home, while we were at this Baghdadi's home, listening to these ... these people, a ... militia group that had been funded and trained by the U.S., that had an unauthorized checkpoint just down the street from this house, came to the house, carjacked the host's car with the host driver in it, and drove away, right out from under the nose of what was the senior U.S. military general and, at that point, the senior U.S. government civilian. And this was, you know, three o'clock in the afternoon, broad daylight. They knew exactly what they were doing, and to whom they were doing it. So you know, the ... the brazenness of the problem was right there in our face.

And the general, the next day, did issue what was essentially a martial law order. One paragraph, very short, very brief. [It was] possibly the first time that we had ever described ourselves as occupiers, or the occupying power, and that in and of itself was ... was fairly dramatic. But [it was] a recognition that as the occupiers, we had an obligation to provide stability and security.

And you know, I don't think I actually talked to the general about this directly, but he did understand that this degree of lawlessness was not just an inconvenience to the Iraqis, but was potentially a major security problem for his troops. And he did try to do, um, a martial law order. And he did step up to the plate and say, We are the occupiers, and we have obligations. And he was not able to get any traction from home, and it basically just kind of withered away, and ... it was never enforced, not in any meaningful way. But it was not because our military did not understand the problem. They did. They just couldn't get the ... the backing to ... to enforce it.

CHARLES FERGUSON: I see. Can you name this general?

BARBARA BODINE: No.

[The general was in fact Army General David McKiernan, in charge of U.S. ground forces in Iraq, and currently the Commanding General of the United States Army, Europe and 7th Army.] Apparently, McKiernan wished to declare martial law but was prevented from doing so by the Pentagon leadership. In my off-the-record interview with a former senior military officer, the officer said that the U.S. military sensed a reluctance on the part of the Pentagon to declare martial law, although the interviewee did not know of any explicit instruction not to do so.

Paul Hughes felt that the Pentagon's reluctance to declare martial law limited the U.S. military's ability to control looting and especially to guard weapons stockpiles:

PAUL HUGHES: Part of the mission order for General McKiernan was to secure all the weapons sites that they found. Uh, the intel [intelligence] count that I had was six hundred and seventy-two sites of concern that had to be secured. Some of them were the size of this suite. Some were twenty-seven thousand square acres, like Al-Tuwaitha. You don't take six soldiers, and say, "I got it, Boss." Some of those sites took battalions to secure. And when you take a brigade of three battalions, and you drop a battalion off to cover that site, or a company off to cover that site, by the time you run into an enemy battle position, you may not have a lot of combat force left. So the American commanders were just quickly looking at these sites, and then they were taking their soldiers and moving on, because they had a battle to fight. We didn't have enough forces in the country.

And when the secretary of defense turned off the deployment of the 1st Cavalry Division, in April, it shocked us. How can you turn off that division? If we had had that division following us into Iraq, we would have stabilized a lot more of Iraq just through our presence.

Seth Moulton agreed that there was rampant looting of weapons depots.

CHARLES FERGUSON: Everybody felt … that a lot of weapons were left unguarded, and so insurgents and criminals could get access to them. Did you have any exposure to that? Was it an issue? Was it not an issue?

SETH MOULTON: It's definitely an issue. There's no question that the Iraqi populace in general is much more heavily armed than anything we're used to in the West. … A lot of that stuff was just … was just never guarded after the war ended. I mean, you had huge ammunition dumps that weren't guarded until, uh, several weeks, if not a couple months, after major combat actions ended. And those places were looted just like the … the schools and the libraries and the museums.

Looting of weapons and ammunition continued for months, largely due to inadequate troop levels. This contributed both to looting generally—because looters increasingly were heavily armed—and also to the growth of the insurgency because insurgents had ready access to weapons and ammunition. As Marc Garlasco traveled through Iraq working for Human Rights Watch, he saw weapons being looted.

MARC GARLASCO: We would find weapons caches. And I'm standing there, watching these insurgents pull out rockets and mortars and bombs from these weapons caches that the Iraqis had, you know, stashed everywhere. And you go to the British, or to the U.S., whoever's there, with your little GPS [global positioning system] receiver, and say, "Hey guys," you know, "we found, like, eighteen thousand million tons of bombs, and there are a bunch of Iraqis there with AK-47s, taking it away. Probably not the best idea. Here's where it's located." And they say to you, "We just don't have enough people to cover it." And it just—I couldn't believe it. It wasn't the right answer. Go there, and ... and take care of it—for your security, for the civilian security, for everybody ...

So I found myself ... Okay, you know, you're there for a specific purpose, but you gotta work on so many other issues, so many different things. And I was just amazed at the breadth and depth of the problems that were going on, you know.

CHARLES FERGUSON: What did you see?

MARC GARLASCO: Total lack of security. And it's, uh, it goes without saying—I mean, it's become so cliché now—but looting of weapons, gosh, it was ... it was just ... it's hard to describe, even. [*sighs*] Utter chaos. Dogs and cats living together. Oh, man. I don't know.

Why Was Nothing Done?

The question of why nothing was ever done to stop the looting of Iraq, particularly in Baghdad, remains one of the most mystifying of the war. Limited capability due to inadequate troop levels clearly played a role, as did the reluctance of the military to assume police functions. But it remains unclear why martial law was never declared; why the military never guarded essential facilities; why the looting was allowed to continue for weeks; and why senior administration officials never intervened. Some interviewees asserted that the Pentagon explicitly ordered the U.S. military not to take action.

JAMES FALLOWS: I've tried hard over the last couple of years to get some kind of satisfactory explanation of why the looting wasn't stopped; why some commander on the ground didn't say, Look, you know, this is terrible, we've got to stop this; why some, some political supervisor of the commanders on the ground didn't say we have to change policy; why the administration in Washington didn't say, all of our gains are imperiled by what ... what's happening in Iraq. I have had no satisfactory answer, and maybe there isn't one.

There do seem to be sort of shards of answers that ... that have come up. One is the attitude which Don, Donald Rumsfeld, so memorably expressed. And I think actually it said something about the administration's point of view, you know: Freedom is disorderly, and people have to sort of blow off steam. I was interviewing Walter Slocombe, who did actually tell me that there was a lot of pent-up energy that people had to sort of get out of themselves, and did you want U.S. soldiers to be there, shooting these recently liberated Iraqis, since, especially, as he pointed out, many of the things they were attacking were sort of symbols of the old regime: you know, by definition, since the old regime had built most of the public infrastructure there. So there was this sense that, well, boys will be boys; you have to let people blow off a little bit of steam.

GEORGE PACKER: Everyone was warning about looting, because looting is what happens, automatically, when you take out a regime. We saw it in Panama; we saw it in the south and north of Iraq after the first Gulf War; we saw it in Bosnia; we saw it in Kosovo. Looting is a given. So no one can claim that they were caught by surprise by the looting. I just don't think they wanted to know. They didn't want to hear it. And I think this administration is set up in a way that, um, unwelcome information cannot penetrate the ... the chambers where the decisions are made.

It is known that before the war, the U.S. military had prepared an order that addressed looting and that ordered ground commanders to stop it. But the order was never issued. Despite asking dozens of people, I have not been able to discover why.

CHARLES FERGUSON: Did the issue of looting come up? Were there any prewar discussions or early-in-the-war discussions about it? Tell me how that went.

JOHN AGOGLIA: Absolutely. From a looting point of view, we sat down and we planners had talked about the challenge of looting in some of these big cities—what we were going to do about it. Again, we were bypassing most of the cities and we were trying to get up into Baghdad itself. But, we put together an instruction for how to deal with looting. It basically came with the idea of dealing with imposing, in a sense, martial law in a region, shutting the place down, and issuing instructions that there is not to be wholescale looting and the population needs to understand that we're not going to tolerate that. We drew up that order.

As we understood it, that order was going to go forth when General Franks went forward to have a meeting with his commanders, and that order was supposed to be issued from Franks to his commanders. We fully thought the order was issued and were sitting there watching the looting going, "Huh?" We were taken aback and found out that the order was never issued, and to this day, I don't know why.

So yes, there was thinking about it. One of my good friends, Will Grimsley, was the lead brigade into Baghdad airport and then probably the second brigade into Baghdad itself, right behind the brigade that did the thunder run. We were just absolutely shocked when I spoke to Will a few weeks later, and he said he never got an order about not looting. We never got that instruction. We went back and checked, and the order was never issued and we were never able to figure out what happened to it. Some of the initial looting—I understand General McKiernan's point that at a certain point of time with the number of troops we had initially, we knew that pushing rapidly up to Baghdad there was going to be some risk that you would have some of that going on. But we also know that you need to get the word out as rapidly as possible that you weren't going to tolerate it and you would arrest those who did it. That just never got out. Both General Wallace and General McKiernan also said they never got it. So, it just never got issued, and I don't know why.

CHARLES FERGUSON: And you don't know whether the change came from the military or from the Pentagon?

JOHN AGOGLIA: I have no idea.

Colonel Agoglia speculated that the decision not to issue the order probably originated from within the military, rather than coming from the Pentagon leadership.

Others, however, say that the Pentagon intervened to prevent martial law from being declared, and ordered the military not to interfere with the looting. I have not seen conclusive evidence in either direction.

Paul Hughes, who regretted the lack of martial law, reported that the looting so alarmed officers of the Iraqi Army that some volunteered to help stop it.

PAUL HUGHES: In his order, he [General McKiernan] was not told to establish martial sec— ... martial law. You know, not once was martial law declared. Had martial law been declared, which would have been authorized under the Fourth Geneva Convention, maybe we would have had a bit more security.

One of the officers that I was working with—one of the Iraqi officers—towards the end of the second or third meeting, when Baghdad was going, it was in chaos, said, "Colonel Paul, I can have ten thousand military policemen for you next week. You just tell me." I took that back to Bernie Kerik's staff, and nothing was done with it.* But ten thousand Iraqi police would have made a big difference; military police would have made a big difference in controlling Baghdad.

Many interviewees blamed the Pentagon for allowing crime to grow even after the initial period of intense looting had tapered off. The Pentagon, they claimed, believed that the looting was not important, did not want U.S. forces to become involved in police functions, and did not want to assume the legal and practical obligations of being an occupying force under the Geneva Conventions.

JAMES FALLOWS: From the military, I think there was, at that time, a kind of sense of, Do we want to get into this police function? One of the big problems of the U.S. military is that as more and more of its duty involves policelike functions and nation-building-like functions, the U.S. military doesn't like that. It likes fighting battles, and not ... not having to deal with civilians. So there's a natural reluctance to become policemen, shooting at ... at individual rioters, who often will be teenage boys, or ... or whatever else.

---

*Bernard Kerik, the former police commissioner of New York, in charge of Iraq's police force for several months starting in May 2003.

You know ... there are some junior military commanders I've spoken with who said they were hoping for orders from higher-ups, saying, look, we have to take responsibility for this. ... To me, the greatest mystery of postwar Iraq involves that month or so after the fall of Baghdad [and] why the U.S. didn't do anything to control the looting. Because in a way, everything that's been a problem since then started in that first month.

In general, I found Richard Armitage to be forthright and frank in his interview, but there were several issues about which he was somewhat evasive, and the looting was one of them. He argued that insufficient troop levels precluded effective action against the looting, but at the same time, he admitted that additional troop deployments had been canceled. Armitage also implied that other forces were at work, but did not describe them. He also refused to describe his discussions of the matter with Donald Rumsfeld, Colin Powell, and the president.

CHARLES FERGUSON: Do you think it was a mistake to allow the looting?

RICHARD ARMITAGE: Well, [*laughs*] obviously.

CHARLES FERGUSON: Do you think something could have been done about the looting?

RICHARD ARMITAGE: It could have been done if you had a sufficient number of troops. But I don't think, given the number of troops that were used in the initial attack, there was sufficient force to prevent the looting.

CHARLES FERGUSON: Okay. When the looting occurred, did you express concerns about it?

U.S. Deputy Secretary of State Richard Armitage, 2003.

Stefan Zaklin/Getty Images

RICHARD ARMITAGE: Everyone expressed concerns about it.

CHARLES FERGUSON: To whom did you express concerns?

RICHARD ARMITAGE: I think everyone in the National Security Council expressed concerns. We sat around the table and expressed the concerns to each other.

CHARLES FERGUSON: Well, it doesn't seem to have resulted in any action.

RICHARD ARMITAGE: It didn't. It's obvious.

CHARLES FERGUSON: How come?

RICHARD ARMITAGE: Insufficient troops on the ground to do much about it while we were still trying to prosecute the war.

CHARLES FERGUSON: Well, as I understand it, something could've been done about that in a number of different respects.

RICHARD ARMITAGE: Yeah, you could've kept the Iraqi Army in place and utilized them, things of that nature. But it didn't happen.

CHARLES FERGUSON: Well, also, Secretary Rumsfeld also canceled the deployment of a major division after … immediately after the war was concluded, did he not?

RICHARD ARMITAGE: Well, that's a matter of history. It was the 4th Division.*

CHARLES FERGUSON: Yep. So, it … Are you saying that everybody in the National Security Council except Secretary Rumsfeld—

RICHARD ARMITAGE: I never mentioned Secretary Rumsfeld. I said we all talked about the looting, expressed concern about it. The … the … Mr. Rumsfeld can speak for himself, and you'll be able to speak to him, I'm sure.

CHARLES FERGUSON: But everybody else on the NSC expressed concern about the looting?

RICHARD ARMITAGE: We all had concerns about it if only for the practical reason that it … that, in Iraq, for the future, is going to need the infrastructure, computers, telephones, wiring, et cetera. Perhaps, the largest concern concerned the looting of the antiquities. This was, perhaps, the biggest concern initially raised.

---

*In fact, it was the 1st Cavalry Division, not the 4th.

CHARLES FERGUSON: So why didn't President Bush order Secretary Rumsfeld to adjust policy in reaction to this situation?

RICHARD ARMITAGE: You'll have to talk to those two.

CHARLES FERGUSON: I see. Did people in the NSC express these concerns to President Bush, personally?

RICHARD ARMITAGE: Well, when you say, "in the NSC," that's a matter of the president's own staff. At the NSC would be in the National Security Council, which are the chief advisers to the president. People at the National Security Council, Secretary Powell, myself, and others—the CIA director—did express concern about the looting.

CHARLES FERGUSON: Did you express any concern to President Bush?

RICHARD ARMITAGE: I was at a meeting where it was expressed by my boss. Generally, when there's two of us there, one speaks.

CHARLES FERGUSON: OK. And, so, tell me what Mr. Powell said at that meeting.

RICHARD ARMITAGE: Well, you know, that's not the way we generally work. Our advice to the president is generally kept that way—private to the president. But I think it is fair to say because it's obvious, on the face of it, that there were [not?] sufficient troops. Had we all come to ... to one mind that the looting was the worst thing in the whole world, there still weren't sufficient troops. Nor was there an ability to get sufficient troops there in a timely enough fashion to prevent the looting.

CHARLES FERGUSON: Well, I have also been told by a number of people, including people who were there doing the fighting, that looting broke out almost as soon as U.S. forces crossed the border into Iraq, and that there was looting continuously all the way up the ... the pathway to Baghdad. And that military commanders were well aware of this. So, that would've permitted enough time to have additional forces deployed.

RICHARD ARMITAGE: No. Additional forces deployed ... Where would they come from? They were all used in the initial assault. The military commanders were, I think, correctly involved in prosecuting the war that was in front of them and not being responsible for civil disobedience and civil dissension and looting in the rear of them. Had we had sufficient forces, which is what I think your initial question was, then we would have had sufficient forces to be able to impose our will.

It was in this context that the lack of prewar military planning for the occupation and the excessively optimistic assumptions of the Pentagon began to bite. Military planning for how to behave once Baghdad was taken seemed to be almost nonexistent. In the face of the rampant looting and crime, the military was apparently uncertain as to how to conduct itself. Seth Moulton and others on the ground experienced the confusion on the receiving end.

SETH MOULTON: After the fall of Baghdad, we had no idea what really was going to happen. And there certainly didn't seem to be much of a plan. So quite frankly, you know, the marines are supposed to be first in, first out. And what we were generally being told is that we'd be getting back on the ships, you know, within a month or two of essentially conquering Iraq. And so that's what we expected to do when we left Baghdad. We instead were told ... We were moved south to Hilla. Which we interpreted to be just, you know, a short stop on the way back to Kuwait and ... and back home. ... My battalion essentially owned most of Babil Province, which is pretty noteworthy, considering how many battalions of American forces it now takes to control that same area. But we owned most of Babil Province, centered in the capital city of Hilla. ... And so I actually worked for the battalion, and, you know, one day the battalion commander called a couple lieutenants in and said, "Lieutenant Martin, you're going to go work with the police department; Lieutenant Moulton, you're going to go work with the Iraqi media." And that was pretty much the extent of my orders.

Barbara Bodine, who was struggling to get Baghdad up and running again, became convinced that the illusions of the Pentagon leadership were preventing any effective response to the city's continuing security problems.

BARBARA BODINE: [The looting and crime affected] our ability to get around, the ability of anyone to come see us, and it was increasingly difficult for Iraqis to go to work. Carjackings were up. The kidnappings of ... of their children. Sabotage. Uh, we would go in and fix something, and ... and the saboteurs would come in and ... and destroy it. And the looting that was reversing almost every attempt we ... we made to rebuild the infrastructure ... It was not only difficult for us to go in and repair it, but it was increasingly more dangerous for the Iraqis to go in and do it, as well. And so ... in the first couple of months, we were falling behind on our ability to ... to repair the infrastructure and get the power and the water and the sewage and everything else in the city up and running again. And the Alice's Red-Queen-race sense [the race in Lewis Carroll's *Through the Looking Glass,* in which Alice must run as hard as she can just to remain in place] that, you know, we were running faster and faster and falling further and further behind was already evident by May, June.

CHARLES FERGUSON: And I assume you told people about this?

BARBARA BODINE: Oh yes.

CHARLES FERGUSON: And?

BARBARA BODINE: And it was ... everyone ... I mean, this was not something that I was the only one dealing with. I mean, it was something we were all dealing with constantly. The State Department certainly knew about it. The CIA knew about it. DOD knew about it. The military did. I mean, they had to live with this every single day. But the decision to commit the kind of political will and resources to fix this simply weren't there. And even as late as the middle of May, when ... when this dysfunctional "race" was already very evident ... while that was going on, and it was being reported with increasing shrillness by everyone, the military was still under orders to accelerate deployment out of Iraq. And Jay Garner was still operating under instructions and assumptions that ORHA would be essentially out of business, completed, by the end of August of '03; that within four months, the U.S. military presence would be reduced to a minimum, and the U.S. reconstruction effort would be essentially over; that we would have returned most ministries to the Iraqis; we would have appointed an interim government; and the security situation would either be sufficiently under control, or we would have brought in enough coalition military support that the U.S. military would be essentially gone. And we were operating on an accelerated redeployment as late as the middle of May. So however much noise everyone was making about the security situation, I, at least, didn't see any evidence that it was affecting the policy decisions.

As it turned out, the initial looting was merely the first symptom of a far more serious security vacuum that generated street violence, organized crime, and militias. The early looting was largely spontaneous and disorganized, but it quickly evolved into systematic, large-scale theft by criminal gangs. Inadequate U.S. troop levels, the absence of the Iraqi police and army, the failure of the Americans to enforce martial law, the pervasive availability of automatic weapons, and the presence of nearly a hundred thousand common criminals on the streets combined to produce an ever more horrifying environment.

NIR ROSEN: Iraq became a dangerous place right after the war. So many guns, so little law and order. Within a month of my being there, I visited the Baghdad morgue ... Prior to the war, the Baghdad morgue received one murder case a month. Within a month, they were getting about twenty-five a day. I got there one morning around nine A.M., and they had already gotten about fifteen bodies, murdered, all of them murdered. And they were seeing rapes often for the first time, rapes and murders. Iraqi girls were being kidnapped. So Iraqi women disappeared [from] the streets. They stopped going to school; they stopped driving; they were relegated to the home. In Baghdad, at least, you could say that under Saddam, if you kept your head down, the violence was ... um, how would I say it? Under Saddam, if you avoided politics, you could in general avoid the violence. The violence was state directed. After Saddam, the violence was every-where. Under Saddam, the Iraqis often said, whether Sunni or Shia, they could walk around the streets at three or four o'clock in the morning. Cer-tainly in the months following the war, this was impossible. Iraq was a scary place to be at night. Criminals rule[d] the streets. And in fact, they continue to do so.

GEORGE PACKER: Chaos. The, the streets were chaotic. People could kill and get away with it. There was no working police force. The Americans were not acting as the police. The Americans were in what they call Force Protection Mode. They were, above all, concerned with their own protection. They were patrolling, but the patrols were more like presence patrols: just, we're here. They weren't really capable of ... of policing the streets of Baghdad. I mean, they didn't know the streets of Baghdad. They didn't speak the language; they didn't have interpreters in sufficient numbers. They didn't have intelligence about what was going on. So it was a free-for-all. And you just felt, there's a ... there's a void here, and it's inevitably going to be filled by people with guns. It's not going to be filled by idealistic students and, you know, Iraqis who've always wanted to have their voices heard.

BARBARA BODINE: If we weren't going to take care of looting and carjacking and ... and the increasing criminality, then we had to support some kind of local police that would. But we were so conflicted over the degree to which we could work with preexisting security, or bring in our own, or what we would do, that we drifted for a very, very long time.

And unfortunately, the ... the criminals in Iraq knew this. And became increasingly bold—kidnappings for ransom, violent carjackings, bank robberies. I mean, these things were happening increasingly before that sort of mutated into an element of the ... the insurgency.

And I think we need to remember that, you know, just before the invasion, Saddam let, I think, like a hundred thousand prisoners out of the jails. Well, those weren't political prisoners. You know, political prisoners didn't last that long in an Iraqi jail. Those were just criminals. And he basically just, you know, took the lid off of the ... the criminal sewer system in Iraq, and these people were all wandering around.

PAUL HUGHES: You also have to remember that what was operating on the streets during this time were, you know, between sixty-five thousand and seventy thousand criminals. In December of 2002, Saddam opened his prisons. Everybody was turned loose. And many of them were armed as they left, because he figured they'll join the Fedayeen Saddam, the irregular force. If you took the hundred and thirty thousand, and said, fifty percent of them were political prisoners, and they're just going to go home and they're just not going to do anything, that still leaves a significant amount of people on the streets. And in the chaotic situation following the collapse of a regime, that is a criminal's heaven. You know, because what do criminals do best?

They commit crimes. You know, they ... I mean, we found cases where women were being picked up off the streets and put into sex slave rings that wound up in Amsterdam. Hello? Baghdad to Amsterdam in a matter of weeks? They had already established that kind of criminal activity. ...

So it's ... it's a terrible problem over there. Those criminals made life hell. The firefights I got caught up in were not firefights where Americans were being attacked. It was Iraqi-on-Iraqi firefights. You'd just be driving down the street, and suddenly, there's a fusillade of fire that just opens up on you. And you're just in the middle of these guys shooting at each other. There's not a thing you can do about it. Which one do you shoot? You know? You know, and if you shoot the wrong one, you're going to have to deal with his relatives.

So it was a real problem for the commanders on the ground there. If we had had more troops, we could have established that martial law, declared curfews, kept people off the streets. ... There was a curfew, but I mean, how ... how well can you enforce a curfew when you don't have troops out there patrolling at night? You know, the Iraqis are not stupid. They know how to move around their own cities. You know.

One of those Iraqis, Omar Fekeiki, agreed that the Iraqi population needed to be placed under military control. Iraq, he said, was spinning into anarchy.

OMAR FEKEIKI: What did they expect? A country this ethnically diverse, religious differences, without a government, without a law to impose. What did they expect to have? Looters in the streets, and we saw ... we saw that.

And it's not ... it's not the first time that happens in Iraq. It happened in the forties and in the fifties. We have a history of ... of people uncontrolled. And we've seen ... History tells us what happened when law disappeared in Iraq.

What we saw after the invasion was everyone goes to the street and does whatever he or she wants. Iraq is not considered in ... The majority of Iraqis are not educated enough to rule themselves, for decades. And I'm not talking now of Saddam Hussein only. Even before that. Since the state of Iraq, we had only dictatorships. Therefore, generations of Iraqis ... are taught how to follow the rules. They weren't taught how to rule them-selves. They weren't told how to plan for themselves. We always had gover— ... Before 2003, we always had governments to tell us what we do. We don't have this mind-set of ... of planning for ourselves, of respecting the law. We had to fear the ... the legislator to ... We didn't abide by the law. We feared the punishment.

And that's what we ... what Iraq lacked after the invasion. There wasn't punishment. Therefore, there is no law. There was ... Maybe there was law, but people didn't abide by it, because there wasn't punishment.

And that was one of the mistakes. We are suffering it still, till now. They thought democracy will make people happy and controlled. But no: De-mocracy needs rules. Democracy means everyone should impose dictator-ship on himself and his family to be democratic to others. I have to be dic-tator on myself, not to break the law, so that my neighbor could ... could enjoy this law, and could enjoy this atmosphere. But they just gave us un-controlled freedom. I like to call it this way. Still, we only ha[d] uncon-trolled freedom.

CHARLES FERGUSON: Otherwise known as anarchy.

OMAR FEKEIKI: Exactly.

> "Think what's happened in our cities when we've had riots and problems and looting. Stuff happens."
> —Donald Rumsfeld, Department of Defense news briefing, April 11, 2003

Everyone I spoke with cited the failure of the United States to respond to the postin-vasion looting as the first enormous mistake of the occupation. Many people in-volved with either the invasion or the occupation felt that the damage done to Amer-ican credibility was even worse than the physical damage done to the country—it undermined Iraqis' confidence in both the intentions and the competence of the coalition forces. In the few short weeks after the invasion, what cautious optimism the Iraqis may have felt had begun to change into disbelief and anger.

CHARLES FERGUSON: How big a mistake was allowing the looting?

GEORGE PACKER: Um, enormous. It's all tied together. The looting was partly a factor of the troop levels. And the sense that Rumsfeld communicated to his commanders—and his commanders communicated down the chain to the platoon and company level—that we were not there to run Iraq. We were there to get rid of the regime, and get out. Which meant no one was going to run Iraq, and there would be a void in which chaos was bound to explode. And Rumsfeld confirmed it when he said, stuff happens, in the middle of the looting.

Beyond the physical damage and the fact that it made the U.S. occupation's task more dangerous and difficult, the looting destroyed much of the fragile trust Iraqis had in the Americans.

GEORGE PACKER: It told the Iraqis several things. One, that their interests were not paramount. We could not be counted on to protect them, or to secure their lives and their fortunes. It told the budding insurgents that we could be ... we could be attacked. It meant that we ... we did not show a strong hand; we seemed weak; we seemed uncertain. It told the middle class, which was our natural constituency, in a sense, for a transformation of Iraqi society, that we didn't care about them, that ... that we were going to allow them to be overrun by criminal elements.

It also just was a tremendous self-inflicted wound, because hospitals, government offices, universities, the ministries were all destroyed. I mean, it was as if ... I heard one Iraqi tribal sheikh say to an American officer—he's quoting, uh, an aphorism: "You don't burn the boat that you're piloting." And I immediately thought of the looting when he said that, because we were going to have to inherit all of this, and work with it, and rebuild it. One CPA [Coalition Provisional Authority] estimate had the cost of the looting, the initial looting, at twelve billion dollars. That was the revenue for Iraq in 2003–2004. That was one year's revenue.

NIR ROSEN: Well, I've said in the past, I've written that the Americans lost the war when they won it. And [at the point of] defeat of the Iraqi regime, they created this vacuum that allowed for the looting. And what followed was this pervasive sense of lawlessness that Iraq never recovered from. And guys with guns took over. And they were the Iraqi guys with guns.

So in a way, they lost the Iraqis right at the beginning, when Iraqis witnessed the looting, and they witnessed Americans standing by. And there was a belief that the Americans actually encouraged the looting or wanted it to happen. The destruction of our country—how could they let this happen? So whether you were Sunni or Shia, you were outraged about the looting. And you blamed the Americans for it.

Years later, people still recalled the looting—and the U.S. failure to stop it—as pivotal. Edward Wong, a *New York Times* reporter I interviewed in Baghdad in 2006, felt that America lost the confidence of the Iraqi population at that moment.

EDWARD WONG: I think the idea of letting the looters run rampant basically undermined confidence in the Americans among a lot of Iraqi people. Even now [in 2006], when I talk to a lot of Iraqis, some of them will bring up the looting. And that was … For them, it was this epochal point in the … in the war, that they looked at this, and saw that there was no power, there was no authority that would come in and actually impress law and order on this place, and that the Americans weren't necessarily here for the good of the Iraqis.

Like people in the Baghdad Museum, for example, went up to American armored vehicles that were nearby, and asked them, "Why don't you just, you know, put your vehicles around the museum?" And [the Americans] said, "We have orders that we can't move from our spots." Things like that really, I think, made the Iraqis question whether or not the Americans were here to help them. And also whether the Americans would be able to keep society together in a way that, uh, Saddam had been able to. Even … even if the Iraqis hated Saddam, a lot of them, right now, are asking, Why have the Americans been unable to keep the fragments together in the way that Saddam was able to?

BARBARA BODINE: I think the statement, you know, [Rumsfeld's] very dismissive statement that, you know, it's just messy—I think that was probably the day that we lost the Iraqis. … And I've talked to some Iraqis since then. And without prompting, they have said the same thing: That's when it became very clear that this liberation really didn't have anything to do with the average Iraqi. It was regime change. It was getting rid of Saddam.

But the needs of the average Iraqi simply were not that high on our prior-ity list. And that was ... That was basically the day that their ... caution turned to skepticism about our commitment to them.

PART TWO

OCCUPATION

CHAPTER FIVE

BREMER BEGINS

The early mistakes of the war and occupation—doing too little planning, disregarding the recommendations and warnings of the prewar analyses, using too few troops, allowing the looting—unquestionably made the occupation of Iraq far more difficult than it otherwise would have been. But Iraq's fate was truly sealed by a series of policy decisions made by L. Paul Bremer and his aide Walter Slocombe, in conjunction with Rumsfeld, Wolfowitz, and Feith, in the Pentagon in early May 2003. The effect of these decisions was reinforced by both men's continuing refusal to reconsider or reverse their decisions despite many warnings, intense opposition, and immediate evidence of dangerous consequences. The three most critical and damaging decisions were to institute a broad purge of the Iraqi leadership, aka "de-Baathification"; to disband the Iraqi military and intelligence services; and finally, to stop the formation of an interim government and instead institute a formal, long-term, open-ended U.S. occupation. Together these decisions provoked enormous animosity, fueling the insurgency at the same time as they crippled the occupation's ability to run Iraq and to provide security.

This chapter examines Bremer's appointment, his early activities, and his first major policy announcement, the de-Baathification order.

Bremer's Appointment

Jay Garner had accepted a six-month appointment as head of ORHA with the understanding that he would be replaced by "a person of stature." In fact, however, the administration began looking for an immediate replacement as soon as Garner arrived in Baghdad. The reasons for Garner's sudden replacement by L. Paul Bremer, and the circumstances surrounding it, have never been completely explained. The change was apparently the combined result of several sentiments: the administration's growing concern about the chaos in Iraq; the sense, shared by many, that Garner was not a forceful or effective manager and that ORHA was floundering (a view that many, though not all, interviewees shared); and, quite importantly, concern about Garner's desire to hold local elections and restore Iraqi sovereignty quickly. These concerns may have been intensified by reservations about Garner's political skills and his known dislike for Ahmed Chalabi.

Some of these concerns, in particular the one about Garner not being a forceful manager and lacking diplomatic skills, were shared by some senior people in ORHA. A number of people I interviewed, some of whom wished to remain anonymous, faulted Garner for his lack of forcefulness, his limited managerial and political skills, and his failure to understand the enormity and urgency of the problems he faced. Others defended him, arguing that he was simply, in George Packer's words, the fall guy for a bad strategy. Nobody questioned the general direction of his ideas or his goodwill. In my own conversations with Garner, I found him to be intellectually sophisticated, but with a strong tendency to think the best of people and to avoid direct conflict whenever possible.

BARBARA BODINE: Garner was in charge of the relief operations for the Iraqis after the first Gulf War. And by everything that I've seen and heard, he did a … an absolutely magnificent job. And I think that he was selected to head ORHA, because the initial fear was that we were going to have a lot of internally displaced people, that it was going to be primarily a humanitarian issue. And so the skills that he had brought to Kurdistan would be useful in … in Iraq. So if you assume that's what we were going to be facing, then hiring someone with his background and his expertise was exactly right.

The problem was that that's not what we faced. We faced a complete breakdown of civil order. We faced a collapse of the bureaucracy and the political structure. Um, this wasn't really a logistician's problem as the relief effort in Kurdistan had been. And so, I think it was a case of very … of bad casting; not a bad person, but just not the right skill sets for what we were dealing with.

GEORGE PACKER: A lieutenant general is brought out of his fishing retirement in Florida, and … and his defense contracting business in Crystal

City, near the Pentagon, to run the postwar outfit. He's never done anything like this. He, Garner, had experience in the humanitarian operation that prevented widespread deaths among the Kurds at the end of the Gulf War in 1991. ...

Garner is excessively maligned. I think he was the fall guy for a bad strategy, rather than the agent of the failure. But he certainly was in over his head and didn't understand the ... the almost historic nature of what he was supposed to do.

There still remains some mystery about why Garner was replaced so suddenly. In fact, it appears that the effort to replace Garner began within a few days of his arriving in Baghdad, and possibly even before he arrived. In his memoir, *My Year in Iraq,* which was published in 2006, L. Paul Bremer observes that the statue of Saddam Hussein, which actually fell on April 9, fell only "a few days" before he was contacted in "mid-April" by Scooter Libby, Dick Cheney's then chief of staff, and Paul Wolfowitz about replacing Garner.

Even less clear was how or why the administration chose Bremer to replace Garner. Bremer was an acknowledged expert on counterterrorism, but he was far from the most prominent or obvious choice for the position. A career foreign service officer, he had served as assistant to Alexander Haig, as ambassador at large for counterterrorism, and as ambassador to the Netherlands. He then became a managing director at Kissinger Associates and later was CEO of the small Crisis Management division of the Marsh & McLellan insurance company. He had never met the president, although he did know Powell, Cheney, and Rumsfeld from previous administrations.

It is tempting to speculate that Bremer's conservative economic views, his religious faith, or both may have played a role in his selection and in the extraordinary power and autonomy he was given by President Bush. In the early 1990s, Bremer, influenced by his wife, Frances, underwent a conversion to extremely conservative Catholicism. In his book, Bremer says that in his first meeting with President Bush, he said, "Mr. President, my wife wants you to know that her favorite passage from your State of the Union speech is, 'Freedom is not America's gift to the world. It is God's gift to mankind.'"

Although an intelligent and cosmopolitan man, Bremer was not well qualified for the job. His only experience with any Muslim society was an assignment in Afghanistan in the 1960s. He had never served in the military, had never worked in the Middle East, had never worked on Persian Gulf issues, spoke no Arabic, had never worked in any postwar occupation or reconstruction effort, had no experience with the oil industry, and had never managed any large budget or organization. He was, as one mutual acquaintance put it to me, a "staff guy" who had spent most of his career in Washington working for other, more prominent men.

In his book, Bremer says that after he was contacted by Libby and Wolfowitz, he spoke with Rumsfeld over the phone. Nine days later, he met with Rumsfeld personally. The secretary of defense told him he would check with "the other members of the national security team" and then arranged Bremer's first, very brief meeting with President Bush the following morning. At that meeting, there was apparently no substantive discussion of either Bremer's qualifications or the job.

Garner was not consulted in this process at all. Here is his description of the transition.

JAY GARNER: First of all, I knew that at some time early on, there would be a transition. Uh, but the … the night I got to Baghdad, after I left up north—and that's the night of the … I think the 23rd of April—Rumsfeld called me, and he said, "Hey Jay, [I] like [how] everything's goin' on; you're doin' a great job, you and your team. Glad you're now in Baghdad, and all that. And by the way, the president is appointing, uh, Jerry Bremer as the presidential envoy."

And I said, "Okay." I said, "Uh, when's he get here?"

He said, "I don't know, but it'll be soon." He said, "I don't know when the announcement's gonna be made, but it could be made tomorrow, and that's why I'm calling you."

And I said, "Okay, when he gets here, I'll go home."

And he said, "No, I don't want you to go home. I want you to stay and transition. And then I'd like for you to remain with him."

But I said, "Well, that's a little hard, because," I said, "what you don't want is the guy that used to be in charge, and the new guy who is in charge, because you send mixed signals out to your people, and they … they have a problem with who to be loyal to." So I said, "The best thing for me to do is go home, but I'll stay until the two of us transition."

And he said, "I'll be over there in another week or ten days, and we'll talk about that." And he came, and we talked about that.

So when Jerry [a nickname for L. Paul Bremer] came, I went and picked him up in Doha, Qatar. And brought him to Basra [in Southern Iraq], and then we came ... went into Baghdad, I guess on the night of the ... 12th, I think, 12th of May. And then he's a ... he's a take-charge guy. I mean, I admire that in him. And he took charge.

L. Paul Bremer (left) holds a press conference as
retired General Jay Garner (right) listens, May 12, 2003.

Actually, Bremer took charge even before his arrival, although he didn't bother to tell either Garner or the military commanders in Iraq. After his introductory meetings with Rumsfeld and President Bush in late April, Bremer started work in an office at the Pentagon. He worked there from May 1 through May 9. On May 10, he left for Iraq, meeting up with Garner in Qatar on May 11, before they flew on to Baghdad, arriving in Baghdad together on May 12.

During his nine days at the Pentagon before leaving for Iraq, Bremer had little contact with Garner, ORHA, or CENTCOM, but he quickly started planning to reverse most of ORHA's basic policies. At the Pentagon, Bremer appears to have focused primarily on three matters: reviewing the situation in Iraq, choosing a staff, and making a series of sweeping new policy decisions. He considered an array of measures whose common goal was to forcefully assert American control and to definitively purge Iraqi society of all vestiges of the previous regime. It appears that these policy goals were also blended, in some complicated way, with a desire to assert and demonstrate his personal control over occupation policy and the organization implementing it.

One of Bremer's first and most damaging decisions was to institute a broad purge of the Iraqi leadership: de-Baathification.

De-Baathification

Garner and ORHA had evolved a pragmatic, nonideological approach to the de-Baathification problem, one with which the military commanders agreed. They would initially recall everyone they could except for the very top regime leadership, then gradually remove "bad guys" over time. Several people also told me that one unspoken element of Garner's policy was a cool, even ruthless calculation that many of the worst Saddamists would simply be assassinated, a process with which, these people said, Garner did not propose to interfere. Not surprisingly, Garner did not mention this in my interviews with him. Aside from this process of elimination in the most literal sense, Garner relied on other Iraqis to come forward with information, and he only fired people for specific, substantive reasons, not simply because of party affiliation.

JAY GARNER: Our unwritten policy in ORHA had been what I'd call a gentle de-Baathification. Our policy was, as you bring back organizations like, say, a ministry, you wouldn't bring back the top guy, and you wouldn't bring back the personnel guy. You'd bring back everybody else. And then over a period of time, the people that you brought back would begin to point out who were the ... who were the bad guys. And we would take the bad guys out, and vet them, one at a time. Which is what we did, in several of the ministries at that time. We removed a dozen or more people in several ministries after people pointed them out. And we went through a ... somewhat of a vetting process to see whether they ... people were just droppin' dimes on them, or were they really bad guys.

Garner and others at ORHA had concluded that while it would be necessary to remove senior regime officials who had been willing instruments of Saddam's dictatorship, it would be crucial to retain competent managers, whether Baath Party members or not, to ensure a functioning government. In dealing with the leadership of the Baghdad municipal government, for example, Barbara Bodine put competence and honesty ahead of party affiliation.

BARBARA BODINE: About the first day, I got in a Suburban … in a four-wheel drive with some key members of my staff. And we drove over to the mayor, mayoralty building, um, where we met with the deputy mayors. The mayor, as a high-ranking Baathi official, was long, long gone. And we met with the deputy mayors and the director generals, who were the technocrats who ran the city, and said to them, you know, "We're here … I'm coordinator for Baghdad and the Central Region. And I need to work with you to keep this city functioning. You are the technocrats who did this before. And we, you know, sincerely hope that you will continue to come to work and do your job, and keep this city functioning, you know, for … for the sake of the Iraqis, the Baghdadis. And let us know what we can do to help you." But I made it very clear that I did not have the resources or the expertise to take over the management of the city. And that wasn't my job. That was … that was their job, and we would be most appreciative if they would continue to do it.

CHARLES FERGUSON: And what did they do?

BARBARA BODINE: Well, I think one of the things that is a testament to their professionalism is, they had been going to work all through this period, anyway. I mean, as the Iraqi government was collapsing and the war was beginning, these people were showing up to work anyway. They were continuing to keep the city functioning anyway. So I think they had already, in my book, proved their bona fides, that … that this is what they were going to do, and they were professionals about it. Those who were political hacks had already left.

So I just accepted them, in a sense, at … at face value. I did tell them early on that I was not immediately concerned with who was a Baath Party member or not. I was concerned with who was incompetent or corrupt or had otherwise abused their position. And if you had done any of that, then you were not going to be able to stay in your job. But that was regardless of your party affiliation. If you were competent and hardworking, and a Baath Party member, you could stay. If you were corrupt, but not a Baath Party member, you were going to leave. And I made it very clear that it was … it was a performance-based evaluation on who could stay and who had to leave.

CHARLES FERGUSON: And how did they do?

BARBARA BODINE: Most of them did very well. They did ask for letters of authorization from us to confirm that they could continue in their jobs. And I did make it very clear in the letter that again, it was performance-based, and the fact that we were asking them to stay in their jobs was not open-ended. And there were one or two letters that we had to pull back, as we discovered that either the person was, you know, egregiously corrupt, or, you know, extraordinarily abusive. And so we did pull back some letters. It was not a carte blanche.

It is possible that dissatisfaction with Garner's moderate and gradual style of de-Baathification played a role in his removal. The Pentagon leadership and ambitious émigrés such as Chalabi preferred a broad, deep purge of everyone and everything connected with Saddam Hussein, the Baath Party, and the former regime.

Douglas Feith drafted the text of the de-Baathification order, which would become Coalition Provisional Authority (CPA) Order Number 1, in early May. In his book, Bremer says that Feith showed him the draft on May 9, the day before Bremer left for Baghdad. Bremer announced the order the day after he arrived in Baghdad.

The de-Baathification order was dramatically more stringent than Garner's policy, and its implementation would be even more so. Anyone in the top four levels of the Baath Party was banned for life from all public employment. Since the government accounted for over 60 percent of all employment, including nearly all important business and professional positions, and since unemployment in Iraq was estimated to be at least 40 percent, the order had the effect of condemning to permanent unemployment anyone affected by the ban. The order also banned anyone in the top three levels of any ministry who had been a Baath Party member at all, even a very low level, nominal member. Exceptions could be granted on a case-by-case basis by a commission to be appointed by Bremer, who chose Ahmed Chalabi to head the commission.

A senior military officer I interviewed in late 2007 told me, off the record, that he and other military commanders had strenuously opposed this new de-Baathification policy and had even opposed using the term "de-Baathification." This officer learned about the proposed order only shortly before it was issued. He expressed his opposition to the policy directly to Rumsfeld, Wolfowitz, and Feith, warning them that the policy would not only cripple administration of the country, but would also alienate the Sunni community and create sectarian strife. He told me that they heard him out, and then told him that they disagreed with him and would proceed.

The text of the order follows on pages 150–151, misspellings and all.

Neither Garner nor anyone else in ORHA was consulted in the drafting of the order. Nor was there any advance consultation with the State Department or the intelligence community. Senior intelligence officers, including the CIA station chief in Iraq, were particularly upset when they learned of it. Here is how Garner found out about it.

CHARLES FERGUSON: What did you think of that order, and had that been discussed with you, and—

JAY GARNER: No. No, I didn't ... I didn't know that that order was gonna be given that day ... I was walking down the hall, and Ambassador Robin Raphel came to me, and said, "Have you seen this?"

And I said, "Uh, what is it, Robin?"

And she said, "It's the de-Baathification order."

So I read it real quick, and I said, "It's ... I don't think we can do this."

She said, "Well, I think you ought to go talk to Jerry." ...

... And the CIA, the chief CIA guy, who will go unnamed, I ran into him, and I said, "Have you seen this?"

He said, "Yeah, that's why I'm coming over here."

So we went to see him [Bremer]. And I said, "Uh, how about letting, uh, letting us go through this, and do the pros and cons, and let's get on the phone with Rumsfeld, and see if we can soften this a little bit."

And he said, "No, I don't ... I don't have that flexibility. I've been given my orders, and I'm gonna execute 'em."

So that ended that discussion.

In a later television interview for *Frontline,* Bremer said he didn't recall the conversation with Garner.

COALITON PROVISIONAL AUTHORITY ORDER NUMBER 1

DE-BA`ATHIFICATION OF IRAQI SOCIETY

Pursuant to my authority as Administrator of the Coalition Provisional Authority (CPA), relevant U.N. Security Council resolutions, and the laws and usages of war,

Recognizing that the Iraqi people have suffered large scale human rights abuses and depravations over many years at the hands of the Ba`ath Party,

Noting the grave concern of Iraqi society regarding the threat posed by the continuation of Ba`ath Party networks and personnel in the administration of Iraq, and the intimidation of the people of Iraq by Ba`ath Party officials,

Concerned by the continuing threat to the security of the Coalition Forces posed by the Iraqi Ba`ath Party,

I hereby promulgate the following:

Section 1
Disestablishment of the Ba`ath Party

1) On April 16, 2003 the Coalition Provisional Authority disestablished the Ba`ath Party of Iraq. This order implements the declaration by eliminating the party's structures and removing its leadership from positions of authority and responsibility in Iraqi society. By this means, the Coalition Provisional Authority will ensure that representative government in Iraq is not threatened by Ba`athist elements returning to power ant that those in positions of authority in the future are acceptable to the people of Iraq.

2) Full members of the Ba`ath Party holding the ranks of 'Udw Qutriyya (Regional Command Member), 'Udw Far' (Branch Member). 'Udw Shu'bah (Section Member), and 'Udw Firqah (Group Member) (together, "Senior Party Members") are herby removed from their positions and banned from future employment in the public sector. These Senior Party Members shall be evaluated for criminal conduct or threat to the security of the Coalition. Those suspected of criminal conduct shall be investigated and, if deemed a threat to security or a flight risk, detained or placed under house arrest.

3) Individuals holding positions in the top three layers of management in every national government ministry, affiliated corporations and other government institutions (e.g., universities and hospitals) shall be interviewed for possible affiliation with the Ba`ath Party, and subject to investigation for criminal conduct and risk to security. Any such persons detained to be full members of the Ba`ath Party shall be removed from their employment. This includes those

CPA/ORD/16 May 2003/01

1

and risk to security. Any such persons determined to be full members of the Baath Party shall be removed from their employment. This includes those holding the more junior ranks of 'Udw (Member) and 'Udw 'Amil (Active Member), as well as those determined to be Senior Party Members.

4) Displays in government buildings or public spaces of the image or likeness of Saddam Hussein or other readily identifiable members of the former regime or of symbols of the Baath Party or the former regime are hereby prohibited.

5) Rewards shall be made available for information leading to the capture of senior members of the Baath party and individuals complicit in the crimes of the former regime.

6) The Administrator of the Coalition Provisional Authority or his designees may grant exceptions to the above guidance on a case-by-case basis.

Section 2
Entry into Force

This Order shall enter into force on the date of signature.

[signature] 5/16/03

L. Paul Bremer, Administrator
Coalition Provisional Authority

CPA/ORD/16 May 2003/01

L. PAUL BREMER: He may have come in and spoken to me at great length about it. I just don't remember it; I honestly don't remember it.

INTERVIEWER: You don't remember these guys coming in and saying this is—

L. PAUL BREMER: Doesn't mean it didn't happen. ...

INTERVIEWER: ... this is [affecting] thirty to fifty thousand people and, my God, what are you doing?

L. PAUL BREMER: [*laughs*] I just don't [remember]. You know I was working twenty hours a day in that period as well, and this wasn't the only thing on my list of things to do the first five days I was there.

Bremer does, however, admit in his book that there was strong resistance to the order from ORHA staff: "There was a sea of bitching and moaning with lots of them saying how hard it was going to be. I reminded them that the president's guidance is clear: de-Baathification will be carried out even if at a cost to administrative efficiency. An ungood time was had by all."

In fact, it is far from clear that the order represented "the president's guidance." Although Bremer does not mention it, the order was drafted and announced with no prior consultation with the National Security Council, the State Department, the CIA, or the chairman of the National Intelligence Council. The order came as an unpleasant surprise to all of these parties. I have been unable to learn whether the president knew of it in advance.

When I interviewed former Deputy Secretary of State Richard Armitage, he suggested that the NSC and the president had already made a decision contrary to Bremer's order:

RICHARD ARMITAGE: We had made decisions. When I say, "we," ... the president obviously makes the decision. The discussion had been unveiled in front of the president about the different levels of the Baath Party, the different ranks, if you will. And [the] determination had been ... presented to the president, which he accepted, to de-Baathify down to a certain level.

So, in other words, there was a recognition, generally, over [at] the National Security Council that some people in Iraq joined the Baath Party simply for the same reason that some people in the former Soviet Union joined the ... the Soviet, the Russian, the Communist party: So they go along to get along a little bit. Not that they were hard-core, the Baathists, ideologically driven people. And this would have allowed schoolteachers and people of that nature to continue in their jobs. However, as Mr. Bremer makes clear in his book, when he went out there, he issued a de-Baathification order, but apparently, the man in charge of de-Baathification was a gentleman by the name of Ahmed Chalabi, and, as I read Jerry's book, he carried de-Baathification through to a much more stringent end than had been envisioned by President Bush.

CHARLES FERGUSON: And when the order was issued, it was a surprise to you?

RICHARD ARMITAGE: Obviously it did; it was a different decision. Not the decision to de-Baathify. ... It was, in my understanding, it was the execution of the de-Baathification order that was flawed and not the de-Baathification itself.

CHARLES FERGUSON: Well, the original order led to the termination, the immediate termination of a number of people that has been variously estimated between twenty-five and fifty thousand. And General Garner has told me—and has said on camera—that he was very disturbed when he learned about it, which was only after the decision had been taken. And that he and the CIA station chief and Ambassador Robin Raphel went to Bremer to try and get him to reverse it. And Bremer said, "I have my instructions and I'm executing them."

RICHARD ARMITAGE: Well, I don't know from whom he had his instructions 'cause his—

CHARLES FERGUSON: Secretary Rumsfeld.

RICHARD ARMITAGE: Well, fine, then. Talk to them about it, because, as I've said, there was another decision made in the ... at the National Security Council.

CHARLES FERGUSON: I see, okay.

RICHARD ARMITAGE: One that I was privy to.

The chairman of the National Intelligence Council, Robert Hutchings, was disturbed by the de-Baathification order, its implementation, and the spirit underlying both. He had not been consulted about the order in advance, and he thought that nobody else in the intelligence community had been, either. After the order was announced, he spoke to Condoleezza Rice, the national security advisor, about it, as well as to the NSC as a whole. He refused to say what Rice's individual reaction was, but he implied that the Pentagon blocked any effort to reconsider the decision.

ROBERT HUTCHINGS: De-Baathification seemed to be based on a very imperfect understanding of what de-Nazification was all about. De-Nazification was a very liberal approach toward officials of the former Nazi regime, most of whom were welcomed back into participation in the political life of the new Germany. Many of them went on to be leaders of the country. De-Baathification, which seemed to be drawing on that same historical source, was much more restrictive. It was basically to try to exclude from political life anybody who had had any ... any reasonable, or any deep association with the Baathist regime—a big mistake, in my view, and I think, in the view of many in the ... in the intelligence community.

I think back to officials who ... people who lived under Communist rule in Eastern Europe, who were members of the Communist Party in a purely nominal way. That was the case for many Baathists as well: To live your life, to operate as a professional person in Iraq, often meant a requirement of being part of the Baathist regime; not necessarily an ideological affinity with that ... with that regime. So there ... I think there was a much ... a too-restrictive approach taken toward officials of the old regime.

CHARLES FERGUSON: Did you make this point?

ROBERT HUTCHINGS: Certainly did.

CHARLES FERGUSON: What happened?

ROBERT HUTCHINGS: [*sighs*] ... I don't have firsthand knowledge here, but I think there was a stronger current of ... of an opinion, a kind of opinion that was given stronger credence by military planners in the Pentagon, and the civilians in the Pentagon, and that was, uh, very anti-Baathist, that to really try to wipe [them] out. And certainly Chalabi and others had this view, maybe as an analytic judgment about what was needed for stability in Iraq, maybe as a more partisan political judgment about what kind of Iraq they wanted to enter into. Whatever the case, I think we made a mistake in taking such a restrictive attitude toward the Baathists.

CHARLES FERGUSON: ... So when you spoke to Condoleezza Rice about this, you know, what did she say?

ROBERT HUTCHINGS: Well, I'm not going to characterize her ... her response. Let me just talk generally about how the administration, as I saw it, was acting in these areas. And that was giving greater credence to those who felt that the remnants of the old Baathist regime had to be eradicated, and that bringing them into government would be both ethically and politically a mistake. And this is, I think, the kind of comments you got from ... from a lot of the emigrés, from Chalabi and others.

Colonel John Agoglia of CENTCOM confirmed Garner's and Hutchings' statements that the CIA and other agencies had warned Bremer that the de-Baathification order was far too stringent. Agoglia was present at several meetings in which the issue was discussed with Bremer.

JOHN AGOGLIA: I was in there when Bremer was talking about going after the top four tiers of the Baathist Party, and folks from other government agencies looked at him and said, "Do you know that's a significant number? Really, all you need to focus in on is the top two tiers, and that's a much smaller number, and those are the real ones you have to be concerned with because an awful lot of folks had to be members in order to be part of the administration, the civil service side of Iraq." You had to be part of the Baathist Party. And to get higher up in the civil service, you had to get into some of those upper tiers of the Baath Party.

They recommended from other government agencies that you only look at the top two tiers, and Bremer didn't listen to them and went for the top four tiers. And you went from about six thousand to about forty thousand to fifty thousand, okay? Very clearly and succinctly, these folks told him that, and he chose not to listen to that.

In defense of himself, yeah, he goes back and says, "Yeah, I think it was the right thing to do on the army and the right thing to do for the Baathists." I'm amazed, but arrogance is amazing, isn't it? It isn't like he wasn't told. I don't know how to say it any better than that.

Moreover, there was the matter of execution. If it had simply been implemented as written, the de-Baathification order would have caused the removal of 35,000 to 50,000 people. But there is considerable evidence that the order was used to execute a far more pervasive purge. Some estimates of the number of people fired range as high as 100,000. In addition to appointing Chalabi, who held stringent anti-Baathist views and who wanted to eliminate rivals for power, to head the de-Baathification commission charged with adjudicating disputes, Bremer also required that he personally approve any exceptions. Very few exceptions were in fact approved. Nearly everyone I spoke with felt that the combined result was a disaster. Even Bremer and Slocombe later conceded a few limited mistakes.

WALTER SLOCOMBE: I have no question that once you got out into the provinces, many more people were disadvantaged and dismissed from their jobs, and so on, because they'd been in the Baath Party. But that was not intended to be the policy. [You could] understand why it happened, but that was not ... that was not intended to be the policy. And it's clear that [there was] overreaching.

Uh, I like to say, it's clear that there were twenty thousand people who were affected by the Baath Party, the de-Baathification order, of whom fifty thousand were high school teachers. I mean, very few high school teachers were ... were actually in the group meant to be affected by the order. But we were told—and I'm certain it was true—that lots of teachers were fired because of their Baath Party associations.

Now some of that may have been because, whether they were at high levels in the party or not, they were unqualified, abusive, corrupt thugs. Some of it may have been because, you know, "Ahmed had the job under the old regime; now my cousin should have the job." Sure that that happened ...

CHARLES FERGUSON: Don't you think that part of the problem might have had to do with the fact that the responsibility for implementing the order was handed over to Ahmed Chalabi?

WALTER SLOCOMBE: Well, responsibility for a special tribunal that was supposed to deal with disputes under it was handed over to Chalabi. The implementation of the order was done ... I mean, it wasn't all ... it wasn't, by any means, all Chalabi.

CHARLES FERGUSON: Uh—

WALTER SLOCOMBE: Uh, it was a mistake, clearly, to put him, or anybody else from the diaspora, in a position like that.

Slocombe admitted that the CPA had no idea how many people were actually fired as a result of the order and the way it was implemented. He did admit that many people were fired even though the order did not in fact apply to them. He suggested that this was not entirely a bad thing.

CHARLES FERGUSON: What was actually the total number of people who were terminated, who were fired, as a result? I've heard numbers ranging from—the lowest I've heard is twenty-five thousand. I've heard numbers up to sixty to sixty-five thousand.

WALTER SLOCOMBE: I've heard numbers in that range, too—

CHARLES FERGUSON: You don't know?

WALTER SLOCOMBE: Well, because we don't ... the ... I know the numbers for the military. The Baath Party total membership was well over a million. And what percentage of those ... I ... I do not know what percentage, outside the army ... I know in the army, because we had the records; we had the personnel records of the military officers, and that included their party status, so we could, you know, virtually get that by a punch of a few keys. I don't know what the numbers were for the Baath Party as a whole. I also know the ... You know, to be ... to be fair ... that ... I think there's no question that things were done, which went beyond the terms of Bremmer's de-Baathification order. That, and that's what most of the post-CPA pulling back is about, rather than the actual ... it ... In many ways, the issue was not, were there twenty thousand or forty thousand or sixty thousand people at the top four ranks in the Baath Party? It's, how do you deal with a problem, which I'm sure happened, that people who were school principals, in fact managers and heads of clinics, and so on—

CHARLES FERGUSON: Got fired, anyway.

WALTER SLOCOMBE: Got fired because they were ... they'd been in the Baath Party, even though technically they weren't subject to. And I think that's a real ... That was not intended, and indeed—

CHARLES FERGUSON: How many of those were there, do you think?

WALTER SLOCOMBE: I don't think we know, because it ... it's the thing that would've happened on a local basis. And I'm sure it happened a lot.

CHARLES FERGUSON: So, fifty thousand? A hundred thousand?

WALTER SLOCOMBE: I wa— ... How ... how could you guess?

CHARLES FERGUSON: Could it be one hundred thousand?

WALTER SLOCOMBE: Could be anything. I ... I don't think we have any way of knowing.

CHARLES FERGUSON: That's a lot of people.

WALTER SLOCOMBE: Oh, sure. Part, not of—

CHARLES FERGUSON: Lot of people—

WALTER SLOCOMBE: ... many of whom—

CHARLES FERGUSON: ... not to know about.

WALTER SLOCOMBE: ... many of whom undoubtedly, richly deserved to be fired. That's a whole different issue.

With one exception—Christopher Hitchens—literally everyone else I spoke with had a far harsher verdict on the order, its implementation, and its consequences.

BARBARA BODINE: I, I think the decision on the broad de-Baathification, and the blanket [military] demobilization were fundamentally flawed decisions. And from those two decisions, so much of what we are still dealing with flowed. I mean, on one level, it ... it was almost a form of collective punishment. It was predicated on this belief that the Sunnis had universally benefited from the previous regime, and were collectively responsible for what Saddam did, and therefore all of them were suspect, and had to be removed. And we basically took the Sunnis as a group, and marginalized them.

Because both of those were done with such, you know, a hammer, we not only got rid of, if you want, the bad Baathis, but the technocrats, uh, the intelligentsia, the elementary school librarian[s], most of the professors. ...

And I've had people ask me, you know, why, for example, does the Oil-for-Food program, the food-rationing program in Iraq, work less well now than it did at the time of the invasion? And one very simple reason is that the technocrats who ran the program before were all fired. You can't ... you can't fire the ... that which operates your state and your society, and not have it collapse. Maybe someday Jerry Bremer will, you know, tell us what he really thought, and why he really did that decision.

Seth Moulton witnessed the de-Baathification order's direct effects on the education system and on the military.

CHARLES FERGUSON: Did you have any personal experience with the consequences of de-Baathification policy, and any view about whether it was handled well, handled badly?

SETH MOULTON: Again, my only experience with this was at a very low level, as a platoon commander. We ... I remember walking, doing patrols. I remember doing patrols around Hilla soon after the invasion. And a lot of schools didn't have teachers, because the teachers were members of the Baath Party, because they had to be, and ... and were not allowed to come back to work. So it certainly seemed like there were some very tangible day-to-day problems with de-Baathification.

But I guess the other thing that occurred to me is, I had just a basic knowledge of, um, de-Nazification after World War II, and my understanding of it was that you had to leave some of the civil servants, professionals, in charge to make things work. I mean, wasn't it Patton who said that, you know, until I can find a non-Nazi who can run the railroads, I'm gonna keep the Nazis running the German railroads? And so it was a little bit surprising to me that this edict was made, to just basically, you know, get rid of everyone in the Baath Party, 'cause I guess I just sort of felt like, well, okay, well who's gonna run things if they're all gone?

CHARLES FERGUSON: Well, everyone in the top four levels of the Baath Party.

SETH MOULTON: Right. But the problem … I mean, so I … Actually I don't really understand this very well. What I've been told is … I mean, which may be just … you can look [into it] further, I don't know. What I … what I've been told is basically that the line was drawn in the wrong place. So it absolutely makes sense to get rid of the top few levels of the Baath Party. But they drew … they put the … they set the bar too high. And just the average person—who had really not necessarily had any serious allegiance to the Baath Party or what it stood for, but simply had to attain a certain level to be qualified to do a wide range of jobs—well, all those people were disqualified as well.

CHARLES FERGUSON: Yep. Yep.

SETH MOULTON: And that was a huge problem. I mean, I'm trying to think of other specific examples. Um. Well, one thing I can speak to is the fact that … is that some of the military commanders, some of the Iraqi security force commanders that I worked with when I was working for General [David] Petraeus, they were members of the Baath Party. And so sometimes people would … Some of the Shiites would say, "Well, you know, we shouldn't have this general in charge, because he was a Baathist." But it was … But these were some of our best generals. These were some of our best leaders, people who were incredibly committed to what America was doing. So they clearly did not hold the ideals of the Baath Party. But they were just … They were there because they were the most competent leaders for the military, for the police. So I guess that's an example of how, you know, if these people had just been summarily thrown out, you would have really lost some of your real talent.

CHARLES FERGUSON: Yep.

SETH MOULTON: And I know that with at least one, with at least two leaders in particular, Ann [Gildroy, another marine lieutenant] and I had to work very, very closely with General Petraeus and some of the leadership in Baghdad to ensure that they weren't just summarily thrown out of their jobs, because they were so critical to the success of the Iraqi security force units where they worked. And yet, there were certainly vengeful people in Baghdad who were just willing to use the … the Baath Party card as a way to get rid of them.

Many participants and observers (Garner, Bodine, George Packer, Chris Allbritton, and Robert Hutchings, among many others) linked the de-Baathification order and the disbanding of the military (the disbanding will be covered in the next chapter) as decisions with similar motivations and effects. One shared motivation the interviewees cited was a desire for ideological purification and collective punishment. Another they described was a calculated desire, among exiles such as Chalabi, to eliminate potential political rivals in the jockeying for power in postwar Iraq. According to the interviewees, the principal effects were the impoverishment of those fired and their dependents, the crippling of the economy, and the stimulation of the insurgency.

JAY GARNER: As early as April, John Abizaid was saying, "What we have on our hands here, we have the beginning of a guerrilla war." And so he … he wasn't taken by surprise; Dave McKiernan wasn't taken by surprise. But all that began to gain momentum, as the months went on, as you got deeper and deeper into summer.

CHARLES FERGUSON: How come?

JAY GARNER: Don't know. Don't know. Probably, possibly because we didn't … we wanted to secure the borders. Possibly because we didn't bring back the army, and you got three hundred thousand guys out there to steal arms. Possibly because de-Baathification was so deep that we weren't able to get the government running as efficiently as we should have, as fast as we have should have, and that you had a lot of disenfranchised Baathists—maybe a lot of those—plus the opportunity that the international terrorists saw to come in the country. ...

Journalist Chris Allbritton summarized the situation well.

CHARLES FERGUSON: And what has been your observation during all this time of the U.S. occupation—the activities of ORHA, the CPA, the embassy, as it now is, since Iraq is ... now a sovereign state?

CHRIS ALLBRITTON: Uh, a collection of missed opportunities and mistakes.

CHARLES FERGUSON: Give us a list.

CHRIS ALLBRITTON: Well, the most obvious is the disbanding of the army, and ... the kind of demolishing of the civil service that was staffed by Baathists [because you] had to be ... you had to be a Baathist to get a job with the government. And a wholesale throwing out of these people into the streets, and cutting off their means of livelihood, and means of pride. There was a real underestimation of the role of pride in Arab culture, and especially in Iraqi culture. ... You know, being conquered, and then losing your job, and ... and not having any means to support yourself or your family was [an] incredibly humiliating experience. Is it any wonder that many of these people ... who almost all had at least some military training, since you had to serve in the army in Iraq—or they were active military—would turn to joining the insurgency, just as a means to feed their family, and as a means of regaining some of that pride?

CHAPTER SIX

ONE FATEFUL DECISION

The Disbanding of the Iraqi Military

On May 23, 2003, L. Paul Bremer publicly announced CPA Order Number 2, which ordered the immediate dissolution of the entire military, security, and intelligence infrastructure of Iraq. The order disbanded the Iraqi Army, the Republican Guard, the Special Republican Guard, various paramilitary and special military organizations, all of Iraq's intelligence and secret police organizations, the Ministry of Defense, the Ministry of Information, the Ministry of State for Military Affairs, and various other organizations. The only security institution of any kind permitted to continue in existence in Iraq was the poorly trained civilian police force.

CPA Order Number 2 stated that to replace the disbanded entities, the CPA would create a new army, which it called the New Iraqi Corps (NIC). (The CPA was unaware that when pronounced, this acronym is an obscenity in Arabic; the CPA later changed the name.) The order called for the total confiscation of all the dissolved entities' assets, including records and information as well as weapons, and stipulated that anyone caught possessing these items would be prosecuted. The order stated that all former ranks and titles, including military ranks, were immediately canceled. It also ordered the immediate suspension of all financial obligations of all dissolved organizations, including all salaries and contract payments, with the sole exception of pensions. The order stated that the CPA would later announce a "termination payment" of unstated size to be made at an unspecified future date for the former employees, officers, and soldiers whose salaries had been canceled without notice. No person who had ever been a "Senior Party Member" would be eligible even for a termination payment, however, and all officers of the rank of colonel and above were automatically designated as senior party members, even if they had never joined the Baath party.

Thus, CPA Order Number 2 immediately rendered unemployed and largely destitute an estimated 500,000 to 800,000 men, approximately 7 to 10 percent of Iraq's total workforce, the majority of whom had extensive weapons training and access to military weapons. This was the equivalent of firing roughly 10 million people in the United States, but in a desperately poor society with an estimated 40 to 50 percent unemployment rate. Most of those who lost their jobs were the sole supporters of large, extended families. More than any other single action, the order created the Iraqi insurgency. Here is the full text of CPA Order Number 2:

COALITION PROVISONAL SUTHORITY ORDER NUMBER 2
DISSOULUTION OF ENTITIES

Pursuant to my authority as Administrator of the Coalition Provisional Authority (CPA), relevant U.N. Security Council resolutions, including Resolution 1483 (2003), and the laws and usages of war,

Reconfirming all of the provisions of General Franks' Freedom Message to the Iraqi People of April 16, 2003,

Recognizing that the prior Iraqi regime used certain government entities to oppress the Iraqi people and as instruments of torture, repression and corruption,

Reaffirming the Instructions to the Citizens of Iraq regarding Ministry of Youth and Sport of May 8, 2003,

I hereby promulgate the following:

Section 1
Dissolved Entities

The entities (the "Dissolved Entities") listed in the attached Annex are hereby dissolved. Additional entities may be added to this list in the future.

Section 2
Assets and Financial Obligations

1) All assets, including records and data, in whatever from maintained and wherever located, of the Dissolved Entities shall be held by the Administrator of the CPA ("the Administrator") on behalf of and for the benefit of the Iraqi people and shall be used to assist the Iraqi people and to support the recovery of Iraq.

2) All financial obligations of the Dissolved Entities are suspended. The Administrator of the CPA will establish procedures whereby persons claiming to be the beneficiaries of such obligations may apply for payment.

3) Persons in possession of assets of the Dissolved Entities shall preserve those assets, promptly inform local Coalition authorities, and immediately turn them

over, as directed by those authorities. Continued possession, transfer, sale, use, conversion, or concealment of such assets following the date of this Order is prohibited and may be punished.

Section 3
Employees and Service Members

1) Any military or other rank, title, or status granted to a former employee or functionary of a Dissolved Entity by the former Regime is hereby cancelled.

2) All conscripts are released from their service obligations. Conscriptions is suspended indefinitely, subject to decisions by future Iraq governments concerning whether a free Iraq should have conscription.

3) Any person employed by a Dissolved Entity in any form or capacity, is dismissed, effective as of April 16, 2003. Any person employed by a Dissolved Entity, in any from or capacity remains accountable for acts committed during such employment.

4) A termination payment in an amount to be determined by the Administrator will be paid to employees so dismissed, except those who are Senior Party Members as defined in the Administrator's May 16, 2003 Order of the Coalition Provisional Authority De-Ba`athification of Iraqi Society, CPA/ORD/2003/01 ("Senior Party Members") (See Section 3.6) .

5) Pensions being paid by, or on account of service to, a Dissolved Entity before April 16, 2003 will continue to be paid, including to war widows and disabled veterans, provided that no pension payments will be made to any person who is a Senior Party Member (see Section 3.6) and that the power is reserved to the Administrator and to future Iraqi governments to revoke or reduce pensions as a penalty for past or future illegal conduct or to modify pension arrangements to eliminate improper privileges granted by the Ba'athist regime or for similar reasons.

6) Notwithstanding any provision of this Order, or any other Order, law, or regulation, and consistent with the Administrator's May 16, 2003 Order of the Coalition Provisional Authority De-Ba`athification of Iraqi Society, CPA/ORD/2003/01, no payment, including a termination or pension payment, will be made to any person who is or was a Senior Party Member. Any person holding the rank under the former regime of Colonel or above, or its equivalent, will be deemed a Senior Party Member, provided that such persons may seek, under procedures to be prescribed, to establish to the satisfaction of the Administrator, that they were not a Senior Party Member.

Section 4
Information

The Administrator shall prescribe procedures for offering rewards to person who provide information leading to the recovery of assets of Dissolved Entities.

Section 5
New Iraqi Corps

The CPA plans to create in the near future a New Iraqi Corps, as the first step in forming a national self-defense capability for a free Iraq. Under civilian control, that Corps will be professional, non-political, militarily effective, and representative of all Iraqis. The CPA will promulgate procedures for participation in the New Iraqi Corps.

Section 6
Other Matters

1) The Administrator may delegate his powers and responsibilities with respect to the Order as he determines appropriate. References to the Administrator herein include such delegates.

2) The Administrator may grant exceptions any limitations in the Order at his discretion.

Section 7
Entry into Force

This Order shall enter into force on the date of signature.

L. Paul Bremer 8/23/03

L. Paul Bremer, Administrator
Coalition Provisional Authority

ANNEX

COALITION PROVISIONAL AUTHORITY ORDER NUMBER 2

DISSOLUTION OF ENTITIES

Institutions dissolved by the Order referenced (the "Dissolved Entities") are:

The Ministry of Defence
The Ministry of Information
The Ministry of State for Military Affairs
The Iraqi Intelligence Service
The National Security Bureau
The Directorate of National Security (Amn al-'Am)
The Special Security Organization

All entities affiliated with or comprising Saddam Hussein's bodyguards to include:

-Murafaqin (Companions)
-Himaya al Khasa (Special Guard)

The following military organizations:

- -The Army, Air Force, Navy, the Air Defence Force, and other regular military services
- -The Republican Guard
- -The Special Republican Guard
- -The Directorate of Military Intelligence
- -The Al Quds Force
- -Emergency Forces (Quwat al Tawari)

The following paramilitaries:

- -Saddam Fedayeen
- -Ba'ath Party Militia
- -Friends of Saddam
- -Saddam's Lion Cubs (Ashbal Saddam)

Other Organizations:

- -The Presidential Diwan
- - The Presidential Secretariat
- -The Revolutionary Command Council
- -The National Assembly
- -The Youth Organization (al-Futuwah)
- -National Olympic Committee
- -Revolutionary, Special and National Security Courts

All organizations subordinate to the Dissolved Entities are also dissolved.

Additional organizations may be added to this list in the future.

———

Nearly everyone I interviewed agreed that while CPA Order Number 1, the de-Baathification order, was a major error, the disbanding of the Iraqi military was much worse—by far the largest mistake made by the American occupation. In all my research and interviews, only a handful of people defended the decision: L. Paul Bremer; his senior adviser for military affairs, Walter Slocombe; his spokesman in Baghdad, Dan Senor; General Paul Eaton, who was in charge of training the new Iraqi army; and journalist Christopher Hitchens. By contrast, dozens of diplomats, policy experts, intelligence analysts, journalists, senior military officers, and ordinary Iraqis described CPA Order Number 2 as an unmitigated disaster that greatly magnified, or even instigated, both the Sunni insurgency and the Shiite militias.

How the order came about is also an extraordinary story, one that I pieced together over the course of two years of interviews and research, and that I present for the first time here. The decision was made principally by Bremer himself, on the recommendation of Walter Slocombe, on Bremer's ninth day at work in the Pentagon, before either man had ever been to Iraq. The decision was made secretly. It was made with no consultation with anyone in Iraq, the military, the intelligence community, the State Department, or the White House, despite the fact that neither Bremer nor Slocombe had any postwar reconstruction, Middle East, or military experience. Before describing Bremer's and Slocombe's procedures and behavior, however, I will consider the merits and consequences of the decision itself.

Dissecting Bremer's and Slocombe's Arguments for Disbanding the Military

To present L. Paul Bremer and Walter Slocombe's arguments, I will principally quote their own words from publications and from my interviews with Slocombe.

Bremer devotes seven pages in his memoir to the disbanding of the military. His clearest argument, however, is found in an op-ed he wrote, which was published in the *New York Times* on September 6, 2007:

> The disappearance of Saddam Hussein's old army rendered irrelevant any prewar plans to use that army. So the question was whether the Coalition Provisional Authority should try to recall it or to build a new one open to both vetted members of the old army and new recruits. General Abizaid favored the second approach. ...
>
> ... the coalition's national security adviser, Walter Slocombe, discussed options with top officials in the Pentagon, including Deputy Secretary of Defense Paul Wolfowitz. They recognized that to recall the former army was a practical impossibility because postwar looting had destroyed all the bases.
>
> Moreover, the largely Shiite draftees of the army were not going to respond to a recall plea from their former commanders, who were primarily Sunnis. It was also agreed that recalling the army would be a political disaster because to the vast majority of Iraqis it was a symbol of the old Baathist-led Sunni ascendancy.
>
> On May 8, 2003, before I left for Iraq, Secretary of Defense Donald Rumsfeld gave me a memo titled "Principles for Iraq-Policy Guidelines"

that specified that the coalition "will actively oppose Saddam Hussein's old enforcers—the Baath Party, Fedayeen Saddam, etc." and that "we will make clear that the coalition will eliminate the remnants of Saddam's regime." ...

Moreover, we were right to build a new Iraqi army. Despite all the difficulties encountered, Iraq's new professional soldiers are the country's most effective and trusted security force.

In my interviews with Slocombe, he explained his reasons for wanting the old Iraqi Army disbanded.

WALTER SLOCOMBE: The expectation before the war had been that ... there would be intact units, which would, partly by prearrangement and partly by the exercise of good judgment, [sit] out the war, and be there in garrison, organized under their officers with their facilities more or less intact ...

And there were various plans for how we would use this capability, which included various kinds of civil works. Um, there were also some problems with that model, but the whole point is that that model didn't pan out, didn't exist, by the time the fighting had started, stopped.

So the issue was—nobody disputed that we were gonna have to create a new force. To the best of my knowledge, the issue was not trying to, quote, recall existing units, but whether you would try to turn the function of creating the new army essentially over to some selected former Iraqi officers, probably mostly people who had been either in external exile or effectively in internal exile, not necessarily the active commanders of the Iraqi Army during the war. That was intensively discussed, and there was certainly an issue about that. My view then, and now, is that any idea of actually recalling units was totally impractical. ... And if it had been practical, it would have been a terrible idea politically.

The reason it was impractical is that the old army was a conscript army, reflecting the character of Iraq under Saddam. Most of the officers—not all, but the overwhelming majority—were Sunnis. Most of the enlisted— again, not all—were Shia. The Shia were not coming back to serve under their old officers, for love nor money. That was simply not gonna happen. It is enough [of a] problem now with getting Shia to serve under Sunni officers, after three years of activity.

So that was one problem. The second problem was that when they left, everybody went home. When they went home, they—the military people—took a lot of the useful equipment and so on with them. What they didn't take was, without exception, looted and destroyed. We know this because when we subsequently … set up the training, we had to find places to do it. We surveyed all the military bases in Iraq, and picked out the ones which were least damaged. But even the ones which were least damaged were in pretty bad shape. So there were no facilities; there were no … to start with the basics, [there were] no uniforms. There were no kitchens; there were no bunks; there were no … uh, barracks with windows in them, and so on. So that there were no facilities to restart.

If you had tried, I have no question that you could probably have organized a few all-Sunni units. If you had tried to do that, it would have been a political disaster of the first order. This country has been difficult enough to try to help with the Shia largely supportive of the effort, and certainly with the Kurds largely supportive of the effort. It is absolutely clear, and was clear at the time, that anointing old Sunni officers, even people who were personally okay, would have had a devastatingly bad impact on the Shia and Kurdish population.

… Insofar as people have in their mind what the term "disbanding the army" suggests—which is sending people who are … in the extreme form, ready, willing and able to go and help, and telling 'em, "You're not good enough, go home"—that just didn't happen. And anybody who believes that it happened is simply wrong on the facts. And I think if you have the image that what happened was that we took people, and told 'em, go home—and I've seen articles by reputable journalists who say this meant that people were suddenly put out of a job, were suddenly sent home, were no longer available—that's just factually wrong.

To assess Bremer's and Slocombe's arguments, I spoke with dozens of people who knew the Middle East and Iraq well; who worked in the occupation for ORHA, the military, and the CPA; or who were involved in recalling the Iraqi Army. None of them felt that Bremer's and Slocombe's arguments had merit. Everyone I interviewed— senior military officers, junior officers on the ground in Iraq, American and Iraqi diplomats, Middle East experts, journalists, executives of nongovernmental organizations—believed that the Iraqi Army was a widely respected, critical national insti-tution. Far from being uniformly Baathist, Sunni, or personally beholden to Saddam, they said, the Iraqi Army was heterogeneous and independent, with the result that Saddam had in fact distrusted it. According to the interviewees, many Iraqi army of-ficers cared about the welfare of their men, and the army did not simply "dissolve," but rather heeded American promises and warnings that if the army cooperated and did not fight, it would be treated with respect after the war. The interviewees also said that recalling the army was both extremely important and eminently feasi-ble and that plans for the recall were well under way when Bremer announced his order. Indeed, many interviewees were not only upset by the decision, but also mys-tified; they could not understand how anyone could make such a decision or could believe what Bremer and Slocombe apparently believed.

Joost Hiltermann is deputy Middle East director for the International Crisis Group, a highly regarded global nonprofit organization that seeks to reduce violent conflict through research and advocacy. Hiltermann, who has lived in the Middle East for many years, speaks fluent Arabic and English in addition to his native Dutch. He is the author of *A Poisonous Affair,* a study of Saddam's use of chemical weapons against the Kurds. I interviewed him in Amman, Jordan, just after I had been in Iraq, and then again in Washington, D.C. I asked him to assess Bremer's and Slocombe's arguments for disbanding the Iraqi Army.

CHARLES FERGUSON: As I'm sure you know, the people who made that deci-sion have advanced four arguments as to why it was the right thing to do. They have said, first of all, the army essentially had already disbanded it-self. Second, that its infrastructure and bases had all been destroyed and/or looted and there was, therefore, no way to reconstitute the army, and make effective use of it and take care of it. Thirdly, that it was a corrupt, politi-cized general officer corps on top of a disgruntled Shiite conscript force. And finally, that the Shiite community, especially Ayatollah Sistani, would have been unacceptably antagonized by standing the army back up. What do you think of those arguments?

JOOST HILTERMANN: Well, I think none of them wash. The army, of course, had not fought, had not resisted the advance of U.S. and other troops in … in March and April of 2003. They had gone home in many cases, but they had not disbanded themselves. They had simply gone home and waited out the war, and had decided not to fight, which you could even read as a sign of solidarity with the invading troops.

And so they were very willing to be called up and to [come] back to the destroyed bases because there was still a command and control structure. There were still commanding officers, who were generally respected. This was not a corrupt army. This was a very professional army. ... Yes, there was of course the Shiite conscript force, but the officer corps was mixed. There weren't just Sunnis. There were also Shiites. And generally there was ... a great deal of nationalism inherent in this Iraqi Army, and [it] enjoyed a lot of popular support for that reason. And it wasn't seen as one of the pillars of the regime. This is one reason why it didn't fight.

CHARLES FERGUSON: Did you talk with Americans about this at the time?

JOOST HILTERMANN: Very much so. I met with American officials in the Green Zone, and we put out a report in early June, around the 10th or 11th of June, that was also used in our discussions in Washington—well, not me personally but my colleagues—and so we certainly made these concerns known. But they were dismissed as sort of sour grapes—people who opposed the war. [They said,] "You know, there of course are problems when you overthrow a regime; there's going to be a bit of instability. But we've just started our reconstruction effort, and everything will be okay."

And the priorities that we identified were not the priorities of the United States government. The main [issue for them] there was force protection—you know, protect U.S. forces and major assets, and everything else will fall in place; we need a political process, and then, once that happens, then the situation will stabilize.

CHARLES FERGUSON: And so, well, first of all, who did you talk to at this time? When you said you spoke to officials in the Green Zone, was it military people? Was it diplomatic people? Both?

JOOST HILTERMANN: I spoke to some officials, both British and American, who were sort of State Department and Foreign Ministry officials. Can't remember, no, whether I spoke to military officials on any of these issues directly. But after we released the report, ... I'm sure that ... But I was ... again, I wasn't in Washington at the time. But there were discussions. I was here later in July, I think. I may have had discussions then. I don't remember now, because I come so frequently and have these discussions.

But in any case, we made our concerns known. I remember in July 2003, of course, I was raising the question of the lawlessness and the lack of electricity. And I said, "Why don't you deploy?"—this was after the Iraqi Army had been dismissed, sent home without any kind of prospect of regaining their former positions, or ... of any kind of salary—and I was saying, "Why don't you bring in the Iraqi Army Corps of Engineers to fix the electricity and to protect the sites?"

In part, Bremer and Slocombe appear to have suffered from a simple ignorance of the structure of Iraq's military apparatus. The Iraqi Army had existed since 1920, and its large officer corps (over 200,000 men) constituted a relatively independent, professional force, except for a few of its most senior and its most political commanders. The army had also suffered enormously under Saddam by being forced to fight his four disastrous wars (Iran-Iraq, the invasion of Kuwait, the first Gulf War, and the 2003 war) at huge human and economic cost, and then having its economic status sharply reduced by the sanctions regime. Saddam recognized this and kept most Iraqi Army units away from Baghdad for fear that they would mount a coup. Other organizations such as the Special Republican Guard were far more favored by, and loyal to, Saddam, but Bremer and Slocombe evidently did not understand the difference. In the seven pages in Bremer's memoir devoted to his decision to disband the entire military, he mentions the Special Republican Guard only once. In my interviews with Slocombe, he demonstrated a similarly limited understanding of the Iraqi military apparatus. Colonel James Torgler suspected their ignorance, too.

JAMES TORGLER: I mean, one of the things that Slocombe said that did not ring true was that—I think I read in his or Bremer's statement—was that the army was discredited, [that] we did not want to put that back on the street. That is true if you talk about the Republican Guard. But every Iraqi I talked to had enormous pride in their army—not the Republican Guard; that was Saddam's thugs—but the army, the base army, because of the history of that army and what it had been able to do from the thirties on. I mean, they did not have a problem with the regular army guys; it was the

Republican Guard, the Special Republican Guard, all those neo-Nazis that worked for Saddam.

There was one respect in which people agreed that Bremer and Slocombe had a point: The Iraqi Army had indeed been involved in some of Saddam's atrocities, including the mass killings of the Kurds between 1988 and 1991 and the repression of the Shiite uprisings of 1991. Still, both Joost Hiltermann and David Phillips, who is also an expert on Saddam's persecution of the Kurds, felt that the disbanding of the army was a disaster and that recalling it was both possible and necessary.

DAVID PHILLIPS: Here again, we should be very clear that the Mukhabarat [Saddam's secret police] and the Special Republican Guard that were responsible for atrocities were viewed by Iraqis as having no place in the new Iraq. But they did recognize that other security structures that were not directly tainted with war crimes or atrocities could be co-opted and turned into partners in security.

CHARLES FERGUSON: Such as?

DAVID PHILLIPS: Such as the Iraqi Army. … So the decision to eliminate the Baath Party leadership, and the decree that was issued by Jerry Bremer and the Coalitional Provisional Authority to get rid of the Iraqi armed forces, directly contravened the advice that Iraqis had developed prior to the war.

Despite the Iraqi Army's prior involvement with some of Saddam's atrocities, nearly everyone shared Phillips' view, for several reasons. First, in Saddam Hussein's regime, to disobey was to be summarily executed. Many in the army hated what they were made to do, but had no choice unless they were willing to die. In fact, when Saddam ordered the repression of the Shiites after the first Gulf War in 1991, thousands of soldiers surrendered to the U.S. military rather than continue fighting for Saddam, in part because they did not want to kill their countrymen. The United States ended up handing these soldiers back to Saddam, and many were executed.

Furthermore, most men in the 2003 Iraqi Army had not been involved in these earlier abuses. The repression of the Shiites and Kurds involved only a minority of the army even then, and the most recent of those actions occurred in early 1991, twelve years before Saddam was deposed. Thus, many of those involved, including all low-level conscripts, had long since left the army.

And finally, in contradiction to Slocombe's claims, most Kurds (and Iraqis in general) I spoke with in Iraq in 2006 felt that disbanding the army had been a disastrous error. Warzer Jaff, a Kurd who was my fixer and personal bodyguard in Baghdad, told me that the disbanding of the army had forced millions of people into destitution. Mahmoud Othman, another Kurd and a member of the Iraqi Parliament when I interviewed him in Baghdad in 2006, pointed out that the disbanding order only pushed the military underground, into the insurgency.

MAHMOUD OTHMAN: What was happening is that the Americans came; they topple the regime. With that, there, the state collapsed altogether. It was something like that. The state almost collapse, the army collapse, the forces collapse, and the institutions, many of them collapse. So the state, which has been there for thirty-five years—whatever state it is; is it totalitarian; it's bad; it's good—nothing was arranged to be replacing that state.

For example, they dismantle the Iraqi Army; there was no force to replace that army. They dismantled many Iraqi [offices]. Nothing was there to replace it. So that's created a big political [vacuum]. And in that, gradually, problems came up. Baath Party, which was toppled then, after one year, they started reorganizing themselves, and coming back to activity. The Iraqi Army, which was disbanded then, they were in the country, gradually, again, they got, uh, organizing themself, and trying to work underground.

Most people I interviewed also disputed the idea that the officer corps was monolithically Sunni, Baathist, or both, and the related assertion that the officer corps had no concern for its rank-and-file soldiers. Colonel Paul Hughes, who was negotiating directly with Iraqi officers in his efforts to recall the army, was able to observe their behavior firsthand.

PAUL HUGHES: Every one of these officers said, "I have no interest in serving in a new Iraqi army. All we want to do is make sure our soldiers are taken care of, because nobody's ever taken care of them before." Now these are Sunni and Shia officers telling me this. So this notion that Walt [Slocombe] puts out, about a Sunni officers corps and Shia soldiers, it's just not true. He's simplifying what was a very complex organization.

After Bremer announced CPA Order Number 2 and the army was disbanded, the U.S. military found personnel records that listed which officers were members of the Baath Party and which were not. The records confirmed that Bremer and Slocombe had been wrong in their presumption that the entire officer corps, or even the majority of it, was Baathist.

JOHN AGOGLIA: Well, sometime ... in June, we found the personnel records of the Iraqi Army at the Ministry of Defense, and we had those computers that contained those personnel records examined by special technical experts. The special technical experts confirmed in fact that the records were authentic and not tampered with. One of the key findings of those records, which was shared with Mr. Slocombe, was that in fact you did not have large-scale Baathist issue in the army until you got to the major general rank, and at the major general rank, fifty percent of the major generals were Baathists and fifty percent weren't. But he [Slocombe] had issued in his proclamation that ... no one above the rank of colonel could join [the new Iraqi Army], because they were Baathists. And we were able to show that it was wrong. And they still wouldn't rescind it. We could show them that ninety percent of the colonels were in fact not Baathist. Seventy to eighty percent of the one-stars were not Baathists. When you got to the two-star rank, fifty percent were Baathists. When you got to the three-star rank, seventy-five to eighty percent were Baathists.

I asked Jay Garner and several other military officers about Bremer's and Slocombe's claim that recalling the Iraqi Army was impossible, given that its bases had been looted and destroyed.

CHARLES FERGUSON: Now, one thing that has been said in defense of the decision to disband the army was that all the army's facilities had either been destroyed or looted; that there was no place to base them; that all their cars were gone, all their trucks were gone, and all that kind of thing. Was that your sense? I mean, what did you think?

JAY GARNER: That wasn't my sense. I mean, down in ... outside Nasiriyah, [Tallil] Air Base was virtually unharmed. And there were a lot of facilities, outside of Baghdad. Now there weren't any facilities inside of Baghdad.

CHARLES FERGUSON: Okay.

JAY GARNER: No, we had ... we had a hard time finding a place for us to stay, inside ... Baghdad. But outside Baghdad, there were facilities.

CHARLES FERGUSON: ... I think this is an important point: In general, your view is that there was sufficient logistical infrastructure available to make use of the army.

JAY GARNER: I think there was.

Colonel Agoglia agreed. He said that in a briefing to Slocombe on May 23, 2003, the U.S. military had made it clear that it regarded the issue as manageable. Others concurred: Despite less-than-ideal military facilities, the Iraqi military could be recalled.

JOHN AGOGLIA: In it [the briefing of May 23], the folks giving the brief laid out the challenges of the infrastructure. In fact, a lot of the infrastructure was destroyed because we did target some of their infrastructure. Others were looted—that sort of stuff. But that was not an obstacle that would stop us from being able to recall the Iraqi Army. It was a challenge, and we would have to get additional logistics in to have base camps for these camps. We could recall these folks.

JAMES FALLOWS: Yes, they'd left the barracks; yes, they'd gone to their hometowns. But these people would come back. For a hundred dollars or two hundred dollars, you could get a lot of them to come back. No, there weren't places to put them in normal bunks and barracks, but U.S. forces didn't have bunks and barracks, either. ... You know, you could do things on the fly.

PAUL HUGHES: You know, the Iraqi officers told me they would have set up tents and lived in the desert, if that's what it took, you know, to work with the Americans. You know, it ... it's just ... he [Slocombe] didn't have anybody on the ground. And he certainly wasn't gonna listen to me.

There was similar unanimity with regard to the claim that the Iraqi Army could not be recalled because it had melted away.

LAWRENCE WILKERSON: One of the things I think Bremer had was carte blanche with the president. So he could, if necessary, weigh in with the president. ... But he made some bad decisions. One was the disbanding of the Iraqi Army. I have it well in hand, from people [who] were there at the time that the Iraqi Army was essentially standing there, waiting. They were waiting for an overture. They were waiting for what they thought would happen—that someone would come to them and say, "This is the plan. And you're integral to that plan. And we need you." No one ever did that. And so they dissolved. And many of them, I am quite confident, became members of the Sunni insurgency.

In our interviews, Slocombe claimed that in a video conference on April 17, senior military commanders, including General Abizaid, had reported that the Iraqi Army had disappeared, and Slocombe strongly implied that the military commanders told him that recalling it was impractical. However, I was able to interview, off the record, a senior military officer who participated in this video conference. He directly contradicted Slocombe's claim, saying that the military commanders made it clear that while the Iraqi Army had disappeared, they believed that the army could and should be recalled.

In fact, shortly after the war, several groups of Iraqi Army officers approached both CENTCOM and ORHA, offering their assistance in reconstituting the army. In part, they were motivated by a desire to see that they and their men got paid. In part, they wanted to help stabilize and rebuild Iraq. Paul Hughes supervised the efforts of two such groups, which, by mid-May 2003, had located and registered 137,000 Iraqi soldiers.

PAUL HUGHES: The fact that a hundred and thirty-seven thousand [men], at least a third of Saddam's army, came and registered tells me the army didn't disappear.

When I confronted Slocombe, he denied that a 137,000 soldiers had in fact registered, or indeed that anyone did.

WALTER SLOCOMBE: Hughes believed that he had an opening to some Iraqi officers who would have been prepared to reconstitute units. I don't—

CHARLES FERGUSON: He already had obtained registration statements from a hundred and thirty-seven thousand—

WALTER SLOCOMBE: No, he hadn't … done that … 'cause nobody could have gotten statements from one hundred thirty thousand anybody for anything in the chaos that prevailed at that point. He may well have been in contact with officers who claimed that they could put together tens of thousands, even a hundred thousand people. I don't dispute that.

CHARLES FERGUSON: Okay.

WALTER SLOCOMBE: But, I mean … did he come into the meeting with boxes of … ? No. … Given how difficult it was to do anything just operationally, organizationally, nobody had a hundred and thirty-seven thousand. He was, in fact, the source of our access to the records of the Iraqi Army, but that was a lot more than a hundred and thirty-seven thousand people, and that was a database, not a … you know … nothing … no; it happened postwar.

When I investigated further, it became clear that Slocombe was wrong. Jay Garner, Colonel James Torgler, and Colonel John Agoglia all confirmed Paul Hughes account, and Colonel Hughes himself supplied further details.

CHARLES FERGUSON: By what date had you acquired a hundred and thirty-seven thousand signatures?

PAUL HUGHES: That was on the 25th of May, when I came back [from a trip to the United States]. And it was actually a combination of two different activities. The Independent Military Gathering had a hundred thousand when I left. My last meeting with them was on the 9th of May, the day before I left.

CHARLES FERGUSON: And they already had a hundred thousand signatures.

PAUL HUGHES: Yeah. This was a nationwide effort. They brought me the … I wanted the printouts, I wanted the disks, and they gave them to me, and I took them back with me to ORHA. I said, "Here we go." And I told Walt and his crew, "I've got these things. They're here waiting for you."

CHARLES FERGUSON: Now, this represented just databases of prior unit forces? Or did it represent soldiers signing up and saying, "I want my twenty-dollar payment; here's who I am, et cetera"?

PAUL HUGHES: It was the latter.

CHARLES FERGUSON: The latter?

PAUL HUGHES: The latter. Remember, I told you, they'd set up shop in the Air Force Officers Club. The reason they were there with all of these computers that they had stolen from the MOD [Ministry of Defense] was so that they could enter these registration forms as they were coming in. So as a representative from a city or a district would come in with a batch, there'd be people there. And they were working twenty-four hours a day. I mean, these guys were adamant that they wanted to be involved; they wanted to produce something for us, to show goodwill. ...

CHARLES FERGUSON: Walter Slocombe told me directly, in our interview, and we have him on camera saying this: that that was not the case, that it was physically impossible for anybody to get a hundred and thirty-seven thousand registrations for anything, for any purpose, in the country at that time because the place was too chaotic.

PAUL HUGHES: Walter wasn't there. He never met with these people. He had no clue what ... You know, he's just saying that. Listen: These people were dedicated folks who wanted to do what was right for themselves and their country and their soldiers. They were willing to undertake extreme danger, to the point that they were stealing from Saddam's own Ministry of Defense, to set this up. You think that they would have stopped that effort because it was too chaotic? They were doing this on their own dime. They were publishing their own registration forms. They weren't asking us for money to do this. They were doing it on the ... by themselves. They had already begun this before they even came to meet me.

CHARLES FERGUSON: I see. And how were they able to reach all these people, all their old units? Were there ... you know ... was mail and telecommunications functioning? ...

PAUL HUGHES: The chaotic part was the lack of mail, the lack of telecommunications.

CHARLES FERGUSON: So how'd they do it?

PAUL HUGHES: By driving from point A to point B. They had a courier system set up that was running around the metropolitan area of Baghdad, of Mosul, of Basra and Kirkuk. They focused on those four, and they would, you know, just tell people. They'd plaster signs up on the street: If you were a member of the military and you want to register, this is where you need to come and fill out a form. Then they would gather these forms, and couriers would take off with them. It wasn't like people couldn't move around Iraq at that time.

CHARLES FERGUSON: That's true.

PAUL HUGHES: We certainly couldn't stop them from moving around Iraq—

CHARLES FERGUSON: Yeah—

PAUL HUGHES: 'cause we didn't have enough troops in there to stop anything at that particular point in time.

CHARLES FERGUSON: So did you tell Slocombe this—that this was going on?

PAUL HUGHES: Yes. He knew this. He and his staff knew this.

Colonel Torgler confirmed this account, saying that the last time he personally checked, fifty-five thousand soldiers had registered, but he knew that the numbers had continued to increase.

JAMES TORGLER: And Paul [Hughes] and I went for a meeting, one of the first meetings with the Iraqi senior officers. I remember we went out to a … It was on the north side of town near hospital city.

CHARLES FERGUSON: The Officers Club.

JAMES TORGLER: Right. At the Officers Club, the old Republican Guard base, and [we] met with those guys and they said, "Okay, we have got ... " I think they said they had, like, fifty-five thousand soldiers that they were concerned about. And the thing, I will tell you, the thing that impressed me, military officer to military officer, is [when] we sat down with these guys, the first question that they asked us is, "Who is securing the borders of our country?" Because they fought in the Iran/Iraq war. And the second one is, "How are we going to take care of our soldiers? How are we going to take care of these people? Their pay had stopped, you know, how do we take care of their families?"

In fact Hughes, Torgler, Agoglia, and others saw great concern on the part of Iraqi officers for their men and their families.

PAUL HUGHES: These officers had all worked in the Ministry of Defense prior to the invasion. And when they knew the war was coming, they all knew they were going to lose. And so they started planning for the aftermath. They removed computers; they removed disks; they removed papers and surreptitiously took them home—something that would have gotten them killed had Saddam found out about it. So quite obviously, these guys were folks that were vested in the future of Iraq. They came to us, at great risk to themselves, because they wanted to take care of their soldiers and their junior civilians and such.

Another argument made by Bremer and Slocombe was that the Iraqi Army had "disbanded itself." That is, they argued that everyone deserted or fled, and that this behavior implied that the soldiers did not want to be recalled. Bremer and Slocombe asserted that finding the deserters would be prohibitively difficult and that conscripts would never return. Everyone I interviewed said precisely the reverse. In fact, some U.S. military planners worried that they would have more people on their hands than they could use, including large numbers of unskilled conscripts. For this reason, the planners felt that a disarmament, demobilization, and reintegration (DDR) program was essential.

CHARLES FERGUSON: When it turned out that a large fraction of the Iraqi

Army did desert and kind of melted away instead of surrendering as an attack unit to the American military, it did not come as a surprise to you?

JOHN AGOGLIA: It was not problematic. We were somewhat surprised that everybody deserted and nobody surrendered. We were kind of surprised by that. We didn't expect that. But the fact that they didn't fight was good and the fact that they had gone away we saw as good. And then, by contacts with the agency [CIA] and others, we were getting told they were ready to come back. They believed [that we could recall them] and they were ready to come back and join us as part of a new army for the new Iraq.

CHARLES FERGUSON: And this is through what kind of contacts?

JOHN AGOGLIA: Through covert means, through special forces, through agency [CIA] folks—those sorts of folks out there. [And] through more direct means—guys coming to reach out to ex–Iraqi generals, guys like Paul Hughes doing that. So, through contacts coming into the military commanders, such as the 101st [Airborne Division] folks up in the north and other folks coming in and offering this. It's coming in from multiple levels that the Iraqi Army is ready to come back in.

Moreover, many people—Hughes, Torgler, Agoglia, Garner, and a number of journalists—pointed out that in large measure, the Iraqi Army had melted away precisely because covert American information had asked them to do so, had warned them not to fight, and had promised favorable treatment to those who cooperated. Several U.S. military officers pointed out that in these circumstances, the Iraqi military did not see itself as a defeated enemy, but rather as a cooperative, but still intact, military force.

PAUL HUGHES: Mr. Slocombe made a comment that we don't pay defeated armies. And I reminded people that there wasn't a single Iraqi officer I had met who said that they had surrendered to the United States military; that in fact, they did what our propaganda campaign had told them to do: put down their guns, and go home. That's what they claimed they had done. That doesn't mean that they're not, you know, going to pick them back up, and do something. They expected us to honor our end of the bargain.

Consequences of Disbanding the Military

Many people told me that it was immediately evident that the disbanding of the Iraqi military and security services had greatly stimulated, or even created, the insurgency.

PAUL HUGHES: These guys [who were disbanded] all knew where those munitions were. They knew how to get to those weapons, and how to use them. And you've just sent them away, and said they don't exist? Common sense tells me you don't do that. And that was one of the things we put in that November 2002 report about dealing with the Iraqi military: Be very careful. ...

... When that decision [to disband the military] came out, that just turned everything upside down. And I told people, we were in for trouble. Up to that point, I had told my officers that, if there had been an attack on an American unit and any of the hundred and thirty-seven thousand people that they had registered turned out to be involved in the attack, that I was going to come and arrest them. I made that promise to them. And they knew I'd keep it. ... But when the army was disbanded, my credibility was gone. So any control that anybody could have had over the Iraqi military up to that point was now gone. Five days later, the night that we were farewelling Jay Garner [in late May], because he was gonna leave Iraq for good the next day, we had two Humvees on the highway, heading out from the Green Zone to Baghdad International; uh, they were ambushed, and two soldiers were killed. And that was when, in my mind, the insurgency began.

My colleagues and I could sit on the balcony, or on the roof, of the Republican Palace at night, and we could watch the tracers throughout Baghdad. We could watch the flares of different colors that went up, marking where American convoys of certain compositions were moving, and being followed by the insurgents. This was a time for the insurgents, those who wanted to resist the American occupier, to learn about us—how we worked, what our modes of operation were—so that when they decided to attack, they knew what to attack. Yeah, it was not a pleasant time, to see all that.

CHARLES FERGUSON: Did you see any evidence that the disbanding of the army had a stimulating effect on the insurgency?

JOHN AGOGLIA: Oh, absolutely. … Shortly after that, we started seeing the first IEDs [improvised explosive devices] going off. Then some ambushes and stuff like that. The activity started to rise. [Brigadier General] Will Grimsley got a group of folks out on a counterambush patrol along Route Irish, between the Green Zone and Baghdad airport. So you've got some guys doing counterambush patrol, and they roll up a group of Iraqis getting ready to lay in an ambush. As they're capturing the guys and doing the initial interrogation, bagging and tagging them and, you know, writing down what's going on on the detention tags, one of the sergeants looks at the soldier and says, "Weren't you just on the side of the road selling me Cokes two weeks ago?" And the guy says, "Yes, I was. I'm a lieutenant in the Iraqi Army, and I believed you when you said you were going to bring me back as part of a new Iraq to serve a new Iraq and not serve Saddam. We deserted because we trusted you. But now you've called us Baathists and cowards and my men have come to me and said you are not to be trusted. You've dishonored us. We cannot trust the Americans. We must fight them to regain our honor, and that's why we're out here fighting you." That was one of the more poignant stories I could tell you, relayed to me by Will Grimsley.

Even after the disbanding order, a group of Sunni army officers tried to negotiate with the CPA, warn the provisional authority about the coming insurgency, and persuade Bremer to change his decision. In December 2007, I conducted an off-the-record interview with a senior military commander who expanded on this. He said that Sunni officers approached him and other senior commanders, including General Petraeus, offering to negotiate prior to joining the insurgency. Petraeus strongly urged Bremer to meet with them, but Bremer refused. The Sunni officers also approached the United Nations, which in turn alerted Bremer. Again, Bremer refused to speak with them.

Samantha Power is a professor at Harvard University's Kennedy School of Government specializing in international human rights policy. She is the author of *A Problem from Hell,* a study of U.S. policy toward genocide in the twentieth century, and

Chasing the Flame, a biography of Sergio Vieira de Mello, the UN special representative to Iraq who was killed in the bombing of the UN headquarters in Baghdad on
August 19, 2003.

SAMANTHA POWER: Sergio Vieira de Mello had a … had his tentacles in
places that the Americans either couldn't reach or showed no interest in
reaching. When Bremer issued the order to demobilize the Iraqi Army, a
number of the most senior generals came to the Canal Hotel, to UN headquarters, and made an appeal to Vieira de Mello to try to prevail upon Bremer to rescind this order, or at a minimum to pay these officers who had
been demobilized.

And they were very explicit that the consequence of letting this order
stand and of marginalizing this incredibly powerful segment of society
would be an insurgency. They were incredibly explicit. One of Sergio's senior aides, a Lebanese diplomat named Hassan Salami, turned to his colleague as the generals walked away after one of their meetings and said, "I
see bullets in their eyes. I see bullets in their eyes." And these generals were
very, very explicit: If, you know, if there was no place for them in Iraqi society; if they weren't able to feed their families; and if there was one—in
their mind, one—source of that marginalization and that misery, and that
was the Americans, they were gonna take matters into their own hands.

Yet Slocombe disputed that the disbanding order had any effect on the insurgency.
Quite incredibly, he asserted that nobody had warned him about such a consequence.

CHARLES FERGUSON: Did anybody warn you that disbanding the army in
this way would—and then was—fueling a major growth of the insurgency?

WALTER SLOCOMBE: Certainly not in those terms.

CHARLES FERGUSON: Nobody said that to you.

WALTER SLOCOMBE: No. I also don't believe it's true, but nobody said it.
Nobody said—

CHARLES FERGUSON: You don't believe it's true?

WALTER SLOCOMBE: No, I don't see … I do not believe it's true.

Slocombe also disputed the economic effects of the disbanding order, claiming that everyone got paid.

WALTER SLOCOMBE: Nobody was … nobody was dismissed or put out of a job as a result of this order. We also said in the order that we would make payments, which we then began to do. We announced we were going to do it in June, and began the payment program in July. Just the mechanics of making those payments, unsurprisingly, turned out to be much more complicated than you might think, and took a lot of time and effort. It was basically a program where we paid former officers, on a continuing basis … we paid them an amount which was essentially … it was meant to be a little bit less than their base pay under the old system, that is, enough to sustain a decent life, but nothing luxurious. We also made a onetime payment to the conscripts.

… If we had it to do over again, we would have announced … What we did announce in the order was that there would be a severance payment to the people who were no longer going to be officers. And it's certainly true that we envisioned that as a onetime payment, a severance payment. Very quickly we began to get lots of demands from former officers that they should be paid. And I think it's clear that if we had it to do over again, it would have been better to have announced at the very beginning that we would continue, and we would make continued payments to former officers. We decided in late June to do that, and started doing it in July. And broadly, that program was successful.

In fact, many people were never paid, and the program was *not* successful. Officers were eventually paid, but only if they were not designated as senior party members. Those who did get paid were paid months late, and in a very disorganized, incompetent way. By the time payments were made, many officers had joined the insurgency. And finally, for the 200,000 largely Shiite conscripts about whom Slocombe professed to be so concerned, their total severance consisted of a onetime payment of $50.

SETH MOULTON: One story was, you know, we're in Hilla. And there's this big problem with unemployment. And it's primarily with the former members of the Iraqi Army. They're all out of a job. And the decision was made, at some level, to pay them.

Now, to be perfectly honest, my first reaction as a marine lieutenant was, you know, this is kind of ridiculous, to be, you know, paying a salary of the guys who just finished fighting us. But I think we realized that, you know, these guys ... these people need to be able to put bread on the table. And there was a certain level of just basic economics, where, you know, it would benefit us in the long run to just help them out for a while, until they found new jobs.

So the decision was made to pay these former Iraqi soldiers. And we weren't really given any guidance about how to do it. ... And our commanders came up with a payment scheme where the Iraqis would go by rank to different payment stations. And we'd have lists of their names, and they'd get issued their twenty dollars or whatever they were ... they were given. And then at the very last minute, the CPA came out with the big plan for how we were going to pay the Iraqis. And they actually gave it to me, because I worked with the Iraqi TV station, to broadcast it. And I remember, the first time I handed this piece of paper to my translator, and he just looked at me like, you know ... Well, first of all, there's all kinds of mistakes in this grand payment plan. I mean, there were just serious mistakes in the translation.

And then we discovered that the scheme they set up was to pay alphabetically, instead of by rank. But the problem is that Arabic naming conventions are entirely different than English naming conventions. And if you ask any Iraqi ... You know, if you ask a group of Iraqis to stand in alphabetical order, they're going to get in order based on their first name, not on their third name. And yet, here the CPA, apparently so knowledgeable about Iraqi culture and, you know, in charge of the reconstruction, had come up with this scheme where we would pay them by their last names. Well, as you can imagine, you know, this just caused tremendous confusion and, quite frankly, rioting in some cases.

Troops assume positions near a crowd of protesting former Iraqi soldiers
in Basra, Iraq, January 6, 2004.

During my interview with Omar Fekeiki in the Baghdad office of the *Washington Post* in 2006, the Iraqi journalist summarized the consequences of the disbanding order.

OMAR FEKEIKI: Dissolving the Iraqi Army was a huge mistake. The Iraqi Army was the only tool for the coalition forces to rule the country … to control the country. Of course, I said that, and they had a government to take over after Saddam Hussein. The Iraqi Army [would have been] linked and connected to that government, and the government could have ordered the army to do whatever they wanted.

Dissolving hundreds of thousands of Iraqis who are members in the army was a huge mistake. … I can't believe they did that. Hundreds of thousands of families [were] dependent on the army. They didn't have an income; they didn't have a source to get money; they didn't have providers. Children, women, wives, sisters, fathers, stopped eating because they didn't have enough money. And that's why I think, I believe, that's why many of the former Iraqi army members joined the resistance. They didn't have another source for money. How could they provide [for] their families? How could they survive the inflation we have in Iraq?

Anyone could come and give a former Iraqi soldier a thousand dollars, just to go and plant an IED. I don't blame them, surprisingly. I don't. Because I have a family to provide [for]. And they have a family to provide [for]. It's nonsense to consider them criminals. No one offered them another job. ... For two years, they didn't have any other source to get bread to eat and survive. No one offered them even any kind of pension. They offer them maybe eighty dollars pension, or something like that, which is ... maybe enough bread for a week. That's just nonsense. Why do we blame people struggling to get food for their families when we don't ... when we don't try, even, to help them?

And when Iraqis tell the government that we need jobs—we were in the army and now we need jobs because we don't have money to survive—they say, "You are insurgents" or "You are not trusted; you have background in the Iraqi Army." Well, millions of Iraqis were in the Iraqi Army, including people who are in the government now. What ... what could they do else? Iraq had no job opportunities. For those uneducated, they had to go to the army, as in any other place in the world. They can't be blamed for that. They can't be blamed for having a job to provide their families. That was a big mistake.

How the Decision Was Made

In some ways, the process by which L. Paul Bremer and Walter Slocombe made their decision to disband the military was even more remarkable than the decision itself. The decision reversed previous policy, which included briefings to, and decisions by, the President, and overrode the policies and plans of ORHA and CENTCOM, which were actively working to recall the Iraqi Army. Moreover, the decision was made secretly, often dishonestly, by a small group of men with almost complete ignorance of the situation with which they were dealing. These men did not consult with or inform the rest of the government, and in some cases, they deceived the people with whom they did speak. Much of this behavior appears to have been driven by the personal characteristics of Bremer and Slocombe.

I tried repeatedly to interview L. Paul Bremer. He initially agreed, but then backed out, stating, via his publicist, that he did not have time. (Around the same time, I ran into a mutual acquaintance of his and mine, the wife of a very senior career diplomat; she told me that Bremer was spending a lot of time giving cooking lessons.) I also tried to interview Dan Senor, Bremer's press spokesman. Senor and I had a long, private conversation in his New York office, at which time he agreed to an on-camera interview. But from that day on, he never returned another e-mail or phone call from me or my office, so the interview never occurred.

I was therefore surprised that Walter Slocombe agreed to a second interview, even after I had uncovered major discrepancies in his account of the disbanding of the Iraqi military. Those interviews were among the most frustrating, and yet interesting, experiences of my life, as I watched Slocombe twist, evade, distort, and occasionally concede the truth.

In light of his refusal to be interviewed, I turn again to Bremer's September 6, 2007, *New York Times* op-ed piece for his description of how he made his decision:

> It has become conventional wisdom that the decision to disband Saddam Hussein's army was a mistake, was contrary to American prewar planning and was a decision I made on my own. In fact the policy was carefully considered by top civilian and military members of the American government. And it was the right decision. ...
>
> ... Walter Slocombe's consultations with Americans officials in Washington and Baghdad showed that they understood that the only viable course was to build a new, professional force open to screened members of the old army. Mr. Slocombe drafted an order to accomplish these objectives. I sent a preliminary draft of this order to the secretary of defense on May 9. The next day I sent the draft to the Defense Department's general counsel, William J. Haynes, as well as to Mr. Wolfowitz; the undersecretary for policy, Douglas Feith; the head of Central Command, Gen. Tommy Franks; and to the coalition's top civil administrator at the time, Jay Garner, asking for comments.
>
> On May 13, en route to Baghdad, Mr. Slocombe briefed senior British officials in London who told him they recognized that "the demobilization of the Iraqi military is a fait accompli." His report added that "if some U.K. officers or officials think that we should try to rebuild or reassemble the old R.A. (Republican Army), they did not give any hint of it in our meetings,

and in fact agreed with the need for vigorous de-Baathification, especially in the security sector."

Over the following week, Mr. Slocombe continued discussions about the planned order with top Pentagon officials, including Mr. Feith. During that same period, Lt. Gen. David McKiernan, the field commander of the coalition forces in Iraq, received and cleared the draft order. I briefed Secretary Rumsfeld on the issue several times, and forwarded a final draft of the proposed order for his approval on May 19.

Walter Slocombe subsequently received detailed comments on the draft order incorporating the views of the Joint Chiefs of Staff and the Office of the Secretary of Defense, making clear that the top civilian and military staff in the Pentagon, as well as the commanders in the field, had reviewed the proposal. Another coalition adviser, Dan Senor, spent the night of May 22 coordinating the text of the announcement with Mr. Rumsfeld's close adviser Lawrence Di Rita. Apart from minor edits to the order, none of the military or civilian officials raised objections to the proposal to create a new Iraqi army or to formally dissolve Saddam Hussein's security apparatus. …

The decision not to recall Saddam Hussein's army was thoroughly considered by top officials in the American government. At the time, this decision was not controversial. When Mr. Slocombe held a press conference in Baghdad on May 23 to explain the decision, only two reporters showed up—neither of them Americans. The first I heard of doubts about the decision was in the fall of 2003 after the insurgency had picked up speed.

As will be described in detail, most of these statements are either false or extremely misleading. First, it appears overwhelmingly likely that Bremer had already made the decision on May 9 and that neither he nor Slocombe had any interest in consulting with anyone. It is equally likely that the consultations that did take place with relevant officials were often deceitful. When some military commanders discovered that Bremer intended to issue the order, they objected strenuously; in response, Bremer and Slocombe sometimes concealed or misrepresented their plans. Bremer and Slocombe may also have concealed from the Pentagon leadership the degree to which General Abizaid, General McKiernan, and other military officers opposed the decision.

The story of what actually happened begins even before Bremer's appointment, with Walter Slocombe. Someone who has known Walter Slocombe for years recently told me off the record that even well before the war, Slocombe already believed that Iraq's military should be eliminated. During the war, the Pentagon leadership appointed Slocombe to head the DOD advisory group that would determine postwar policy for Iraq's military. For reasons that are explored on the following pages, Slocombe was the sole departmental senior adviser to remain behind in the Pentagon after the end of the war.

L. Paul Bremer was appointed to succeed Jay Garner in late April. After Bremer started work at the Pentagon on May 1, 2003, Slocombe began to urge Bremer to disband Iraq's military and security apparatus, even including the Ministry of Interior and the civilian police. This view meshed well with the Pentagon leadership's desire to purge Iraqi society of all remnants of the previous regime. It also appealed to Bremer's desire to demonstrate and assert American control through dramatic, strong new policy decisions, and possibly Bremer's desire to demonstrate his personal control as well. On May 9, Bremer's last day at the Pentagon and the same day that Feith gave Bremer the text of the de-Baathification order, Bremer sent a memo to Rumsfeld recommending the disbanding of the military, saying that he would make a final decision after he arrived in Baghdad. In fact, the evidence strongly suggests that Bremer had already decided and had no interest in researching anyone else's opinion on the matter.

In the following section, I reconstruct this complicated sequence of events, which lead to the formal public announcement of CPA Order Number 2 on May 23.

Reconstructing the Decision

Before the war, Jay Garner had briefed the National Security Council and President Bush on his intention to recall and use the Iraqi Army after the war. Then, shortly after the war, CENTCOM and ORHA began to plan the recall. The U.S. Army and intelligence officers with whom I spoke all contradicted Bremer's September 6 op-ed contention that General Abizaid thought the Iraqi Army could not and should not be recalled. All the interviewees who had spoken with Abizaid about the subject told me that he strongly supported recalling the army throughout April and May 2003.

My off-the-record interview with a senior military commander who was involved in these issues, and who was aware of Abizaid's opinions, supports this conclusion.

JAY GARNER: The Iraqi Army didn't surrender in this war, like it did in the first Gulf War. It just evaporated, you know. They took off their uniforms, and just folded themselves back into the civilian population. So that when we got into Baghdad, John Abizaid, Dave McKiernan, were constantly telling me, "How 'bout hurrying up? Let's get the army back. Let's get the army back 'cause we need to use them."

Army Colonel James Torgler, who was working for Garner at ORHA, had started collaborating with CENTCOM on recalling the army only days after Baghdad fell. Shortly after the end of the war, he participated in a conference call that included both General Abizaid and Walter Slocombe. During that conference call, Slocombe gave no hint that he was considering disbanding the army. In fact, Torgler said, Slocombe encouraged the ongoing recall effort.

JAMES TORGLER: We had the conference call with General Abizaid, Slocombe, Paul [Hughes], myself, and, for a brief moment, Wolfowitz came into the room while we were talking on his end. And I have got pretty detailed notes on that. But the upshot was General Abizaid wanted to ... they were just ... they were starting to capture or uncover units. ... The number we were talking [about recalling] was around forty thousand. And Slocombe, as I recall, said, "Yes, great, wonderful idea. Yes, we have got to do this." And he cautioned us that he had not been officially named yet, so anything he had to say was truly advisory; he was not in charge of anything. And we are like, "Okay, fine."

And then Wolfowitz came in, ... and he talked briefly about the fact that, yes, we had all these people [Iraqi troops] and, you know, we should use them for something. I will have to look at my notes, but there was no push back on creating the security force. ... It had to have been the third week of April that we were having this discussion.

Colonel Torgler said he also received encouragement for his work on the DDR (disarmament, demobilization, and reintegration) program to screen the Iraqi military as it was recalled.

JAMES TORGLER: One of the things I knew from working Afghanistan is we were going to have to have a DDR process in place—

CHARLES FERGUSON: Yes.

JAMES TORGLER: Okay, you know what DDR is.

CHARLES FERGUSON: Yes.

JAMES TORGLER: In fact, I had ... we had a contractor who had developed the concept of what it would take on site. And I remember giving Garner and Bates the briefing and saying, "Okay, this is how you would do it," and talking with General Strock. We were going to use ... There was a division based in the south of 51st Division, I think, just outside of Basra, that would work, [where] we would pull these people together. And so we had plans. And so we continued that planning. And about that time, Slocombe got named and then Gardner—Gregg Gardner was his [Slocombe's] military assistant. And we started talking on the phone and I explained to him where we were going. And I got nothing but encouragement—encourage, encourage, encourage.

Paul Hughes, who was in charge of the Iraqi Army recall effort, had a similar experience. On May 9, the very day that Bremer recommended the disbanding of the Iraqi military to Rumsfeld, Hughes spoke with Slocombe on the phone. Hughes says Slocombe did not breathe a word about Bremer's recommendation. In fact, there is no evidence that either Bremer or Slocombe even mentioned the idea of disbanding the Iraqi military to anyone in ORHA, CENTCOM, the Joint Chiefs of Staff, the State Department, the CIA, the National Security Council, the White House staff, or any other part of the U.S. government prior to Bremer's memo to Rumsfeld recommending this policy on May 9.

CHARLES FERGUSON: So [Slocombe] didn't say that he had already come to the tentative conclusion and recommended to Bremer to dissolve the army?

PAUL HUGHES: Absolutely not, because had he said that, I would have been on Jay's doorstep posthaste to say, "We've got a change in policy." You know ... back during Desert Storm, how sensitive we were to policy issues, policy pronouncements, and such. You know, that kind of stuff, you know, you don't hear a civilian official say, and just blow it off. You immediately go let the boss know, "We've got a change in plans," you know. So at that particular point in time, there was no indication whatsoever that there was any kind of inkling of thought in Washington that they were going to abolish the military.

Yet that same day, May 9, was the day that General Paul Eaton received a phone call, telling him that he was being chosen to train a brand new Iraqi army.

CHARLES FERGUSON: Tell us the first time that you had any involvement with Iraq, of any kind.

PAUL EATON: P. J. and I were traveling down—P. J. is my bride of, uh, over thirty years—and we were traveling down Victory Drive, which is this great institution outside of Fort Benning, Georgia: [a] classic military post entryway. And we were in the convertible, headed down to see the Chattahoochee River that had busted out of its banks.

Cell phone went off. And it was my boss, telling me that, uh, I'd been selected to go command the Coalition Military Assistance Training Team, otherwise known as CMAT, which was the outfit destined to train the … new Iraqi army.

CHARLES FERGUSON: What was the date?

PAUL EATON: That date was 9 May 2003.

The following day, Bremer left for Iraq, stopping in Qatar along the way, where he received a briefing at CENTCOM from CENTCOM deputy chief of planning Colonel John Agoglia. The briefing included, very explicitly, CENTCOM's plans for recalling the Iraqi Army.

JOHN AGOGLIA: I briefed Bremer in Qatar. When he came in to me, Franks, and Abizaid on the 10th of May in Qatar, I was the one who briefed him. One of the key parts of our postconflict plan was recalling the Iraqi Army, and [I] highlighted that to him and told him that was something we were working on. We already had been working with Mr. Slocombe and had already been working with Wolfowitz and Feith. And Abizaid chimed in as well.

He [Bremer] knew this was a key part of the plan. There was at least that time frame to know about it. And some of the discussions with Slocombe, I don't remember specifically, but I'm confident it came up for discussion. I couldn't be as confident as I am that I know I had these discussions with Slocombe, but Bremer knew what the military concept was for recalling the Iraqi Army and the critical part of the plan that was. He understood that, because I know I personally explained that to him in the presence of General Franks and General Abizaid, who also continued to emphasize that piece of why that was so critical.

Colonel Agoglia said that during the briefing in Qatar, Bremer gave no indication whatsoever that he was considering, much less planning on, disbanding the military.

CHARLES FERGUSON: Garner says that a couple of days—one or two days—after Bremer arrived in Baghdad, that he [Garner] received a memo (which was in fact sent to all the senior people at ORHA, so it was sent to Garner and Paul Hughes as well, although Hughes was in the United States at the time), but Garner received a memo which was from Bremer and [which] said, "I understand that senior people in ORHA have been in contact with members of the Iraqi military, and I order all these contacts to stop immediately." And Garner says that he went to Bremer when he read this memo and said, "Look, we have to communicate with these people because we're in the process of recalling them." Bremer said to him, "That's not going to happen." And that was the way that Garner found out for the first time that the army was not going to be recalled. So this would be on, like, May 14th, or something like that.

JOHN AGOGLIA: Interesting. First I've heard that. I can't say I doubt it. Amazing. Just another example of folks coming in, nodding their heads up and down, and saying, "Yeah, yeah. We understand. Yeah, we support you," when in fact they're not being totally truthful and honest with the folks they're talking to. If he knew that on the 14th, then I'm assuming he knew it on the 10th. He sure as shit didn't say that to Franks or Abizaid. So once again we have an example of a guy coming in and saying, "Yeah, yeah,

yeah," and nodding up and down as if these generals are a bunch of idiots and they have all the goddamn answers and the generals don't. To me it's just amazing. It's just typical of the way they operated, unfortunately.

In my December 2007 off-the-record interview with a senior military officer, I learned that when Bremer was in Qatar, he did mention to a very few of the most senior commanders the possibility of disbanding the Iraqi Army. They told him that they thought that this would be a bad idea, and that on the contrary, they felt that it was important to proceed with their plans to recall the Iraqi Army as quickly as possible.

Even after Bremer arrived in Iraq on May 12, he informed very few people of his plans, and there is no evidence that he seriously consulted with anyone prior to announcing CPA Order Number 2 on May 23. By May 14, when Bremer circulated the memo ordering ORHA to cease contact with the Iraqi military, ORHA and CENT-COM already had their recall plans well in place. They were planning to recall 100,000 members of the Iraqi Army within nine months, in groups of three divisions at a time every ninety days, for a total of nine divisions. This force would be constructed through the recall of an even larger number of personnel, who would then be filtered through the DDR process that ORHA was preparing to create.

It appears that the first time anyone in Iraq learned that Bremer had definite plans to disband the Iraqi military was when he circulated the aforementioned memo, one or two days after his arrival in Iraq. The memo itself mentioned nothing of Bremer's plan to disband the military. But when Jay Garner read the memo, he went to see Bremer. He told Bremer that ORHA needed to be in touch with the Iraqi military in order to organize its recall. Bremer replied that he was canceling the recall and would disband the army. I interviewed Garner once, long before Bremer's op-ed article in the *Times,* and twice more shortly afterward. In the first interview, I asked him about his reaction to Bremer's reply.

CHARLES FERGUSON: When you learned of the decision to disband the army, was that a surprise to you? Had this been discussed?

JAY GARNER: Yeah. No, it hadn't been discussed. It was a surprise. A big surprise.

CHARLES FERGUSON: Really?

JAY GARNER: Uh-huh.

CHARLES FERGUSON: So Mr. Bremer never talked to you about this.

JAY GARNER: Well, Mr. Bremer made that ... Bremer made that decision, I think, the second day he was in Baghdad.

CHARLES FERGUSON: Uh-huh, sure, but you know, telephones exist. He never called you up from—

JAY GARNER: No. No. I was ... That was a surprise that, I ... I didn't know that.

CHARLES FERGUSON: What was your reaction? What did you think?

JAY GARNER: I thought it was a poor idea. I thought we needed to bring them back.

In our second interview, Garner described his meeting with Bremer—and a similar meeting with Walter Slocombe—in more detail. It was clear to Garner that Bremer already regarded the decision to disband the military as final at this point—approximately May 15.

JAY GARNER: I went to see Slocombe around the 15th or 16th ...

CHARLES FERGUSON: When you went to see him, did you speak with him about the disbanding of the Iraq Army at all?

JAY GARNER: I talked to him about that and about a memorandum from Ambassador Bremer that said ... Bremer had put out a memorandum that went to the staff, and a copy was furnished to me, and it said something like that he was aware that members of ORHA had been talking to members of the Ministry of Defense, the Ministry of Interior, and also talking to former army officers and that he wanted that to end until he and Walt Slocombe could come up with a policy.

So I went to see him, and we ... and I don't remember the exact conversation. I remember some of it, not verbatim. I said, "You know, Jerry, we have to continue to talk to the Department of Defense, because we're going to bring ... we're bringing the army back, so that's why we're talking to these people."

CHARLES FERGUSON: You mean the [Iraqi] Ministry of Defense.

JAY GARNER: The Ministry of Defense, I'm sorry. "And we've set the money aside to pay the army as we bring it back and give them their back pay." And he said, "Well, I don't think we're going to do that." And I said, "Well, the plan all along has been to bring the army back." And he said something like, "We're not going to do that anymore. We're going to start with ... ," I think, "We're going to start a new army" or, "We're considering starting a new army," or something like that. And I said, "Well, Jerry, you know, you can get rid of an army in a day, but it takes you years and years to build one back up because it's the process of training it, sustaining it, paying it, medicating it, taking care of the families, that type of thing. It's institutions that have to be built. It's not the trigger pullers."

And he said, "Well, we're going to come up with a policy, and I don't think we're going to bring the army back." And it was clear he didn't want to talk about that any more. And I said, "Well, in the Ministry of Interior, you talked yesterday about how important the police were." He said, "They are." And I said, "Well, the police are all the Ministry of Interior. If you shut off conversations with them, they'll all go home." He said, "Well, go see Slocombe and tell him to take the Ministry of Interior out of the ... out of our policy we're doing."

So I went to see Walt Slocombe, and I said, "Hey, Walt, all of the police are in the Ministry of Interior. You can't shut that down, because the police will go away." And he said okay. And [I] said, "Why are you trying to get rid of the army?" He said, "We think we need a new army. We don't think this army is what we want." And I told him the same thing: You can get rid of it in a day, but it's going to take years to build it back. And we just kind of ended that conversation. And that was around the 15th or 16th of May.

Incidentally, Slocombe later professed not to know that Garner opposed the disbanding decision:

CHARLES FERGUSON: He's said publicly, and he [Garner] also said to me, that he was in favor of recalling the Iraqi Army and using it as a kind of public works, WPA [U.S. Works Progress Administration] kind of instrument.

WALTER SLOCOMBE: Um, if that was his view, that was his view. He certainly did not express that to me at the time.

In fact, a number of military officers, including a senior officer I interviewed off the record in December 2007, told me that Garner had in fact objected to disbanding the military at the time. Bremer and Slocombe also claim that they sent copies of their draft order to Garner, CENTCOM commanders, and others for "clearance," and that no serious objections were made. Garner and others, however, say that they never received or saw any draft order, but that they certainly did object when they learned what Bremer and Slocombe were planning to do.

CHARLES FERGUSON: Okay. Now, the decision to disband the army and security services: Did you and/or Ambassador Bremer discuss it in advance with General Abizaid, General McKiernan, General Garner, General [Peter] Pace, or Colonel Hughes?

WALTER SLOCOMBE: Not Pace. Not Pace.

CHARLES FERGUSON: Okay, but with the others?

WALTER SLOCOMBE: Well, certainly with McKiernan. And I, of course, I don't know who Bremer would have discussed it with. There were several meetings with McKiernan on the general subject: what to do about the army and how to move forward.

There were discussions with Abizaid, which were premised on the proposition that there was no Iraqi Army left, and therefore, the issue was, How do we rebuild an army? There were certainly those discussions. And the … I'm sorry, the other was … oh, Colonel Hughes. Well, Paul was around. I assume he was involved. I don't know.

CHARLES FERGUSON: General Garner?

WALTER SLOCOMBE: Oh, Garner for sure.

CHARLES FERGUSON: Okay.

WALTER SLOCOMBE: 'Cause the drafts that were circulating internally went to both McKiernan and Garner.

CHARLES FERGUSON: Yeah, this is a bit mysterious, because we have General Garner and Colonel Hughes, both of them on camera, saying that the dissolution of the army came as a complete shock, both to them and also to

General Abizaid and General McKiernan, and that all of them were extremely disturbed by it and opposed it.

WALTER SLOCOMBE: I'm sure that what you tell me is true. But I know that the drafts were sent to them.

CHARLES FERGUSON: Well, if—

WALTER SLOCOMBE: And we ... got back comments from them, and McKiernan cleared on the order. Now clearing, as you probably know in the bureaucracy, clearing doesn't necessarily mean "I think this is the best idea I've ever heard," but it certainly means "I've been informed and if I thought this was a terrible idea, I have the opportunity now to say it."

Garner, for example, raised some questions about it, not on the fundamental issue, but about details. See, we sent the draft around to the different offices, so that there were questions about cost and so on.

When I spoke with Garner, however, he denied that he had ever received a draft of the order.

CHARLES FERGUSON: When you saw this document [Bremer's memo ordering ORHA to stop all discussions with the Iraqi Army], which then led you to go see Ambassador Bremer, that was the first that you had heard—

JAY GARNER: Yes, because Paul Hughes—up to ... I think probably up to twenty-four hours before that—had been talking to large ... large numbers of the former Iraqi Army, and we were planning on bringing them back. And I think I told you, when you and I talked before, we had ... a contracting force that was going to assist in training and bringing them back and that type of thing.

CHARLES FERGUSON: So did you ever see the draft order that Bremer says he circulated starting on May 10?

JAY GARNER: No, I never saw that. I saw what he said in the paper, but I never saw that article, that draft, and I was never asked for comments on it.

CHARLES FERGUSON: I see. Okay.

JAY GARNER: To this day, I haven't seen it.

CHARLES FERGUSON: I see. And did Bremer ask you to comment on the substance of the issue at any time other than this one conversation?

JAY GARNER: No. That's the only conversation we ever had. It was clear to me at that point … It was clear to me the decision had been made.

CHARLES FERGUSON: So he was not asking for your comment then, either?

JAY GARNER: No, not at all.

Furthermore, it appears that Bremer had not informed either General Abizaid or General McKiernan that he had reached a final decision to disband the Iraqi military. When Bremer told Garner his intentions, Garner called the generals and found them both unaware of what was going on.

CHARLES FERGUSON: Did you speak with any of the senior military commanders about this question at that time?

JAY GARNER: You know, some time after that, I talked—maybe that day or the following day or so—I talked to Abizaid and McKiernan. And I said, "They ought to bring the army back." And they were surprised.

CHARLES FERGUSON: They were surprised?

JAY GARNER: Yes … they were surprised because they had been putting a lot of pressure on me to bring the army back as fast as we could for all of the reasons that you already knew about.

CHARLES FERGUSON: So you had the impression, or more than the impression, that Abizaid wanted the Iraqi Army recalled?

JAY GARNER: Well, Abizaid talked to me continually about when are we going to bring the army back. So sure, he wanted it brought back.

CHARLES FERGUSON: And …

JAY GARNER: And when I read in the *New York Times* article [Bremer's op-ed article] that Abizaid had agreed with that [the disbanding], maybe he did. If he did, I did not know that.

CHARLES FERGUSON: Okay.

JAY GARNER: And Abizaid and I were pretty close. I mean we ... we talked almost daily and saw each other quite a bit.

CHARLES FERGUSON: And how about McKiernan?

JAY GARNER: McKiernan always wanted to bring the army back because he needed the force.

CHARLES FERGUSON: And he said that to you?

JAY GARNER: Charles, we had all kinds of meetings, and bringing back the army always came up as "When can we get them back?" You know, "How soon can we do this?" And they were kind ... In fact, I'd say McKiernan and Abizaid were a little upset with me that I couldn't ... I wasn't getting them back any faster than I was, you know, that I hadn't already brought a substantial number of them back. So I think they were a little anxious about that, and they were a little disappointed that I hadn't been able to do a better job of bringing them back. That was my impression.

Meanwhile, Walter Slocombe arrived in Iraq for the first time on May 15. Paul Hughes had been urging Slocombe to come to Iraq for several weeks. He had become increasingly disturbed by Slocombe's reluctance to leave Washington.

PAUL HUGHES: Every department went over with us, except for the Office of the Secretary of Defense, ironically. They were the only ones not to send a team with us. And that had consequences. That had consequences. And I'm not sure why that team didn't show up until June, or I guess late May, early June. But they didn't show up until after the disbanding of the Iraqi Army was ordered, which was a ... a real shock for a lot of us.

CHARLES FERGUSON: That's crazy.

PAUL HUGHES: I'm sure that they probably had their reasons. But it certainly wasn't something I would have done. I urged them time and again, in my conversations with them from Baghdad, that they needed to get over there, because there were people waiting on them, and on one man in particular, to show up so he ... he could make decisions, and get the ball rolling. In his absence, I was left with the duty of having to deal with the Iraqi Army, just to keep contact with them.

Several others suggested to me privately that Slocombe stayed behind in part because he was concerned that he wouldn't be comfortable enough in Baghdad. It was also an adroit political move, for it allowed Slocombe to work with Bremer in the Pentagon during those nine crucial days, May 1 through May 9, when Bremer's most important—and devastating—policy decisions were made. In my interviews with Slocombe, he was clearly sensitive about the issue of his staying behind in Washington. He also seemed somewhat evasive about the exact dates of his travel to Iraq, and sought to imply that he had arrived in Iraq earlier than he had.

WALTER SLOCOMBE: Well, at that point [in late March 2003], there was already a substantial number of civilians out in ORHA, deployed forward. They were actually in Kuwait. And General Garner was out there at that point, as well as quite a few other people. And I said, "I don't see any reason to go out there. I can get ready better here in Washington than sitting in a hotel in Kuwait. And you know, we have telephones, [and] so on." So I spent the time from then until early May virtually full time in the Pentagon. I wasn't, at that stage, a government employee, but I was basically working virtually full time, uh, talking to people, reading stuff, going out to the agency, talking to people at AID, talking to people who were familiar with Iraq, talking to g— ... There was this, I've forgotten what the initials are now, but there was a group of Iraqi exiles, mostly Iraqi Americans—"exiles" is probably not the right term; many of them were citizens—who had been brought together to advise and be helpful in getting the planning started, and I talked to them; talked to other people ...

... At any rate, in early May, I did go out. I went out. I got there a couple of days after Bremer. And started talking to people, figuring out, working with the CENTCOM people to get a practical plan for doing the training. We put together that plan, in part, over the course of the time I was out there. I was out there for about two weeks.

Actually, Slocombe arrived in Baghdad on May 15, not "early May," and he was there for eight days, not two weeks. He left on May 23, immediately after announcing the disbanding order, and he did not return to Iraq until June 12.*

---

*In my film, Paul Hughes erroneously says that Slocombe arrived on May 16 and stayed for four days. I discovered the error long after the film was released and posted a correction on the

Slocombe suggested that Paul Hughes' presence in Iraq was a reason that he, Slocombe, could remain in Washington. When I pointed out that he had not consulted with or even informed Hughes of his views and had made his first major policy decision contrary to Hughes' judgment, Slocombe became tense.

Walter Slocombe, the senior advisor for security sector and defense affairs to the Coalition Provisional Authority, 2003.

CHARLES FERGUSON: I was told that you were the only ministerial adviser, and the DOD, Department of Defense, Ministry of Defense advisory group, was the only advisory group that stayed behind in Washington. That every other Iraqi ministry's advisory group went first to Kuwait and then was in Iraq for two weeks before you arrived.

WALTER SLOCOMBE: I don't know … I don't know. But the going to Kuwait struck me, and struck a lot of people, including some people you've quoted, as a mistake. To try to send the whole body, as opposed to having a few people out there.

CHARLES FERGUSON: And how about the time in Iraq?

WALTER SLOCOMBE: I'm sorry, I don't know what you mean.

CHARLES FERGUSON: The time in Iraq that they were there when you guys hadn't shown up.

film's Web site. In every substantive issue for which I have any evidence, Hughes' comments seem accurate, and most have been confirmed by others, including his description of ORHA and CENTCOM contacts with the Iraqi military and their plans to recall the Iraqi Army.

WALTER SLOCOMBE: Well, I mean, there's always an advantage to be on the spot, I don't dispute that.

CHARLES FERGUSON: And don't you think that there's a—

WALTER SLOCOMBE: On the other hand, it is also true that basically, people who are out there aren't getting anything done. We can't talk to anybody, we can't go out on the … we can't deal with people. Now Paul [Hughes] was doing a good job. One of the reasons was, it seems to me, was that it's better to have Paul, people like that, out there, and me back here with Bremer. And … and, there's certainly a lot of people who—

CHARLES FERGUSON: If you are trusting him, then why did you make your first major decision in a way that directly—

WALTER SLOCOMBE: You know, we've been over that. … Your questions and my answers to that are the same as they were before.

CHARLES FERGUSON: Well, but if you didn't trust him—

WALTER SLOCOMBE: And I really do have to … I really do have to get going. If you have a different subject … I mean, neither of us are going to convince the other, but, I mean, we've been through that.

CHARLES FERGUSON: Well, if you didn't agree with or trust his judgments about these matters, don't you think it was important for you to be there to be able to form a judgment yourself?

WALTER SLOCOMBE: Well, I believe I was there as soon as I could do anything very useful, given that there were people there. I mean, you know, there was a lot of stuff to be done in Washington as well.

Several times during his first trip to Iraq, from May 15 to May 23, Slocombe met with CENTCOM officers, who told him of their plans to recall the Iraqi Army. At least twice, Slocombe commented that he thought that he might disband it instead and listed his arguments for doing so. In each case, military officers vehemently disagreed with him and warned him that his beliefs were wrong. When confronted with these objections—and when explaining his disbanding proposal to others—Slocombe adopted a combination of two complementary strategies. In some instances, he appeared to back down and told the military officers to continue their efforts. In other cases, he portrayed the disbanding decision as just a formality, saying that the dissolution of the formal organizations was independent of the question of how Iraq's actual future military should be constructed.

Apparently, CENTCOM commanders also found it difficult to take Slocombe seriously. Thus, between May 9 and May 23, the military continued, and in fact expanded, its plans for recalling the Iraqi military.

JAMES TORGLER: I got to Baghdad to stay, I guess, the end of the first week in May, and started working away, started ... You know, at that time, the whole point was we were going to stand up. And the number kept getting bigger of how many—

CHARLES FERGUSON: Tell me about that.

JAMES TORGLER: We were talking; the forty thousand [Iraqi troops] soon got to be a hundred thousand. How can we do this, one hundred thousand? And well, we got it. It is all throughput. I mean, if you've done any sort of military logistics, your constraining factor is, Okay, how much of your product can you move through?

The first time Slocombe mentioned any dissatisfaction with the army recall effort was shortly after he arrived in Iraq on May 15. When Colonel Agoglia heard Slocombe's views, the colonel expressed his disagreement directly to Slocombe.

JOHN AGOGLIA: Slocombe shows up in theater about the 16th.

CHARLES FERGUSON: Yep, 15th, I believe.

JOHN AGOGLIA: Okay. So he shows up, and one of the first things he asks me is, "Hey, John, how can we call on an Iraqi Army that didn't have the courage to stand and fight, that were a bunch of cowards and deserted? Will the American people stand for us recalling an army that was so cowardly that they wouldn't stand and fight?"

I thought he was kidding. I mean, I was flabbergasted. I looked at him and said, "Mr. Slocombe, Sir, we asked them [the soldiers] to do that. They did exactly what we asked. Yeah, we expected more to surrender, but they didn't. But they did what we asked them to do. They're waiting to be recalled. We've been executing this operation against them since June or July of last year. Guys in uniform like me think it's a good idea they didn't stand and shoot and fight. We think that's a good sign. We think it's time to recall these guys and bring them back on board. We need to develop those plans."

He looked at it and said, "Ahhh, I don't know."

I said, "Sir, come on. The fact that they didn't fight is not a bad thing. The fact that they deserted—okay, got it, there may be something there. There may be some folks who have other motives for why they deserted, but a majority of them, from what we understand from the intel, they deserted because that's what we asked them to do." ...

Then we started getting feeds that the Saddam Fedayeen ... is also able to threaten the soldiers who would think about ... or the families ... if they thought about surrendering. So the soldiers now feel that their families are threatened. So they can't surrender, because Saddam Fedayeen will take action against their family. So they're going home to take care of their family. We are starting to get that information coming on in. Now, when exactly that started coming on in, I don't know. Someone asked me that question the other day. But I think we had that information by the time May rolled around. ... We had that information, we're talking May, so by the time April was around, that information was coming on in. So that's another piece to pass on to Mr. Slocombe, say, "Look, it looks like most of these guys deserted because there were tip-offs and leaks about the outreach we were making to the army to desert and to surrender, and their families were threatened by this organized group of thugs, and they felt they had to go home and protect their family. So again, they've done what we would have done."

He said, "Okay, well, maybe." But the point is, he had no idea about what we had been doing in terms of planning against these guys to get them to do exactly that. He comes in with this mind-set that they're a bunch of cowards. That's his mind-set that then drives the way he approaches this. The next piece that's in his head is that they're all Baathists. We're like, "We don't have any credible evidence that they're all Baathists. Better yet, they at least all have guns, so why not call them back in? We know that they're a symbol of unity and nationalism for Iraq. So why don't we recall them and sort out those that are Baathists and those who aren't? We will probably be able to figure that out. Let's bring them together and sort that out rather than having them dispersed with weapons all throughout the country. Let's bring them in, you know, like we said we would—keeping our part of the promise and bringing them together— and then we'll sort out who's a Baathist and who isn't, as time goes on. But that's not the most important thing right now." He couldn't quite comprehend that.

When confronted with objections from military officers, Slocombe tended to back down and portray the proposed disbanding of the military as a mere formality that would not interfere with the military's plans. This may account for why the senior military commanders continued to behave as if the army would be recalled. One senior military commander, with whom I spoke off the record, believes that Tommy Franks objected to Rumsfeld about Bremer's plans, but the senior officer with whom I spoke was not present during the conversation.

JOHN AGOGLIA: For a guy like McKiernan, he's got a shit[load] going on. There's this discussion by this guy Slocombe, who seems just totally out of the net on what's going on with recalling the Iraqi Army. So when you have this discussion about we're going to disband these pieces of it, we're going, "Yeah, but we're going to recall the Iraqi Army." In fact, we had CENTCOM planners sitting with CFLCC [Coalition Forces Land Component Command] planners in Kuwait, planning on the recall of the Iraqi Army. So [from] McKiernan's point of view, this discussion about CPA Order 2 is noise. That's noise to him. "Got it, go do what you've got to do. I'm developing a plan with CENTCOM folks at the direction of General Abizaid, who is also talking with Wolfowitz, Feith, and Slocombe about recalling the army." Everyone thinks this is what we're doing. Everybody just assumes we are recalling the Iraqi Army because that's what the plan is. No one understands that Slocombe is actively undercutting this planning and this assumption. Nobody understands that, including myself. We thought he understood what we were doing and why. We thought that, okay, he had some initial questions about it, but that was questions based on a lack of understanding of what was going on. So no one takes him seriously when he's walking around, saying he's not sure we're really going to do that. ... And I'm telling Abizaid [about] these discussions I'm having with Slocombe—

CHARLES FERGUSON: You were talking to Abizaid about this?

JOHN AGOGLIA: Yes, because Abizaid is coming in on the security team to do the discussion with the security process and the weapons cards and who is going to carry weapons and those things.

CHARLES FERGUSON: So what was Abizaid's view of recalling the Iraqi Army?

JOHN AGOGLIA: Abizaid thinks we're recalling the Iraqi Army. I would participate in the VTC [video teleconference] with Abizaid in mid-April in which Wolfowitz, Feith, Slocombe, Abizaid, Paul Hughes, were all in, and had this discussion, and Abizaid was very much on board with that.

I'm telling Abizaid in May now that Slocombe is asking these questions. He's talking about CPA Order 2, disbanding Saddam's army. And I told him my view is we go along with CPA 2 because it makes sense to disband these elements as long as [we] know we're going to recall the Iraqi Army, not the Republican Guards and not the SRG [Special Republican Guard]. And he says, of course. So he's in agreement with me, and he sees this issuance of CPA Order 2 as a necessary evil, but it doesn't impact on our plan to recall the Iraqi Army. ...

CHARLES FERGUSON: I assume you mean you were taking the same people, the same structure, and standing the army back up.

JOHN AGOGLIA: Right, but they would not be Saddam's army. They would be a new Iraqi army, serving a new governance body, whatever that governance body was going to be.

CHARLES FERGUSON: Okay, so the same force that is reporting to a different governance.

JOHN AGOGLIA: Right, because Saddam's army was gone and with it anybody who was in that army under just rank or privilege because of Baath Party association. That sort of stuff was not going to be stood. But you know, we don't know who those folks are. We got some indications of some of those folks. We're going to recall those soldiers.

CHARLES FERGUSON: It's important to be precise about language here because I'm going to want to quote you, and you're going to want to be quoted appropriately. Maybe slow down a little bit. So, your intent was, and the intent shared by the CENTCOM planners—by McKiernan and Abizaid—was that you were in fact going to recall the Iraqi Army with eventual vetting of that army to remove Saddamists and extreme Baathists, but you were going to recall that army and put it back in place under a new governance structure, a new Iraqi government.

JOHN AGOGLIA: Yes, absolutely.

CHARLES FERGUSON: So, did Slocombe explicitly tell you that this was okay and that CPA Order Number 2 was just going to be a formality?

JOHN AGOGLIA: To me, he did. ...

CHARLES FERGUSON: And you think that he clearly understood that this was not creating a new army from scratch?

JOHN AGOGLIA: Absolutely. Now it turns out he didn't agree with that. But he did understand that. There was no doubt.

Colonel Agoglia was not the only one to whom Slocombe feigned agreement—or at least declined to state his real intentions—when confronted with resistance. On May 22, the day before CPA Order Number 2 was announced, Slocombe was in a meeting with Colonel Torgler. Here is Torgler's account.

CHARLES FERGUSON: I assume you know that Walter Slocombe and Jerry Bremer have since argued that one of the reasons that the army had to be disbanded is that it was basically a corrupt Sunni officer corps, corrupt Baathis, Saddam officer corps.

JAMES TORGLER: Yes.

CHARLES FERGUSON: And a disgruntled, unhappy, oppressed, abused, Shiite, enlisted, draftee, soldier base.

JAMES TORGLER: Yes.

CHARLES FERGUSON: You did not see signs of that?

JAMES TORGLER: No. What Jerry Bremer and Walter Slocombe are telling you is that they did not know anything about the Iraqi Army. When they tell you that, what they are talking about is the Republican Guards. And Walt and I had this discussion. About a week later, I am doing the planning and I talked to the lawyers and I talked to the money guys. We are down to the point where we are trying to figure out how much and where. We are probably ten days out from going and having this meeting. I talked to these people, and they had agreed that for twenty dollars—one thin twenty-dollar bill—they were going to register, they were going to turn in their weapons, and they were going to sign a proclamation that said they were not a Baathist or fundamentalist and that they recognized the Iraqi state. Because my position was, if I keep them in the army, I know where they are. I can control them. ...

... So he [Slocombe] is getting all these briefings, and he casually mentions that it is the administration's position—he did not say who, but the position of them—that we needed to get rid of all the Baathists and disband the army. And I think my reaction was one of horror and incredulity. I was stunned. ... I do not think I actually asked him if he was insane, but I ... You know, I was still in uniform, a lieutenant colonel; I was a lot less cynical than I am now. But I did not understand what was going through. And he rolled that line out at me: "Well, they are all Baathis, and they are all this and that."

And I said, "No, no. Respectfully, you are dealing with an army that is organized along Soviet lines. And I have some experience in this, being in Germany for six years, getting ready to fight the Russians. And talking to these fellas, your hard-core Baathists are your general officers."

But even then, you have got to remember, I mean the stories we heard. If you wanted to exist in this society in a level of comfort, you had to be a Baathist. Yes, I mean I talked to doctors who were required ... you know, what they did to deserters in the army ... They cut off their ears and they used military doctors to do it ... And if the doctors refused, then they killed them and their family. So truly a Hobson's choice. Do I become a

Baathist and live, or do I stand on my principals and my entire family is dead in the street? You know.

CHARLES FERGUSON: Yes.

JAMES TORGLER: So, there was not a lot of give and take like that. So, I took that whole Baathist thing with a grain of salt …

And then he [Slocombe] said, "Well, why would we call them back? They are a defeated army."

And that set me off again: "No they are not. We told them; we made a bargain with them that said, if you stand down, if you stand aside, you will be part of the solution." In fact, more than one [Iraqi] colonel told me that. He did not actually show me the flyer, because it was written in Arabic, but he said, "You told us on the radio that if we stand down, if we pulled our units out of the fight, we would be part of it." And they fully expected to be part of the solution, which … made perfect sense to me.

And then he [Slocombe] said, "Well, we have to get rid of the Baathists."

I said, "Well, I am not disputing that. But we have a moral obligation to take care of these people. We took over this country." And said, "If you take down the army, where is the infrastructure to feed the widows and orphans? Who pays the disabled vets? Who pays the retirees? Who does what? Oh, and by the way, Sir, if you disband the army, you lose control of two hundred thousand people with guns. If you DDR them, you register them, you sort out who you want to keep. And then life is good."

And at the end of that discussion—which he thought was going to take fifteen minutes, but by my watch, it took about two hours—the last word that he said to me was, "Okay, continue your planning to pay the army."

He got on a plane and flew away, and about thirty-six hours later, they put out the proclamation disbanding the army. And oh, by the way, did not tell any of us. And so they put it out, as I recall, on a Friday. Now, if you know anything about the Muslim world, what happens on Friday?

CHARLES FERGUSON: Yes.

JAMES TORGLER: … I get this message back on Friday that said, we put this out, and do not talk to the Iraqis any more. What?! And … on Saturday morning, I had a meeting scheduled. And so what I was told to do was go out and meet with them [the Iraqis] at the gate, read them the proclamation, do not bother to answer any questions, and then go back in. And so this horse's ass had to go do that. I am a little irritated. Yes, and you can probably understand my irritation, because the Iraqis did not react well.

CHARLES FERGUSON: Well, what a surprise.

JAMES TORGLER: Yes, in fact I have an e-mail that I can share with you that I sent my wife. And as a Cassandra, I said [to my wife], "I think a lot of people are going to die because of this, because, in their eyes, we promised them something and then pulled it back, and did not care, and they were humiliated." ...

CHARLES FERGUSON: What he [Slocombe] said is that he announced the dissolution of the army on the 23rd at a sparsely attended press conference and immediately thereafter flew away back to the United States.

JAMES TORGLER: Then it would have been the evening of the 22nd.

CHARLES FERGUSON: Okay.

JAMES TORGLER: It would have been that night before he flew away and made his announcement.

CHARLES FERGUSON: And prior to that, none of you had any idea that he was going to disband the army?

JAMES TORGLER: It was like a thunderbolt out of the blue. ... My first meeting with him was that discussion. I had talked to him on the phone, but the first time I had actually been in the same room physically with him was that day when we had that two-hour meeting. I talked to his military assistant, Gregg Gardner, many times, and he was there through all of that. We were doing our planning for the new Iraqi army. In fact, he was building a staff to do that support. I mean, it was like a thunderbolt out of the blue. All of a sudden, poof! "No, we are not doing that."

On May 23, the day after the release of CPA Order Number 2, the same thing happened again. On his way out of Iraq, Slocombe stopped in Kuwait, where he received a briefing from a group of military and intelligence officials, who included Agoglia and Admiral James Robb, CENTCOM's chief planner.

JOHN AGOGLIA: On May 23, I was on a plane with him later that afternoon, and we flew down to Kuwait, and he received a briefing on the plans to recall the Iraqi Army.

CHARLES FERGUSON: Okay.

JOHN AGOGLIA: ... The idea was to recall three divisions every ninety days. ... Clearly, the briefing was to him to recall the Iraqi Army, and talking about how they were going to do it. And Admiral Robb was there from CENTCOM. I was there. We had agency folks there who could talk about the vetting of the generals—they could go out and get the right command structure and have guys come in that could be trusted agents for us to help us recall the Iraqi Army and stand the army up. This is the stuff he is getting told. Everybody is working towards this plan of recalling the Iraqi Army. General Abizaid thinks its on track; he's briefed it on up to Wolfowitz and Feith. I mean, we're moving forward. CPA Order 2 is seen as a formality as a sense in our eyes.

CHARLES FERGUSON: What was Slocombe's reaction to this briefing?

JOHN AGOGLIA: He was, "Got it, got it, got it." And he just said, "Roger, understood," and basically directed them to continue with the planning. It wasn't a decision brief. It was an information brief; it was a status brief; it was an update. We weren't asking for a decision, because we all assumed that decision was made. This is what we were doing, including Admiral Robb. So, we are giving an information briefing, an update, a status update, the challenges we are going to face, but what they are doing to overcome the challenges, actions other organizations are doing like the agency, the vet people. These are things he's getting told so he has an understanding of how far along we are on the planning. He then left on that day, and he was gone for about two weeks.

On May 22, Bremer sent letters to Rumsfeld and to President Bush stating his intention to disband the Iraqi military and to issue CPA Order Number 2 the following day. On May 23, Bremer publicly announced and distributed the order. He held a meeting with his own staff to announce the new policy. An intelligence officer who was present at the meeting, but who will not speak on the record, told me that much of Bremer's own staff was surprised and objected to the decision, and that several told Bremer so directly and immediately.

Even at this point, nobody in the CPA or the Pentagon—not Bremer, Slocombe, Rumsfeld, Wolfowitz, or Feith—had consulted with or even informed anyone else in the government about the decision—not the State Department, the CIA, the National Security Council, the National Intelligence Council, or the Joint Chiefs of Staff. Most learned of it through the news media. Deputy Secretary of State Richard Armitage was also surprised by the announcement.

CHARLES FERGUSON: When did you first learn of the order disbanding the Iraqi Army?

RICHARD ARMITAGE: At a meeting at the NSC. We had had many discussions about this. But, as Mr. Bremer's book makes clear, the original decision, I believe, was to ... disband echelons above battalion and keep battalion below as a force to be utilized, to provide security, et cetera. But, for reasons described in Mr. Bremer's book, he and Secretary Rumsfeld apparently made another decision.

CHARLES FERGUSON: And so what date did you learn about—

RICHARD ARMITAGE: Well, I ... Come on. You've gotta give me a heads up to ... I don't remember which date. You have to give me a heads-up so I can look up in my diary.

CHARLES FERGUSON: Well, okay. It's ... it's not ...

RICHARD ARMITAGE: It was ... it was shortly after the invasion, obviously. But, I don't remember the date.

CHARLES FERGUSON: Okay. Well, let me tell you why I'm asking. It's not so much a matter of, you know, was it nine, ten, or eleven. But there's a staging question. Ambassador Bremer, greatly to my surprise, I have to say, says fairly openly in his book, that based on advice from Walt Slocombe, he made the recommendation to disband the army to Secretary Rumsfeld on

May 9. And the reason the date's pertinent is that was before either Slocombe or Bremer went to Iraq for the first time. ... And it's also fairly clear that they didn't discuss this with any of the senior military people or with General Garner, all of whom opposed it. Were you aware of any of that?

RICHARD ARMITAGE: No. I had said that we had discussions that came to a different conclusion at the National Security Council—and that was one to keep echelons, as I recall, battalion and below.

CHARLES FERGUSON: Right.

RICHARD ARMITAGE: So, this idea to disband the entire army was one that came as quite a surprise to me.

CHARLES FERGUSON: I see. What was your reaction when you learned of it?

RICHARD ARMITAGE: I thought we had just created a problem and had a lot of out-of-work soldiers. ...

CHARLES FERGUSON: Who ... who did you express to that concern to?

RICHARD ARMITAGE: A lot of us at the National Security Council sat around and talked about it. Secretary Powell certainly knew it. He ... he found out about it as I did.

CHARLES FERGUSON: Which was how?

RICHARD ARMITAGE: Just as we found out. One day, Jerry [Bremer] announced that he disbanded the army.

CHARLES FERGUSON: OK. And [laughs] did any of you say anything to the president about this?

RICHARD ARMITAGE: We'll keep our advice to the president quiet. The president already made a different decision, which was to keep battalion and below, in force.

CHARLES FERGUSON: Earlier, yes ...

RICHARD ARMITAGE: Well, within ... I mean, in a couple of days proximity.

CHARLES FERGUSON: Yes. Yes. That's right.

RICHARD ARMITAGE: So, from my point of view, that decision had been made. And we moved on to the next decision. And it was a surprise, I think, to most of us, to find that the army had been disbanded.

CHARLES FERGUSON: To most of you? So, is this—

RICHARD ARMITAGE: I can't say. I don't know what the president ... if he had any discussion with the secretary of defense about it. Jerry, in his book, makes it clear that he talked to the secretary of defense.

CHARLES FERGUSON: Yep.

RICHARD ARMITAGE: But, beyond that, I'm unaware of whom else Secretary Rumsfeld talked to. I just know he didn't speak with my boss.

CHARLES FERGUSON: And, and when you say, "us," I thought you were referring to the National Security Council. Was ... was Cond—

RICHARD ARMITAGE: Many, many of us, both staffers and ... and principals. I was not a principal except when my boss was gone, I would be there to support him. I think most of us were caught relatively unaware or completely unaware by this disbanding of the army.

It appears that nobody in the intelligence community was consulted, either. Here is National Intelligence Officer Paul Pillar:

CHARLES FERGUSON: Tell us whether anyone asked you in advance about the merits of dissolving the Iraqi Army. Did you have any discussions with anybody about that before it occurred?

PAUL PILLAR: We were not asked; we had no such discussions. ... In brief, our judgment was, with regard to some of the organs that were closest to the regime, and that Saddam had relied on most heavily for the continuance of his own power, such as the Republican Guard, the Special Republican Guard, and the various Iraqi intelligence services, those really could not be trusted at all. With regard to the regular Iraqi Army, we thought that there was indeed a potential for them to be of use in contributing to security in the postwar situation. But again, it wasn't our job to make a specific judgment about disbanding or not disbanding.

CHARLES FERGUSON: No, fair enough. But presumably it was within your purview to say something about, you know, if you do this, then the consequences will be that.

PAUL PILLAR: The implication of what, yes. That is a ... It is a proper intelligence function to talk about—and we are often asked these sorts of questions—to talk about the likely consequences of the U.S. doing this or that. We were not asked specifically about the consequences of disbanding the army.

The military was caught unaware as well. Apparently, Bremer and Slocombe told McKiernan and Abizaid about the proposed order at most a few days before issuing it. It also appears that, as with Colonel Torgler and Colonel Agoglia, Bremer and Slocombe may have tried to soften the blow by representing it as primarily a formality, which would not preclude the rapid construction of a large new army mainly based on the old one. (I have been unable to learn exactly what Bremer told Abizaid and McKiernan at this point.)

Whatever he had been told, McKiernan was plainly unhappy with the decision. On May 23, the day the order was issued, McKiernan held a press conference in Baghdad. He carefully avoided making any direct statement disagreeing with the order, but nevertheless implied his concern:

> There is a large number of, uh, former Iraqi soldiers that are unemployed now. That is a huge concern, not only from a security standpoint, but from an economic standpoint. They're not earning an income right now.

As described earlier, Slocombe maintained that Abizaid, McKiernan, and Franks had been sent the draft order for clearance, had been informed of Bremer's intentions before the order was issued, and had no disagreement with the order per se. But he did not give an exact date on which McKiernan was given the draft order, and revealingly, Slocombe said that he spent his last day in Baghdad—May 23—rushing around to obtain clearance signatures, which suggests that Abizaid and McKiernan either had not yet seen the draft or, if they had seen it, had not approved it. Slocombe conceded that McKiernan and Abizaid disagreed with him on the substance of what to do—whether to recall the army or build a new one from scratch.

Slocombe also asserted that Garner had been similarly consulted and had contributed comments. Garner denies this. McKiernan, who is still on active duty, has not agreed to be interviewed.

WALTER SLOCOMBE: Yeah, it was in that period. I mean, I can remember vividly spending the day. I mean, it was like being back in the Pentagon except you were doing it in Baghdad, running around and making sure 'cause we were trying to get it out, running around trying to make—not physically, [but] phoning people and so on—trying to make sure that we had the clearances from the people that we needed to get clearances [from], and that included the command and General Garner.

CHARLES FERGUSON: Now, General Garner—

WALTER SLOCOMBE: You couldn't very well have been there without knowing that this was going on, 'cause we were talking about it.

CHARLES FERGUSON: Well, what he says is that he learned of it after the decision had already been made. And the first he learned of it was a memo that stated that the decision had already been made.

WALTER SLOCOMBE: Well, I mean, that's a little different from saying he didn't know it was gonna happen. There's no question that Bremer was inclined to do this from before when he went out, before he went out, before he left Washington. And I can understand how somebody who didn't think it was a good idea could have thought, "Well, I don't ... I won't make a fuss about it, 'cause it's already been decided. I'm not gonna ... I'm not gonna fall on my sword over it." I can understand that, and if that's what Garner means, then I ... I'm sure that that's what he felt and what he meant.

CHARLES FERGUSON: No, that's not what Mr. Garner means.

WALTER SLOCOMBE: But—

CHARLES FERGUSON: What Mr. Garner means, and we have him saying this on camera, and he said it to me again at considerable length in a telephone conversation two days ago, is that he first learned of the dissolution of the Iraqi Army by being told—

WALTER SLOCOMBE: First of all, he first learned of the dissolution of the Iraqi Army when it happened. I interrupt on this point—

CHARLES FERGUSON: The formal dissolution—

WALTER SLOCOMBE: The formal, the proposal to issue the order, which was finally issued, the substance of which never changed.

CHARLES FERGUSON: The formal dissolution of the Iraqi Army.

WALTER SLOCOMBE: Okay. All right, right.

CHARLES FERGUSON: He learned of the formal dissolution of the Iraqi Army by a memo, which stated that it had already been decided. And he further said that he spoke with General McKiernan and General Abizaid, who were both also quite shocked and surprised—

WALTER SLOCOMBE: Well, this … I mean, they may have been. But let … let's get straight the … the fundamental sequence of events. I don't in any way dispute that Bremer was inclined to do this before he went out. But he sent out … he sent Rumsfeld a memo saying, in substance, "I'm inclined to do it, but I will discuss it when I get out there."

Now, that undoubtedly means he would require some persuading not to do it. I know that there were discussions, most of which were not about issuing the order, because nobody thought rightly … nobody thought that issuing the order was a big deal.

McKiernan's comments on May 23 certainly do not suggest that "nobody thought that issuing the order was a big deal." Nor do Garner's. The senior military officer I interviewed in December 2007 told me that he thought the order was a major mistake, and said so at the time. And, interestingly, although General Tommy Franks made no public comment on the order, he chose May 23 as the date on which to announce his retirement from the military. Richard Armitage implied that he, too, had expressed his disapproval of the decision to Bremer, but that it was too late.

CHARLES FERGUSON: Do you think that recalling the Iraqi Army would have been a good idea?

RICHARD ARMITAGE: I thought that disbanding the Iraqi Army to the extent we did was a bad idea. So obviously, recalling at, you know, the lower echelons, I thought would have been a good idea. It would have gotten them off the street and kept them employed, as it were.

CHARLES FERGUSON: Did you ever express these concerns to Ambassador Bremer?

RICHARD ARMITAGE: These were done things. I don't … I saw Bremer several times in Baghdad, and certainly talked to him on the phone and in SMTs [satellite media tours] meetings, but, if you'll review the situation, you're going to find the events proceeded pretty rapidly. And it was very difficult to get the mercury back in the bottle.

As for the secretary of defense and the President, it is hard to know how they really felt about the decision. When I asked Jay Garner if he ever mentioned his concerns to them, he replied that he had discussed the issue with Rumsfeld, but not the president, after he returned to the United States in June:

JAY GARNER: Well, to my memory, what I said was something like, "You know, Mr. Secretary [Rumsfeld], I think we've made three bad decisions—or three tragic decisions—and one was the de-Baathification; the second one was getting … was not bringing back the Iraqi Army; and the third one was the removal of the leadership group that we had put together. But it's not too late to reverse those, and we still have time to reverse them." And he thought for a minute, and he looked at me and he said, "Well, I don't think we can do that because we are where we are." …

CHARLES FERGUSON: Did he indicate that he agreed or disagreed that those decisions had been—

JAY GARNER: He did not indicate one way or another.

CHARLES FERGUSON: But he clearly heard you say that you thought there were mistakes.

JAY GARNER: Yes, but this is then—Charles, this is around the middle of June, the second week of June.

CHARLES FERGUSON: Yes. Okay. When was the last time you spoke with President Bush?

JAY GARNER: You know, I don't know that they ... It was that day that I talked to Rumsfeld. Rumsfeld and I then went over to the White House and spoke to the president.

CHARLES FERGUSON: And did you mention the—

JAY GARNER: I did not, no.

CHARLES FERGUSON: Okay. Did you mention any comment about Bremer's policies?

JAY GARNER: No. ...

CHARLES FERGUSON: Okay. Can I ask how come you didn't feel it was worthwhile raising the army issue to the president?

JAY GARNER: Well, I worked for Rumsfeld, and I told Rumsfeld what I thought. He was my boss, and I told him what I thought, and, you know, I'm an army guy. [I] go up to the guy I work for and tell him whether I agree or disagree, and he says, "Well, the decision is made," and that's it. So I did not say anything to the president about it.

It does seem, however, as if the military were somewhat less concerned at this point than it should have been, probably because Bremer and Slocombe continued to conceal the full extent of their intentions. Not only did they intend to disband the Iraqi military, but as we will see shortly, they did not intend to construct a new one of any significant size. This decision apparently came as a surprise to the senior military commanders when they learned of it in June.

Creating a New Iraqi Army

On May 9, 2003, General Paul Eaton received the phone call informing him that he was in charge of creating and training a new Iraqi army. Eaton had a series of meetings in Washington, D.C., with Walter Slocombe and others. Both he and Slocombe flew to Iraq in mid-June. It was apparently only then that General Abizaid and the other CENTCOM commanders were informed of the decision that the new army would be quite small, and constructed slowly. In place of CENTCOM's plans to recall nine divisions, that is, approximately 100,000 Iraqi soldiers, within nine months, Bremer and Slocombe proposed a new Iraqi army of only three divisions after two years, and virtually no active force within six months.

JOHN AGOGLIA: When he [Slocombe] comes into theater [in mid-June], when he comes in, he has with him Major General Paul Eaton, and Eaton's going to be the guy who is gonna be in charge of retraining the Iraqi Army. As the head of the U.S. Army Infantry Center, a very good choice. So, he comes in; he's going to go talk to Bremer about his meetings in D.C. I get to sit in on his debrief to Bremer about the decisions on the Iraqi Army. So, he starts talking, and Bremer says, "Listen, we're going to recall the Iraqi Army, but we're not going to do it in three months; we're going to do it in two years, and we're only going to recall three divisions over those two years." And I looked at him. I said, "Does General Franks know about this?" And he said, "It doesn't matter, John." And I said, "Yes, it does matter." And he said, "No, it doesn't. The decision has already been made." And I said, "Who the fuck made the decision?" "Secretary of defense did." "Does General Franks know?" He said, "It doesn't matter, John." And I guess I ended up cursing again because Ambassador Bremer asked me to leave. I was pretty upset because that was the first time we'd heard that. I was like, "Excuse me? We're going to recall this army, three divisions only over two years?" And I immediately was concerned. So I went outside and I picked up the phone and I called Qatar. I got ahold of [Colonel] H. R. McMaster, who was the executive officer for General Abizaid. [I] spoke to H. R. and asked him if General Abizaid heard any of this, and he said no and put General Abizaid on the phone. And I explained it to General Abizaid and said, "Hey, Sir, here is what Mr. Slocombe just brought back here—this decision made in D.C., and he's in support of it. He's recommended it, and the secretary of defense has made this decision." General Abizaid was not happy. I don't remember his exact words, but he was not pleased. He asked some pointed questions. He was upset. And he said, "Got it. I'll get back to you." Then he hung up.

The plan to create a new Iraqi army from scratch meant that all the prior planning of ORHA and CENTCOM had been in vain. And since Eaton had only been appointed on May 9 and had only arrived in Iraq in mid-June, progress would necessarily be slow. Furthermore, Eaton was given very few resources—few people and little money. Even Eaton, who defended the disbanding order, was disturbed.

PAUL EATON: The fact that the man charged with standing up the Iraqi Army, let alone the Iraqi security forces, received the mission as late as 9 May, which is … a week after the president declared "end of mission" on the aircraft carrier deck, my first reaction was, uh, we're a little late. And when I started getting into the middle of it, what we had was a twenty-slide PowerPoint decision brief that had been approved by the secretary of defense, to embark upon a very slow rebuild of the Iraqi armed forces, which actually really addressed the Iraqi Army, not the air force or the navy. And it was an attempt to do it as a true economy-of-force action. Total budget was less than two hundred million—

CHARLES FERGUSON: Total budget was less than two hundred million dollars?

PAUL EATON: Correct.

CHARLES FERGUSON: Isn't that crazy?

PAUL EATON: And this is going after the security forces for a nation of some twenty-five million people. So we were absolutely not focused on this … The civilian Pentagon leadership level had not focused on the preparation of Iraqi security forces to [fill] the vacuum that the coalition forces created when they took down the government, took down the Baath Party, and took down the Iraqi Army. So, you know … this situation lies absolutely at the feet of the Rumsfeld-Wolfowitz-Feith trio.

CHARLES FERGUSON: If this had been done properly, when would you have been given this mission?

PAUL EATON: I'd be speculating. … And part of this is, everybody can be a Monday-morning quarterback. And we could not have seen clearly into the … nature and seriousness of the insurgency that … that's ongoing right now. A lot of us could have speculated about it. But again, history is gonna be the judge on all this.

The postconflict phase team of Garner and all the men who would have assisted him in this … I don't know when it was built; I don't know how well resourced it was. But when I got there, it was five guys borrowed from the CENTCOM staff and Eaton sitting down in a villa that had been [Saddam Hussein's son] Uday's, trying to figure out the way ahead for a twenty-five-million-inhabitant-country's army. That was it. And it was a little late in the day to get after the security forces' redevelopment phase for this country.

CHARLES FERGUSON: So you don't have any particular sense of when it should have been started.

PAUL EATON: I would have expected … You know, it … again, hindsight, twenty-twenty. When you sit down to take down the country, and plan on its takedown, it's a continuous operation. And it's Phase IV of an operation. … And the development of a robust Phase IV is just as important as the development of a robust Phase III. And the resourcing of that plan is part of that drill. So, certainly in '02.

I asked Eaton about the plan he developed in May and June 2003 after he was appointed.

CHARLES FERGUSON: What was the plan at that point? What was contemplated in terms of dates, schedules, size of the Iraqi Army?

PAUL EATON: The original plan was a PowerPoint briefing of a little over twenty pages that laid out for a nationally recruited, representative force of all the ethnicities and the religions of the country that would be locally employed for the defense of Iraq from enemies from without. So the intent was to develop Iraqi army units that reflected the society, to train them to defend the country from external aggression. That's how we recruited this force. The intent was to build nine light-motorized infantry battalions in the first year, and nine each in the next two years.

CHARLES FERGUSON: So that's a total force of what size in each of those years?

PAUL EATON: The intent was … Numbers take on a meaning of their own very quickly in Washington, D.C. And the figure of forty thousand was put on the table. And that is roughly a small … That is a small corps. And some of the terms associated with this project was the "New Iraqi Corps." Well, that acronym is an offensive word in Arabic. So it quickly morphed into other terminology: The New Iraqi Army is what it quickly evolved to.

The chosen policy was to have a private company, Vinnell, select recruits, and to have all recruits undergo a new training program. The first training cohort did not go well.

PAUL EATON: The intent was to recruit a thousand soldiers, with officers and noncommissioned officers from the former Iraqi Army; to bring them into the recruiting stations; and then to move them forward to Kirkuk, the training base that we selected, that is twenty kilometers from the Iran-Iraq border, about ninety kilometers northeast of Baghdad. And, it's out in the middle of nowhere. It is just an austere base that Saddam had built during the Iran-Iraq War—never occupied, heavily looted—that we need to refit. …

We started with a very small group. That did not go well. And the intent was to bring some forty-five former lieutenant colonels of the Iraq Army— old Iraqi Army—and have them vet our training, provide advice, feedback, and they would be the officer corps of the first battalion of the New Iraqi Army.

They came in. We brought them in. And these were all men who had been recruited by British and U.S. military units. They showed up on the 15th of July. And we, General Crocker and I, welcomed them to the installation, congratulated them on their decision to be the … the vanguard of this New Iraqi Army. And we then had them go to their barracks. We waited a couple hours, to bring them back for the first meal. And General Crocker came up to me and said, "Paul, we've got a problem. They've got demands."

So I met with a group. And this group of forty-five former lieutenant colonels in the Iraqi Army said that "We want our old rank back. We want more money, and we are not working for the coalition." And we took the forty-five men, put 'em back to their barracks. I assembled them the next morning at eight. And said, "Get on the bus, gentlemen; you're going home." And they were a little bit set back. They were surprised by that action. And we sent them back home.

After this initial effort, Eaton modified his recruiting goals and found a thousand recruits to train. A few months later, Eaton negotiated an agreement with Jordan to have the Jordanian army train the officer corps of the New Iraqi Army. Meanwhile, the insurgency was gathering strength. As the security situation deteriorated, the goals and needs for the new army increased.

CHARLES FERGUSON: When did you first think that the plan for the New Iraqi Army—its planned size and capabilities—might not be adequate to Iraq's security needs?

PAUL EATON: I sat down with General [Ricardo] Sanchez and General Abizaid in August. And we talked about the need for acceleration of the development of the security forces in Iraq.

CHARLES FERGUSON: August of 2003.

PAUL EATON: Uh, 2003. Correct. And Generals Abizaid and Sanchez were embarking upon a plan to locally recruit, locally employ units throughout the theater, throughout the country. And this was kind of an Iraqi national guard, that was called the ICDC, the Iraqi Civil Defense Corps. And these units were to be raised locally, trained by coalition forces, and equipped to the best of our ability. This was something done by Combined Joint Task Force 7, commanded by General Sanchez. All of this [was] to augment and to develop security forces in a much more rapid sense throughout the country.

It also became apparent that we needed to increase the, uh, the through-put, if you will, in the training and the manning for the Iraqi army. And the eye of the needle was the development of infrastructure to provide barracks for these soldiers. It's a volunteer force. You need barracks to bed these men down. The option of tents and so forth—we explored all venues. And we kept coming back to, we've got an infrastructure drama before we can increase the size of the army. ...

Again, the army, at this point, is destined for defense of the country from enemies from without. And when I was asked, in one interview, in one press conference, in October of '03, how long before Iraq will be able to stand on its own? my reply was, in a perfect world—which means you are not employing this force, you have virtually unlimited resources, and you have a ready population to provide the manpower to outfit the force— between three and five years, for between six and twelve divisions. ... So my answer then was three to five years. That's where you are building the force, training the force, and you are not employing the force. This is a force that's training in a vacuum and not being employed in an insurgency, and not being affected by an insurgency.

All those factors changed over time. When we began to look to the Iraqi army to fight the insurgency within the country—which is not what these first battalions signed up for; they didn't sign up to fight their fellow Iraqis ... and this problem will come to a head April of '04.

So the answer to the question is, all those factors: in a vacuum, three to five years to develop a force that can defend Iraq from attacks from Iran or Syria or Turkey, whatever ... whatever scenario you outline. What we proposed to the secretary of defense was, we'll build three divisions, in one year, under the new system, with a bill of 2.2 billion dollars, to build out the infrastructure north to south, the beginnings of a navy and the air force; and we will put to the field the nucleus of what will become the future Iraqi armed forces, realizing that the basis of any army is a light infantry. And from that, you build your tanks regiments, your artillery formations, your signal outfits, your military police organizations. But you start with the infantrymen and then move forward. That's what we laid out to the secretary of defense. He approved that plan on 5 September.

But the plan kept changing, and it was very difficult for Eaton to keep pace. In addition, Pentagon politics and bureaucracy sometimes interfered.

PAUL EATON: The deputy secretary of defense—at that time, Wolfowitz— withheld 253 million dollars from infrastructure rebuilding in order to put some pressure on the CPA, apparently—or, uh, [I'm not] sure where he was trying to put pressure, but what it did was put pressure on me. And it didn't aid the development of the police program at all. What it did was substantially delay the barracks development up in the north. That held up a division's worth of barracks. So—

CHARLES FERGUSON: This was for the army or the police?

PAUL EATON: This is for the army.

CHARLES FERGUSON: The army.

PAUL EATON: So this was ... this was money that the secretary of defense had cut over to the CMAT program to develop the army, and in an arbitrary fashion, in January ... of '04, Wolfowitz withheld this money, which seriously delayed the building of barracks up in the north of the country. ... I ... had this stray electron from the Pentagon withholding money to delay the development of the barracks.

CHARLES FERGUSON: You gotta be careful. That's gonna be in the film. [*laughs*]

PAUL EATON: Well, it had a serious impact; it made no sense, and we ultimately got the money. But it caused ... it fractured the timeline that we had because we had men, equipment, coming on line. And they needed barracks before we could assemble the whole unit. The pipeline was filled with men, but we didn't have a place to put them. And it was a serious problem. Basically, we had to warehouse Iraqi leaders, awaiting barracks development. And it was—

CHARLES FERGUSON: Did you protest this? Did you say, you know—

PAUL EATON: Basically, I got thumped pretty good by the Joint Staff ... that they were working it. And ultimately, they broke it out after six weeks ... So we had to rebuild the construction crews. It was a real load of sand in the gears to do this.

Eaton also said repeatedly that neither he nor other American military commanders had enough resources to do their jobs properly, and that the occupation of Iraq had never received the degree of national commitment that it required.

CHARLES FERGUSON: You've said many times, "Not enough troops." The other thing that you've also said a few times is that the level of effort devoted to training internal security forces was vastly inadequate. So those two things, you think, are the two core contributors to—

PAUL EATON: It's still inadequate. We are still [inadequate], now, when you take a look at national interests and what the country, what the United States of America, really gets after. And if you start looking at what security forces we are truly paying attention to outside of our borders, what comes to mind: Israel, Egypt, South Korea. Those armies are intensely important to the interests of this nation. If you start—and I just offer this as an opportunity for analysis—if you start comparing the amount of money that we are spending to sustain the Israeli army, the Israeli security forces, the IDF [Israeli Defense Forces]; and, on the other side of the canal, the Egyptian army; the South Korean army is pretty much on its own feet now, but past expenditures may deliver the true tone of what we're doing in Iraq right now. What are Iraqi security forces driving around in today, compared to their American and British colleagues? And how are we doing with the provisioning of the Iraqi police forces today?

CHARLES FERGUSON: Today being early 2006.

PAUL EATON: Correct. So, when I was there, and working the police program, towards the end of the stay that I was there, I had American leadership up in Mosul lay it very clearly to me: Here we are, the best army in the world, outfitted with very sophisticated weaponry, and body armor and vehicular armor. And we have these brave Iraqi policemen and soldiers in thin cotton shirts, out in front of us. That's what was happening. That was what was happening back in spring of 2004. And today, it's a lot better. I see a lot of Iraqi army units under body armor. We still don't have the requisite vehicular armor in the ... in the hands of the Iraqi security forces.

Between 2004 and 2006, writer James Fallows undertook to understand the effort to build the New Iraqi Army and attempted to assess its progress. When I spoke with him about his findings, he provided a discouraging overview. The subsequent performance of the Iraqi military suggests that he was correct.

JAMES FALLOWS: One strange area of convergence—right-left convergence, Iraqi-U.S. convergence, convergence of almost everybody, except maybe the extreme Sunni insurgents—is that it would be much better for everyone if Iraq had a viable security force than if it did not. Because if Iraq had a viable force of its own to maintain public order, and prevent civil war or mass communal slaughter, then the U.S. wouldn't have to be there, or wouldn't have to be there in such numbers. ... Why, several years after the fall of Baghdad, is there so little sign of an actual viable Iraqi force? The answers seem to be, in a way, a paradigm of all the rest of the puzzle of postwar Iraq. ...

It's hard [to train an army] anyplace; it's hard in Iraq. It's particularly hard when it's being done under combat circumstances. And given that it was—how hard it was—the U.S. then, for about a year or so, paid no attention to it. You know, the first year or so was basically wasted in the effort to bring up an Iraqi force, and it was compounded by the decision to dismiss the existing Iraqi Army a couple of months into the occupation. So you have one of the most important, and one of the most difficult, feats of managing postwar Iraq, that for a long time was ignored, or ... or sort of countermanded, even. And the U.S. is now trying to cope with the consequences of that.

Since the middle of 2005, by most estimates, the effort has become more successful. The U.S. sort of learned better how to do this. But it learned better how to do it at a time when the insurgency was getting bad at a faster pace than the military was improving. So if anything, the U.S. has been losing relative ground in being able to leave things to the Iraqis.

CHAPTER SEVEN

THE POLICE, CRIME, AND THE SECURITY VACUUM

By late May 2003, the poorly trained Iraqi national police force was literally the only remaining organization in Iraq available to provide security and order in the country. The American military had been ordered not to intervene in looting, crime, or domestic security problems, and on May 23, L. Paul Bremer had disbanded all of Iraq's military, paramilitary, intelligence, and secret police organizations, along with the ministries that operated them.

Unfortunately, the Iraqi police and judicial system were weak institutions with major internal problems. They were also severely neglected by the U.S. occupation. As with policy toward the Iraqi Army, U.S. policy toward the Iraqi police eventually changed, but it was too late. The growth of crime, corruption, militias, police death squads, and insurgency outpaced U.S. efforts at police training and oversight, and by 2006, the police and Interior Ministry had become heavily controlled by fundamentalist Shiite groups—particularly the Badr Organization and the Mahdi Army—and also by apolitical criminal gangs. To simplify: In 2003, the Iraqi police were inadequately trained, inadequately equipped, and timid; by 2006, they were still inadequately trained, but they were very dangerous.

The Police

Under Saddam Hussein, the Iraqi police had been the least powerful, least professional, and least favored of the major security forces. The national police force numbered between 100,000 and 150,000. It performed few patrols and even fewer investigations because there was little crime in Iraq, and because some major crimes such as bank robbery were treated as security threats and were therefore investigated by the secret police and intelligence services rather than by the civilian police. The police were known to have used harsh tactics. However, prewar U.S. intelligence about the police was extremely limited and in some cases erroneous. In his memoir, Bremer asserts that most Baghdad police stations had "rape rooms," an allegation that none of the other interviewees concurs with, although everyone agrees that the police had sometimes been brutal. Even so, interviewees who had worked with the Iraqi police just after the war also found officers and commanders who were well intentioned.

CHARLES FERGUSON: In Bremer's book, he says that the police were deeply involved in torturing people and in brutality both to political prisoners, and also, in a completely nonpolitical way, he says in his book, most Baghdad police stations had a rape room, where women were raped. Is that what you saw? What did you see of what the police … were like, what they had been doing under the previous regime?

JAY GARNER: Well, I don't know the actual answer to that. I think that the police could be very brutal. That wouldn't surprise me, although I'll say this: Most of the police stations I saw were pretty small to have rape rooms. Now some, yeah. And I went into a lot of police stations.

CHARLES FERGUSON: Okay.

JAY GARNER: So, I'm not denying that. I'm just saying I don't know about that.

CHARLES FERGUSON: You didn't see any evidence of it?

JAY GARNER: No, no I didn't.

Everyone, however, agreed that the Iraqi police badly needed professionalization and training. Despite this, prior to the war the Pentagon leadership rejected the Justice Department's recommendations for deployment of a postwar police advisory force of 6,000 to 10,000 persons. Then, in March 2003, before leaving Washington for Kuwait, Jay Garner separately requested a force of 2,500 to 5,000 advisers to help supervise and train a postwar Iraqi police force. National Security Advisor Condoleezza Rice's aide, Frank Miller, objected; Garner persuaded Rice to hold her potential veto in abeyance until Garner could report from Baghdad. Garner's request remained pending as the security situation in Iraq worsened.

JAY GARNER: I briefed many times in February. I briefed on the necessity to bring back the police and the amount of money that it would take for law enforcement restoration, the amount of money up front. And I briefed that to Dr. Rice, to Rumsfeld, to a lot of people. We also had a team, a Justice Department–State Department team that had done quite a bit of work, prewarfare work, on what it would take. And then an initial plan. And if I remember right, Charles, [it] called for about twenty-five hundred advisers, administrators, trainers, for about a hundred thousand police. And then they would always say their leader-to-led ratio should be about one to fifty. Now, they also said that twenty-five hundred advisers to them was the minimum, but there might be a necessity for another twenty-five hundred. And so what we needed was some up-front money to determine the actual size of the footprint that we were going to need in order to bring back and retrain the Iraqi police.

The problem with the Iraqi police is they were really the last link on the security food chain. They had a police academy, but they didn't send all their policemen to a police academy; only a few went to that. And they didn't patrol; they essentially stayed in stations. So that if you wanted to be a policeman, you went down to the head room and they gave you—if you were in the right party—they gave you a uniform, and you became a policeman that day. So, we recognized that. And so, when I got there, I guess, gee, Charles, about the 28th or 29th of April, I began going on the radio and announcing for the police to return, and some had already trickled back. So there was a concerted effort on our part, all through this process. Well, you had to bring the police back; there was no other way to do it.

CHARLES FERGUSON: And at this point, what had happened to your request for the large training and advisory group? Had that been approved?

JAY GARNER: No, it wasn't approved. It was held in abeyance. Frank Miller, who worked for Condoleezza Rice, did not agree with that. He didn't think—and whatever reasons I never quite understood—but Frank Miller did not believe that we needed that large footprint. And so I went to see

Dr. Rice probably in March—I don't remember now—and essentially briefed her on the difference between what I thought was the right footprint and what Frank Miller thought was the right footprint. And I asked her not to make a determination against me at that time; just leave it open, and when we got there, I would call her and I would report back and give them a realistic number.

During the war, the police force deserted and disappeared, as the army had done. In the chaos and looting that followed, most major police facilities were looted and destroyed. After the war, ORHA began to recall them. Eventually, about 40 percent of the prewar police force would return to work, but when Jay Garner arrived, there was a total absence of police on the streets.

Ray Jennings has spent his career working for nonprofit organizations doing community development work in postconflict countries. He arrived in Baghdad in May 2003. One of the things that struck him was the large amount of loose weaponry readily available on the street.

CHARLES FERGUSON: I remember the first time I spoke with you. ... You said then that one of the first things that you saw that struck you was that there were weapons everywhere, and that in every bazaar, you could outfit a small army with what you could buy there. Tell us about that.

RAY JENNINGS: Yeah, that's quite true. And in fact, at that time you probably had many organizations that would later become micromilitias do just that. Because of the looting, because of perhaps lack of anticipation, the arms would be easy to come by by Western military forces. These were freely available. And this was AKs [AK-47s, Soviet-designed automatic or semiautomatic assault rifles]. It was RPGs—rocket propelled grenades. Grenades were a favorite, of especially youth, who would buy them and then use them in the course of their play. Dropping them off buildings was something they took great amusement in—

CHARLES FERGUSON: Dropping grenades off buildings?

RAY JENNINGS: Yeah, off the sides of buildings, from the roofs. ... You have to understand, at the time, the disorder that was present in the city ... It didn't raise too many eyebrows because at this time, you have to remember, the looting had just happened, in early May, throughout the month of May, when you had looting continue on one scale or another. Many of these weapons were actually procured through looting. There are ... several significant stories of arsenals that were looted while Western forces did look on, because it was not part of their mandate to control this. And so many of these arms did come through these venues and found their way to the market, where they could be sold to provide liquidity for the people who had procured them, and now had sold them, perhaps resold them.

So the place was awash in weapons, and in many ways, it's not too unusual. Many postconflict environments, you'll see the same thing, and it's primarily because of a lack of security that many people did just that. If they didn't already have a weapon, they certainly bought one. If they already had a weapon, and could afford it, they'd buy another. And personal security was high on people's agenda in Baghdad in May 2003.

Shortly after Bremer was appointed to replace Garner, Bernard Kerik was hurriedly appointed as the senior adviser to Iraq's Ministry of Interior, in charge of all police forces in Iraq.

Bernard Kerik is a complicated man. He is widely regarded as having been dedicated, effective, and courageous as a special narcotics detective in New York City, as commissioner of corrections, and as New York's police commissioner under his mentor, Rudolph Giuliani. In my interview with Kerik, I found him to have a practical street sense that was impressive. At the same time, he wasn't entirely trustworthy; although he emphatically assured me that he would not be indicted on corruption charges, approximately one week later, he was. While Kerik has many virtues, he also has a long history of unethical and illegal conduct, including the use of his official positions for purely personal ends. He abandoned his young girlfriend and child in Korea when he was a military policeman there. He was fired from a private security job in Saudi Arabia following an investigation by the Saudi secret police. He repeatedly had sex with his mistress and book publisher, Judith Regan, in an apartment that had been donated for the use of exhausted 9/11 rescue workers. He used his official position in an attempt to obtain favorable treatment for businessmen who had supported him financially. He has pleaded guilty to conflict-of-interest charges, and in November 2007, he was indicted by a federal grand jury on tax evasion and corruption charges.

I asked him—and Michael Moss—how Kerik was hired to supervise the policing of Iraq. Moss is one of several *New York Times* reporters who began investigating the police force after many people, including U.S. military officers, said that it was a huge, underreported, problem.

BERNARD KERIK: The first week of May, I was contacted by the White House liaison for the Pentagon—and I forget his name—to ask me if I would come down and meet with Secretary Rumsfeld's office to discuss policing policies in Iraq. ... I think I got the call on a Wednesday and went down to the Pentagon on Saturday. ... I met with one of Rumsfeld's assistants and a few other people that briefed me about the interim sort of ministers that were being appointed to go into Iraq, people that would take over the various offices. And we discussed basically the Ministry of Interior and reconstitution of interior—what the interior consisted of, what the prior offices were, an estimated number of police and border controls, and other things. Some information they had; some they didn't have during the course of the brief. I went through that for several hours, probably three or four hours. And then at the conclusion of that, sometime around the time I was ready to leave, I met with Ambassador Bremer. Bremer was on the way to Iraq. In fact, he probably left the next day. ...

I came back home that Saturday. I want to think ... I went back to ... I went back to the Pentagon the following Thursday. And I left for Kuwait the following Sunday. I think I got into Kuwait on the 18th [of May] if I'm not mistaken. ...

MICHAEL MOSS: Bernie Kerik had been a very successful police official in New York City, and was thought very highly of by people who were advising Secretary Rumsfeld. And he was closely connected to Rudy Giuliani, who also has ... was very close to the administration. And they saw in Bernie a quick fix, if you will. ... And so they called Mr. Kerik down to the Pentagon. And he went down, and talked to them. And they said, "Great, you're our guy. Can you be there in ten days?" And he basically had ten days to prepare. He had had some experience in Saudi Arabia, but hadn't been to Iraq; knew little about it; and, in part, prepared himself for the job by watching A&E documentaries on Saddam Hussein.

Kerik says he faced immediate internal pressure from Walter Slocombe to disband the police. Kerik asserts that he didn't like the idea—and that he disapproved of Bremer's and Slocombe's decision to disband the army as well. His assertion is consistent with the available evidence. In fact, Slocombe's initial draft of CPA Order Number 2 included the dissolution of the Interior Ministry, which supervised the police. As we learned, it was only Jay Garner's intervention with Bremer that prevented this from occurring.

BERNARD KERIK: There was an internal momentum—not by me, by others … to abolish the Iraqi police … like they did the Iraqi military …

CHARLES FERGUSON: Who was this?

BERNARD KERIK: Slocombe. It was Slocombe. When I first came in, I reported to Slocombe. On the table of organization and the CPA, they had me under Slocombe … Slocombe was a nice man. I liked him personally. I did not agree with … We had disagreements. …

CHARLES FERGUSON: So tell me about your disagreements with … or your discussions. What happened between you and Slocombe?

BERNARD KERIK: Oh, I can't say exactly when, although I probably could—I would bet I have the change of the organizational chart—when Bremer basically took me out from under Slocombe. He said, "You're going to report to me directly." I don't know when that was. But the disagreement, I think, primarily was I disagreed with the military being disbanded.

CHARLES FERGUSON: You [did] not agree with the military being disbanded?

BERNARD KERIK: No, I didn't think they should have been disbanded. I mean it—

CHARLES FERGUSON: And you told Slocombe that?

BERNARD KERIK: Well, I said I didn't think it was the right move. It was after the fact because it had already happened. You know, it was a process that had already happened. I wasn't involved in the process, but I did not agree with it. I think I probably made it vocal to him or others. But there was sort of a momentum to do the same thing with the police. You know, look, we're in Iraq. The U.S. military is the only thing right now securing the ground. You had probably, depending on who you listened to, you had between seventy-five and a hundred and fifty thousand national police that are out there somewhere. They know the people. The people will listen to them, you would hope. And you have a war going on, but you also have this … you know, people coming in that are victims of crimes: "I got carjacked," you know, "here." "They just sent me my son's ear. They kidnapped him."

Okay, you know: Who's doing that? Because the military isn't doing it. The military is, like, they're in a war right now. There's a lot of stuff going on they got to do. Who's doing the local policing and addressing the real issues for the people? So my thing was, if you abolish the Iraqi police right now, it's going to take you … you know, it'll take you an extra three years to get them up and running. … Like that's, you know, it's crazy. And to me, the thing that stuck out to me in the back of my mind on the military … And look, these guys had information and intelligence I didn't have, and maybe there's some reason to do it that I didn't know about it—but my thing is, you know, for two months prior to going into Iraq, we dropped leaflets all over the place. We told all these military guys, "Look, we're coming. When we get there, you surrender. You'll be taken care of. We're coming to help you and your country," and all this stuff. Okay, you have a half a million military guys, and then you come [and], you know, basically, you say, "Fuck you, you're fired." Okay, well, that's a problem because you now have a half a million guys that are from the military. They're familiar with weapons; they have weapons; they're familiar with explosives. It could be an issue down the road, which I think eventually, it was an issue.

CHARLES FERGUSON: Did you tell Slocombe this?

BERNARD KERIK: In those … the way I'm saying it now?

CHARLES FERGUSON: Yeah.

BERNARD KERIK: No, no. I mean I … Basically, you know, we didn't … I didn't have these discussions with him. No, I didn't discuss the military stuff with him. You know, but on the police end, that was my thing. "Look, we need them now. We need twenty times what we have right now." So why would you give up? Why would you just say, "All right, everybody's fired; let's start fresh"?

CHARLES FERGUSON: So what did Slocombe say? Why did he want to disband the police force?

BERNARD KERIK: I don't know.

CHARLES FERGUSON: He didn't tell you?

BERNARD KERIK: The Baath Party, you know; start fresh. You know, it was pretty much the same reasons as, you know, disbanding the military for the same types of reasons.

The Iraqi intelligence service met with a fate similar to that of the army; the service was disbanded. For Saddam's secret police—a truly horrific organization that had tortured and killed many thousands of people—very serious vetting would obviously have been required, and complete disbanding was perhaps merited. But little was done to create a replacement. The lack of intelligence services allowed organized crime, militias, and the insurgency to grow unchecked, as there was no risk of their being penetrated by undercover agents and the U.S. possessed very little knowledge of Iraq. (American intelligence operations were initially quite poor, with few Arabic speakers and virtually no native Iraqis.) Bremer was apparently in favor of constructing a new Iraqi intelligence service, but either he did not regard it as important or he was blocked by Washington.

CHARLES FERGUSON: You had the intelligence service as well?

BERNARD KERIK: They fell under the Interior ... [but] we did not reconstitute the intelligence.

CHARLES FERGUSON: It was disbanded, but did you have jurisdiction over what became in effect the new secret police, the new intelligence service?

BERNARD KERIK: I would have if I'd stayed. They weren't even up; it wasn't even reconstituted by the time I left.

CHARLES FERGUSON: Was anybody talking about doing that?

BERNARD KERIK: Yeah. The guys that were talking about doing it was … I was talking to the station chief for the agency—for the CIA—at the time, and I personally, I think they had a phenomenal plan for bringing these guys in. And they had the right … they had the right attitude, if you will. … I said this from the time I came back from Iraq: "We're not going to win the war in Iraq based on pure combat missions. We're going to win the war in Iraq based on intelligence, because if you don't know who the enemy is, then we can't find them. If we can't see them, we can't fight them." And at the end of the day, when I first came back, they said, "more troops, more troops, more troops." I disagreed. I think in some areas, you needed more troops—like the military police were spread thin because the Iraqi cops, they need OJT [on the job training] partners; they need somebody to work with them; they need personal trainers; they need stuff like that. But overall more troops? Personally, I don't think it was necessary. I think if you had an adequate intelligence service—an Iraqi intelligence service that worked—I think half of our problems would have been eliminated.

CHARLES FERGUSON: Why didn't that happen?

BERNARD KERIK: I don't know.

CHARLES FERGUSON: You don't know.

BERNARD KERIK: No.

CHARLES FERGUSON: Was Bremer in favor of it?

BERNARD KERIK: Yeah, I think Bremer was in favor of it.

Michael Moss found no evidence that Bremer had pushed hard to obtain more support for the police, although Moss could not exclude the possibility. Similarly, Bremer may have favored the creation of a new intelligence service, but there is likewise no evidence that he pressed hard for it. (Bremer does not mention the issue of a new intelligence service at all in his book.) Moss felt that while Bremer wanted more U.S. military forces to restore order, Bremer also wanted Iraqi security forces to remain weak, purged of all hints of prior institutions, and to be constructed from scratch.

MICHAEL MOSS: You know, Ambassador Bremer says that he cared very much about the Iraqi police and made it a significant, if not top, priority for his own efforts, and ran into resistance at the Pentagon, in that he didn't have the resources to make it happen. It's questionable how hard he pushed for that. I mean, it's questionable how much of that is his recollection now, after the fact. We found no sort of strong memos written by him, and could find no meetings where he is standing up and demanding the kind of resources that he says he was wanting. So I think it's probably a combination of those two. ...

... [Kerik] went there as part of this early group of ... fifty police, Justice Department advisers who were struggling to reconstitute the police, and very quickly found himself totally overwhelmed by the job. And [Kerik] was there for a very short time, and critically, during the time he was there, there were reports, new reports prepared, which were even more alarming than the prewar reports. Because these people now were seeing firsthand ... the incredible job they were facing in redeveloping the police force: the incompetence issue, the exposure to corruption. And they called for as many, if not more, police advisers to be brought to Iraq immediately, to help out. Bernie Kerik says that he endorsed that idea and pressed for it with Ambassador Bremer at the time, but [Kerik] left Iraq before those plans could be dealt with.

One of the early police advisers was Gerald Burke, a retired major in the Massachusetts State Police, who would eventually became the senior adviser to the Baghdad police chief. He shared his early impressions of the Iraqi police force.

GERALD BURKE: Well, we went into Baghdad on May 15, 2003. We drove up from Kuwait, which was a little bit of an adventure in itself. It was about a nineteen-hour ride. ... The team that I was with was Department of Justice. There were six retired American police officers, three retired American corrections officers, and about a dozen American judicial types. I think one was an assistant district attorney; maybe a couple of them were assistant U.S. attorneys. One was a court ... I guess you call him a clerk magistrate. And then I think we had three or four retired judges in the group as well. And the original team went up to Baghdad with the mission of doing an assessment of the Iraqi criminal justice system.

CHARLES FERGUSON: ... When you got to Baghdad, did you in fact participate in an assessment?

GERALD BURKE: Yes we did. We arrived, as I said, on May 15th. It was about nine or ten o'clock at night before we got into Baghdad, about a nineteen-hour ride. And the next morning, uh, the police team—the six of us—we drove over to the Baghdad police academy. And we met up with, at that point it was the 18th MP Brigade, Military Police Brigade. ...

The assessment took us about two to three weeks to write. It wasn't difficult. The condition of the Iraqi police service was so bad that they needed everything. So the executive summary almost could have said that, you know, the Iraqi police service need everything: they need equipment; they need their stations repaired; they need weapons; they need new recruits; they need training for veteran officers; they need training for the leadership element. The top command staff of the police service didn't return to work. Those who probably had a more guilty conscience didn't return to work. So we need to train everybody, and reequip everybody, from the stations to the vehicles to the weapons to the uniforms.

Burke and his team generated a list of recommendations. They were remarkably similar to the prewar recommendations made by Robert Perito at the Justice Department and the separate recommendations made by Jay Garner.

GERALD BURKE: The primary recommendation was for about six thousand international police trainers to come into Iraq to run the police academies, and to go out into the field to work in the police stations, where they would be advising the day-to-day operations, and in some ways, to make [sure] that what the officers and the policemen were learning in the academy—[that] they were actually practicing [in] the field.

[The] number six thousand was not, you know, not just taken out of thin air. It was a number that was extrapolated out from other missions. The team that I was on, the six police members, three or four of us had

had previous international experience. One of the members had been in about forty or fifty countries working on police training, over about [a] fifteen-year period. The team leader had been doing international police advising since the eighties. So he'd been at it for about fifteen years as well. And we extrapolated out the number of trainers based on sort of the population of Iraq and the geography of Iraq. A simple extrapolation would have been too many people; it would have been up around twenty thousand advisers. So we did have to back off of that number. And we came up with about a six thousand number. And that was based on missions like Haiti, East Timor, Bosnia, Kosovo, and some other countries. So we recommended about six thousand. ...

... Well, we sent the recommendation up our chain of command. And at some point, I imagine, it got to Bremer, and maybe to Washington ... the Department of Justice is who we worked for.

I asked Kerik about the number of police advisers recommended by the assessment.

CHARLES FERGUSON: Let me go back to the recommendations of the assessment. [Had] the assessment also recommended anything else about what the United States' policy should be? I've been told, for example, that one of the recommendations was a six-thousand-person advisory and training force, an oversight force.

BERNARD KERIK: Yup.

CHARLES FERGUSON: Can you tell me about that?

BERNARD KERIK: I don't know if it was six thousand, but it was a high number, though. There was a difference of opinion between the State Department guys, which is there from the INL [International Narcotics and Law] Program, and the Justice Department's guys, which is the IntTap Program, the International Police Training Program. The INL Program, they wanted a very limited number.

In mid-June, the Pentagon denied the request for the large advisory force to assist in the recall and reorganization of the Iraqi police. For the next year, there would be only fifty police advisers for the entire country.

GERALD BURKE: Well, we got two additions to the team. They came in July. One of whom was on a ninety-day contract. He was on a leave of absence from his department. About September, I think we got another two officers. But by that time, three members of the original team had decided that they didn't want to continue the mission, and they went home around September or October. By October, November, we still had less than a dozen American police advisers in the Baghdad area. The Brits had about a half a dozen down in the Basra area, and the Danes maybe had four or five working with the Brits down in Basra. But in the Baghdad area—the city of six million people, six or seven million people—we had about, well, less than ten, I guess.

Michael Moss confirmed this.

MICHAEL MOSS: And at that point in time, there were maybe, in [the] country, a couple of dozen police advisers trying to reconstitute the entire police force.

CHARLES FERGUSON: A couple of dozen.

MICHAEL MOSS: Yes. Through the first year of the war—again, when the insurgency was still, uh, in its infancy and/or not even developed yet in some parts of the country—there were approximately fifty trained police advisers in [the] country, trying to create what ultimately is turning into a police force of a hundred and fifty to two hundred thousand officers.

Nonetheless, using a few dozen U.S. military police and his small group of advisers, Burke began recalling the Baghdad police and then training them.

GERALD BURKE: Well, when we first went in and started working with the military police in May of '03—and we were working on the assessment— the military police were recalling the Iraqi police back to work. And the Iraqi police, perhaps because of their heritage of the regime, were obedient. Many of them did return to work. We got back probably eight or nine thousand by July, August of the summer of '03.

And we had put together a training program for those officers returning to work. [The] transition program was called the TIPS Program—Transition Integration Program—where we would introduce some concepts, like policing in a democracy, human rights, you know, how to handle prisoners, women's rights, things like that. So we started that program in June, late June of '03. It's about four, five weeks after we got in the country, we were actually able to get the first training program started. It was a three-week program, as I said, for veteran officers returning.

One of the problems, however, is we didn't have enough instructors. As I said, we only had about a half a dozen at that point. So, working with the MPs, we got a detachment of reserve military police officers from California. Fortunately, because they were a reserve unit, about a third of them were police officers in the real world. So we had a [corps] of people—you know, it was about forty-five, uh, MPs, about a third of them, fifteen or so, who were police officers or sheriffs in the real world. So we used those for that training program, the initial training program.

CHARLES FERGUSON: And how did it go?

GERALD BURKE: Very well. It was a small effort, and it was gonna take forever to train the eight or nine thousand police officers that returned to work. In addition, we were probably [going to] have to recruit another ten thousand to get the department up to, you know, the strength of about eighteen, twenty thousand people. But the training went well. It was just gonna take forever to train those eight to nine thousand people with only forty-five instructors.

Iraqi police patrol the streets of Baghdad, 2004.

Then, in early 2004, because police training had lagged and the security situation had dramatically worsened, General Eaton was placed in charge of training for the entire Iraqi police force, while still also being in charge of training the New Iraqi Army. Eaton had no prior experience in training civilian police forces, which is radically different from training soldiers.

PAUL EATON: And the lines of communication between Baghdad and the individual police stations were problematic. They were not positive—a lot of friction and a lot of suspicion. ... So in fact, the police chiefs [were distrustful of] that lieutenant colonel of [a] coalition army, who is providing him the support and the sustenance that he needs to be able to do his mission.

So we went in there to reorganize—to assist the minister of [the] interior to reorganize the lines of communication, the chain of command, which were, pardon the expression, Byzantine, and to identify the requirements for the police: what cars, what radios, what weapons, what uniforms, what body armor did they need. And then to provide for the training of the leaders.

So we had to bump up the leader training. We went into a full-requirements mode. It was catch-as-catch-can, down at the station level. ... There is a fund available to the commanders on the ground, the Commanders Emergency Relief Fund. And they were using these moneys that would periodically dry up and then be awarded back. So we had an incoherent funding line to assist local units to develop police forces. We didn't have a coherent requirements identification system at a national level, where we could say, "Okay, we need fifteen hundred armored cars; we need eighty-five thousand pistols; we need so many rifles, machine guns, to support the police." Yet on 5 September in '03, the secretary of defense clearly understood that the police forces were his first priority, but in fact, an unsupported priority.

CHARLES FERGUSON: How come?

PAUL EATON: I would have to see into ... the machinations between Ambassador Bremer and the secretary of defense. I didn't see into that. All I saw was the result: Whereas we had made terrific progress with the army from June to March, we had made little progress, little coherent progress, at the national level, in development of a coherent police structure. You'd have to ask Walt Slocombe what happened between him and Bernard [Kerik] in the beginning, and what the requirements were, because [Kerik] ostensibly had that mission in the beginning.

CHARLES FERGUSON: Yes.

PAUL EATON: I saw no evidence of … of any kind of, uh, coherent program nine months later, when I stepped into it.

In fact, as late as 2004, it appears that Rumsfeld and the Pentagon civilian policy leadership continued to resist recommendations to have American police trainers become more heavily involved in supervising and training the increasingly corrupt, politicized, and dangerous Iraqi police.

CHARLES FERGUSON: Was anybody making a strong argument about that issue—the security issue, the policing issue, the chaos issue—early on?

MICHAEL MOSS: Well, we know that Colin Powell cared very much. And sort of the entire State Department [was] very concerned about that. But the problem was that the Pentagon, Department of Defense, was running things in Iraq. And you know, while there were discussions, the power rested with Secretary Rumsfeld, who, you get a real sense from, especially in that time, didn't want to be in Iraq and did not want to see this as a long-term situation and didn't want to see this as a developing, you know, insurgent conflict. And for those reasons, you know, [Rumsfeld] imposed that will on people below him, and … resisted.

Again, one of the ironies here is that it was, you know, law-and-order experts in this country who were brought in to advise [the] Justice Department and State Department and involved themselves in maintaining and reestablishing law and order from a civilian perspective in Iraq, whose advice and pleadings, ultimately, were ignored, which is … which is sort of astounding.

So I think at the highest levels—I mean, I can't tell you what went on in Secretary Rumsfeld's office—I think that some of these arguments got there. And I know that at one point, that he himself made a decision in the spring of '04 to reject a proposal that would have given the police trainers the power to make arrests and actually impose and involve themselves in situations, which they very much wanted because they would see corrupt police officers doing things, and they would have no ability to deal with that person—to either hold him and detain him and/or arrest him. They wanted those powers. And Secretary Rumsfeld—and/or ultimately President Bush, I should say—rejected that proposal.

CHARLES FERGUSON: Do we know the extent to which President Bush was aware of, or involved in, these debates, these questions?

MICHAEL MOSS: That's the only issue that I'm aware of that went to President Bush directly—again, [it] was [a] notion of empowering police trainers with the power to arrest.

The Security Vacuum

After the U.S. returned sovereignty to Iraq in late June 2004, there arose far more serious problems than inadequate resources or the U.S. advisers' lack of power to arrest Iraqis. First, as the insurgency worsened, police stations became frequent targets of attacks, including suicide bombings, making the job of being an Iraqi police officer one of the most dangerous on earth. And second, following Iraqi elections and the formation of a government, a new pattern of government structure began to emerge. In this new structure, Iraqi coalition governments allocated control of specific ministries to specific political parties. The Interior Ministry and police were quickly claimed by Shiite extremists aligned with the Supreme Council for the Islamic Revolution in Iraq (SCIRI) and its militia, the Badr Brigade. (In 2003, the Badr Brigade changed its name to the Badr Organization in an effort to avoid the CPA's effort to disband militias. In May 2007, SCIRI changed its name to the Supreme Islamic Iraqi Council (SIIC). The removal of the word "Revolution" from the organization's title was intended to reflect the changing situation in Iraq, as there was no longer any need to overthrow a secular Baathist government. (Despite the group's name change, this book will continue to use the more familiar SCIRI designation, and will insert "SCIRI" in brackets whenever an interviewee refers to the group using shorthand such as the "Islamic Council" or the "Supreme Council.") The Mahdi Army, the large and heavily armed militia controlled by the radical Shiite cleric Moqtada al-Sadr, also penetrated many police units, especially in Baghdad, and both militias used the police to form death squads that engaged in sectarian killing on a large scale. At the same time, large-scale criminal gangs formed, some of them within the police, and engaged in kidnapping, extortion, and smuggling. In addition, political and administrative controls were weak, with the result that enormous abuses occurred. These ranged from the creation of large units outside the normal command structure, to the wholesale inclusion of Shiite militia units into the police, to the illegal trade in police uniforms, which often made it impossible to know who was a legitimate police officer and who was an impostor. Meanwhile, violence grew: revenge killings, kidnappings for ransom, killings generated by business rivalries, ordinary murders, and the insurgency. Eventually, the Pentagon reacted, but it was too late. By late 2005, many Iraqis regarded the police as criminals and killers— merely another source of the violence that surrounded them.

MICHAEL MOSS: For the first year of the war, after the invasion, when the insurgency was still rather small and contained to isolated places in the country, and was still sort of developing the power that it has today, there was an incredible opportunity to develop the police, at that point in time. What you had was a vacuum. And into that vacuum stepped tribal chiefs, sectarian interests, who saw the police as their own route to power.

And we paid especial attention to Basra, in the south of Iraq, and documented—by interviews and records and speaking to both Iraqis and British troops who were there, and the few American advisers and British advisers who went to Basra—that what you saw there was a pattern that replicated itself later elsewhere in Iraq. [It was a pattern] where you had, again, criminal interests, tribal chiefs, sectarian groups, all vying for power and appointing their own representatives to the police force, which became this incredibly dangerous and fractured and anything but what you might imagine a police force should be in a country. And so, it was that vacuum, it was ... By our absence, we created the opportunity for these other interests to use and manipulate the police force for their own ends.

CHARLES FERGUSON: So let's continue chronologically. After this first year, tell us what happened, A, inside the Interior Ministry and the Iraqi police, and B, to American policy.

MICHAEL MOSS: You know, through the first year, what you saw was the police force reconstituting itself for the most part. You had a large amount of nepotism going on. You had tribal chiefs and, as I mentioned, sectarian leaders appointing their own people to the police force. You had a lot of patronage appointments going on. So you had a sort of incompetent sort of police force becoming gradually more and more corrupt.

The first sort of permanent interior minister—a gentleman named Falah al-Naqib—in the summer of '04 was very concerned about security in Baghdad, and hugely concerned about the police force that was developing. And [he] decided, on his own, to basically reject the police force that the Americans were in charge of reconstituting. And ... hired and built his own commando forces to act as police officers in Baghdad. And it was a very interesting move because it was essentially sort of the first step toward militarizing the police because by that point in time, the insurgency was growing and beginning to rage. And Naqib said to us that, you know, "I had no choice. I basically had incompetent and/or untrustworthy police officers trying to defend Baghdad residents from suicide bombers, and it was an impossible situation." So he created these commando forces, largely staffed by Republican Guard members under Saddam Hussein—Special Forces officers, who were incredibly competent.

And another thing that happened in the summer of '04 was that the Pentagon finally realized that it needed to seize control of the Iraqi police force development. Up until that time, it was largely State Department, Justice Department officials who were working on the training and development of the Iraqi police, but in the summer of '04, after reviewing the situation, Secretary Rumsfeld decided he needed to pay especial attention to the police because at this point, they also realized, finally, that they needed the police to fight the insurgency.

Again, more than Iraqi soldiers, you know, a well-trained, competent police force is out in the community, knows what's going on in neighborhoods, is closer to the people who know what's going on, and is far more able to get ... intelligence on [insurgents'] whereabouts and plans than an Iraqi army force that was also being developed.

So the Pentagon realized it needed a police force. And the general in Iraq at the time, who was put in charge of developing an Iraqi police force [General Paul Eaton], saw the development of the commando units and said, "This is fabulous; let's do this." And they threw their resources, training, and equipment into developing more of those police commando units in order to use them to help fight the insurgency.

CHARLES FERGUSON: And then what happened?

MICHAEL MOSS: ... That essentially was a deal with the devil because while these commando units were efficient—they knew how to fight; they knew how to kill—they were also beholden, in many cases, to sectarian groups. And at this point, you had the Shiites in power, and they were hiring Shiite-predominant members of these commando units. And at the same time—and this was happening also when, you know, you've gone from an insurgency to the beginnings of a civil war—and both Falah al-Naqib, to some extent, but also his successor, Mr. Jabar, the subsequent interior minister, felt very strongly that he needed Shiites in his police force to protect him from Sunnis.

CHARLES FERGUSON: And were these the same people who had formerly been in the Special Republican Guard or the Republican Guard, or—

MICHAEL MOSS: Yes, absolutely ...

CHARLES FERGUSON: So in other words ... it was not the case that the Republican Guard and Special Republican Guard were completely Sunni.

MICHAEL MOSS: Yeah, no, not at all. Right. And beyond that, too, just sort of finding people who would be loyalist to the Shiite party. So, suddenly, you had police units made up almost entirely of Shiites who were deemed loyal to the Shia parties and willing to do their bidding, which then developed into the death-squad activity, uh, starting last year.

Again: the deal with the devil. You know, starting summer of '05, we started hearing of horrendous atrocities. There's a case in the summer of '05 where thirty-six Sunni men were grabbed in a suburb of Baghdad, and their bodies were found a few days later on the Iranian border, I believe, scarred by acid and disfigured and dismembered. And the residents at the time ... There were witnesses who saw the kidnapping, and it was, by all reckoning, a police commando group, who called themselves the Volcanoes.

CHARLES FERGUSON: Okay. Where do you think the situation is now? Do you think that it's irretrievable? Or do you think that there's some possibility that the police can be purged, vetted, brought under control, professionalized?

MICHAEL MOSS: Well, starting last fall, the police story entered sort of a third phase. So, the first year was sort of a vacuum of doing very little to reconstitute the police. Second year, if you will, sort of the militarization of the police, where the Pentagon saw an opportunity to use the police in the insurgency. The third phase now is sort of a recognition, finally, by the Pentagon, that it needed the police, but a competent force. And it needed to do something about the corruption and the infiltration. And so starting this year [2006], the Pentagon began sending large numbers of police trainers out into the field to work with the police officers. It's basically what the plan was, originally. And as of now, there are something like three thousand police trainers throughout Iraq, working with the Iraqi police.

One of the things I should mention is that training police is sort of a two-step process. And in this country, you know, an officer in New York City will go to an academy, I believe, for as long as six months. But then subsequent to that, for as long as a year, there will be a trainer with that officer out in a car, on patrol, in order to ensure that the lessons learned in the school play out in the field. And that's what was not going on, to a large extent, in Iraq. They were getting academy training, but not the field training. So starting this year [2006], the Pentagon embraced this notion, which had been advocated from the beginning, which was to put a large number of police trainers out in the field. Whether that's too little too late, as some people fear, it's hard to say. I mean, it's very, very difficult to go in and clean up a force that is corrupted to the extent that it is.

I mentioned Basra in the south. Again, one of the horrendous things they found was that it was not just the Iraqi police force, but the unit that was assigned to police the police—the internal affairs division—was so corrupted that they essentially decided they had to start over. And they disbanded the unit and went to neighboring provinces to hire new police to become the new police-policers, if you will, in Basra. One of the complications, though, also, is the sovereignty issue. The governor of Basra has resisted efforts to clean up the police in Southern Iraq, including Basra. And that's been very frustrating to American, British, and/or Iraqi officials who are trying to do that. [There's] a very sort of difficult political question to deal with there.

Matt Sherman, who was deputy senior adviser to the Interior Ministry under the CPA, painted a rosier picture than Moss did. But even Sherman admitted that the police and Interior Ministry became dangerously politicized in mid-2004.

MATT SHERMAN: The Iraqi commandos were created in June and the beginning of July of 2004 by Minister Falah al-Naqib. This was under the Allawi government. And Minister al-Naqib was a Sunni, someone who came from a military family. His father used to be chief of staff of the army in Iraq. A very proud military family, which then fled Iraq during the regime. ...

And he saw a situation, when he became minister, of a growing insurgency. And also of wanting to create a force that would then be able to combat this insurgency. And so what he did was he created the Iraqi commandos. And this is more or less a paramilitary force. And it was initially made up of a lot of former Ministry of Defense and army personnel who had deserted. And his logic was, Why recreate the wheel when the wheel is mainly already there? We just need to put it back together.

And so what he did—with his uncle, who is a sheik, who was detained by the regime for a coup and was sentenced to death and was spared his life—was then create these commando units. And they were, for the most part, a Sunni force that was then designed to fight a Sunni insurgency. And they proved to be incredibly effective. They were independent in many ways of multinational force in Iraq. They weren't under the operational control of them, like the Ministry of Defense forces are. ...

What shifted, then, was then you had another minister. After Falah Naqib stepped down, a new Jaafari government came on. You then had a new minister who came on, who was a Shia. And he then had his own interests in wanting to deal with the commandos. And I think there was a conscious decision by the members of SCIRI—the Shia party—that they wanted to kind of gain control of the commandos.

SCIRI, during the January 2005 elections, was the most successful party throughout the country. They were most dominant, and they did incredibly well, but they only went for one ministry. They could have really had any position they wanted, any ministry they wanted. But they only went for one. And they went for the Ministry of Interior. And I'm of the opinion they went for that ministry because it's a powerful ministry, but more importantly, to gain influence and control, in many ways, of the commando units. Again, these were units that had free rein throughout the country; they weren't under the operational control of the coalition government. And they were effective. And I think they saw them as a unit that they could then ... use for their own political ends ... [and] as a defensive mechanism in order to target some of the Sunnis who may have targeted them during the regime. ...

And so you saw a real strong politicization of the commandos. And as a result, you had lots of these stories come to the forefront about targeting Sunnis, about death squads, about really acting outside of the rule of law. And thus you have the situation that we have now, where their reputation has been tarnished, and there's lots of questions about what to do with the commandos.

CHARLES FERGUSON: Well, is it just a matter of rumors and tarnished reputations, or is there reason to be concerned about them? My impression is that they actually are quite dangerous.

MATT SHERMAN: Uh-huh. I think there are lots of dangerous people within them. Um, again, it's a question of, Is it the entire force that's tainted? I don't believe it is. But it definitely is a significant portion of it. And it's another situation, again, which goes to the power of rumor within Iraq, and really having difficulty trying to be able to tell the difference [between] fact and fiction. You know, no matter what environment you're in, there are many shades of gray. But there are many, many more in Iraq.

... The coalition and the military have been trying to take real steps ... to embed advisory teams in with the commandos, and also, soon, with the police. So, trying to monitor and restrict them from doing these sort of things. There were issues, you know, human rights issues, I'm sure, that they witnessed that they didn't try stopping and reporting. ... But [they] need to be able to, right now, more so than any time else, to provide even greater advisory services and monitoring to make sure these sort of things really stop.

Another problem they also have is that the uniforms that they've used just proliferated all over the place and were copied, duplicated. And so you really have lots of rogue elements and people that are using or working under the guise of the security services when really they're after their own political agenda or [the] political agenda of their militia party, or whatever.

Crime

As the security situation in Iraq deteriorated between 2003 and 2007, conditions in the country went through several phases. First was the looting. Then, shortly afterward came the spread of weapons and crime, including organized gangs engaged in smuggling and kidnapping. In late 2003 came the addition of the insurgency; then, beginning in late 2004, the penetration of the police by sectarian death squads and major criminal gangs; and finally, beginning in 2006, the rise of large-scale sectarian killing, ethnic cleansing, and near civil war.

By mid-2003, much of the prewar Iraqi police force had been recalled and Gerald Burke was supervising their training. He found the Baghdad police force completely overwhelmed. There was already simply too much crime to keep up with. Other interviewees agreed.

GERALD BURKE: My job, at that point, was to meet with the chief [Baghdad's chief of police]. We had a weekly citywide command staff meeting, where he brought in his commanders and went over current events. And then we had an east side and a west side, similar meetings. And we'd talk about what was happening. One of the biggest problems at the very beginning was revenge killings. We had people who had felt offended—their honor had been affected by the regime. They took that opportunity to try to find the people within the regime and go out and kill those people. And we were finding sometimes ten, twenty bodies a day that were probably along the lines of revenge killings and honor killings.

Another problem we had was some kidnappings. Very early on, there was a lot of kidnappings, particularly young girls, school-age girls. And we worked with the Baghdad police on trying to set up a sort of school resource officer program, where police officers, Iraqi policemen, would be assigned to the various schools' security at the schools.

Then we also had some kidnappings for money—businessmen or people who may have been involved in the regime were kidnapped for … probably because they were suspected of having money or valuables. And people were kidnapping them, thinking that they had participated in the looting of the banks.

So initially we had quite a little bit of a spree of crime—of kidnappings and murders at the very beginning.

PAUL HUGHES: Kidnapping in Iraq is just rampant. My Iraqi colleagues tell me it's just a life-and-death situation about whether the wife goes to the market or not because you don't know if she's going to come home. Kids go into school; you don't know if they're gonna come home. A kid kidnapped from a middle-class family over there—that's five thousand dollars to get the kid back. And the price goes up. And if you're a kidnap victim by one gang, if they don't think they're going to get a good ransom, they'll sell you to another gang, and you get moved around like that, until, uh-oh, you get sold to somebody that belongs to al Qaeda, and now you are in deep trouble.

CHRIS ALLBRITTON: Kids will be kidnapped, and you know, [their] parents will get a ransom note, and they'll somehow have to raise this amount of money in a week. And, you know, sometimes they'll be let go; sometimes they'll be killed. It happens with adults, too. Our office manager has had his uncle and cousin kidnapped. The uncle was tortured to death. The cousin was also tortured, but he was let go. The ever-present threat of … hard-core crime is always there.

Some of the kidnappings were political, performed by militias such as the radical cleric Moqtada al-Sadr's Mahdi Army. With some of the kidnappings, it was hard to tell who was behind them.

CHRIS ALLBRITTON: There was also a rash of kidnappings in August [2004]. Several of my friends were kidnapped and … all but one got out okay. One of them—an Italian journalist—was killed. He was kidnapped not by Moqtada al-Sadr's people, but by the Iraqi … uh, I believe it was the Secret Islamic Army in Iraq. And—

CHARLES FERGUSON: The others were kidnapped by al-Sadr's—

CHRIS ALLBRITTON: The others, well, al-Sadr wannabes, by and large. James Brandon was kidnapped by al-Sadr wannabes, down in Basra. They kidnapped him because they said they wanted, you know, the Americans to end the military attack on Najaf. And Moqtada al-Sadr said, "He's a journalist; let him go." They let him go after twenty-four hours.

Another one was Mike [Agaron], who was held for a week. Again, that was like … just kind of like … the gang that couldn't shoot straight. It was just kind of embarrassing how bad these kidnappers were, because the negotiations were very protracted, and it involved things like, they wanted to be reimbursed for the water he drank, and these were kind of stumbling blocks to letting him go. But he was treated fine while he was with them.

Two Frenchmen were abducted, also, by the Islamic Army, I believe it was. And that took four months to get them out. And then the Italian was killed.

Many people described kidnappers acting with complete impunity:

JOOST HILTERMANN: You know, you talk to people, and they were afraid. They were afraid to go out in the street. I mean, people were out in the street during daylight hours, but women, for example, who used to drive to work were no longer doing that, because they were afraid of carjacking, which had become a serious problem. And people felt threatened in their own homes by armed people. Of course, in Iraq, many people have a weapon. And so the fact that there was no effective police force in the streets meant that these people could go around and get what they wanted.

And this, over time, had an added element, which was the kidnapping for ransom of Iraqis. I remember my colleague … We were staying at a hotel in the Karada neighborhood of Baghdad. In the middle of the day—I wasn't there at the time—but she witnessed the kidnapping of a small boy right in front of the hotel. You know a car just stopped, grabbed the boy, and drove off. This was in January 2004. This was already a serious problem, and there was absolutely nobody who was preventing this from taking place.

Most kidnappings weren't reported, and even those that were reported were rarely investigated, much less solved. I asked Gerald Burke about the lack of police intervention.

CHARLES FERGUSON: What fraction of kidnappings get investigated or cleared?

GERALD BURKE: ... Close to zero. Even the police themselves would recommend to families of kidnap victims that it was best to negotiate with the kidnappers and to try to talk them down into the amount of the ransom to release. Even the police commanders who had family members kidnapped would wind up negotiating the price down. You know, they'd frequently ask for outrageous amounts of money, you know, a million dollars, half a million dollars. And it would come down to in the five-to-ten-thousand-dollar range, that somebody would be released. And the families would collectively find the money amongst them, you know, at the tribal level.

Matt Sherman also described the surge in kidnappings and the inability of the Iraqi police to handle their number.

MATT SHERMAN: One of the ways lots of these [insurgent] groups make money is through kidnappings, and we saw a steady increase in Iraqi kidnappings that were going on. For every one Jill Carroll [an American reporter kidnapped in 2006] that's kidnapped, there are hundreds of Iraqis that are kidnapped. And there were situations where we, in our office, not only had to deal with just trying to do the planning, but then we also had to try putting out fires. And many times, there were situations where certain Iraqis were kidnapped that were brought to our attention, that we then tried to assist in the investigation, not only unilaterally on the coalition side, but to do it with the Iraqis, with the police, with the major crimes unit there.

And again, it's a situation where ... You know, it's not where you just have one or two or three kidnappings, but you have hundreds. And you get overwhelmed—the Iraqis do, particularly. Where to begin, because you just have a deluge of individuals who are asking for help, or soon don't ask for help anymore, because they just don't think that the police would be able to provide any type of service to them, because they're just overwhelmed with the number of cases that they have to deal with. And so you're caught in the situation of where to focus your resources, and how individuals can bring about, you know, some success.

CHARLES FERGUSON: What fraction of kidnapping cases were satisfactorily cleared, you know, where—

MATT SHERMAN: I honestly don't know. I don't know. Because, I mean, under my situation, there were, you know ... members in the ministry or deputy ministers ... directors general had family members that were being kidnapped, and they asked us for assistance. There were other lower-level members with the ministry that other people that we had worked with, be it families that provide translating service, that came to us, and say [they have family] members that are being kidnapped, [and] what can you do to help?

And so we went about, trying to go about these things on a case-by-case basis, to do what we can, be it through wiretapping services, be it through utilizing our intelligence sources, [or] by using other types of means. ... But again, the numbers just kept growing, and the resources just aren't adequate to deal with those numbers.

In addition to being overwhelmed by rising crime, the police were being attacked in their own stations.

GERALD BURKE: There were about eighty police stations between the municipal police, the patrol police, and the traffic police. And I'd go in and I'd sort of sit down with the station commander, find out what his needs were, what his complaints were, and do a little bit of a site visit—an inspection of the station, particularly the cell blocks to see what kind of prisoners they had, what they were being charged with, what the condition of the cells were—so, uh, spot inspections. And in doing that, I visited every police station in Baghdad many times.

Starting around July, we also had a lot of the stations were being attacked, sometimes with direct fire, like small-arms fire, and rocket-propelled grenades, and sometimes indirect fire, with mortar attacks on stations.

Like kidnappings, virtually no bombings were solved or even investigated.

CHARLES FERGUSON: So what fraction of bombings in Baghdad are cleared or resolved? What percentage of the time is a bomber apprehended, or is an attacker against a government installation, such as a police station, apprehended?

GERALD BURKE: Close to zero. If at all ... They usually get away with the crime.

CHARLES FERGUSON: Okay. And why is that?

GERALD BURKE: Again, partly because of the volume of attacks, that they don't have the ability to investigate them if they're not caught at the moment of the crime. And if they're in a car with a car bomb, they detonate it, kill themselves, and, you know, the people around them, so there's nobody to arrest in that situation. The person is dead, committing the crime.

CHARLES FERGUSON: Well, but such people, you know, they never do it themselves. They always have—

GERALD BURKE: Right.

CHARLES FERGUSON: ... lots of people supporting them—

GERALD BURKE: Yeah.

CHARLES FERGUSON: ... helping them, et cetera.

GERALD BURKE: Yeah. No investigation's conducted into [it].

According to Burke, any investigations that did occur were hampered by the lack of crime laboratories, equipment, and trained personnel—as well as by the sheer amount of crime.

GERALD BURKE: There were some technicians in the crime lab that had some skills in ballistics and forensics. But the crime lab had been looted, and all of the equipment had … most of their equipment had been stolen … when the regime collapsed. So a lot of what skills they had, they didn't have the equipment to practice it. And at some points, the attacks were coming so frequent and so numerous, that they wouldn't be able to investigate them, just by sheer volume of the number of attacks. Every police station was attacked frequently. And some of them were blown up. I'm talking about total collapse of buildings. So, [to do] a crime scene like that would take, you know, days. And they just did not have the time or the resources or the manpower to do those kind of investigations.

Falch Kheiber/Reuters/Corbis

Car bomb in central Baghdad, June 14, 2004.

Ironically, one reason the police were unable to cope was that under Saddam Hussein's dictatorship, there had been very little crime in Iraq. And so the police were unprepared to handle the crime wave after his regime fell.

MATT SHERMAN: It's really the common crime that affects the Iraqis, which is most debilitating to the average person on the street. It's not just the car bombs that we read in the newspapers [and] see on the television—the organized crime, the burglaries, the rapes, the retribution killings, and things like that—but really, the types of things that are affecting Iraqis, day in and day out. And that's what the Iraqis used to tell me all the time, saying, you know, "The car bombs are devastating, but it's really just common crime, which is starting to cripple the trust that people have in the government." Because you have to remember that during the regime, there wasn't that much crime. There was some, but it really wasn't anywhere near the level that it is now.

CHAPTER EIGHT

THE CIVILIAN OCCUPATION AND THE CPA

In addition to de-Baathification and disbanding the Iraqi military, Bremer and the Pentagon leadership made a third critical decision in early May 2003. They decided to reverse existing U.S. policy, which called for rapid formation of an interim government, and instead to institute a long-term U.S. occupation. Here we examine that decision and the administration's policy toward Iraqi sovereignty and political structure more generally. We also look at the operations of the Coalition Provisional Authority under Bremer and the authority's management of reconstruction and economic reform in Iraq. By most accounts, all of these efforts were badly mismanaged.

Governance, Sovereignty, and Iraq's Political System

During his nine days at the Pentagon before leaving for Iraq on May 10, 2003, L. Paul Bremer and the Pentagon leadership made one further change in U.S. policy. They decided to halt Jay Garner's effort to form an interim Iraqi government; they also decided to cancel the local elections that had been scheduled in several Iraqi cities and to institute a long-term, open-ended U.S. occupation. As with the de-Baathification order and the disbanding of the Iraqi military, Bremer was making a major change without consulting the U.S. military, ORHA, or the State Department, all of which were then actively engaged in negotiations to form a provisional Iraqi government. Bremer also sharply limited the role that Iraqis could play in decision making. No Iraqis were permitted to work at senior levels in the CPA, and CPA orders became the supreme law of Iraq, overriding any decisions taken by Iraqi ministries or other entities.

The people I interviewed offered a legitimately wide range of opinion about the proper path for restoring Iraqi independence and establishing a new government in Iraq. Nearly everyone, however, agreed on three things: First, that it was imperative to give Iraqis a major role, both symbolically and substantively, in political decisions and policymaking. Second, they considered it important to set a clear date for the restoration of sovereignty and to avoid both the appearance and the reality of being a long-term foreign occupier. And third, they believed that overreliance on exiles such as Ahmed Chalabi was unwise. Not everyone agreed that ORHA under Jay Garner had governed well, but everyone agreed that the series of decisions concerning political control of the country, taken by Bremer in the critical period of early May 2003, and instituted over the next few months in Iraq, were deeply misguided.

Mark Danner is a journalist specializing in U.S. foreign policy and a MacArthur Fellow who has written extensively for *The New York Review of Books*. He began covering Iraq in 2003.

MARK DANNER: Among the many mysteries, when we look back at the occupation, and look at the occupation now [in 2005], and try to ask ourselves, where did things go wrong, and why did they go wrong? is the apparent inability, or certainly the apparent failure, of the Bush administration to make clear decisions about what sort of government they wanted to install in Iraq, and what kind of political transition they wanted to have.

When General Garner, in his brief tenure, was the ruler of Iraq, in April and early May of 2003, it's clear that he intended to establish very quickly an interim government, made up essentially of exile politicians, including Ahmed Chalabi, including Mr. Hakim of SCIRI, including Mr. Jaafari of Dawa—all of the politicians who we've come to know as the leading exile politicians. This is what he planned to do.

When he was fired, after several weeks, and L. Paul Bremer came and replaced him, these decisions were reversed. And in effect, L. Paul Bremer installed an American occupation and was eventually persuaded, under great pressure from Iraqis, to create a governing council that would advise him, but that had no real power, made up of those same Iraqi politicians.

So a dramatic change was made in the spring of 2003, from absolutely transferring some power to Iraqis, right at the beginning, to the decision to have a long-lasting occupation, the end of which was not in sight. That is, when Bremer came in, there was no clear notion of when power would be restored to Iraqis.

Just as had happened with the disbanding of the military, Richard Armitage was taken aback by Bremer's actions to institute an American occupation. According to Armitage, neither the State Department nor the National Security Council was consulted about these decisions in advance. I have also been told by an extremely senior military officer that these decisions took the military by surprise as well. Only shortly before, the administration's assurance had been that most U.S. troops would be withdrawn a few months after sovereignty was returned to an interim government controlled by Chalabi and other exiles.

CHARLES FERGUSON: Were you aware in advance of Ambassador Bremer's decision—and I frankly don't, myself, know whether it was just his decision or not—to reverse General Garner's and ORHA's policy of preparing for the creation of provisional government and instead institute a long-term U.S. occupation?

RICHARD ARMITAGE: We found out about it. It wasn't just General Garner's [policy]. ... They had held, as I recall, two sort of ... for a lack of a better term, the Afghan term is a *loya jirga*. That was sort of large meetings to try to get the Iraqis themselves to come together and have a provisional or temporary government. And the last of these was to be held in Baghdad. And I think Jay Garner was certainly supportive of that—to get some governing body of Iraqis. But this was done away with on the way to Baghdad. And I didn't think ... Jay Garner [knew] about it beforehand. And nor did I.

CHARLES FERGUSON: Isn't it rather astonishing that these incredibly sweeping decisions were made by Ambassador Bremer, A, without wide consultation of the government and, B, before he had ever set foot in Iraq for a single day?

RICHARD ARMITAGE: ... I won't accept the term "astonishing." I'll say it's surprising to me. But what discussions may or may not have been held with the president, I don't know. So it could be astonishing if the president didn't know anything about it. Or it might be perfectly normal. As I said, he's the one elected leader, nationally elected leader. And he does make the decisions.

CHARLES FERGUSON: Well, but that the deputy secretary of state, the secretary of state, the National Security Council, was surprised by these decisions? Such fundamental decisions?

RICHARD ARMITAGE: I would [say] I was surprised. But I can't tell you who else was. But some of the [members] at the National Security Council were surprised. Others clearly weren't. The secretary of defense wasn't. But, as I say, the president will make these decisions. And what he knew or didn't know, I can't say. ... I can only speak for myself on that because that happened outside of any meeting that I saw. And I just know it was a surprise to me because we had one of our officers out working right alongside—an excellent Arabic-speaking officer, one of our more senior now-ambassadors to Pakistan—so we were certainly surprised when he was thanked for his service.

Along with many others, Professor Samantha Power was critical of Bremer's efforts to exclude Iraqis from the decision-making process. In place of an interim government, Bremer created a largely powerless committee, the Iraqi Governing Council, whose members were appointed by Bremer, with seats allocated by sectarian quotas. Power noted that the UN Special Representative Sergio Vieira de Mello had tried to impress upon Bremer the importance of giving real power to the Iraqis in the council, but that he was unable to do so.

SAMANTHA POWER: Sergio was the person who came up with the name "governing council." He said, "You got to put the word *govern* in the title of this thing, ..." because Bremer initially wanted to call it the advisory council or the advisory board. And Sergio said, "No. You've got to signal that these guys are actually in charge of the country's destiny." So Bremer changed the title, but didn't change the functions. He kept it as an advisory board, as a rubber-stamping board, but called it a governing council. And of course it was that disconnect between the title and the manifest lack of power of this council that discredited the governing council in the eyes of Iraqis very, very quickly.

So Sergio had, you know, some impact in terms of the composition of the council; he was responsible for the name change—changing the name from an advisory council to a governing council—but what he never really succeeded in doing is prevailing upon Bremer or impressing upon Bremer the indispensability of handing over executive authority sooner rather than later. He simply could not communicate that. And that was a lesson that Bremer ended up having to learn himself at the cost of incredibly precious credibility. And at the cost of a year in the life of Iraq, perhaps Iraq's most important year of existence.

At the same time that he stopped the formation of an interim government, Bremer also canceled local elections. Journalists Yaroslav Trofimov and Nir Rosen and Professor Larry Diamond discuss the consequences of this decision.

YAROSLAV TROFIMOV: Canceling local elections in places like Najaf was also very unpopular because, immediately, the questions arose as to the truthfulness of the American message. People said, "Well, you came here saying you will bring freedom and democracy. Now we want to have a vote, and you're banning us from doing that." And from then on, people like Ayatollah [Sistani] started pushing for rapid elections. And rapid elections were the [mainstay] of the demands of the Shiite parties, especially.

NIR ROSEN: I think that, well, right after the war, you had Iraqis—Sunnis and Shias—calling for elections, calling for autonomy from the Americans. And of course, the American fear was if we have elections, hand over the country to religious leaders, or former Baathists ... that Iraqis weren't ready for it. So they postponed the elections by a couple of years. And the same people won: religious leaders and, among the Sunnis, former Baathists, or former Baathists who had reconstituted themselves as religious leaders. So we had a couple of years of war, fighting, and sectarianism for nothing, really.

LARRY DIAMOND: On the cancellation or vetoing of local elections, I see no evidence that Bremer thought that was a mistake. He may have, but I don't know. And of course, the biggest decision that was taken in May of 2003 was the decision to have an American occupation of Iraq; to establish a coalition provisional authority; to have America be, under the guise of a coalition provisional authority, the ultimate ruler in Iraq and at the time, with no termination date in sight.

Now, the sign that we realized that the indefinite nature of that occupation was a mistake came in November of 2003, when we implemented the November 15th plan to bring a clear end to this political occupation, and to give Iraqis a fairly spirited timetable for political transition. But whether any element of the Bush administration has really reflected upon the fundamental strategic error of having an American occupation of Iraq, I don't know, and I haven't seen any evidence of.

The November 15 plan emerged as the U.S. occupation came under increasing pressure derived from the unpopularity of Bremer's decisions, the deterioration of Iraqi living conditions, and the growing insurgency. Bremer apparently envisioned a very long term U.S. occupation, perhaps many years; this angered Iraqis and made the Bush administration increasingly nervous. Condoleezza Rice, who was national security advisor at the time, finally intervened to force Bremer to declare a schedule for Iraq's political future, including the restoration of sovereignty. But Bremer's earlier decisions—de-Baathification, disbanding the military, instituting a long-term occupation, and appointing the powerless Iraqi Governing Council—had deeply alienated the educated Sunni minority of Iraq, who boycotted the political process for over a year. This meant that constructing a new political order in Iraq would be much more difficult and would take more time.

Most observers agree that Bremer and the United States badly mismanaged the political restructuring of Iraq. Here is an extended analysis from Larry Diamond. As a Stanford professor and an expert on democracy, Diamond worked on governance and constitutional issues for the CPA in 2003 and 2004. He explained the effects of the time pressure placed on the political reform process.

CHARLES FERGUSON: What do you think of how the process of creating a new Iraqi government has gone on? What do you think of both the way it was done and its results?

LARRY DIAMOND: I think that it would have been much better to have a political transition in Iraq led by an Iraqi interim government, as happened in

Afghanistan. So I think the processes of having a political transition under American political occupation, as the Coalition Provisional Authority, was a mistake.

Putting that aside, I think one of the major flaws in the November 15th plan, which has continued to be implemented in its timetable, was the timetable itself. And here I take, as a political scientist, a rather strong exception to the Bush administration's characterization of this timetable as a great triumph for the United States. Superficially, we've seen at these various moments—the January 30th, 2005, parliamentary elections; the October 2005 constitutional referendum; the December 15th, 2005, elections—moments of victory of democratic participation, and even triumph, superficially. But if you look beneath the surface, you see very serious problems in each event.

On January 30th [2005], the country went to the polls, largely without the Sunni population, who boycotted the election because they thought the electoral system was going to be unfair to them. They didn't think the country was ready, and they thought they were gonna wind up being excluded. Now, it was a wonderful, moving thing that Iraqis voted in the numbers they did. It was necessary to have elections pretty soon because that was part of the bargain that was struck with Ayatollah Sistani and the Shiite political parties. But there was—as we would see in the months following the January 30th elections, when the insurgent violence and the terrorist attacks ramped up in number and intensity very dramatically— there was a huge price to be paid for going ahead without the Sunnis, in essence. And I think that the insurgency gained a new level of momentum as a result of that. From then on, we have been struggling to repair and balance a deeply flawed political terrain that was distorted by the lack of organic presence of Sunni political parties and leaders.

[U.S. Ambassador to Iraq Zalmay] Khalilzad tried his level best, having arrived in July of 2005, under very difficult circumstances with this process already very far along, to correct these flaws. When he arrived on the ground in late July, Iraqis were already negotiating the permanent constitution. And ... Sunni Arabs had been added to the constitution drafting committee. ... Fifteen of them had been added to the then fifty-five-member drafting committee, which initially had not included any Sunni

Arabs at all. So they had some representation, but not as voting members, because they weren't members of parliament. And as the August 15th deadline for completing the Iraqi constitution began to draw near, it became evident to most of the Iraqis involved in the process that they weren't gonna be able to reach agreement on time.

Now, here we come to one of the acute flaws in the November 15th transition timetable, which I had struggled against, advised against, and tried to buffer against. As a political scientist who has followed democratic transitions around the world, both in peaceful situations and in conflict situations, I felt strongly that the timetable we had for the year 2005, requiring three elections in the space of twelve months, was far too ambitious; that it would not allow time for Iraqi parties and factions to forge the compromises and understandings that would be needed to create a stable Iraq in the future; and that just logistically, it was gonna be very difficult to pull this off.

Partly as a result of my pleading—and I tell you, I pleaded with my American and Iraqi colleagues—and partly because, I think, many wise Iraqis themselves worried and recognized the dangers of this, a provision was written into the interim constitution to allow for some breathing room. It enabled the Iraqi parliament to vote a one-time, six-month extension of the deadline for drafting a constitution, from August 15th of 2005 to February 15th of 2006, if they felt they were making progress, but they needed more time. This extension would have had, by the interim constitution, to be adopted by August 1st.

In late July, the chairman of the Iraqi constitution drafting committee, and by all accounts I've seen, the vast majority of members of the committee, [including] key factions [of] the Sunnis and others, had come to conclude they just weren't going to cut a deal within the remaining sixteen or seventeen days that were left; that if there was going to be a viable, consensual constitutional compromise that was going to help to stabilize this country, it was going to take more time—at least two or three more months—[and so] they needed the constitutional extension.

That extension was blocked by one country and, really, one man: And that's the president of the United States.

Now, President Bush can be admired for his resolve, for his commitment, for his unwavering devotion to a vision of a democratic Iraq that would emerge in spirited fashion, according to this timetable that he and the Americans had devised. But as I said at the time and continue to feel, there's a very fine line between Churchillian resolve and blind stubbornness. And here in Iraq, in the face of a constitutional debacle that was looming before us, in the form of a failure to adopt a constitution that all major sections of Iraq felt they could accept and buy into, the president insisted, and the Iraqis yielded. And the result was a constitutional agreement, on August 15th, that was for the Iraqi Shiite religious parties a great triumph because it enabled them to form one massive Shiite superregion across all nine southern provinces that would implicitly have significant control over future oil and gas revenue. But [it] left the Sunnis in particular feeling deeply, deeply aggrieved.

In many policy decisions, the United States also emphasized sectarian identity, favoring Shiites and apportioning power or voting along sectarian lines. Many Americans and Iraqis told me that this had the effect of creating or widening sectarian differences rather than reducing them. Diamond and many others felt that the combination of Bremer's early decisions and the subsequent mismanagement of the political process contributed significantly to the rise of sectarian conflict in Iraq.

LARRY DIAMOND: In the final days before the [constitutional] referendum, again, a very able, adept, pragmatic American ambassador, Zalmay Khalilzad, pulled a kind of rabbit out of the hat in the form of a compromise agreement. ... This was enough to bring two Sunni political parties on board in support of the constitution, but not to win many Sunni votes for the constitution, as a result of which over ninety percent of Kurds, and over ninety percent of Shiites, I estimate, voted for the constitution in the October 15th [2005] referendum, and probably about the same percentage of Sunni Arab Iraqis voted against it.

So we had, from January to October, [and] through the December 15th [2005] elections, an increasing polarization of the political process around ethnic and religious identity; an accumulated feeling of grievance on the part of Sunni Arabs that their interests have not been injected into, represented in, the unfolding democratic political process; and a danger that if the country produces a government and a constitution that does not have broad support in the country, that ultimately, this could trigger the slide to civil war.

So I have been, from the beginning, deeply concerned about the pace of the transition—which I think has been too rapid, too inflexible, and too heavily dictated by our own political needs in the United States—and deeply worried about the process of political polarization that this, with some degree of predictability, has unleashed.

During his time in Iraq, Diamond became progressively more alarmed at the situation. In 2004, he decided to convey his views directly to Condoleezza Rice.

LARRY DIAMOND: In the middle of April of 2004, I decided, after a brief visit back to the United States, that I wasn't going to return to Iraq. By then, we had had twin insurgencies break out in Fallujah, where the Sunni-based insurgency had ... developed, in a way, its headquarters, and in the Shiite south, where Moqtada al-Sadr was now in full-scale rebellion against the United States, the occupation, and the whole emerging political order. And I felt my effectiveness had really come to an end—that I wasn't really being listened to in the Green Zone. And it was clear, with this new drama, that I wasn't going to be able to travel outside the Green Zone, so there wasn't much point in returning.

But I did feel that there was some point in conveying my views to Dr. Rice. And so I sat down and tried to integrate everything I felt about what lay ahead and where we'd been going wrong into a single memo, which I wrote, and sent her on April 26th ... 2004, shortly after I decided not to return.

In this memo, I tried to both present a perspective and a series of concrete policy recommendations. The perspective was that we faced—as we had from the beginning in Iraq [and] continued to increasingly, I think—a huge legitimacy deficit, not only in terms of our international legitimacy for what we were doing, but frankly, we just were not trusted and respected by the Iraqi people. Many of them believed—and not just the Sunni Arabs—that we were there for the oil, that we were there for ulterior motives, that we were there to occupy and control the country, and that we

were going to be there indefinitely. So I felt we needed to—if we were going to get control of these insurgencies—we needed to do a number of decisive things, both on the political front and on the military front.

On the military front, I just felt flatly, as I had from the beginning, that
we needed more troops—a lot more troops—and that we needed to get
them there quickly. I know that many military officers in Iraq agreed with
me, even if they couldn't say it. I also felt very strongly that we needed to
proceed vigorously with plans that we had drafted for the demobilization
of the different political party and religious militias that had been operating on the ground in Iraq. We had what was called a disarmament, demobilization, and reintegration plan—DDR is the lingo for it in postconflict
work. It was called formally, when it was announced in early May, a transition and reintegration plan. I felt we really needed to put a lot of money,
and frankly, a lot of military muscle into the effort to see that these militias
really disarmed and demobilized, so that there would be a political climate
on the ground in Iraq where competing political parties could campaign
and mobilize without the fear, intimidation, and violence that would otherwise be inflicted upon them by these political party militias. So I urged a
vigorous, continued effort to confront, demobilize, and disarm the major
political party militias, particularly in the Shiite south. And I urged a significant increase in the number of American troops.

On the political side, which was really my specialty, I urged Dr. Rice
and the administration to address the legitimacy gap we faced, and the suspicions that Iraqis had of us. In particular, I repeated something I'd said before: I really strongly urged the administration to make a clear, emphatic,
declaratory statement that we were not seeking permanent military bases
in Iraq, and would not seek them. Because this was one of the major suspicions of the Iraqis, and it has been since 2003, up to the current moment,
one of the factors that has been driving the insurgency: the belief that their
country is under occupation, that we seek to be there indefinitely, to use it
as a platform for indefinite American military power projection in the
region.

Secondly in this regard, I felt strongly that the United States needed to
work to establish some sort of time frame for American military withdrawal. Not necessarily a deadline, but at least a vision of how long we

thought we might be there so that if we were to declare that, you know, we thought we could be out of there in three years, but that this depended on circumstances on the ground in Iraq, the burden would shift to the Iraqi resistance that claimed it was fighting to drive us out of Iraq, to cooperate in building a peaceful political future so that we could achieve what everybody wants, which is [an] Iraq that is free and sovereign again—or at least what everybody says they want.

I urged that we distance ourselves from some of the exiles who Iraqis had suspicions of and create a broader political landscape. And I reiterated again a concern I had raised with Ambassador Bremer and my colleagues in the CPA: that elections were approaching now, within a year, not that far on the horizon, and that if we didn't find a way to strengthen moderate and secular political forces to enable small, new political parties that were forming to compete and get the attention of the Iraqi electorate, that it was really not going to be a free and fair election in January, that it was going to be dominated by the few political forces that would have the money—whether from Iran, from the treasury of the Shiite mosques, from the Kurdistan regional government, or from other supporters in the region—to campaign. And so I urged the creation of some kind of transparent political parties' fund that would give a variety of new political parties that were forming in Iraq ... resources with which to campaign and guaranteed airtime on the television and radio media.

So basically, I was concerned to begin to create a framework in which the insurgency could be negotiated down by political means. I also raised the problem of Iraqi detainees that needed to be addressed, where Iraqis didn't know what was happening with their loved ones. This was just before the Abu Ghraib scandal broke, but I was hearing a lot of complaints from Iraqis. And I urged that we try and, through political means, address some of the grievances that were driving the insurgency, and bring a lot of the people that were supporting the insurgency into the political process.

CHARLES FERGUSON: So what did you do with this document?

LARRY DIAMOND: I e-mailed it to Dr. Rice's assistant.

CHARLES FERGUSON: And?

LARRY DIAMOND: I called the next day, and I was told that she had received the document, and it had been given also to her principal deputy for Iraq, Ambassador Robert Blackwill.

CHARLES FERGUSON: And?

LARRY DIAMOND: That was the last I heard.

The CPA

It did not help Iraq's political transition that the Coalition Provisional Authority was it-self extremely inefficient. The CPA acquired a bad reputation almost instantly. In part, this derived from factors beyond Bremer's control, such as the absence of ear-lier planning and inadequate troop levels. But it also reflected the organization's—and Bremer's—own deficiencies, which by all accounts were numerous and severe.

Although L. Paul Bremer took control of the occupation on May 12, 2003, the day after his arrival in Baghdad, he did not retain ORHA's structure or most of its per-sonnel. Instead, he built a new organization largely from scratch, using only a rela-tively small number of ORHA's more than four hundred employees. Most people I interviewed described the CPA culture, as it evolved under Bremer's leadership, as dysfunctional. The military quickly coined the joke that CPA stood for "Can't Provide Anything."

CHARLES FERGUSON: What did you think of the CPA's ability to adapt to the situation in Iraq as it changed?

YAROSLAV TROFIMOV: The CPA's ability to understand Iraq, first of all, was very limited. And the way it was structured made it impossible for them to adapt to anything, because most officials there were on three-month con-tracts. They would come into the country, spend the first couple weeks adapting, work for a month, and then spend the last few weeks [unintelli-gible]. So there was no institutional memory in it. So it was ... it was really just a permanent learning curve that never ended. [Over time], a few se-nior officials stayed longer, for a year or six months.

CHARLES FERGUSON: So most people working for the CPA stayed there for only ninety days.

YAROSLAV TROFIMOV: Yes, absolutely. Most people working for the CPA stay for ninety days. Officials, such as governors of provinces, who were the viceroys of a huge swath of Iraq, they would come in there, often with no understanding of Iraq or Arabic or any knowledge of the Middle East, you know; rule the place for three months; leave. Then somebody would come back and start from scratch because all the relationships would just disappear. And all that accumulated knowledge—whatever knowledge could be accumulated in three months—would be gone. And at the end of that stay, many of them didn't even learn basic Arabic phrases like "good morning" and "thank you." And the ones who were staying in the Green Zone, in the international zone, lots of them never left it. They just stayed there and went to the mess hall and to the PX and talked about themselves with other Americans. So their idea ... their idealistic ideas were implemented without them actually understanding the effects of them.

While Trofimov, as a journalist, was an observer of the CPA, General Paul Eaton experienced its deficiencies from the inside the occupation.

PAUL EATON: The CPA ... was never properly resourced. It wasn't just boots on the ground, but it's Ambassador Bremer, and the revolving door that came out of the State Department and other agencies, where as soon as somebody would develop the appropriate relationships with the Iraqis, in ninety days, a hundred days, a hundred and twenty days, they'd go home. So, whereas you have Ambassador Bremer, who comes in in April, and stays until June the next year, his staff is just constantly changing. And that is a terrible way to run an organization.

The CPA didn't supply body armor. Some CPA employees got their own.

LARRY DIAMOND: So I took basically what I would need for most of six months: clothes, toiletries, some music, my notebook computer, um ... Phoebe Marr's book on Iraq, things like that.

CHARLES FERGUSON: Body armor?

LARRY DIAMOND: No. In my naïveté, I assumed that that would be provided. So of course, we land in Kuwait, in the airport, with its hot pink

signs and bureaucratic informality. We're taken to the Kuwait Hilton, …
and there, you check in with KBR—Kellogg Brown and Root, a division
of Halliburton—and you're processed, and you're equipped. You're given
desert boots, a combat helmet, and a flak jacket. I didn't feel I really needed
the desert boots. [I] didn't know that they were gonna be kind of de
rigueur as a result of Bremer's own sartorial style.

And I thought, well, I had a flak jacket, I'd be fine. And I must confess,
it was only until I had been in the Green Zone for some number of days,
that I learned by chance that a flak jacket is not a bulletproof vest. It will
stop, you know, stray flak. But if somebody fires a bullet at you, it's gonna
go through the flak jacket. And as I started going out of the Green Zone to
lecture and meet people, to engage Iraqis, I was uncomfortable with the
fact that I did not have, and could not be provided by the Coalition Provisional Authority with, a bulletproof vest—even though each and every one
of our British colleagues in the Green Zone had not only a bulletproof
vest, but the highest-quality bulletproof vest, the kind that have thick ce-
ramic plates in front. … So that was one extreme, and the other extreme
was the Coalition Provisional Authority saying to its American employees,
"Here's your flak jacket, eh, good luck."

L. Paul Bremer,
2004

AP Photo/Bullit Marquez

The CPA's telephone, computer, and e-mail problems persisted for months.

RAY JENNINGS: The interesting thing about what would happen in the palaces [is that] around lunchtime, you'd have everybody come out of their cubicles and then meet in the cafeteria, and that's when you would see people you wouldn't normally see, you know, during the rest of the day. And so the central meeting area was this food service area, where, if you wanted to get some business done, or find somebody—especially in the early days, when phones weren't working, and there wasn't an easy ability to contact people—that's where you'd find them. So that's often when I would go to the palace to find people—is go there during lunch, and cruise the tables, and find who you needed to talk to ... Until there was a phone system, it was really hard to find people. It was just part of the inefficiencies of doing this work.

CHARLES FERGUSON: How long was it before there was a phone system?

RAY JENNINGS: There wasn't a reliable phone system until probably end of July, maybe August [2003]. Even then, only certain people had phones. So it was very hard to contact them.

CHARLES FERGUSON: Why?

RAY JENNINGS: The difficult part of trying to have an efficient operation without basic necessities like phones was that you could spend half a day trying to find the person you needed to reach by trying to track them down in person. Or, if you knew somebody who had a phone—because there were only a limited number of phones when phones were first handed out—you could call that person and have them try to run the person down that you needed to find. And that alone was a source of inefficiency in the early days. Um, there were satellite phones; they were so oversubscribed that you were constantly dropping a signal ... They weren't an easy answer 'cause it would depend on who you wanted to reach having a satellite phone. And there was some difficulty in having different satellite systems work over Iraq. And then there was the additional complication in that satellite signals were often interfered with when the military engaged in certain kinds of activities in Iraq. So between all that, there was a pretty enormous amount of frustration for communications in those early days.

CHARLES FERGUSON: How long was it before things actually kind of worked?

RAY JENNINGS: It was far more reliable … you had far more reliable cell phone service by late fall of 2003.

CHARLES FERGUSON: But there was, like, six months, at least, when people did not have good telecommunications.

RAY JENNINGS: Yeah, certain implementers, such as the contractors— for-profit contractors—were able to get access. Certainly State Department; certainly principals amongst the U.S. military. Although you have to bear in mind that oftentimes, one of the hazards—or one of the complications—is that the military was rarely on the same communications grid as the implementers. So if you're trying to contact a colonel who's out in the field to say, "Look, our folks [are] gonna be out there, working," they're using a different communications system.

Even Walter Slocombe agreed that telephone and e-mail problems were serious, although he tried to excuse them.

WALTER SLOCOMBE: We actually had … Curiously enough, we had computer connectivity pretty early on, back to Washington. But we didn't have internal computer … There were no phones, and you couldn't send an e-mail … from one office to another, unless you had a private AOL account, or something.

CHARLES FERGUSON: Isn't that kinda crazy?

WALTER SLOCOMBE: Oh … it was very, very awkward …

CHARLES FERGUSON: Well, obviously it was awkward. That, I think, we can take that for granted. But isn't it also, like … insane that a military occupation of a country, you can't communicate—

WALTER SLOCOMBE: Oh, there's no question that we did not have, at the beginning, the kind of support and resources, which we got pretty quickly, but we didn't have them at the beginning. Now part of the problem is no amount … to some degree, no amount of advance planning would have solved that problem. You're always gonna have problems. …

When Larry Diamond arrived in early 2004, he found that there were still many re-source problems.

LARRY DIAMOND: It was clear that we were just under-resourced in every re-spect. We didn't have enough troops; we didn't have, as I have already indi-cated, enough body armor. We were overwhelmingly short of armored cars to move people around; of security details to protect people; of helicopters, which were really the safest and most efficient way of getting people around; of civilian staff; of virtually everything you could imagine.

And then there were the personnel problems.

CHARLES FERGUSON: Tell us about life in the Green Zone.

RAY JENNINGS: There has been much written about it. Let me tell you about the palace, which was the main building where most of the CPA at the time did its work. I mean, it always struck me that the … CPA was a bit of an aquarium, in that … many of the people who moved around in it—including myself when I would work in it—in and amongst colleagues in that building, we were all underwater … that we would … it would be slow motion … that we would be trying to get things done, but the ineffi-ciencies were monumental in the CPA.

CHARLES FERGUSON: How come? Or give us an example, and then say how come.

RAY JENNINGS: Well, I mean, let me tell you of a story about what I en-countered there: I also teach at Georgetown University. I have several stu-dents who are graduates, masters-level students, who when they get out of the program, they go right to work in developmental venues. During the course of my time in the Green Zone, when I was in the palace, I bumped into one [who had] just graduated and I asked her what she was doing. And she said, well, she couldn't believe her luck. She'd just been appointed to … asked to come to Iraq, and asked to work on the transport sector, es-pecially in Baghdad. I said, "Well, in what regard?" And she said, "Well, I'm being asked to do the traffic plan for the city." And I asked her if she had any training in municipal planning, and she said no.

So she's fresh out of school and had been put in charge of something quite, quite complicated, to say the least. And being out in Baghdad traffic, the need was apparent for doing something on this scale that was good.

Colonel Paul Hughes saw the same thing.

PAUL HUGHES: We were getting new people in, after Bremer showed up. Kids, right out of college, you know. They'd have a baccalaureate degree; just got it the fall, the previous spring. Daddy made a contribution to the campaign, so the kid gets a chance to go over and experience some fun travel and adventure. Pretty boys, that's what I called 'em. They sat around Bremer's front door and did nothing. They were useless. And when you were on restricted rations, you know, you didn't want somebody sitting around eating food, drinking your water, who wasn't contributing to the mission. And I had real problems with those guys.

We had expatriate Iraqis being shoved down our throat by the Department of Defense—coming from the U.K., from the United Kingdom, and the U.S. to help the ministry advisory teams. And these folks were coming faster than we had places to put them. And there were days on end when you'd see the lobby of the Al-Rasheed Hotel just filled up with these guys 'cause they had nothing to do. They'd sit there all day, and jaw-jack with one another, and smoke cigarettes. All the time, drawing U.S. pay for jobs that weren't being done.

Very few people within the CPA, even at senior levels, either spoke Arabic or had any experience with the Middle East.

YAROSLAV TROFIMOV: I remember, one of the most senior officials in the CPA in Tikrit, Saddam Hussein's hometown, was a navy dentist who was sent there because she happened to be of American Lebanese origin. So they figured out that being American Lebanese, she can, you know, she at least has the Arabic last name.

CHARLES FERGUSON: How many of the CPA senior officials spoke Arabic?

YAROSLAV TROFIMOV: Virtually nobody in the CPA … spoke Arabic. Maybe five or six among the top forty, fifty, seventy, officials had Arabic knowledge ... There were some Arabists. And there were some people from the State Department towards later days of the CPA. In the same city of Tikrit, I remember staying with the governor there, who was a career State Department official, and who had spoken Arabic very well. He actually translated a book by an Egyptian author, about Israel, into English once. But that was an exception; that was not the rule.

CHARLES FERGUSON: And how many of the senior people in the CPA had previous experience with the Arab world?

YAROSLAV TROFIMOV: The number roughly corresponds, I think, with the number of those who speak Arabic. And some of them did have experience in the Arab world. But ... very few of them had an experience of running anything, especially running a government. So it was very easy to come with these ideas of how things should be, but if you don't actually know how to run the very basic organizations, it's very hard to put them into reality.

Some of the personnel problems were the result of deliberate choices, in particular the choice to subject CPA employees to political and ideological questioning, and to favor those who had been active in Republican politics, even if they had no relevant experience.

PAUL PILLAR: [Well] a lot of people went to work in CPA, as I understand it, with the main qualification for getting their job being that they were on the mailing list of the American Enterprise Institute, or more specifically, the Heritage Foundation. I think you need something more than that, as qualification to do the difficult work that CPA was trying to do.

Often these people were very young and inexperienced, leading to absurd situations. Barbara Bodine described the issue and gave an example:

BARBARA BODINE: One pattern that began to emerge—although I don't think we fully understood how far it would go, but [it] began to emerge even in the spring of '03—was the replacement of technocrats with people who were, um, politically close to the administration; ideologically comfortable, but not necessarily coming with the experience that was needed in order to do the job. And one example was the person who is responsible for public health—and that obviously was a major issue in a country like Iraq—who had tremendous experience, and had gone into Iraq well before any other civilian had … was replaced by someone who had been a state public health official, but in a state that had never had this kind of a crisis—someone who was very personally close to the administration. And, you know, one [replacement] would happen, and you don't really notice it. And two happened, and pretty soon, after a while, you realize that there is this slow, progressive replacement of technocrats with ideologues.

CHARLES FERGUSON: And how far did that go?

BARBARA BODINE: It went all the way. I think one example is that during the drafting of the transition administrative law—the precursor to the constitution—um, the Iraqis who were involved in that … many of them were very, very senior, well-experienced lawyers, political scientists. These people brought an enormous amount of experience to the table. And the person who was the primary liaison to the drafting of the constitution from our side missed a key meeting because he had to go take the LSATs [Law School Admission Tests].

In 2005, I interviewed Matt Sherman, the good-natured, well-intentioned, slightly befuddled man who had been the deputy senior advisor—i.e., the number two U.S. official—for the Iraqi Ministry of Interior in 2004. Mr. Sherman had held an extremely important position—probably one of the five or ten most important positions in the U.S. occupation and unquestionably one of the most complex and difficult. He was responsible for U.S. policy toward the Iraqi police and the intelligence services, which were increasingly infiltrated by Shiite militias, death squads, and criminal gangs, while he was being ordered to combat the growing insurgency. Sherman described how he came to have his job:

CHARLES FERGUSON: Just out of my personal curiosity, when you were working on [George W. Bush's] 2000 campaign, who were you working with?

MATT SHERMAN: I was working with Dr. Rice. She had put together a small team of individuals who were mainly her former Ph.D. students, or had worked with her in the past, who were younger—who were mainly thirty-five or younger—who she wanted to be able to throw ideas off of to be able to kind of just—a sounding board, I guess you could say—to discuss issues that were potentially coming up with the campaign, and to just get some fresh perspectives. And we'd assist in that when we could and provided position papers and things like that. It was an advisory position. It wasn't necessarily a full-time position.

CHARLES FERGUSON: Okay. So now tell us how you came to show up in Iraq.

MATT SHERMAN: Well, I had ... again, I worked on the campaign, and I was in law school at the time, down in North Carolina. And I had completed law school, and went back to New Jersey, which is where I'm from, to practice law. And [I] was doing that for a few years, for about two years or so, when we had the situation [in] Iraq.

And there's always been ... again, my background has always been international relations and politics and things of that [nature]. So there was a strong urge to get involved in a mission in Iraq. It was something that I believed in; it was something that I thought, you know, we were moving down the right path; it was something I wanted to take part in.

So I then reached out to people who I'd worked with before and asked if there was a way that I could participate and help out and lend my background and energy to. And so, after a number of months, I was appointed to work at the ministry in December of 2003, and arrived on the ground in January of 2004.

The CPA's inefficiencies became legendary.

LAWRENCE WILKERSON: "Can't Provide Anything." That's what "CPA" meant in the minds of military officers. Um, having talked to Drew [Erdman, then in charge of the Education Ministry] at length about some of the operations and some of the things that were happening, I understood why that was the case. Because the military officers would often be out in the field, expending the small amount of funds that they had for immediate action to, say, clean up the street, effect some temporary improvements in the sewage system, maybe get a generator running, that sort of thing— the kinds of things that would have made a difference to the Iraqis [*snaps fingers*] just like that. ... And once the military had expended its small amount of money to do that, it would come back to CPA. And it would say, "I've got this, this, this, and this to do in Mosul and Kirkuk, in Basra, wherever ... and it's gonna cost this much," and so forth. And it [the request] would disappear. It would simply disappear. Two weeks later, the captain or the major or the colonel or whatever would come back and say, "What happened to my request?" "Uh, what request?" And this happened over and over again.

You don't have to do that too often to the can-do guys in the military, and you become "Can't Provide Anything." And that's what CPA stood for with regard to these young, hard-charging officers who were trying to get things done out in the hinterlands of Iraq.

Seth Moulton was one of those officers on the ground.

SETH MOULTON: I ended up working more closely with the CPA when I got involved with the Iraq media because I would go to them and collaborate with them on, um, on some of the media projects.

There were some great people who worked for the CPA and some very interested and motivated people. But they were sometimes the exception, not the rule, and you definitely got the ... I got the impression that the military was doing a lot more to ensure the future of Iraq than the CPA was in terms of the level of effort ... in terms of the tangible accomplishments that we made.

In addition to its personnel, skill, and resource deficiencies, CPA decision making suffered because most CPA employees had almost no contact with Iraqis. The CPA created a miniature America within the 3,600-acre Green Zone, which most CPA employees rarely if ever left. As time went on, this isolation worsened because the insurgency, kidnapping, and other violence made it increasingly dangerous for Americans to function without extremely heavy security. As a result, most CPA employees had very little exposure to, or understanding of, the realities of life in Iraq.

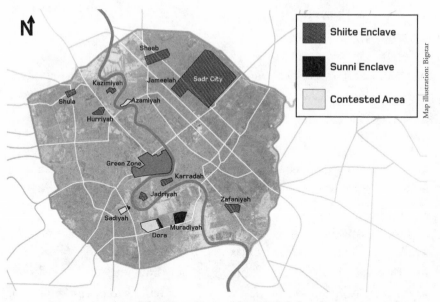

The Green Zone within Baghdad

PAUL HUGHES: I began to realize that CPA really wasn't too concerned about what the people in Baghdad knew; it was about what the people inside the Beltway believed. You know, Bremer wanted to make sure everybody inside the Beltway understood Baghdad was going to be a glowing success. Meanwhile, we're putting up more T-walls [precast concrete walls] and concrete barriers, and hemming ourselves in.

Now, I absolutely hated the Green Zone; I got out every chance I could. I would fly somewhere else in Iraq, and go visit people, go visit Iraqis. I'd meet with journalists. That's how I would go downtown at night, to meet with Iraqis, and sit in their homes and hear their complaints and their thoughts. And I would come back and tell Dan [Senor, Bremer's press spokesman], "You have a problem. You're not communicating to the Iraqis." And I'd get this cold look from him, saying, we don't need to talk to the Iraqis.

CHARLES FERGUSON: He said that?

PAUL HUGHES: He didn't say that, but his actions essentially said that. The person who said that to me was the deputy director of the Office of Global Communications at the White House.

The CPA's isolationist behavior, as well as rising security problems, served to both keep Iraqis out of the Green Zone and to keep the Americans in—a problem that affected the U.S. military as well as the CPA.

YAROSLAV TROFIMOV: I remember, there were huge lines of Iraqis—engineers, public officials, people just willing to help, to translate—standing in line at the gates of the palace, where the new administration, the American administration, had just taken hold. Made to wait, and not being received by anyone. Just, oh, "Go away. Don't come back." And you know, these people came there, and tried once, and two times, and three times. And then they gave up. And then, some of them thought, "Well, you know, maybe the insurgency is the option." So this refusal to accept advice, or help—this mixture of ignorance and arrogance—was what really did undermine this effort.

CHARLES FERGUSON: What happened when you spoke to CPA officials about these problems?

YAROSLAV TROFIMOV: Some of them were reluctant to acknowledge that there are problems. Some of them were saying, "Well, you know, we know what's best for them." And obviously, there were all sorts of excuses because, you know, there is a security that has to be maintained.

And this focus on security was not really necessary in the very early days, because in the early days, there was no insurgency. But from the very early days, there was a huge distance between the CPA—the American sort of governors of the country, and you know, the masters—and the subjects. And it was virtually impossible for an Iraqi who had a grievance to relay it to the Americans.

I remember going to meet Iraqis. I met some officials in [Karbala]. And they told me, "Look, you know, there was this huge weapons stash in the school here. We've been trying to get hold of the Americans for the past several weeks, going to the base, but they wouldn't talk to us. And you know, we're afraid to go there because they started shooting at people who approach the base."

So that lack of contact, lack of interaction, was what really doomed the effort, at the end.

Getting into the Green Zone was difficult even for American journalists. George Packer remembered his first trip to Baghdad in July 2003.

GEORGE PACKER: Looking back, these are all incredible things to remember, that you could just show up in Baghdad, drive around, and find a hotel, and check in. Um, I knew it was dangerous, but I had the feeling I could move around and work there. And so I began to do that. I had two names in the American occupation authority. They were sort of midlevel civilians—young Americans from the State Department. I got their names from a friend, and I just tracked them down and began to talk to them. It was difficult because they were inside the Green Zone, across the river from my hotel. And it wasn't easy. Now it's ... you know, it's almost impossible. But then it was not easy to get inside not just the Green Zone, but the palace where they were headquartered.

A. Heather Coyne, Army Civil Affairs officer for the city of Baghdad, also commented on the Americans' initial openness and then subsequent retreat to the Green Zone as security worsened.

A. HEATHER COYNE: We were in the Green Zone, unfortunately. So it wasn't really Baghdad, and it wasn't really Iraq. But at the beginning, for the first year and a half or so, I was still going downtown two or three times a day on missions. And we felt that we were just as much a part of the city as anyone living downtown. It was only after a year or more that the Green Zone started becoming so fortresslike and so difficult for Iraqis to come into and so difficult for us to leave.

Packer related the isolation of the Green Zone to the illusions the CPA harbored about the state of affairs in Iraq.

GEORGE PACKER: Inside the Green Zone, things seemed to be going pretty well in March of 2004. They were deep in negotiations over the interim constitution, known as the TAL: Transitional Administrative Law. And from within a bubble, you can imagine, if you can only get these people sitting around this table to agree on a document, you've basically solved the problem; you've laid out a timetable for the return to sovereignty and the election of a government, and the writing of a new constitution.

Um, the problem is, the bubble was getting smaller and more and more airtight, so that the news from outside the Green Zone was not penetrating. And that news was [that] this Iraqi body called the governing council, which the American authorities set up, had almost no real legitimacy or visibility outside the Green Zone. So if the Coalition Provisional Authority and the governing council negotiated a wonderful document, by way of an interim constitution, and got everyone inside that room to sign off on it, it might actually not make much difference out in the streets.

And that was clear to me in March because I could see more. I had more understanding myself. I knew more people. I had been watching it for a longer time. And I could see the great gap between what those inside the halls of power were doing, and what people out on the street were feeling.

L. Paul Bremer in his office in the Green Zone

Bremer's Personality and Its Impact on CPA Policy

The CPA had difficulty working with the professional military, the CIA, the UN, and the State Department. To some extent, this problem derived from the larger ideological and power struggles between the Pentagon (to which the CPA reported) and these other organizations. In significant measure, however, these difficulties seem to have stemmed from Bremer's personality and leadership style.

Nobody I interviewed ever questioned Bremer's work ethic, his dedication, or his courage. People praised his commitment, saying that he drove himself extremely hard. While he was in Iraq, Bremer was probably the most heavily targeted, and most heavily protected, person in the world. He was the object of multiple assassination attempts, yet continued to work and travel without interruption. At the same time, the overwhelming majority of those with whom I spoke also felt that Bremer was rigid, authoritarian, ideological, arrogant, and unwilling to listen to ideas contrary to his own.

LARRY DIAMOND: I was deeply impressed with the energy, tirelessness, commitment to cause of Ambassador Bremer and with many of his leadership qualities. He's a charismatic individual. He's an impressively eloquent individual. He's a real take-charge guy. He is, um, a deep believer in certain principles, and worked very hard for them.

But at the same time:

LARRY DIAMOND: I think Bremer, in his administrative style, was too centralized. This was something that I came to realize only gradually and that I became more fully acquainted with only later, after I interviewed, for my book, a number of my CPA colleagues, who described to me their own piece of the puzzle of how the CPA operated, and their own frustrations.

He did tend to stovepipe most matters—fragment them into separate lines of authority, coming directly to him. And therefore, different elements of our operation, of our civilian administration in Baghdad, didn't adequately know what each other was doing unless they really sought out the information. And they were frustrated.

There was a very narrow circle around Bremer. It didn't adequately include the several career American ambassadors who were there with decades of collective experience in the region. It relied excessively on a cluster of rather young and inexperienced people, some of them quite talented, who became my friends—and in some ways, I have come to have great respect for them—but who didn't have the experience and the savvy for such an awesome and complicated political mission and therefore, I think, made some mistakes as a result of this, and who, frankly, alienated a lot of the Iraqis they were dealing with by their youthful brashness. This is a society that deeply values age, wisdom, mutual respect, politeness. And we had twenty-four-year-old kids, sometimes essentially ordering about very senior and respected Iraqi intellectuals and statesmen.

Lawrence Wilkerson was more direct and more critical.

LAWRENCE WILKERSON: Despite Ambassador Bremer's book, I would have to say three or four things about him that probably the book attempts to counteract: One, he was not necessarily the right person. And I say that because the right person needed to be someone like our current ambassador, Khalilzad, someone who understood the tribal, ethnic culture, and could immerse himself in it and deal with it as painstakingly, as meticulously, and as slowly as that has to be done. We had a man who was more or less cut out of the Jonathan [Howe] mold. Or the "I'm in charge and everyone will do what I say and that's it, understand?" And that's kinda the way L. Paul Bremer came across to me, and kinda the way he came across to others who were around me, who were advising me, and with whom I discussed the matter. So that's the first problem: much, much, much too hard-core; too unaccustomed to that kind of environment; and too mission-driven to see that, for example, his exclusion of the Iraqis early on from major participation in the decision-making process was a grievous error … grievous error. So that's the first problem: the personality of Bremer.

Apparently, Bremer's personality also alienated Army General Ricardo Sanchez, who had come to Iraq in May 2003 to take charge of U.S. ground forces. The alienation was so intense that the two men had difficulty working together. This lack of communication worsened an already significant problem, namely, the unclear division of authority between the CPA and the military. Neither organization was clearly in charge, with the result that decisions either did not get made, or were made and reversed repeatedly.

LAWRENCE WILKERSON: There was another facet of the first thing I gave you—his personality, his character—that also, I think, troubled the situation greatly, and that also conflicted with the personality and character of the initial commander, General Sanchez, because the word I was getting from Baghdad was that they didn't even talk to each other, that they hated each other. Now, I don't know whether it was as strident as they hated each other, but they didn't talk to each other. So there definitely was not unity of command, which is, as you may know, in the military a principle of war, a principle of doing anything. You need one man in charge, and that man needs to be the person the president wants in charge, and that man needs to be empowered. There were two people in charge: Sanchez in charge of the military operations, and Bremer in charge of the CPA. ... So it's clear to me there wasn't unity of command. And it's clear to me that Bremer and Sanchez didn't get along very well. And I have ample evidence of that. So that was a tremendous problem, too.

Bremer also alienated UN envoy Sergio Vieira de Mello and other senior UN diplomats. Once Bremer had successfully pressured Vieira de Mello into helping to obtain Iraqi support for the Iraqi Governing Council, Bremer brushed him aside. Samantha Power, who has written a biography of Vieira de Mello, commented on Bremer's attitude.

SAMANTHA POWER: Initially, Sergio was able to play a kind of in-between role—in between American interests on the one hand and the interests of a variety of Iraqi factions on the other. But as soon as the governing council was assembled, as soon as Bremer had made use of Sergio, had made use of the UN, he had almost no time for the United Nations.

And so, on issues like detention policy ... hoodings was one of the issues that Sergio raised again and again with Bremer and with General Sanchez—the hoodings of prisoners. At that time, there was no knowledge of dogs and torture. But Sergio was, very early on, onto the recognition that if there were no procedures—if you had contractors who were unaccountable; if you had no clear command and control; if there were no organized visits by international human rights organizations—excesses were gonna happen. Bremer would hear none of it. I mean, Americans, of course, weren't capable, in Bremer's mind, of committing atrocities of the kind that were later revealed.

What Sergio lived through was two months of in effect being used as a vehicle to get to certain segments of the Iraqi society. And then for his last month, what he endured was not having his phone calls returned and being treated as precisely as irrelevant as the UN Security Council had been treated in the run-up to the war in Iraq.

Bremer was generally unwilling to change his opinions or behavior, and according to Professor Power, he would blame Washington for his own intransigence.

SAMANTHA POWER: One of the things that Bremer did often was invoke Washington as grounds for explaining why he couldn't actually do what Sergio was asking him to do. You know, the overreliance on the exiles, which is something that Sergio pointed out to him early on. You know, Bremer would just sort of [say], "Well, you know, I have my orders from Washington. You know, there's almost nothing I can do. These are the handpicked favorites already. You know, there's only so much we're gonna be able to mix, to tinker with this equation."

The Reconstruction Effort

The management—or mismanagement—of the effort to restructure Iraq's economy and rebuild its infrastructure is an extraordinary, still inadequately understood story. The available evidence strongly indicates that it was an utterly dysfunctional effort.

In fact, there were two parallel and largely separate "reconstruction" efforts. One was the reconstruction effort that was funded by federal appropriations and which was often bureaucratic, slow, misguided, and extremely wasteful. The other effort was the unofficial one, which was wild, corrupt, and often secret.

This second, parallel effort used frozen Iraqi assets that had been in the custody of the Federal Reserve Bank since economic sanctions were imposed on Saddam's regime in the early 1990s. After Bremer became head of the CPA, a large amount of this money was released to CPA custody under the auspices of the Development

Fund for Iraq (DFI) and disbursed to both U.S. and Iraqi organizations, which ranged from private military contractors to Iraqi ministries. In the slightly more than one year of Bremer's tenure as head of the U.S. occupation, $12 billion in cash was shipped from the Federal Reserve Bank in the United States to the CPA in Iraq in planeloads of hundred-dollar bills. This money was disbursed with extremely weak, sometimes nonexistent administrative and financial controls. Approximately $9 billion of it remains unaccounted for.

CHARLES FERGUSON: What do you think of how the CPA and the United States handled the economic and infrastructural reconstruction of Iraq?

YAROSLAV TROFIMOV: Okay, the idea was—as in many other aspects of the occupation—to transplant ready-made American solutions to Iraq, and to treat Iraq as a tabula rasa, discounting any local experience and local knowledge there, and not asking the Iraqis themselves, what do they want? I mean, nobody bothered to go and ask the Iraqis, "Do you want the power station built [here]? Or that part of this [road] cleared up?" So, what was done is to try to build the most expensive, the most top-of-the-line facilities with American taxpayer money, instead of using infinitely smaller amounts to get the Iraqis to fix what was already there. And, of course, all these facilities would take years of lead time to be developed. And in the meantime, the insurgency had started, and a growing share of that budget had to be spent on providing private armies to guard the installations and the Western executives and workers themselves.

Paul Pillar laid the bulk of the blame for the poor reconstruction efforts on security problems.

PAUL PILLAR: Reconstruction has fared poorly above all, because of the security situation. And what the lack of security, which has meant the diversion of major resources to provide security ... Many of the things in budgets that ostensibly are for reconstruction really are for security, in the sense of hiring guards and so on. And a substantial chunk of that eighteen billion dollars that was appropriated some time back actually has been formally diverted to security purposes: building prisons, and so on.

In addition to that, there are other nonmonetary but substantial hindrances, everything from just the difficulty in getting a truckload of goods from one part of the country to another, the difficulty in getting employees to reliably come to work when they have their own security concerns about whether it's safe even to leave their homes—all sorts of things like that. That's by far the biggest impediment.

I think there have been other impediments that had to do with the way the reconstruction issue was approached. There clearly was an inclination on the part of some of the people involved, some of whom went to work for the Coalition Provisional Authority, to make Iraq a kind of laboratory for, uh, a laissez-faire economy. It was the wrong place to try to do experiments in political economic ideology, in my view, and I think we're seeing some of the ... some of the results now.

Sam Gardiner, a retired military officer and a consultant to the Joint Chiefs of Staff, and many others, including Richard Armitage, noted that the reconstruction effort's emphasis on large-scale new construction by U.S. firms cost time and money that could have better been spent on repairing existing Iraqi systems.

CHARLES FERGUSON: Do you have an estimate of how much money it would have taken to be properly prepared?

SAM GARDINER: Well, actually—now, that's an interesting thing—it would have cost less. It would have cost less money to be prepared than it was the way we ended up doing it. Now that sort of gets into the problem of managing the postwar situation. But the solution that was adopted after we took Baghdad was a solution of having big contractors and big projects. That wasn't the way the Iraq infrastructure was built. Iraq was small plants, serving small numbers of people. Had we been prepared to fix the things that were there, we could have continued the system that was in place. But in essence, by having the notion that you had to have big contractors, we overrode that, replaced it with the large construction projects, and in ways, delayed the time to do it, and it ended up costing more.

CHARLES FERGUSON: Some people I've spoken to have made the argument that in fact, Iraq's infrastructure was so dilapidated that there was no point in trying to fix it.

SAM GARDINER: Not true. ... Probably the best example is in the water system. There were a group of American veterans who had adopted projects to go to Iraq and fix these small water plants. And they had a lot of data on [what was needed] to fix them. Now [the Iraqis] had experience on how to fix them. Nobody ever asked them; nobody ever thought of adopting that system. It was fragile, but the people of Iraq knew how to keep it together. You know, it was baling wire and chewing gum, but they had kept it together with baling wire and chewing gum. All they needed was a wrench and some new wire. You know, but we went down the path of saying, "Oh no, you've got to have a big water plant."

Seth Moulton and another military officer, Ann Gildroy, offered an example from their own work.

SETH MOULTON: Ann and I used Iraqi engineers, and we worked very, very closely with the Iraqi security force commanders ... to build their facilities. So, when we went to build border forts, instead of, you know, just going to the Army Corps of Engineers to come up with some grand design for a border fort, we would actually go to the Iraqis and talk to them about what they needed, and then use Iraqi engineers to sit down with the commanders. And between them and us, design the best border fort possible.

So there was a story—remember that story of the border fort down [by the] Saudi border that the Army Corps of Engineers built for, I think, 1.3 million dollars? And they handed over the keys in this great ceremony to the Iraqi commander. And he was so unhappy with what they had built— just because, for all the money they had spent, it wasn't what he needed in a border fort—that he refused to take ownership of it. And in contrast, we built border forts for about two hundred thousand dollars apiece, on the Iranian border, that they ended [up using] the design—

ANN GILDROY: Well, they—

SETH MOULTON: They duplicated the design elsewhere in Iraq—

ANN GILDROY: Yeah.

SETH MOULTON: ... Right? I mean, they—

ANN GILDROY: And I mean, our guys really came up with the design. I mean it—

SETH MOULTON: Yeah, I mean, it wasn't us. It was because we had been willing to work with the Iraqis. And so, they brought down their commanders from Baghdad to show this thing off and say, "This is the kind of border fort that we need everywhere in Iraq." And yet it cost two hundred thousand dollars. And it also was done by two marine lieutenants, essentially. That was the American component. Because the Iraqis did it ... did everything else. They did the engineering; they did the supervising; they did the construction. And, I mean, one of the reasons why it came out well is because you actually had Iraqi engineers out there, supervising these contractors: Iraqi engineers who knew how the contractors would try to scam, versus Americans who might get out there once a month at best.

We were building these forts right next to forts put up by the Army Corps of Engineers through that big conglomerate, Parsons. And I mean, we had our forts designed and constructed and dedicated in a period of about probably five months. And I think when we left, the Bechtel forts, which had been started maybe a year before we arrived—

ANN GILDROY: Exactly—

SETH MOULTON: ... were still not finished. And you can imagine the cost. And yet, when we did this, we would get friction because, you know, the people in Baghdad, they trusted their Army Corps of Engineer buddies, and that's where they wanted the money to go, and that's who they wanted to see running this stuff. Again, just really no understanding of how things actually worked out on the ground.

Ray Jennings reported similar problems when the U.S. military worked on civilian projects.

RAY JENNINGS: Several military contingents in Baghdad, for example, did undertake a school rehabilitation program. Um, this was seen as being a great set of projects that could enhance community relations for local commanders. Normally, what kind of developmental groups would do is they would go in, develop parent-teacher associations, and kind of work with communities to identify where the school goes; how the school should be built; how many students are there; what the parents want to see [at] school; and develop, represent, what should be taught there—in Bosnia and other venues. And in Iraq, the military spent much of the funds that it had at its disposal in Baghdad—a good percentage of them—building schools that didn't refer to the community. They were decided as priorities by a very small number of local elites and a local military commander. The schools were built, often with no transparency with local contractors. And they are often built for far, far more money than was required. Now, the schools that I saw built by many nonprofits were built for thirty to thirty-five thousand dollars. Many of the military schools were built for eighty to eighty-five thousand dollars. And the results were far inferior to the projects that were done by the NGOs.

CHARLES FERGUSON: What accounted for that difference?

RAY JENNINGS: Mainly contractors who skimmed, or a lack of monitoring of the project itself. Normally, what the NGOs would do is get the community involved in watching the contractor do its work, and making sure that the community saw and recognized they had a vested interest in a good school resulting from this investment.

It's easy to see how ... military civil affairs folks could have thought that, "Look, we'll do the work; people will see us doing the work; and it'll endear us to the community." The other side of that, though, is that if you don't get the community involved, they don't feel invested. Why should they care if the military and a local contractor are doing the work, and they have never been asked, "Should the school be built there again?" Maybe it's built on a swamp. "Should there be a night watchman?" Well, many places, there wasn't, and as soon as [the] ceiling fans were put in, they were gone by the next morning. Um, oftentimes, NGOs would volunteer somebody to watch the building site so things didn't walk off. In other cases, what often happened was, in terms of expediency, civil affairs contingents would ask a local self-appointed mayor, "What contractor should we use to get the school done?" And in too many cases, it was often a relative, and the price was too high.

Even when the CPA did try to locate and use Iraqis, it often had a hard time.

RAY JENNINGS: It was difficult initially because many Iraqis weren't sure what or how they would be treated—whether they would be subject to arrest. Um, they weren't sure whether or not their exposure in being involved with these kinds of activities of the CPA would subject them to personal danger.

Also, I mean, under the Baathist ... leadership, centralized management was the management style. And there was no central order, coming down, ordering people to come back to work, either. So, you had experts who eventually were able to be contacted by the CPA. But what's interesting is that once the transitional ministries were set up, the new Iraqi ministers found it far easier to find these people than the CPA ever did.

CHARLES FERGUSON: So the difficulty wasn't with finding these people per se; the difficulty was with the CPA finding and employing these people?

RAY JENNINGS: Yeah, in part because the CPA didn't have a ready-made mechanism for locating, reassuring, and ordering people back to work.

Then, as the security situation deteriorated in 2004, a vicious circle took hold. High levels of crime meant that many small, decentralized projects could not be adequately protected. The vulnerability of these small projects reinforced the tendency of the CPA and U.S. contractors to concentrate on large, expensive, centralized projects, leaving existing systems to deteriorate. Furthermore, the CPA became ever more reluctant to use Iraqi contractors, because to do so would require dealing directly with large numbers of Iraqis, which it was not equipped to do and which became increasingly dangerous.

RAY JENNINGS: Well, I mean, USAID [U.S. Agency for International Development], as in many of the places that it works, had a tremendous challenge to operationalize itself quickly. And USAID, more so than many of its implementing organizations—the organizations it gives money to do these projects—had very restrictive security constraints upon it. And that made it quite difficult for USAID personnel to get out on their own and look at the projects that are under way, [and] build refinements into the directives they were giving their implementing partners. They gamely did as best they could under these constraints, but I think you'd find, in talking to many USAID people who were there, that over time, it became increasingly harder for USAID personnel to get out to the project sites that they were funding.

A. HEATHER COYNE: I was a graduate student in international relations at Johns Hopkins School of Advanced International Studies. And I came out of grad school with a dream job in mind that worked with development in conflict zones and looked at the liaison between civilian and military and security forces. And [I] realized, after calling around to a bunch of NGOs, nongovernment organizations, that nobody did this job. And then in my position at OMB, the Office of Management and Budget at the White House, I was in charge of terrorism and special operations programs, and [I] stumbled across, in my work on special operations, a description of civil affairs, which is the army branch that does nation-building. But we don't use the N-word.

I looked at it for a little while and thought, "Oh, you know, how ironic: There's my dream job; it actually does exist, but it's in the army." And then I caught myself thinking, "The army." I said, "No, no. I don't ... I don't join the army. I'm from California. [*laughs*] I'm a bleeding-heart liberal. I can't join the army." And about a week later, I was calling the recruiters.

So it took another couple years of weaseling my way into the army, another year after that, weaseling my way into civil affairs, which is a specialty branch and is a little tough to get into directly, and then [I] volunteered for Arabic language school. And when I graduated from Arabic language school, we deployed to Iraq a couple months later ...

When I first got to Iraq, most of my unit, and me in particular, we were on a high because we really believed in what we were doing. We were very excited about it. We thought we had the preparation and the skills necessary to make a difference. And I personally had been waiting to go to Iraq for about sixteen years, ever since the chemical weapon attack on Halabja. I thought the international community needed to intervene, needed to tell Saddam Hussein that that wasn't acceptable. We didn't, but for me, it was sort of a question of better late than never.

But what Lieutenant Coyne found when she started working in Baghdad did not please her.

A. HEATHER COYNE: So when we got there, I was full of enthusiasm and excitement and hope for what we could accomplish. And it took several months before I started realizing that we didn't have any of the preparation that we needed, any of the training, any of the expertise, not even the equipment to move around [in] and do our job. So as things started becoming more difficult and more frustrating and more—we ... we weren't seeing progress; in fact, we were seeing a lot of backsliding—I started really analyzing what it was that we were doing as civil affairs and as the coalition. And [I] realized how little of a capability the U.S. government and the international community, more widely, have to do this mission. ...

CHARLES FERGUSON: So tell us very specifically, what your experience was. What happened? What began to indicate to you that we were not prepared, that things were not going well?

A. HEATHER COYNE: There are so many. And I actually kept a book the entire time and wrote down everything we did wrong. It's a pretty long book. There's one anecdote that sums this up for me. ... I had just recently started working at the CPA as the civil society officer for Baghdad and was in an office that was also dealing with the local government project, developing local councils to serve as the interface between Iraqi citizens and the national government.

And at one point, the colonel who was in charge of the programs for Sadr City—the heavily Shia area that we had so many issues with—came to us to report on some of the work he'd been doing with the district council there. And he told us that they had stumbled finally, after a lot of false starts, on this program that had a lot of potential to clean the streets: Give ten dollars to everybody who showed up to help that day, and just get the streets back in order. They were so excited about this program. It was working beautifully. The streets were getting cleaner. People had money in their pockets. They were feeling good about the whole program until, the colonel said, he had somebody ask the participants what they thought of the program. And the participants said, "We love this program. This is a great program. Our streets are better. Our communities are better. And we're so grateful to Moqtada al-Sadr for this program." And the army did a double-take and said, "What do you mean Moqtada al-Sadr? This is the district council funding the program." And they said, "No, no. It's Moqtada al-Sadr." And the colonel said, "Well, why do you think that?" And they said, "Well, because Moqtada al-Sadr told us that he was funding the program." So it turns out that Moqtada al-Sadr, the arch nemesis of the process that we were trying to put in place, had taken all the credit for this program simply because his information campaign was better than ours.

So I looked at the colonel. I said, "Well, that's terrible to hear, but why don't you just hand out, with the ten dollars at the end of the day, a certificate that says, 'Thank you for participating in the reconstruction of your country. This is a small step, but it's the first step in a longer process.' Sign the certificate, 'Your friendly neighborhood district council.' And put a PS: 'Your district council meets every Wednesday at two. Citizens are encouraged to come in and talk about this program and their other priorities for the community.'"

And the colonel looked at me and said, "Well, that's a great idea. But we don't have any ability to print certificates." Not realizing, you know, our entire psy-ops [psychological operations] army capability is down the street. Not to mention that you could just go out to any Iraqi print shop and give them an order for several thousand certificates, and they'd have them to you the next day, and, you know, you've improved business for them, anyway.

This summed it up for me: that we didn't have any idea what we were doing. We were making things up from scratch. We were not looking at the resources or the effect of our programs. We weren't considering impact. We didn't have the creativity and flexibility to deal with the situation. And we didn't have trained people who were steeped in the ideas and the best practices from all the other experiences we've been through around the world, other interventions. None of that institutional memory had been transferred to the people who were working in Iraq. It was … I refer to it as "amateur hour" in Iraq.

The majority of reconstruction efforts and funding for Iraq was to have been based on congressional appropriations. In October 2003, Congress voted to appropriate $18 billion for the reconstruction of Iraq. This money was in addition to the Development Fund for Iraq, described earlier, and the funds used for U.S. civilian and military operations in Iraq.

One year later, only $1 billion of the $18 billion had been spent. The U.S. reconstruction effort was plagued by an almost endless list of problems, including the overuse of U.S. versus Iraqi contractors, the need to divert 25 to 40 percent of reconstruction funds to security as the insurgency worsened, misguided priorities, bureaucratic delays, and corruption.

The lack of U.S. response to corruption and waste in the reconstruction effort has been striking. One Iraqi defense minister personally stole $1 billion before escaping to London, where he lived openly for months before moving to Jordan. An electricity minister jailed on corruption charges escaped from an Iraqi prison in the Green Zone with the aid of U.S. private military contractors and now lives openly in the United States. After Congress established the office of the Special Inspector General for Iraqi Reconstruction, which was given responsibility for monitoring reconstruction spending, the Bush administration attempted to abolish the organization.

Perhaps the worst problems, however, were bureaucratic and political. Linda Bilmes, a former assistant secretary of commerce, is now a professor at Harvard's Kennedy School of Government. Specializing in government budgeting, she has studied economic and financial issues related to the Iraq war since 2004.

LINDA BILMES: The story of the reconstruction money in Iraq is one of the greatest tragedies of this entire story. It's one of the places where this really, really went wrong. ... This is now money that became available on October 1, 2003. At that time, the security situation in Iraq had not yet deteriorated. And this was the moment at which the Iraq people were looking for the electricity to go back on, and for the lights to go back on, and for the water to be running, and for all those basic services to go back on, and for life to go back to normal. But due to a series of, um, unfortunate events, the money was not spent until much, much later. And let me go through a series of events that unfolded.

First of all, the money was given to the Pentagon to spend, even though most of the projects were civilian, like painting schools and redoing water projects and things, which were not really the Pentagon's area of expertise. Secondly, the Pentagon procurement process is extremely slow. But most importantly, the Pentagon was required by Congress to go for competitive bids on any contracts that were given out for reconstruction. And when they had initially done work in Iraq, earlier in 2003, the Pentagon had gone to sole-source contracts. In other words, the contracts had gone to a few contractors they already knew. Now in this case, they were required by language that had been put in by the congressional committee to have a competitive bidding process for the contracts. And if they didn't do that, it was required that Secretary Rumsfeld personally sign a letter to the committee chairman explaining why it was not possible to have a competitive bid on the contract.

Over the next six months, the administration was not willing to sign a letter. They were also not willing to launch into a competitive bidding process. And so the request for proposals, which are the thing that needs to be written before a contract can be sent to competitive bidding, dragged on for a long, long time. And it wasn't really until March of 2004 that some of these requests for proposals were finally being issued in a competitive manner. By that time, and in those six months, the security situation had deteriorated. By the time many of these contracts were awarded, in the spring and the summer of 2004, [the] security situation had completely unraveled. Many of the bidders were no longer able to actually provide services or do the work for the cost that they had anticipated, because of the need for additional security costs.

In addition, during this period of time, there was a very strong preference by the Pentagon to have American companies doing the work. And there are numerous instances that have been documented where local Iraqi contractors proposed that they could do pieces of work for much, much less than, in fact, the American contractors could have done. But the policy was basically that American contractors needed to do the work.

So the combination of not using the local work force, which was right there and cheaper; of delaying over this competitive bidding squabble; the slowness of the Pentagon procurement; [and] the inexperience of the Pentagon at being able to do this kind of civilian work resulted in the fact that here we are now, in December of 2005, and Iraqis still don't have functional electricity, water supplies, water treatment, sewage treatment, and all of those things for which the administration had actually gone and asked for money early on in 2003.

A second issue is the fact that the money that was originally allocated was not spent in that first year, and so some of it was then [taken] back. The Office of Management and Budget, seeing that there was a pot of money that was not being used, immediately said, "Oh, we're gonna take five billion dollars of that back." … [The eighteen billion dollars] that was made available on October 1, 2003, simply was not spent in the 2003–2004 period. Actually, in the first year, only around a billion dollars of that money was actually spent.

So in that very immediate time, when we needed to win the hearts and minds of the Iraqis by providing basic services—and the money was there—we were not actually able to get the money out the door to restore these services. … It is really one of the tragedies of the entire financing of the war. … After the money became available on October 1, 2003, one of the several reasons why the whole bidding process was delayed was that the Pentagon had not wanted to use the competitive bidding process. They had balked at using the competitive bidding process. However, Secretary Rumsfeld had also not wanted to write a letter, saying that they wanted to use a sole-source contracting. So—

CHARLES FERGUSON: Why didn't he want to write a letter?

LINDA BILMES: The question as to why he didn't want to write a letter is something that I don't know. … My sense was simply that this was a cat-and-mouse game between the administration and the committee over whether they were having sole-source contracts or competitive contracts. Congress always likes competitive contracts because in their districts, they have more chances of getting a piece of the action. The administration, particularly the Pentagon, likes sole-source contracts 'cause they go to somebody they know and they think can get the work done. So it was a kind of standoff. But the tragedy was that because of this sort of bureaucratic wrangling between the appropriators and the administration, the money was just not gotten out the door. So you had the people sitting in Baghdad in the Coalition Provisional Authority, saying, "We've got contractors; we need this money. We've got the money—it's there in the budget—we need the contracts; we needed to get this stuff out the door." And they were simply not able to get the money out the door fast enough. And by the time they got the money out the door, it was too late.

The State Department also dragged their feet on getting the reconstruction money out the door, because they knew that after the Coalition Provisional Authority was dissolved, when it would be dissolved, then the money would revert to the State Department. So twenty-one billion dollars is a nice chunk of money. The State Department felt—with some justification—that they had more expertise in doing this kind of work. So they wanted the money. And they had wanted it in the first place. But the money had gone to the Pentagon. So you had the Pentagon, which was slow and dragging its feet on getting the contracts out, and you had the State Department, which really didn't intervene to get the money out any more quickly, because they were hoping that they would get the money and then they could do the project. Which they did, but by that time, it was too late, because the security situation had deteriorated.

Journalist George Packer reported that it was often the soldiers on the ground who felt the brunt of those policy decisions; their hands were tied.

GEORGE PACKER: American soldiers should have been able to hand out fistfuls of money very early on to jump-start projects in the cities: urban renewal, garbage pickup, reconstruction, and, you know, we'll do the accounting later. But it should have been done really quickly, and with a lot of resources. And instead, the red tape was already in place. And soldiers were frustrated by the occupation authority, the CPA, because it didn't get the money out fast enough. And John Prior [an army lieutenant Packer interviewed] was frustrated. He told me, "My hands are tied. The most frustrating thing is I can't do more for them." And it was frustrating to see that, and to see the goodwill of soldiers like him blocked by essentially, um, great errors of judgment made at much higher levels than the level he was at.

In addition to managing the reconstruction effort, the CPA also attempted to restructure the Iraqi economy. It did this with relatively little advice from serious economists and followed an ideological program of privatization and closing of state-owned enterprises. It is clear that most of Iraq's state-run enterprises were extremely inefficient, by the standards of the industrialized West. These enterprises, however, accounted for the majority of Iraq's nonoil economy and employment; closing them abruptly was yet another contributor to unemployment, resentment, and the insurgency.

Brad Setser is an economist specializing in emerging economies and international economics. He is the author of many articles and books, including *Oil and Global Adjustment* (2007), and is a Geoeconomics Fellow at the Council on Foreign Relations.

BRAD SETSER: The U.S.—and particularly those who wanted to create a new model for the Arab world—arrived with grand plans to remake Iraq: de-Baathification, disbanding the Iraqi Army, ending all subsidies to state-owned enterprises. The net result was to dismantle existing mechanisms for injecting Iraq's oil surplus into the economy. Soldiers—particularly career soldiers—were left unemployed and without any income. Workers in state-owned enterprises were in the same position. The existing institutions for, in some sense, spending the cash generated by Iraq's oil were dismantled far in advance of the creation of any new institutions to serve the same function. The basic problem most oil-exporting economies face is that oil production is hugely capital intensive, not labor intensive. Most local jobs don't come from the production of oil, but rather from spending all the income generated by selling oil that can be produced fairly cheaply at the global market price.

No doubt Iraq's old institutions were inefficient. But those inefficiencies created jobs and provided income. Those on the payroll of the army and Iraqi state-owned enterprises couldn't, and didn't, become entrepreneurs overnight. In the short run, they were just unemployed. Ending the sanctions that had insulated Iraq's economy from the global economy had a similar effect: Anyone who had cash could now buy foreign goods rather than Iraqi goods. No doubt that led to large benefits to many, who now had access to higher-quality goods at a lower price. But those who had built businesses supplying Iraqis with locally made goods that were hard to obtain during the era of sanctions were basically out of work. It was effectively economic shock therapy—and a shock that stemmed from the decisions of an outside actor, not one from a domestic decision that the old economic system wasn't working and needed to be changed. Stage one of the economic shock is a big increase in unemployment. Only after wages "adjust"—meaning fall—and time elapses will new sources of economic activity emerge.

The overall result seems to have been a lot of economic disruption, and certainly more economic disruption than would have been the case if existing institutions for distributing the oil surplus had been maintained in some form. And the economic disruption certainly seems to have made it harder to achieve a host of political goals.

By all accounts, the management of U.S. reconstruction efforts improved after Iraqi sovereignty was restored and L. Paul Bremer left Iraq. But as with many other aspects of U.S. policy in Iraq, the change came too late. By the time U.S. policy and its administration improved, a combination of security problems, political issues, and corruption had crippled the reconstruction effort. By late 2007, many indicators of Iraqi economic performance and infrastructure capacity remained at, or even fell below, prewar levels.

CHAPTER NINE

INSURGENCY, MILITIAS, AND SECTARIAN VIOLENCE

The first signs of resistance to the U.S. occupation came in two forms simultaneously: the early, scattered assaults of the Sunni insurgency, and the initially more organized actions of the fundamentalist Shiite militias, particularly Moqtada al-Sadr and his Mahdi Army. Both problems appeared in April 2003 in embryonic form, but for the first several months of the occupation, Baghdad and Iraq were fairly safe for American military personnel and other Westerners. Looting and street crime were serious problems, particularly at night, but the victims were Iraqi; criminals and looters did not attack U.S. forces. Nearly everyone I spoke with, even Yaroslav Trofimov and others who tended to view the war and the American presence very critically, agreed that the insurgency was not primarily an immediate, inevitable result of the U.S. presence, but rather a response to specific U.S. actions that alienated the population, particularly Sunnis.

CHARLES FERGUSON: So you think that there was a period of time after the initial conquest of Baghdad, of Iraq, when the Iraqi people were sort of watching and had an open mind.

YAROSLAV TROFIMOV: Absolutely. In the first … three or four weeks after the fall of Baghdad, that was still very, very safe. We could go anywhere. … Virtually nobody among the U.S. military was killed in the first month after the fall of Baghdad. And the reason was precisely the fact that many Iraqis were suspending their judgment; they were giving the Americans the benefit of the doubt, trying to see: Will the electricity come back? Will the water come back? Uh, will the salaries start flowing again? And most importantly, will the Americans show any signs of leaving? Will [they] show any signs of transferring power to the Iraqis?

The early, scattered insurgency was emboldened by the failure of U.S. forces to control looting and to impose order. The continuing chaos allowed insurgents to operate freely. It also signaled to them that U.S. forces would not be able to stop them.

YAROSLAV TROFIMOV: By being un[able] and unwilling to restore order, they [the American military] really showed themselves to be weak. And that encouraged the insurgency because this myth of an omnipotent American army was shattered. [The] myth that was so carefully nurtured in the first Gulf War was destroyed in the second.

GEORGE PACKER: It [the military's allowing the looting] told the budding insurgents that we could be attacked. It meant that we did not show a strong hand; we seemed weak; we seemed uncertain.

When U.S. troops did respond, their actions were often mistaken or overly aggressive. Several interviewees linked the early insurgency to errors made by the military, particularly the killing of civilians during political demonstrations. Trofimov and others cited one particular incident that occurred in Fallujah, a predominantly Sunni city in the Iraqi province of Al Anbar, roughly fifty miles west of Baghdad. On April 28, 2003, U.S. troops fired on a demonstration there, killing approximately a dozen people.

YAROSLAV TROFIMOV: The troops there responded. And they responded as if the war was still going on. So they responded with the big fifty-caliber machine guns. And they killed many of these teenagers, more than ten on that day. And they killed people in the houses in front of the school because big … bullets, they go right through the mud walls of the houses. … And I saw bullet holes going through the fridge in the back of the house, in the kitchen, piercing through several walls inside the house.

And that really turned people against the U.S. there. Uh, you should remember that in Iraq, especially in the Sunni parts of Iraq, the culture is still very tribal. The notion of blood feud is very strong. And so, if somebody is killed, his entire extended family has an obligation to avenge that. And so they did. And Fallujah became the very first place where the insurgency started against the United States. This was the very first place where just two weeks later, they started putting improvised roadside bombs and firing rocket-propelled grenades, against the American patrols there.

The Sunni insurgency gathered force after L. Paul Bremer's crucial May 2003 decisions, which provoked Iraqi resistance while simultaneously crippling the occupation's ability to control it. These U.S. policy decisions also dramatically increased Iraq's unemployment rate, leaving an additional several million people, perhaps 10 percent of the total population, without income. Most of the people I spoke with felt that these decisions, particularly the disbanding of the military, were the driving force behind both the Sunni insurgency and the growth of the Shiite militias.

When General Paul Eaton arrived in Iraq in mid-June 2003, he still felt that Baghdad was safe. But within a few weeks of his arrival, the security situation had deteriorated palpably.

CHARLES FERGUSON: When did you begin to realize that there was a significant insurgency in Iraq?

PAUL EATON: It was a building event. Uh, the first day that I was in Baghdad, I was able to drive outside of the Green Zone without body armor, and without apparent weapons, no bodyguards. And we did not have a two-vehicle [rule] at that time. And that was the 14th of June. Uh, we got a lot of upbeat interaction with the Iraqis—every once in a while, some hard stares, but by and large, a very positive reaction on the part of the Iraqis. Uh, the insurgency, the security situation started to deteriorate, really, in a couple of weeks. And what you've got—

CHARLES FERGUSON: A couple of weeks?

PAUL EATON: A couple of weeks. The odd assault of an American soldier ... the first incident that I remember is a civil affairs soldier in line to buy a CD. And an Iraqi guy comes up and, uh, and shoots him in the back of the head, execution style. And that was the first casualty of an American soldier that I recall, postconflict, while I'm there, in an apparent peaceful environment. He's buying a CD from a sidewalk stand and gets a bullet in the back of the head.

So immediately, you go into ratcheting-up the security concerns, the security steps: Impose the two-vehicle rule; that you are always armed; that you are wearing your body armor; that you are now in an environment that is not necessarily safe …

… We kept seeing an increase in the number of incidents on the road of small-arms attacks. And after a couple of months, we started seeing a more aggressive use of what would become the real killer, and that's the improvised explosive devices, the so-called IEDs. It was a while before we started seeing the vehicular-borne improvised explosive devices.

Nearly everyone I interviewed agreed that the Pentagon and the U.S. military initially discounted the possibility of a serious insurgency. Rather than using counterinsurgency tactics, which emphasize protecting the civilian population, the military's primary response was to launch missions to hunt for insurgents through raids, searches, arrests, and detentions. Since the military's intelligence was poor, these measures were ineffective and frequently targeted innocent people. The military also used mass detentions as a substitute for precise knowledge. Moreover, troop levels were insufficient to ensure the safety of the Iraqi population. As a result, many Iraqis were not convinced that cooperating with the United States was safer than doing nothing or cooperating with the insurgency.

GEORGE PACKER: Well, the military, having gone in with too few troops, having misconceived the mission, which was not simply to take out the regime, but to take control over the country, to impose security on the country, to create conditions where positive change could occur … the military didn't understand that these roadside bombs, these RPG [rocket-propelled grenade] attacks, these constant small-arms fire that the troops were continuing to receive, even after the fall of the regime, were not just the deeds of a few dead-enders, as Donald Rumsfeld called them, but were essentially the start of a new war, which was a continuation of the war. And it was going to be a much more difficult war to fight. It was gonna be an insurgency, which America has never been, um, very skilled at fighting, and which no power has ever had an easy time defeating. In fact, it's extremely difficult to defeat an insurgency. It took months and months—you might even say it took almost two years—for the U.S. military to acknowledge that this was a full-blown, serious insurgency. A guy I know who's a retired special forces officer went to Iraq in January of 2004, and he was there as one of General Abizaid's aides, kind of consultants. And he was just going to see how things were; he's a counterinsurgency expert. He was at the palace where the CPA is headquartered. And he was talking to an army colonel, whose desk was right outside Bremer's office. And he said he used the word "insurgency." And the army colonel held up his hand and said, "There is no insurgency in Iraq; there is a high level of domestic violence," which clearly was just the party line. Rumsfeld himself had said, "The reason I don't use the word 'guerrilla' war is because there is none."

So there was almost this willful blindness that was a continuation of the blindness going into Iraq about the seriousness of the forces that were starting to undermine the American project. And so we never got serious about counterinsurgency. We never ... for almost two years, uh, maybe a year and a half, seriously tried to train Iraqi security forces that would be capable of defeating this insurgency.

Barry Posen is a professor of political science at MIT, where he specializes in defense policy and is director of the MIT Security Studies Program.

BARRY POSEN: And it didn't take very long to see that there was some kind of organized insurgency in the country, right? Journalists saw it; officers on the ground saw it; people in the intelligence business saw it. But you weren't really allowed to say it, right? And Rumsfeld wouldn't let people use the word.

So there's three or four months of—maybe more—of essentially self-delusion about what was happening in the country, right, which allowed the insurgency to get, I think, a little bit ahead of us. And then, once we began to understand that there was some kind of violent opposition, we categorized the opposition in our own way, and approached it with techniques that were comfortable. Which is to say, we ran conventional ops—conventional operations—in the country to try and hunt down and run down people who we thought were bad guys. And of course, this is the phase of the war where you have a lot of the most disturbing films of Americans searching houses, of mistakes made in terms of crowd control, all this kind of thing, um, which, again, helped the insurgency make its case to its constituency that the Americans were occupiers, not liberators.

So there's a kind of a self-induced fog that happens for the first several months of the insurgency—a mental fog that I think allows the insurgency to get away from us. And the fact that we ... that Rumsfeld and company had so limited the troop size in the hopes of, I guess, of trying to demonstrate some new form of war left us with too few assets in country to be able to do what in the first instance, you know, people who study counterinsurgency will tell you to try and do, which is at least try and put a wet blanket on the thing. Even if your intelligence is bad, even if you don't quite understand what the insurgency is about, even if people hate you, right. If you don't know much, at least try and get enough force into the place so that the key areas have a lot of guards and a lot of eyes so that the insurgents just can't have much freedom of action. That's ... the minimum you're trying to achieve. And that the people who live in those areas feel like if they don't want to join the insurgency, they don't have to, right, that they'll in some sense be protected. So we weren't even really in a position to do that.

Nobody in the administration asked the intelligence community to conduct any estimates of the insurgency in 2003 or 2004. Consequently, the National Intelligence Council decided to start conducting them itself and to send the numbers to senior policymakers.

CHARLES FERGUSON: Let's take the immediate postwar period, the spring–summer of 2003. Why don't you tell us what you were involved with with regard to Iraq during that period?

ROBERT HUTCHINGS: Well, we were chronicling what was a deepening insurgency. I can't remember when the I-word was first used, but I know when George Tenet [then director of the CIA] introduced it, it caused some consternation on the policy side. He used a term that had been surfacing in our own analyses—ours at the National Intelligence Council and others around the intelligence community—but to first call it an insurgency was kind of an unwelcome bit of news on the policy side.

CHARLES FERGUSON: Okay. So you were looking at the insurgency.

ROBERT HUTCHINGS: Right.

CHARLES FERGUSON: What did you conclude?

ROBERT HUTCHINGS: That it was deepening, it was broadening, and it was not limited to foreign fighters or disaffected Baathists, that it was a much broader-based phenomenon. And these things all … sort of crystallized in a national estimate we did in the early fall of '03, which talked about the spreading insurgency and spoke about the underlying causative factors that were allowing this insurgency to grow. There was a kind of tendency on the military side, understandably, to look for enemies that could be shot at or apprehended … There was a kind of a tendency to look for former Baathist officials, or foreign fighters, so that they could target those who were deepening the insurgency. And it was a kind of a disinclination to pay as much attention to what we thought was a more profound phenomenon: a broadening social discontent as the economic situation was deteriorating, as people's personal security was becoming weaker, and as resentment of the American occupation was growing.

These foundational aspects were what we were more focused on. It's not that the policy side disregarded them entirely, as that they didn't give them the same weight that we would have … I think they were more convinced that it was foreign fighters and diehards within the old Baathist regime who were trying to recapture power. So they, in some ways, drew precisely the opposite conclusion … The deeper the insurgency, the more convinced they were that they had to route out the remnants of the old Baathist regime.

CHARLES FERGUSON: But if I recall correctly, there was no evidence to support those beliefs.

ROBERT HUTCHINGS: Oh … I imagine they could have found some evidence for those beliefs. It's a matter of interpretation of a lot of events. There certainly were disaffected Baathists who were eager to regain power. That's unassailable. It's a question of the weight you give to these things, and we had an interpretation and an analysis that gave greater weight to the damage we were doing by not allowing Baathists to return to political life and to facilitate a quicker handover of authority to Iraqis.

Even after Bremer disbanded the army and the insurgency began, former army officers affiliated with the insurgency contacted the United Nations and offered to negotiate with the Americans. Bremer refused.

LARRY DIAMOND: The only other thing that I think needs to be explored that the media has, strangely, largely missed, in part, perhaps, because it's intrinsically so difficult to penetrate, is that there is this fact that beginning around the fall of 2003, elements of the Iraqi insurgency, through international intermediaries, sent signals to the United States that they wanted direct talks; they wanted to negotiate in the presence of international mediators, particularly the United Nations. These entreaties, or feelers, went largely unanswered for a long period of time. And I think in the process, again, we missed an opportunity to at least explore what might have been done through political means to wind down this insurgency, and to give significant elements of an aggrieved Sunni Arab population an incentive to suspend violent struggle and play the peaceful political game.

Against the advice of some of his senior staff, the UN special envoy, Sergio Vieira de Mello, decided to support Bremer's proposal of July 2003 to create the largely powerless figurehead body, the Iraqi Governing Council. Vieira de Mello traveled around Iraq and the region, trying to persuade important Iraqis, including potential members of the insurgency, to support the proposal. Other UN diplomats warned Vieira de Mello that he risked becoming an ally of the American occupation in the minds of insurgents. But Vieira de Mello felt that he needed to support Bremer if he was to have any hope of influencing Bremer's decisions in other matters. It was a dangerous gamble: That summer and fall of 2003, the insurgency was growing more and more deadly.

    Jamal Benomar is a senior UN diplomat who speaks fluent Arabic as well as English. He was Vieira de Mello's senior political adviser in Baghdad. I interviewed him in New York in early 2006.

JAMAL BENOMAR: So it was part of our job, you know, to make sure that we develop this broad contact with all representatives of Iraqi society.

CHARLES FERGUSON: Uh-huh. And when you started speaking with members of the insurgency—and when the insurgency started to appear with increasing force—what did you find? Who were they? What did they want? How did they think?

JAMAL BENOMAR: Well, definitely, we spoke with many people who supported the insurgency. We spoke with many people who claim that they are associated with the insurgency, and others. And what was very clear is that, you know, the insurgency was in the making at that time. And we were becoming convinced that it's going to be a very tough and long struggle. And it was not going to go away, you know, within weeks or months.

You know, we started to see various signs of organizing, fund-raising, training. And what we saw is the development of a broad movement that is not structured in the traditional, hierarchical way. What we started to see signs of were various groups spontaneously emerging in various parts of the country, not operating completely independently from the other, but you know, they are joined by networks that rely on kinship and tribal connections. And the one thing that was common to all these groups is the presence of Baathists and very senior military officers. And that trend evolved. And the violence increased. And the statistics can show all this. It started very slowly in June, July 2003, but by the fall, this had become already a full-fledged insurgency in various parts of the country.

CHARLES FERGUSON: And did you speak with the Americans about this?

JAMAL BENOMAR: Sure. Our discussions covered the security situation in the country. And we were very concerned that the security situation was worsening. And in fact ... the turning point [that] had taken place is when the UN compound itself was bombed, and you know, we lost many colleagues in that bombing. And I think it was, you know, the sign that something dramatic had happened in the country: The insurgency had become very lethal, full-fledged, and ready for a long struggle and long fight with the coalition forces.

Vieira de Mello had tried to preserve a balance between his need for access to Bremer and his need to appear independent and open to opposing views from Iraqi society. One measure he took was to decline U.S. offers to provide military forces to guard the UN compound. The UN's own security, however, was extremely poor, with the result that the UN compound was left essentially unprotected. Senior UN personnel complained to Kofi Annan about this in 2003, but nothing was done. On August 19, 2003, Vieira de Mello's attempt to show openness and independence proved fatal.

SAMANTHA POWER: One of the things that Sergio did that is very, very poignant in retrospect is that, seeing that the United States had boarded itself up in the Green Zone and was not accessing the Iraqi street, seeing that it was taking instructions from the Pentagon, but not actually being solicitous of Iraqi opinion, Sergio created a structure in Iraq that was precisely the opposite of the Green Zone. You might call it the anti–Green Zone. And he made UN headquarters the hub of Iraqi complaint. There would be long lines of people outside the Green Zone, but they couldn't get in in order to register their complaints about missing family members or about, you know, tanks that had bulldozed through their homes, or about low-flying helicopters, or about the demobilization of the army, de-Baathification complaints. You'd have these long, long lines right outside the Green Zone, but they could not make their complaints felt. In the UN compound, by contrast, it was incredibly porous. If you wanted to complain, the UN was very, very eager to hear your complaint. And Sergio saw it as his role to relay those complaints to Bremer at the highest levels in the hopes that some of these things would get tended to before an insurgency took root.

And unfortunately, that very accessibility—the fact that, you know, Iraqi generals who had been disbanded and weren't being paid, people whose family members were in detention and who were complaining about torture and so on—the very ease with which they were able to access UN officials within the UN compound, that ease made it also very, very easy for a suicide bomber to access Sergio and the compound itself.

And on August 19th, 2003, in what is now known as the UN's 9/11, a large Russian-made truck pulled right outside Sergio Vieira de Mello's window and set off just a huge amount of explosives. The entire southwestern corner of the UN building collapsed; twenty-three people were killed. Sergio was under the rubble and alive for more than three hours awaiting rescue. But of course ... even though the United States had predicated its war in Iraq on a link between Saddam Hussein and terrorism, no prewar planning had been done for a terrorist attack on a civilian target. None. So there was no search-and-rescue capacity whatsoever in the U.S. military. Everything was made up on the fly on the day of the attack itself. It was the first attack of any consequence on a soft target. And so Sergio and others paid the price—in Sergio's case, with his life—for the shoddy or nonexistent American planning. And with that attack, the UN presence in Iraq was scaled way down. Other civilian institutions that might have been tempted to come in and try to mitigate the effect of the occupation … mitigate some of the suffering in Iraq … they began to think about packing their bags.

The UN headquarters in Baghdad after the bombing of August 19, 2003.

As the insurgency grew, suicide bombers targeted other civilian and NGO (nongovernmental organization) targets, driving most nonmilitary foreigners out of Iraq by the end of 2003. Journalist Mark Danner witnessed this shift.

CHARLES FERGUSON: When did you first go to Iraq?

MARK DANNER: I first went to Iraq in October 2003.

CHARLES FERGUSON: And what did you see?

MARK DANNER: [*sighs*] When I first went to Iraq in the fall of 2003, you could still travel fairly freely in the streets. Uh, you could get out of your car, and go into a shop and buy a book. You [could] talk to people on the streets. You could still—although many reporters at that time didn't—but you could still go into a restaurant, have lunch, talk to people. Um, you might have been a bit nervous—look at the door all the time; make sure no one is coming in who might be inclined to shoot you or kidnap you—but you could still actually be out in the world.

And looking back on it now, from the present conditions in Iraq, where reporters absolutely cannot do that, and where Westerners—or foreigners, put it that way—absolutely cannot do that, because they risk being killed or being kidnapped, and they also put at risk any Iraqi associates who might be seen to be talking to foreigners ... And looking on that moment now [it seems like a] kind of paradise because you could actually get out, talk to people, and feel some degree of confidence that you ... might have a sense of what was going on in the Iraqi street.

At the time, in the fall of 2003, the insurgency was getting under way and had reached a point where it was undeniable that this was a movement, an actual organized insurgency. The Americans were still essentially rejecting this. ... In fact, I was driving one morning to interview ... an American intelligence officer in Iraq, and going down a main street when suddenly, the car lurched up in the air. I didn't hear this enormous explosion, but I heard the aftermath, which is often the case when a very big explosion happens near you: You don't actually hear it. The first thing I heard was the tinkling of the windows in their sashes along this street. And then [there was] an enormous eruption of oily black smoke about a block away. And my driver, at my urging, rushed over to this. We're about the first person on the scene of this horrific scene, where [there were] enormous, uh, sort of pillars of flames and the bodies strewn on the street. People running everywhere; sand and glass everywhere. It turned out that this explosion had knocked down a wall of sandbags. And it killed twelve people, at what, I found out later, was the Red Cross [Iraqi Red Crescent] compound. And this was a day on which there were four successive suicide bombings within forty-five minutes. And it was the beginning of Ramadan. This is now known as the Ramadan

Offensive, but it was really the announcement of the insurgency as an organized, tightly controlled—at least in some of its aspects—movement.

The day before, the insurgents had succeeded in a rocket attack against the Rasheed Hotel, in which they had come within a room of hitting then-deputy secretary of defense, Paul Wolfowitz. They killed a lieutenant colonel in the room beneath him. And this was an extraordinary thing, because the Rasheed is in the middle of the Green Zone and the rockets had been launched from fifty yards in front of an American checkpoint. It was an extraordinarily audacious attack. But it was, in a sense, the announcement that the insurgency had arrived in a big way.

Ghaith Abdul-Ahad is an Iraqi journalist. Now working for the *Guardian* newspaper in England, he has also been published in the *Washington Post* and other newspapers. Abdul-Ahad studied architecture in Iraq, but went underground when he was called up for military service upon graduation. He lived covertly in Iraq for five years, despite many attempts to leave. During the 2003 war, he was arrested for taking photographs in Baghdad while also in possession of a shortwave radio, and he escaped execution only by bribing his interrogator. Since 2003, he has worked as a photographer and journalist covering the Iraq war and occupation. He now lives in Beirut, but continues to work in Iraq. When I interviewed him in New York in late 2007, Abdul-Ahad told me that he thought that some level of scattered resistance would inevitably have occurred in Iraq, no matter how the Americans had behaved. But, also he said, the rise of large-scale, organized resistance was largely a product of Bremer's decisions and the Americans' mistakes.

GHAITH ABDUL-AHAD: The first insurgent I met was in, I think, August, September, 2003, north of Baghdad, in a place called Hawija. And he was fighting out of pride, out of nationalism. Then I met lots of insurgents, 2004, 2005, 2006. I remember one of them, who lived north of Baghdad … was telling me he was an officer in the Iraqi Army. And then Baghdad fell, and he was just like someone hit on his head and running around … I don't know, with no map in his hand. He doesn't know what to do; he's just lost. He told me—he was crying—he couldn't go back to his home, because he couldn't face his wife. And he has been so defeated. The Americans are in Baghdad, so he can't go to his wife. So he roamed the streets until he found a group of Syrians and Arab Mujahadeens, who were still fighting. He went with them. They hit a Humvee with an [RPG] or something … but he took back the fighters with him to his house, and he gave them shelter. By that time, he cannot sort of regain his honor, regain his—

CHARLES FERGUSON: This is when?

GHAITH ABDUL-AHAD: You know, May 2003.

CHARLES FERGUSON: Before or after the army was disbanded?

GHAITH ABDUL-AHAD: Oh, before the army was disbanded. Before the army was disbanded. And I've heard a lot of these stories in different forms. So I think the first [night] of the insurgency was this natural reaction towards occupation—very nationalistic, dominated by Sunnis, maybe because they were in the army … but also lots of Shia who were fighting. That was the first reaction. The Arabs were a lot [of] the Mujahadeen. And then, after an initial period of—

CHARLES FERGUSON: When you say "Arabs," you mean non-Iraqi Arabs?

GHAITH ABDUL-AHAD: I mean non-Iraqi Arabs. I mean Syrians, Jordanians, Saudis. The initial insurgency—based on small cells of resistance dominated by nationalists, but with … some Islamic ideology attached to it— prevailed up until late 2003 [to] early 2004, when the Americans started counterinsurgency. And then [the insurgents] realized that this one was not working, and they needed help, they needed support, they needed bigger organizations, they needed money, they needed weapons. And then the small cells start melting into bigger organizations. Then Islam became the most dominant ideology, because Islam was a very good way to get funds from … al Qaeda. … And suddenly, lots of people who did not approve or accept al Qaeda's ideology or methods or everything had to work with them because they had the organization; they already had the structure. … I think in every insurgency and every militia organization, the structure is the most important thing. Weapons can come and go; training can come and go. It's the structure, and how do you build that structure. It took the Iraqis two years to build that structure, and al Qaeda already had that structure, you know, built in.

CHARLES FERGUSON: So the current structure of the Iraqi insurgency is—

GHAITH ABDUL-AHAD: ... Now it's totally different. I think if we speak about ... based on my interviews—and I'm talking now about ... definitely dozens of insurgents I've met: al Qaeda, Islamic Army, Mujahadeen, Shia insurgents, Shia nationalists in the south of Iraq—in all my interviews, I think the insurgency went through this initial reaction against an occupation, mainly by army officers, soldiers, villagers, young men, old men; people had a reaction against an occupation. Then it went into organizations, into cells, smaller cells. The smaller cells became a bigger organization.

The Rise of the Shiite Militias

The two largest and most powerful Shiite militias to emerge after the war were the Badr Brigade, which was trained by the Iranian Revolutionary Guards, and the Mahdi Army, which was created and controlled by the populist, anti-American cleric Moqtada al-Sadr. These militias fought against Sunni groups, sometimes against U.S. forces, and increasingly against each other, particularly for control of oil-rich Southern Iraq. In 2007, a large splinter group from the Mahdi Army formed a political party with a third militia, the Islamic Virtue Party, which now controls Basra, the Shiite southern city around which is found much of Iraq's oil.

PAUL EATON: Why do militias exist? And why do we have a neighborhood watch here? We have a neighborhood watch because we've got a threat to the neighborhood, and so citizens band together to provide for security. Eventually, we call them police forces and armies. And we've looked at the fractured nature of Iraqi society, and the fact that you got a Sunni-dominated army that imposed Saddam's will on Kurds and on Shia. So, like a neighborhood watch, you develop your own protection force; you develop your *peshmerga*; you develop your Mahdi armies; you develop the militias to provide your guys a sense of security. Which is exactly what the *pesh* did, up in the north.

CHARLES FERGUSON: That's not quite what the Mahdi Army is, though—

PAUL EATON: Well, the Mahdi Army's a little bit different, but still, it's men banding together to support, in this case, a cleric—

CHARLES FERGUSON: Well, I'm sure you know that a lot of the Shiite militias, of which there are now a considerable number, now operate with a kind of de facto approval of the Shia-controlled Interior Ministry, and have been associated with death squads, executions, a lot of, you know, very unpleasant behavior. Did you see that when you were there? Did you see the growth of that? Did it concern you?

PAUL EATON: I was aware that ... it was a fact. When I got there, the militias were in existence, and we had a substantial [DDR] program to bring them down in number. But at the same time, we hadn't solved the security drama. So I saw no ... potential for success of eliminating militias until we were able to provide a national and local security program.

Radical Shiite Muslim cleric Moqtada al-Sadr, 2003.

From the very first, American policy toward the Shiite militias was ambivalent and unsteady; it alternated between attempts at suppression and attempts at co-optation or negotiation. On April 10, 2003, for example, a mob of Moqtada al-Sadr's militia, the Mahdi Army, assassinated an important pro-Western Shiite cleric, Sayyid Abdul Majid al-Khoei, by stabbing and hacking him to death in the city of Najaf. An Iraqi judge issued an arrest warrant charging al-Sadr and eight of his men with murder, but the Americans had the warrant sealed and it was never executed. Then in 2004, the Americans tried to arrest Moqtada al-Sadr, only to back off again after

Bearing a poster of Moqtada al-Sadr, Iraqis attend Friday prayers
in Baghdad, December 2, 2005.

encountering both military and political resistance. This pattern continued for years
as al-Sadr, his political movement, and his militia continued to gain power.

By 2004, the Mahdi Army controlled Sadr City, the huge Shiite slum in Baghdad.
Nobody could enter Sadr City without gaining permission and passing through
Mahdi Army checkpoints. As Sunnis were forced out of other parts of the city, the
Mahdi Army came to control more and more of it, as well as portions of Southern
Iraq. Militias enforced their own rules, performing police and social functions while
also eliminating Sunnis and rival militias from neighborhoods they controlled. Fre-
quently, they also abused their power for personal gain, seizing houses and prop-
erty from those they forced out. They also enforced fundamentalist Islamism, often
violently, for example by burning down liquor stores, kidnapping or killing secular
Iraqis, and assaulting women in Western dress.

When Seth Moulton returned to Iraq for his second tour of duty in mid-2004, he
and his platoon were sent to the Shiite holy city of Najaf in Southern Iraq, where
they found that the Mahdi Army had taken over the entire center of the city.

SETH MOULTON: I think a lot of Iraqis in Najaf—a lot of whom were not
supportive of the militia, really, because ... they were really ruining their

lives—were going to their militia buddies and saying, you know, "You guys better watch out, 'cause the marines are in town now and you're not gonna be around much longer."

Unfortunately, it wasn't that simple. The militia was far more powerful than the marines had expected. Also, combat occurred in the middle of the city, endangering civilians and Muslim holy sites.

SETH MOULTON: For several nights, we would get stood up in the middle of the night because there were threats that the Iraqi police station downtown was being taken over. And so we would essentially get a platoon or two ready to go down and reinforce the police station. And the first couple times it happened, things fizzled out and nothing came of it, and we just went back and went to sleep. And maybe the third or fourth time, I remember, we went down, and we actually staged at the Iraqi Army base. And Lance Corporal Young, who was driving my vehicle, you know, said, "What's goin' on, Sir?" And I said, "Well, quite frankly, it's probably just another one of these … you know, we're gonna get all ready to go out with the Iraqis, and things will calm down, and we'll be home in a couple hours."

Instead, things did not calm down. And a couple hours later, we were in the middle of the worst combat that I'd ever seen in Iraq. … We started driving down towards the police station, and it was really an amazing scene. It was kind of what you would imagine this new-generation warfare is, because you have a tremendous number of civilians all around. You hear all the gunfire up ahead of you, including rockets from some of the Cobra helicopters that had already been called in. Uh, mortars start to land. And all these civilians are just running down the street—of course running away—and we're running, you know, towards this. So there's civilians running by, and you know, telling us, in broken English, or just in Arabic, where the militia are, you know, "Watch out for the roof"—stuff like that. There's this guy with a video camera running alongside me, who, you know, took some footage, I think, that ended up on CNN that evening.

And uh, we went down to the center of the sort of main square in Najaf, where the main police station was. And it was probably about five hundred meters from the famous Imam Ali Shrine, the big mosque, which was essentially the ground zero for the militia occupation of the center of the city. And uh, it was pretty intense. I mean, there [were] a lot of bullets flying, a lot of mortars, a lot of rounds flying, a lot of mortars landing. And my platoon was the first into the police station, which was kind of the center of the attack. And we just took up positions alongside the Iraqi police, and defended it from the militia.

But, you know, it was at that point that I kind of just took a minute, and stopped, and thought, you know, well, I left Iraq in September of 2003, thinking that probably I'd never be back and that things were going so well that by this time, you know, there would be probably few Americans even left in Iraq. And here I was, in the middle of combat that was far worse than anything I had seen during the invasion or during the "war," as we knew it at that point. ...

We had always known about this cemetery, this infamous cemetery in Najaf, which was supposedly a stronghold of the militia. It's the place that we expected to assault with the Iraqi army in the October, November, December time frame, later in the year. And the decision was made at that point that we should just ... you know, we were already in the middle of this, and we should just finish it. And so, as soon as we left the police station, we went back and kind of restaged for all of about ten or fifteen minutes, and then just entered the cemetery. And a platoon of tanks and my platoon, quickly followed by several other platoons in the company, went into the cemetery and essentially just got online and started clearing through there, which was unbelievably difficult. I mean, it was like the worst possible environment that I could imagine as far as, you know, trying to clear. Because these cemeteries are nothing like the cemeteries we know in the States. There are all these tombs that are essentially aboveground and essentially on top of one another. So even just walking through the cemetery is difficult, let alone trying to root out people who are hiding in there and shooting at you. And we did that for the next couple days. And you know, I think by that time, the Americans realized that this was not just a one-battalion operation to get the militia out of Najaf. And so they had to call some other battalions in, and they had to rethink things. So after about three days, we actually pulled out of the cemetery and would spend the next month or so going back in there and repeatedly advancing and attacking the militia. But it wasn't until the end of August that we actually did a full-scale assault on the Old City of Najaf and took it over. So it was really a month. Basically, the entire month of August was just fighting in Najaf.

Moulton felt that the Mahdi Army had primarily negative effects on the population, and that most of Najaf's citizens were grateful to the marines for removing them.

SETH MOULTON: Because the militia was making life difficult for everyone, not just for the Americans; security improved dramatically once the militia was gone. And then—

CHARLES FERGUSON: Say more about that. How was the militia making life difficult for everybody?

SETH MOULTON: Well, the militia controlled the center of the city, and so obviously, you know, coalition forces weren't allowed in there. But there were also a lot of restrictions on the movement and activities of just everyday Iraqis. I know for awhile, you had to have a militia ID card just to enter the center of the city. And so a lot of the citizens in Najaf weren't able to go to the mosque, and weren't able to go to their businesses and just live life as they always had. So I mean, there's no place in Iraq where the insurgent activity makes security better, nowhere at all. And so the average Najafi citizen was really happy to see the militia gone.

The benefit provided by the marines' assault, however, was temporary. Combat was ordered to halt as a result of one of the many reversals of U.S. policy toward the Mahdi Army's leader, Moqtada al-Sadr, who was allowed to escape.

CHARLES FERGUSON: And do you think that you dealt Moqtada al-Sadr's forces a significant military setback or not?

SETH MOULTON: Well, we definitely dealt them a significantly military setback. But I think that a lot of us feel that the way it ended—with essentially a truce—was ... uh, you know, it was difficult. So we certainly dealt them a significant military setback, in that we, you know, killed a lot of them, and certainly ruined their confidence, and unquestionably kicked them out of Najaf. So from that sense, it was very successful. But I think that [there was] a lot of question as to whether we should have just completely finished the job, right up to the steps of the mosque, versus stopping about halfway through the Old City.

When asked about the failure to neutralize Moqtada al-Sadr, Richard Armitage replied that insufficient troop levels were primarily responsible, but that the decision to stop combat had probably come from the civilian Pentagon leadership. Others have said, however, that the State Department also oscillated in its views and, in order to obtain a negotiated settlement with Moqtada al-Sadr, sometimes pressed for an end to the 2004 assault.

CHARLES FERGUSON: Were you part of the deliberations about whether to capture or kill Moqtada al-Sadr?

RICHARD ARMITAGE: Yes, I was.

CHARLES FERGUSON: And what did you feel about that? And why was the decision taken—

RICHARD ARMITAGE: Well, as Jerry [Bremer] … I think I must have indicated, he wanted to do this. He saw Moqtada al-Sadr and the Mahdi militia as a real problem early on. … It gets back, in my view, to the matter of troop strength—that the U.S. military didn't want to be diverted from their major mission to go after what would have been a probably short-term but difficult and, I'm sure, bloody battle. And ultimately, that's what won out. We had supported Jerry, as I think he indicates.

CHARLES FERGUSON: Okay. So you think it was a mistake not to eliminate Moqtada—

RICHARD ARMITAGE: Well, you use terms that I don't use, such as "eliminate," which would indicate to me that you had to kill him.

CHARLES FERGUSON: Right.

RICHARD ARMITAGE: I think we wanted to … take care and disband the Mahdi Army, which we'd need to capture or, if they fought, perhaps to kill.

But the term "eliminate" is not one you use in government with any ... I mean it's not precise to say what you want to do.

CHARLES FERGUSON: Okay.

RICHARD ARMITAGE: Did we want to disband the Mahdi Army? You bet. Just like Jerry Bremer wanted to. We [saw] Moqtada al-Sadr as a trouble-maker and a thorn in the side, absolutely. And we wanted to arrest him.

CHARLES FERGUSON: I see. And it was the military who said no.

RICHARD ARMITAGE: Well, the military and the Department of Defense. I don't—

CHARLES FERGUSON: Ah.

RICHARD ARMITAGE: I mean ... on the ground they're not gonna turn around and tell Jerry, "No, no, hell no," but—

CHARLES FERGUSON: Right. So this was a decision made by Secretary Rumsfeld.

RICHARD ARMITAGE: Well, I don't know that it was, but I suspect it was.

By mid-2004, the Shiite militias numbered in total perhaps a hundred thousand armed men. After the United States returned sovereignty to Iraq in late June 2004, their strength only grew.

The growth of the militias was closely intertwined with mosques, charities, and political parties. The Badr Brigade was affiliated with the largest and most powerful Shia party, the Supreme Council for the Islamic Revolution in Iraq (SCIRI).* Moqtada al-Sadr, leader of the Mahdi Army, inherited a vast network of mosques and Islamic charities from his father, a famous Shiite cleric who was assassinated by Saddam Hussein.

NIR ROSEN: Very quickly, the mosque came in and filled in the vacuum that the Americans created by getting rid of Saddam and leaving nothing in its place. This was apparent to me as soon as I got there. Shia clerics, in partic-

---

*In May 2007, SCIRI changed its name to SIIC, the Supreme Islamic Iraqi Council.

ular, just took over as much of Baghdad as they could, providing social services, providing security, preventing looting from going on. Looting was still going on. Looting went on for a few weeks, of course, but in Shia neighborhoods, they very quickly established control, in particular the clerics associated with Moqtada al-Sadr, who took advantage of his father's network of clerics and mosques throughout the country. They distributed aid, water, oil, food; provided security; and established an Islamic order.

And in areas where they weren't in control, perhaps Sunni clerics were in control or criminals were in control. But very quickly, the vacuum the Americans created was filled by Iraqis, whether criminals, tribal leaders, or religious leaders.

Like SCIRI itself, SCIRI's militia, the Badr Brigade, was created in Iran. It was trained by the Iranian Revolutionary Guards, and despite—or because of—its strong Iranian connections, it is somewhat less radical, less nationalist, and less anti-American than the Mahdi Army. Nonetheless, by 2005, SCIRI controlled the Interior Ministry, and the Badr Brigade had infiltrated the Iraqi police, which was increasingly linked to death squads, kidnappings, and sectarian killings of Sunnis. In 2006, the Badr Brigade renamed itself the Badr Organization in an attempt to portray itself as a peaceful enterprise.

In 2006, I interviewed the head of the Badr Organization, Hadi al-Amiri, in Baghdad. He had only occupied the position a short time—his predecessor had recently been assassinated—yet he exuded arrogance and brutality. His minions were clearly afraid of him.

As was typical of Baghdad meetings, my crew, my personal bodyguard, and I were asked to surrender our weapons before the interview began. We were also asked to surrender our mobile telephones, likewise a typical request, because they could be used to signal an attack or to detonate a bomb remotely. We noticed that the others present had removed their shoes, and did so ourselves. When al-Amiri entered the room, he noticed that we had taken our shoes off, even though two of us were Westerners. He grew furious at the guard, who was clearly terrified. When our translator watched the footage we had taken during this incident, he commented in the margin: "This reminds me of the Saddam time."

HADI AL-AMIRI [*to guard*]: Why you made them take their shoes off?

HADI AL-AMIRI [*to camera crew*]: Wear your shoes. Wear your shoes … No, no, wear your shoes. That's fine; I am wearing mine.

HADI AL-AMIRI [*to guard*]: Did you tell them it's not allowed to take off their shoes anymore? Tell me who did it! What's your name? I have told you a hundred times, no one is allowed to take his shoes off! I have told you this a hundred times! Go and call the guards for me now.

CAMERA CREW: No one told us to take off our shoes. But we saw the gentleman here took off his shoes, and we did the same.

When al-Amiri turned his attention to us, he embarked on a rote lecture on the peacefulness and success of his organization. He spoke in Arabic through our interpreter; this is our later, exact translation.

HADI AL-AMIRI: We are proud that when it was necessary to carry weapons, we carried weapons. And we are proud that when Saddam's regime collapsed in April 9, 2003, we let down weapons with our full will without any exterior power asking us to do so. Now we are a political organization and we have a wide public representation. We have participated in last year's provincial elections. And now more than six or seven provinces are controlled mainly by us. And six of these provinces, the governor is from us, including Baghdad. Anyhow, in the current parliamentary election, we have participated. We have more than fifteen members from the Badr Organization in the current new parliament. And we believe in democracy, multiplicity, and the peaceful transfer of power through ballot boxes.

Lest we had misconceptions about his organization's peaceful intentions, al-Amiri concluded his opening statement with this:

HADI AL-AMIRI: Despite the rumors against us of being a militia organization, we are proud that we were of those who called for the dissolution of the militias. And we seriously worked with Order 91 [a CPA order that mandated the disarming and dissolution of extralegal militias; like many CPA orders, it was never enforced] for Ambassador Bremer regarding the militias' dissolution.

I asked al-Amiri about the Mahdi Army and how to handle it.

HADI AL-AMIRI: Now when you come to the Sadr movement, it's a reality in the political field. I think if there was a wise dealing with the Sadr movement, there [wouldn't have been] two wars with the Sadr movement. And there are others who are not Americans, who are Iraqis, who are pushing the Americans to finish the Sadr movement. Or they are pushing them to finish a certain party. I remember I told General [Barbara] Fast, who is the head of the American military intelligence during General Sanchez's time—the leader of American forces in Iraq—I told her that you are going to make a mistake if you fight the Sadr movement and that Sadr should be contained instead of being targeted because these are public movements; as far as you pressure it, they get wider and wider. And I told her that Saddam Hussein pressured us for twenty years. And whenever he increased his pressure, we were deeply rooted. I also advised her to open a discussion with the Sadr movement instead of going into a confrontation with them.

And now you see that the Sadr movement is part of the political process. And we must keep containing it in the political process. And even the Mahdi Army, we should deal with it by what's called the law of integrating the militias—and it's possible to contain them—so we can avoid a direct confrontation with them.

Myself, I believe that the armed forces should be the only power that holds weapons. And there should be no weapons at all; only in the hands of the army forces. And my hope is that the security situation would progress for better. And even our personal security guards, we would relinquish it.

CHARLES FERGUSON: Do you think that the Mahdi Army should disarm itself now?

HADI AL-AMIRI: I think—and this is my belief—that there should be security first. And also there should be timing of the strengthening of the security forces and at the same time the process of containment of what's called militias and paramilitaries.

There are two ways to contain the Mahdi Army. First is a battle with the Mahdi Army and removal of Mahdi Army weapons by force, which I think

[is] a wrong way, which will lead to more casualties and more sacrifices, and it will make the Mahdi Army more consistent in keeping its weapons. And the other way is to win them to our political process and make them let down their weapons voluntarily. And we tell them that it's banned to have any armed people in secure areas. I don't think they will disagree.

Interviewing Hadi al-Amiri, head of the Badr Organization, 2006.

Frequently, al-Amiri simply lied.

CHARLES FERGUSON: So do you believe that women should have legal rights in all areas?

HADI AL-AMIRI: In the Shiite community, there is a great development in women's rights. She has the right to be a scholar in religion and even a scientist in religion. And she can do whatever she wants in regarding science. But yes, we have some conservancy on that she should be well covered … but she has the right to be everywhere.

In reality, the rise of the Shiite political parties and their militias was leading to a massive reversal of women's rights in Iraq, partially due to religious fundamentalism and partially due to traditional tribal behavior.

NIR ROSEN: In fact, this was one thing that was quite depressing about Iraq in general, was the abominable treatment that women suffer—not only religious restrictions, but tribal restrictions. Honor killings were quite common—honor killings based on the mere suspicion that your sister had perhaps spoken to another Iraqi male. She had dishonored your family. You had to wash the shame, as the expression goes, by killing her. And especially in poorer Shia neighborhoods, this was quite common. And the men who did this were actually admired and respected, in many places.

CHARLES FERGUSON: I see.

NIR ROSEN: None of my friends, of course.

CHARLES FERGUSON: So you're not optimistic about what the future holds for Iraqi women.

NIR ROSEN: No, quite pessimistic, in fact. Perhaps you could say that things were better for them under Saddam, in a way. Now, with the release of tribal and religious forces, reactionary, conservative—atavistic, in fact—the status of Iraqi women is completely like chattel. They very quickly disappeared from the streets.

The militias used violence often and casually to enforce their dictates. Increasingly, they operated as criminal gangs reminiscent of the Revolutionary Armed Forces of Colombia (FARC) and other organizations that combine revolutionary politics with organized crime. While the FARC depends principally upon the cocaine traffic, militias in Iraq derive their income primarily from smuggling, extortion, political corruption, and large-scale kidnapping. The militias became the enforcers of fundamentalism as Shiite political parties sought to roll back the cultural modernity that had characterized Iraq since the 1960s. Saddam's regime was predominantly secular, women's rights were generally well-protected, and fundamentalist interpretations of Islamic law did not decide disputes. Alcohol, movies, music, and Western clothes were openly available and widely consumed. But as the Shiite militias, and particularly the Mahdi Army, tightened their grip, displays of Western dress, makeup, music, romantic affection, or alcohol became potential capital offenses. While I was in Baghdad in March 2006, my bodyguard and fixer, the Kurdish journalist Warzer Jaff, told me the following story:

WARZER JAFF: [My friend was] telling us, [it] just happens a couple of days ago in … Baghdad. He says he was there, and he saw a guy with his girlfriend—a guy who had, like, a Western haircut, and his girlfriend, she was wearing [pants] or, like, some modern clothes. And two cars full of Mahdi Army guys, they stopped there, and they didn't like the idea—a guy with his girlfriend, you know, walking around. They wanted to give him a hard time, so they start telling the guy, "Why you [look] like that, blah, blah, blah." So the guy [said], "I mean, I didn't do anything." ... They start beating him. So they really [hit him] very hard, he says. And his face became bloody, his body. His girlfriend, she was screaming; she was crying. So they throw him in the trunk of one of the cars. They close the trunk. And the guy starts yelling, ... "Please let me out! I cannot breathe, I cannot breathe." And one of the guys, he just went to the trunk, and he starts beating the trunk. Like, you know, "... Shut up. Shut up, motherfucker." And then they took him. And they left his girlfriend on the street, screaming and crying.

Since the leaders of SCIRI had lived in Iran for the twenty years before Saddam was deposed, and the Badr militia was trained in Iran, I was curious as to how al-Amiri would respond to questions about Iran. He proved quite adroit.

CHARLES FERGUSON: Tell me, should Iran develop nuclear weapons?

HADI AL-AMIRI: They say, "We don't want weapons." That's what they say. What do they really believe? Your answer should be as good as mine. They say, "We want nuclear power for peaceful purposes and under the supervision of international agencies." That is what they say in public. As to what their real intentions are, you might know better. I believe those who have the closest relations to Iran are the Americans. They have an old, extensive, and deep-rooted relationship. In fact, I should be the one asking you about the Iranian question, because you Americans are better experts on Iran than us.

Sometimes, al-Amiri displayed a refreshing truthfulness when it suited his interests. He seemed honestly puzzled and angered that the Americans were proving so inept at securing Iraq, and he was quite direct with his criticism when the affected areas were Shiite or mixed, and therefore of interest to his organization. He was particularly puzzled that the Americans were failing to control Baghdad and the roads between Baghdad and other critical areas.

CHARLES FERGUSON: The supreme council [SCIRI] complains that the Americans are preventing them, and prevent security forces in Iraq, from

pursuing the terrorists, and that they are also protecting some of the terrorists. What do you think about that?

HADI AL-AMIRI: We say that there are some hot areas, and until today, we
don't have a clear sight about these sites. Why these hot areas are not targeted? All agree that car bombs come from areas at the edge of Baghdad,
starting from Tarmiyah and ending in Mada'in. We have discussed the issue with them for about a thousand times so far. We asked them to control
these areas, but they did not until this day.

I don't think it's difficult to control Baghdad. According to my info, the
south provinces are relatively secured. And Kurdistan provinces Duhok,
Erbil, and Sulaimaniyah are secure. Anbar is calm these days, according to
my info. And the real battle is in Baghdad and Diyala. And I don't think
there is difficulty in controlling Baghdad and Diyala if there is a plan and a
real will to bring security. I think if there is a will and a plan, it won't be
difficult to control Baghdad.*

CHARLES FERGUSON: If it's easy to control Baghdad, why do you think the
Americans aren't doing a proper job?

HADI AL-AMIRI: I didn't say it's easy. ... I did not say it's easy, but I said it's
possible to control the security of Baghdad and it's not difficult. I will give
you two examples—

CHARLES FERGUSON: If there is a possibility, why aren't the Americans doing it?

HADI AL-AMIRI: ... Now they are doing what is called "favoring" for the political process. The Americans think that through political balances, they
can bring on security.

---

*Tarmiyah is a rural area in north Baghdad with a predominantly Sunni population, much of it
comprised of former regime intelligence and security forces. Since the fall of Baghdad, many of
its people were assassinated by Shiites, who often accuse the Badr Organization of these assassinations. American attempts to cool the area and eliminate the insurgency in Tarmiyah have
failed so far. As for Anbar Province, we read of Seth Moulton's experience of insurgency there in
Fallujah. Diyala Province, in particular the city of Baqubah, is reported to have come under
Sunni insurgent control in 2006 and 2007.

I will give an example: the road between Baghdad, Latifiyah, Karbala, Najaf, and Hilla; the road from Baghdad to Kut through Mada'in area. This area is now converted into what is called "death triangle." There is no single day passes without the killing of more than twenty to thirty people, in addition to burned cars. And this road has become a hell road. In the middle of the day, terrorist groups come and control the road and kill anyone they want to kill ... and steal what they want ... and leave without any punishment. We explained to them [the Americans] that you can control these roads with only one battalion. And now it's true that only one battalion has controlled the whole area. For more than a year so far, I think no single operation has occurred in the road. And the road to Latifiyah as well, there were few limited terrorist operations. And now the security situation is very good in this road. To bring security, I don't think it's only the military operations can bring it. ... When I say it's possible to control Baghdad, it is possible to control Baghdad ... through comprehensive planning.

Entrenched Insurgency

Between 2003 and 2006, the Sunni insurgency became a major and popular force. In addition to the initially nationalist Sunni insurgents, who were often former army officers, a fundamentalist branch arose. Led by al Qaeda in Mesopotamia, this branch grew to become a major force in Baghdad and the Sunni triangle. The nationalist and fundamentalist groups were increasingly at war with each other as well as with the Americans. Foreign fighters also joined the insurgency. While foreign fighters never accounted for more than 10 percent of insurgents, they constituted a disproportionately high fraction of suicide bombers.

As the insurgency progressed, the Bush administration and the military began issuing estimates of its size, the number of insurgents in detention, and the number of insurgents killed, in a manner eerily reminiscent of the body counts of the Vietnam war.* While there is wide skepticism about these figures and their meaning, even these official and semiofficial statistics indicate a steep, continuous growth of

---

*Please see the back of the book for several tables estimating the size and impact of the insurgency.

the insurgency since mid-2003, despite the large number of alleged insurgents killed, captured, and held in detention. As we will see later, these same statistics suggest that the 2007 troop surge has had a noticeable but limited effect on the general level of violence.

Some feel that the insurgency was and is far larger and more popular than the official figures suggest. Here is what Gerald Burke said about the situation as of late 2005:

GERALD BURKE: Well, I think you have to understand that ... the insurgents really [are] in four categories. And it's hard to say they're insurgents when they're on opposite sides, in fact. The insurgents range from former Baath Party people: people who were in Saddam's government structure, people who were in his secret police organizations, people who were in [his] army, people who had a vested interest in the power base that Saddam had within the government of Iraq. And there could potentially be a couple hundred thousand people in that core portion of the insurgency, especially when you consider the army—

CHARLES FERGUSON: A couple of hundred thousand people?

GERALD BURKE: A couple hundred thousand former Baath Party and government employees, who had a vested interest in the regime staying in power.

CHARLES FERGUSON: And who are participating in the insurgency?

GERALD BURKE: Well, they're no longer part of the government, and most of them are unemployed. They're not participating in the insurgency full time, but they're available to participate in the insurgency if they're given some money to do it. ...

CHARLES FERGUSON: And you think that that many people are, at some level perhaps, very—

GERALD BURKE: They're supportive of—or they're participating in—some of that activity.

CHARLES FERGUSON: A couple of hundred thousand.

GERALD BURKE: Yeah, former soldiers in Saddam's regime, former government employees, former members of the secret police organizations, Saddam's Fedayeen Republican Guard: several hundred thousand people potentially in that core of Saddam's supporters.

CHARLES FERGUSON: Well, potentially or actually?

GERALD BURKE: [*sighs*] I think ... the supporting side, ... actually ... that they will harbor fugitives, that they will supply safe houses for them. And a lot of it is tribal. A lot of 'em will go to members of their tribe, and the tribal members will know that Cousin So-and-so is probably participating in anti-American, anti-new-Iraqi-government activity, and they will harbor him.

CHARLES FERGUSON: I would assume that you're familiar with the U.S. military's official estimates of the size ... of the insurgency.

GERALD BURKE: Yeah.

CHARLES FERGUSON: That it's—

GERALD BURKE: Well, that's only one part of it. That's only one part of the insurgency ... of the anti-Iraqi activity that's going on over there ... is the Baath Party. You also have foreign fighters. You have guys like [terrorist Abu Musab al-] Zarqawi coming in from Jordan, and others coming in from across North Africa and other Arab countries, that are coming in particularly for participating in the car bombings, the suicide car bombings. And there potentially could be a thousand to two thousand of them at any given time, that are in Iraq, you know, scouting out new targets, training for how to set up a car bomb. But the danger there is that it's a pipeline [so] that they can continually replace the people who die in these car bombings and suicide bombings. So that's the second part of the insurgency. You got the Baath Party; you got the foreign fighters.

A third element is former criminals. Just prior to the invasion, Saddam released about a hundred thousand prisoners—common criminals—from the jails. Most of them had no job skills, except how to commit crimes. Many of them [were] probably former soldiers 'cause everybody was in the service at one point, in one of the government military organizations. So, for short money, they would be willing to go out and plant explosives, or to take pot shots, or to fire an RPG, or to launch a mortar at American targets. So there's another hundred thousand criminals that are available to participate in the anti-American activity.

Insurgents in Fallujah.

Several analysts pointed out that Iraq's poverty and extremely high unemployment rate contributed to the problem, simply because the insurgency provided people with an opportunity to make money. Insurgency became a significant source of employment for otherwise unemployable young men.

Sarah Leah Whitson first traveled to Iraq in the aftermath of the first Persian Gulf War to study the effect of the sanctions regime. She is now Middle East director for Human Rights Watch.

SARAH LEAH WHITSON: It's become an employment option. You know, for millions of twenty-, twenty-five-year-old Iraqi men, there are no jobs; there is no place to work. And you can actually get a little bit of money being an insurgent. It might even be less risky than being a police officer in Iraq.

Whitson's comment about the relative risk of being an insurgent and a police officer was not sarcastic. By late 2007, over 7,500 Iraqi soldiers and police officers had been killed since the beginning of the occupation. Being an Iraqi police officer is indeed a very dangerous job.

As the insurgency grew, it targeted not only the U.S. military but also Iraqis—professionals and intellectuals essential to the functioning of the country, wealthy Iraqis supporting the Iraqi government, political leaders, and journalists. The apparent goal of these assassinations was to cripple the functioning of the government, of essential services, and of Shiite institutions. By 2007, for example, the majority of Iraq's doctors had fled the country. The insurgency also formed relationships with criminal gangs and began to engage in criminal actions—robberies, kidnappings, smuggling—as a means to fund itself. Insurgents would also pay criminals for political killings and for kidnapping services. Thus, the insurgency contributed to the general feeling of insecurity and chaos in Iraq as well as to specifically anti-American attacks.

Omar al-Dumlaji, a professor of civil engineering at Baghdad University, became Iraq's interim minister of construction under the American occupation. I interviewed him in Baghdad in March 2006. He had left his normal home and was living in another house for fear of being killed. He no longer went to the university campus, for the same reason.

CHARLES FERGUSON: I was told recently that since the war, almost twenty percent of the professors at Baghdad University have been assassinated. Is that true?

OMAR AL-DUMLAJI: Well, we have been receiving lists of people who were assassinated. And in fact, many of them were personal friends of mine. For example, only a couple of weeks ago, the dean of the college of engineering at [unintelligible] University, which is another university inside of the city of Baghdad, was assassinated. He was in fact abducted. And a ransom was paid for his release. Yet he was killed, instead of being freed alive. And … he was my classmate at college. And … we led a long life together through our mutual profession.

And many people are being killed: not only professors from universities, but the experts at large. I mean, for example—

CHARLES FERGUSON: Why are they being assassinated?

OMAR AL-DUMLAJI: … I think because of the loss of the minimum requirements for security inside of this society, probably some would want to evacuate this society from knowledge and expertise. And by that, we will never have any sort of real development in this country.

CHARLES FERGUSON: Who's killing them?

OMAR AL-DUMLAJI: Who is killing them? Some of them are only ordinary criminals … who would want to ask for money in return for their release. This is part of it. And there is this other part, where it has got a political dimension. There are some of the political groups who are working inside of this society, who think that they are at war with the West in general, and with the United States in particular. And they wouldn't want to see this new experience, this new political experience inside of Iraq to succeed. By doing that—I mean, by assassinating people with knowledge and expertise in general—they would want to make them leave the country, so that there'll never be any sort of real development in this country. How would any government function without having expert people around inside of the society?

Well into 2004 and even 2005, the White House and the Pentagon continued to minimize the significance of the insurgency. For the first year of the insurgency, the administration did not even request any intelligence assessments of the insurgency. However, the National Intelligence Council (NIC) continued to conduct them on its own and sent them to senior administration officials.

ROBERT HUTCHINGS: We were ... analyzing the deepening insurgency as it unfolded during the year [2004]. We waited until the following summer [after the NIC's original intelligence estimate of the fall of 2003] because, you know, that was when we felt that there was a fundamental shift that ... suggested we ought to take a brand new look in a national estimate on where the insurgency was now.

CHARLES FERGUSON: Caused, I would assume, by Fallujah and the al-Sadr uprising?

ROBERT HUTCHINGS: Right.

CHARLES FERGUSON: Okay. So why don't you tell us about that?

ROBERT HUTCHINGS: ... It was basically a new estimate, but it was called a memorandum to holders because it referred back to the 2003 estimate, also looking at the state of the insurgency. And there again, we found a deepening insurgency and signs of incipient civil war. And one of the worries we had ... was that there was a civil war that was buried inside the insurgency and sometimes the manifestations weren't easily distinguishable. So that we felt that if the insurgency somehow miraculously ended tomorrow, that there would still be a civil war. And we were looking at activities in the Kurdish north, where, to my mind, having lived through the disintegration of Yugoslavia, it was reminiscent of the Slovenes in the Yugoslav federation: the Kurds finding ways to establish a de facto separate state, economically, in security terms, in everything but name, while the violence between Shia and Sunni was beginning to become a real worry.

CHARLES FERGUSON: Okay. So that estimate was produced when?

ROBERT HUTCHINGS: That was the beginning of the summer. I can't remember the exact time. Probably June.

CHARLES FERGUSON: All right. And who read it? To whom was it sent, and who read it?

ROBERT HUTCHINGS: I can't say who read it. It was sent to the most senior officials. I think it was fairly widely read. It was sent to the president, vice president, and the National Security Council principals and deputies, and on down the line.

CHARLES FERGUSON: Secretary of defense and state?

ROBERT HUTCHINGS: Sure.

CHARLES FERGUSON: Okay.

ROBERT HUTCHINGS: There was a second sort of companion estimate, which was done later in the summer—August [of 2004]—which was a fresh look at the situation, and not just the security situation, but the situation in Iraq as a whole. And ... this one was one that ... unfortunately, it was ... I think it was published in August. It was leaked to the *New York Times* in September, I believe; it could have been October. But it then became a cause célèbre because it came out in ... the early stages of the presidential election season.

CHARLES FERGUSON: Uh-huh. And what was the response of the high-level administration officials to those two estimates?

ROBERT HUTCHINGS: Well, the second one, the president called it "guesswork." And his press spokesman called it "hand-wringing and nay-saying." What was really revealing to me was the president hadn't read it—not even the one-page summary, over which we worked so hard, to reduce these findings to a single, readable page.

CHARLES FERGUSON: The president had not read even the executive summary?

ROBERT HUTCHINGS: Correct.

By 2005, it had become extremely dangerous for Iraqis to work for Americans, because Iraqis were targeted by insurgents for that reason. Even working for American journalists became dangerous. For fear that he would be killed, my own interpreter in Baghdad, who had been an emergency room doctor, lied even to his parents and immediate family, telling them that he was still practicing medicine. Seth Moulton acknowledged the dangers that cooperative Iraqis faced.

SETH MOULTON: There's an Iraqi contractor I worked pretty closely with in Babil Province, who was killed. ... And he was just stopped on the side of the road and hauled out of his car, and shot. And that's tough 'cause, of course, you know that the reason why he was killed is because he was working with us. And so you develop these pretty close relationships with these people, and everyone knows this can happen, just like marines go over there knowing that they can get killed. But it's still tough. It's still tough.

By 2006, the climate of fear among Iraqis working for the Americans was so intense that it affected even the U.S. embassy and its employees. In June 2006, Ambassador Zalmay Khalilzad sent a secret cable to Condoleezza Rice, detailing the strain. The document was leaked to the *Washington Post* and is reproduced here in full.

```
R 121430Z JUN 06
FM AMEMBASSY BAGHDAD
TO SECSTATE WASHDC 5042
INFO IRAQ COLLECTIVE

UNCLAS   BAGHDAD 001992

E.O. 12958: N/A
TAGS:   PHUM, PREL, ASEC, AMGT, IZ
SUBJECT:  Snapshots from the Office:   Public
Affairs Staff Show Strains of Social Discord

SENSITIVE

1.  (SBU)  Beginning in March, and picking up in Mid-
May, Iraqi staff in the Public Affairs section have
complained that Islamist and/or militia groups have been
negatively affecting their routine. Harassment over
proper dress and habits has been increasingly pervasive.
They also report that power cuts and fuel prices have
diminished their quality of life.  Conditions vary by
neighborhood, but even upscale neighborhoods such as
Mansur have visibly deteriorated.

Women's Rights
--------------

2.  (SBU)  The Public Affairs Press Office has 9 local
Iraqi employees. Two of our three female employees
```

report stepped up harassment beginning in mid-May. One, a Shiite who favors Western clothing, was advised by an unknown woman in her upscale Shirrte/Christian Baghdad neighborhood to wear a veil and not to drive her own car. Indeed, she said, some groups are pushing women to cover even their face, a step not taken in Iran even at its most conservative.

3. (SBU) Another, a Sunni, said that people in her middle-class neighborhood are harassing women and telling them to cover up and stop using cell phones (suspected channel to licentious relationships with men). She said that the taxi driver who brings her to work every day to the green zone checkpoint has told her he cannot let her ride unless she wears a headcover. A female in the PAS cultural section is now wearing a full abaya after receiving direct threats in May. She says her neighborhood, Adhamiya, is no longer permissive if she is not clad so modestly.

4. (SBU) These women say they cannot identify the groups that are pressuring them; many times, the cautions come from other women, sometimes from men who say they could be Sunni or Shiite, but appear conservative. They also tell us that some ministries, notably the Sadrist controlled Ministry of Transportation, have been forcing females to wear the hijab at work.

Dress Code for All?
----

5. (SBU) Staff members have reported that it is now dangerous for men to wear shorts in public; they no longer allow their children to play outside in shorts. People who wear jeans in public have come under attack from what staff members describe as Wahabis and Sadrists.

Evictions
----

6. (SBU) One colleague beseeched us to weigh in to help a neighbor who was uprooted in May from her home of 30 years, on the pretense of application of some long-disused law that allows owners to evict tenants after 14 years. The woman, who is a Fayli Kurd, says she has nowhere to go, no other home, bu the courts give them no recourse to this new assertion of ower. Such uprootings

may be a response by new Shiite government authorities
to similar actions against Arabs by Kurds in other parts
of Iraq. (NOTE: An Arab newspaper editor told us he is
preparing an extensive survey of ethnic cleansing, which
he said is taking place in almost every Iraqi province,
as political parties and their militias are seemingly
engaged in tit-for-tat reprisals all over Iraq. One
editor told us that the KDP is now planning to set up
tent cities in Irbil, to house Kurds being evicted in
Baghdad.)

Power Cuts and Fuel Shortages
a Drain on Society
----

7.   Temperatures in Baghdad have already reached 115
degrees. Employees all confirm that by the last week of
May, they were getting one hour of power for every six
hours without. That was only about four hours of power
a day for the city. By early June, the situation had
improved slightly. In Hai al Shaab, power has recently
improved from one in six to one in three hours. Other
staff report similar variances. Central Baghdad
neighborhood Bab al Mu'atham has had no city power for
over a month. Areas near hospitals, political party
headquarters, and the green zone have the best supply,
in some cases reaching 24 hours. One staff member
reported that a friend lives in a building that houses a
new minister; within 24 hours of his appointment, her
building had city power 24 hours a day.

8.   (SBU) All employees supplement city power with
service contracted with neighborhood generator hookups
that they pay for monthly. One employee pays 7500 ID
per ampere to get 10 amperes per month (75,000 ID = USD
50/month). For this, her familiy gets 6 hours of power
per day, with service ending at 2am. Another employee
pays 9000 ID per ampere to get 10 amperes per month
(90,000 = USD 60). For this, his family gets 8 hours
per day, with service running until 5 am.

9.   (SBU) Fuel lines have also taxed our staff. One
employee told us May 29 that he had spent 12 hours on
his day off (Saturday) waiting to get gas. Another
staff member confirmed that shortages were so dire,
prices on the black market in much of Baghdad were now
above 1,000 Iraqi dinars per liter (the official,
subsidized price is 250 ID).

Kidnappings, and Threats of Worse
----

10.   (SBU)   One employee informed us in March that his
brother in law had been kidnapped. The man was
eventually released, but this caused enormous emotional
distress to the entire family. One employee, a Sunni
Kurd, received an indirect threat on her life in April.
She took extended leave, and by May, relocated abroad
with her family.

Security Forces Mistrusted
----

11.   (SBU)   In April, employees began reporting a change
in demeanor of guards at the green zone checkpoints.
They seemed to be more militia-like, in some cases
seemingly taunting.   One employee asked us to explore
getting her press credentials because guards had held
her embassy badge up and proclaimed loudly to nearby
passers-by "Embassy" as she entered.   Such information
is a death sentence if overheard by the wrong people.

Supervising a Staff At High Risk
----

12.   (SBU)   Employees all share a common tale of their
lives: of nine employees in March, only four had familiy
members who knew they worked at the embassy.   That makes
it difficult for them, and for us.   Iraqi colleagues
called after hours often speak Arabic as an indication
they cannot speak openly in English.

13.   (SBU)   We cannot call employees in on weekends or
holiday without blowing their "cover."   Likewise, they
have been unavailable during multiple security closures
imposed by the government since February.   A Sunni Arab
female employee tells us that family pressures and the
inabilitiy to share details of her employment is very
tough; she told her family she was in Jordan when we
sent her on training to the U.S. in February. Mounting
criticisms of the U.S. at home among family members also
makes her life difficult.   She told us in mid-June that
most of her family believes the U.S. -- which is widely
perceived as fully controlling the country and
tolerating the malaise -- is punishing populations as
Saddam did (but with Sunnis and very poor Shiites now at
the bottom of the list). Otherwise, she says, the

allocation of power and security would not be so
arbitrary.

14. (SBU) Some of our staff do not take home their
American cell phones, as this makes them a target.
Planning for their own possible abduction, they use code
names for friends and colleagues and contacts entered
into Iraq cell phones. For at least six months, we have
not been able to use any local staff members for
translation at on-camera press events.

15. (SBU) More recently, we have begun shredding
documents printed out that show local staff surnames.
In March, a few staff members approached us to ask what
provisions would we make for them if we evacuate.

Sectarian Tensions Within Families
----

16. Ethnic and sectarian faultlines are also becoming
part of the daily media fare in the country. One Shiite
employee told us in late May that she can no longer
watch TV news with her mother, who is Sunni, because her
mother blamed all government failings on the fact that
Shiites are in charge. Many of the employee's immediate
family members, including her father, one sister, and a
brother, left Iraq years ago. This month, another
sister is departing for Egypt, as she imagines the
future here is too bleak.

Frayed Nerves and Mistrust in the Office
----

17. (SBU) Against this backdrop of frayed social
networks, tension and moodiness have risen. One Shiite
made disparaging comments about the Sunni caliph Othman
which angered a Kurd. A Sunni Arab female apparently
insulted a Shiite female colleague by criticizing her
overly liberal dress. One colleague told us he feels
"defeated" by circumstances, citing the example of being
unable to help his two year old son who has asthma and
cannot sleep in stifling heat.

18. (SBU) Another employee tells us that life outside
the Green Zone has become "emotionally draining." He
lives in a mostly Shiite area and claims to attend a
funeral "every evening." He, like other local
employees, is financially responsible for his immediate
and extended families. He revealed that "the burden of

responsibility; new stress coming from social circles who increasingly disapprove of the coalition presence, and everyday threats weigh very heavily." This employee became extremely agitated in late May at website repots of an abduction of an Iraqi working with MNFI, whose expired Embassy and MNFI badges were posted on the website.

Staying Straight with Neighborhood
Governments and the 'Alasa'
----

19.   (SBU) Staff members say they daily assess how to move safely in public. Often, if they must travel outside their own neighborhoods, they adopt the clothing, language, and traits of the area. In Jdariya, for example, one needs to conform to the SCIRI/Badr ethic; in Yusufiya, a strict Sunni conservative dress code has taken hold. Adhamiya and Salihiya, controlled by the secular Ministry of Defense, are not conservative. Moving inconspicuously in Sadr City requires Shiite conservative dress and a particular lingo. Once-upscale Mansur district, near the Green Zone, according to one employee, by early June was an "unrecognizable ghost town."

20.   (SBU) Since Samarra, Baghdadis have honed these survival skills. Vocabularly has shifted to reflect new behavior. Our staff -- and our contacts -- have become adept in modifying behavior to avoid "Alasas," informants who keep an eye out for "outsiders" in neighborhoods. The Alasa mentality is becoming entrenched as Iraqi security forces fail to gain public confidence.

21.   (SBU) Our staff report that security and services are being rerouted through "local providers" whose affiliations are vague. As noted above, those who are admonishing citizens on their dress are not known to the residents. Neighborhood power providers are not well known either, nor is it clear how they avoid robbery or targeting. Personal safety depends on good relations with the "neighborhood" governments, who barricade streets and ward off outsiders. The central government, our staff says, is not relevant; even local mukhtars have been displaced or coopted by militias. People no longer trust most neighbors.

22.   (SBU)   A resident of upscale Shiite/Christian
Karrada district told us that "outsiders" have moved in
and now control the local mukhtars, one of whom now has
cows and goats grazing in the streets.   When she
expressed her concern at the dereliction, he told her to
butt out.

Comment
----

23. (SBU) Although our staff retain a professional
demeanor, strains are apparent. We see that their
personal fears are reinforcing divisive sectarian or
ethnic channlels, despite talk of reconciliation by
officials. Employees are apprehensive enough that we
fear they may exaggerate developments or steer us
towards news that comports with their own worldview.
Objectivity, civility, and logic that make for a
functional workplace may falter if social pressures
outside the Green Zone don't abate.

KHALILZAD

NNNN

The Rise of Sectarian Conflict and Ethnic Cleansing

Although sectarian tensions had clearly existed in Iraq for a long time, they were contained for most of the country's history. This was partly the result of simple repression, but also the result of government policy and of real tolerance. Under Saddam Hussein's dictatorship, there were many mixed marriages in Iraq. Among educated people, it was considered impolite even to ask whether someone was Sunni or Shiite.

The removal of Saddam and the institutionalization of an American occupation, however, led to a gradual but eventually dramatic increase in sectarian tensions. In part, this was simply because Saddam's repressive brutality evaporated and people were free to express themselves. In large measure, however, it seems to have been the unintended result of American policy choices. As discussed earlier, Bremer's early decisions deeply angered and alienated the Sunni elite, which saw extremist Shiite groups taking power. In addition, the rise of crime, anarchy, and then insurgency led people to seek protection, which was offered primarily by fundamentalist militias. Concomitantly, the U.S. occupation began allocating power and money along sectarian lines, something Saddam had never done, even though the regime leadership under Saddam was disproportionately Sunni. Thus, for example, the Iraqi Governing Council had proportional allocations of Sunnis, Shiites, and Kurds. Some portions of the Sunni insurgency specifically targeted Shiites; al Qaeda in particular sometimes chose targets specifically to incite sectarian violence. Then, as sectarian tensions and the insurgency intensified, the process became a vicious circle, with repeated cycles of violence and retaliation. Sunni insurgents, al Qaeda, and Shiite militias waged war for control of geographical areas, and when one group obtained control, it would begin forcing out members of other sects. This was often done violently and somewhat randomly, creating enormous refugee flows and increasingly segregated neighborhoods.

OMAR FEKEIKI: Well, I hear them talking about a possible civil war. But in fact, it started a year ago. Since the [Ibrahim al-Jaafari] government took place, if we go back to our archives, we'll see how assassinations according to ethnic backgrounds and religious backgrounds increased—since late April 2005.

The only thing I think will increase is that the civil war will be more obvious and people will talk about it more. Now, Iraqis' pride prevent them from talking about the civil war, because the term is just ugly ... Iraqi community and society is very mixed through marriage, through work, whatever. And that's why they don't want to talk about [the] possibility of people fighting each other. But in fact, they are fighting each other.

Although it's not the same civil war we've heard about in Lebanon, it's now more—I don't like to call it civil war—it's ethnic cleansing. It's militias [who] belong to a certain ethnic background or religious background, killing the other side. And it's increasing: average of ten to twelve bodies found in Baghdad alone every day; for unknown people, their hands tied and blindfolded and shot in the head or the chest.

CHARLES FERGUSON: Yes. In fact, tell us what happened in your neighborhood two days ago, four days ago. ...

OMAR FEKEIKI: It's not my neighborhood. It's close to my neighborhood,

adjacent to my neighborhood. ... I read in, um, I believe a British newspaper, quoting a police officer in [the] other neighborhood: Fourteen bodies were found, and their IDs were attached to their chests, and all their
names were Omar.

Omar is a very Sunni name. Although some Shiites name [their sons]
Omar, but not to the extent we say it's a Shiite name. It's a very Sunni
name in the Islamic history. And to hear that Omars were killed because
they were Omars—their names were Omar—what else we could call ethnic cleansing? What else we could call? The situation has become ... like,
impossible to solve.

... People are now being killed for months now. We hear people saying,
and political parties saying, people are being killed according to their iden-
tifications. Fake checkpoints in the streets stop driving cars or whatever,
people passing, and looking to their IDs and see if they were Shiites, Sunnis, Kurds, Arabs. And then either kidnap them or kill them in the same
place. That's just not the Iraq we expected in March 2003.

While it is unclear exactly who killed the fourteen men with Omar identification papers, the murderers were probably members of a Shiite militia trying to send a signal to the Sunni insurgency and more broadly to the Sunni population of Baghdad.
The incident occurred two days before my interview with al-Amiri. I asked him about
it; he lied.

CHARLES FERGUSON: Two days ago in Baghdad, fourteen dead bodies of men
named Omar were found in a street. Who do you think killed those men?

HADI AL-AMIRI: I wonder how you knew their names. We know that their
names are unknown, unknown people, so how did you know that their
name is Omar? Why won't these fourteen bodies of people called Ali [a
Shiite name]? Who knows? Is it written in their blood test or in their DNA
that their name is Omar?

The problem that we have here is that the reality is that the number of
Shiites assassinated is way much more than the number of those killed
from the brothers, the Sunnis. There is an obvious sympathy with the
Sunni brothers, but there is no sympathy with the Shiite bloodshed. And
they deal with Shiite blood as water and not blood.

In one of the meetings with General Casey, he asked, "Who is assassinating the Sunnis in Baghdad streets?" I answered him, "I hope that your question was who is responsible for killing Iraqis, whether Sunnis or Shiites. So if you know who is killing the Shiites, then come and tell us. And then we will cooperate to find out who is killing Sunnis." That was first. And secondly: "You are responsible for the security. You, General Casey, you have the security file in your hand for all of Iraq. If I were responsible for the security file, then you have the right to ask me this question. Therefore I have the right to ask you who is responsible for the killings of Shiites. And also to ask you who is responsible for the killings of Sunnis. And as you are responsible for security in Iraq, then you have an obligation to answer this question. … You, as a security official in charge, you should provide me with an answer, and not ask me."

Whitson and Hiltermann described how violence in Iraq became increasingly sectarian.

SARAH LEAH WHITSON: I guess now, in December 2005, the insurgency has evolved. While the leadership of the insurgent groups still are unified, no matter what their political bent and no matter what their goals—whether they're, you know, radical Islamists, seeking to establish or reestablish the Caliphate in Constantinople; or whether they are Arab nationalists, seeking, you know, just to restore the sovereignty of Iraq—their goal remains one of liberating Iraq from foreign occupation. But for the membership of the insurgency—and the reason the numbers continue to grow and have stayed as strong as they are—it's also now become, unfortunately, tragically, a sectarian divisional thing, where now, you know, if you're a Sunni, the insurgents are your team and you have to be on that team because there's no other option. The other option is the Shiite team or the Kurdish team. And that's how it's broken down now.

JOOST HILTERMANN: Well, Iraq today, in May of 2006, is on the verge of civil war. And I guess it could still be prevented if X, Y, and Z happen. But X, Y, and Z are very difficult to accomplish. I'm speaking in particular about the creation of a genuine government of national unity. That may happen, but that in itself will not be sufficient. I'm talking about a substantive review of the constitution, and that is unlikely to happen, even though attempts will be made to revise the constitution. And the building up of security forces, as has happened in the past couple of years, that are led by nonsectarian commanders. And I think that was going to be very difficult because these security forces have been infiltrated over the past year by armed militias and their commanders. And to reverse that process is going to be extremely, extremely difficult. So if these things do not happen—as I think may be too difficult to accomplish—then there's very little there to prevent the country from sliding into all-out civil war. We've already seen a degree of sectarian fighting between various groups—insurgent groups, militias, government forces. We've seen some sectarian cleansing of neighborhoods and mixed areas.

After A. Heather Coyne left the army, she became the manager for the Iraq program of the U.S. Institute of Peace (USIP), a position subsequently held by Paul Hughes. She went to Baghdad for USIP shortly before the February 2006 bombing of the Samarra mosque, a major Shiite holy site. The bombing brought Iraq to the brink of civil war, where it has remained ever since.

A. HEATHER COYNE: I'd been back there about a month when the Samarra bombing [happened], and that [had] been my nightmare scenario for a long time: that the insurgents or the foreign fighters—whoever was behind it—would hit something, either something so holy or with such a mass casualty effect that the Shia militias would have to come forward and say, you know, "We're gonna retaliate. We can't stand for this. We're not gonna put up with it anymore. We're striking back." And then they'd take the gloves off. And on the Sunni side, the civilians would feel even more vulnerable and targeted and realize they had no place in the new Iraq, and were always going to be a vulnerable minority, and that violence was their only option. They'd decide that. And then the whole thing would spiral out of control.

... The note I left them [the Iraqis] on when I left Iraq in February [2006] was a different one. The tone had changed again. I guess I'd call it reality setting in, that the Iraqis were beginning to realize that there are no quick fixes in setting up a representative and functional government. And no quick fixes in managing what's now clearly a deeply divided society.

Shiite family members, killed by suspected insurgents, lie dead on the road near Baquba, 2006.

By mid-2006, the overall security situation in Iraq was desperate. It was no single problem. In fact, one extraordinary thing was that there were so many ways one could die in Iraq—some of them political, others not. There were insurgent attacks with small arms, mortars, and rocket-propelled grenades (RPGs), improvised explosive devices (IEDs), car bombs, and vehicle-borne IEDs (VBIEDs). There were suicide bombers using explosive vests under their clothing. There were fake checkpoints. There were accidental killings by Americans when they raided or assaulted suspected insurgents, traffic killings by American forces and private military contractors, killings at American and Iraqi traffic checkpoints by nervous soldiers. There were kidnappings for ransom, political kidnappings, targeted assassinations, killings in the course of carjackings and robberies, personal revenge killings, killings of business or political rivals, honor killings of women, and sectarian killings of Sunnis by Shiite militias and vice versa. There were murders by police death squads or by others impersonating the police. There were sectarian killings of Shiites by Sunni in-surgents and murders by fundamentalists of those who offended Islamic norms by selling alcohol or dressing stylishly. And so on. By 2006, killings were so numerous that most were no longer reported, and it became increasingly difficult to assess the level or the source of violence.

CHARLES FERGUSON: What's the crime rate in Baghdad?

GERALD BURKE: I don't think anyone really knows what the crime rate is. We hear about the violent bombings, but I don't think we even have a good handle on those. You'll hear that, you know, Baghdad has ten, fifteen bombings a day. And it's maybe, uh, fifty KIA [killed in action]. But I sus-pect that's drastically underreported. I know that on a couple of occasions, when police officers were killed … even when police officers were killed … that the bodies were immediately put in the back of a pickup truck, wrapped up in sheets, and not taken to a morgue, not taken to a police sta-tion, but taken back to the family. Where the family would prepare the body for burial, and within a few hours at most, the body would be in the ground, and there'd be no autopsy. And if it wasn't for the fact that they were police officers being killed, there'd probably [have] been no report to the police. So I think a lot of people mistrust the police, first, and get a sense of futility. Why bother telling the police, 'cause they're not gonna in-vestigate it, anyway. So they don't even report the murders and deaths to the police.

CHARLES FERGUSON: Okay. So there are published numbers about, you know, death rates, civilian death rates in Iraq and in Baghdad. If you had to make a wild guess, the actual rate of violent deaths is what fraction higher than the reported numbers?

GERALD BURKE: We're probably capturing a third of what's actually occur-ring, at least in the Baghdad area that I'm very familiar with.

CHARLES FERGUSON: So you think that the—

GERALD BURKE: If we're reporting fifty, we're probably getting a hundred and fifty a day KIA, killed in action.

Also by 2006, the Iraqi government clearly no longer possessed any coherent control over its own security forces. Through a combination of the control of the Interior Ministry by SCIRI and the Badr Organization, corruption, the formation of criminal gangs within the police, penetration of police units by the Mahdi Army, and other factors, it truly became impossible to trust the police—or those who were dressed as the police.

MATT SHERMAN: The coalition and the military have been trying to take real steps by [trying] to embed advisory teams in with the commandos, and also, soon, with the police ... so trying to be able to monitor and restrict them from doing these sort of things. There were issues, you know, human rights issues, ... I'm sure, that they witnessed that they didn't try stopping and reporting and doing that much. But [they] need to be able to, right now, more so than any time else, to provide even greater advisory services and monitoring to make sure these sort of things really stop.

How one provides "advisory services" to death squads Sherman did not say. Aida Ussayran was the deputy human rights minister of Iraq when I interviewed her in Baghdad in 2006. She had spent twenty years in the anti-Saddam Iraqi resistance, living underground in Iraq and later in England.

AIDA USSAYRAN: For example, if you want to go and put somebody in prison, the detainees, you must have the warrant for them, through their judges or the Ministry of Justice. And we went to court with the Interior Ministry. We succeeded to have this warrant that it's forbidden to arrest anybody without this warrant that you have from the ... judicial people. And now they abuse this. Now you can see people arrested by many sources. We don't know who they are—some people wearing black shirts, some people ... the Interior Ministry's people ... some people are from the brigades that we have, the militia. We have so many kinds of militia. I don't know all the militias. You have the Mujahadeen militia; you have the Badr militia; you have many militias in this country. And they all are very democratic in arresting people and killing them.

The police situation grew so out of control that when I was in Baghdad in late March 2006, Iraqi television broadcast a remarkable announcement: "The Ministry of

Defense advises Iraqi citizens not to obey instructions from Interior Ministry personnel unless they are accompanied by coalition forces." I asked reporter Michael Moss
about it.

CHARLES FERGUSON: As a brief side note, by the way, I don't know if you
heard about this—I never was able to verify it conclusively myself—but
when I was in Baghdad in late March, I was told that while I was there,
there appeared a notice on Iraqi television, very late at night, on an Iraqi
program. There was an announcement which said: The Ministry of Defense advises Iraqi civilians not to obey orders from Interior Ministry or
Iraqi police personnel unless they are accompanied by coalition forces. Did
you ever hear about this?

MICHAEL MOSS: Um, yeah, that's in fact true. Our Iraqi news staff in our
Baghdad bureau saw the same notice. I think it ran more than once. And
the warning was particularly to be alert and be fearful at night because
many of the death squad attacks and kidnappings for ransom occur at
night. And people were specifically warned to not open your door if the
Iraqi police, quote unquote, came knocking, and to not cooperate and not
obey any orders that they might give them, especially at nighttime.

One of the problems is that it's really hard to tell who is who. And not
only has the official Iraqi police force been infiltrated by militia and thugs
and just outright criminals, but people are using Iraqi police uniforms—
stolen uniforms—to pretend that they're police. So that's one of the very
difficult things for civilians, and one of the reasons why it's such a crisis
now, is that they can't trust their own government, if you will, the police.

In fact, Moss told me that when he was in Baghdad, the guards at the *New York
Times* compound (there are dozens of guards, armed not just with AK-47s but also
with belt-fed machine guns mounted in towers) refused permission when Iraqi security forces sought to enter the compound, and at least once were on the verge of
combat with them.

By 2006, Baghdad had descended into near chaos, with the majority of the city controlled by various militias. In October 2006, the *New York Times* surveyed the city and constructed a map showing who controlled what areas. It demonstrated graphically what Nir Rosen told me around the same time, namely, that the U.S. military had lost control of Iraq and had been reduced to the status of "just another militia." The U.S. military controlled the Green Zone and the area around Baghdad airport, but little else. Some areas were controlled by Iraqi security forces, but the Mahdi Army controlled the largest area, including Sadr City. Various other neighborhoods were controlled by the Badr Organization, Sunni militias, and local militias or neighborhood watch groups. Large areas were essentially controlled by no one.

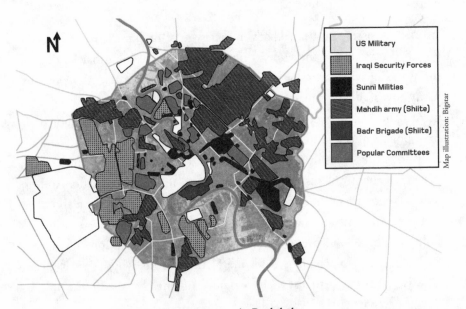

Insurgent areas in Baghdad.

Eventually, the Pentagon and the military responded and began an aggressive effort to train and monitor the Iraqi police. But it was too late.

When I spoke with Iraqis during my trip there in 2006, I made a point of asking them whether any of their friends or family members had been kidnapped or killed. Nearly everyone said yes, and some had had as many as a dozen members of their family killed. My interpreter, Omar X, lost over a dozen family members to an array of sources—kidnappings for ransom, sectarian killings, in some cases killings without apparent motive. Omar himself had been able to enter the United States in 2007 on a Fulbright scholarship.

OMAR X: We had an ordinary life. I mean we were like middle-class people that we were living fine till the last year, when things became really worse in Baghdad and we started to face problems. First, my older brother was kidnapped and they shot him in the head, and luckily, he survived. He didn't die, but he lost his one eye and he lost the sight of the other eye. And then my younger brothers were kidnapped in January; they took them when they get out from the school, and also I did my best to get them back. I started to call some people I know from my works and some political people and also I get them back. But in last June, my father was kidnapped, and really, I wasn't lucky to get him back. He was killed there the same day they took him, according to the police, and we find his body a week after at Baghdad morgue.

CHARLES FERGUSON: Do you know who kidnapped and killed your father?

OMAR X: Well, according to the witnesses that they saw, the people who took him, they are in the militia because they are controlling the neighborhood where he was and also because there's no reason to kill him, unless it's the sectarian things, because he was sixty-years-old man and he wasn't doing anything. ... So I think the reason for that is sectarian thing.

CHARLES FERGUSON: Why were your younger brothers kidnapped?

OMAR X: They had school that day, and after they finished the school, they were walking, trying to come back home, and they took them from the street in front of their school.

CHARLES FERGUSON: Why? Was that sectarian, or was it for money?

OMAR X: Well, actually, I have no idea. I mean, I think it's maybe because ... I mean, there's a lot of things, but I'm not sure from any. Maybe because of money, but then they realize that you don't have so much money. I doubt it much because of my job, but you know, they were targeting not my work ... But, you know, Charles, in Baghdad you can't find a real explanation for every accident, because they are just too many and sometimes it happens for no reason.

CHARLES FERGUSON: Your older brother getting shot, why was that? What happened there?

OMAR X: That was also sectarian, because they took him with seven other people from the shop where they were working, and they shot the whole seven people. He was the only one who survived. Because the hospital that day received seven bodies, and they discovered that he was still alive and among them.

CHARLES FERGUSON: Is that why you decided to leave—because everybody in your family was getting kidnapped and killed?

OMAR X: … Yeah, I mean, it's really difficult for me to live more in Baghdad. But the Fulbright thing, it was applied like a year and a half ago, and it just came at the right time. Sometimes, I feel that I was lucky that I applied and have been enrolled in this scholarship. Otherwise, where would I go?

CHARLES FERGUSON: How about your family leaving? I assume that your family left because—

OMAR X: Because we lost our house, Charles. After my father was killed and after my brothers were kidnapped, we started to plan to leave, at least for them to leave Iraq. But it took a very long time for them to get the passports. I mean, they got their passports, like, two weeks after my father was killed, so it was already a plan, you know, for them to leave Baghdad, because after they were kidnapped, we stopped them from going to school and they were spending time hiding at home. So they really became depressed, and they felt like their lives stopped at that point. So I was trying to get them out, but because of the passports, we were late and we lost our father.

CHARLES FERGUSON: Why did you lose your house?

OMAR X: Because we left the house and, you know … most of the neighborhoods in Baghdad [are] under the control of the militia, and any empty house, they take it. So when my father was kidnapped, my mother and my younger brothers had to leave the house. And like a week after, they [the militias] came and they broke into the house and they took it.

CHARLES FERGUSON: Took it, meaning that somebody else moved in?

OMAR X: Well, I don't really know. We lost contact in the area. But at first the neighbors were telling us, they broke the outer door and they took ... Everything was in the garden. Then two days later, they came and they went inside and they stayed and they took a lot of stuff. Well, that's also, I thought, very dangerous for my family or for me to go back, because I think now they saw a lot of evidences of my work or, you know, other things ... There's a computer there, there's some footage, other things. ...

CHARLES FERGUSON: How about the rest of your family—your cousins, your grandparents?

OMAR X: Also scattered. Some have left the country, especially the young people—some of them are in Jordan, some in Syria, some managed to reach Europe, to Sweden. But mainly the older people are still in Baghdad.

CHARLES FERGUSON: The older people.

OMAR X: Yeah, I mean like my aunts, who are very old women like in seventies, they still living at their houses in Baghdad, despite the risk. They think that they will not be hurt, because they are old women. But they managed to send their sons, their daughters, outside Iraq or outside Baghdad. Some are living in Kurdistan; some are living in the southern provinces like Najaf, where it's considered to be safe. So it's kind of very scattered.

CHARLES FERGUSON: Is your entire family Sunni?

OMAR X: No, we are mixed. I mean, my mother is a Shiite.

CHARLES FERGUSON: But that did not provide any protection from the Mahdi Army?

OMAR X: No, no. Those militia are really just killing. The Shiite militias kill Shiite people, and the Sunni kills Sunni people. It's just by name [that] they are representing a sect, but in reality … I mean, I'm a Sunni, but I can't get protection from Sunni militia or from the insurgent. They will kill me for stupid reasons, like the way I dress, the way I cut my hair, or even if they know I'm working on something. So it's not like if you are a Sunni and you are with the Sunni insurgents, that you are in [a] haven and they're gonna protect you. It's not like that.

On a Baghdad street in 2006, I interviewed a fruit vendor, whose opinions of the occupation were typical of many other Iraqis with whom I spoke. Life, they said, was better under Saddam.

CHARLES FERGUSON: Ask him how he feels about life, his life since the Americans came.

TRANSLATOR [*in Arabic*]: He asks you: What has changed in your life, for better or for worse, since the occupation?

FRUIT VENDOR [*spoken in Arabic, translated by translator*]: Well, under the occupation—and this is the opinion of most Iraqis—we expect that every day will be worse than the one before.

CHARLES FERGUSON: And is that in fact his experience, that every day is worse than the day before?

TRANSLATOR: He asks: Is it affecting your personal life this way? Do you feel that every day is worse than the one before?

FRUIT VENDOR: In terms of our quotidian life, it has become habitual. Not only does it affect me, but also my family and everyone around me. Why? Because of how it affects the market, the streets, the lack of security. We can no longer go around as we please, as was the case before. Before was the time of Saddam. It is true that Saddam was fighting "us." Saddam used to fight us in the past, that is true and an undeniable fact, but who replaced him was worse than him.

CHARLES FERGUSON: Did anything happen to him personally, or his family?

TRANSLATOR: Did something tragic happen directly to you or to your family?

FRUIT VENDOR: Okay, listen. Imagine the distance between here and the cart—around twenty-five meters—a car exploded that far away from me. Me and my father and my brother were standing around. My brother got killed; he was martyred. And all my friends who were in the market got killed.

PASSERBY [*intervenes in conversation; spoken in Arabic, translated by translator*]: In the past, they used to say that you risked death at the hands of the state, under torture and interrogations. Today, you risk dying from bombings, explosives, armed thugs; the paths to death are numerous nowadays. Death has become trivial.

FRUIT VENDOR: I will tell you about the past. In the past, my parents and my siblings used to operate this store. I am a taxi driver. I used to work until two or three A.M. At the time, Baghdad used to be busy and glittering until the morning. Now, at seven, everyone closes shop and goes back home. That is because of the security situation.

TRANSLATOR: Do you want the Americans to remain or leave?

FRUIT VENDOR: Honestly, them leaving would be merciful for the Iraqi people. Why? Because it seems to me, honestly, that they are trying to drag the Iraqi people into sectarian war. They want to transform us into Bosnia or Lebanon.

TRANSLATOR: Thanks, dear.

FRUIT VENDOR: You are welcome.

CHAPTER TEN

THE MILITARY OCCUPATION

In 2003, the U.S. military had neither planned sufficiently for postwar Iraq nor was prepared for what postwar Iraq became. There were several reasons for this. The first was the military's own serious neglect of postwar (Phase IV) issues, including its neglect of the excellent prewar analyses that had warned of the likely challenges facing the occupation. Second, the Bush administration, having predicted a short, clean occupation and a quick withdrawal, had instructed the military to behave accordingly. Third, U.S. intelligence had inadequately understood the degree to which Iraq's government, society, and infrastructure had deteriorated under the sanctions regime and the extent to which Iraq was flooded with unguarded, unregulated weapons. And finally, prewar planning for the postwar period had assumed that the Iraqi state bureaucracy would be kept intact rather than "de-Baathified," that the Iraqi Army would be recalled rather than disbanded, and that other nations such as Turkey would contribute more troops than were ultimately forthcoming.

Lawrence Wilkerson and James Fallows commented on the absence of prewar military-industrial mobilization and its continuing absence even after the occupation and the insurgency had begun.

LAWRENCE WILKERSON: We didn't do anything after 9/11. I would submit to you that on 9/12, we had ample opportunity to convince the American people that we needed, for example, a war tax. We needed some sort of mobilization. We needed some sort of consideration, at least to begin the possibilities of conscription. We needed to mobilize industry, as Harry Truman did so adroitly for the Korean War. We needed to consider things like the conflict we're contemplating in Afghanistan and the one we're contemplating in Iraq are not going to be short-term affairs; therefore, we need to alert industry to this.

What would industry be alerted to do? Build more Hummers, more vehicles with armor on them; do the kinds of things that you could contemplate you were gonna have to do if you got engaged in a long-term insurgency, which clearly you were gonna get engaged in, in both Afghanistan and Iraq. None of these things were done.

JAMES FALLOWS: It does seem, with a couple years' perspective, as if that first year after the fall of Baghdad had … one blunder of either omission or commission after another. … I mean, for example, it now seems clear, in retrospect, that General Tommy Franks, the head of the Central Command, CENTCOM, at that time, really had no interest at all in what would happen to Iraq once Saddam Hussein was kicked out. There are countless bits of testimony by his subordinates and colleagues that he was very much invested in the war plan, and then that was it. You know, this Phase IV stuff of peacekeeping wasn't interesting to him. And so there was that problem.

There was the division of authority problem, all the way along, between the military leadership in CENTCOM and the civilian authority, whether it was a Jay Garner or L. Paul Bremer. … It's startling now to remember that it was … less than a month after the eviction of Saddam Hussein that President Bush was on his aircraft carrier, with the "mission accomplished" ceremony. So there was this idea, from the U.S. public and the administration: Okay, this is done. You know, major combat activities have ceased. And so there was that kind of diminution of real intensity.

President George W. Bush's "Mission Accomplished" speech
aboard the USS *Abraham Lincoln,* May 1, 2003.

Failure to Provide Security

The U.S. military had not adequately prepared for widespread looting, civil disorder, large-scale criminality, a major insurgency, and extralegal militias comparable in size to the U.S. military presence. The Americans were not ready for a long, difficult occupation of Iraq. This was apparent in innumerable ways, ranging from large-scale policy issues to very specific implementation details. There was no attempt to increase the size of the military or to raise the readiness levels of the military re-serves or National Guard. U.S. troops received little instruction concerning the Ara-bic language, Iraq, Islam, or the Arab world. The initially deployed force contained very few interpreters, Arabic speakers, Civil Affairs officers, or military police. Most U.S. military transportation vehicles were unarmored, and no provision was made to increase the production of armored vehicles. Few if any U.S. troops were given counterinsurgency training. The Defense Department's procurement and purchas-ing systems often remained slow and bureaucratic.

Somewhat more puzzlingly, once it was in Iraq, and even after the magnitude of the occupation's problems became apparent to many observers, the U.S. military often did not react well. While troop levels were clearly inadequate, it seems equally clear that even with the forces it possessed, the U.S. military could have done more to stop the looting, to guard critical buildings, and to guard or destroy weapons caches. Instead, the military focused on protecting its own forces, searching for weapons of mass destruction (WMD), Saddam Hussein, and other wanted regime officials.

JAMES FALLOWS: For the three or four crucial months after the fall of Bagh-dad, the two main things the U.S. military was doing on the ground were looking for WMD supplies and looking for Saddam Hussein. And it seems now, in retrospect, that those were really damaging things to do, not sim-ply because they didn't find a WMD and did eventually find Saddam Hus-sein, but because the process of those searches—busting in the doors at night; rounding up people; taking them to Abu Ghraib; having mass ar-rests; not being able to distinguish very clearly who you were, who you should keep or not—had a really embittering effect on the population. It was when the insurgency began to get going.

So the three or four months when public order might have been restored, and a sense of people's daily life getting better, instead were typified first by looting, then by the breaking-in-the-doors regime. And so, one after another, you had these sort of short-term decisions, which, by the end of 2003, meant you had a country with an insurgency under way.

When the United States occupied Iraq, the country was awash in weapons. The active duty military, of course, possessed many weapons, which soldiers often took with them when they deserted. But there were also the weapons controlled by Saddam Hussein's irregular forces, such as the Fedayeen Saddam. These enormous stockpiles of weapons, ammunition, and explosives were spread throughout the country—in schools, open fields, warehouses, markets, everywhere. In addition, many private Iraqis possessed automatic weapons, a situation that Saddam had tolerated and in some cases encouraged. The U.S. military's failure to identify and guard these weapons was seen as a major error that worsened both the insurgency and ordinary crime.

YAROSLAV TROFIMOV: Weapons were lying around everywhere after the war. I remember going to the zoo in Baghdad with an American lieutenant colonel who was responsible for that part of the city.

CHARLES FERGUSON: The zoo.

YAROSLAV TROFIMOV: The zoo. And the colonel was concerned because there were lions in the zoo. And there were wolves, and looters would come in and, you know, kill lions and kill the wolves and [take] them for food. So he would send a detachment there to protect the animals once in a while. It didn't help, because, you know, the soldiers weren't there all the time, so that when the soldiers were away, more and more animals would be stolen and eaten.

But what struck me was that there was this huge meadow in the middle of the zoo. [It] was just blanketed with weapons. There were mortars and grenades and rocket launchers and just boxes of Yugoslav-made ammunition and bullets. And nobody thought of securing this. It was just there. And you know, week after week, you would go there, and there would be a little bit less, little bit less. I mean, people [would] just come and take and put it away.

And the same was happening everywhere, you know, because the Iraqis' stocks of conventional weaponry were enormous. And there were not enough U.S. troops to secure them. There was [not even] an attempt to secure them. Under the highway overpasses in Baghdad, the Iraqis had left these big antiaircraft rocket launchers. These big trucks with huge—I'd say ten-foot-long—rockets on them, fully armed. And I remember kids playing … and you know … these things were exploding once in a while. And local communities … would often try to get the U.S. military to help to remove those things. And they had no way of reaching the U.S. military. Or when they did reach the U.S. military, the U.S. military had other priorities.

The same happened at the nuclear facilities, where lots of radioactive material on the side of the Iraqi nuclear program was looted. And people were getting sick because they were using heavy metal sinks—and they were highly radioactive—for storing the milk and the water.

So all those weapons that the insurgency is using today were there. And a fairly limited effort to get them under control would have diminished the insurgents' ability to strike.

CHARLES FERGUSON: Do you think, then, it would have been possible to limit the flow of weapons around Iraq—limit the availability of weapons to the insurgents?

YAROSLAV TROFIMOV: Yeah, absolutely. It would have been possible to limit the amount of weapons that they have. It's not so much as a flow of weapons. It's the fact that the weapons were there, lying in the open, and if the U.S. didn't remove it, someone else did. And the people who did remove them stored them and used them later.

In Basra, the riverfront … was just strewn with enormous amounts of weaponry there. And the British soldiers were there … They didn't receive orders to remove any of that. [So it was] just there, lying abandoned.

———

General Paul Eaton agreed about the lack of security, which was caused, he said, by the lack of available troops.

Weapons found by U.S. forces.

CHARLES FERGUSON: What did you think of the occupation of Iraq by the time you'd spent, let's say, a month in Baghdad? What did you think of what you saw around you?

PAUL EATON: I saw a terrific number of absolutely great Americans, and great members of the coalition working very hard. They were substantially undermanned to do the job that they had to do. It was an evolving situation on the ground. And what I found were my peers and the youth of America doing some very, very hard work, trying to hold things together. And there just were not enough soldiers on the ground to execute the security function for the country of Iraq.

Marine Lieutenant Ann Gildroy was one of those soldiers working hard to improve the security situation in Iraq. During and after the operation to clear Najaf of the Mahdi Army, she worked on the training of Iraqi security forces. Although she found that CPA policies had impeded the effort and that the new Iraqi army recruits were initially unreliable, she nevertheless made enormous progress before the general conditions of the country overwhelmed her efforts.

ANN GILDROY: When I arrived [in 2004], quite frankly, people were correctly focused on getting the marines that were on the front lines what they needed. And ... it worked to my benefit. I met the operations officer at the time, who was a lieutenant colonel, and I said, "I want to be out with the

Iraqi security forces." And I sort of put together this quick little sales pitch about how I felt I could help them, and why I felt I had the right skill sets to get out there and help them.

It was sort of a far-fetched thing. Most people, especially females, are kept more behind the fence line. So ... there were a lot of different steps that fell in place that allowed me to have a position there, where, one, I could exploit some of the talents I have and, two, get a very unique experience. And one of the things that enabled me to do that is just the mere fact that everybody was so—correctly—engaged in fighting Moqtada al-Sadr's militia. And so people were really too busy to focus too much on who was going where, and, you know, was a female going to the right position versus a male? And so, lo and behold, I got my wishes, and I went over to Diwaniyah, where the commanders of the Iraqi security forces were located.

... At the time, when I first arrived on the ground, we had one brigade. Not even, really. It was one brigade, and one of our infantry companies was training one of the battalions in Najaf—or that was what they were supposed to be doing before the battle broke out. You know, [the battalion] was only on the ground for a couple weeks before real fighting broke out. And so the original mission sort of went to hell in a handbasket, and we adapted. ... One rifle company trained a battalion in Najaf; the other rifle company, that I worked with, Alpha Company One-Four [First Battalion, Fourth Marines], they trained a battalion in Diwaniyah.

The command for the Iraqi security forces was located where I was, so I had access to them because they were colocated right close to our base, right outside the fence line. So it wasn't, as in some circumstances ... a great amount of travel to get to them. We could be over there at two in the morning, discussing, you know, what had gone on that day, what we could do.

... Everything I'm saying is completely about Iraqis; I had nothing to do with focusing on issues for American marines. So from pretty much forty-eight to seventy-two hours once I arrived in Najaf, my entire focus from that point on would be on Iraqi security forces. So anything I'm saying, I'm just prefacing with the fact that it's all Iraqis.

... By the end of, I think, week two, [we] had faced a sixty percent desertion rate with the Iraqis. So our units completely fell apart, due to the fighting. At that time, we had just arrived. They didn't have the right amount of ammunition or the right equipment to fight that battle. I mean, it was a helluva fight, even for the marines and the army, much less for a newly founded Iraqi army without the proper training and equipment.

… At first, some marines would get frustrated with Iraqis running away from the fight, deserting. And it's sort of like if you took us, our first couple weeks in OCS [Officer Candidate School], and you put five rounds in our magazine, and you told us, with no flak jacket and no helmet, and knowing that nobody was gonna come medevac us out when we got hit, and you said, "Well, go anyway."

… The CPA had put together these units based on sort of a very American way of doing things, which was, Here's a pie, and we're gonna say that all Iraqi units need to be split equally among all the various political parties. And so the units were constructed in such a way that served to help them fall apart when fighting came, because they had no allegiance to the ground they were standing on, and not necessarily to the leaders that were in charge of them. So that was one of the first things we changed. We sat down with the Iraqis, and we said, "Hey, why are your guys running away? Okay, we get the equipment, but is there no allegiance or loyalty, and why aren't they standing up?"

And they said, "Hey, you know, the first thing is that these aren't the guys we would have selected ourselves."

And so we said, you know, "You're the Iraqis; you pick them. We're gonna work with you. We'll establish physical training standards, we will get medical checks, but you're gonna vet these guys, and you're gonna tell us where the best guys are gonna come from."

And so that was really a switch for us because it threw the power into the Iraqi commanders' hands. And, you know, they know their country best. And it's always a fine line in Iraq: How much do you say, "Hey, we have the military experience, so we're gonna take the final vote here," and then when do we actually grant the power to them?

In this case, we said, "This is the time to let the Iraqis exercise more power if in fact we're gonna get them to stand on their own feet." And it worked phenomenally well. Now, one year later, when I left, the 8th Iraqi Army Division is arguably one of the strongest divisions in Iraq, and we went from one brigade to a full division with some incredible commanders and, I think, some very, very loyal troops. But that was one of the first serious problems. And I looked back at some of the things I wrote in e-mails and diaries, and I was very pessimistic at that point. I really felt like there was no hope, and it was hard to put a hopeful, positive face on when you went to see the Iraqis. But they have a lot of tenacity. They've been through a helluva lot over the past few decades. And so we worked together, and we made it an equal playing field. If we're sitting in a meeting, it was Americans and Iraqis, and the Iraqis had just as much sort of prowess and say as we did, and that proved to be very, very helpful in our working relationship. And I think we came out with a better overall Iraqi force.

... [In addition,] we created a special elite unit within the Iraqi forces. I'm not sure if other people were doing that across the country. We sat down—when I say "we," I mean me and this company I worked for, this incredible company, Alpha Company, and their leadership—and we tried to figure out what to do. And one of the things was Falcon Company. Alpha Company's company commander came up with this idea, and it was great because it really gave the people who wanted to stay and fight something to strive for. So we started to piece this unit back [together], one by one. It took a long time. And then, by October, we had our first graduation of another company. And we had Prime Minister Allawi come down ... and General Petraeus and [Iraqi Joint Forces Commander, General Babakir] and some others ... and we had a big ceremony. And from there, things sort of started happening. ...

By December, the area that I was in, in Diwaniyah and Najaf, was doing very well. And so we moved up to Karbala, which was having some more problems. ... It was under the same command, but had not received any sort of direct attention. We went up there, and we again began training the Iraqi battalion there. We completely refurbished all of their facilities. We brought in totally new equipment for them.

One thing I worked a lot on is getting the Iraqis up to Baghdad to get their own equipment from American bases and start to count their own weapons and keep their own tallies of equipment to farm out from, say, the division brigade level down to the battalions. That sounds obvious and simple, but it's very difficult because in Iraq, a lot of the logistics at that time belonged to the Americans. So, multinational forces were controlling the movement of weapons and equipment through the country. And what would happen is it would undermine the authority and legitimacy of the Iraqi commanders because all of a sudden, weapons would show up on the doorstep of one unit, and another unit didn't get it. And the commander had absolutely no say in how to farm out his equipment—no responsibility. And so a lot of equipment was disappearing, and people were wondering why, and it's because it was never put in their hands. Nor were they charged with the responsibility of it in the first place. So that was one of the first things we changed. And I actually would go with them and escort them up to Baghdad to actually load weapons onto trucks that looked like they couldn't make it down my driveway. But somehow we managed to get up to Abu Ghraib and offload lots of equipment and bring it back.

These were small steps with big meaning. And so our units ended up being very, very self-sufficient. They started to submit reports to us when they needed things. We could simply notify a warehouse that an Iraqi convoy was going to come and pick their gear up. And that was sort of unheard of in other parts of the country. Iraqis didn't typically have enough coordination to go up and pull their own weapons stores from American bases, and get it back safely. And now we have units that were transporting and delivering very high-value weapons and equipment to all units across central-south Iraq. And it proved to be very, very effective.

Unfortunately, Ann Gildroy's story proved more the exception than the rule, both with regard to how the U.S. military behaved in training Iraqi forces and with regard to how Iraqi forces performed.

Alienation of Iraqis

While the U.S. military did some very important, helpful, and productive things, including collaborative efforts with the New Iraqi Army such as those described above, it also employed many measures that alienated the Iraqi population. U.S. behavior could be strikingly crude. The military reacted to the early insurgency with punitive and indiscriminate actions, including mass arrests, raids, detentions, and, of course, the torture and abuse at Abu Ghraib prison. Because the Americans were very slow to improve their Arabic language and intelligence capabilities, many errors were made and innocent people were arrested or killed. The U.S. military was even slower to provide armored vehicles and body armor to its own soldiers. It often neglected to employ best-practice counterinsurgency techniques, which focus on protecting the civilian population and gaining the trust of the population so that civilians will report insurgents. The military—and even more so the thousands of private military contractors who flooded into Iraq—has killed large numbers of innocent Iraqi civilians since 2003, particularly in traffic and checkpoint incidents.

The Americans' problems with the Iraqi population started immediately and worsened as the occupation hardened and the insurgency grew. While it is impossible to know—and the U.S. military has released no statistics with regard to this question—the anecdotal evidence suggests that the military's error rate was quite high in its dealings with Iraqis, both friendly and hostile. Raids, arrests, detentions, confiscations, and shootings seem to have been frequently indiscriminate or misguided, often through a lack of both understanding and intelligence, but sometimes also through arrogance and a lack of discipline or accountability. Other innocent casualties resulted from the fog of war and the military's understandable need to protect itself when attacked. As with traffic killings, the ratio of innocent Iraqis to insurgents or criminals arrested, imprisoned, killed, or injured is impossible to know, but most people with whom I spoke believed that it was high. If one combines raids, arrests, detentions, and shootings of civilians, it seems likely that by 2007, U.S. military conduct had directly affected, wounded, or killed over 100,000 Iraqis, and possibly well over 200,000.

In addition, lesser problems such as delays caused by curfews, checkpoints, checkpoint searches, traffic stoppages caused by convoy movements, and other such issues clearly affect most Iraqis' daily lives. When I drove overnight from Erbil to Baghdad in an armed convoy operated by a private military contractor in 2006, our convoy was forced to slow or stop numerous times by U.S. military convoys or patrols. This made our trip approximately 50 percent longer than it would otherwise have been. It was also more dangerous, because traffic near U.S. convoys can often be caught in insurgent attacks. Of course, by reducing the number of insurgent ambushes and improvised explosive devices (IEDs), those same U.S. patrols were critical to making our journey possible at all, but it was clear that living with U.S. military behavior on a daily basis was difficult and could provoke great resentment.

Seth Moulton felt that the military's intentions were overwhelmingly good and that serious efforts were made to avoid killing civilians. But even he acknowledged that the situation was difficult.

CHARLES FERGUSON: You've spoken several times about respects in which American conduct made Iraqis grateful: liberating Iraq in the first place from Saddam, removing Sadr's militia from Najaf, and other things. And I've certainly heard people say those things to me.

SETH MOULTON: Uh-huh.

CHARLES FERGUSON: I've also, though, heard a lot of people say that there were a lot of arbitrary searches, arrests, detentions made with, you know, not much sensitivity; that very few of the Americans spoke [Arabic]; that American convoys and checkpoints would, with disturbing regularity, shoot at, sometimes kill, Iraqi civilians who approached too close, didn't stop, were coming too fast, tried to pass a convoy. I'm sure you've heard these things said, at least in the press. What's your experience with all that? What do you think of all that?

SETH MOULTON: Most of the American units that I've … spent time with have tried very, very hard to always do the right thing, and to not kill anyone or injure anyone they haven't intended to or needed to. But there's no question that wars are messy. And this one in Iraq, with the way the insurgency is being waged, is particularly so.

Most nonmilitary observers, including Americans who had worked for the occupation and journalists, were far less circumspect. Journalist Yaroslav Trofimov spoke about the killing of innocent civilians by the U.S. military.

CHARLES FERGUSON: What would be your estimate of the ratio of civilian casualties to insurgents killed by American forces?

American soldiers pass a dead Iraqi while patrolling Baghdad.

YAROSLAV TROFIMOV: It's very hard to answer this question because the U.S. military policy is, We don't count their bodies. Which means that there are not statistics that are reliable of how many civilians are killed. But just from personal experiences and from witnesses, so many incidents, I can say that there are significantly more civilians that have been killed than insurgents or guerrillas or Iraqi soldiers in the actual conventional fighting phase of the war. So the civilians are paying the main price for this conflict.

Trofimov mentioned a number of specific incidents, including the following:

YAROSLAV TROFIMOV: The question of how many civilian casualties are there is very hard to answer. If you ask the U.S. military, anybody they kill is a terrorist. It's very, very rare for the U.S. military to acknowledge that they made a mistake. But I had some practical experience with this. I remember, one of the first major operations [of] the U.S. military in late May 2003 was in the … [Balad] triangle north of Baghdad. They announced that they killed seventeen insurgents there. And so I went to the villages … to find out what actually happened, the next day. And I remember that in one of the areas, there was an attack on an American tank. Nobody was killed on the U.S. side. And the U.S. announced that, you know, they killed seven insurgents who were involved in that particular attack. So I went to the village and the neighboring village. And it turns out that this was on the road between a Shiite and a Sunni village. So in the Sunni village, the local imam, who was very young—thirty-something years old—and his friend had organized the attack. The two of them [had] put a bomb in the road. They were sitting in the ditch and waiting. But they put the bomb next to the Shiite village because they didn't want [Major Brazels?] to come their way. So what happened is, once the U.S. troops came under attack in that village, they shot these two. But they also started shooting flares so that people in the nearby base would see them and come to the rescue. And one of the flares had fallen onto dry grass right next to a flock of sheep of one of the Shiite farmers in that village. And the sheep were the main possession. So that farmer, who was seventy-something years old—an old grandfather—was roused by his wife, who said, "You should go run and save our sheep." So he took all his children—I think he had five sons—and they all ran to save the sheep. Obviously, people running at you at night are seen by the U.S. military, by a soldier who has just come under attack, as enemies. So they were all mowed down and killed and announced to be terrorists, even though they came from a Shiite village, and Shiites were not involved in the insurgency.

Trofimov noted, correctly, that sometimes, even Westerners had been wounded or injured by U.S. forces.

YAROSLAV TROFIMOV: We know about lots of incidents where civilians are killed, the Iraqi ones. There is a much bigger number that we don't know about, because nobody bothers to report it. But just on the example of Westerners getting killed—I'm an Italian citizen, and there was the Italian ambassador to Iraq, who was a minister of culture in the CPA. So he was driving on the road to Baghdad, and his car—clearly an SUV that doesn't look like an Iraqi car—was trying to bypass [a] convoy on the road, and one of the cars waved him through. And then the next convoy, they panicked, and they shot at his car. So they wounded him, you know, this ambassador, who was almost eighty years old. And they killed his interpreter.

And of course, we all know what happened on the airport road ... in Baghdad, early in 2005, when the kidnapped Italian journalist was being taken to freedom in Italy, and the U.S. military shot at their car, and killed the Italian secret service agent who was trying to rescue her. So this sort of mistaken identity shootings are extremely common.

And I remember talking to an American diplomat, who lives in the Green Zone in Baghdad and rarely leaves it. And his comment to us: "If I get to die in Baghdad, it's probably because some marines will kill me." So it's a war, and you know, once you're a soldier, your main priority is to survive. And there are no penalties for shooting civilians. Virtually no penalties.

CHARLES FERGUSON: Hm. What happens when a civilian is killed, or civilians are killed? Is there an investigation, typically, or not?

YAROSLAV TROFIMOV: Typically, the troops do have to file a report at the end of this, a sort of postaction report [an "after-action report"]. But very rarely, there is an investigation that actually leads to something. Human Rights Watch, early on in Baghdad, had produced a report about dozens of shootings of civilians at checkpoints with details and times and actual ... you know ... there were women and children in the cars that were shot at checkpoints and killed for no reason. There were no weapons; there was nothing. And I remember, we were asking General Sanchez for [information] on this for weeks and weeks and weeks. And he would [promise] a press conference to get back to us. And never did. So it's extremely rare that investigations that occur actually lead to some sort of disciplinary action.

Nir Rosen contended that U.S. military conduct played a significant role in provoking the insurgency. He spoke about what it feels like to be occupied.

NIR ROSEN: In a way, the Americans provoked the resistance. It was a very brutal occupation. Um, it's difficult to understand what it feels like to be an occupied ... to feel like these foreigners can take your life at any moment now. They point their guns at you from their Jeeps; they stop you when you're driving. You're constantly aware that these big, scary white guys with guns can take your life in an instant. Everywhere you go, whether you're sitting in traffic or whether you're on line to get into the Green Zone, you have guns pointed at you, whether it's M-16s, or even larger, scarier, fifty-caliber, or the larger, scarier tanks; you constantly feel that foreigners, who don't speak your language and don't understand what you want, can kill you. And of course, it's happened often. Iraqis would not understand instructions given to them at traffic checkpoints. They wouldn't understand what the Americans wanted. They would approach too quickly. They would get shot and killed. The Americans didn't know Arabic, so they assumed all the Iraqis were the enemies.

While Rosen is, in my experience, sometimes dogmatically leftist, his comment about traffic killings was supported by many other interviewees and press reports. Many people, including some Americans, spoke to me about the problem of traffic killings. There are two basic kinds: shootings by convoy guards as convoys move on the roads, and shootings at checkpoints. In both cases, it appears that the error rate is very high. When I was staying in Baghdad, an American reporter told me at dinner one evening that an American soldier had fired a "warning shot" at him earlier that day; it came within a foot of him.

Iraqis who did not understand U.S. rules were often summarily shot if they approached too rapidly in their cars, if they did not stop when ordered or when signs or lines indicated, if they came too close to a convoy, if they failed to move aside when a convoy wished to pass, or if the vehicle simply looked suspicious. Most people with whom I spoke felt that the overwhelming majority of Iraqis killed in traffic incidents were innocent civilians. This would represent several thousand deaths, and possibly over ten thousand, since 2003.

One reason that so many Iraqis are killed is that the U.S. military keeps its rules of engagement secret for fear that insurgents will respond by appearing to behave properly. But this also means that Iraqis do not know how to behave, particularly if they cannot understand the hand signals or the sometimes inaccurate Arabic used on signs at checkpoints. Furthermore, many Iraqis are illiterate, and thus cannot read the warning signs at checkpoints even if the signs are written in correct Arabic.

There was also the problem of raids, searches, arrests, and detentions, which frequently produced errors.

American troops on patrol.

GEORGE PACKER: There was also just a sense [that] the Americans were making mistakes. And some of them were inevitable. You're always going to arrest the wrong person, from time to time, and bust down the wrong door, if that's the way you're conducting operations. But the mistakes were far more frequent … and stupid than they need to have been, because the Americans were always sort of reacting; they were always behind.

Gerald Burke described the impact of such operations on the Iraqi populace.

CHARLES FERGUSON: Did you deal with the issue of the American military's searches and detentions of potential insurgents, which were, you know, in a certain way, quasi-police operations, but—

GERALD BURKE: I would argue that they weren't police operations, that they were much more along the lines of military operations and internments, rather than arrests—

CHARLES FERGUSON: Okay—

GERALD BURKE: ... where people [were] being rounded up without any semblance of probable cause, even the Iraqi standard of a reason to suspect. If you happen to be a military-aged Iraqi in an area of operation where the American military went into, there was a good chance you were gonna be ... arrested or interned as a suspected insurgent—just for being a military-age man in that area of operation.

CHARLES FERGUSON: Really.

GERALD BURKE: Yeah.

CHARLES FERGUSON: And you witnessed this.

GERALD BURKE: Witnessed this. Witnessed it and heard of it from Iraqis complaining of it to me frequently.

CHARLES FERGUSON: I see. Okay. That presumably did not endear them to the American forces.

GERALD BURKE: Well, in many occasions, you take the Iraqi man of military age out of his family, you're taking the breadwinner, the person who is bringing home the money and the food.

CHARLES FERGUSON: So you get a lot of angry Iraqis.

GERALD BURKE: Yeah. You anger not just him, but you anger an extended family 'cause he's probably supporting more than his immediate family.

Suspected insurgents at a Baghdad detention center.

Many Iraqis I interviewed reported having difficult personal experiences with the U.S. military or hearing of close relatives or friends who had had such experiences, which suggests that these difficulties were quite common. Anna Edward is an Iraqi from a mixed Kurdish-Christian family in Basra. She joined the Kurdish Communist party and became an anti-Saddam activist as well as an activist for women's rights. After years in the Kurdish underground, she left Iraq and spent several years in Communist East Germany. In 2003, she returned to Iraq and founded an Iraqi NGO devoted to women's issues. I interviewed her in Baghdad in 2006, asking her principally about political and social conditions in Iraq. Though she remains a devoted Marxist, I found her honest and reliable in answering my factual questions. In the middle of the interview, while discussing the problems of crime and kidnapping, she pointed out that not all violence came from these sources.

ANNA EDWARD: One of my cousins, just last week, the Americans, they enter his house at night. And they beat ... they have beaten him. He is over seventy years. He and his wife ... he's a Christian. And they beat him. And they didn't listen. He knows English. And he was trying to explain to them. [They said,] "No, you have two children. Where they are?" He said, "I don't have children! Never, I have a child!" But after one hour, they discover it was false [information that they were fed]. But after when they have, you know, broken everything in house.

This is in Baghdad. So I believe, when they enter people's houses, like in the rural areas, [they do it] in a brutal way. And ... we condemn it. I believe that they [the Americans] are scared, of course. But they should consider very well the reports they get from others because I believe that certain groups, they are playing with Americans to give them false information.

Ali Fadhil was trained as a doctor. He was hired as George Packer's interpreter in Iraq and then became a journalist in his own right. Like many educated Iraqis, particularly in Baghdad, he comes from a mixed family; his father is Sunni and his mother is Shiite. I interviewed him in New York in 2006. He and his family had just been forced to leave Iraq as the ironic, indirect result of his mistaken arrest by U.S. forces.

CHARLES FERGUSON: I remember when we met for the first time. You said that just before you left Iraq, the Americans had arrested you and searched your house. What happened? Tell us about that.

ALI FADHIL: Yeah. On January 7th, Miss Jill [Carroll, a reporter for the *Christian Science Monitor*], she was kidnapped by insurgents in a neighborhood called Adel neighborhood. ... The same night at midnight, twelve-thirty, American forces raided. They came to my neighborhood, they raided my house.

... I was sleeping with my wife and two kids on the same bed in my room upstairs in her family's house, and there was a sudden explosion. All the windows of the house were broken. All were fallen down. We thought, there's a mortar or kind of plane landed on the house, on top of the house. But within seconds, a rifle came through the door and shot the bullets inside the room where we are sleeping and I threw myself on my kids and wife, trying to protect them. In seconds then, three American soldiers rushed into the room. They were surrounding the bed.

They took me out of the bed. They laid me on the ground. They were shouting things like, "Go around! Go around!" Things like that—really, nothing that I could understand. Maybe it [was] military terms or something. The only thing I hear at that time [was] my daughter Sarah, who's just three years, shouting and crying. Also my son Adam, ten months, crying, and my wife shouting. "What's happening?" she was shouting in Arabic. "What's happening, Ali? What's wrong? Tell them you're a journalist and you're working for a British TV."

After that, they banded my hands. ... They took me downstairs, where I saw American soldiers searching the house. There were about twenty or so searching the house. They were gathering all the cell phones that we have in the house. They took me into the living room. They made me sit on a chair, and after that, a captain came to me, American captain, and he interrogated me. He had a piece of paper and he said, "Do you know this lady?"

I said, "I don't know her, but probably she is Jill Carroll ... because I saw her on the news tonight." And he said, "She's in this house." And I said, "No way. She's not in this house." ... And he said, "No, this is Mujahadeen house." Mujahadeen is a Sunni tribe.

And [I] said, "How come it's a Mujahadeen house? Go into the sitting room, into the other room ... and see there is a big picture of Imam Ali." Imam Ali is a Shia figure—the holiest Shia figure for the Shiites.

And he went there and he came back asking about my identity. I explained to him that I'm a journalist. I'm working for British TV, Channel Four, and the *Guardian* in London. He wasn't convinced, though.

In minutes he brought a camera. I have a small camera, a handicam camera. And there was a tape inside it that I was logging ... And he brought it from the kitchen with the tape inside that showed me talking to the camera and the Green Zone behind me. I was at the fifteenth floor of the Palestine Hotel, talking to the camera for the last film I did, "Iraq Missing Billions." And there were some shots like close-ups on some buildings inside the Green Zone like pans—things that we thought we [were] gonna use in the editing, and we did.

CHARLES FERGUSON: But filming of the Green Zone is prohibited.

ALI FADHIL: It's not prohibited.

CHARLES FERGUSON: It's not prohibited?

ALI FADHIL: No, it's not at all. ...

CHARLES FERGUSON: It is now, by the way.

ALI FADHIL: Well [it is] if you are moving inside the Green Zone. That's what it is. You can't put the camera and set it on the corner of the street inside the Green Zone.

... I was in the ceremony inside the Green Zone for the anniversary of the Iraqi Army just two days before the raid. And I was inside with my camera, and I was filming the Green Zone, everywhere around. In fact, I didn't think I will have this opportunity. I filmed, and there were American soldiers. There, the U.S. ambassador came, and I filmed him, and I filmed all around from inside the Green Zone.

And the funny thing is, the captain told me, "Can you explain to me ... why you have these shots?" And I said, "Well, because we are doing this film. It's about reconstruction. I was trying to save the Green Zone, CPA, things like that."

And he said—I remember his face and he's coming closer to me—and he's saying, "Do you know that these places were targeted a few days ago?" And [I] said, "No way. I'm a journalist, and I know these places weren't targeted, and I was inside the Green Zone two days ago and I filmed these places. And there's another tape, if you want to see it, from inside the Green Zone." And that was shocking for him. And from that time, everything changed—the mood how he dealt with me. Everything changed. Then he started saying that "We need to take you somewhere to interrogate you in a better way so we can have better information about this lady." He didn't say the name, by the way.

There was another man in the paper he showed me. It was a man with a beard, and he asked me, "Do you know this guy?" I said, "Yes." And he said, "How do you know him?" I said, "Because I see him every day in the Green Zone when I go to cover a conference or something." ... His name is Mahmoud Mashhadani. He was the sheik of a mosque in my neighborhood. He was wanted [by] the Americans in mid-2004. They came to my house in 2004, and they asked for the same guy, and we told him that this is not his house and he's not living here; he's living somewhere else in the neighborhood, but we don't know where. And it's a fact: We don't know where he's living. He might be living somewhere, like a few blocks.

Then they took me ... They threatened me with the dog. They slipped something on my head, a kind of liquid—I didn't know what it was—and that's what that dog was barking and barking [at]. It might [have been] a kind of stimulus to the dog or something. After that ... they hooded my face.

They took me in a Bradley, I think, an armored vehicle, in a tank or something. And they drove for, like, maybe three-quarters of an hour or something, somewhere right and left, right and left. At that time I was sitting and ... I was thinking about, There'll be an IED; there'll be an RPG on the tank. And one time I get tired. I ... rest back on the side of the tank, and then I get anxious and I leaned forward again.

So ... they drove until I found myself in a small room with wooden walls and a young American soldier with a pistol tied on his leg. And he was guarding me. I tried to ask him questions where I am, but no answer. Minutes later, two American civilians came inside the room. They were asking me a question like "Mr. Fadhil, do you know why you're here?" I said, "To interrogate me? I don't know why I'm here." And they said, "No, it's because it was a mistake. There was a mistake in the address, and we apologize for that." And that was a kind of a shock for me, but at the same time, I just

remembered all of the stories of the other people I met ... And I was thinking this: that this is the time I'm thinking the same way they [did]; they
thought there was these kind of things—the raids and detention.

And they said, "We apologize for what happened." And [I] asked them,
"... And so [you're] not going to interrogate me about the reporter?" They
said, "No, and we're gonna release you tomorrow morning as soon as possible." And I asked them about the conversations before the house, because
they smashed the whole furniture of the house. And they said, "Yes, other
people [will] come in the morning and ... they will talk about the conversations." And they gave me a bed with a blanket. It was cold at that time. I
slept. The poor American soldier was sitting on the chair and looking at me.

In the morning, two American civilians came inside. They were looking
like the private security people, wearing a vest and all kind of guns everywhere around. They were [saying], "Mr. Fadhil, we apologize for what happened, but now we are going to release you, and we have some money for
the compensation." I said yes. They opened one envelope with one thousand dollars. They said, "This is the thousand dollars for the damages of
the house," and then another envelope with the five hundred dollars. "This
is," they said, "This is for the time you spent with us in the Green Zone."
[It] was the highest salary I've ever got in my life. I took the money. They
said, "But we need to fold [your] eyes again."

They put bandage on my eyes, and they took me outside the room. And
I managed to see that they put me in a civilian car. And they drove me
around somewhere, I didn't know, right and left, right and left, until later
on ... they released me between two very high barricades, like three meters
high. And I walked outside the concrete barricades to find myself in the
south gate of the Green Zone, the place that I never imagined I would be
someday, because it's the worst place in Baghdad to be.

You know, I was wearing pajamas and going out of the Green Zone
wearing these pajamas. Even there was a hole in the pajamas. And I walked
out from the Green Zone. People were looking: This guy's walking out
with civilian clothes from the Green Zone. And hardly I found the taxi,
and he drove me back to the house, looking at me in a weird look, you
know. And thank God I arrived at my neighborhood, which was closed at
that time when I arrived. And I had to walk across the bridge towards the

house, where I found the whole family terrified and crying. And they didn't believe that I arrived in the morning and that day, because the stories that they hear—that we hear—that people got taken for months and, if they are lucky, for weeks. And from that time, the problem started for me, as new security problems started in the neighborhood.

CHARLES FERGUSON: How so?

ALI FADHIL: There were three other houses raided at the same time my house was raided. And they detained the people inside of these houses, like three people from one house, four people from the other house, two people from the other house. All of them, they were taken and they never released them the same day, the next day, a week later. They never released them, and people started questioning: "Why was this guy released, why the others not?" Two days later, the news about an Iraqi journalist working for British media were in the local news. And I had a kind of security issue. I received a phone call from a friend telling me that "Some people know that you're living in Gazalia, and it's not good for you to stay. You have to leave." So I had to leave the place. I took my family. They lived in the hotel for a few days before they left for Jordan. And myself, I stayed there for two weeks before I left Iraq. I had to do my last interview with the American ambassador, which was very difficult, until we got in.

And the Abu Ghraib prisoner abuse scandal affected Americans, including military officers, as well as Iraqis.

A. HEATHER COYNE: What changed my mind and made me stop fighting the decision [the army's decision to redeploy her out of Iraq] was Abu Ghraib. When that came out, I didn't want to be in uniform anymore in Iraq. I was still committed to the Iraqis and to this project and to the whole operation, but I ... I was embarrassed to be in a uniform.

And I realized I wasn't getting anywhere with the resources and support I had, anyway. It would make more sense to go home and come back as a civilian to try and do things in a way that made a little bit more sense. What hit me hardest about Abu Ghraib was that for a year, when Iraqis came up to me saying, "Oh, my family member has disappeared or has been arrested by the Americans, [and] I'm really worried [about] them," I could always respond [with an] absolutely clear conscience, "Don't worry. They're in an American prison, and it's too bad that they're separated from you, but they're being treated well, they're being taken care of, and they'll be back soon. Once it's proved that they weren't involved in an act of terrorism, an act of violence, they'll be coming home to you."

And I realized that every time I'd say that over the last year, I had no idea whether those people were being treated well or not. I assumed they were because that's what I expected from my country and my military. And I was telling these people to rest assured, when I didn't know how their family members were being treated.

So that was kind of the last straw for me. And I said, "It's okay. I'm going to go home. I'm going to accept the fact that the military's sending me home. And I'm going to find an organization to come back with that does a better job at this." ... Even before I'd left Iraq, I had already made arrangements with the U.S. Institute of Peace to turn around and come back a few weeks later as their chief of party.

A U.S. soldier watches as detainees are released at Abu Ghraib prison, October 1, 2005.

Everyone I spoke with, however, agreed that the U.S. military conducted itself far better than the approximately forty-five thousand private military contractors operating in Iraq. In general, the military behaved with some degree of care, and soldiers were subject to at least some degree of discipline and accountability. In contrast, the contractors were effectively accountable to nobody, and it showed.

This was not inevitable; it was a product of U.S. policy. L. Paul Bremer issued a CPA order that exempted all U.S. contractors from Iraqi law. Private military contractors working for the U.S. military usually signed a contract that made them subject to the Uniform Code of Military Justice, but few were ever investigated or prosecuted. Contractors working for the U.S. State Department—and there were many, including those hired to protect U.S. diplomatic personnel—were not subject to U.S. law at all.

SETH MOULTON: It's kind of sad when you see all these civilians who come over to work for the private contractors, who are doing so much of the work with the reconstruction, really just because we don't have enough troops. And you just don't get the impression that we're really sending the best and the brightest to do this work. We're sending the guys who really need a paycheck.

Some of them are great, and there are some amazingly patriotic Americans who can't serve in the military or something anymore, and so they sign up to be a contractor and work for KBR or something. But by and large, the great talent of this nation to make Iraq work is not being used. And I think that's going to have to change if we're gonna win.

Moulton commented on contractor killings.

SETH MOULTON: Of course, there are some good ones, but I've seen an awful lot of civilian contractors who have been particularly violent and very shortsighted in terms of what they're doing. You know, in terms of having no problem shooting at vehicles if they enter their convoys, and thinking solely about the immediate security situation and not what shooting at that might do to the long-term security situation.

And there were times when we, as marine units, would essentially have to clean up the mess from civilian contractors coming through and shooting at vehicles, you know, without really due cause. Because then, all of a sudden, the civilian populace in the area would be angry, and we'd have to deal with it.

I remember going to a meeting with the State Department in Kut one time, and the first hour of the meeting was simply spent in paying reparations to a young Iraqi who had been shot up by the Blackwater crew that protected the State Department. I mean, what a waste. Here the State Department is going to Kut to try to work with the Iraqi governor there— who is not easy to work with at all—and yet, the first priority, and a good chunk of time, had to [be] taken up by simply paying off this poor Iraqi who had been shot by Blackwater.

Blackwater tries to do a good job, but I don't think they're nearly as professional as the military, from what I've seen, at least.

Gerald Burke agreed that the contractors often operated as renegades.

GERALD BURKE: I don't think there's anyone on the coalition side investigating the private military contractors. It's very difficult. I mean, they're driving in unmarked SUVs. And the vehicles all look alike ... And no one has to coordinate when they go out, or where they go.

I know that [at] one point, a member of the Iraqi police intelligence division was walking across the street near an Iraqi police checkpoint and a convoy of PMC's went by, and for some reason, somebody in one of the vehicles shot at this civilian—he was a policeman, but he was in civilian clothes near a checkpoint—and killed him. And we talked to Iraqi police who were manning the checkpoint, and they were adamant, every one of them—as we did, you know, sort of an informal investigation with the Iraqi Ministry of Interior—that there was no justification for the shooting. But we couldn't determine what company or whose convoy it was.

Life on the Ground

U.S. personnel on the ground were clearly under extreme pressure. They often had difficulty distinguishing friend from foe, and were often misled by Iraqis who had political or personal agendas. Most Americans in Iraq did not speak the language or understand the culture of the country in which they found themselves. Since their lo-cal knowledge was so limited, it was extremely difficult for them to know whom to trust and when they were safe. They therefore developed an understandable ten-dency to distrust everyone, everywhere. Furthermore, while it may be politically in-correct to mention this, it is relevant to note that there were no sexual outlets. Be-cause of the combined effect of the language problem, Islamic norms, and the insurgency, U.S. personnel had no opportunity to form sexual relationships with Iraqis, and U.S. forces are prohibited from having sexual relationships with their col-leagues. Iraq is full of young, sexually unsatisfied men, both Americans and Iraqis, carrying automatic weapons.

Also, physical conditions in Iraq can be extremely difficult. Electricity, water sup-plies, sanitation, refrigeration, heating, and air-conditioning are vastly inadequate. To give an unpleasant but instructive personal example: When I was in Baghdad in 2006, I lived in conditions that were palatial by normal Iraqi standards. Yet in the fourteen days I was in Baghdad, I had very severe diarrhea four times. Needless to say, U.S. soldiers on patrol cannot always choose when to spend two hours on a toi-let. Moreover, summer temperatures regularly exceed 120 degrees Fahrenheit, whereas winters can be very cold. And although major U.S. bases are relatively comfortable, for U.S. forces on patrol, conducting operations, or stationed outside of such bases, Iraq can be an extremely harsh place.

U.S. military personnel also suffered from a lack of sufficient armor, particularly for vehicles, but also body armor for people.

CHARLES FERGUSON: The armor issue: You probably know that at least in the American press, there's been a lot of discussion of the insufficient sup-ply, the slow response of military contractors and the Pentagon to supply-ing armored vehicles and body armor. Did you see that? Was that an issue? Was it not an issue?

SETH MOULTON: Yes, absolutely. As a marine infantry battalion, we proba-bly were given some of the highest priority for issuing the [small arms pro-tective insert (sappy) plates], for example—the bulletproof plates that you insert into your Kevlar vests. The first time I ever saw one of those in my life was just before we left for Iraq. We got issued them, but there weren't enough to go around for the entire battalion. So most of the guys in rifle platoons would have two, but then there were some who only had one, and then I think some of the staff officers and whatnot, you know, may have had none. I'm not sure. I think that they issued some more once we got to Kuwait. But I don't know that we really were fully outfitted for quite some time.

We certainly had no armor on our vehicles, though that was an issue that really didn't show itself until later on in the war, although I guess, from what I'm told—I've never been to Kosovo—but they've been using armored Humvees in Kosovo for some time, so it seems like it would be only natural that you'd think maybe we might need some of those if we're gonna invade Iraq.

In general, I just think it's another example of how America is really not committed to this effort. I mean, if the administration really wanted to … if the administration had insisted that we—I shouldn't say that. I mean, if America had insisted on getting armor to the troops, then absolutely, we could have done it. And I think that there are some stories someone told me about how, a few months after the fall of Baghdad, President Bush proudly announced that we had turned out two hundred armored Humvees. And putting that in context, you know, the same time frame after December 7th, 1941, we had already produced twenty thousand airplanes or something.

… The priority is just not there. I mean, gosh, we have automobile plants closing down in America. I'm not a factory expert, [but] just retool them to produce some armored Humvees. That shouldn't be that difficult. I mean, it's taken forever to get them there. We never had a single armored Humvee while we were in Iraq, throughout 2003. We went to Iraq in 2004 with unarmored Humvees, and they were given armor kits in Kuwait, which were just sort of cutout doors with no windows and a bulletproof windshield, and that's about it. And it wasn't until I started working for General Petraeus in the army, actually, that I ever had a fully armored Humvee. And that was in January of 2005.

CHARLES FERGUSON: I see. And was this a significant issue with regard to your operational flexibility and/or casualty levels?

SETH MOULTON: Well, for most of the fight in Najaf, we were not in Humvees. There were certainly some lives that were saved by the armor plating we did have—the bullet marks attested to that. So what we had helped, without question. But ... in this case, more armor would definitely be better. And I'm sure that for other units that were in combat that involved more vehicle types of things—ambushes and whatnot—of course it was an issue. It just wasn't as much for me in the particular issues of Najaf. Now, when traveling around Iraq later on, working with the Special Forces and whatnot, I don't think they would have even let us go in their convoys if we didn't have a properly armored vehicle, because of the IEDs and everything else.

I interviewed half a dozen wounded Iraq veterans in late 2005. Two of them said that the armor issue had directly affected them. Hugo Gonzales was in an unarmored Humvee.

CHARLES FERGUSON: How were you injured?

HUGO GONZALES: Okay, Sir. The night I got injured, it was the night of the 21st of June, 2004. We went out on a combat patrol because we got a confidence that in the town of [Gadir], a very bad town in Baqubah, they were building bombs. So we go up there, trying to surprise them, trying to make some raids, trying to get some information, and go inside houses to see what is going on in there.

That night, I was lucky because I was assigned to a cruiser weapon. That was gonna make me stay in a vehicle, taking command of a cruiser weapon all night. I didn't have to go walking and go inside houses. ... But I was in the bucket. The bucket is a nonarmored vehicle that we have in there, and we take to convoys, and we take everywhere we go. But to be in the bucket has an extra inconvenience, and an extra [sighs] ... an extra thing because anything that happens, you're gonna get it. So nobody wants to be in there.

That night, when we get down there ... the lieutenant ... started to ask some questions, [looking for] some information. And we start to ... [get] the sense of something bad is gonna happen. For example, they shut down the lights ... to disturb us and make us ... blind in the eye [by shining a bright light at us]. But nothing happens there. That was the perfect time to attack us, when they turn off the light again. Nothing happened then.

Then we saw there were a lot of people gathering. Then we saw the men kicking women and boys ... literally, actually, kicking them. ... That's another thing that let us know that there is something gonna happen; they are taking the women out; they are taking the kids out.

So everybody was saying the same thing, and the sergeant[s] say, "Okay, we're gonna go." When we were leaving, at the entrance of that town, the [unintelligible] go out. I suffer the blast almost directly, Sir. And then I came, I start hearing the firefight. From the far to the closest: *ba-ba*. We started firing.

As a consequence of that blast, I suffered a penetrating traumatic brain injury. And I lost the perception of light in my right eye. I suffered a pellet in my left eye that gave me a [macular] hole in the retina. But we fight. We fight until we hear the cease-fire. It wasn't that long. It was only, like, ten or fifteen minutes, no more than that.

But I knew I was hit. I can feel the warm and the wet of my blood in my hand. And at that point, I just call for my mother. I feel a little bit dizzy. But my sergeant helped me get out of the bucket.

Over there in the floor, they gave me the first aid. When they laid me down, I lost conscious. ... I wake up [*sighs*] in Baghdad. They practice a craniectomy. They take out a piece of the skull from my frontal lobe— [temporal] and parietal—they took out a big piece. Because of the penetration that my brain suffered, the brain starts swelling and it didn't have any room to go, so they have to make room to [let it] out. It was swelling very bad because of the wound. And they placed that piece of skull in my belly. They make me a marsupial wound so I can take care of my own bone. ...

CHARLES FERGUSON: How long were you in the hospital?

HUGO GONZALES: Two years.

In contrast, David Yancey was in an armored Humvee, and his unit had been issued adequate supplies of both body and vehicle armor.

CHARLES FERGUSON: How did you get injured? What happened?

DAVID YANCEY: We was pullin' just a routine convoy escort. And our Humvee struck an IED. And it was a hundred fifty-five round that we ran over the top of, and it just blew our Humvee apart. I was a gunner. And my driver lost both his legs. And it ejected me out. And I suffered a fractured femur, nearly lost my right arm, and collapsed lung, and [closed head] wounds and shrapnel wounds. And me and my driver were both sent back to Walter Reed [Army Medical Center in Washington, D.C.].

CHARLES FERGUSON: I see. And when did that happen?

DAVID YANCEY: The explosion happened March 29th of 2005, and we got to Walter Reed by April 1st.

CHARLES FERGUSON: So, very quickly.

DAVID YANCEY: Very quickly.

CHARLES FERGUSON: Hmm, okay. And I should ask this question: Was your Humvee armored?

DAVID YANCEY: Yes it was.

CHARLES FERGUSON: So even though your Humvee was armored—

DAVID YANCEY: It was a big IED that we ran over.

CHARLES FERGUSON: Wow.

DAVID YANCEY: A big IED. And just tore it apart. But it was an armored Humvee.

CHARLES FERGUSON: … If your Humvee hadn't been armored, what do you think the damage from that IED would have been?

DAVID YANCEY: I think it would have been deadly.

CHARLES FERGUSON: I see. So you think that the fact that your Humvee was armored saved your life?

DAVID YANCEY: Right.

CHARLES FERGUSON: I see. Okay. And the armor question: I'm sure you've seen lots of discussion of this.

DAVID YANCEY: Uh-huh.

CHARLES FERGUSON: What do you think about that? What did you see in Iraq with regard to that question?

DAVID YANCEY: What I saw, we were heavily armored. We had [up-armored] Humvees before we went out on the mission. Going in and out, we had heavy armor[ed] Humvees. And we had body armor. We were supplied body armor before we ever left the States. And we were already wearing it and gettin' used to it.

CHARLES FERGUSON: Uh-huh.

DAVID YANCEY: So from what I seen and what I can count for, we had plenty of armor.

CHARLES FERGUSON: And do you think that it made a difference?

DAVID YANCEY: I think so.

CHARLES FERGUSON: So did you see other cases where people were hit by IEDs or gunfire, and you think that—

DAVID YANCEY: Oh, I know it made a difference. I saw other Humvees come in off of missions that had survived IED attacks.

The Defense Department was extremely slow to remedy the armor shortage, a situation that generated enormous anger throughout the military. During one infamous town hall meeting held in Kuwait on December 8, 2004, a soldier confronted Donald Rumsfeld.

SOLDIER: Yes, Mr. Secretary. My question is more logistical. Now why do we soldiers have to dig through local landfills for pieces of scrap metal and compromise ballistic glass to up-armor our vehicles and why don't we have those resources readily available to us? [Applause]

DONALD RUMSFELD: I talked to the general coming out here about the pace at which the vehicles are being armored. They have been brought from all over the world, wherever they're not needed, to a place here where they are needed. ... I think it's something like four hundred a month are being done. And it's essentially a matter of physics. It isn't a matter of money. It isn't a matter, on the part of the army, of desire. It's a matter of production and capability of doing it.

As you know, you go to war with the army you have. They're not the army you might want or wish to have at a later time. Since the Iraq conflict began, the army has been pressing ahead to produce the armor necessary at a rate that they believe—it's a greatly expanded rate from what existed previously—but a rate that they believe is the rate that is all that can be accomplished at this moment.

General Paul Eaton believed that the Pentagon leadership was insulated from the harsh reality on the ground in Iraq.

PAUL EATON: It was all hard. It was all hard. You know … if you ever ask a soldier if he has enough of anything, he'll say no. I mean, a soldier never has enough ammunition, batteries, food, water, soldiers, stuff. You never have enough stuff. But it got redefined in the Coalition for Provisional Authority … We didn't have any up-armored vehicles available to CPA, outside of a few for Ambassador Bremer and a couple other guys for VIP visits. Everybody else traveled around in thin-skinned SUVs. That's how we got around. And it was only until there was a very high probability of getting engaged that we'd see that get fixed.

CHARLES FERGUSON: How come?

PAUL EATON: Well, to paraphrase somebody: You go to war with the army you have.

CHARLES FERGUSON: [laughs] Right, but that can get changed, you know.

PAUL EATON: It sure can. And just means that you've got to act very quickly. First you have to recognize you got a problem. And then you've got to act on your analysis. And … [the] Pentagon was five or six thousand miles away.

CHARLES FERGUSON: Did people try and educate the Pentagon?

PAUL EATON: Yes.

CHARLES FERGUSON: They failed.

PAUL EATON: And distance provides its own filter. When you're that far away and that secure, you can listen to … I mean, I would be in teleconferences, and I'm sitting in the little room in the Republican Palace and I'm looking at the room on the far end in the Pentagon, and it's a different planet. And I'll guarantee you that the Pentagon was and is operating at a hundred percent strength plus.

In order to continue the occupation, it became necessary for the U.S. military to rely more heavily on the National Guard and reserves. The training and equipment of these part-time military groups were clearly inferior to their active duty comrades.

SETH MOULTON: There's certainly great differences among military units. I mean, the National Guard in Iraq is overall very ill prepared and not well trained enough to deal with the level of combat that they're experiencing. And you know what? They'll tell you that. I expected, when the Mississippi National Guard arrived to take over Najaf from the 11th Marine Expeditionary Unit, of which I was a part, I expected them to be kind of like cowboys—rather arrogant. And the experience I had with them was exactly the opposite.

I mean, the first thing that the platoon commander said to me—the platoon commander who was doing a direct turnover with my platoon—the first thing that platoon commander said to me was, "Listen, dude, I'm a farmer. I don't know why I'm here, and I'm not ready for it. Please just tell me whatever you can so that I can make it through the next year."

And we did. We tried to do the best we could. And we dedicated a lot of time, during a very short turnover period, to just doing whatever we could to try to set up the National Guard for success. But like I say, they were the first to tell you that they weren't prepared for what they were being thrown into. And you know, if you're not prepared for that, I mean, there are gonna be mistakes. And that clearly happens in Iraq. There's always gonna be some mistakes. Some of it's unavoidable, but some of it is avoidable.

By all accounts, the military occupation since the insurgency gathered force in 2004 has been a contest between forces of improvement and forces of deterioration. In

general, the forces of deterioration were victorious. The U.S. military gradually began to adopt proven counterinsurgency techniques, increase its Arabic language
and intelligence capabilities, deploy a greater number of armored vehicles, and otherwise adjust to the realities of a long-term occupation faced with serious resistance. At the same time, the insurgency and the Shiite militias continued to grow,
and the gulf between the military and much of the population worsened as conditions in Iraq deteriorated; and so the strain on the military grew as well. By early
2007, the U.S. military had effectively lost control of the country, which had become
a quasi-warlord society with several low-level civil wars under way simultaneously.

PART THREE

WHERE DO WE GO FROM HERE?

CHAPTER ELEVEN

CONSEQUENCES

As of late 2007, the balance sheet for the Bush administration's intervention in Iraq appeared approximately as follows: The intervention did remove Saddam Hussein and his regime from power and installed, in a limited form, a democratic political system in Iraq. There is also substantial freedom of speech and communication, with widespread cell phone use and Internet access. The intervention also provided increased freedom and prosperity for Iraq's Kurds. At the same time, however, the war has had enormous costs. It has caused approximately 4,000 American deaths, 60,000 to 80,000 American wounded, and an unknown but large number of Iraqi deaths, perhaps a quarter of a million. It has generated over 4 million refugees and internally displaced persons. Iraq's government services, infrastructure, and nonoil economy have deteriorated sharply, and its current political leadership is universally regarded with contempt. Iraq has fractured into a quasi-warlord society ruled by multiple, competing armed groups that often engage in criminal behavior and in armed combat with each other. For everyone except Kurds in the north and political dissidents, Iraq is now far more dangerous than it was under Saddam Hussein as a result of terrorism, insurgency, crime, political assassination, and sectarian conflict, as well as the deterioration of public health. The war has also proven expensive. Total economic costs to the United States appear to exceed $2 trillion; worldwide economic costs are far larger. Most analysts also believe that the situation in Iraq could destabilize the Persian Gulf region, even leading possibly to regional war, and that the occupation has weakened U.S. diplomatic, economic, and military leverage with regard to Iran, North Korea, and the Arab world. Many, though not all, analysts believe that the war has substantially increased the long-term risk of terrorism against the United States and other Western nations.

Iraq continued to deteriorate through 2007. The question of whether progress has recently been made as a result of the troop surge and other U.S. policy initiatives that began in mid-2007 is a complicated issue, one that is discussed and debated in chapter 12. For now, we take a closer look at the balance sheet items just enumerated.

What Iraq Has Become

As of late 2007, Iraq is a quasi-warlord society with a paralyzed central government whose individual ministries are controlled by various political parties and militias. The country is dominated by four regional power struggles, which often approach open warfare, conducted through a combination of politics, corruption, crime, and militia violence. Three rival Shiite militias and political parties (the Badr Organization, the Mahdi Army, and the Islamic Virtue Party) are struggling for control of the south; the Mahdi Army is fighting Sunni militias, al Qaeda, and sometimes the United States for control of Baghdad; secular or nationalist Sunni groups are fighting with al Qaeda in Iraq and foreign fundamentalists for control of Sunni regions; and the Kurds are fighting with Arabs for control of Kirkuk and its oil resources. Thus Iraq is in a state of near civil war, which is barely contained by the American military presence. The country suffers from an extremely high level of criminal violence and pervasive corruption. The south and Baghdad are predominantly controlled by fundamentalist Shiite militias and their affiliated political parties. American occupation forces have been progressively marginalized. The recent American troop surge is generally regarded as having produced a substantial but unsustainable reduction in violence, without altering the fundamental processes under way in the country, including continuing ethnic cleansing, geographical segregation along sectarian lines, deteriorating infrastructure, and political paralysis.

Political Structure

By the time sovereignty was officially restored to Iraq in June 2004, the collapse of the Iraqi state was well under way. As the power of both the Americans and the prior institutions of the Iraqi state continued to decline, a new political structure and balance of power emerged in the country. After three elections and much political bargaining, the central government fell under the control of loose, unstable alliances of primarily Shiite politicians and parties backed by heavily armed militias, especially SCIRI (Supreme Council for the Islamic Revolution in Iraq, which was renamed SIIC, for Supreme Islamic Iraqi Council, in May 2007) and Moqtada al-Sadr's followers. The political leadership of the central government grew increasingly paralyzed, corrupt, and irrelevant. Journalist Nir Rosen described what he saw as the disintegration of the country.

NIR ROSEN: I think it's been going very consistently in the same trajectory since the end of 2004, which is … the disintegration of Iraq. The increasing insignificance of central government, growth of militias, local militias, even the disintegration of militias—Moqtada al-Sadr's militia is no longer very cohesive or disciplined; it's becoming more and more local.

CHARLES FERGUSON: Who is going to run Iraq—

NIR ROSEN: … That's been decided [since] 2005, and it's been clear who is going to run Iraq: It's Shia—sectarian Shia militias. Nobody has been threatening their power at all. So there is violence between those militias, perhaps a little bit, but [it will get] much worse in the future. But it's quite obvious who is running Iraq, to the extent that anybody can run it because events in Baghdad don't necessarily run anything else outside of Baghdad.

CHARLES FERGUSON: So, is there an Iraqi army? Is the Iraqi army controlled by the central government?

NIR ROSEN: It is a little bit, but it's not entirely. The Kurds in the army are loyal to Kurds, the Shiites are loyal to Shia parties, Sunni to Sunnis. There are very few units that, as far as I can know, are integrated or work together, and mainly those are the ones that are controlled by the Americans. And security forces are loyal to sectarian or ethnic militias. The army is majority Shia, anyway, so who are they going to be loyal to?

Nobody I spoke with had anything good to say about the political leadership or the central government. Here is a long, cool, detailed assessment by Juan Cole, a professor at the University of Michigan. Cole has studied the Middle East, and particularly Shiite Islam in Iraq, for over two decades. Like Nir Rosen, Cole is a left-wing thinker, but neither man is crudely or predictably so—for example, as we will see later, Cole does not support U.S. withdrawal from Iraq—and Cole and Rosen's basic view of the Iraqi government is shared by nearly all the knowledgeable Americans and Iraqis with whom I spoke. I found Cole very accurate on factual matters and analytically incisive.

JUAN COLE: Well, of course any generalization about a large group of people is probably flawed. There are certainly people in the Iraqi government who are brave and patriotic and risking their lives to try to do a good job. But there are substantial problems with the way the Iraqi government is run. It is a weak government. It is not clear that any order given by the prime minister affecting provincial policy would necessarily be obeyed by provincial authorities. It is not clear that the bureaucracy is entirely under the prime minister's control. Many of the ministries were given out to the parties that supported [prime minister of Iraq, Nuri] al-Maliki in a kind of spoils system of a sort that used to exist in the United States in the days of Andrew Jackson. So that the Ministry of the Interior—which in Iraq is not about managing trees, but is rather a security ministry; it's more like our FBI, our Homeland Security—the Interior Ministry is under the control of the Islamic Supreme Council of Iraq [SCIRI], a hard-line Shiite fundamentalist party formed in Tehran, the paramilitary of which, the Badr Corps, was trained by the Iranian Revolutionary Guards. And obviously, the special police commandos of the Interior Ministry are specially recruited from the Badr Corps, and so the Sunni Arabs feel that this Ministry of the Interior is a bastion of Iranian Shiite influence [and] that the commandos have been involved in ethnic cleansing of Sunni Arabs and attacks on Sunni Arab leaders. So that's not a national ministry if it's being viewed as sectarian and indeed is under foreign Iranian control. That's an exaggeration, but there is something to it.

And then there's the whole question of whether it is involved in receiving arms from Iran—the ministry itself—whether it has storehouses of them, and whether they get sold off behind the scenes or stolen, and so contribute to the insecurity. The Ministry of Petroleum, likewise, is under the control of the same party and again, it is alleged that Badr Corps thugs are involved in the national petroleum industry as a result. Since we're trying to convince the Sunni Arabs that they're going to get a fair shake from the National Petroleum Ministry, [the fact] that it is under the control of a very sectarian Shiite fundamentalist party is not helpful in that regard. The Health Ministry had been, before they resigned, under the Sadr movement, and it had been alleged in summer of 2006 that the Sadr movement was actually using the hospitals as a tool; that is to say, if Sunni Arabs who were wounded checked into them, they would be viewed as Sunni guerrillas and the Shiite authorities would then deal with them as enemy combatants.

So the government consists of ministries that have been captive to sectional political party interests and have even, in 2006, engaged in a kind of warfare amongst one another. It appeared to be the case that Interior Ministry commandos captured—kidnapped—employees of the Ministry of Higher Education who were Sunni Arabs, perhaps suspecting them of, behind the scenes, being involved in the Sunni Arab insurgency.

So the ministries are sectarian; they are party driven. They are sources of patronage for the parties, who provide employment to their party members. And remember, a lot of these parties are family affairs, so you're talking about nepotism and cousins getting jobs as well as party clients. And they're very corrupt. There's a great deal of embezzlement. The Islamic Virtue Party in the south controls the provincial petroleum apparatus. Petroleum is nationalized in Iraq at the moment, so there's a federal component [and] there's a provincial component to the petroleum industry. It is estimated that between gasoline smuggling and outright embezzlement from government offices that some two billion dollars is being drained off of the petroleum industry in the Basra area by parties and their militias. And this transfer of wealth from what should be the government to these parties and their gunmen has caused the security situation in Basra to be extremely tense with firefights among the militias of the parties that sit in the provincial council. So you have an unconventional, low-intensity war going on amongst the very parties that are supposed to be running the province.

So the government is more or less a failed state. I mean, the parliament can barely get a quorum. To my knowledge, the parliament has passed no significant legislation in all the time that it's been there since it passed the constitution itself, and it seems to be deadlocked over all of the important issues that face the country. It's been able to forge no sort of national com-promises that might mollify disgruntled parties and bring them into the process.

In Cole's view, paralysis at the top guarantees that little will change. His assessment is widely shared among both Iraqis and American observers.

JUAN COLE: Two major Shiite factions, the Islamic Virtue Party, which is based in the south in Basra, and the Sadr movement, led by Moqtada al-Sadr, have formally pulled out of the al-Maliki coalition, have had their ministers resign from the cabinet, and are now in the opposition. So even within the Shiite block, al-Maliki is much weakened. And then the Iraqi Nationalists, led by former-appointed prime minister, Ayad Allawi, has pulled out of his government. And the Sunni Arab block, the Iraqi Accord Front, led by Mr. al-Dulaimi, has pulled out, and this is a party—or a coalition—to which the Sunni vice president, Tariq al-Hashemi, belongs, and al-Hashemi has repeatedly threatened to resign. Al-Hashemi, the Sunni vice president, maintains that for a long time in spring of 2007, he simply couldn't get an appointment even to see al-Maliki. So the hopes that al-Maliki as prime minister would reach out to the Sunni Arabs and bring more of them into the political process has been forlorn. He has lost the Sunni Arabs who were willing to sit in parliament with him and be part of his national unity government, and who were willing to provide cabinet ministers to him in his government. Those are now gone. They're in the opposition. They're attempting to form alternative parliamentary coalitions and bring down his government.

It's not easy to bring down a government as the constitution is designed. Unlike, say, in Britain, where you can call a snap vote of no confidence and the prime minister could fall if he doesn't win it, in Iraq, the constitution insists that the prime minister fall by a simple majority. That is to say, that it's not just a majority of the quorum, but you would need 138 votes out of 275. And since the security situation is still not good, and since so many parliamentarians don't live in the Green Zone and find it difficult to come to parliament—since so many parliamentarians actually live in Ahman, Jordan, or in London—getting a quorum of 138 is difficult; getting a vote of 138, I mean, it would almost be a unanimous vote nowadays. So it's very difficult to unseat al-Maliki. But these political forces that had been in his government as the national unity government are now seeking to undermine him and to replace him.

Most Iraqis I spoke with were far more direct, at least when discussing the political leadership—the prime minister, ministers, and parliament members. Some felt that the central government bureaucracy was still reasonably effective, given the circumstances, but nobody had a good word to say about the political leadership. Here is Omar Fekeiki, first commenting on Prime Minister Maliki:

OMAR FEKEIKI: When Nouri Maliki came to power, he promised to reconcile between the Shiites and Sunnis and he's been talking about this since … April or May 2006, when he came to power.

CHARLES FERGUSON: Do you think that he's sincere in trying to do that?

OMAR FEKEIKI: No, no, no, no. … What Maliki is doing is basically [similar to] the Baathification of Iraq in the sixties and seventies. What Maliki is doing is the Dawafication of Iraq. It's basically, he's filling the government posts with people from the Dawa Party [a large Shiite party in the United Iraqi Alliance], and the latest evidence of that is his nomination of the minister of health, who is a member of Dawa Party, [though] he nominated him as an independent and he passed the nomination illegally in the parliament. Have you heard of this?

CHARLES FERGUSON: No.

OMAR FEKEIKI: … Remember when the Sadr group and the Sunni group and the Ayad Allawi group ministers boycotted the government months ago? Since then, Maliki was trying to fill the posts with the new people. He promised in every single statement and in every single press conference that he was going to fill them with democrats and independent people. Five days ago, Maliki nominated two people. One of them is a member of Dawa Party, and he nominated him for the post of minister of health, and he said he's an independent. The parliament had to vote them in the government, and there were only 110 members of the parliament present at that session, and they passed the nomination, which was totally illegally, because they needed to have a majority and the parliament is 275 members. But they passed, anyway, and Maliki said, "Those are my ministers," including a Dawa Party member, which is totally illegal. So he lied to the government. He lied to the people. Now there is an investigation, and Maliki said the ministers will stay in their positions until the investigation proves whatever it's going to prove, and that means they're going to totally ignore it and forget about it.

Then Fekeiki commented on the Iraqi parliament's behavior in 2007.

OMAR FEKEIKI: ... Let me tell you one thing that is documented. The oil law in Iraq has been pending for a long time, and the Iraqis have been under this situation for four years now. The Iraqi parliament two weeks before its recess, two weeks before September 1st, the Iraqi parliament with all what Iraq is going through, with all the bodies found in Iraq, with all the car bombs, the Iraqi parliament was trying to pass a law that allows them to issue themselves, the Iraqi parliament members, and their families, diplomatic passports, so they can go during the recess and go to Europe ... And they passed it a week before the recess. And the second law that was passed a week before the recess was a law to allow ... the parliament members to retire a year after they join their parliament and still keep eighty percent of their salaries. Those are the only two laws that were passed in the Iraqi parliament in the last year. Can you imagine this?

Feisal al-Istrabadi did not fundamentally disagree, but noted that political stabilization took the United States a long time, and Iraq probably needed even longer. When I interviewed him in October 2007, Istrabadi had just resigned as Iraq's ambassador to the United Nations, though the Iraqi government had responded that it would not accept his resignation. Istrabadi was back teaching at the University of Illinois.

FEISAL AL-ISTRABADI: I said to [U.S. Ambassador to Iraq] Ryan Crocker, whom I knew from our days in the opposition, I said, "Look, if the French had made it a condition of their support for you [during the American Revolution] that you have a permanent constitution, which adequately dealt with the issue of slavery according to then current European standards; if they had insisted that you had legislation to create the Bank of the United States; if they had demanded that you had resolved the issue of federal consumption of state debt," I said, "you'd still be a British colony today." These things took time. It took thirteen years for the United States to come up with its constitution after independence, including going through a functional constitution. It wasn't called that in those days, which created a very weak central government in which each state had essentially sovereign powers. Does that sound familiar? That's what we have. We've created a weak confederal system, in which the regions and/or the governors basically enjoy all sovereign power. Guess what: It didn't work for the United States; it's not working for us. But it took the U.S. thirteen years to sort all that out. We are expected to do it by September 1st so that General Petraeus can say, "My, my, it has all been done and it's all in a nice pretty bowl." It's crazy.

After the rise of the insurgency, large-scale kidnapping, and the Shiite militias, the United States belatedly tried to build an enormous new Iraqi army and police force with little result. Numerically, the Iraqi security forces (including the army and police) are now larger than they were under Saddam in 2003, but they are generally regarded as inefficient, unprofessional, politicized, and corrupt. They are politically controlled by various regional tribal leaders, militias, and political parties, rather than by the central government. As a result, ethnic cleansing and sectarian violence continued to escalate in Iraq until the 2007 troop surge. As we will see shortly, since the surge, these processes have been temporarily slowed but not reversed.

Nobody I spoke with had anything good to say about the Iraqi security services. Many people said that the army is somewhat better than the police, but even the army is regarded as sectarian and incompetent. Omar X and Ali Fadhil both said the police are utterly untrustworthy and incompetent, despite the police's American training.

OMAR X: The Iraqi government and the Iraqi security forces are really not neutral, efficient government or forces. They all belong to parties; they are all working according to external agendas; and they have their own plans that they want to implant. You can't create a neutral, safe world or a secured Baghdad with such people—such a government and such security forces—and that's what the Americans rely on. I mean, they paid a lot of money to train the Iraqi forces and to recruit them, but what benefits? If they were good forces, we would have had security a long time ago, but now they don't do that. I mean, in my neighborhood, there were Iraqi police checkpoints. When the fighting was starting, they were riding their cars and trying to escape because they think, "We don't want to fight. We can't fight them—the insurgency—and we don't want to fight the militias. And we might be killed. We might be killed, so why bother? We are working only for half salaries." So they fled away. And that is what happened when the shooting started, when the clashes started. They just disappear and they come back when things are calm.

ALI FADHIL: As far as I know, and as far as I can tell you from my observations in Baghdad, the Iraqi army is really unprofessional, to the extent that they are incapable of doing anything, even manning a checkpoint. ... It's a joke in Baghdad, by the way, about the Iraqi army becoming the most advanced army in Iraq. This is a joke in Baghdad.

And you ask why [it's a joke], and they say because [the army has] robots in the checkpoints. ... They're having their cell phones in one hand ... and the other hand, they're just showing their fingers to get cars to pass through without looking even at the driver or the car ...

... They [the enlistees] are actually poor people coming from poor neighborhoods such as Sadr City, such as poor areas in the south, and even poor areas from the Sunni areas. And everyone is looking to the other person with a suspicious eye and thinks that they are against him, or this is not a real job; this is just a job for money and that's it. Or as happened in many occasions, they in fact have relationships with other militias and insurgents.

CHARLES FERGUSON: And who has political control over the army? Is it the national government? Is it regionalized? Does it depend on individual units?

ALI FADHIL: No, it's basically individual units, and it basically belongs to whoever the officer is. So if the officer is from the Sadr office, this unit or this platoon belongs to the Sadr office. If the officer is from the Supreme Islamic Council [SCIRI], they belong to the Supreme Islamic Council. And this is how it works. ... It's less sectarian than the police, but still they obey the orders of their political leadership, by which I mean their parties, their militia leaders ... So basically, in the neighborhoods, the people prefer the army rather than the police because the police are really sectarian. It's worse than the army in terms of being very unprofessional and also full of gangs and thieves.

Here is Cole's view of the real power struggle under way in the country:

JUAN COLE: In my view, three wars are being fought, [and have been] fought all the time that the U.S. has been there. There's a war for control of Basra, the oil port city in the south, amongst Shiite militias and parties. There's a war between Sunnis and Shiites for control of Baghdad and its hinterland, which the Sunnis were winning in 2004 and 2005 and which the Shiites are now winning. And there's a war in the north for control of Kirkuk, the northern oil-producing area, between the Kurds on the one hand and the Arabs and the Turkmen and the Christians on the other. Those wars have been being prosecuted while the coalition has been there. They will go on being prosecuted when the coalition leaves. They will be fought either to a conclusion or to a standstill.

Life in Iraq Now

All the Iraqis I spoke with said that life in Baghdad was unbearable. When I interviewed Ali Fadhil on September 23, 2007, he had just spent most of the summer in Baghdad. His comments are very similar to those made by other Iraqis who have family members in Baghdad or who have visited or worked in the city recently. (For reference, readers can refer to the back of this book for statistical information on Iraq's services and economy.)

ALI FADHIL: It's been exactly twenty months since I left Iraq, when I came back to Iraq this year. ... And twenty months, this is like a huge time in Iraq's calendar. And I was hearing, reading, seeing the news about Iraq, you know, myself being very interested in the news coming from Iraq. And also making all these phone calls throughout the year before I went to Iraq. And hearing from friends and relatives. You know, I lost some friends as well, and some relatives were killed. When I arrived, I was shocked by seeing the situation even worse than what they told me. Baghdad streets are completely, completely devastated. It's like a war being there for thirty years—not four years, thirty years.

Streets are like death streets. You see the garbage everywhere. You see the dust everywhere, and everything is gray. All the color has disappeared from Baghdad. I can assure you about this. There are no colors anymore in Baghdad.

Then seeing the people and their lives; they are having more troubles than ever this year. They have problems with electricity, which is worse now. They have problems with water, which is now contaminated and they have to boil it or buy water from the Department of Water, which is expensive compared to their salaries.

Omar X agreed with this assessment when I interviewed him in October 2007.

CHARLES FERGUSON: How are government services, electricity, water?

OMAR X: Till the day I left Baghdad, there was no electricity. We had water, like, two hours per day. No services. The garbage was filled in the street like, you know, mountains of garbage. And sewage was flooding the streets. No government services at all on all the basics. I mean, that's another problem that makes your life miserable in Iraq. It's not only the security. It's not only you are scared that you will lose your life at any moment. I mean, the concept of living in Baghdad is trying to survive the day. But what makes it hard for you is the lack of services. The temperature in summer reaches very high, like fifty degrees Celsius, and you have nothing to cool the room that you are sitting in. I remember, I was sleeping at night, sweating, all my body is sweating, and I feel my brain is boiling, and there is not even cold water to drink. And when I got to the water catcher, there's no water. And I have to use the water from the tank, this old tank over the roof, which was under the sun for the whole day and the water's really, really hot and you can't drink it. So it's lack of services ... actually there's no services at all.

CHARLES FERGUSON: And this is continuing to get worse?

OMAR X: It was getting worse, I told you, and I don't think it's improved now. I mean, I've left Baghdad two months, less than two months now, and I have never heard from anybody there that things have improved. Twenty-four hours: no electricity, no water.

Iraqi children search through garbage.

Ali Fadhil, Omar X, and others mentioned that the failure of government services forced people to use far more expensive alternatives, which deepened the nation's already pervasive poverty.

ALI FADHIL: They're having problems with the prices. Baghdad is more expensive than Beirut. ... Maybe not the most expensive, but it's an expensive city in the Middle East. Baghdad is really expensive.

You need eighty dollars to fill your car with gas from the black market because it's impossible—nearly impossible—to get it from the gas station, which is crowded and most of the time closed because there is no fuel. The tanks can't come from the refineries, because the road is closed or it's dangerous. Besides, also the smuggling and the black markets are going on.

Also the problems of the schools; kids are finding it difficult. Many of the Iraqis have actually just told their kids to stay home because it's difficult and just they don't know if their kids will come back or not.

And I think that's a brief description. There's a lot more of what's going on. Life is really difficult in Baghdad right now; it is really difficult compared to twenty months ago.

Omar X and others confirmed that the combination of religious fundamentalism and violence was driving educated, secular people from the country. Indeed, most professionals, including the majority of doctors, have already left Iraq.

OMAR X: Most of Iraqis who are secular or well educated ... either they've been killed or they left the country because they just can't live the life of militia.

JUAN COLE: Health care seems to have collapsed, and medicines are short in supply. The physicians have often fled; the nurses have fled. There have been outbreaks in the north of Iraq of cholera because of poor sewage treatment. The U.S. military seems to be interdicting shipments of chlorine, which are essential to water purification, because they also have military purposes.

People noted another major change since 2004: As the balance of power and terror shifted in favor of Shiite militias, particularly the Mahdi Army, Baghdad was ethnically "cleansed," resulting in increased ethnic segregation within Baghdad and the exodus of Sunnis from it. By early 2007, most of the city was controlled by the Mahdi Army or splinter militias derived from it. Thus, one reason that there is less violence in Baghdad now is that there are fewer Sunnis left to kill or to be killed.

JUAN COLE: Well, the first thing to say is that when the U.S. took Baghdad in 2003, it was probably about fifty-fifty Shiites and Sunnis. In January of 2007, the Shiites were sixty-five percent.

There had been a seesaw war probably in 2004, 2005. The Sunni forces were making a push on Baghdad and ethnically cleansing Shiite neighborhoods, and the Shiites began fighting back in a big way after the Samarra bombing of February 2006. So by January of 2007, the city was sixty-five percent Shiite. And then the troop escalation began and the U.S. acted especially against the Sunni Arab guerrillas in the capital. And by July of 2007, Baghdad was seventy-five percent Shiite. So while the surge was going on, there was a massive ethnic cleansing of Sunni Arabs from the capital. This is a big change for a city of some six million to have a ten percent shift like that. You're talking about hundreds of thousands of people being displaced. And that was happening while the surge or the troop escalation was going on. And my own suspicion is that precisely because the U.S. disarmed or chased out Sunni Arab guerrillas from the capital that it gave an opening to the Shiites to act behind the scenes. It left the Sunni Arabs more vulnerable. So some of the decrease in violence—this is not a point that is original with me—probably comes from the lessened number of mixed neighborhoods. That is to say, there are neighborhoods that used to have Sunnis and Shiites who fought with one another who now just have Shiites, so no reason to fight.

Casualties: The Dead, the Wounded, and the Disabled

More than 1.2 million men and women, over 90 percent of them American, have now served in the Iraq war. As of December 2007, more than 4,200 coalition soldiers, including more than 3,900 Americans and approximately 175 Britons, have been killed in Iraq.

Somewhere between 40,000 and 80,000 soldiers have been wounded. The uncertainty over the number of wounded arises because there is reason to believe that official Defense Department statistics severely underestimate the true number, counting as "wounded" only those injured by combat or hostile action. If a soldier in Iraq is run over by a truck, is blinded by sand, suffers heat stroke, or attempts suicide, he or she is not listed as "wounded." Including such noncombat injuries, the number of wounded Americans is already over 60,000. In addition, in November 2007 USA Today reported that more than 20,000 soldiers returning from service in Iraq, and not listed as wounded, had tested positive for brain injuries in medical examinations conducted by the U.S. military.*

---

*Gregg Zoroya, "20,000 Vets' Brain Injuries Not Listed in Pentagon Tally," *USA Today,* November 22, 2007, available at www.usatoday.com/news/military/2007-11-22-braininjuries_N.htm.

Stefan Zaklin/epa/Corbis

Memorial for an American soldier.

The effects of the war were clearly present in the wounded veterans I interviewed. The effects of their injuries would last for life. As described earlier, David Yancey nearly lost his right arm, suffered a collapsed lung, and received head wounds and shrapnel wounds from an IED. He could no longer serve in the military, and would be unable to perform many normal tasks.

CHARLES FERGUSON: What do you think about the future? Are you able to stay in the army? Do you want to stay in the army? Do you have an idea what you're gonna do next?

DAVID YANCEY: Uh, due to my injuries, I [will] be forced to get out of the military and try to pursue a good career, civilian career job.

CHARLES FERGUSON: Do you have an idea what you want to do?

DAVID YANCEY: I'm thinking about [a] federal job. Postal service, et cetera.

As we learned earlier, Hugo Gonzales was severely injured when his unarmored Humvee came under attack.

HUGO GONZALES: Right now, as a consequence of [the attack], Sir, I am suffering from posttraumatic migraines and posttraumatic epilepsy. Sometimes I have bad memories about what happen, but I am not scared of them. I face them. I have some dreams with my mother with me in the theater, right there, in the middle of a mission, and me, you know, getting very anxious about what are you doing here—my mother and my family.

And here we are. I am going forward, Sir. There are things that are gonna be there with me, with all my life. But they are there for a reason. What is the reason? What's the meaning? Only God knows. God is the one that have a purpose. And He know where He want me to go. I mean, His [hands see] the 21st June in 2004, Sir ...

CHARLES FERGUSON: Do you think that you'll be able to handle life outside of the military?

HUGO GONZALES: That's another question mark because what I'm living right now is not the real life. I am not ... this is not real life. Real life is gonna be going out there, [encountering] people that maybe they are not in a good mood that day. My tolerance to frustration is not the same right now. I am not ... I am not—my vision is not the same. My wife has become my new pair of eyes. And I don't know how I'm gonna handle the struggles of life anymore, because I am not exposed to those struggles anymore.

For those soldiers who aren't seriously physically injured, there is still the enormous long-term impact of having been in a war, particularly a terrifyingly foreign war in an extremely strenuous environment. Summer temperatures in Iraq frequently reach 120 degrees Fahrenheit, and soldiers in full combat gear in such temperatures are frequently operating near human physical limits. In addition, the emotional impact of inflicting or witnessing civilian casualties is great, as is the constant risk of attacks from apparent civilians, such as suicide bombers. Although troop levels are far lower than they were in the first Gulf War of 1990 to 1991, long-term emotional and physical effects are expected to be far greater, because of the length of the war, the long deployments of many troops, the greater use of depleted uranium munitions, and the conditions of irregular, guerrilla warfare and terrorism. Linda Bilmes, a budgeting expert at Harvard's Kennedy School of Government, has studied the economic and medical impact of the war on the troops.

LINDA BILMES: Well, when people come back from the war, the reason they claim disability payments is they find they're just not quite the same. They can't hold down a job; they have joint pains; they have memory lapses; their marriage is deteriorating. They find that things are just not quite the same as they were. They have temper tantrums; they have unexplained nightmares; they have sweats; they have things that they used to be able to do that they can't do anymore.

And the big amount of cost, in terms of veterans' disability, is not for those who have been really severely wounded, but it's for the many hundreds of thousands of people who come back and they find that they can't work and hold down a job in the way they used to, because they're just not quite the same as they were before.

Moreover, there appear to be substantial deficiencies in the way veterans' medical problems and disability claims are handled. When I interviewed Hugo Gonzales in early 2006, he had been in Walter Reed Hospital for two years, and he was medically able to leave, but he was still there:

CHARLES FERGUSON: Do you know when you'll get out?

HUGO GONZALES: No, Sir. Right now, the future is a little bit uncertain. … I have plans. I have what I wish to do. But I cannot tell you something specifically, because I don't know when I'm going out. My case right now is stuck since October the 12th, 2005.

CHARLES FERGUSON: What do you mean, stuck?

HUGO GONZALES: Stuck means that I already finish [but not] all my bureaucratical process. I already have a ninety percent disability, they offer me. But [it] is stuck, and they are trying to figure it out—what are they gonna do with me because they have questions. Nobody knows.

CHARLES FERGUSON: So when you say "stuck," what you mean is that since October of last year, they just haven't decided—

HUGO GONZALES: Haven't decided, yes. I was about to go out, and then the case went back. This become an extraordinary case, from one moment to another. And that means I am over there, playing the waiting game.

Hugo Gonzales's case was caught in the immense backlog of veterans' disability claims. Here is a reproduction in full of the written Congressional testimony of Professor Bilmes on the subject of veterans' claims before the House Committee on Veterans Affairs on May 23, 2007:

Chairman Filner, Members of the Committee, and Colleagues:

Thank you for inviting me to join this important discussion. As you know, I testified to this committee on March 13th, so I have not prepared new testimony. What follows are some key points from my previous statement.

I believe we are all well familiar with the problems facing our veterans and the Veterans Benefits Administration. These include:

1. A backlog of more than 400,000 pending claims now in the queue, with 200,000 others "in process";

2. An expected influx of at least 1.6 million additional claims within the next two years, including some 200–400,000 from OIF/OEF [Operation Iraqi Freedom / Operation Enduring Freedom] soldiers;

3. A system that incentivizes veterans to apply for disability compensation so they can obtain access to VA medical care;

4. An average waiting time to process a claim of 6–24 months;

5. Thousands of experienced claims adjudicators who are eligible to retire, thus an urgent need to retain high performing employees and to recruit and train new ones;

6. Increasingly complex claims—with an average of 5 separate conditions per claim;

7. A complicated system for ascertaining whether a veteran is disabled, using a non-monotonic rating scale for each of thousands of conditions;

8. A high rate of errors, discrepancies and inconsistencies in how these scales are applied to individual veterans cases;

9. A convoluted disability claims form that is 23 pages long; and

10. Difficulty in implementing the Benefits Delivery at Discharge program due to lack of coordination and data-sharing with the Defense Department.

11. A lack of state-of-the-art IT systems to expedite the process for veterans and to capture information.

As large as the toll of the war on American soldiers may be, the toll on Iraqis has obviously been enormously greater. The overwhelming majority of Iraqis who have died since the occupation began have been innocent civilians, not soldiers, insurgents, or terrorists, most of them killed by other Iraqis. It is impossible to know how many Iraqis have died since April 2003, but the number is vastly higher than semiofficial public estimates, such as those provided by Iraq Body Count. Of Iraqi deaths, it appears that approximately 90 percent are the result of insurgent attacks, suicide bombings, kidnappings, assassinations, criminal violence, and sectarian killings perpetrated by other Iraqis or, particularly with suicide bombings, by foreign fighters. Thus, while American forces have clearly killed many innocent civilians—certainly thousands and possibly tens of thousands—killings by U.S. forces are a small minority of total violent deaths in Iraq.

As of November 2007, Iraq Body Count had documented approximately 80,000 violent deaths of Iraqi civilians since the beginning of the war.* This is clearly a severe underestimate, as it counts only deaths publicly reported by at least two sources. Other estimates of the Iraqi death toll are much higher. One study commissioned by the MIT Center for International Studies and published in *Lancet,* a British medical journal, estimated that by October 2006, Iraq had suffered 655,000 excess deaths.† Another recent estimate was even higher. While the methodology of the *Lancet* study, which is based on household surveys, has been questioned, it is the most rigorous assessment to date. It is generally agreed that the majority of violent deaths in Iraq are no longer reported officially nor mentioned in the media at all.

The number of Iraqi wounded and disabled is likewise impossible to know, but the entire society has been deeply traumatized. I saw it myself when I was there. Many people I interviewed spoke of the effects of the war on themselves, their friends, and their family. Here is one sample from my translator Omar X:

---

*Updated statistics of the number of dead are available on Iraq Body Count's Web site, www.iraqbodycount.org.

†For information on the MIT *Lancet* study, see David Brown, "Study Claims Iraq's 'Excess' Death Toll Has Reached 655,000," *Washington Post,* October 11, 2006, available at www.washingtonpost.com/wp-dyn/content/article/2006/10/10/AR2006101001442.html.

U.S. Marines "clean" a house after a raid in Fallujah.

CHARLES FERGUSON: How's your family?

OMAR X: They are fine. They moved to Syria and they're trying to restart their lives there. My mother's really depressed and she became really short-tempered, which makes my younger brother suffering so much from her. But they understand what she went through. Also my brothers have just started to go to school again, and they're trying to accommodate themselves there and to learn how to live in a new, safe area.

CHARLES FERGUSON: I'm glad they were able to get out, and I'm glad that you were able to get out, Omar.

OMAR X: Yeah, I mean it's been a really difficult time for my family and, well now, we're just trying to go through the life.

Here is Ali Fadhil's succinct comment on the same issue:

ALI FADHIL: I mean, I remember that we're sitting and we're saying that people who died got lucky, but people living like us in Iraq—when we were in Iraq—they are dead while they are alive.

There is almost no mental health or psychiatric treatment available in Arab Iraq, and even medical treatment for serious physical problems is increasingly difficult—and dangerous—to obtain. Most medical professionals have fled the country, the health ministry is controlled by Shiite fundamentalists, and security in hospitals is poor. When Omar X's brother was shot in the eye and blinded, he was kept at home rather than taken to a hospital, for fear that he would be identified and assassinated en route to or in the hospital.

The Refugee Crisis

By late 2007, approximately 20 percent of Iraq's total prewar population had become refugees. More than three million had left the country, mainly for Jordan and Syria, and another two million had been displaced internally, changing the ethnic composition of Iraq. External refugees are overwhelmingly Sunni, with the result that Arab Iraq (i.e., Iraq excluding Kurdistan) is now perhaps 80 percent Shiite (versus 60 to 65 percent in 2003), a trend likely to continue and to reinforce Shiite political and military dominance. Nir Rosen outlined the various refugee populations.

CHARLES FERGUSON: I assume the overwhelming majority of the refugees in both Jordan and Syria are Sunni.

NIR ROSEN: That is correct ... In Syria you have a lot of Christians as well, and Shiites, but the overwhelming majority are Sunnis.

CHARLES FERGUSON: So basically, Shiite refugees are internally displaced within Iraq, whereas the Sunnis leave ... So that would suggest that actually the total population of Iraq is now much more Shiites than it used to be, maybe 80 percent or more now.

NIR ROSEN: You have a million [refugees] in Jordan; you have two million in Syria; you have not that much, a hundred and fifty thousand, in Egypt, at least when I was doing the research; forty thousand in Sweden; a few hundred in the U.S. But nobody knows exactly what the sectarian breakdown of the refugee populations are.

CHARLES FERGUSON: But if there is over three million of them, and if they are overwhelmingly Sunni, then that suggests there has been a significant change in the total ethnic composition.

NIR ROSEN: Oh yes, yes. And you have a few hundred thousand that fled up north to Kurdistan as well.

CHARLES FERGUSON: Interesting. So Iraq is now overwhelmingly a Shiite country—no longer a mixed country in the way it was.

NIR ROSEN: And there are almost no mixed neighborhoods as well.

Iraqi refugee camp in Al-Ruweishid, Jordan.

Many more Iraqis would clearly leave if they were able to do so, but in late 2007, Jordan and Syria closed their borders, and many nations, particularly the United

States, have implemented extremely restrictive policies toward Iraqi immigrants. Iraqi Kurdistan was also experiencing increasing pressures as an estimated 200,000 Arab Iraqi refugees moved there for safety.

Many, though not all, observers fear that the refugee situation could destabilize the region even more than the war. The United States has thus far refused to provide any financial assistance to refugees or to the governments admitting them. Syria is regarded as a hostile power by the United States for a number of reasons, including its potential nuclear weapons program, anti-American policies, support for Hezbollah in Lebanon, and suspected role in assassinating prominent Lebanese Christian politicians. Jordan, conversely, is far more moderate and pro-American, but its stability may be even more at risk as a result. Nir Rosen was among the most pessimistic regarding the refugee crisis in both countries.

CHARLES FERGUSON: What would destabilize Jordan?

NIR ROSEN: Well, King Abdullah is already sort of flimsy and fragile, lacking legitimacy, backed only by the CIA. There is a very strong Salafi [a variant of fundamentalist Islam] type of movement in the country. And I have written about the presence of another million Iraqi refugees, in addition to half the country already being Palestinian. I don't give them more than five years.

CHARLES FERGUSON: I see.

NIR ROSEN: I hope, as well, that they will be gone in five years, but that's not the point. I just think the regime is very flimsy, increasingly corrupt. It is the same problem as it is in Syria. The [Iraqi Sunni] resistance movements have their leadership based in Jordan and Syria. Many among the population in Jordan and Syria sympathize with the plight of Sunnis in Iraq and the resistance. And being so close to the U.S., I think, is committing suicide. ...

CHARLES FERGUSON: Okay. And Syria?

NIR ROSEN: Syria: majority Sunni country with a history of Sunni Islamist opposition to the regime. And the regime is dominated, or seems to be dominated, by Allawites, who are kind of like Shiite, and they have a good relationship with Iran and the Iraqi government—the people who are killing Sunnis in Iraq right now—so that's contradiction as well. [There is] a lot of sympathy among much of the Syrian population for the plight of Iraqi Sunnis. The majority of the two million Iraqi refugees in Syria are Sunni.

CHARLES FERGUSON: I didn't realize that it [the number of refugees] was that large.

NIR ROSEN: The Syrians had to close the border because they have been overwhelmed.

CHARLES FERGUSON: Okay. I thought it was about a million now.

NIR ROSEN: It was a million. It was over a million when I was doing my research on the refugee issue in Syria in January and you had three thousand Iraqis going in every day. ... Just the presence of the refugees is a huge burden. Syria subsidizes everything, so every loaf of bread in an Iraqi refugee camp is being paid for by the Syrian government. Both in Syria and Jordan you see tripling of rent prices, food, things like that. And Syria ... [is] fragile internationally. ... We must regard the sectarian tensions, the status of militias, and economic burdens that just break the backs of already fragile regimes.

Joost Hiltermann, who lived in Amman, Jordan, for several years and who, like, Nir Rosen, speaks fluent Arabic, was less pessimistic about the impact of refugees on the stability of neighboring countries, at least Jordan.

CHARLES FERGUSON: And what do you think will be the consequences of the refugee flows—the large number of refugees in Jordan and Syria, lesser numbers in other places? What do you think is going to happen as a result of the presence of those refugees?

JOOST HILTERMANN: Well, the situation there is fragile, but stable at the moment. Jordan is not letting in any more refugees. Some may already have left, may have moved on to Egypt or other places. Not many, but in any case, no new ones are coming in. Syria has also put new restrictions in place, so it's harder for Iraqis to move to Syria. Should the situation deteriorate sharply in Iraq, new refugee flows will move towards the borders, but very likely the borders will be sealed closed, and refugees will be stranded in the desert, where they will either have to turn back or move into internment camps that the international community would facilitate. So, I don't see refugees destabilizing the neighboring states at this point.

CHARLES FERGUSON: And how about their long-term presence? It's difficult for me to imagine that large numbers of those people are going to want to go back to Iraq anytime soon. You know, most people that I speak to think that the people who already left and are now living in either Jordan or Syria are likely to remain there for years, possibly decades. Do you think they are going to have any effect on those societies, and if so, what do you think that effect will be?

JOOST HILTERMANN: It's very hard to say. I mean, of course these regimes will try to gradually assimilate these populations into their own. That has happened with the Palestinian refugees as well. Of course there's still camps and there are still problems, but by and large, the Palestinian refugees in Jordan and in Syria have become part of the landscape. And it may even be a positive thing for Jordan, for example, that there are Iraqi refugees. They will dilute the majority Palestinian population in Jordan, which is an existential threat, in some ways, to the Hashemite regime and to the trans-Jordanian presence. So it's not necessarily a negative thing. It's the process—it is how it is accomplished that is difficult to manage, and this is where the Jordanians will want to act very carefully.

As of late 2007, the United States has provided essentially no financial support either to the refugees or to their host nations. Nor has the United States admitted into its borders more than a few refugees itself—less than a thousand by early 2007, and at most a few thousand more by late 2007. The nation of Sweden has admitted several times more Iraqi refugees than the United States has.

Terrorism

Many people I spoke with feared that the war in Iraq would, both directly and indirectly, increase the risk of terrorism against the United States and other Western nations. The people expressing this concern ranged widely across the political spectrum and included persons who had been in favor of the war. Here is Amazia Baram, a conservative Israeli policy analyst who has consulted informally for the Bush administration:

CHARLES FERGUSON: Tell us what you thought about what issues, what problems Iraq would pose in the postwar period.

AMIZIA BARAM: [*sighs*] The problem is this: that if the coalition—or actually America—fails in Iraq; if Iraq disintegrates and becomes an arena of civil war, I see serious problems because much of it will become like little Afghanistan. That's my fear. It's not just Iraq, which is bad enough. It's where terrorists all over the world will find refuge. And so in a strange way, somebody in the West will have to come back and reconquer the place.

Harvard lecturer Jessica Stern, an expert on terrorism, spent five years studying and interviewing religious terrorists for her book *Terror in the Name of God:*

CHARLES FERGUSON: And what do you think of the insurgency in Iraq and the development of terrorism in Iraq after our invasion?

JESSICA STERN: The United States has facilitated the next iteration of that international *jihadi* movement. We have given that movement the best possible training. We have provided war games for them. They are now trying to fight against the best-trained military on earth.

And they will not stay there. That's very clear. This is not a kind of roach motel, where we gather the world's international *jihadis* and kill them in Iraq. They will escape from that motel, and we've already seen that in Jordan—they are now very well-trained and very angry. And I believe we will eventually see them on Western streets.

CHARLES FERGUSON: And why don't you believe the assertion that the administration has made: that in fact this is a place where large numbers of terrorist *jihadis* will be caught and/or killed by American forces, and that this represents a disaster for them?

JESSICA STERN: One of the problems with the Bush administration's thinking about this issue, in my view, is that we're not talking about a definite number of *jihadis*; that you just kill three, and there are three less. We're talking about a movement that continues to grow. We should be thinking about the flow of new *jihadis* into the movement. ... So when the administration touts its purported successes by bragging about the number of known members of al Qaeda who have been captured or killed, without thinking about how many new ones have been created, I get quite distressed. It seems to me that the more we kill, the fewer we have turned. We should be trying to bring them over to our side, and use them to undermine the movement, rather than capturing or killing them. This represents an intelligence failure, when we capture or kill them, or when we incarcerate them or kill them, rather than turning them to our side.

And moreover, the more important element is how many new ones are being created. And the war in Iraq has really facilitated [Osama] bin Laden's efforts to continue to spread that *jihadi* movement internationally. And it's become a kind of virtual movement, where it doesn't require active recruitment. It's just become a kind of fad to become a *jihadi*, fighting the West, largely, in my view, as a result of what's happened in Iraq. Or I should say, greatly facilitated by what has happened in Iraq.

CHARLES FERGUSON: And what do you think, if anything, the administration or the United States could do now to arrest or reverse this development?

JESSICA STERN: Sometimes when you make a really bad decision, all options available are unattractive. And I'm afraid that that's the situation we're currently in. ...

CHARLES FERGUSON: ... You said earlier that we're providing war games for the resistance, for the insurgence, for the *jihadi* movement. Could you say more about that?

JESSICA STERN: In Iraq today, former Baathist military personnel, intelligence personnel, are now working together with ordinary criminals and international *jihadis*, getting the best possible training that they could ever hope to get: fighting against the world's best-trained military. They're getting to work together and practice. And this is a fabulous opportunity for them.

CHARLES FERGUSON: Now, if it's the best-trained military in the world, why is it a fabulous opportunity for them, as opposed to a disaster for them?

JESSICA STERN: ... It's a disaster for those who are killed. But those who survive ... are world-class terrorists. They will have extraordinary skills and expertise that they will be able to take with them into future *jihads*.

Stern, who had also studied and worked on WMD issues in academia and at the National Security Council under the Clinton administration, thought that the net effect of the Iraq war was to reduce the security of the United States. She made the following comments to me in late 2005, before the public transportation bombings in London and Madrid:

JESSICA STERN: There were very, very good reasons to want to take that [the Saddam] regime out. But the way we went about it, it seems to me, is very dangerous for the West, and very dangerous, in particular, for Americans, because of the way it has enhanced the capabilities of the *jihadi* movement, and enhanced the mobilization strategy of al Qaeda beyond its wildest dreams.

CHARLES FERGUSON: And do you think that this in fact poses an increased risk of terrorism in the West and in the United States?

JESSICA STERN: I believe that the war in Iraq has greatly increased the risk of terrorism in the West and in the United States. One reason for that is that some of the *jihadi* volunteers are coming in from Europe. They are coming in from Europe with European passports, and they're going back to Europe. We know this is already happening. Those people with European passports will have much easier access to the United States than people from Iraq, for example. I think it's just a matter of time before *jihadis* who have been trained in Iraq end up in the West, bringing their *jihad* back to us. ... God, I sound like such an alarmist. But I really do think this ... Do I sound too alarmist? I probably do.

CHARLES FERGUSON: You sound very alarmist. ... It's whether you really believe this or not, Jessie. If you really believe it, then—

JESSICA STERN: I do.

CHARLES FERGUSON: Okay. Do you think that the West, and in particular, the United States, and even more particularly, the current administration, are preparing adequately for this possibility?

JESSICA STERN: I think the Bush administration is taking this threat seriously.

Economic Effects

The economic costs of the Iraq war appear to exceed $2 trillion for the United States and an unknown but clearly very large amount for the rest of the world, including Iraq and the region. Iraq-related oil price increases have cost the United States substantially (several hundred billion dollars), but have cost the rest of the world economy far more—probably over $1 trillion since 2003. Only a few nations and industries, primarily those related to oil and the defense industry, have benefited. Some of the largest costs, both economically and in terms of effects on human welfare, have been borne by the poorest nations, due to increased oil prices. Other large costs borne by some poor nations are associated with the large refugee flows from Iraq, which have caused economic stress in Jordan, Syria, and, to a lesser extent, Egypt and Lebanon.

As of early 2008, the United States will have spent approximately $500 billion directly on the war in Iraq. The real, total cost of the war, however, is far larger. First, military operating costs will continue at over $75 billion per year until the United States begins substantial withdrawals. Second, the war leads to substantial future military expenditures due to increased recruitment and training costs, equipment replacement, and so forth. These costs are estimated to be in the region of $200 billion. In addition, Army Reserve and National Guard deployments reduce U.S. economic output by removing people from the civilian economy—roughly 100,000 at any given time since 2003. Moreover, some fraction of the increase in oil prices since 2002 is clearly attributable to the war. While one can debate the size of that fraction, its effect on the United States alone is clearly in the hundreds of billions of dollars.

In addition, there is an enormous long-term economic repercussion caused by the emotional and physical effects of war on soldiers. Professor Linda Bilmes has studied this issue extensively. She made the following comments to me in late 2005, when the number of U.S. personnel who had served in Iraq and the number of U.S. casualties in Iraq were only about half the levels reached by early 2008:

LINDA BILMES: In the first Gulf War, there were just over a hundred individuals killed, and about four hundred and fifty wounded. Despite that, we are paying now a hundred and sixty-nine thousand veterans for disability claims. Those claims came into the Veterans Administration for a variety of things which have been, by the veterans, associated with their exposure to depleted uranium during the bombings in the initial Persian Gulf War. The VA has accepted the premise and the principle that a wide variety of conditions, ranging from memory loss to joint pains to depression to Lou Gehrig's disease and others, are in some way a result of the service during the first Gulf War. So we are currently paying two billion dollars a year in payments to veterans of the first Gulf War. Which is kind of an extraordinary figure, because it is generally assumed that that was a war for which the United States did not bear a cost, because the allies paid for the operating costs at the time.

When you think about the implications of that for the current war, the cost projections are really quite astounding. I mean, we now have a war that has gone on for nearly three years, with fifteen thousand wounded, as opposed to four hundred, and again, with close to six hundred thousand Americans who have served in that war. And many of them have served not for one month, but for eighteen months or more. So we can anticipate a significant number of claims related to the service in this war. [Bilmes' numbers are from 2005. Estimates of U.S. wounded now range from forty thousand to over eighty thousand, and over one million Americans have now served in Iraq.]

In addition, according to the Pentagon, the amount of depleted uranium which was used in the bombings of Baghdad during the Iraq war exceeded the amount that had been used in the initial Persian Gulf War. Estimates vary about how much the amount of depleted uranium increased, but in the modern weapons that were used, there was a significant increase. So we can anticipate that many, if not all, of the servicemen who were present during the initial bombing campaign would have grounds on which to successfully claim for disability.

And when we talk about disability claims, it's important to realize that we're not only talking about the ... wounded. We're talking about claims which everybody who has served is eligible to make, for any condition which may have been related to something that happened during their service. So it is certainly reasonable to expect that for people who have been serving in very difficult situations, for [an] extended period of time, that many, many of them will have a variety of problems related to physical or mental disabilities, which they can claim successfully were a result of this. Not all of those people would be receiving a hundred percent disability payments, but a very significant percentage of them will be receiving some disability payments for the next thirty-five to forty years.

Global economic effects are difficult to compute. The first attempt at estimating such effects is documented in a book by Linda Bilmes and economist Joseph Stiglitz.* It is clear that increased oil import costs have had a significant effect on both industrialized nations such as European countries and Japan, and also substantial effects on poor, agricultural nations without domestic energy resources in Latin America, Asia, and Africa.

There are, however, two notable categories of economic actors who have benefited from the war enormously: the oil industry and oil exporting nations. Popular media attention on corporations benefiting from the war has been focused primarily on defense and engineering contractors such as Halliburton, Bechtel, and SAIC, as well as private military contractors such as Blackwater, Triple Canopy, and Dyncorp. While these firms have certainly benefited greatly from the war, the amounts involved are utterly dwarfed by the increased profits of the U.S. and global oil industry, which have received little public attention. The graph on the following page shows the revenues and profits of the largest U.S. oil companies since 2001.

The other major global beneficiaries of the war have been oil exporting nations. Since the price of oil has approximately quadrupled since the beginning of the Iraq war, nations such as Saudi Arabia, Iran, the United Arab Emirates, Kazakhstan, Nigeria, Chad, Venezuela, and Russia have benefited enormously from the situation. In several cases, these nations are corrupt dictatorships whose domestic or

---

*Linda Bilmes and Joseph Stiglitz, *The Three Trillion Dollar War: The True Cost of the Iraq Conflict* (New York: W. W. Norton, 2008, in press).

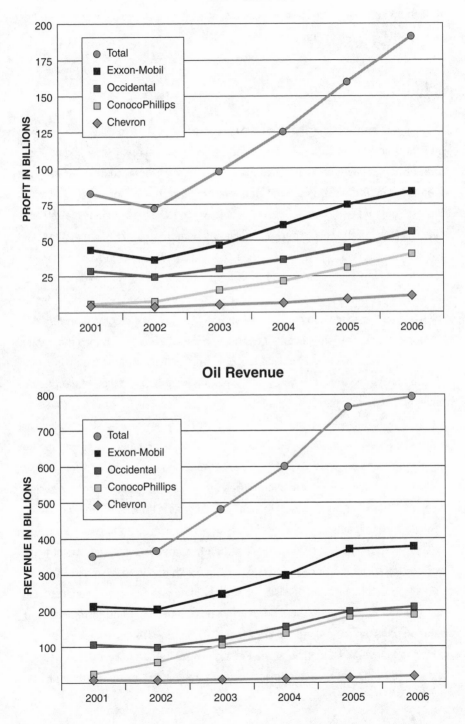

foreign policies, or both, are opposed to those of the United States and the West. Among these, one nation deserves special attention for the role it plays in the Iraq war and the Gulf region, namely, Iran.

Iran

I spoke with many people about the impact of the war on Iran, on U.S. relations with Iran, and on Iran's relationships with Iraq and other nations in the Middle East. There was complete unanimity that the mishandling of the occupation of Iraq had greatly strengthened Iran, to the detriment of Iraq, the region, and the United States. Some interviewees believed that this would have been the inevitable result of any U.S. invasion, while others felt that it was primarily a consequence of the mishandling of the occupation. Most people thought that it is now in Iran's interest to keep the United States pinned down in Iraq, and that the combination of high oil prices and the collapse of Iraq left Iran in a remarkably strong position with regard to its nuclear weapons aspirations, its leverage in Iraq, and its regional power.

Iran has long been suspected of operating a covert nuclear weapons program. A December 2007 National Intelligence Estimate (NIE) concluded that Iran had stopped nuclear warhead design in 2003, just after the U.S. invasion of Iraq, apparently out of fear that the United States might attack Iran to eliminate its nuclear program or even remove the regime. However, while Iran apparently stopped its warhead design effort, the NIE reiterated that Iran has continued work on uranium enrichment, a heavy-water reactor capable of producing plutonium, and ballistic missiles. Since plutonium and ballistic missiles are virtually useless except for nuclear weapons production and delivery, respectively, it appears likely that Iran is continuing to develop a nuclear weapons capability, if not yet the weapons themselves.

Both despite and because of this fact, nearly everyone I interviewed felt that it was imperative for the United States to negotiate with Iran in order to stabilize Iraq.

Professor Ashton Carter, assistant secretary of defense for international security policy in the Clinton administration, had advocated invading Iraq to remove Saddam, primarily on the grounds of WMD risks. The Iraq weapons inspectors had reported to him when he worked at the Pentagon, and he had believed that Saddam possessed WMD. He offered this comment on Iran when I interviewed him in late 2005:

CONSEQUENCES 443

ASHTON CARTER: Iran is, oddly, given how much we dislike the Iranian regime, the single greatest beneficiary of the war in Iraq for the simple reason that we eliminated Iran's great antagonist, Iraq. American policy in the decades before 2003 was to balance Iraq and Iran: A pox on both their houses; let them slug it out in the war that they had between them. And at the very moment we're concerned about Iran's nuclear program, we continue to have, and justifiably so, very negative feelings about the regime that took Americans hostage. [And yet,] we eliminated their historic enemy for them and put them on top in the Persian Gulf. I don't think we've seen that dynamic play out yet. But in effect, inadvertently, but totally predictably, the United States did Iran a huge favor by eliminating Saddam Hussein.

CHARLES FERGUSON: Now, I assume you realized that that would happen when you yourself supported this war. What did you think about that calculation before the war?

ASHTON CARTER: Well, the downside of going to war was the loss of life and the fact that we would end up having conquered Iraq [and] having to run it, having eliminated a brutal but coherent state in the center of the Middle East. That was the downside.

The upside, we thought, was that we were eliminating weapons of mass destruction of Saddam Hussein. That was the compelling upside, the reason why we felt this had to be done. We now know that that reason was based on faulty intelligence. But the downside was always there and was apparent to me, at least, all along. Although others who supported the war suggested otherwise: that running Iraq was going to be easy—was gonna automatically be a good thing for the American position in the Middle East—that never seemed plausible to me.

CHARLES FERGUSON: So you did realize, before the war, that there was a substantial risk that it would embolden Iran and increase Iran's potential influence in the region.

ASHTON CARTER: Yes. It was apparent to me, and I think it was apparent to anybody who understood the Middle East, that if, in the wake of the war, we proved unable to govern Iraq and to leave behind a strong unitary state, that the winner would be Iran because we would have shattered Iran's historic enemy.

Abbas Milani, a policy analyst specializing in Iran at the Hoover Institution at Stanford, observed that in 2003, the United States had enormous leverage over Iran, but failed to use that leverage, whereas now Iran possesses enormous leverage over the United States through Iran's ability to influence events in Iraq. He also believes that as a result of this U.S. failure, the West no longer can prevent Iran from acquiring a nuclear weapons capability.

ABBAS MILANI: In the immediate aftermath of the war, when the war had just been won, when the U.S. had, in a week, defeated the army that Iran could not defeat in a decade, the regime in Iran was very, very anxious. It had heard the stories about Tehran being where real men go and Baghdad being play for boys, and it had heard of threats that the next stop is Tehran, so it was very willing to make a deal at that time. ... At that time, the regime in Tehran was in its weakest point. It had economic problems. It had political problems at home. And it had the United States fresh as neighbors. If there ever was a time when the United States needed to talk to Iran and put the things that they have at stake on the table, it was then. That opportunity was lost, and with every passing day, it became very clear to the U.S. that victory was temporary, that there were problems on the rise, and you could almost do a mathematically accurate graph—[with] the number of casualties in Iraq ever increasing, the belligerence, the self-assuredness, the cockiness of the regime in Tehran increases with it parallel. And that moment was lost. And not only nothing came of that moment, but then very soon, developments in Iraq offered the [Iranian] regime an opportunity—a great opportunity—to enhance its power and its position both in Iraq and in its relationship with the United States.

CHARLES FERGUSON: And what kind of deal do you think the United States could have made with Iran in 2003?

ABBAS MILANI: I think at that time, the regime was willing to ... It had suspended uranium enrichment. It was willing to suspend the enrichment activities. A reformer was in power, and he was willing to make political concessions to the United States. I suspect they were willing to negotiate at least on their support for groups like Hezbollah in Lebanon in return for some semblance of security from the United States that they would not be attacked. At that time, I am convinced that they were willing to make this deal. I'm sure you have heard about the story about how they sent this letter at the time and the letter said that they are willing to do everything under the sun if the U.S. just makes this promise. I have never believed that that letter came from someone who had the power to deliver. My sense is that that letter came from somebody who wanted to act as a go-between, who was delivering promises, pies in the sky that he or she could not deliver. But my reading of the Iranian situation was then that it was the moment to talk with them. It was a moment to make clear what the United States expects, what the United States will do, and what it expects of them, and what they can expect of the United States.

They would have had the support of the Iranian democratic movement at the time. There was a very viable democratic movement. Students were in the street. Everything was truly set for concession from the regime—a concession that would have benefited not just the United States, but a concession that would have benefited the democratic movement in Iran. And I ultimately believe that the only way the problem of Iran will be solved is if we help the Iranian people themselves, not do it for them. Get a democratic regime in place. The solution to the Middle East will come if there is democracy in Iran, and democracy in Iran can only be made by the Iranian people for the Iranian people of the Iranian people. But the U.S. and Europe and Russia and China can [play] and could have particularly in 2003 played a very, very important, helpful role. They didn't. Now oil is at one hundred dollars. The regime is cockier. [Mahmoud] Ahmadinejad is in power. The Iranian regime has thousands of its agents doing everything from business to political shenanigans in Iraq, and it feels like it can talk from a position of power.

I've never seen them speak from as much point of weakness as they were in 2003, and [now] I've never seen them speak from as much a point of cockiness. And a dangerous point of cockiness, because in these tense moments, where there might be a confrontation between the two—Iran and U.S.—that cocky self-assuredness can, I think, lead to a miscalculation on their behalf. It can lead to the assumption that under no circumstances can the U.S. muscle their will or their might to hit, attack. And I think that's a bad assumption for them [the Iranians]. I see dangerous signs that they are near that stage where they think they can really do no wrong and that there's nothing that the West in general can do to them …

I don't think the nuclear issue has a negotiated solution left, anymore. I think the regime is way beyond the point of being willing to give up their nuclear program. They might have been willing to give it up four years ago. Now they think they're close enough, and they have milked it nationally and internationally.

Although nearly everyone I spoke with felt that Iran was a dangerous regime bent upon obtaining nuclear weapons, or at least a weapons capability, Juan Cole felt that Iran was much less of a problem than generally believed. He is nearly alone in believing that Iran's nuclear intentions are purely peaceful. However, he is far from alone in believing that the United States has misread and misrepresented Iran's role in Iraq. While he views Iran's role in Iraq more favorably than most specialists, several interviewees concurred with his view that Iran was not contributing heavily to violence in Iraq.

CHARLES FERGUSON: What do you think of the argument or the proposition that it's in the Iranians' interest to keep Iraq unstable and violent because it keeps the United States pinned down and dependent on Iran—to some extent—and that, in fact, Iran will therefore continue to find it in its interest to keep the situation bad?

JUAN COLE: Well, I'm unpersuaded by the American claim that Iran is any significant element in the unstable situation in Iraq. I think the Iranians have by and large played a positive role in stability in Iraq, and I think it's fairly easy to trace their influence. The party in Iraq that is closest to them is the Islamic Supreme Council of Iraq [SCIRI], led by cleric Abdul Aziz al-Hakim, who lived in Iran as an expatriate for over twenty years. The Supreme Council was formed at the suggestion of Ayatollah Khomeini. Its paramilitary was trained by the Iranian Revolutionary Guards, and some maintain that the Badr Corps still is on the payroll in Iran. So if any force were indicative of Iranian influence, it would be the Badr Corps and the

Islamic Supreme Council. And we know what they've been up to, because they won the provincial elections in so many of the provinces of Iraq in January of 2005, so they control Muthanna Province and they control Nasiriyah, they control Najaf, they control Karbala, they control Diwaniyah, and those have been relatively quiet.

Cole, alone among those with whom I spoke, also expressed skepticism that Iran was intent upon developing nuclear weapons. Here is our initial exchange:

CHARLES FERGUSON: What, if anything, do you think the United States could accomplish by speaking with the Iranians? And what do you think the role of Iran's nuclear weapons program has in any discussions that could or should occur?

JUAN COLE: Iran does not have a nuclear weapons program, to anybody's actual knowledge.

CHARLES FERGUSON: Mr. Cole, really now.

JUAN COLE: It doesn't have a nuclear weapons program. There is no evidence for it.

CHARLES FERGUSON: Okay.

JUAN COLE: It has a civilian nuclear energy program, which is being actively inspected by the International Atomic Energy Agency, which has been visited numerous times, in which canisters have been opened and facilities examined. There has never been any evidence of highly enriched materials that would be suitable for—

CHARLES FERGUSON: That's not true. That is not true.

JUAN COLE: That is true.

CHARLES FERGUSON: Highly enriched uranium has been found in Iran.

JUAN COLE: Yeah. In Iran, there was one incident in which they found a bit, and when it was investigated, it was very clear that this was contamination, because they had imported some equipment from Pakistan. There's never been any evidence. And, you know, Mr. [Mohamed] El Baradei [director of the International Atomic Energy Agency, which monitors the Nuclear Non-Proliferation Treaty] has repeatedly said these things, issued them in his reports, and so forth. What he says is that he is frustrated that the Iranians don't seem to be a hundred percent cooperating with him. And so there is an element of uncertainty here. He can't give a hundred percent assurance that there's nothing going on behind the scenes, but he can't find it. There's been no positive indicator of any weapons program. And he has stated these things repeatedly, and I can pull out the text for you, if you like. He said them as recently as August, and the reason for which he was not eager to go forward with further United Nations sanctions and basically sabotage the Bush administration attempt to apply for their sanctions on Iran in September [was] because he can't find the evidence to prosecute with. And, you know, I just … I really insist on this, [because] it is continually said in the U.S. media that Iran has a nuclear weapons program. That may be true; I can't completely rule it out, but it's not in evidence. It's not something that we can say, "Yes, we know this is happening. We know where it's being done. We know that it is being done."

And there are all kinds of counterindications to it. For instance, the Supreme Jurisprudent of Iran, Ali Khamenei, who is the chief theocrat, has given a very clear *fatwa*, and it follows the one given by Ayatollah Khomeini, that nuclear weapons are illegal in Islamic law because Islamic law, like Roman Catholic canon law, you know, has a law of war. And in the Islamic law of war, it is not permitted to kill innocent noncombatants, which any nuclear exchange clearly would do. Now you can't complain that Khamenei is an absolute dictator and a theocrat and he's regimenting his society in these unpleasant religious ways, on the one hand, and claim that he's going around giving *fatwas* that are completely ignored or are basically false on the other. I mean, either it's an ideological state or it isn't. And while it's not impossible that Khamenei is lying, nor is it impossible that people in the Iranian government would do something and sort of hide it from him. I mean, things like this are never instant. And, you know, the Iranian authorities' repeated announcements that they don't believe in nuclear weapons and don't want one and aren't trying to get one are never quoted. And indeed, the U.S. press keeps talking about the nuclear weapons program and the Iranians' desire for a nuclear bomb that the Iranians have never expressed. There is no Iranian leader who has ever said, "We want a bomb," and they all say, "We don't want one."

Every other expert with whom I spoke—over a dozen people—completely discounted Cole's initial arguments concerning Iran's "peaceful" nuclear program. They pointed out, correctly, that the president of Iran has denied the existence of the Holocaust, that the Iranian regime has told many public lies, that it has killed large numbers of innocent civilians despite the supposed religious prohibitions on such killing, and that other *fatwas* provided exemptions from Islamic law for those pursuing *jihad*. The analysts also pointed to Iran's record of obstructionism in nuclear inspections and Iranian popular and elite political support for developing nuclear weapons.

Shortly after the publication of the December 2007 National Intelligence Estimate, Cole and I had an e-mail exchange about the subject. He began the exchange by mentioning the estimate and suggested that it conceded that Iran did not have a weapons program. I demurred, and we had an exchange. Here is part of my e-mail to him:

[The December 2007 Intelligence Estimate says that] the Iranians WERE developing a warhead until 2003, which means that they most definitely did have a weapons program until that time; they still are developing plutonium production capability and ballistic missiles, neither of which has any conceivable peaceful purpose. In fact ballistic missiles are not even militarily cost-effective unless armed with weapons of mass destruction, and nuclear warheads are far easier to employ in this way than chemical or biological warheads. The fact that they [Iran] stopped warhead development in 2003 is interesting, perhaps perplexing, but it does not prove, at all, that the Iranians have never had a nuclear weapons program, that they aren't still developing a weapons capability, or even that they aren't still interested in developing weapons themselves. Once you have weapons-grade fissile material and delivery systems, warhead design and production is relatively straightforward, and if they wanted to continue with minimal interruption and reduced risk of attack from the U.S., suspending warhead development until they have the material and delivery systems was in fact rational. The question is why they didn't announce it. I don't know, but one possible answer is that this would have involved admitting that they previously HAD a warhead design effort, which they have always denied.

And here is Juan Cole's response:

I have all along agreed that it was possible that the Iranians were working on a bomb.

What I had said was that El Baradei could not find evidence of such a program (diversion of materials, suspicious sites, Iranian-generated plutonium signatures), and that I felt that the Washington consensus was altogether too categorical that there was such a program as we spoke (in October of 2007) in the absence of any real proof of it.

I was talking to a retired nuclear physicist who used to work at Los Alamos about all this, after our conversation. That person said that the secret experiments, which later came to light, of the 1990s, suggested that the Iranian scientists had gotten interested in some weapons-related issues and had been curious enough to do some relevant experiments. This person actually put it that way, as a matter of the scientists' own curiosity.

It is possible that there were such occasional experiments until fall 2003. We do not know enough to call them a program and we do not know that the experiments were authorized by Khamenei.

What we seem to know is that we intercepted in summer of this year the conversation of a high ranking Iranian official who was upset that those particular experiments were halted in fall of 2003. For all we know, they had come to the attention of Khamenei, who shut them down, to the dismay of hawkish officers (not everyone in the government likes Khamenei). And, certainly, they could not have been formally shut down without Khamenei's approval.

The Iranian government is extremely vague and complex. It is sometimes not clear who is responsible for what, and where the buck should stop for particular decisions. It is personalistic and often opaque. The American way of looking at things, where there are demarcated institutions and individual accountability, is misleading in this context.

So I'd be a little less categorical about what exactly we now know about a "program." That there were occasional weapons-relevant experiments, and that Rafsanjani seems to have been interested in a bomb, was already known. That is not necessarily the same as a Manhattan Project authorized and funded at the highest levels of government.

Cole may or may not be correct in his characterization of Iran's warhead design effort as "experiments." But Iran's heavy-water reactor project, which will give Iran a plutonium production capability, and its ballistic missile program are extremely large-scale programs that are surely authorized and funded at the highest levels of the Iranian government.

Bushehr Nuclear Facility, Iran.

Interestingly, however, Cole is definitely *not* alone in doubting some of the other accusations that the Bush administration has made about Iranian behavior in Iraq. For example, Cole, Nir Rosen, and others expressed deep and intelligent skepticism that the Iranians have supplied technically advanced IEDs used to attack U.S. convoys and armored vehicles, as the Bush administration has alleged. Cole doubted that the Iranian regime was supplying most of these devices, and said that if it was supplying any of them, it would be to corrupt Shiite militias, who then resold them to Sunni insurgents.

CHARLES FERGUSON: The Iranians are at least said to have been ... supplying IEDs and funding for insurgence of various types and kinds. What do you think of that?

JUAN COLE: I think it's mostly American propaganda.

CHARLES FERGUSON: Oh, so you don't think that these advanced penetrator devices actually come from Iran?

JUAN COLE: No, or certainly not all that are alleged to come from Iran come from Iran. I mean, the American argument is that the Iraqis can't make the explosively formed projectiles, and that's ridiculous. The technology that's involved is actually used in the Iraqi petroleum industry. The U.S. invaded Iraq because it was afraid of how high-tech the Iraqi capabilities were, right? And then it turns around and says they can't make a roadside bomb? I mean, it's frankly ridiculous. And if you trace where these explosively formed projectiles have been deployed, they've often been deployed in west Baghdad or in Al-Anbar or Diyala Provinces, clearly by Sunni Arab forces. And there is no way on God's green earth that the Iranians are giving these to Sunni Arab guerrillas.

CHARLES FERGUSON: Oh, you don't think that there's a good argument that it's in their interest to just destabilize the situation and keep the Americans pinned down, and so that actually it would be in their interest to supply everybody?

JUAN COLE: No. It's a brain-dead argument, frankly, Charles.

CHARLES FERGUSON: Well, that's exactly what the United States did during the Iran-Iraq War, so it's not like it's a strategy that nobody's ever tried.

JUAN COLE: Well, yes. But, you know, what the United States did during the Iran-Iraq War didn't involve inflicting damage on U.S. troops. Let's just back up here. The proxy for Iran in Iraq is the Badr Corps, and this keeps being forgotten by everybody, because the Badr Corps is allied with the United States and so you never see the Pentagon come out and denounce the Badr Corps.

CHARLES FERGUSON: Right.

JUAN COLE: Well, that's weird because the Badr Corps is a very major paramilitary force in Iraq, which has been involved in death-squad killings. It's sometimes been quite unhelpful to the security situation on the Shiite side, and yet it's never denounced by the U.S., because it's disciplined, it's generally allied with the U.S. against the Mahdi Army of Moqtada al-Sadr, and it's generally allied against the Salafi Sunnis that the Americans call al Qaeda and so forth. And so, because it's a U.S. ally, it gets a pass. And the Iranians depend very heavily on it to advance their interests in Iraq. They are not going to give Sunni Arab guerrillas the means to blow up the Badr Corps. The Sunni Arab guerrillas try to blow up the Badr Corps, try to assassinate its commanders, try to kill its foot soldiers, try to kill its political leaders every day. That would be brain-dead for the Iranians to enable the killing of their own guys. And I don't believe it's being done. I mean, there's no evidence for it. So the Iranians are not giving IEDs to the Sunni Arabs. I mean, that's just crazy.

And again, you know, if something is being alleged that makes no sense, I have a rule that you need more evidence for it than less. And what I find is when things are alleged that are counterintuitive, usually much less evidence and much vaguer evidence is offered for it than is the case when things make sense. So I think to the extent that the Iranians are giving anybody anything with regard to training and weaponry, they're probably giving it to the Badr Corps. And the Badr Corps is corrupt and inefficient sometimes, and I think they're probably storing the Iranian-made weapons that are given [to] them in warehouses in Baghdad, and they get stolen off from there or they get sold off from there. And there's a very lively arms market in Baghdad, so it could be that some of this stuff is actually coming in from Iran to the Badr Corps and then leaking into Baghdad. But why are the Iranians giving it to the Badr Corps? Not to destabilize Iraq, but rather to ensure that their guys come out on top in the long run.

And so I think a lot of what the Americans allege about Iran just makes no sense on the one hand, and some of it is probably a jealous-girlfriend story. That is to say, the Americans want the Badr Corps for themselves. They would like to detach the Islamic Supreme Council [SCIRI] and the Badr Corps from their Iranian mooring and make them uniquely American allies. And I think they put pressure on the Supreme Council in various ways to lessen their ties to Iran. So they arrested the son of Abdul Aziz al-Hakim, Ammar al-Hakim, one time when he was coming back from Iran. They raided the compound of Abdul Aziz al-Hakim and arrested five Iranian visitors, whom they charged with being spies. These were the guests of the leader of the major block in parliament. So, you know, the Americans keep trying to tie the Iranians to the insurgency or to the kind of scruffy, Iraqi nativist Mahdi Army; well, none of those things make much sense. And where we know the Americans have actually taken action against actually existing Iranians in Iraq, they've been in the compound of the Supreme Council or they've been with the Kurds, who are American allies. So the evidence seems to me to be that the Americans and the Iranians have a tacit alliance in Iraq that they have very similar interests and that they have the same allies. And it seems to me what's really going on—the real source of American complaints against Iran—is that the Americans are having to compete with the Iranians for the allegiance of their own allies in Iraq. That's what's going on.

Nir Rosen tended to agree with Cole.

NIR ROSEN: I'm skeptical of anything they [the Bush Administration] say. They might believe it, but that doesn't make it true. Americans have been blaming foreigners for their problems in Iraq and Afghanistan ... for a long time. I think just because the American military official[s] say it, it doesn't make it so. In fact, that only makes me suspicious given their track record of (A) stupidity and bad intelligence and (B) just lying.

And in all my time in Iraq, I have never seen any evidence of this Iranian military interference in Iraq, and nor has any journalist that I respect and trust. And I think we are much better aware of what's happening in Iraq than the military is. At least, many of us speak the language.

Regardless of the truth of the Bush administration's allegations about Iranian-supplied IEDs, nearly everyone agreed that it was in Iran's interest to keep Iraq sufficiently unstable to force the U.S. to remain bogged down there, though not unstable enough to incite a full-scale civil war that might destabilize Iran itself or drag it into a regional war.

ABBAS MILANI: They want this government of Iraq, the Maliki government, to succeed. They want a Shiite-dominated government. That's what their hope is. Yet that's where the points of convergence would end. Where the points conflict is that they don't want the U.S. to get out. They don't want a very viable, working, secular, democratic Iraq. They don't want a democratic Iraq where women have equal rights, for example, and might make the situation tempting for Iranians to use Iraq as a model, particularly now that there is Turkey. So keeping the U.S. pinned down, but not pushing the U.S. so far as to lead to a civil war is, I think, where the policy has been.

And they have done it very successfully so far. They have pushed and they have pulled back. They have pushed and they have pulled back. They have shown their muscle when they want to. I think you might remember one time some Iranian diplomats were taken hostage—twelve of them, I think—and out of nowhere, about a hundred and forty Iranian special forces appeared, attacked the place where the hostages were kept, released the hostages, and then disappeared into the crowd. And from reports of American officials who were there, CIA officials who were there, is that they were shocked. They didn't know where the hell these people came from. They were extremely well trained, and they disappeared. That infrastructure is there, and they plan to use that infrastructure to consolidate hegemony if nothing happens, and then to hit at the U.S. if the U.S. pushes them or hits them.

Effects on the Persian Gulf Region and the Rest of the Middle East

Interviewees mentioned four somewhat related processes by which the war in Iraq places the stability of neighboring countries, the Persian Gulf, and the rest of the Middle East at risk. The first, already discussed, is the refugee crisis. The second is the increased risk of regional nuclear proliferation. The third is widespread ethnic conflict and civil war that could lead to a regional war. The fourth is increased *jihadist* activity and terrorism in the region.

Several analysts commented at length on both the likelihood and the consequences of a regional war. They tended to agree that the likelihood of a regional war would be greatly increased by an American withdrawal or the outbreak of full-scale civil war within Iraq. In such a war, Iran would support Shiite groups, while fears of Shiite dominance would lead Saudi Arabia, Syria, Jordan, and possibly Egypt to intervene on behalf of Sunni groups. Conflict might also break out between the Iraqi Kurds and their neighbors, especially Turkey and Arab Iraqis.

Everyone I spoke with agreed that neither Iran nor Saudi Arabia wanted to see full-scale civil war in Iraq, nor to be drawn into a regional war. Everyone agreed that the consequences of such a war could be dire for the region and the global economy. There was a wide spectrum of opinion, however, on the question of whether a full-scale civil war was likely, and how widespread it might be.

CHRIS ALLBRITTON: It's not the end of the world if Iraq splits up into three, or two, kind of separate little entities. It very well might be the end of the world if it splits up violently. Um, and that's not entirely hyperbole. I mean, when you have massive civil war—violent, nasty civil war on top of twenty percent of the world's oil supply, that will probably engulf other regional players—Iran, Saudi Arabia, Jordan, Syria, maybe even Egypt, and possibly Turkey. Then you have an entire disruption of the world's oil supply, or a good proportion of the world's oil supply. And oil prices are already spiking. Do you really want them to go up higher? Do you want to see those costs go through Western economies? Do you want to see these economies slow down? It could be very, very, very, very bad, and with huge repercussions.

What are the chances of it ending peacefully? Like I said, I don't know. I couldn't calibrate it exactly. But I think the way the trend lines have gone—in which everything gets more and more violent—what's happening is that the politics of the street and the politics of the Kalashnikov are going in one direction and becoming more intense. ...

CHARLES FERGUSON: What would you put the odds of (A) full-scale civil war, (B) continuation of roughly the current level of insurgent violence, (C) an improvement of the situation to some reasonably stable state?

CHRIS ALLBRITTON: Well I think C will eventually happen: the stabilization. But it could be generations away. Full-scale civil war is a very real possibility.

Juan Cole, Joost Hiltermann, and most others felt that a full-scale civil war would be inevitable if the United States withdrew completely from Iraq. At the same time, Cole said that both Iran and Saudi Arabia were thoroughly aware of this risk, that both nations wanted to avoid it, and that they would negotiate with each other in an effort to prevent it.

JUAN COLE: The Saudis and the Iranians have somewhat resisted this American attempt to foment a kind of Middle Eastern cold war [against Iran]. They have visited one another and kept lines open.

Cole did not estimate the likelihood that American withdrawal and a resultant full-scale civil war would produce a regional war, but he and many others clearly felt that the possibility was very real. (This possibility and its policy implications are considered in detail in chapter 12.)

Abbas Milani was more skeptical about Iran, although he agreed that Iran did not want a full-scale civil war. He said, however, that Iran wanted to keep Iraq destabilized to keep the United States pinned down in Iraq.

CHARLES FERGUSON: Say a little bit about what you think Iran's interest is with regard to America's position in Iraq. We spoke about this a little last time, and I think that you agreed at that time that Iran viewed it as in its interest to keep the United States pinned down in Iraq and to keep the Iraqi situation sufficiently unstable that the United States felt committed to remain there in large numbers.

ABBAS MILANI: Yes. I think the Iranian situation—in terms of their view of what the U.S. should be in Iraq—is very sophisticated in the sense that it is tense and very precise. They don't want a civil war. I don't believe they want a civil war, because, as I said, a civil war would cost them dearly. Hundreds of thousands might migrate to Iran. Iran [would] have a refugee problem. They [would] have to get involved on the side of the Shiites, and the Saudis and the rest [would] likely get involved on the side of the Sunnis. Iranian Kurdistan would get involved in any civil war that will engage the Kurds of Iraq. They [the Iranians] don't want a civil war. They don't want a partition, because partitions will again fan the flames of ethnic independence in Iran. Iran is an ethnic quilt: twenty-five percent Turk, ten percent Kurds, five percent Baluchis and Arabs, and one percent Turko-man. If the borders tend to at least begin to be redivided along ethnic lines—which would be a tempting possibility after an independent Kurdis-tan—Iran stands to lose. So they don't want a partition.

Several people also noted, however, that a civil war or a regional war involving Iran, or both types of conflicts, could result from purely intra-Shiite conflict, with the Iran-ian-financed Badr Brigade facing off against nationalist, pan-Arabist Moqtada al-Sadr and his Mahdi Army. Cole noted above that this intra-Shiite conflict for control of the south was one of the three civil wars under way in Iraq. Allbritton believed that serious intra-Shiite conflict could draw in Iran.

CHRIS ALLBRITTON: They [the Shiites] are angry, uneducated. … Moqtada al-Sadr … exploited that and formed the Mahdi Army. It could easily, eas-ily turn bad if they decide they don't want to take part in a government be-cause Moqtada al-Sadr is opposed to Iran. He's much more of a … pan-Arabist Islamist, if you can imagine such a beast. He considers himself very Arab, and not Persian, and wants to have Najaf and his people, and Sadr City, as the basis of Arab Shiism. Whereas Iran, being Persian, they want to control the world of Shiism.

And I think this potentially explosive situation has been utterly unfore-seen by the Americans, which is why you see Iran now with so much power. They really exploited the Shia position in Iraq. … The Americans didn't see that coming. They should have. But they didn't.

CHARLES FERGUSON: So you think that there could be a lot of conflict within the Shiite south between those who support Iran and—

CHRIS ALLBRITTON: There is some evidence that there is some conflict within the kind of Iranian-backed aspects of Shia and the … Iraqi-based Shia. Groups such as the Supreme Council for Islamic Revolution in Iraq, and the Badr organization, and Dawa—who are the main power brokers in the Iraqi government—they're all Iranian-backed. They spent time in Iran; during the Iran-Iraq War, they were nurtured by Iran, especially the Supreme Council and Badr Organization. On the other hand, you have the kind of Arab Shia, who are represented by Moqtada al-Sadr, who stayed in Iraq. They weren't exiles. They have a very strong kind of Arab identity.

The possibility of a regional war between Iran and the Sunni nations, combined with Iran's nuclear program, raises the possibility that civil war in Iraq could stimulate a regional nuclear arms race, with Iran on one side and Saudi Arabia, Egypt, and Syria on the other. Syria apparently had a covert nuclear program—on September 6, 2007, Israeli aircraft secretly bombed a suspected Syrian nuclear facility, which was allegedly built with North Korean support—and at various times, Saudi Arabia and Egypt have exhibited some inclination or effort to develop a nuclear weapons capability.

Several experts also argued that the U.S. preoccupation with Iraq had impeded nonproliferation efforts globally, including efforts against North Korea.

CHARLES FERGUSON: What do you think the effects of the Iraq war have been on other potential proliferators of WMD?

ASHTON CARTER: [*sighs*] Well, the preoccupation of the United States, and especially this administration, with Iraq, has caused us both to take our eye off the ball in North Korea and Iran and also, now, to be in a disadvantaged position with respect to both of them. The North Koreans, during this whole period of the quest for Iraq's weapons of mass destruction that weren't there, the North Koreans, who we know have weapons of mass destruction—nuclear weapons, not chemical and biological weapons— they've been running amok, for the last five years, reprocessing plutonium. And so, during the period when we're supposedly at war with terror and at war with weapons of mass destruction, the most bizarre regime in the world, and the one that might be a source of weapons of mass destruction to terrorists—namely, North Korea—has proceeded unchecked. And … we've put ourselves in a position where we have less leverage against the North Koreans. First of all, they've been emboldened by the fact that they've gotten away with murder for five years and the United States hasn't done a thing about it. And second, our position with respect to our allies is weaker than it was five years ago. And third, the North Koreans know we're bogged down in Iraq, and therefore, they feel that they have a freer hand. So you put all those factors together, and you have: Not only are the

North Koreans further along in the nuclear program than they were five years ago, but we're in a less good position to stop them now than we were five years ago. So there's no question that the preoccupation with Iraq has caused us to pay a price in our national security elsewhere around the world. No question.

Lawrence Wilkerson made a similar point and said that he had witnessed the effect firsthand when he worked for Colin Powell in the State Department.

CHARLES FERGUSON: What were you doing ... January through March of 2003? How were you spending your days? Who were you meeting with?

LAWRENCE WILKERSON: I was monitoring the situation with regard to Iraq as closely as I could, but there were many other problems around the world, too. One of the things that you learn quickly ... is when you have an issue like 9/11, followed by military operations in Afghanistan, followed quickly by military operations in Iraq, it sort of sucks all the energy out of the room. You don't have a lot of time for other issues. And other issues suddenly get relegated—just human nature—they get relegated back to the back bench.

Well, one of the things I was doing was trying to watch these other issues. ... The other issue that I was watching, very, very closely—because it also happens to be my area of expertise—was North Korea, and the situation in North Korea. So I was trying to keep my hands and my mind around North Korea, which I considered to be even a more dangerous situation than Iraq, at the same time my secretary and the State Department were becoming increasingly focused on Afghanistan and Iraq, and the major challenge that we saw there.

In a similar vein, several observers argued that the U.S. occupation of Iraq, and the failures of occupation policy, have stimulated anti-American, anti-Western, and *jihadist* sentiments throughout the Middle East, compromising America's ability to play a useful role in resolving the Israeli-Palestinian problem, the conflict in Lebanon, and other conflicts in Somalia, Pakistan, and other Muslim nations. There have also been criticisms of U.S. policy in Somalia, which in some regards has been similar to U.S. policy in Iraq. Professor Joseph Nye commented as follows:

CHARLES FERGUSON: What do you think the effects of our invasion and oc-cupation of Iraq have been on the region and our relations with the region?

JOSEPH NYE: Well, I think the net effect has been negative, not positive. There were some people, after the first election in Iraq, who said, "See, this is transforming the region." You had, you know, [Hosni] Mubarak in Egypt talking about letting opposition run in the election. You had the Saudis holding some very limited local elections. But that euphoria, I think, has worn off somewhat. ... And in the meantime, the reputation of the United States—our attractiveness or soft power—has declined quite precipitously. If you look at public opinion polls in Jordan and Pakistan, which are both frontline states in the struggle against terrorism, polls show that Osama bin Laden is more popular than George W. Bush. That's not healthy for us.

Not everyone agrees that the Iraq war has caused a vast increase in anti-American sentiment or that it has weakened America's global position. Here is Richard Armitage:

CHARLES FERGUSON: Do you think that this entire episode—the invasion of Iraq, the way it was done, the way occupation policy was carried out, the way the United Nations was treated—do you think that that's had a mate-rial cost in American diplomatic standing in the world?

RICHARD ARMITAGE: ... I think the actual cost was less in the invasion of Iraq than in the fact that it didn't seem to go as well as we'd hoped. But the reason that we're enjoying in some areas of the world a low popularity, if you will, is much more complex than that. And it seems to me part of it is that some people in the world don't like our policies. Some people, in addi-tion to that, might not like our leaders or the way they carry themselves. To some extent, they may not like the fact that the United States still is—notwithstanding the difficulties of Iraq and Afghanistan—still a country who can go it alone and has been relatively immune, notwithstanding 9/11, from the great neuralgia that has affected almost every other part of the globe, protected as we are by our two great oceans. And finally, I think that in some parts of the world, we enjoy a low popularity rating because it's very fashionable and allowed to criticize the United States, but criticism of their own governments is not allowed. So I think the sum total of those four elements—and maybe some others—are the reason for some of our present difficulties.

Armitage is, however, in a distinct minority here. Jessica Stern, who is generally hawkish on terrorism issues, echoed Nye's sentiments.

JESSICA STERN: In a way, the United States fell into a trap. It was as if bin Laden set a trap for us, that we should go and attack a Muslim country. Iraq is, of course, an extremely important Muslim country. And we did exactly what bin Laden would have wanted us to do. And indeed, he has pointed this out in his statements: that President Bush has really assisted him in his effort to decimate the U.S. economy and make the *jihadi* movement thrive.

CHARLES FERGUSON: How so?

JESSICA STERN: Bin Laden is interested in proving that the United States is out to humiliate the Islamic world and destroy the Islamic world. And we went into a country allegedly because of its weapons of mass destruction, which we still have not found, and humiliated the Muslim people globally. He has been able to argue that. He has been able to use our adventures in Iraq as proof that that was our goal. And of course, the pictures coming out of Abu Ghraib really helped him in that regard.

CHARLES FERGUSON: Hm. And what do you think the effect of the American invasion of Iraq has been on general Arab public opinion, not just bin Laden's supporters?

JESSICA STERN: As soon as it was clear that we were going to invade Iraq, the bottom fell out in support for the United States in the Islamic world, according to polling by Zogby [International, a polling firm]. And then, once we did invade, poll after poll showed that in Muslim-majority countries, the United States had lost all respect. And indeed, in Jordan and in Pakistan, majorities claimed to have more confidence in bin Laden than in President Bush.

CHAPTER TWELVE

CURRENT AND FUTURE U.S. POLICY IN IRAQ

This chapter considers, first, recent U.S. policy toward Iraq, particularly "the surge," and, second, the question of U.S. policy going forward. Assessments of U.S. policy since early 2007 are somewhat more favorable than assessments of Bush administration policy from 2002 through 2006. There is also a consensus that the sharp decline in violence reported by the Bush administration and the Iraqi government is real, not a fabrication. Nonetheless, for reasons described shortly, most interviewees remain sharply critical of recent policy and extremely skeptical that this reduction in violence will last, or that the military surge of 2007–2008 will bring long-term benefits to Iraq.

In early 2007, the Bush administration reacted to the continued deterioration of security in Iraq by a collection of three policy measures. The first was the military surge itself: increasing U.S. troop levels and patrols, particularly in Baghdad and Sunni-dominated provinces. The second was providing money and weapons to Sunni groups, including some that had previously been part of the insurgency. Although not widely known in the United States, the recent U.S. practice of creating and funding the "Sunni Awakening" and "Concerned Citizens" councils, that is, Sunni militias, is a critical element of U.S. policy, arguably more important than the troop surge. These Sunni groups currently number over seventy thousand armed men. Most observers believe that if the U.S. either withdraws its troops or stops supporting these militias financially, the militias will become extremely dangerous contributors to civil war and sectarian violence. The third element of recent U.S. security policy has been the implementation of extremely stringent security measures such as curfews, prohibitions on private driving, and neighborhood traffic controls in Baghdad, Fallujah, and other areas. In addition, and arguably in response to the

U.S. troop surge, Moqtada al-Sadr announced a temporary cease-fire, and ordered the Mahdi Army not to initiate violence against U.S. or Iraqi government forces.

The administration also engaged in some limited diplomatic initiatives with Iraqi political groups, Syria, and Iran. Many facets of U.S. policy and behavior, however, have not changed. The surprising level of skepticism that I found with regard to recent U.S. policy thus comes from two sources: first, doubt that the surge and the arming of Sunni groups will provide lasting security gains, and, second, a belief that the long-term structural forces behind Iraq's deterioration, including much of U.S. policy, remain unchanged or are even continuing to worsen. In addition, most people I spoke with thought that the United States had mismanaged its relationship with Iran so badly between 2003 and 2007 that it would be difficult or impossible for the United States to secure greater Iranian support in managing Iraq, or to prevent Iran from developing nuclear weapons, if it ever chose to do so.

With regard to future policy, there is a wide spectrum of opinion concerning such questions as whether the United States should withdraw from Iraq; whether the United States should support the central government or current political leadership; optimal policy toward Iran; whether negotiations with Iran would prove fruitful; and whether a U.S. military presence is required to prevent civil war in Iraq or regional war among its neighbors. The preponderance of opinion appears to be that a complete U.S. withdrawal would be extremely dangerous, although some argue that remaining in Iraq would be even more so.

Recent Administration Policy and the "Surge": A Summary

As of late 2007 and early 2008, the principal elements of Bush administration policy in Iraq could be characterized as follows:

- Continued commitment to a long-term, open-ended U.S. military presence in Iraq until U.S. forces are no longer needed to maintain security or to train Iraqi forces
- Opposition to any mandatory withdrawals of U.S. forces from Iraq or to setting any date for complete withdrawal
- Temporarily elevated troop levels (the surge), whose stated goals are to

reduce sectarian violence and to enable the Iraqi central government and the principal political groups in Iraq to reach agreement on critical policy issues such as the division of oil revenues, Sunni participation in government, and constitutional reform

- Continued employment of U.S. forces in Iraq to perform counterinsurgency operations, to provide security to the local population, to train Iraqi security forces, and to contain ethnic violence from both extremist Sunni insurgents (e.g., al Qaeda in Iraq) and Shiite militias
- Direct financial and military support for local, provincial, and tribal militias (i.e., bypassing the central government), primarily arming groups in the Sunni Awakening or Concerned Citizens programs to combat al Qaeda in Iraq and to limit Shiite militia violence against Sunni populations in Baghdad and other cities
- Implementation of stringent security measures, such as traffic controls and curfews, to reduce insurgent and sectarian violence
- Partial or substantial reversal of some earlier policy decisions, for example, through large training programs for Iraqi army and police forces, the relaxation of de-Baathification policies, and the construction of a large army employed principally for internal security
- Continued public support for—and pressure upon—the Maliki government and Iraq's principal political parties to reach compromise agreements on major policy questions
- Support for Shiite political groups, particularly SIIC (formerly SCIRI), who are opposed to Moqtada al-Sadr and the Mahdi Army, combined with some pressure on these groups to restrain their violence and to reach agreements with moderate Sunni and Kurdish groups
- Continued U.S. support for training, equipping, and deploying the existing Iraqi security forces, primarily the army and the police
- Refusal to provide financial or other support for Iraqi refugees in Jordan, Syria, and other nations; refusal to admit substantial numbers of refugees into the United States; some very limited military assistance to facilitate safe internal refugee flows and migration
- Continuation of confrontational policies toward Syria
- Aggressively confrontational policies toward Iran, including public criticism and diplomatic, economic, and, sometimes, military pressure, targeted both

at Iran's nuclear program and at Iranian activities in Iraq; arrests of Iranian
officials visiting Iraq; and low-level negotiations with Iran over conduct in Iraq,
possibly with positive though limited results

Publicly, the Bush administration continues to maintain that progress is being
made in Iraq, although the U.S. statements have become less frequent and less
specific. Its most detailed recent statements pertain to the surge and argue that the
surge policy is yielding progress both in immediate security and in the administration's announced "political benchmarks." Here is an excerpt from President Bush's
speech on Iraq, made on September 13, 2007:

One year ago, much of Baghdad was under siege. Schools were closed, markets were shuttered, and sectarian violence was spiraling out of control. Today, most of Baghdad's neighborhoods are being patrolled by coalition and
Iraqi forces who live among the people they protect. Many schools and markets are reopening. Citizens are coming forward with vital intelligence. Sectarian killings are down. And ordinary life is beginning to return.

One year ago, much of Diyala province was a sanctuary for al Qaeda and
other extremist groups, and its capital of Baqubah was emerging as an al
Qaeda stronghold. Today, Baqubah is cleared. Diyala province is the site of a
growing popular uprising against the extremists. And some local tribes are
working alongside coalition and Iraqi forces to clear out the enemy and re-
claim their communities.

One year ago, Shia extremists and Iranian-backed militants were gaining
strength and targeting Sunnis for assassination. Today, these groups are being broken up, and many of their leaders are being captured or killed.

These gains are a tribute to our military, they are a tribute to the courage
of the Iraqi security forces, and they are the tribute to an Iraqi government
that has decided to take on the extremists.

Now the Iraqi government must bring the same determination to achiev-
ing reconciliation. This is an enormous undertaking after more than three
decades of tyranny and division. The government has not met its own leg-
islative benchmarks—and in my meetings with Iraqi leaders, I have made it
clear that they must.

Yet Iraq's national leaders are getting some things done. For example, they have passed a budget. They're sharing oil revenues with the provinces. They're allowing former Baathists to rejoin Iraq's military or receive government pensions. Local reconciliation is taking place. The key now is to link this progress in the provinces to progress in Baghdad. As local politics change, so will national politics. ...

Americans want our country to be safe and our troops to begin coming home from Iraq. Yet those of us who believe success in Iraq is essential to our security, and those who believe we should begin bringing our troops home, have been at odds. Now, because of the measure of success we are seeing in Iraq, we can begin seeing troops come home. The way forward I have described tonight makes it possible, for the first time in years, for people who have been on opposite sides of this difficult debate to come together.

Our troops in Iraq are performing brilliantly. Along with Iraqi forces, they have captured or killed an average of more than 1,500 enemy fighters per month since January. Yet ultimately, the way forward depends on the ability of Iraqis to maintain security gains. According to General Petraeus and a panel chaired by retired General Jim Jones, the Iraqi army is becoming more capable—although there is still a great deal of work to be done to improve the national police. Iraqi forces are receiving increased cooperation from local populations. And this is improving their ability to hold areas that have been cleared.

Because of this success, General Petraeus believes we have now reached the point where we can maintain our security gains with fewer American forces. He has recommended that we not replace about 2,200 marines scheduled to leave Anbar province later this month. In addition, he says it will soon be possible to bring home an army combat brigade, for a total force reduction of 5,700 troops by Christmas. And he expects that by July, we will be able to reduce our troop levels in Iraq from 20 combat brigades to 15.

General Petraeus also recommends that in December we begin transitioning to the next phase of our strategy in Iraq. As terrorists are defeated, civil society takes root, and the Iraqis assume more control over their own security, our mission in Iraq will evolve. Over time, our troops will shift from leading operations, to partnering with Iraqi forces, and eventually to overwatching those forces. As this transition in our mission takes place, our troops will focus on a more limited set of tasks, including counterterrorism operations and training, equipping, and supporting Iraqi forces. ...

Realizing this vision will be difficult, but it is achievable. Our military commanders believe we can succeed. Our diplomats believe we can succeed. And for the safety of future generations of Americans, we must succeed. ...

We should be able to agree that we must defeat al Qaeda, counter Iran, help the Afghan government, work for peace in the Holy Land, and strengthen our military so we can prevail in the struggle against terrorists and extremists. ...

Some say the gains we are making in Iraq come too late. They are mistaken. It is never too late to deal a blow to al Qaeda. It is never too late to advance freedom. And it is never too late to support our troops in a fight they can win.

Good night, and God bless America.

Two prominent analysts agreed with the administration's claims. On July 30, 2007, the *New York Times* published an op-ed article by Michael O'Hanlon and Kenneth Pollack, two Brookings fellows who favored the 2003 invasion but subsequently criticized some occupation policies. The article, "A War We Just Might Win," described the authors' week-long visit to Iraq, and argued that the military surge was working: "... we were surprised by the gains we saw and the potential to produce not necessarily 'victory' but a sustainable stability that both we and the Iraqis could live with. ... Everywhere, army and marine units were focused on securing the Iraqi population, working with Iraqi security units, creating new political and economic arrangements at the local level and providing basic services—electricity, fuel, clean water and sanitation—to the people. ... American advisers told us that many of the corrupt and sectarian Iraqi commanders who once infested the force have been removed."

These sentiments appear to be widely shared within the U.S. military, and to a lesser extent among American journalists and analysts. In December 2007, Marc Garlasco, with Human Rights Watch since 2003, told me that friends of his serving with the U.S. military in Iraq were optimistic that with the surge and the "Sunni Awakening," the U.S. occupation had "turned a corner" with regard to the security situation. A CBS News correspondent who has been visiting Iraq since the 1980s said the same thing, also in December 2007. However, these views, which I do not discount (in my experience Garlasco is accurate, reliable, and judicious), do not appear to be widely shared by the Iraqis I have interviewed or by U.S. journalists who speak Arabic and who travel in Iraq independently of U.S. forces. Everyone agrees that violence has declined. However, my Iraqi and journalistic interviewees were strikingly, almost shockingly unanimous in saying that this effect is temporary, unsustainable, and being accomplished through policies that will make Iraq more dangerous in the long run. These observers believe that the structure and content of administration policy is intended primarily to keep the harsh reality of the dire situation in Iraq at bay through the fall 2008 elections, in the same way that Richard Nixon's "Vietnamization" kept South Vietnam from collapsing until after the 1972 elections. They pointed to the 2008 timetable for ending the surge and predicted that violence in Iraq would resume thereafter. They also were unanimous in asserting that infrastructure and essential services had continued to deteriorate. Moreover, none of my interviewees believed that the surge or its security gains have produced any domestic political progress in Iraq. Nir Rosen felt that even the term "surge" was absurd; he doubted that the increase in U.S. troops could have had any significant effect.

NIR ROSEN: I don't think there was a surge. ... I think it was more of an ooze ... It was a very slow increase of the troops by, I think, fifteen percent.

Perhaps most striking is the observers' stunningly unanimous opinion that the surge is producing no lasting military or security benefit whatsoever, for reasons discussed shortly. All Iraqis I spoke with, except for Feisal al-Istrabadi, are harshly critical of the surge and the claims made on its behalf. This included Sunnis and Kurds as well as Shiites, and also Iraqis who were initially extremely supportive of the war. For example, when I re-interviewed Omar Fekeiki in November 2007, he said that even if security had improved in Iraq, infrastructure and services had continued to deteriorate. He told me that his family in Baghdad, with whom he spoke almost every day, hadn't had running water for two months. The insurgency and the militias were just waiting the Americans out, he said.

OMAR FEKEIKI: What happened is what they called "the surge," which, before it started, I predicted it's not going to work. They'll just take over some neighborhoods and then the insurgents will kind of hide, so they'll declare that it's quiet and safer, which is what happened, and we all know it's not true. I get my information from inside Baghdad, unlike other White House statements or unlike other newspapers or TV stations, who are doing propaganda for the surge. I think what happened is a hundred percent worse than it was before. It's not going anywhere towards improvement.

… Before the surge, I said it wouldn't work, because Bush said, "We're going to start the surge. The additional American troops are going to hold the areas; they're going to fight the insurgents." [What actually happens is] they'll go into a neighborhood, and the classical thing the insurgents do is to stop fighting the Americans, to deceive them and make them think that the insurgents left. So I predicted what was going to happen is the Americans go and take over these neighborhoods, the Bush administration announces the victory or the successful surge, and then says, "Okay, we can withdraw our troops." I thought about this in November 2006, and that's exactly what happened. Now the Americans … Every single newspaper you read now, especially in the last three weeks, they've been talking about how kind of normal the life in Baghdad is.

Professor Juan Cole pointed out that security gains were being obtained largely through unsustainable measures, such as banning all private car traffic in cities, with severe economic and social consequences.

JUAN COLE: For instance, Al-Anbar Province was 1.1 million or so persons, although so many people have fled to Jordan that it's maybe less than that now. That's what it was in 2004. One of its major cities … is Fallujah, which, of course, the U.S. invaded and largely destroyed. Two-thirds of the buildings in the city were damaged, and it was emptied out. … A lot of people from Fallujah are still living in tent cities with poor sanitation in the desert, but the people who have been allowed to come back to Fallujah since late May of 2007 have been forbidden to drive their cars. There's a little bit of public transportation and some official truck transportation for getting goods into the city, but basically the people of Fallujah are walking. The unemployment is estimated at eighty percent as a result. So if you've got—oh, it could be, you know—upwards of a fifth of the population of the province immobilized like that in a very artificial way that obviously cannot be sustained, then you're going to produce a statistic that shows improved security, but it's a very artificial statistic.

Another pillar of the surge has been U.S. financial and military support for Sunni tribal groups who are fighting al Qaeda in Iraq in Sunni provinces, and similar support for Concerned Citizens militias in Sunni neighborhoods in Baghdad. Here is Joost Hiltermann's comment, made in December 2007, on the effect of supporting the Sunni tribes, the so-called Sunni Awakening:

JOOST HILTERMANN: Our [the International Crisis Group's] position on the Sunni groups has been ... that this was a particularly poor way of solving the problem of instability in Iraq. ... The problem with the Sunni groups—some tribal elements as well as former insurgent groups—is that from their perspective, they face both a tactical enemy and a strategic one. The tactical enemy is al Qaeda in Iraq (AQI); the strategic one is Iran. AQI was a problem for many of these people because it tried to enforce its will through killings and other forms of intimidation, and was moreover recruiting young people from underneath their noses. They have long been itching for revenge, but they were weak and the U.S. was fighting them as well; this often forced local groups into tactical alliances with AQI. The surge offered these groups an opportunity to fight back, which they seized.

The surge is a temporary phenomenon, however, designed to allow the Bush administration to complete its tenure without any major outbreak of violence. The surge was meant to create space for the leadership of Iraq's divided communities to reach a new national compact, but so far nothing has happened, and I expect very little on this front. The Bush administration does not seem to have the appetite for brokering such a deal, and as long as it can keep violence at acceptable levels, it knows it does not really have to work on political progress.

Once the surge comes to an end, these Sunni groups will face a new situation. They will have been empowered, and they will face an Iraqi government, also strengthened, that they associate with Iran.

Iran, to them, is the real enemy. Supported by Arab states, minus Syria, they will confront government forces and allied militias, especially as these forces continue to push Sunnis out of mixed areas in Baghdad and elsewhere. At that point, AQI can be expected to bounce back—it has not been defeated, only weakened and displaced—and it will be in the forefront of fighting "the Iranians." These groups then will face a choice: Join up with AQI, or fight on their own. But in the latter case, they will sooner or later be killed, forced into exile, or be compelled to join AQI after all.

In short, current U.S. support of these groups is tantamount to empowering them for the eventual fight against the U.S.-backed government—assuming there will not be a political agreement before the surge ends.

In November 2007, Iraqi journalist Ghaith Abdul-Ahad wrote a newspaper article about one of the Concerned Citizens groups in Baghdad. The Guardian article is a chilling portrait of a quasi-psychopathic, quasi-criminal local warlord.* I asked Abdul-Ahad about the security gains in Baghdad and the apparent return of some degree of normalcy in Baghdad life.

GHAITH ABDUL-AHAD: Charles, I think it's very easy to fall into the trap of "Happy News euphoria." Remember what happened in 2005 after the elections, when everyone started cheering for the happy democracy flourishing in Iraq? I do believe that as long as Iraq is a country under the rule of militias and armed groups, progress is still far away. Increasing the number of U.S. troops, dividing Baghdad into walled cantons, and paying local gunmen to secure the streets will reduce the number of casualties—with a hefty price of creating fiefdoms ruled by warlords. But without a proper political process and a functioning parliament, the civil war in Iraq will continue. ...

I have just come out of Iraq. I spent time in West Baghdad, Sadr City, Latifiyah, Mahmoudiya, and Basra. And in all these places, I found people fighting over power and influence, arming themselves to take back villages or towns from other factions and sects, or just preparing themselves for the day when the Americans will leave.

Warzer Jaff, my Kurdish bodyguard and fixer when I was in Baghdad and now a freelance journalist working for the New York Times, agreed. He argued that the United States was purchasing short-term safety for American troops by further destabilizing the long-term situation.

WARZER JAFF: You can tell that the security situation is a little bit better. But at the same time, I don't think that it's going to last for a long time, because, I think, the United States has changed some of their policies in Iraq.

---

*Ghaith Abdul-Ahad, "Meet Abu Abed: The US's New Ally Against al-Qaida," available at www.guardian.co.uk/Iraq/Story/0,,2208820,00.html.

For example, supporting the Sunnis in different ways, like what's happened in Anbar Province or in other neighborhoods in Baghdad. For example, in Ameriya, which was a dangerous neighborhood, there is a connection between the Sunni fighters from that neighborhood and the Americans. And the guy who's leading the Sunni fighters—they were like former Sunni insurgents, basically—the guy was one of the Islamic Army's leaders. They [the Americans] armed and they're financially supporting three hundred people in Adhamiya and other Sunni areas also. But I think that policy is not going to be a good thing for Iraqis and the Iraqi government, because I think the Americans, they're not doing that to stabilize Iraq. I think mostly they're doing that to make the American losses in Iraq low, to make the attacks on Americans be low, so that the Americans, they don't read every day in the news that several American soldiers were killed. Because what Americans are doing with the Sunnis right now, they are doing it without coordinating with the Iraqi government. So those groups, they have direct contact with the Americans. And they don't care about the government. And the government, they don't have any power over what's going on. So if the United States leaves in one month, what's going to happen to those guys? I mean, they're militias; basically, they're former insurgents. And so it's going to be, I think, a problem between the Iraqi government and those armed Sunni groups who are supported by American militias. I'm not against dealing with Sunnis, but not like this. I mean, the way they do it, I think, it will create problems in the future.

CHARLES FERGUSON: What kind of problems?

WARZER JAFF: Problems that those groups—they don't belong to the government; they're basically militias and tribes. They're dealing directly with the Americans—American generals or American armies. And the government is weak. So, basically—

CHARLES FERGUSON: I see. So, essentially, you think that the current American policy during the surge is supporting and creating more militias?

WARZER JAFF: Yes.

CHARLES FERGUSON: I see. And so that when the Americans withdraw, the

Iraqi government will be even weaker and there will be even more conflict between the various militia groups?

WARZER JAFF: Correct.

Ali Fadhil agreed with Jaff, and added—as did several other interviewees—that as the Mahdi Army had consolidated its power in much of Baghdad and Southern Iraq, the area had become a feared fundamentalist Shiite police state of its own.

CHARLES FERGUSON: So people in Baghdad feel the surge has had some beneficial effect, but they fear that it won't last, or they believe that it won't last.

ALI FADHIL: They are confident it's not going to last, because this is not the first time. And they know ... it's right now there for a while, and then it will go. They know that very well. ...

What happened really in the streets—which is something the American intelligence in Baghdad knows about, but they just don't tell the media and they're keeping it away from everyone—but what's happened really in the streets of Baghdad: The Americans prevented the militias and the gangs from appearing constantly on the streets, on the main streets, but it's there on the side streets. They're everywhere. They're filling the neighborhoods. You can't get in the neighborhood without seeing the militias or the gangs. They run checkpoints in the side roads; they leave the main road to the Americans and to the Iraqi army. Some people said even [that] the Iraqi army sees the militias and they know where they are, but they reached an agreement: Leave us alone, and we will leave you alone.

So the militias are on the side streets. They're controlling the neighborhoods. You can't move from one neighborhood to another if you're displaced by Shiites or Sunnis without getting permission from the militias or the Sunni insurgency in that neighborhood.

For example, in Baghdad streets right now, the feared word is "the office." When people say "the office" to me, ... they whisper "the office." They don't say "the office." They whisper. And I said, "Why?" And they say, "You don't know why? These people are killing Shiites and Sunnis. They are the new Mukhabarat.* That's what they are."

---

*The Mukhabarat was Saddam Hussein's extremely brutal and ruthless secret police.

And what's happening right now is "the office" is the new Mukhabarat. "The office" is a code name [for] the Sadr office and the Mahdi Army militias in the neighborhoods. You can't get into the neighborhood, move with your family, unless you go to "the office" first and get permission from them to move. And they will give you the permission after they make sure who you are and [that] you're a clean person—you're not a Sunni or you're not working with the Americans. If you want to take your furniture out of the neighborhood, you'll have to get permission as well, because you will be stuck at the checkpoints. If you want to buy a house, you can't unless you have permission from "the office." So it's like … It's another government, which in fact, to be honest with you, is a real government. It's the real government. It's governing the lives of the Iraqis inside Baghdad, and I believe it's the same in the other provinces in the south, if not worse.

Joost Hiltermann is somewhat more optimistic about the surge's immediate effect of reducing violence. He argues that the surge has produced some real benefits, such as the cessation of ethnic cleansing in Baghdad—temporary though that might be. He also believes that if the Americans leave completely, a bloodbath will follow.

JOOST HILTERMANN: Baghdad remains an intensely mixed city until today. It's just wrong to say that there is a Shiite victory. I think there is a potential Shiite victory, and I think if the surge hadn't happened, that Shiite victory might already have occurred. … I think, thanks to the surge, the Shiite militias have been unable to accomplish their plan to totally cleanse the city, not ethnically, but in a sectarian way, religiously, of … Sunnis. The mosaic that Baghdad used to be has changed dramatically, but it has become a different kind of mosaic. Now people are not intermingled in neighborhoods, but people have consolidated in their own neighborhoods, which, however, remain commingled throughout the city. There is no line you can draw—well, no single line you can draw—through the city that divides Sunnis from Shiites. They remain totally intermingled. That is a good thing, but it's also a highly fragile situation that could easily come to an end. Certainly, the Shiite militias could then push forward and complete the task, which is still going to create a lot of bloodshed and a lot of fighting.

The surge was designed to create space for the various Iraqi parties to make political deals that are to restabilize the country. And this was done by a military effort that suppressed, or meant to suppress, the most violent Iraqi actors or also, in some case, even non-Iraqi actors—on the one hand al Qaeda in Iraq, which is a foreign leadership, and the other hand, the Mahdi Army, the JAM [acronym for the Jaish al-Mahdi, the Arabic name for the Mahdi Army]. And what is happening now is that the military effort has in fact succeeded in reducing the level of violence in Baghdad, and it slowed down the sectarian cleansing that we saw there very heavily in 2006. But at the same time, we have seen absolutely no progress on the political front. And so we are in a holding pattern. And General Petraeus has now succeeded in extending the surge by a number of months until next summer [2008] essentially, but just like an airplane circling above the airport before it must come down and can be refueled even, eventually the plane must come down one way or the other; it will either have to have a soft landing, or it will crash.

Hiltermann warned further that even arming the Iraqi security forces could promote violence over the long term, because the security forces are often beholden to sectarian and regional factions rather than to the national government. He therefore felt that the security issue could not be handled in a sustainable way without regional negotiations, in which the United States has thus far refused to engage.

JOOST HILTERMANN: To the extent that the Americans are building up Iraqi security forces, they are basically arming potential factions in the civil wars that will break out or escalate, or whatever term you want to use.

CHARLES FERGUSON: Now I would include the Iraqi army in that statement not just—

JOOST HILTERMANN: Very much so. Not just the police, but also the army. I think the Bush administration has recognized this and therefore has started to focus on making local deals and building up local forces, but the risk of that strategy is that in fact you are promoting warlordism, especially because you don't have a long-term political strategy for Iraq, again because there is no regional framework. And so what is happening now is that some Sunni sheikhs are being empowered and the Supreme Council is being empowered.* But this is only going to lead to further intracommunal conflict, and it is not doing anything to generally bring down the levels of violence. And so again, I don't see a viable internal strategy unless it is wedded to a viable regional strategy.

Here is Juan Cole's assessment of progress, or rather lack of it, relative to the administration's political benchmarks:

JUAN COLE: It was hoped that the government would reach out to Sunni Arab leaders outside of government. It was hoped that a law would be passed that would mollify the Sunni Arabs—would assure them that they would get their fair share of the nation's petroleum income, something that's not assured to them under current conditions where they have no developed fields in their areas and the big fields are in the Shiite south and at Kirkuk, which is increasingly claimed by the Kurds in the north. So the Sunni Arabs are afraid of being cut out of the deal, especially since there's a move towards provincial confederacies amalgamating the various provinces of Iraq into superprovinces of an ethnic caste. So the Kurds have their Kurdistan, which is three provinces in the north, which are now really no longer three provinces, but just one state. And there's a move by the Shiites to make a superstate among eight provinces in the south. And the constitution guarantees that all new oil finds, all new mineral finds in those regional government areas, would belong to the regional government and not to Baghdad. So the Sunni Arabs can see a push whereby resources are being claimed that they would view as national resources by these ethnic groups, by the Kurds and the Shiites. And one Sunni politician said that, you know, "We'll be left with the sand around Fallujah." So there were these hopes that the troop escalation and the counterinsurgency techniques of General Petraeus would calm the situation down to the point where the hard political work of reconciliation could be tackled. That hasn't happened. Not only has there been no progress on any of the four major benchmarks announced by the Bush administration in January of 2007—benchmarks that were supposed

---

*Hiltermann refers to the Supreme Islamic Iraqi Council (SIIC), formerly the Supreme Council for the Islamic Revolution in Iraq (SCIRI), the largest Shiite party, which controls the Badr Organization militia and much of the central government.

to have been achieved by June of 2007—not only has there been no progress on any of those, [but] the constitution hasn't been looked at again with regard to the regional governments [and] the push for the kind of confederalism "con-sociation" government is still on. Not only hasn't the al-Maliki government reached out to Sunni Arabs outside the political process and brought them in, but actually the al-Maliki government as a parliamentary force and as a cabinet force, which was a national unity government, has largely collapsed. I am not sure that al-Maliki could survive a British-style vote of no confidence in parliament were it called at this point.

Among those I interviewed, the only very partial and limited defense of the current Iraqi national leadership and of continued U.S. support for it came from former UN ambassador, Feisal al-Istrabadi.

FEISAL AL-ISTRABADI: Well, they have done a bit too little too late with the surge. The more troops is better than less troops—that needs to be followed through—but again, there is going to be, because of the campaign season, an impetus to reduce the number of troops, say, in March [2008], certainly well in advance of November of 2008. ... The most important thing, I think, is to give the political class in Iraq, such as it is, room to maneuver and not to insist on these silly benchmarks, which have really nothing to do with making political progress in Iraq; they've everything to do with the political debate in Washington. Too much of the political transition has been dictated by Washington's political needs ... And it may all be too late, anyway. That's entirely possible.

Even Istrabadi, however, acknowledged deep problems with the current Iraqi leadership and the failure of Iraq's political process. Like a number of other Iraqis with whom I spoke, he seemed painfully ambivalent about whether there was anything in the current situation that could be saved, or even that there was anything left that was worth trying to save.

FEISAL AL-ISTRABADI: About a year and a half ago, a friend of mine who had never lived a day outside of Baghdad, said the United States should withdraw every single soldier, wait twenty-four hours, and then invade again and just start all over again. ... I don't know if, you know, it's humpty-dumpty now or whether it's salvageable. I am not an optimist by nature. I have always tried to work as though I were, but I suppose my leaving my former position is perhaps statement enough of where I think things are headed.

What Should the United States Do Now?

Future U.S. policy toward Iraq must contend, at a minimum, with the following issues:

- What level of military presence to maintain in Iraq, ranging from elevated (surge) levels to complete withdrawal
- How much support to provide to the current central government and its constituent elements, including its current leadership, its principal political parties, and the Iraqi security forces, relative to provincial, local, and tribal groups or even, according to some, a military coup and martial law
- Which goals and policies to pursue with regard to division of oil revenues
- Which structure(s) of political power and constitutional provisions to support, for example, with regard to partition versus centralization and the independence of Kurdistan
- What posture to adopt toward Iran, including both its nuclear program and its role in Iraq
- Which policy to maintain toward Iraqi refugee policy

In addition, the United States must grapple with many other Middle East–related issues, including some that may appear peripheral to Iraq, but are themselves major concerns, such as the Israeli-Palestinian question, America's use of torture and extraordinary rendition, U.S. policy toward other Middle East nations, and U.S. energy and oil policy.

Finally, there are long-term issues for the United States itself as a result of the war: the effects of incurring $2 trillion in war-related costs; the need to rebuild the morale of the military; the importance of reevaluating U.S. policy toward the Persian Gulf and the rest of the Middle East; the need to improve U.S. and international competence with regard to nation-building, postwar reconstruction, and counterinsurgency operations; and, not least, the need to care for over 1 million veterans who have served in Iraq.

In what follows, interviewees debate and comment on each of these issues.

Withdrawal

Even those who opposed the war from the outset are sharply divided on the question of U.S. withdrawal. Many consider withdrawal essential; some reluctantly advocate withdrawal in the absence of political progress. But many others feel that the United States must keep significant forces in Iraq indefinitely. The principal argument of those advocating that the United States remain in Iraq is that if U.S. forces withdrew, there would be a horrific bloodbath, followed probably by regional war as the Saudis, Syrians, and Jordanians intervened to support the Sunnis while Iran intervened to support Shiites. Juan Cole, whose politics are generally liberal and who was opposed to the original use of military force to remove Saddam, made that argument clearly.

JUAN COLE: Those wars [the multiple civil wars under way in Iraq in 2007] have been being prosecuted while the coalition has been there. They will go on being prosecuted when the coalition leaves. They will be fought either to a conclusion or to a standstill. And probably the presence of the U.S. troops, which are not present in large numbers either in the south or the north in Baghdad, has kept people from fighting set-piece battles with large militia forces on each side.

I lived in Beirut in the early years of their civil war in the mid-seventies, and I saw that kind of firefight between standing militias who came out and opposed one another. There were actual lines and conventional battles. You haven't had so much of that in Iraq, because the United States would bomb them from the air if they tried to do that, and stop them. But if the U.S. isn't there, then people would organize themselves into large-scale militias, and they would fight these three wars. And so Iraq would certainly be engulfed in massive violence, were the United States not present.

And the problem with a situation like that is that it can spin easily out of control even further. So it would be very bad for Iraq to undergo such a tripartite war, but it would also potentially be bad for the Gulf region in general. It could bring the Saudis and the Iranians into a proxy war, similar to what happened in 1980 through '88, when you had the Iran-Iraq War, except that the Iran-Iraq War was a war between states. It was a war between Saddam's Iraq and Khomeini's Iran, and so there were some constraints on what could be done. And, for instance, they didn't destroy each other's petroleum facilities, because a kind of mutual-assured destruction operated—both of them would have been reduced to fourth-world countries if they had done that. They did attack each other's facilities sometimes, but there was a restraint there.

If Iraq falls into this massive guerrilla war—Sunnis and Shiites are massacring one another, and the pictures are in the press—the sentiments could rage in Saudi Arabia and Iran that would force those governments to intervene in some way, even if only by allowing volunteers to go in and fight or sending in covert forces. And the danger of a proxy war between Iran and Saudi Arabia is that pipeline-sabotage guerrilla kinds of actions could then spread to Saudi Arabia and Iran to Kuwait, and so forth, that really would potentially take oil production off the market for some period of time. International petroleum supplies are tight. There is rapidly increasing demand from China and India. We already have historic highs, as I speak, in the petroleum markets. And for the Persian Gulf to go into flames, for a regional guerrilla war to break out, it seems to me, could have very dire consequences for the world economy and for the American economy.

So Iraq is not like Vietnam, where the U.S. could withdraw precipitately and altogether and let the chips fall where they may and suffer no real economic or political consequences from that. The U.S. has destabilized the cockpit of the world economy. The plane is now spiraling down.

Feisal al-Istrabadi and Joost Hiltermann agree with Cole. When I asked about the consequences of a withdrawal, Istrabadi answered me with a rhetorical question, and Hiltermann had a lengthier answer.

FEISAL AL-ISTRABADI: Do you want to withdraw American troops and have Iran, Saudi Arabia, and Syria come in?

JOOST HILTERMANN: It depends on when. If it [the United States] withdrew now, today [in late 2007], the situation would immediately dissolve into total chaos and mayhem. Civil war would take over. There would be in fact three or four civil wars—one is a Sunni-Shiite sectarian one, one an intra-Sunni one, one an intra-Shiite one, and one possibly a Kurdish-Arab one, along the boundaries of Kurdistan. That would be inevitable and immediate. If the United States forces were to withdraw after a period of time, it would depend on what they left behind ... Now if American forces withdraw [soon], we can easily see a recurrence of the sectarian conflict, or an intensification of the sectarian conflict, but I don't think we will see a disappearance of the intra-Shiite conflict. I think this, in fact, is something that's going to be defining the Iraqi future, this intra-Shiite conflict. And we may see a realignment within the Sunni camp to defend Sunnis against what is seen as an Iranian onslaught through the Shiite militias. And a Kurd-Arab conflict may take place as the Kurds see an opportunity to push when the central government collapses totally in the wake of an American withdrawal.

But many Americans and even some Iraqis favor either unilateral, simple withdrawal or a withdrawal after a final ultimatum to the Iraqi leadership to find a negotiated solution. Some observers argue that a bloody civil war would not necessarily result; others feel that there is no alternative—that while the result of withdrawal might be horrific, the consequences of continued U.S. presence are even worse.

Ghaith Abdul-Ahad argued for a timed, gradual withdrawal. Precisely because the Iraqi political leadership is so selfish, he said, it would make real progress only if it realized that it would no longer be able to rely on U.S. protection.

GHAITH ABDUL-AHAD: The United States should announce a timetable and begin negotiations with all sides, inside and outside Iraq. Only when the United States is leaving will Iraq's leaders take seriously the need to reach an agreement.

Ali Fadhil agrees that violence would increase if the United States withdrew, but feels that the United States is so incapable of behaving competently in Iraq that the Western nation should withdraw, anyway.

ALI FADHIL: I think the Americans should leave. That's what I think. I think there is no way they can help. Anything they do right now will be wrong. Any government they will be right now will be seen by everyone as a product of the Americans, even if it's a new dictator.

Nir Rosen was more ambivalent, as many are. He agreed that violence would increase if the Americans withdrew. But he also believed that the risks of sectarian violence and regional war have now been mitigated by the refugee flows and internal migration that have produced a segregated society in which not much further ethnic cleansing remains to be done. And finally, he felt that because the United States is so incompetent and makes so many mistakes, the U.S. presence causes enormous damage even though it prevents much killing.

CHARLES FERGUSON: What do you think the United States should do now?

NIR ROSEN: I don't think it matters, one way or the other, in terms of Iraq.

CHARLES FERGUSON: So you don't agree with the argument that if the United States pulled out, that there will be a real bloodbath?

NIR ROSEN: The people that make that argument, I would like to hear what they call what's happening now. That's already happened, to a large extent, because the ethnic or sectarian cleansing has been very successful ... so there aren't that many mixed neighborhoods. You aren't going to have a Rwanda scenario just because there are no Tutsis left for the Hutus to get. I mean, that's not completely true; there are parts of Baghdad that would be overrun faster if the Americans leave. No matter what, this process is going to happen, but it's been happening at a slower rate and a less bloody rate— people leaving as opposed to people getting massacred. So, if the Americans were to leave now, you would see the Sunnis of Baghdad certainly getting finished off quick. I am not saying it's an argument for the Americans to stay. If the Americans were to leave, you would also see sort of a surge of Iraq's neighbors. They would have a more direct involvement in events in Iraq—backing militias that they have backed, whether Sunni or the Shia. But this is all happening, anyway.

CHARLES FERGUSON: And so, you don't think that things in Iraq would be dramatically worse if the Americans were to leave?

NIR ROSEN: It could be a little worse. I mean, there was a time when I said that if the Americans leave, that could prevent a civil war. Now I do think that if the Americans left, from the Iraqi point of view—from the point of view of, at least, the Sunnis of Iraq or other minorities—things would get much worse. But the majority of the refugees are already Sunni, and the Sunnis of Iraq have basically been finished off—as well as anybody with brains and money who was left—have been killed. I spoke to Omar X a few months ago, and he said that if the Americans leave, then they would all be killed in his neighborhood; the government would kill them.

CHARLES FERGUSON: Yeah, I know.

NIR ROSEN: And that's a view that many Sunnis who might have supported the resistance have had for the past year or so.

CHARLES FERGUSON: Yeah.

NIR ROSEN: … An American departure might expedite destabilization in Iraq's neighbors, [but] I don't think the Americans have that much power and influence anymore, since it is one more militia. Certain things are going to happen. It is just a question of sooner or later.

CHARLES FERGUSON: Okay. And what do you think is the likelihood of a really intense regional war with the Iranians intervening very directly, and the Saudis intervening very directly, and so on?

NIR ROSEN: Iranians don't have to intervene too directly unless the power of their proxies are threatened. And the Saudis don't have the ability to do that, and the Sunni militias do. Only the Americans can really block—or even they can't—but the only potential militia that could threaten the Shia militias would be the U.S. army. And that's not likely. So I think that the Iranians are content that their proxies fight in Iraq rather than them.

Barry Posen, director of the MIT Security Studies Program, strongly favors complete U.S. withdrawal. He argues that the risks of withdrawal can be mitigated by linking withdrawal to political and military decentralization, refugee assistance, and an international regime that collects and distributes oil revenues, if necessary without the permission of the Iraqi government.

BARRY POSEN: There's certainly a risk that whatever the level of violence is, American disengagement may create the permissive conditions for more violence, but that's not necessarily true. Just as the folk who advocate staying in Iraq don't particularly have a theory that's going to tell us how staying in Iraq is going to reduce violence very much in the near term. If you believe [General David] Petraeus, there has been some decrease in the kinds of violence we count in the places where [they] have a lot of troops.

But if that doesn't seem to do much for violence in other places and the other shoe hasn't dropped yet, we don't know how permanent this will be.

I think the arguments against disengagement have tended to take the following form: If the Americans leave, then the following four or five or six disasters will happen. And my view is, if the Americans just got up and left, those six disasters *might* happen. The question is, Can we have a strategy for leaving that buffers ourselves against the possibility of those disasters, tries to lower their probability or lower their intensity, and in end, leaves us in a situation that's a bit better than the situation that we're in?

One of the things that irritates me is that Petraeus and [Ambassador Ryan] Crocker's testimony did not generate an actual conversation about a change in strategy, about alternative strategies. What it descended into, unfortunately, is just a discussion about numbers. Can we pull out five thousand troops or ten thousand troops or fifteen thousand troops or twenty thousand troops? But not a question of, If the strategy that you're on is a strategy for success, is there some other strategy that might be better?

Now, I think we should have had the discussion about alternative strategies. And, I think, it's reasonably clear now that there is an alternative strategy bouncing around. A lot of people, not just me, share that strategy. Among those who talked about it early on was [former president of the Council on Foreign Relations] Leslie Gelb. Senator [Joseph] Biden has now talked about it. In a subtractive way, Senator [Richard] Lugar sort of talked about it. Many of the columnists in [the] *New York Times,* right and left, now subscribe to the strategy. And it all basically has to do with beginning to accept that the president's dream of a unified, democratic Iraq is not a very likely outcome. And we could chase this dream for a very long time at a very high cost without too much chance of success. Instead, we have to look at what the actual trends are in Iraq. If you read between the lines of Petraeus and Crocker's testimonies, you can even see that they themselves are sort of hinting at it: The actual trends are towards decentralization in Iraq. That doesn't have to mean partition, because there's no particular reason why we have to recognize independent countries in the different pieces of Iraq, but the decentralization of political power and, as near as possible, fixing it so that the various communities and factions have a high degree of political control over their own lives, as well as the ability to secure themselves. That's the direction we need to go, not chasing this unified dream that the president wants to chase.

And to do this, there's a lot of things we need to do, some of which, interestingly enough, Petraeus and Crocker have been doing.

CHARLES FERGUSON: The list of things that you think we have to do?

BARRY POSEN: Well, one: We have to fix it so that the different groups can defend themselves, which, I think, is what we've been doing by allowing these Sunni neighborhood protection societies [the Concerned Citizens program], or tribal protection societies, or whatever you want to call them. We have not only allowed them to organize themselves, but we're actually sort of legitimating them by giving them sort of kind of legal status as part of the Iraq security forces. So that's one thing: to fix it so these groups can defend themselves.

I pointed out to Posen that many others warn that this strategy of arming Sunni groups is producing dangerous militias. When I showed him Ghaith Abdul-Ahad's article, he agreed that the Concerned Citizens strategy was dangerous. Thus, it is not clear that Posen's argument here holds up well.

BARRY POSEN: [Ghaith Abdul-Ahad's article] ... is one of the clearest and most honest depictions of what is going on that I have seen. It is consistent with everything else I have seen and thought. I think a lot of people understand this is going on. ... But few are inquiring into the downside risks, as this is the method by which we have improved the statistics, which have helped get Iraq off the front page. It looks to me like we are creating a situation that only we [the United States] can run, and which is unstable in any case. The question is Why? Is this Petraeus and Crocker freelancing? What are their motives? Does the White House understand? Et cetera.

Other principal elements of Posen's proposed strategy for facilitating U.S. withdrawal are support for refugee relocation and international control of Iraqi oil revenues.

BARRY POSEN: Second is, to let people know when we're going to leave the country, and that that time is going to come, whether it's in eighteen months, or two years, or whatever. And that people who are still left living in places where they suspect that they are threatened by other groups, they should consider whether or not they want to keep living in those places. And if they don't, they should move, and they should move while the Americans are in a position to assist them in the move by protecting them, by providing economic resources when they try and resettle in other parts of the country. Now, some of that we're doing now; some of it we're not. If you read between the lines of some of the newspaper stories, our forces have sort of protected people while they've left places.

Now, this is not a pretty thing, but I think—based upon what we know about Iraq—this is what, in fact, had been happening. And nobody has a theory about how to reverse it. I think we should make it more humane—accept it, work with it, and try to provide economic resources for the people who have moved, had to abandon homes, and begin to develop a bit of an economy in other parts of Iraq. If you believe the United Nations, a half a million people have relocated themselves within Iraq since the surge began, which doesn't suggest to me that we're bringing a lot of security to the places where they are. But it does suggest to me that they have a sense of where they can find security. Now, this has not produced perfect ethnic boundaries, and probably nothing will. But this is in the general direction that, I think, we have to move.

The other thing we have to do is figure out a way to make the resource share more reliable and more equitable over the long term. Even if you look at the people who advocate partition, they mention some magical thing—I think [*New York Times* columnist] Tom Friedman uses the euphemism that the Baghdad government is going to be an ATM for everyone else. Well, the Baghdad government can't be an ATM for everyone else without making everyone else want to fight to control the Baghdad government. So the Baghdad central government can't be the ATM. It can't be the agent for distributing oil revenues. Someone else has to do that. And there have been editorials written about this. I think that Hillary Clinton wrote one. We did, successfully, collect most of Iraq's oil revenues for several years in the oil-for-food program. Most of the corruption was in the for-food side of it, not in the collection of revenue. So we could set up some kind of exterior organization that would collect most of Iraq's oil revenues and then sign checks to the provincial governments on a per-capita basis.

CHARLES FERGUSON: Well, how do you think we're going to get the Iraqis to agree to that?

BARRY POSEN: They don't have to. It doesn't matter whether they agree to it or not. They didn't really agree to it the last time. ... Look, the transactions happen abroad. This is the beauty part of the oil business, of being a one-crop economy. It shouldn't be any harder to set up an oil-for-peace program than it was to set up an oil-for-food program. It should be much easier to implement it.

So I think this is something we can do, but it shouldn't be us. ... These observations about how we need to have international diplomacy and regional diplomacy to help end this, well, what are some of the things that regional/international diplomacy could do? One is—if Iraq is, in part, a struggle for wealth—basically trying to assure all parties that they are going to get some fair share of the wealth. The scheme that I've laid out would be a way to do that. But you would need a lot of international legitimacy to try and manage such a thing.

Larry Diamond favors using the threat of withdrawal to force all the interested parties, including Iran and Saudi Arabia as well as the major Iraqi groups, to the negotiating table. In the event that negotiations fail to produce real progress, however, he too advocates withdrawal.

LARRY DIAMOND: I think unless we get a political consensus among the principle Iraqi parties on what the rules of the game and the constitutional structure are going to be on these and related realms, there is no chance of stabilizing the country. And the most that we can do is what we are doing there now, which is basically become the police force for the country—they certainly don't have one—and hold up the floor. Essentially what we have been doing at the national level—I'll come to the local level in a minute—is holding up the floor so these different Iraqi political parties, factions, militias, incipient warlords and whatnot, can seek to corner power and resources in the uncertainty of the current situation and with the extraordinary greed that characterizes political and military actors in this situation.

And I have long since come to the conclusion that I don't want any more American lives being lost, any more American treasure being wasted, so that we can enable these different Iraqi actors to simply loot the national treasury. You know, divert the oil to their spot market or whatever, and pursue their private and sectarian projects. If that's all that's going to happen, sooner or later we are going to get out and the situation is going to collapse. And in that case, we might as well make the hard assessment that the battle is lost—that Iraqis won't assume, at the national level, responsibility for their own future—and get out sooner rather than later.

Now, I just want to insert the caveat here, Charles, that there's a lot of positive things happening, tactically and on the ground. I recognize that casualties are way down, or at least partially down, because of the surge. There have been real elements of progress in Anbar Province, in turning back al Qaeda, and getting people to assume more responsibility at the local level, and getting cooperation from locals, and eliciting people to come forward and assume some responsibility to rebuild their communities. But the problem is essentially twofold. First of all, this is not sustainable militarily. Everybody knows that the surge is going to be wound down probably, at the latest, by spring [of 2008]. And once we start withdrawing that kind of twenty-thousand-troop surplus and pulling a lot of the troops back to their bases, if we haven't generated the more organic political sustainability of this thing, a lot of the progress we made tactically on the ground is going to quickly unravel.

That's the first thing. The second thing is a lot of this local stuff is not cumulating up nationally into these broader understandings and agreements that could stabilize the macro political picture, and I think in that sense, as well, it isn't sustainable. So, what I would do is gather the principal Iraqi political parties, infractions, military, religious, political, and so on, together into a Dayton-style peace conference. I would do so with the intensive cooperation of the United Nations and the European Union, which I think would be ready to cooperate with us on this.

It would take probably a number of weeks, maybe three to four months, of dialogue within Iraq and in the region to prepare the meeting and identify the parameters for what needs to be talked about and begin to scope out … what exactly the critical issues are that need to be addressed and what the possible compromises are. Then we bring people from Iraq, but also from the region, together for what would be a very difficult and intensive dialogue. We don't come with preconceived ideas on what the solution should be. I think that the [U.S.] Senate vote was a big mistake in that re-gard. It's not for the United Sates Senate to decide what the future struc-ture of Iraq is going to look like. But [we should be] signaling, probably in general terms, this publicly as well: that if they can't come to an agreement of some kind, if they are unwilling to make the compromises that are nec-essary to save their country, we are out of there. They can have their civil war. And we are not going to indicate, at that time, who we are going to help and how we are going to position ourselves. We are only going to in-dicate that we are not going to stay there indefinably holding up the floor for them, losing several hundred American lives a year, spending what is 10 billion, 20 billion—I have lost track—per month on this war so that they can have the space to maximize their wealth and power, rather than build something for the future of the country.

And then we have to be prepared to follow through. If we are not pre-pared to let go of this thing and cut our losses, we are going to stay—oh, I'm absolutely convinced of that—because we will not have the leverage to in-duce the political compromises that would have some chance, in my judg-ment (at this point a fairly small chance, but at least some chance) of sal-vaging the situation. If it comes to that, I don't think we simply withdraw a hundred and fifty thousand troops from the entire region and say, "Well, this is going to be a cataclysm; now it's your problem." We have to be more tactical and strategic than that. We would have to keep troops in Kuwait; we would have to keep troops elsewhere in the region; we would have to shore up Jordan; we would probably have to position ourselves maybe in a sub-stantial way in Kurdistan; we would have to continue our alliances with some of the Sunni tribes to ensure that al Qaeda doesn't get deeply en-trenched there again. There would be a larger battle. But I think that's com-ing in any case sooner or later if we don't stabilize this situation politically.

I asked Diamond about the substance of what might contribute to, and constitute, a satisfactory outcome. Like Posen, he feels that international control, and equitable distribution, of oil revenue are crucial.

LARRY DIAMOND: Oil is clearly a national resource. Although provinces or regions can join jointly with the center in negotiations with companies on the exploration and production of oil in their territories, nothing can be done without the agreement of the center in that regard. Oil revenue and gas revenue, as it comes more on stream, will be paid into an international trust fund. And then there will be a formula, as there is in Nigeria, for the distribution of the oil and gas revenue between the center and the regions and provinces, and ... among the different sub-national units. And the money will be paid. This is part of what could reassure the Sunnis and bring them into this: The money will be paid directly from the International Trust Fund to the regions and provinces so the center can't, you know, abscond with it or hold it back as a political weapon.

In many regards, Istrabadi and Hiltermann agree with Diamond's views. But they both responded quite strongly when I asked about simple, unilateral withdrawal.

CHARLES FERGUSON: Now there are, of course, many people—primarily Americans, but not only Americans—who say that the United States should simply withdraw anyway. ... Yes, it will be bloody when the United States leaves, but by staying we are only postponing the inevitable. There is nothing that the United States can do that will fundamentally change the structure of the situation, and so it's better to leave now, rather than later, because in some ways, the United States presence makes things worse. What do you think of that view?

JOOST HILTERMANN: ... These are people who, like me, probably were against the war in the first place. But as such, if you were against the war and against the Bush administration, why take your anger out on the Iraqis? The fact is that in April 2003, the situation in Iraq totally changed because of the U.S. invasion, and whether we like it or not, the war did happen, and U.S. forces were on the ground. ... Now they are there, and to withdraw them now would be extremely dangerous because the situation has changed. And so I find it highly irresponsible; it [being in favor of withdrawal] ... has nothing to do with the well-being of Iraqis. ... I'm very concerned with what happens to Iraq and what happens to Iraqis who were the victims in 2003 and will be the victims again now.

I mentioned to Larry Diamond Joost Hiltermann's criticism of Americans who advocate withdrawal.

CHARLES FERGUSON: I asked essentially the same question a few days ago to Joost Hiltermann.

LARRY DIAMOND: Smart guy.

CHARLES FERGUSON: And he gave an answer that was very similar to yours in most regards, with, I think, one very significant divergence, which is that he said, you know, "Look I, Joost Hiltermann, was opposed to this war, but now that we are here, even if negotiations fail, it would be irresponsible of the United States to just completely pull out, because there would in fact be a bloodbath and, you know, having troops in Kuwait, having troops maybe in Kurdistan, would not prevent that bloodbath. That bloodbath can only be prevented"—

LARRY DIAMOND: Oh, absolutely, I agree. And I agree analytically that the bloodbath would happen.

CHARLES FERGUSON: But you think that it has to? That it's just not tenable for the United States to keep a hundred thousand troops indefinitely in Iraq?

LARRY DIAMOND: Yes, I think it is not tenable for the United States to keep a hundred thousand troops in Iraq for, you know, what? Two years, five years, ten years, twenty years—how long are we going to stay there? At what price to our other national interests around the world? At what price to the kids who are going to lose their lives, lose their limbs, come back shell-shocked with one or another version of posttraumatic stress disorder? Some of them will blow their brains out. At some point, we have to resolve that we have discharged our moral responsibility to this place, that the Iraqi actors have to assume responsibility, and that sometimes the only way you get a new form of political stability in a place is by going through a very ugly period of warfare and somebody wins.

I don't say this cavalierly, Charles. You know, it weighs on me very heavily. I think that the nightmare that Joost Hiltermann envisions is going to come sooner or later, anyway, if we don't get a political settlement. And the failure of imagination of the morally committed people like him is to see that in [such] a situation, we are just completely trapped and at the mercy of much more unscrupulous forces that understand our moral commitment and are exploiting it as a shield or a crutch behind which they just loot the national treasury and, you know, savage the country's institutional future.

Of those I interviewed, only Christopher Hitchens argued that continued escalation of U.S. force was necessary or would be productive. Here is our exchange, which occurred in September 2006.

CHRISTOPHER HITCHENS: Some generals say we're more worried by the civil war than by the insurgency now, making a distinction without a difference. The civil war was the tactic of the insurgency. Civic strife, I'd rather call it. Sectarian strife was the method and the aim of the insurgency. To that extent, they have succeeded. We face defeat at the hands of a very well-organized campaign initiated by an extremely fascist and theocratic minority largely imported to Iraq, [a country] which has no tradition of bombing and suicidal tactics.

CHARLES FERGUSON: Well, again, but—

CHRISTOPHER HITCHENS: So the question is, Is the United States Army going, therefore, to surrender to a group that you say is so negligible? Should it withdraw in the face of something that can obviously be outlasted since it's apparently so small?

CHARLES FERGUSON: What do you think the United States should do now?

CHRISTOPHER HITCHENS: It should make Iraq into a killing ground for *jihadists*. It should make it absolutely plain that they will never have Iraq and that their tactics will never make us leave.

CHARLES FERGUSON: And that should be done how?

CHRISTOPHER HITCHENS: Well, more ruthlessly than it currently is being. It should be made ... it should be made a statement by all Americans—anyone who can possibly be the president of the United States—by both houses, by such intellectuals as we have left. ... For whatever reason, this has become the place of arms between us and the enemies of civilization. It will not be the place where they win. We can deny them a victory there and we will, as we intend to do, everywhere else that they try.

CHARLES FERGUSON: You've become quite the neoconservative.

CHRISTOPHER HITCHENS: I don't see what's conservative about wishing to deny theocratic genocidal psychopaths the right to ruin another country and use it to threaten our friends and ourselves.

CHARLES FERGUSON: Well what do you—

CHRISTOPHER HITCHENS: It is a clash of civilizations—

CHARLES FERGUSON: What do you think of the—

CHRISTOPHER HITCHENS: … which ours has to prevail.

CHARLES FERGUSON: What do you think of the nature of popular opinion in Iraq with regard to the continued presence of the American army?

CHRISTOPHER HITCHENS: Well, I would be in favor of a referendum in Iraq on the single question of either a date for, or the principle of, a withdrawal by the coalition because I don't think that otherwise any of us can quite know what we're fighting about. And I think it also would be very interesting to analyze which province in which area reported in. And I think there's a strong case for conducting some such test of opinion. For the moment, I don't think we can be forced to do so, because the Iraqis have voted three times for parliamentary representatives and their own constitution … and no party ran with any success on the demand for an immediate withdrawal. The party that did the best is the most hostile in the Iraqi parliament to the coalition presence. Moqtada al-Sadr's party ran only on the demand that a date be given for a withdrawal, which is not a nonnegotiable demand, but not an immediately concede-able one either. I think that many Iraqis are somewhere in the middle, as are certainly the majority of Americans. I think it would concentrate the mind very much to be more certain about this question.

CHARLES FERGUSON: And—

CHRISTOPHER HITCHENS: But we are not, we can't pretend that we're only in Iraq for the sake of the Iraqis. We never have pretended that. We were also there to make sure that Iraq does not become another rogue and failed state, which can become a platform for the launching of attacks on our allies, on ourselves, on what I prefer to call civilization. We have the right to deny them that, even if they all do want it.

While Hitchens is the only interviewee who advocates long-term intensification of the U.S. military effort, most American and nearly all Iraqi interviewees agree that a U.S. withdrawal would precipitate a slaughter and civil war, with a subsequent regional war likely. Some analysts, however, including Larry Diamond, Barry Posen, and Zbigniew Brzezinski, feel that American withdrawal would not necessarily yield a wider regional war. In this view, which appears to be in the minority, regional war would be avoided because it is not in the interest of either Saudi Arabia or Iran to be drawn into it; they understand that their own regimes are fragile, and their rational self-interest would prevail.

LARRY DIAMOND: I think that none of the regional actors want or can afford this full-scale civil war, including Iran. And this is the most intriguing angle of it that I think people have not seriously thought through. Iran is a multinational country—fifty-one percent Persian—and they have been, to some extent, shored up by having the U.S. there, threatening the regime, giving the regime an excuse to crack down and rally the country around them. And I think that it's a gamble, but if we pull out and they have to take responsibility for this, it has the possibility of being very destabilizing for the Islamic Republic of Iran. The prospect of it being very destabilizing for them could, first of all, induce them to put pressure on the various Shiite parties to be more flexible and make more compromises. And second of all, [it] could lead to a turbulent political situation in Iran that might swing the country back, at a minimum, towards more reformist dynamics that were prevailing during the first term of President [Mohammad] Khatami. I say so, because there's already restlessness in the Kurdish section of Iran—not very well reported or paid attention to—but that's restive. The [Arab] minority is restive, the Azerbaijan minority is restive, and the economy of the country is in very bad shape.

This is a very cynical statement, but, you know, we are at a pretty bad place there now. If Iran has to watch the country of Iraq disintegrate while we, to some substantial extent—I don't say completely—draw back and say, "We have discharged our responsibility; no one inside the country originally is assuming responsibility; good-bye, it's your problem now," this is going to put a lot of stress on the Iranian regime, both in terms of the spillover effect of a disintegrating Iraq and the financial and military burden of having to worry about the insecurity on their border and figure out ways to stabilize it. Then, also, you have got different factions in Iran backing different factions in Iraq, and those divisions could widen when mistakes increase inside Iraq.

Iran and Iraq

Joost Hiltermann, Larry Diamond, and many others agree on the importance of regional negotiations that would include Iran. And all the interviewees agreed that although the optimal time for negotiations was 2002 to 2003, and that the United States will now negotiate from a position of weakness, such negotiations should still be attempted. There is, however, a range of opinion on their potential benefit. Most analysts feel that Iran wants to keep the United States pinned down in Iraq with its military and diplomatic energy drained by a continuing counterinsurgency struggle that it cannot win. In this view, Iran would be as alarmed by a U.S. withdrawal as by a now-improbable U.S. victory. Thus, paradoxically, the threat of complete withdrawal may constitute the strongest leverage that the United States has.

CHARLES FERGUSON: My own impression, actually, is that the Iranians like having us being tied down.

LARRY DIAMOND: Yes.

CHARLES FERGUSON: Do you think that they could or would try to do things to make it impossible for us to withdraw, even if we had stated our desire and commitment to do so in the absence of a grand agreement?

LARRY DIAMOND: That is one of the most interesting questions I have heard anybody ask. It's very shrewd. ... Yes, I think that's entirely conceivable. ... Then you've got to think through: Well, what might they do, and how do you respond? And, you know, you can't be trapped by them, precisely because it's so well-serving their interest. This is one of the strongest reasons why I want to take a different approach. I think that they are just doing so well, having us bogged down there, bleeding there strategically. ... And so we have got to reshuffle that deck.

Joost Hiltermann advocated a final attempt to reach a negotiated agreement through a regional conference including the major Iraqi groups and the neighboring countries, particularly Iran, with the hope that this could yield a new, more legitimate and more competent Iraqi government. Hiltermann admitted that a broad agreement with Iran was necessary for such a regional negotiation to work. He also admitted that this was unlikely to happen.

JOOST HILTERMANN: There is no solution with the current Iraqi parties in power. They are too weak, too divided, too dysfunctional, and, frankly, too unwilling to make the kinds of political deals that we are looking for to bring about a sort of new national compact that would replace the constitution, which is clearly also a sectarian document, with something that is more inclusive. And so we have recommended taking the conflict a step further and away from internal issues, to a regional level, simply because whenever the United States puts pressure on the Shiite parties—Shiite Islamist parties, that is to say—to reach out to their opponents across the divide, say, Sunni insurgent leaders, these Shiite parties run back to Iran and say, "Help, help! We are under pressure." And the Iranians are more than willing to spoil any kind of American attempt to stabilize the situation in Iraq, because as long as other issues are not resolved, from the Iranian point of view, they are not going to let the Americans gain any kind of advantage in Iraq. And so we need to take the Iranians out of the equation or bring them into the equation in a different posture. And this will require serious negotiations between United States and Iran. But this cannot possibly be limited to the Iraq question and would have to include the more broader issues that divide the two countries, including, of course most importantly, the nuclear question. So this is not easy, but we think that short of a change in the Iranian posture, the situation cannot be resolved in American's favor in Iraq.

When pressed, Hiltermann admitted that it was quite unlikely that the Iranians would agree to help the United States in this endeavor. But he felt that it was not completely impossible and therefore had to be tried. He argued that in the mean-time, the United States must remain in Iraq.

CHARLES FERGUSON: What do you think the prospects are for the United States actually being able to effect some change in the internal Iraqi situation in a way that leaves behind—or creates—a more stable structure, so that if and when the United States withdraws, either partially or totally, that there will be a stable government and there won't be a civil war?

JOOST HILTERMANN: Well, it will be extremely difficult, and it may well fail. But unlike the critics, I don't say that failure is inevitable. I only say that a precipitous withdrawal would inevitably lead to further chaos and the breakup of the country, which would then lead to a regional war, which would then force the United States to come back in greater numbers. So it doesn't serve American strategic interests to withdraw, from that point of view, either. But I do think that as long as there is even a glimmer of hope that things can be somehow stabilized in Iraq, then we should try that. But at the same time, I believe that the United States should indicate that it has no-long term intentions to remain in Iraq. At the same time, it shouldn't probably give a narrow timetable for withdrawal, because to box itself in is also not wise. But the principle has to be clear that the United States has no interest in staying in Iraq and that, in fact, it wants to withdraw from Iraq and the rest of the Middle East and leave political matters to be decided by the people of the Middle East.

But in this interim period, as long as a security vacuum exists, the United States continues to play a role. And this would have to consist of working with Iraq's neighbors to set up a regional security framework and an alliance of neighbors that have one thing in common, which is that none of them wants Iraq to fall apart. All of them would be harmed grievously if Iraq fell apart. This is a very important basis to work on, and they could do so if the willingness was there. But then we go back to the one real issue that is aggravating existing conflicts in the Middle East, and that is the U.S.-Iranian rivalry. And so we must see some kind of solution to some of the key questions on that front. If that fails, then I think all hope is lost for Iraq and then there would be no more reason for the United States to keep forces on the ground there. But we are not there yet. That issue remains unresolved, and I think a concerted effort should be made not to bomb Iran, but to find a negotiated solution to the very difficult question of its nuclear program.

Hiltermann added the following comment, which he made before the December 2007 publication of the National Intelligence Estimate that assessed that Iran had suspended weapons development in 2003, although it was continuing to develop uranium-enrichment capacity that could eventually be used for weapons development.

CHARLES FERGUSON: And how do you think that could be done? I mean, I am personally extremely skeptical that there is anything that the United States or the West can offer the Iranians that would induce them to stop.

JOOST HILTERMANN: Well, that is not clear. The Iranians have in the past given clear indication that they were ready to talk about these things and even willing to talk about a grand bargain. I am not saying that had those talks begun, they would have led to a grand bargain, but at least there was a willingness and it was an initiative of the Iranians. It was rejected in 2002 by the Bush administration as it was preparing for war with Iraq, the purpose of which, I think, was to send a signal to the Iranians that they should desist from developing nuclear weapons. The signal was lost because of America's failure in Iraq, and now the Iranians are much stronger than they were five years ago.

Abbas Milani, conversely, felt that negotiations with Iran should concentrate solely on Iraq and regional issues. He argued that Iran was determined to develop at least a nuclear weapons capability, if not actual weapons, and there was nothing the United States could do to stop the Iranians in this regard. On the other hand, he said that Iran and the United States did have some limited but significant shared interests in Iraq.

ABBAS MILANI: I don't think the nuclear issue has a negotiated solution left, anymore. I think the regime is way beyond the point of being willing to give up their nuclear program. They might have been willing to give it up four years ago. Now they think they're close enough, and they have milked it nationally and internationally. But there is a possibility of slowing down the process, slowing down the enrichment, increasing the IAEA [International Atomic Energy Agency] supervision. That can only be done through negotiation.

If there is a possibility of increasing cultural trade between the two countries—which I think is absolutely necessary—if there is a possibility of establishing diplomatic ties, which I think is to the benefit of the United States, the regime would be very reluctant to do it, but nevertheless there is pressure on the regime at home to do it. This is not a regime that is completely free to do anything it wants. It has a disgruntled populous, a restless populous that might explode anytime, and that population clearly is in favor of improved relations with the U.S. We have empirical overwhelming evidence of that, so it could do that. It could open economic ties with Iran.

CHARLES FERGUSON: Do you think that any of this could have any benefit vis-à-vis Iraq? What do you think the United States could achieve vis-à-vis Iraq by negotiating?

ABBAS MILANI: Oh, vis-à-vis Iraq, absolutely. I think if the Iranians [obtain] some satisfaction in terms of their own deals with the U.S., they will decrease their support for the insurgents. They will decrease their support for the forces that have been destabilizing the United States. We see evidence of this already, for whatever reason. Petraeus thinks the Iranians have weapons support that they were offering to the Iraqis and said [that] it is now time for us to sit and negotiate. Clearly they [the Iranians] can help in this sense. Clearly they can tighten the faucets or open the faucets. ... The Badr Brigade is their creation. I've never believed that the Badr Brigade would do anything that the Islamic Republic tells it. The Badr Brigade is, after all, primarily Arabs. And Arabs primarily—even when they are Shiites—hate Persians, and Shiite Persians hate Arabs. But is there a possibility for them [the Iranians] to convince the [Iraqi] Shiites to put down their arms and cooperate with the U.S.? I think there is, and there's evidence for it. The dismantling of Moqtada al-Sadr's Mahdi Army that's slowing down help to the Shiite insurgents, I think, are clearly indications by the regime that they can deliver on these things.

CHARLES FERGUSON: What do you think the United States could, should, offer them in return?

ABBAS MILANI: My sense is that the United States should offer them uncon-ditional negotiations. It should offer them the chance to have trade. But here I think it's very crucial, because that's where my view differs from many of the other colleagues who say the U.S. should have relations with Iran. My sense is that if the U.S. is to keep the goodwill of the Iranian peo-ple that the U.S. now enjoys—and I think it's a very worthy capital; it shouldn't be squandered—if it is to keep that intact while negotiating with the regime, which is what the great bulk of the Iranian people have said they want and almost every Iranian democrat inside Iran has said they want, almost everybody in these two categories, the Iranian people and the democrats [whose statements] I have seen or have talked to, they also say, "We don't want the U.S. to sell the farm to these guys. We don't want the U.S. to forget about the human rights issues. We want the U.S. to talk with them, but talk with them from a position of principled disagreement on human rights and on democracy." The model—again, I think you might have seen, I've written this several places—the model I think would be Reagan and the Soviets after '82, where they talked business, but they also talked human rights; they talked Helsinki and they talked SALT II [Strategic Arms Limitations Treaties II]. That kind of a combined negotia-tion is, I think, what Iranians would want and what Iranians would em-brace. The U.S. would get much out of it and would not lose that very im-portant thing that I referred to—that goodwill that I think it must make every effort to keep.

CHARLES FERGUSON: And you think that negotiations and trade agreements of that kind would be sufficient to induce the Iranians to change their be-havior vis-à-vis Iraq?

ABBAS MILANI: I think so. I think so. I don't think it's enough to change their view on the nuclear issue, but I think it is on Iraq, because what they want from Iraq they already, more or less, have. They wanted Saddam to go. They wanted Shiite domination. They wanted no partitions. They wanted not a full-fledged democracy, but a Shiite democracy. All of these things they have gotten. They wanted to embarrass the U.S.; they got it. They wanted to show their goodwill, help the Shiites and the rest of the Muslim world assert themselves; they've gotten it. From now on, it's downhill, because if they push Iraq to civil war, if they push it into partition—any of those things are things that they would not want. So I think they would have a lot to gain from having a kind of negotiated settlement to the tense relationship with the U.S.

Laith Kubba, former spokesman for the Iraqi government now working at the National Endowment for Democracy in Washington, was more optimistic than most with regard to the potential benefits of negotiating with Iraq's neighbors, particularly Iran.

LAITH KUBBA: The neighbors are the key, it is obvious, but the Bush administration refuses to open regional negotiations for two reasons. First, this would require admitting that it must deal with Iran, and that it has mishandled Iran in the past. And second, this would also be an admission that the present Iraqi government—the government they have constructed and supported—is a failure.

It is obvious that the present Iraqi government is incapable of resolving the problem. In fact, the players in power in Iraq benefit from the chaos and corruption, and because the United States does not understand the region well, they [the Iranians in power] can manipulate the situation. But the regional powers—principally, Iran, Saudi Arabia, and Turkey and, secondarily, Jordan, Syria, and Kuwait—they understand the situation and they can put very effective pressure on the Iraqis. But the United States must be involved for the simple reason that only the U.S. can calibrate the balance of power between Iran and the Sunni nations in order to generate a sustainable peace. If the United States adopts this approach, I think that Iraq can remain a unified state and can be stabilized. And a strong Iraq is absolutely necessary if the United States wishes to contain Iran. It is true that Iran might wish to keep Iraq unstable now in order to penalize the United States. But if the United States agrees to treat Iran as a serious regional power, this will throw the regime off balance and will allow the United States to engage with multiple competing groups within Iran, some of which are very pro-American. I believe that Iraq can be stabilized.

Few were as optimistic as Kubba, but nearly everyone agreed that, whatever the outcome of regional negotiations, it would be very unwise to attack Iran militarily. In mid-

2007, Joseph Nye advocated making a deal with Russia in order to secure Russian cooperation for severe sanctions on Iran. Nye argued that the United States should be willing to delay its planned deployment of antimissile systems in Europe, a move strongly opposed by Russia, for as long as Russia supports Western diplomacy regarding Iran's nuclear program. Milani, as quoted above, believes that it is probably too late and that, in the long run, an Iranian nuclear weapons capacity must probably be accepted as long as the current regime remains in power. Both Milani and Larry Diamond think that Iranian regime change from within is the best option and that internal pressures within Iran can best be supported through a combination of American engagement and continued pressure. At the time of our last interview in November 2007, shortly before publication of the December 2007 National Intelligence Estimate, Diamond still feared that the administration might launch an attack on Iran. I asked him what he thought the results of such an attack would be.

LARRY DIAMOND: I am just totally opposed to it [attacking Iran]. I'm very, very worried about their nuclear program. I realize that it's just a frightening possibility for them to get a nuclear weapon, but I feel that the only way to securely put that program out of business is to change the regime. And I think we are much more likely to get regime change, say, in the next five to seven years' span, by a patient, vigorous, creative, internationally mobilizing strategy of tightening the sanctions, tightening the news, mobilizing comprehensive regional and international pressure, and condemnation, rather than another unilateral bombing that would turn the world against us, make us the bad guy, make Ahmadinejad the victim.

Both Abas Milani and Omar Fekeiki agreed that bombing Iran would be foolish, but they differed on the issue of sanctions. Milani felt that sanctions could be maintained without incurring the anger of the Iraqi population toward the United States. Fekeiki, conversely, held that sanctions were just as bad as a military attack. He pointed to their earlier effect on Iraq: impoverishing the population without weakening the regime.

OMAR FEKEIKI: The American policy towards Iran is, again, arrogant and based on emotions. This is the problem. If you are dealing with a country, go talk to the people in the country. Don't talk to exiles only, because the exiles are not living inside the country. You're talking with what they call

"Iranian experts" who left Iran forty years ago, when Khomeini was in charge. [Ayatollah Khomeini assumed control of Iran in 1979, twenty-eight years before Fekeiki's comments.] And those exiles don't know what Iran looks like now, and that's why they can't figure out how to deal with Iran. ...

America made a mistake in Iraq. They killed five hundred thousand Iraqi children, and they're doing the same thing in Iran now. They're making the Iranians suffer. They're losing the few friends they have in Iran now, because that's what they did in Iraq—they lost their friends because of sanctions. No one is going to say the UN imposed sanctions on Iranians. They'll all say America imposed sanctions on Iranians, and that's the truth.

Joost Hiltermann did not completely rule out the use of military force against Iran, but suggested that it should be considered only as a last resort, after all attempts to negotiate had been exhausted.

JOOST HILTERMANN: Again, we go back to the one real issue that is aggravating existing conflicts in the Middle East, and that is the U.S.-Iranian rivalry. And so we must see some kind of solution to some of the key questions on that front. If that fails, then I think all hope is lost for Iraq and then there would be no more reason for the United States to keep forces on the ground there. But we are not there yet. That issue remains unresolved, and I think a concerted effort should be made not to bomb Iran, but to find a negotiated solution to the very difficult question of its nuclear program.

At the same time, the Iranians are acutely aware of being encircled by pro-American regimes or countries with U.S. boots on the ground. And so they have a need to develop weapons such as nuclear weapons. The Iranians will need certain guarantees. They also want to be readmitted into the international community in various ways. A grand bargain is still a possibility, but I think that as long as we have Dick Cheney in the White House and, you know, other neocons still putting pressure on this administration, any kind of negotiated solution to the Iran question is in fact impossible. Maybe we have to wait for a new administration to come to power—unless somehow the tipping point is reached within this administration and serious talks are begun. I don't see it.

CHARLES FERGUSON: Do you speak with people in the United States government about these things?

JOOST HILTERMANN: Of course, on an ongoing basis.

CHARLES FERGUSON: And what do they say when you tell them what you said to me?

JOOST HILTERMANN: There might be a sort of pained recognition of the realities that are upon us. I found this now for the last year or two, and this is true wherever I speak, which is at the State Department—where I give roundtable discussions where officials of the State Department, but also the Pentagon and various agencies, are present—at the National Security Council, and on the Hill. And so, I find a ready audience for my analysis, and I find also the response, "Well, what can we do? We are locked into a very difficult situation."

CHARLES FERGUSON: When you advocated engaging with the Iranians?

JOOST HILTERMANN: I certainly find an echo, but there are still very powerful forces that are opposed to that. Or they say that it's just not possible, or that it is not realistic, or, as you say, that the Iranians are not particularly interested in coming to a deal on the nuclear issue. They [the American officials] may be right; you may be right. I don't know, but I think it should be tried, because if we don't, then I think the consequences will be dire.

CHARLES FERGUSON: And what did they say when you say, "Yes it is bad, it is difficult, it might not work, but you have to try." What's the response?

JOOST HILTERMANN: It's hard to say. Generally, the officials I meet with, they accept the analysis. They may quibble with certain points, with certain ways of looking at it. I think they prefer to continue to work through the current government of Iraq and the constitution, mostly because they have invested so much in it. We say that it's time to depart from that approach and take it to a regional level. So I think, generally, that we tend to agree on what ails the place, but the current preference is to go with the security plan of Baghdad, with the surge, with Petraeus, with working with the current government as it has some chance of success.

A Military Coup?

A surprising number of Iraqis believe that the United States has one and only one productive move left in Iraq: to support a military coup to remove the current political leadership and institute martial law. Most Iraqis with whom I spoke said that there was still some residual capability in the Iraqi state bureaucracy, but that the political leadership was so hopelessly corrupt, selfish, and incompetent that Iraq was doomed if it remained in power. Omar X held that a U.S. withdrawal would yield a slaughter, but that the United States had to use force to remove the current government. This view is surprisingly popular among educated, secular Iraqis. When they object, their concerns are pragmatic—Could it work?—rather than principled. The underlying source of their feelings is clear: utter despair over the current situation.

CHARLES FERGUSON: So, what do you think the United States can or should do now? Or is there nothing the United States can do?

OMAR X: Well, now I don't think they can do anything. I mean, the only thing—and I know it might be impossible, but I was speaking with my friends and with the people I know when I was in Baghdad—[is for] the United States [to] make a war again on Iraq and occupied Iraq as it did at first time when they removed Saddam. If they did that again and they removed those corrupted parties and they removed this government and started to do the things the right way, maybe they will change something. But I know that's impossible and the United States will never do it. And it might also not happen, because now we have so many militias, we have so many gangs, we have so many insurgents. I mean, we have so many fighters getting money and weapons from outside Iraq. It's not like what it was in 2003.

Well, I think there's nothing the United States can do anymore to improve things in Iraq, and I think they are going to leave Iraq soon. At that time, the disaster will happen, and that's what I'm seeing for my country. I see a really bad picture for it. I don't think I'll ever see the old Baghdad that I know. I never think that I'll see it again.

CHARLES FERGUSON: Do you think that maybe in five, ten, years—

OMAR X: No, no way, Charles, just because so far, we still have the destructions and the killings. The killings increase the hatred—the sectarian gaps between the people—and now everybody seeks revenge. Everybody wants to know what's happened to his loved one that was killed, and he wants to get revenge. So we need a long time for this to stop, and after that, you will need a long time to reconstruct and rebuild this destruction. So I don't know, maybe fifty years or so, but it depends on when those people in Iraq will have enough from the killings and they will get satisfied by the blood that's been dropped so far.

Ali Fadhil, Omar Fekeiki, and even Feisal al-Istrabadi voiced variations on these sentiments, with slightly different reasons for feeling that a coup might be the only, best option left.

ALI FADHIL: I would say, anything the United States would do in Iraq will be wrong. I would say, there is nothing the United States can do that is right. It's because, basically, they don't understand the situation there. … They have come and they have dealt with the situation the wrong way. It's not going to be solved until they go back to point zero. Probably the coup might make a huge difference, of course. Would it be successful? Maybe. It's not a bad idea. Going back to the dictatorship definitely would help.

CHARLES FERGUSON: Do you think that there are military leaders in Iraq who would be capable of mounting such a coup and running the country?

ALI FADHIL: Well, this is another problem. I've never heard of someone, but usually, reading the history of Iraq … those who led the coup against the government in 1958, '63, '73, and even in '76, none of them was really famous at that time.

So probably anyone can do the job, I think. Any military leader. Any officer who has spent thirty years in the army is probably vicious enough to be a dictator, I think.

Omar Fekeiki has specific ideas about who a coup leader would need to be:

CHARLES FERGUSON: If the United States did care about Iraqis, what would it do?

OMAR FEKEIKI: Change the government.

CHARLES FERGUSON: If necessary by force?

OMAR FEKEIKI: It has to be by force at this point, yes.

CHARLES FERGUSON: So essentially invade again?

OMAR FEKEIKI: Invade it from the inside, yes. And I don't think it's only my personal opinion. I'm sure it's supported by many evidences. This government has failed, and it's proving failure every single day. They have to change the government, and they shouldn't replace it with another Shiite government. They should replace it with another Shiite leader who is secular.

And finally, Istrabadi, who wondered whether a coup could work and doubted that the Americans would permit it, agreed that it might be the last remaining possibility. It was astonishing to hear Iraq's former UN ambassador discuss a coup against his own government in such matter-of-fact terms.

CHARLES FERGUSON: Several Iraqis have said to me that they would welcome a military coup and martial law if it was enforced in anything approaching a reasonable way. Do you think if that happened, anything would come of it?

FEISAL AL-ISTRABADI: It's not impossible. I mean, a year ago, you would have laughed because there was no Iraqi army. Now there is. I would have to think that if you are a military officer looking at this political class unable to make basic decisions—I mean, basic decisions that secure the capital—I would think the temptation must be great to think you can't do it any worse.

CHARLES FERGUSON: And you think that there is an army that is cohesive enough that it—

FEISAL AL-ISTRABADI: That's the question. I don't know, I don't know. And what about the American army? Would they sit by and let a coup happen in Iraq? That's tough; it's tough to see that.

I will tell you, some Iraqis tell me they want the Americans to do it.

Now that's not going to happen. That's a failure of people understanding the American system and what the American system would tolerate politically here. If you are telling me that you're speaking to Iraqis who are saying they want a coup and they want a strong man to provide them with security and basic services, I will tell you I'm hearing the same thing.

Most non-Iraqis, however, were extremely skeptical that a coup could work. Larry Diamond, Joost Hiltermann, and others believed that the destruction of the former Iraqi Army, the fragmentation of the new Iraqi security forces, the increased power of Shiite militias, the purging of senior Sunnis from the government, and the scattering of Sunni officers meant that an effective, clean coup was impossible, even if it were desirable. They also were skeptical that the best-positioned leaders of such a potential coup would represent much of an improvement.

CHARLES FERGUSON: Some people I have spoken to, including some educated, secular, usually democracy-prone Iraqis, have advocated a military coup and the imposition of martial law. What do you think of that as an idea?

JOOST HILTERMANN: Well, who would carry out a coup? The only army in Iraq is the American army. There is no Iraqi army that is strong enough to carry out a coup. As I said, the army will fracture immediately into warring factions. The coup proposal, which was popular actually more than a year ago and has now largely faded, was being bandied about especially in Jordan and maybe some other places among secular Iraqis, educated ones, clever ones, mostly Sunni ones, but not exclusively so, who very much wanted … Their argument was that Iraq could not be a democracy and that the only viable option was a Saddam regime without Saddam, one that was not as cruel, more like Jordan. And, you know, it's the Arab regimes that have argued for the same. Their favorite person is Ayad Allawi, who is in fact a little Saddam, but who has proven to be completely incompetent, totally corrupt, and totally discredited among the Iraqi people inside Iraq.

There is no clear alternative to that. … There is no one who could bring about such a coup. There is no organized military force that could do it except the Americans. And the Americans have already made their choice.

CHARLES FERGUSON: So you think that there is no way that, for example, former army officers now in Jordan and Syria would be able to command enough support in the existing Iraqi army to be able to insert control over the country?

JOOST HILTERMANN: Absolutely not. The only support they have is with the insurgency groups, because that's where their colleagues are. Very few of their colleagues are in the New Iraqi Army. The Iraqi army consists now of former Badr militia members and Kurds. Some Sunnis have been brought back in, but these are the minority, and they could never carry out a coup. Never.

Partition

Nearly everyone I spoke with favored some degree of decentralization in Iraq. There was, however, surprisingly strong and uniform opposition to partition, especially among Iraqis.

FEISAL AL-ISTRABADI: I am starting to think about some of the screwy ideas that are coming out of Washington, such as soft partition or hard partition or medium partition from [Delaware Senator Joseph] Biden and Michael O'Hanlon [an analyst at the Brookings Institution] and these other people—

CHARLES FERGUSON: You think that those are crazy ideas?

FEISAL AL-ISTRABADI: Absolutely silly.

CHARLES FERGUSON: How come?

FEISAL AL-ISTRABADI: Well, first of all, nobody in Iraq is fighting to partition the country. I defy Joe Biden or Leslie Gelb or Peter Galbraith [a lobbyist for Kurdistan] to identify for me a group which is fighting to partition Iraq—soft, hard, or otherwise. There isn't one. Even the Kurds. Every time there is as little bit of unpleasantness on their border vis-à-vis Turkey and Iran, they come running to Baghdad for help because they know they can't stand up to them alone. Now that's number one.

Number two: If you start partitioning Iraq on ethno-confessional basis, why stop at Iraq? Why not partition Saudi Arabia the same way? Why not partition Kuwait the same way? Why not partition Bahrain and the whole Gulf the same way? And how are you going to stop the populations in those parts of the Arab world from thinking to themselves, "Why just for the Iraqi Shia? Why not for me?" The petroliferous area of Saudi Arabia happens to be the eastern province. The eastern province is overwhelmingly Shia. Why are the Shia in Saudi Arabia going look across the borders and say, "Oh, it's good for them, but not good for us"? I mean, you begin to open a Pandora's box that anyone with a rational mind who can look beyond the next election would recoil from in horror. And I understand Biden is running for secretary of state, but there has got to be a better way to secure that post than to destroy the Middle East, to relegate it to unending misery for the next century.

Many other Iraqis concurred that despite all of Iraq's tribal, ethnic, and religious divisions, nobody in Iraq wants partition and that it wouldn't work, because populations and families are so mixed. The sense of Iraqi national identity was far stronger than I had expected. Given this sentiment, there was a wide range of opinion concerning the effective, practical degree of centralization or decentralization that should be pursued. In part, this hinged on whether the analyst thought that it was still possible to construct a workable central government. Nir Rosen, for example, questioned whether the central government even existed.

CHARLES FERGUSON: I spoke with Feisal al-Istrabadi yesterday. ... He made the point that most Iraqis still want one Iraq with at least some degree of central government and they don't want a partition of the country.

NIR ROSEN: That's correct. ... Nobody is starting to secede from Iraq. But it doesn't mean that there is not fighting to exclude the other from Iraq—remove them from the center of power, get them as far away from each other as possible, control resources, things like that. I mean the Supreme Council or Supreme Islamic Iraqi Council [SCIRI]—whatever they are called now—it certainly wants a super–Shia State in the south, but they too aren't trying to secede from Iraq. I don't think anybody makes that claim.

CHARLES FERGUSON: Okay. So, your description would be, then, that the contest for control of central government is over; it's controlled by the Shiites. And all that's left now is kind of fighting at the fringes for control regions and mixed areas.

NIR ROSEN: Well, you are assuming that the central government exists. I mean, it exists in name, but it is not a government. It doesn't provide any services. It doesn't even have a monopoly on violence. So, there isn't really a kind of a control of central government. I mean, there was the election, but power was never in the hands of the government; it's in the hands of militias.

Some American analysts seemed resigned to such a high degree of decentralization that it would amount to partition or something close.

BARRY POSEN: When Crocker was asked point blank about partition, he denied it. But, you know, the old joke that a diplomat is someone who lies for his country ... Crocker just boldly said, "That's not what we're doing," but it is what they're doing. And I think that they know that Bush is a wasting asset, and that Bush is not going to pull out of Iraq in the next eighteen months. And they are trying to find something progressive to do, something that's actually practical.

Refugees

Many Americans and Iraqis expressed disgust at the U.S. failure to aid Iraqi refugees and the administration's consistent refusal to admit more than a tiny number of Iraqis to the United States. One American, whom I will not name, suspected that the administration's motives were directly political and related to the 2006 and 2008 elections: that if large numbers of Iraqi refugees entered the country, they would begin broadcasting their plight and Iraq's true condition, making it more difficult for the administration to ignore or spin the truth. Many analysts argued that the United States had a moral responsibility to assist those whose misery it had created, and particularly to help those whose lives were in danger because they had worked for the Americans. Several interviewees linked America's responsibility to help refugees to the likely bloodbath that would accompany an American withdrawal.

SAMANTHA POWER: As you know, there are already internal checkpoints, ... I mean, people can't even move internally right now. So, as part of the withdrawal strategy that has civilian protection as its centerpiece, you announce this date [and] you basically work as best you can with the authorities, as obstinate as they are, to facilitate safe transfers and movement. You drastically increase, of course, the number of refugees you let into this country. ...

It's two million people now in neighboring countries and almost no extra bilateral assistance given to either Jordan or Syria or Lebanon. ... You're talking about six million Sunni who are the people who are most vulnerable. I mean, [in] Shiite territory, you're going back to some version of militant tyranny and intertribal conflicts, and assassinations, and all of that. But it's really the Sunni population that's going to be rendered the most vulnerable.

OMAR FEKEIKI: If the United States wants to stay in Iraq, they have to change the Iraqi government. They have to start all over again because if they want to stay in Iraq, they have to have a mission. Their mission should be protecting the Iraqi government until the Iraqis start to trust the government and support it themselves. And with this current government, the Iraqis don't trust the government. Why should I tip the insurgents to the government? Why should I call the 911 line and say there is an insurgent in my neighborhood? This insurgent is protecting me against the Shiite militias. The government cannot do that. So they have to change the government. They have to bring a secular government and stay in Iraq to protect the government for six months, for a year, for no matter how long. If they want to leave, it's going to be hell. It's going to be hell. But if they want to leave, they have to accept every single Iraqi refugee, because if they [the Americans] leave, the Sunnis will be killed in their provinces.

Private Military Contractors

In late 2007, following an incident in Baghdad in which Blackwater PSD guards killed seventeen unarmed Iraqi civilians, a wider public debate opened in both Iraq and the United States concerning abuses committed by, and the lack of oversight and legal accountability of, private military contractors in Iraq. After the Bush

Administration declined to make contractors subject to legal action through U.S. courts, in November 2007 the Iraqi Parliament moved to revoke the legal immunity granted to all U.S. contractors in Iraq by L. Paul Bremer and the CPA. At least some observers feel that if private military contractors are subject to Iraqi law but not to U.S. law, the result will be the withdrawal of nearly all private contractors from Iraq. Given the extremely heavy dependence of the U.S. occupation on private military and civilian contractors, this would have a devastating effect on both the security of U.S. personnel and remaining reconstruction operations. At this writing, the issue remains unresolved, although in late 2007, the State Department agreed to develop a stronger set of controls over its private military contractors.

Iraqi Comments on the American Political Debate

Several Iraqi interviewees made very caustic remarks about the political debate in the United States. As already noted, some found the timing of the troop surge to be suspiciously close to the 2008 presidential election. However, far from confining their criticism to the Bush administration, they were often equally scathing about the Democrats and the presidential candidates of both parties. For example, in mid-2007, I was invited to screen portions of my film for the Democratic Policy Caucus of the U.S. Senate. I invited Omar Fekeiki to join me; he was then in Washington, D.C., spending the summer working at the *Washington Post*. There were approximately twenty senators in the room. Here is his reaction, which I must, regrettably, say is factually correct:

OMAR FEKEIKI: You remember when we went to that meeting.

CHARLES FERGUSON: Yes, talk about that.

OMAR FEKEIKI: They didn't even mention … They did not say the word "Iraqis" in plural in that meeting, talking about the situation in Iraq. I wrote about it on my blog. They did not say the word "Iraqis," and they had an Iraqi in the room. They were talking about what to do in Iraq, and they did not even mention the word "Iraqis," and they did not care about an Iraqi in the room. They don't care. Those are the decision makers in the U.S.; they don't care about Iraqis. And that's why I'm saying if they withdraw or not, Iraqis are irrelevant now. In America, Iraqis are irrelevant now in this issue. I mean, it struck me that day that they had a meeting to discuss the situation in Iraq and how to go forward, and they invited an American who made a movie about Iraq, and they thought that that's it, what they hear from the director of that movie is enough, although they've had an Iraqi in the room. That struck me. And that day, I realized how correct I am when I think the Americans don't care about Iraqis. They just don't.

American Veterans

There is mounting evidence that the long-term problems of returning veterans will be serious, and that the U.S. Department of Veterans Affairs is not well prepared to meet them. Here I quote the primary policy recommendations made by Linda Bilmes in her congressional testimony of 2007:*

To fix these problems—and I want to stress that unlike some of the more intractable problems we face in the war, these problems can actually be solved, to a large extent—I urge you to enact sweeping bipartisan legislation that would, at minimum, do the following:

I. Change the presumption for eligibility to favor the veteran. The current system places the full burden of collecting evidence and medical records on the veteran. The solution is to reverse the paradigm and have VBA [Veterans Benefits Administration] grant presumption of eligibility. There are several ways to implement this concept. A veteran presenting with a disability could be guaranteed a minimum disability stipend for at least two years—in the same way that we offer free health care for two years—during which time the claim can be fully processed. A sample of claims can be audited to deter fraud.

II. Require that all servicemen have a complete physical examination at the time they separate from the military, which would form the basis for presumption. DOD must be required to provide complete medical records

---

*Linda Bilmes, testimony before U.S. House of Representatives Committee on Veterans Affairs, VA Claims Roundtable Hearing, May 23, 2007, Washington, D.C., available at www.ksg. harvard.edu/ksgnews/OntheHill/2007/bilmes_052307.html.

for all soldiers to the VA [Veterans Administration, former name for the department] immediately on discharge.

III. The BDD [Benefits Delivery at Discharge] process should be expanded and extended to members of the Guards and Reserves. All veterans should have the right to a medical examination prior to discharge conducted by the VA, and the VA should be readily available to do this.

IV. Streamline and simplify the disability process to a 4-step rating (not disabled, low, moderate and severe disability); and simplify the form by creating a "short-form" like the IRS [Internal Revenue Service] does for taxes. Veterans applying for known presumptions using the short form should be able to waive the 60-day notification period and receive benefits in 30–45 days.

V. Extend free VHA health care to 3 years or longer in order to relieve the pressure on veterans to file disability claims. Ideally, this should be extended to 5 years, but we must provide higher funding for VHA and give it much greater flexibilities to hire personnel quickly and to re-allocates [sic] money in its facilities depending on local needs.

VI. Develop a "fast-track" claims adjudication process for all older claims, with the objective that 75% of claims already in the system be resolved within the next fiscal year. This could be done giving VBA hiring flexibilities to temporarily hire more retirees, to increase pay for VA claims officers, to bring on civil servants from other government agencies who want to help (for example, loans of other civil servants, postal workers, and teachers) as well as by increasing the use of temporary contractors.

VII. Place one or two claims specialists in each neighborhood Veterans Center and in mobile vet centers to assist veterans and their families in filling out claims forms.

REFLECTIONS

In this concluding chapter, a range of analysts and observers address broader questions: whether a war to remove Saddam was justified; what the actual record of the first five years of occupation was; whether various individuals conducted themselves ethically; whether the effort could ever have worked pragmatically; why so many mistakes were made in conducting the occupation; and finally, what, if any, lessons can be drawn from this experience.

Paths Not Taken: The First Five Years

The Bush administration itself seems largely to avoid the question of whether it mismanaged the occupation of Iraq. When it does address its record since 2003, it largely defends its decisions, although sometimes it allows for an oblique admission of error. The most striking comment of this sort was made by President George W. Bush to Robert Draper, who interviewed the president extensively for his book *Dead Certain.* Here is the comment as reported in the *New York Times.* His comment is consistent with my impression from many interviews: that President Bush was remarkably disengaged from the policy decisions being made in his name.

> Mr. Bush acknowledged one major failing of the early occupation of Iraq when he said of disbanding the Saddam Hussein–era military, "The policy was to keep the army intact; didn't happen."
>
> But when Mr. Draper pointed out that Mr. Bush's former Iraq administrator, L. Paul Bremer III, had gone ahead and forced the army's dissolution and then asked Mr. Bush how he reacted to that, Mr. Bush said, "Yeah, I can't remember, I'm sure I said, 'This is the policy, what happened?'" But,

President George W. Bush briefs the press with Secretary of Defense Donald Rumsfeld (left) and Vice President Richard Cheney (right), January 13, 2005.

he added, "Again, Hadley's got notes on all of this stuff," referring to Stephen J. Hadley, his national security adviser.*

A small number of primarily neoconservative analysts continue to defend the administration's record. Most commentary, however, has been damning, including that from retired senior military officers and diplomats who worked on the occupation. On April 13, 2006, a group of six recently retired U.S. Army and Marine Corps generals called for Donald Rumsfeld's resignation, an unprecedented event. My own interviews often produced similar sentiments, even among former administration officials. For reasons of length, I will quote only a few here, starting with Richard Armitage, whom I asked to grade the quality of the administration's Iraq policy.

RICHARD ARMITAGE: I bifurcate it. ... As it turns out, the audacity of the original military plan was very significant, and it was conducted with a rel-

---

*Jim Rutenberg, "In Book, Bush Peeks Ahead to His Legacy," *New York Times,* September 2, 2007, available at www.nytimes.com/2007/09/02/washington/02book.html?pagewanted=print.

atively minimum of civilian causalities. I think the occupation, up 'til the Iraqis took over, was a C-minus at best.

LAWRENCE WILKERSON: The way we moved, from January to March [2003], and the way we deployed forces, and the diplomacy we exercised, was probably as good as you could put together in that short a time frame. But the decisions we had made earlier about the size of the force that would go into Iraq, about the makeup of the force that would go into Iraq, about the postinvasion planning and so forth, were basically inept. In fact, I think historians will judge this war planning that preceded the actual invasion of Iraq in March of 2003 as some of the worst war planning in the history of our country, if not the worst in the history of our country.

What I saw was a haphazard, ill-planned effort to move from the situation where it was absolutely clear to everyone that we were going to war, to the actual execution of that war: the euphoria that accompanied the end of major military operations, and then the deer-caught-in-the-headlights kind of attitude of the national leadership when it didn't prove to be a cakewalk, as most of them, I'm convinced, thought it was going to be.

GEORGE PACKER: We've never been serious about this. That's the thing that historians are going to be baffled by. We rolled the dice on Iraq in the biggest way imaginable. Bush gambled his presidency on it. And we weren't serious. We didn't come close to going in there and to taking it on with what we needed. And I cannot say why.

LAITH KUBBA: It did not have to be this way. ... If the state had not been destroyed, if the army had not been disbanded ... if the Sunnis had been treated with respect, you would not have seen this insurgency, this sectarian conflict. ... There would have been problems, of course, but you would have had an Iraq that was basically stable, peaceful, and intact.

Analyst Anthony Cordesman offered a particularly damning assessment.

CHARLES FERGUSON: Give us a grade. How did we do?

ANTHONY CORDESMAN: Essentially, we did not. It wasn't an F. If you go back historically, we had no aid plan for Iraq; it was assumed that the surplus of oil-for-food money and Iraq's oil income, export income, would solve its problems. We did not worry about the government; we assumed that the exiles and the people left over from Saddam would be an effective government. We brought in General Garner, under ORHA, to provide a transition with a ninety-day contract. When we then went further, and brought in Ambassador Bremer, it's important to note that we still had no plan to provide economic aid and no clear concept of what Ambassador Bremer should do.

In addition to the sort of triumph of hope over reality from the neocons—that somehow we'd get rid of Saddam, there'd be this marvelous transition, and Iraq would change the region—we had the practical reality that the U.S. military was not organized for counterinsurgency and was not organized to provide stability operations in Iraq, and was never given that mission. The problems were compounded by the failure to be able to move troops through Turkey, but that didn't really explain what happened.

The State Department, in the interagency process, often described all of the problems that might emerge. But it was equally clear that the State Department—and other branches of the U.S. government—had no operational capability to plan what should be done. AID [USAID, U.S. Agency for International Development], a branch of the State Department, basically had no concept at all of what kind of aid would need to be provided in Iraq, but in fairness, also was never tasked with trying to figure out what it should really do. And this failure was not a matter of being something you can grade; it was an absolute.

CHARLES FERGUSON: Well, it sounds kinda like an F to me. Why wouldn't you give them an F? ...

ANTHONY CORDESMAN: You give people grades who are making an attempt to do something. [Here,] you have not something you grade, but just a basic conceptual and policy failure. It isn't a matter of giving it grades.

CHARLES FERGUSON: So kind of "no attendance."

ANTHONY CORDESMAN: I think what you had were people who truly believed that somehow this would work out. They had almost no area expertise. Most of them had no real experience with foreign aid, with peacemaking. People who did often had very, very strong ideological convictions. And I think, in many cases, you had a failure institutionally to really provide the administration with meaningful advice to the alternative.

From former Iraqi Ambassador to the United Nations, Feisal al-Istrabadi placed much of the blame on L. Paul Bremer.

FEISAL AL-ISTRABADI: Bremer systematically took apart the state of Iraq as though it were a Lego set that he could just take apart and put back together at will. But that isn't how it works. ... I mean, a lot of it was rotten, granted. But instead of building on the fact that there were institutions and, over time, pruning that which is rotten, he just decimated the whole thing and was going to start all over again. A year later, he left Baghdad to give lectures at fifty thousand dollars a pop.

And finally, with memorable directness, Ambassador Barbara Bodine:

CHARLES FERGUSON: And how much different do you think Iraq would be now if the occupation had been planned properly and conducted properly?

BARBARA BODINE: ... I would have a hard time figuring out how it could have been any worse. When we were first starting the reconstruction, we would sort of joke that there were five hundred ways to do it wrong, and two or three ways to do it right. And what we didn't understand is that we were gonna go through all five hundred.

There was another area of strikingly broad agreement concerning U.S. policy since 2003: the mismanagement of relations with Iran. Nearly everyone agreed that the Bush administration had made two enormous mistakes in handling the Iranian regime. First, the administration failed to capitalize on its leverage immediately following the war, and second, the administration had greatly underestimated Iran's ability and inclination to affect postwar events in Iraq through its Shiite proxies.

FEISAL AL-ISTRABADI: The time for the United States to have negotiated with Iran—it seems to me—was in 2003, when it looked like they had cleaned Saddam's clock in six weeks and got control of the whole country.

And you didn't have an Ahmadinejad in those days. Instead, the neocons started talking about a left turn or a right turn. So that means, instead of convincing Syria and Iran that Iraq was a one-off, regardless of what they [the Administration] may have been planning, they started threatening Syria and Iran. They gave these countries every incentive to contribute to an American failure in Iraq. But now what do you have to offer Iran? You are on the verge of being defeated in Iraq.

Of the hundreds of people with whom I spoke, only two tried to claim that the present situation in Iraq was an improvement over life under Saddam: Richard Armitage and Christopher Hitchens. Even Armitage expressed some ambivalence.

CHARLES FERGUSON: Why didn't you resign?

RICHARD ARMITAGE: Pardon me?

CHARLES FERGUSON: Why didn't you resign?

RICHARD ARMITAGE: I think, at heart, the feeling that you express when you ask a question like that is that we were opposed to the war. I'll speak for myself; Secretary Powell is able to speak for himself. As I said, I wasn't opposed to the notion of removing Saddam Hussein. I had questions about the timing. And I recognized that there's only one nationally elected leader in this country, and that's the president. Second, this was not—as I said, since I didn't oppose the war—for me, it wasn't a matter of principle. Third—and this is a common, I think, Washington dilemma that you feel, and maybe you fool yourself to some extent—that you are involved in many other things, many of which were going quite well and that you had some responsibilities for. So, from my point of view, as long as it wasn't a matter of principle or a matter of morality, there was not need for me to resign.

CHARLES FERGUSON: Don't you think that, at a certain point, if, you know, incompetence causes the country to fall apart [and incurs] one hundred thousand deaths, that becomes a matter of principle?

RICHARD ARMITAGE: I don't know where you got the figure a hundred thousand deaths.* And when the country falls apart, I think ultimately Iraqis will decide whether they want a better future or not. But if you're suggesting that I'm incompetent, you're welcome to your opinion.

CHARLES FERGUSON: No.

RICHARD ARMITAGE: And we'll discuss it later. [*laughs*]

CHARLES FERGUSON: Not that you're incompetent—quite the contrary—but that the occupation of Iraq was incompetent.

RICHARD ARMITAGE: It was very troubled and very flawed. Whether it's incompetent, I say, ultimately, we'll see. But there's no question, I don't think one could make any other judgment. ... Talking about it, reducing it to numbers, is stupid, and it's unworthy. It's unworthy for the Iraqis who died. It's unworthy for anyone who dies. The point of the matter is, there's been a lot of deaths. Also the point of the matter is that the initial attack by the United States and coalition forces in Iraq was conducted with extreme care for civilian casualties. You didn't have much whining or carping about it, because they were so careful. The majority of the deaths have been accomplished by Iraqis killing Iraqis. I don't think there's any question about that. One can say that had you not invaded, then Iraqis wouldn't be killing Iraqis. Well, that would be not true. Saddam Hussein was killing Iraqis. But in addition, Saddam Hussein was occupying his neighbors and invading both Iran and Iraq. And he'll never do those things again.

So it's a bad, messy situation. Any administration official who told you otherwise, I think, would be casting doubt on their own credibility. By the same token, there are some things that we know will never repeat them-

---

*I got the figure of 100,000 deaths from the first survey of Iraqi civilian deaths commissioned by the MIT Center for International Studies and published in *Lancet,* a British medical journal. As of late 2007, even the most conservative estimates of civilian deaths in Iraq are well over 100,000, and two peer-reviewed surveys have reported estimates of over half a million excess deaths since 2003. For an excellent survey of these studies, including links to the original papers, please see http://en.wikipedia.org/wiki/Lancet_surveys_of_mortality_before_and_after_the_2003_invasion_of_Iraq.

selves. I'd say the rape of Kuwait and the horror of the Marsh Arabs, for that matter.

CHARLES FERGUSON: We agree on that. How much differently, though—and this was the point of my question; it wasn't primarily about the merits of using force to dispose Saddam ... How different do you think this would have been—including the level of civilian causalities in Iraq, but many other things as well—how different do you think this could have turned out if it had been done competently, as opposed to the way that it actually was done?

RICHARD ARMITAGE: Well, I'm not accepting your terminology of "incompetence." But had there been more troops there—significant number of troops—had we sort of overwhelmed the playing field with soldiers, we could have done what I suggested earlier, which is both bend an enemy to our will and to take and hold ground. So I think it would have been significantly different.

But I think there would also have to be several other things in place, such as the ability to flow in immediately infrastructure, and perhaps rethinking some of the decisions that were taken in a somewhat murky fashion from my point of view; that's the [disbanding of the] army and the de-Baathification.

The preceding interview was conducted in 2006, and Armitage may feel differently now. Christopher Hitchens was another matter; he agreed that Iraq is in collapse, but argued that (A) without the war, Iraq would have collapsed, anyway, and (B) the current situation was still far better than Saddam's regime.

CHRISTOPHER HITCHENS: I personally think that there was nothing that was going to save Iraq from something like the implosion that it's now undergoing. In fact, if I hadn't believed that, I wouldn't have thought that the prudential reasons for criticizing the invasion could be overruled, because the prudential reservations had to be taken very seriously. I mean, it's possible you could make it worse, right? We can think of ways in which Iraq would be better off without Saddam Hussein—we've got a clear case on this and other things—but what if it brings in the roof? Obviously, an objection like that could paralyze any policy wants in Iraq, but it had to be taken seriously. Well, my argument was—from observation of Iraqi society and conversations with Iraqis—that the roof was coming in, anyway, and that we would be very lucky to stop it, you know, burying everybody. So, interested as I am in the what-ifs and the might-have-beens, and strong as my opinion is that Chalabi was right, there should have been a much earlier transfer of sovereignty and a much earlier election, I don't think it would have prevented the intervention of al Qaeda, which was already under way before we got there; the incitement of sectarian warfare; the werewolf policy of the Baath Party remnants; and the struggle for power between sectarian groups. I don't believe that is the result of the intervention. I believe those things were in our future, in any case.

... I am reminded of how, until very few years ago, the entire country [Iraq] was privately owned by a psychopathic crime family and there was only one voice that could be heard in the entire country. And I continue to regard the present situation as an improvement on that.

CHARLES FERGUSON: Most Iraqis I've spoken to don't, which is an astounding fact. I mean, these are not people who love Saddam Hussein.

CHRISTOPHER HITCHENS: It doesn't matter what they think.

CHARLES FERGUSON: Because?

CHRISTOPHER HITCHENS: Because they couldn't have kept Saddam going, even if they'd wanted to. Even if they had voted for him a hundred percent. ... their opinion would still be irrelevant. You can't in fact keep a one-man crime-family dictatorship going. They'd have had to live in the post-Saddam era at some point, anyway. They can wish it all they like. It's like believing in God or heaven or hell; it doesn't make it true. So we would have had to deal with a post-Saddam Iraq, whether they wanted to or not, or whether they've become dependent on it or not.

Hitchens also continued to defend many U.S. policy decisions and the arguments used to justify them, particularly those advocated by his (self-declared) friend Ahmed Chalabi. Only a very few people still advance these arguments; even prowar neoconservatives such as Ken Adelman and Richard Perle have since condemned the incompetence with which many occupation decisions were made. Hitchens started out quite unrepentant, although when pressed on specifics, he began to retract. In this section of our interview, he had just stated that he felt that the dissolution of the Iraqi military was "the correct decision."

CHARLES FERGUSON: You do?

CHRISTOPHER HITCHENS: Yes. Well, it was—well, not correct; it was necessary, inevitable. Iraq doesn't need armed forces that size. … So it was essential to wean the country off this banana republic military system. …

CHARLES FERGUSON: Pretty fast weaning, don't you think?

CHRISTOPHER HITCHENS: I think the most important thing was for the United States to make it absolutely clear that this was not going to be one of the countries where we govern through a military caste. The CIA strategy for Iraq, as you know, was for a long time—still is, as far as I know—to rule by proxy through a coup, to decapitate the Saddam regime, replace it or rather preserve it. … That would have been a disgraceful betrayal of the aspirations for regime change of the Iraqi people—and a very typical CIA maneuver. That's what we did in Chile, Brazil, Indonesia, Greece, Cypress, and so on. We've got a military we can rule through; we discard this; we publicly show you we're not going to run the country that way; we take the risk of the consequences. I think it was probably a mistake to dismiss so many people so soon. That's very hard to argue. …

CHARLES FERGUSON: So if I understood correctly the last remarks you made, you believe that they [CPA Order Numbers 1 and 2] were important things to do in principle and were correct in principle, but you would agree that perhaps a few mistakes were made in how they were done? Or not?

CHRISTOPHER HITCHENS: … There are very few things that ought to have been done in Iraq—or that Iraq needed to have done—that have been done in a timely or an apt or an intelligent manner since the liberation. And by all means, this general remark comprises or covers de-Baathification of the society—and not just the system, but the society itself; the de-Baathification, if you like, as a mentality—and the dissolution of the Iraqi armed forces. I could be more specific if you like.

CHARLES FERGUSON: Please.

CHRISTOPHER HITCHENS: I have a friend called Kubat Talabani—he's the son of the current and only ever elected president of Iraq—who said to me very early on in the proceedings, before the intervention, in fact, said, it's not a matter of how many soldiers that was then being discussed; what they need to send is about half a million psychiatrists. The country is diseased; it's sick. I mean, these are people who were forced, not very long before the overthrow of Saddam Hussein, to vote in the claimed number of one hundred percent, or a hundred percent turnout, and come out and dance. Not just to vote, but to celebrate and applaud that dictator. Picture the humiliation of that, and signing ballots in their own blood, and so forth. Picture the self-hatred of this. People were forced to applaud at the executions of their own family members. They were forced to inform on them or made to degrade themselves in every conceivable way. That's why some of them now act so courageously—was they know they won't get what they would have done if they'd acted as oppositionists in the past. They're overcompensating. They're showing what little courage they have left.

This can't be undone by an official stroke of policy ... but has to be begun somewhere. And it seemed to me right that when former friends of mine, who've been in prison and in exile and tortured and had their families murdered, were pointed to new jobs—say, in one particular case I know about very well, in the foreign ministry or at an embassy overseas—that the goons in the embassy or the guys on the door, the guards, shouldn't be the same people who'd been the enforcers of the previous regime. You would expect them not to be there, anymore. That's a minimum demand.

As for the removal of the extraordinarily parasitic armed forces that had been consuming so much of Iraq's national product, only used as an aggressor against other nations and neighboring states and as an internal police force, it was imperative to break the spine of that, to say we're going on without it for several reasons: One, its parasitism and its political record. Second, the masking role it played in preventing Iraq from facing the backwardness of its economy and the soaking up of unemployment by

conscription: just keeping people off the streets by making them into bul-
lied soldiers at the mercy of a Sunni oligarchy. And third, to show that
there would not and could not be a military coup, as had been the curse of
Iraq in the past, and the United States wouldn't rule through a proxy
regime as had been the plan of the CIA.

So, in concept, the proposal for demilitarization and de-Baathification
are essentially the same. And if [they had been] applied in, say, 1991—if
Saddam Hussein had been removed from office power at that point—I
think would have been very salutary. What unfortunately happened in the
intervening period—the period of underreaction to Baathism and to Saddam's aggressive promiscuity with weapons and terrorism—was twelve
years of sanctions plus Saddam, in the course of which the population was
made to live on rats and dirty water while a palace was built in his name
and a mosque in every province of the country. And that created in Iraq
what there hadn't been before: a kind of lumped underclass, dispossessed,
unemployed, ... underpaid, easy prey for mullahs. ... This is part of what
we're confronting now. This is all the problem of the legacy of our underreaction to this hateful and evil regime and the far-too-long postponement
of the reckoning with it. ...

CHARLES FERGUSON: Well, as regards the in-principle desirability of doing
these things, yes. But I asked you about the way that they were actually
done.

CHRISTOPHER HITCHENS: Well, after a certain point, the way in which
they're actually done, um, will be if you like ... No, wait. I mean, I have no
comment on the way they were actually done. I mean, I'm simply not well
enough informed. Strike the question. I haven't got an answer. I mean,
here's my rule.

CHARLES FERGUSON: Mr. Hitchens, this is an historical first.

CHRISTOPHER HITCHENS: Yes, well you should know my rule: Whereof I'm
not well-informed, I do not pronounce.

Nobody else I interviewed argued that the result of the war was anything short of a
disaster. Everyone mentioned the same things: the hundreds of thousands of Iraqi

dead, the 4 million refugees, the lack of water and sanitation and electricity, the 4,000 American dead and 50,000 American wounded, the toll on a million returning veterans, the $3 trillion economic cost, the damage to American standing, the strengthening of Iran, the weakening of the U.S. military, the likelihood of Iraq's falling prey to a combination of Islamic fundamentalism, warlord rule, anarchy, and civil war, as well its becoming as a haven for terrorism. They weighed the risks of wider regional conflict. I heard this list recited literally dozens of times.

YAROSLAV TROFIMOV: That fundamental justification of [engaging in war to protect] human rights, of course, is hard to apply now, when tens of thousands of Iraqis have been killed by American troops. And the basic human right, the right to life, is more precarious now than it was under Saddam. ...

CHARLES FERGUSON: And what did they [people in the Arab world] think that Iraq would be like after the war? Did they think it would be chaotic, that there would be civil war? Did they think it would be peaceful and orderly?

YAROSLAV TROFIMOV: People did expect things to be chaotic and tense. I don't think anybody expected things to get as bad as they are now. And frankly, the scenario that we see now is much worse than the worst-case scenario that anybody had imagined back then.

... The whole fate of the Middle East, and even the world, resides on what's going to happen in Iraq. If Iraq is lost, and if Iraq goes back to some sort of Islamo-fascist regime like we had under the Taliban in Afghanistan, then we are back to September the 10th, 2001, except on a much larger scale and, you know, with billions of dollars of oil money at their disposal.

Could It Have Been Different?

A wider range of views, however, existed with regard to another question: whether a war to remove Saddam could have produced a stable, peaceful Iraq. Approximately 80 percent of those I asked, including both proponents and opponents of the war, answered that U.S. intervention could have been successful, at least in the sense of producing a stable Iraq at peace with its neighbors, if the occupation had been competent and pragmatic. Many held that immediate, full Western liberal democracy was unrealistic, but that a regime with some democratic elements and substantial freedoms had been feasible. Others believed that an invasion and occupation was doomed under any circumstances, because of a combination of Iraqi nationalism, anti-Americanism, internal sectarian tensions, the absence of democratic traditions in Iraqi culture, and Islamic fundamentalism. Nearly all Iraqis with whom I spoke, a generally elite group of educated, secular people, felt that the occupation could have worked; the most extreme skeptics were primarily American liberals in the academic and intelligence communities. Barbara Bodine, who had opposed the war as being unnecessary and contrary to U.S. national interests, told me that if the administration had simply been less ideological, it could have obtained most of what it said it wanted in Iraq. Here is Yaroslav Trofimov, consistently among the most critical and skeptical of those I interviewed:

YAROSLAV TROFIMOV: Well, we all came into Iraq with this idea that the U.S. government would be competent. And we expected a basic ability to deal with the situation. I mean, the U.S. is a superpower, so people everywhere—in Iraq, in the Arab world, and in Europe—thought that the U.S. would be able to restore order fairly quickly, and provide basic services. ...

CHARLES FERGUSON: I'm sure that you have read and learned, as we all have, about the fight between the Defense Department and the State Department that took place before the war about who would control postwar occupation policy administration. Did you know about that beforehand, and did you understand what its implications and its effects would be?

YAROSLAV TROFIMOV: We all saw on the ground that, from the very first phase of the occupation, anybody with State [Department] links was marginalized and not sent into the CPA. There were very, very few people there with State Department links, up until the end of 2003. That happened to change because as the need for local, Arabic-speaking experience became more and more acute towards the final month of the CPA, the State Department people started appearing there. ... Had these people been involved in Iraq in the very, very first days, then the results might have been different.

CHARLES FERGUSON: How different do you think it could have been?

YAROSLAV TROFIMOV: I think we would not [have] avoided the insurgency altogether, but there is insurgency and insurgency.

George Packer spoke regretfully of lost chances:

GEORGE PACKER: I will not ever forget how much yearning there was on the part of Iraqis to believe that this was going to be good, that this was going to change their lives for the better, at long last, after so much suffering. And there was a lot of goodwill among Americans, especially the soldiers who were seeing Iraqi suffering, driving around in the slums and seeing just how ugly and brutal Saddam's rule had been. So it was a kind of a poignant situation, where you had these two different peoples, each of them wanting to believe the best about the other and to make it work. But it was not at all clear that it was going to work, and there were already a number of worrying early signs. But to those who say that this had to fail, this was bound to fail, this failed out of historical inevitability, I would simply say, I was there at the beginning and there was a chance of success. That's my assessment of how it stood in the early weeks.

CHARLES FERGUSON: So this could have worked.

GEORGE PACKER: … It was a terribly difficult project, especially given the fact that the U.S. had so few allies, but the chances of success were radically diminished by the way in which we did it, not the fact that we did it.

Chris Allbritton was among those skeptical of the possibility of implanting democracy In Iraq.

CHARLES FERGUSON: How different do you think it could have been?

CHRIS ALLBRITTON: Well … it may be that Iraq is ungovernable, in a democratic sense; it may just be that Iraq needs a strongman. I don't know that I completely buy that. I know a number of Iraqis who have genuine democratic impulses and really want their country to be a Western-oriented, secular, democratic model with rights for everyone. But it's a tough place. It's a really tough place in a tough neighborhood.

Paul Pillar was among the most skeptical about the potential for any successful occupation of Iraq.

CHARLES FERGUSON: How much of a difference do you think it would have made if this occupation had been done competently, as opposed to the way that it was done? Was it a totally doomed endeavor, no matter how effective you were? Or could this have turned out much better?

PAUL PILLAR: We are likely to have debates for years and years between those who say it was a fool's errand and those who say it was a matter of faulty execution. I note that some of the most vigorous critics of how well the policy has been executed were those who were in favor of the war in the first place, and I suppose that's one way to relieve one's cognitive dissonance.

I think there's no question there have been major flaws in execution from the standpoint of troop strength, to the approach toward economic reconstruction, to things like the de-Baathification and army dissolution decisions. We can go on and on about those.

But I think one of the implications of the sorts of assessments that the intelligence community made before the war about the awesome challenges to be faced afterwards—again, assessments that reflected the views of experts on Iraq on the outside—is that no matter how expertly the policy had been executed, the challenges and problems would have been immense. Those analysts and those experts whose views those assessments reflected had no reason to factor into their assumptions an assumption of lousy execution. And so I think the lesson I take away from that is that no matter how perfect the execution has been, we would have had a deep, deep difficulty to deal with. And I think on balance, that tilts the argument in favor of the fool's-errand position.

Here are extended comments from A. Heather Coyne, the former army officer in charge of Civil Affairs for Baghdad, among the most optimistic about what could have happened, and also among the most critical about what actually did happen:

CHARLES FERGUSON: Two questions. One is, having seen all that you've seen, what do you think now, having been in Iraq? And second and relatedly, how much of a difference would it have made if it had been done competently, as opposed to—

A. HEATHER COYNE: It makes all the difference in the world. I still believe that this could have worked. If you'd really had the capability, and the materials, and the relationships, and the expertise, and the trained staff, and the equipment, and everything else you needed before you ever went across the berm.

If we'd already had a plan for women's centers and how they were going to be set up, and a contractor who had bought into our plan for it, and had prepared staff and resources and materials to get them running as soon as we moved in, or training materials for the Iraqi NGOs, or a plan for a cell phone system that actually united the country instead of dividing it. The list is infinite of the things that could have been repaired and worked out before we ever went in. You can't think that you can go into an effort of this magnitude without having the staff, the equip, the resources, the capability to do it right. Because if you do it wrong, it's worse than if you had done nothing.

It had the potential to be transformational. But it will never have that potential if you can't back it up with the equip and the resources.

CHARLES FERGUSON: What do you think of those differences and of the possibility that they were bound to explode when Saddam was removed?

A. HEATHER COYNE: A lot of people have the Balkan Ghost mind-set, which is that these people have hated each other for centuries and they've fought each other for centuries and you'll never stop them hating each other and fighting each other. I don't buy into that. That sounds more like an excuse than an explanation. Quite frankly, the English and the French and the Spanish and the Germans hated each other for centuries, too, and that doesn't mean that the EU can't be a successful organization. I don't think sectarian violence was inevitable at the level that we see it.

Of course, there's sectarian tensions. There were always sectarian tensions under Saddam, certainly after he targeted ethnic groups and religious groups because of their opposition to him, both the Kurds and the Shia. But that's just the clay to work with. You have to have political actors who

have a permissive environment, who can exploit and manipulate those underlying tensions in a way that creates a sectarian identity that overpowers
all other identities that Iraqis might have. Part of the problem certainly was
the way CPA managed programs and exacerbated a lot of the tendencies
that were already there—or made the permissive environment for Iraqi
leaders to exploit and take advantage of the tension. ... For instance, the
mobile phone system. CPA ... ended up creating a southern network, central network and northern network that were not interoperable. So if you
were a Shia in the south, you couldn't make a call to a Kurd in the north.
Talk about getting the exact opposite result to what we wanted.

CHARLES FERGUSON: Yeah. That doesn't seem very bright.

A. HEATHER COYNE: And there were lots of things that weren't very bright
that CPA did that exacerbated the problems. But I put most of the blame
on leaders who saw sectarian identity as the best way for them to profit in
the new system and to take power in the new system.

I had mentioned that Saddam had eliminated any form of civil society
other than his own Baath Party. The one area that people could continue
to mobilize and continue to be a community outside Saddam's system was
the mosques. The mosques, therefore, when Saddam fell, were the only institution that could mobilize the Iraqi people quickly and efficiently. So
that sets the playing field for all these returning exiled parties. The ones
that were going to do best in the new Iraq are the ones that needed to mobilize through the mosques—namely, the sectarian, religious-based parties.
All the other parties that came back—and there were some secular or func-
tionally based—didn't do as well, because they didn't have any mobilizing
institutions that worked for them the way the mosques did for groups like
SCIRI and Dawa [Shiite parties].

So those groups had a running start on everybody from the beginning,
and they used CPA's bad judgments and CPA's preset idea that this was
Bosnia all over again, and they exploited that. They pushed policies. And
they pushed laws and decisions that would allow them to then bolster their
own power in the new system. For instance, the de-Baathification law: The
de-Baathification law might have been badly thought out, but even more
importantly, it was badly implemented. The person implementing it was

using it to eliminate rivals in the system. So a de-Baathification law that already exacerbated some of the sectarian tensions was then used by Iraqi leaders to further exacerbate them and to make everything that much more clearly framed in terms of sectarian identity.

So no, I don't think that the violence at the level that we've got to is inevitable, but it would have taken very careful management and very thoughtful management from the beginning by the international community in order to avoid and restrict those Iraqi leaders from abusing the trends and the current in order to push their own advantage. And we didn't manage it.

All of the educated and secular Iraqis with whom I spoke felt certain that things could have been vastly different after Saddam was deposed. They too differed as to whether a fully democratic government was realistic, at least initially, but they all thought that basic stability and a regime that respected basic human rights would have been easy to obtain. In general, exiles, such as Laith Kubba, were more optimistic about the potential for democracy, while Iraqis who had been living under the regime believed that at the very least, a period of martial law was necessary before any democratic transition.

LAITH KUBBA: In retrospect, I may have made a mistake when I advocated immediate, full democracy in 2002. I think perhaps it would have been best to start with local elections, then provincial elections, and wait for national elections until the country was stabilized and the population had some experience with democracy. Local elections would have been easy because people know who their natural local leaders are; they know them personally. National elections needed more time. But I have no doubt that if the United States had not destroyed the Iraqi state, had maintained law and order, that Iraq would be a stable and peaceful nation now.

Omar Fekeiki held an intermediate position. He felt that if the United States had behaved intelligently, a period of martial law would still have been necessary but also sufficient to ensure order. He believed that once order and stability had been restored, a democratic transition would have been possible.

CHARLES FERGUSON: What kind of government do you think they should have set up or facilitated in Iraq after an invasion?

OMAR FEKEIKI: Eight months of martial law—that could have taken care of everything, martial law in Iraq. How can you disband an army and police, and let the imprisoned Iraqis—who were imprisoned and suffering for forty years—let them loose? Martial law, I thought. And that's what we talked about when we were waiting for the Americans to come into Baghdad. We thought there would be martial law. We were prepared to accept the martial law in Iraq.

This is the thing: They [the Americans] did not know where they were going into. They just didn't know. They had no idea what Iraq looks like as a community and as a culture. Martial law in Iraq for eight months; anyone who commits a crime will be executed, according to the Iraqi constitution. I'm not being a dictator; that's my constitution. According to the Iraqi criminal law, if you kill an Iraqi, you can get the death sentence. That's what should have been done in Iraq.

CHARLES FERGUSON: And then after that, what kind of government, do you think?

OMAR FEKEIKI: We had a secular government. I mean, we had secular leaders. Ahmed Chalabi, who they hate and most Americans hate—and I don't know why they hate him. They tell me he's a crook and he's corrupt, but who isn't? ...

CHARLES FERGUSON: But I would have thought that Chalabi embodies the idea of the disconnected exile, and you felt that it was important to have Iraq run by people who had lived there and understood the country.

OMAR FEKEIKI: This is the problem. They should have had a government ready, and during the first year, the first two years, they should have had a government. You can't ask Iraqis to vote. What I'm saying is, eight months of martial law with a secular government. And then, when it's safe to have elections—when I can nominate myself to an office, to a post, and I go nominate myself, the Iraqis will know me, safely go and vote for me. That did not happen.

When I first interviewed Feisal al-Istrabadi about these issues, he had just been appointed deputy ambassador to the United Nations. His comments were remarkably frank for a diplomat, yet at the same time I could sense his impatience, his desire to say more. He spoke first about the West's misconceptions about ethnic tensions in Iraq.

FEISAL AL-ISTRABADI: You see, Iraq is not Yugoslavia. And the mistake a lot of Westerners make is in analyzing us as Yugoslavia. In the former Yugoslavia, there were Croats, Serbs, and Bosnians. In Iraq, there are Kurds, Shias, and Sunnis—never mind the other twenty-four ethnic and confessional groups in Iraq. And so that becomes a wonderful jumping-off point: We are exactly the opposite of Yugoslavia.

[In] Yugoslavia, Marshal Tito was, by Stalinist standards, at least, a comparatively benign dictator who held a country together consisting of people who fundamentally didn't like one another. He papered over those differences: people who historically, in fact, had killed one another. Iraq is the exact opposite of that. First of all, we didn't have a comparatively mild tyrant; we had one of the most despotic tyrants from the last half of the twentieth century, and one whose name goes down with the tyrants of the twentieth century—no small thing—who assumed power over a country in which the various ethnic and confessional groups had lived to a very high degree of amity. There are, for instance, with the exception of the mistreatment of Iraq's Jews, not a single example of one group in Iraq rising to butcher another—the Kurds rising to butcher the Arabs, or the Arabs the Kurds, or the Shias the Sunnis, or whatever it is. What you have are examples of a malevolent central government massacring the Assyrians, or a central government massacring the Kurds, the central government massacring the Shia, but you never have communal violence in Iraq. You've never had that. Instead, you had a tyrant who created and exacerbated fissures. This is part of his legacy that we have to live with.

Somewhat later in the same interview:

CHARLES FERGUSON: You may not feel comfortable talking about this; I'll let you decide. How much different do you think it could have been if the occupation had been planned and conducted competently?

FEISAL AL-ISTRABADI: Um, look: I'm a diplomat.

CHARLES FERGUSON: [*laughs*] Fair enough. Okay.

FEISAL AL-ISTRABADI: I'm a trial lawyer by training. I deal with facts. As a trial lawyer, I can't make my facts. I do the facts as they are dealt to me. ...

CHARLES FERGUSON: No problem.

FEISAL AL-ISTRABADI: This is how things went. ... By the way, I will say this: Some of the problems we are having I think were inevitable—not all of them—and I think the road was made more difficult by some of the mistakes that were made. But again, you are never going to have [a tranquil place like] Minnesota unfold in Iraq on April 10th. It's going to take time. There will be problems. And I will tell you this: On April 9th, I was still practicing law in northwest Indiana. I stayed home to watch the statue in Firdos Square being brought down. As it was happening, two thoughts occurred to me. First of all—and I thought this was a perfect metaphor—the Iraqis weren't able to bring the statue down by themselves. It took the Americans to bring it down. Number two: When it actually came down, I felt absolutely no euphoria, because I knew that, and said to myself: The hard work begins now.

So those who thought that it was simply going to be a picnic, I think were fooling themselves at the time. You can't have gone through what the Iraqis have gone through and not have real issues to confront in the rebuilding of the country.

CHARLES FERGUSON: When did you decide that you were going to go back and participate in the—

FEISAL AL-ISTRABADI: Well, the statue came down April 9th. On April 27th, I was in Baghdad.

Two years later, al-Istrabadi cut loose, perhaps because he had just left the government.

FEISAL AL-ISTRABADI: I don't think it's an accident that [it is] the same political class that the United States looked to ... [and that controlled the] Iraqi Governing Council ends up governing now. And that's what the U.S. did; it created a political class that had nothing to do with competence, but had everything to do with ethno-confessional allegiances. I would argue they never understood Iraq and they sort of doomed the enterprise [to] failure, mostly through ignorance.

Should Saddam Have Been Deposed in 1991?
Were the Sanctions Wise?

The majority of interviewees thought that Saddam should have been deposed in 1991. Iraqis were particularly bitter about how the United States left them to be brutalized by Saddam after pushing the Iraqi military out of Kuwait. Even many Americans, including some who opposed the war in 2003, considered 1991 a missed opportunity. Moreover, nearly everyone—even those who felt that the United States was correct in not deposing Saddam in 1991—believed that the ensuing sanctions were extremely unwise and damaging. Ellen Laipson was the national intelligence officer for the Middle East when Saddam invaded Kuwait.

CHARLES FERGUSON: Looking back on it now, do you think that it was a wise thing, or do you think that it was a mistake to have allowed Saddam to retain power, to not have done the combination of things that would have deposed him, ranging from going further into Iraq, suppressing, destroying more of his military, not allowing him to suppress the rebellions—you know, all the—

ELLEN LAIPSON: Well, that's a very loaded question. I mean, it depends a lot on what your own political values are. I would say, in hindsight, adding all of the attributes of Saddam—source of instability in the region, gross human rights abuser, et cetera—I wish that we had stuck with it and brought this unhappy chapter to a close earlier. I do think that the 1990s ... We were living on borrowed time; we were running out of things to do to keep Iraq in its cage. But all of that containment of Iraq was never really addressing the gross humanitarian and human rights problems that were occurring in Iraq all the time.

But again, you know, you have to be in the shoes of the president at the time. The first President Bush [George Bush Senior] decided that his war aims were to get Iraq out of Kuwait, full stop. Now that is, I think, hugely

540   NO END IN SIGHT

in debate. In hindsight, I think a pretty wide swath of the political spectrum says, we should have solved the problem then once and for all. Our Arab friends had told us at the time: If you're gonna do it, go all the way. Finish the job.

CHARLES FERGUSON: Really?

ELLEN LAIPSON: Oh yes. The Saudis and others were rather exasperated that we stirred up the hornet's nest and didn't finish the job. It was a strong Arab preference that we ... finish the job at the time.

CHARLES FERGUSON: I'm sure you realize that in public debate about this issue, there have always been two considerations that have been advanced as the reasons not to have finished the job then. One was that if we went all the way to Baghdad, then we'd end up owning and occupying the country, and we'd have a lot of the problems that we have now. Or at least that was the assertion, the concern. The other was that we'd lose the coalition partners, because the Arab countries in the coalition wouldn't want us to go all the way to Baghdad, wouldn't want Saddam to be deposed. Do you think that that is not the case?

ELLEN LAIPSON: I think that in the Middle East, it's very, very often the case the leaders of nondemocratic countries tell us things privately that may be different than what their public posture is. But I do think that the coalition would have fallen apart. ... I think that some of the European countries that joined in the coalition may indeed have balked at the idea of regime change. They may not have been as ambitious as at least some on the American side were to bring about change in Iraq.

So your point about the coalition may be true. But it's not exclusively an Arab issue. I think the Arabs, of course, were nervous about whatever we did. Everything we do is intruding in their space, is creating great uncertainties for them. So they can simultaneously wish [that] if we're going to come in, we'd finish the job, but also worry hugely about what are some of the consequences and reactions in their own societies. It is, I think, in the judgment of many that watch the Middle East closely, these nondemocratic regimes usually have more capacity to manage their domestic affairs than they themselves may believe. ...

But I am one hundred percent sure that Arab leaders expressed to us privately that if we were going to come in and disrupt the local order as much as we did, it would have been better to finish the job. ... Now that doesn't mean that they themselves would have taken responsibility for helping Iraq post-Saddam. But just to go back on your other point, I think there was a belief that you could have gotten rid of Saddam and simply picked another Baathi general—you know, a sort of Saddam Lite. ... If it had been done in the early nineties, there would not have perhaps been quite as much ambition to sort of say [that] the only alternative after Saddam is full democracy. The alternative after Saddam might have been another centrally controlled, nondemocratic system, but at least without Saddam.

In my first interview with him in late 2005, Feisal al-Istrabadi argued forcefully that sanctions and the U.S. failure to depose Saddam Hussein in the first Gulf War had proved disastrous for Iraq.

FEISAL AL-ISTRABADI: The failure to remove Saddam Hussein and the Baath tyranny in 1991 must rank as, I think, one of the greatest blunders in the history of diplomacy, assuming whoever it is that said that war is diplomacy by other means.

In 1991, the first President Bush exhorted the people to rebel, to overthrow the Baathist regime. They did. Fourteen out of Iraq's eighteen [governorates] were under rebel control when General [Norman] Schwarzkopf allowed Saddam Hussein to use helicopter gunships to massacre the rebels—men, women and children. When the ground war began in 1991, there was a sense of euphoria in Baghdad because no one believed that Saddam Hussein and the regime would be allowed to survive. What occurred in Iraq in 1991—allowing Saddam to massacre the Kurds in the north and the Marsh Arabs, who were primarily Shia, in the south—was something the Iraqis never forgot and, unfortunately, I think, is a part of the history which contributed; it was a betrayal, in fact. And that betrayal was never forgotten by the Iraqis. And it has contributed to the history, I believe, of some of the difficulties, which ensued in the 2003 completion of the 1991 war. You know, some historians—and I'm by no means an authority—argue that the Second World War was the conclusion of the First World War. 2003 was the conclusion of business left unfinished in 1991, after a period of time in which the misery that was visited on people of Iraq has yet to be adequately described. This was a period when the middle class in Iraq—which was the largest middle class, probably, of any Middle Eastern country, at least of the Arab Middle East—this period of sanctions was the period in which that middle class was completely destroyed. Completely, thoroughly, utterly destroyed, so that, for instance, you had college professors who had lived a very high standard of living before, [who] were now using their personal cars after hours as taxis. People were selling their furniture, their silverware, their books, which were the last items to be sold from people's houses. This was the period during which time Saddam Hussein built his famous hundred-some-odd palaces. It was during this period of time when the country was under sanctions; supposedly, the regime was under sanctions.

And I have to say, at the time, I was living, practicing law in northwest Indiana, in sort of a suburb of Chicago. I was watching a discussion between a professor at the University of Chicago and Senator Dick Durbin, who is, of course, still in the U.S. Senate—a Democrat from Illinois. And the professor was saying, "Well look, these sanctions, they're hurting the people of Iraq." And in the only sort of honest moment of the entire discussion on sanctions, Senator Durbin said, "They're supposed to hurt the people of Iraq." Well, they did. And the people of Iraq didn't forget that. And why should they?

CHARLES FERGUSON: What do you think the United States should have done during that period?

FEISAL AL-ISTRABADI: Well, Saddam shouldn't have been in power during that period of time. ... The whole policy, I think, was wrong. The whole policy was wrong. Allowing him to survive was wrong. The sanctions were wrong because they allowed him to consolidate his power. He became weaker vis-à-vis his neighbors, but he didn't need to be stronger than his neighbors to survive; he needed to be that much stronger than the people of Iraq, and he managed that quite beautifully. It was just a disaster. That entire policy of containment—dual containment, I think it's called—it was just a complete disaster, viewed from the perspective of the region and from the perspective of the Iraqis in particular, because what it meant was that the people of Iraq were, in essence, cannon fodder for higher political considerations.

Some Americans resisted the proposition that the United States should have deposed Saddam in 1991. Their arguments were primarily based on the "realist" view of U.S. national interests and on the pragmatic difficulties of occupying and managing Iraq. Often, those who made these arguments pointed to Iraq's current condition as evidence that it had been wise not to depose Saddam in 1991. Because Saddam was containable (in their view), the United States did not need to involve itself with internal Iraqi affairs. Here is Lawrence Wilkerson, who during the first Gulf War was special assistant to Colin Powell, who was then the chairman of the Joint Chiefs of Staff:

CHARLES FERGUSON: In retrospect, what do you think of the way the United States handled the conclusion of the first Persian Gulf War and its aftermath: the decision not to go towards Baghdad, the decision not to completely destroy the Iraqi military and the Republican Guard, not to intervene when the Shiites rebelled and then were repressed—all those things?

LAWRENCE WILKERSON: ... I have to look at it from what I call a very dispassionate perspective of the academic. At the same time, I'm looking at it from the perspective of a soldier and a person who was involved in it.

From the academic perspective, what I saw happen in 1991 was, in foreign-policy terms, I think, an excellent decision. And I say that for several reasons. First, I would refer you back to the Korean War. The Korean War was a bloody, almost interminable—to the people involved in it—conflict. Even though it went from '50 to '53, it seemed interminable at the time, if you read the newspapers and so forth. And one of the things that made it that way was—as much as I have infinite respect for Harry Truman and his abilities—was the mission creep that took place, if you will. The United Nations mandate, as it were, was to expel the invader. Well, we didn't just expel the invader, we decided to increase that mission considerably, and essentially attempt to reunify the peninsula. And we went north, and we went to the Yalu, and as everyone knows, hundreds of thousands of Chinese joined in the conflict, and made it bloody, and made it almost a stalemate for three horrible years. So that historical precedent is enough to caution any president, once he has a UN mandate, not to go beyond it. ...

Well, whether or not we had taken the Iraqi Army down to the point that it was no longer a threat to its neighbors, critics can question. But we made the decision—I say "we"; President George H. W. Bush made the decision, and I thought at the time, and still think, it was a very sound decision—that we had degraded the Iraqi Army's conventional capability to the extent that it would no longer be, for some time to come, a threat to its neighbors. And that was implicit in the UN mandate as well. ... So we had accomplished the United Nations mandate; we had accomplished the mission we set out to accomplish. And moreover, President George H. W. Bush understood, I think instinctively, if not intellectually—and I think he understood from both dimensions—that increasing the mission in this case, making the mission different, widening it, going to Baghdad, much as going to the Yalu in 1950 was a mistake, would have been a mistake of the same proportions. And [he] knew that he was not prepared, nor was America prepared, for the years and years of effort that would be required to fix Iraq if one went to Baghdad and therefore owned it afterwards. And so the decision was made—and as I said, I think it was a very sound decision—that we would stop where we had ended, and that was successfully fulfilling the United Nations mandate.

Even Wilkerson, however, concurred that the sanctions were unwise.

CHARLES FERGUSON: Okay. And what do you think of the sanctions period—

LAWRENCE WILKERSON: ... A personal viewpoint that I have about sanctions: they're worthless. There are some exceptions, but the exceptions more often than not prove the rule.

How and Why Was the Occupation Mishandled So Badly?

Richard Armitage evaded the question as to why the occupation of Iraq was mishandled, and why the president did not intercede to correct the administration's mistakes. This exchange occurred in mid-2006, several months before Donald Rumsfeld's resignation:

CHARLES FERGUSON: I'm not asking about what you said to the president, or what he said to you, or what Secretary Powell said to him, or what he said to you, but what's ... what is your sense of why the president didn't do something about all this? You know, ...the troop-level question? Why the looting didn't affect him more? Why the growing chaos in Iraq, the kidnappings, you know, all that?

RICHARD ARMITAGE: I think the president ... Clearly, he must have been fairly happy with his team. And he keeps the team ... on the team that's in existence today. So you'd have to come to the conclusion that at least the only nationally elected leader is satisfied with the team and the advice he's getting from them. I don't know what other conclusion you could come to.

CHARLES FERGUSON: But why do you think that is?

RICHARD ARMITAGE: I, listen ... you've ... I'm not the president. I'm not him. I walk in my boots, and he walks in his, and you'll have to ask the president. He's a man, the only one, who's judged by the nation. In a way, we have that judgment almost every day, as every poll is run. And some days he's down, and some days he's up. That's the way we do things. And he'll be judged by his actions. And, as I say, he clearly has to be satisfied with the advice he's getting, because he's got the same team.

I asked Jay Garner both about the fumbling of the occupation and about his own behavior.

CHARLES FERGUSON: Why do you think all those mistakes were made?

JAY GARNER: I don't know. I have no idea.

CHARLES FERGUSON: Hm.

JAY GARNER: Puzzling.

CHARLES FERGUSON: What would you say maybe you would have done differently, in retrospect?

JAY GARNER: Ah ... [sighs] I don't know what I'd have done differently, because I don't know that if I had done anything ... It would have fallen on deaf ears. ... The predicament I was in [was] that when things happened, the decision was made, and I wasn't in on the planning process of that. ... My mistake was probably not finding a way to get myself more involved in the planning process of things.

CHARLES FERGUSON: I see.

JAY GARNER: Yeah.

CHARLES FERGUSON: So that the dissolution of the army wouldn't have been a surprise—

JAY GARNER: Right.

CHARLES FERGUSON: ... for example.

JAY GARNER: Well, and I could have raised hell about it, you know, and had my day in court. I may have lost, but I'd've had my day in court.

Others cited various combinations of four factors: the political freedom granted to the administration in the wake of the 9/11 attacks; the fact that a small group of strongly ideological, religious, ruthless, and arrogant people controlled the government; the lack of relevant Middle East, military, and postwar occupation experience on the part of this group; and the combination of inexperience, arrogance, and disengagement on the part of the president.

My own sense from the public record and from my interviews is that two factors were critical. The first was the ignorance, inexperience, and disconnection of the president. The picture of President Bush that emerged from my interviews was of someone unaware of, and quite unconcerned with, the decisions being made in his name. He was apparently blithely confident either in his own instincts or in the abilities of his advisers. Over and over, I heard the same things: The president didn't read documents; he didn't investigate assertions; he approved unquestioningly whatever his immediate circle recommended. The second critical factor, I believe, is that the administration, and its policy in Iraq, was controlled by a very small number of people with certain shared personal, psychological characteristics. I do not think that ideology or political forces alone can explain the irrationality of occupation policy and the administration's reluctance to correct mistakes. Cheney, Rumsfeld, Wolfowitz, and Bremer appear to share a combination of arrogance, religiosity, intellectual rigidity, impatience, and inexperience with postwar occupations that, in this situation, proved fatal. Condoleezza Rice seems to have done whatever she thought those in power wanted. Powell and Armitage were too loyal and too ambitious to rebel once their objections had been heard and dismissed.

Here is a selection of comments on these subjects. I begin with George Packer.

CHARLES FERGUSON: Why do think that the occupation was so poorly planned?

GEORGE PACKER: The planning fiasco ... was one part supreme arrogance on the part of officials who had no idea of how it would go, and no concern that it might not go that way, and no other plan if it didn't go that way. It was one part ignorance, because they really didn't know the country that they were about to take over, and yet they thought they did. I think that to Paul Wolfowitz, Iraq was gonna be like Poland in 1989 or Germany in 1945. I think those were his historical analogies.

It was one part presidential abdication. President Bush was ... missing in action on the planning for the postwar. In Bob Woodward's book *Plan of Attack,* Vice President Cheney is quoted, or paraphrased, saying, the president understood where to put his focus. And in the months leading up to the war, he [President Bush] zeroed in on the military plan. And what I learned was, when it came to the postwar, Bush was ... not involved. Not only not involved in making decisions, like what are we gonna do with the Iraqi Army and the Baath Party, and what transition to Iraqi self-rule is going to happen?—all those key policy questions—but he deferred to his vice president and his secretary of defense the control over those decisions. There was a great war within the administration between the vice president's office and the Pentagon on the one hand, and the State Department and, to a lesser extent, the CIA on the other. It was up to the president and his national security adviser, Condoleezza Rice, to resolve that conflict, to hear out the arguments and resolve them. And instead, the conflict continued, unresolved, all the way through the occupation. I mean, people were still being kept from going to Baghdad because of their bureaucratic affiliation and supposed ideological leanings after the fall of the regime. And in the absence of Bush and Rice forcing a resolution, Donald Rumsfeld and Dick Cheney used their tremendous skills as infighters to essentially win dirty, to simply seize control and take it away, and to freeze out Colin Powell and the State Department, even on matters where the State Department obviously was the go-to agency. ...

Donald Rumsfeld had no interest in postwar Iraq. He wanted to get out. And so the plan was essentially, we'll stay for three or four months; we will install a government made up of exiles and led by [Ahmed Chalabi]; and then, in August or September of 2003, we will begin a drastic reduction of troops; we'll go down to thirty thousand. That was the plan. That was Rumsfeld's plan as executed by Wolfowitz and Feith.

And it was a ludicrous plan. It was a plan that didn't begin to grapple with how difficult and dangerous and complex these postwar situations are. We learned that in the nineties; we learned it in Somalia, in Bosnia, in Kosovo; we learned it in Afghanistan, under this administration. But Donald Rumsfeld and the officials under him decided that they were not going to be deterred by history, that that was sort of the history of failure. That was failure-thinking. They were gonna do it a different way. And it was gonna go the way they said it was gonna go. They weren't going to be saddled with the failures of others. They had found a new way to do it: without nation-building; without deep, long commitments; without quagmires. And I think they convinced themselves that they were right; it would go that way.

CHARLES FERGUSON: You don't think that there was also an element of just sheer callousness about the fate of Iraq and the Iraqi people?

GEORGE PACKER: I think on Donald Rumsfeld's part, there was indifference to the fate of the Iraqi people. When he saw the looting on TV, and said, stuff happens, and free people are free to make mistakes and do bad things, that showed a really shocking degree of callousness.

I think for Paul Wolfowitz, it's different. I think he cared enormously about what would happen in Iraq and felt a real sense of commitment to Iraqi democracy. And I think Paul Wolfowitz was a man operating in good faith. But I think he was a classic study of, you might say, the best and brightest who turn out to be fools because he so wanted it to go the way he thought it would go that he couldn't imagine it going any other way. That was actually his word. ... I think for him, it was not a failure of his heart; it was a failure of his imagination, which is quite tragic because Iraq will always be his war; it will always be his project. His reputation is inextricably tied to it, and his place in history. He's the one member of the administration who I think must have trouble sleeping at night, because I think he knows what's happened and why. He must.

CHARLES FERGUSON: Have you spoken to him about it?

GEORGE PACKER: Not on the record.

CHARLES FERGUSON: Okay. Have you spoken to any of the principals about it?

GEORGE PACKER: I spoke to Douglas Feith, and I got a lot of justifications—

CHARLES FERGUSON: A lot of horseshit.

GEORGE PACKER: Yeah, I didn't hear anything that told me that he was capable of understanding what had happened and why, and what his own role in it was. He was a lawyer. He practiced law for many, many years. And I think his approach to talking about Iraq is that of a lawyer trying to essentially snow the jury. Feith was a very weak link in the chain of command because he was in a key position; his office was in charge of planning for postwar Iraq, and they utterly failed to. But at the same time, they were very successful in winning these intramural policy wars, and they almost seemed to think that if they could just win the war against the State Department, then Iraq would be just a footnote—an afterthought.

They were very ideological people. They came up in the seventies and eighties and nineties—and I'm speaking generally of what are called the neoconservatives as ideological warriors, who felt that the established institutions in America—the universities, the courts, the bureaucracies, the media—were corrupt and spineless and self-hating and inimical to American greatness. And no one epitomizes this type of neoconservative as insurgent as much as Richard Perle, who I did interview, and who wasn't a key official in the Iraq war, because he was out of government. He was the chair of the Defense Policy Board, which is an advisory body, but he was not technically a member of the administration. But he was the chief impresario and advocate and propagandist for the war.

And I think for Richard Perle and for Douglas Feith, who got his job at the Pentagon through the intervention of Richard Perle, and for others at lesser levels under them, Iraq was always part of a larger war, which was essentially an American political war for control over our own institutions of governance and of democracy and of culture. And in a way, I think they took their eyes off Iraq very quickly. If you read, for example, the *Weekly Standard*, which is the house organ of neoconservatism, in the days immediately after the fall of Baghdad, the leading writers of the *Weekly Standard* were already looking to the next phase of the war. Now, obviously, that means the war on terror, which meant Syria, Iran, North Korea, but it also meant the war at home. They were already essentially declaring that the liberals, the Europeans, the Arabists—all of their political enemies—had suffered a tremendous defeat in Iraq and that they would go on suffering defeats because history was on the side of the neoconservatives. Although I don't want to say that they're profoundly antidemocratic, 'cause I think they operate within a democracy by the rules of a democracy, there is something of a kind of vanguard quality to them, a kind of a Leninist quality, in the sense that they do believe that a small group of people leading from the front, absolutely uncompromising, taking no prisoners, and holding true to some core principles, can move history in a certain direction. And that they don't need the humdrum institutions to be on their side. They don't need, you know, those thick-headed appeasers in the State Department and the CIA. That the press is part of the problem and that the media is part of the problem. So, in a sense, Iraq was, to them, part of a much larger struggle. And in April of 2003, they thought that they had won that battle. And they moved on.

From Lieutenant Seth Moulton:

CHARLES FERGUSON: What are your feelings about the way the high levels of the government have conducted this war, and conducted themselves in this war?

SETH MOULTON: Personally, I feel the war would be going differently if you had leadership that really understood, number one, what it's like to be on the ground—had actually served in the armed forces—and number two, really had a good managerial grasp of making this thing work.

Now I'm speaking as a twenty-seven-year-old lieutenant. So all I can speak from is my experience on the ground. And [I've] read a few history books about how wars have been run and mismanaged or managed correctly in the past. And there's always gonna be mistakes. But it just seems like so many of the mistakes that have been made in this war are pretty obvious ones, are the same kinds of mistakes we made in Vietnam and supposedly learned [from]. And yet it hasn't changed.

I also think that … the fact that America has really not been called to serve since September 11th significantly impacts the war in Iraq. And I think that if we had a different style of national leadership—I think that if President Kennedy had been leading America on September 12th, he would have asked a lot more of Americans, and America and the war effort would be a lot better off as a result. Now that's just pulling one person out of history, or whatever, but I think that's a big problem.

… It just seems to me, it doesn't help that so many people in our national leadership, from the administration to the Congress, have never really served, themselves, at the ground level. I don't think that you need to be in the military to be president. I mean … that's not America; that's not the kind of society we live in. But there's no question that in the middle of a war, that kind of experience would help.

A number of people commented on the impact of poor intelligence and on the systemic failures of the intelligence system. Here is part of my interview with James Bamford, who has studied the U.S. intelligence system for the last twenty years and written several books about it.

CHARLES FERGUSON: Why do you think the intelligence community has performed so poorly?

JAMES BAMFORD: Well … what time period are you covering here?

CHARLES FERGUSON: … If you think there's a different explanation for the prewar period as opposed to the occupation period, then answer them separately.

JAMES BAMFORD: Yeah, it's performed poorly, actually in both situations for different reasons. It performed poorly in the first situation because they had nobody over there, and they had very little capability in terms of understanding what was going on inside the country. And it performed poorly after the war began, because the people they put over there didn't have much of a capability to deal with the local population. I mean, if you're dealing with human intelligence, the whole idea is to recruit people, and they haven't had much success in recruiting people in the insurgency. They've never had anybody recruited, at least far as I know, that are close to the leadership in the insurgency. ... They don't even know how big the insurgency is. So for two different reasons, they were performing poorly before and after.

CHARLES FERGUSON: And is there anything that they could have done about either of those? Before the war, could they have done more to penetrate Iraq, to recruit Iraqis, to—

JAMES BAMFORD: They could have done a lot more. Starting [in the] early nineties, after the end of the Cold War, and after the first attack on the World Trade Center, they should have seen the writing on the wall that terrorism is an area that they should be focusing on, to some degree. I mean, not entirely, but they should be beginning to look for people who have some indigenous knowledge, people who can speak the language. There's 280 million people in the United States. If they can't find thirty people that can infiltrate some of these organizations, then what is the use for these intelligence agencies?

I think the CIA had huge amounts of money. I think they had a huge amount of brain power in there. I just don't think they had ... either motivation or skills necessary to figure out that that's what they have to do. When I interviewed one of the senior officials over there for *A Pretext for War,* I asked him, "Why didn't you recruit somebody, recruit a few people ... that actually looked like they belong over there, and spoke the language, and had some cultural knowledge of what's going on, and then train the person in how to infiltrate? ... The deficit here is a person that's not gonna have a eight-bedroom house paid for by the government and a chauffeur-driven car, which is kind of what a lot of the Foreign Service people kind of expect a lot of places. They're gonna live in [a] cave, or they're gonna live out in the sand 'til they establish their bona fides, which may take a couple years." And you know, he looked at me like I was crazy, like, "We don't do those type of things. That's not what we do. We're the CIA." ... And that's what they needed to do.

Other agencies do things similar to that. The DEA [Drug Enforcement Agency] infiltrates Colombian drug dealers, and ... if you want to talk about dangerous groups, they're very dangerous groups. They do it. The FBI infiltrated the Mafia with their own people. J. Edgar Hoover, when he was director of the FBI, had a policy where FBI agents never went under-cover; they never got their fingernails dirty; they never rolled up their sleeves; they never even took off their white shirts. So that was sort of the attitude at the CIA: We just don't do those kind of things. Well, they should have started doing those things a long time ago, starting at least post–World Trade Center I. And maybe by the time, you know, 2000 rolled along, they'd have some actual people inside terrorist organizations or inside Iraq. And I think that's the key problem with the CIA: They just didn't do that.

CHARLES FERGUSON: Hm. And now, after the war, during the occupation, what was going on there? Why didn't they recruit people who understood Iraq? Why didn't they place people into Iraq who understood Iraq, who spoke Arabic?

JAMES BAMFORD: I think it was too late. I mean, you need ten years' worth of planning for things like this. And throwing some people who've learned Arabic in the last couple years at University of Minnesota or something, you know, and they look like they're quarterbacks for Notre Dame or something—that just doesn't work. You gotta be really professional about it, or give it up. And they weren't very professional about it. They had peo-ple over there ... they don't look the part; they don't sound the part; they don't fit in; they don't really know the cultural heritage. And from what I understand, almost none of 'em ever leave a compound, unless they've got an eight-car convoy around 'em. How are you supposed to recruit people like that? I mean, the proof is in the pudding: The insurgency has grown ever since this has happened.

I've never seen any indication that they have anybody anywhere near the leadership in any of these organizations that is giving them information.

Once in a while, they'll find some courier that will have a message on him or a computer disk or something. I think that's the best that they've been able to do so far. I mean, they aren't even able to find who's given all these videotapes from al Qaeda and bin Laden and his deputy and so forth. ... They've been giving out these videotapes for the last four years, and we haven't even been able to trace one of 'em back. That doesn't sound like great intelligence work to me.

CHARLES FERGUSON: Hm. And you think that it could in fact be much better; that it's not just that it's a very difficult problem?

JAMES BAMFORD: Obviously, it's a difficult problem. There's lots of difficult problems in the world. It's a very difficult problem. But they haven't attacked it like they should. They haven't attacked it like the DEA attacks the Colombian drug problem to some degree ... Not that [the DEA have] been great successes, but at least they've tried by doing the right things: finding people who fit in, infiltrating organizations with their own people. ... I haven't seen that from the CIA. They're people that sit back there, and ponder things, and write reports. And they have people out in their embassies there that wander out and try to recruit people that aren't very successful. And [this is] what you have: You have ... huge areas of the world where we have nobody penetrating.

And now two excerpts from Robert Hutchings, former director of the National Intelligence Council (NIC). The first describes the impact (or lack thereof) of his assessments of the insurgency in 2004. The second excerpt describes his more general thoughts about the administration. First, the reaction to his second National Intelligence Estimate on the insurgency, which the NIC produced in mid-2004:

ROBERT HUTCHINGS: I don't think it made much of a dent on their thinking. ... This is where the real breakdown between policy and intelligence was revealed, I think. These kinds of gloomy assessments were really pretty much dismissed on the policy side. We were accused [at] the National Intelligence Council, in a *Wall Street Journal* editorial, of running an anti-Bush insurgency, a second insurgency. So, somehow the messenger was being conflated with the message. We took no joy in delivering such a gloomy message, but the messenger was not welcome in some circles, so there's a kind of tendency to dismiss a priori, out of hand, analysis that was this gloomy.

CHARLES FERGUSON: I see. Did it ever occur to you to resign or to speak out publicly about the situation?

ROBERT HUTCHINGS: No. Those things [weigh] on one's mind. I mean, I've been in public life long enough to have thought about these things from time to time. And I actually thought about it before I went into this job. For this or any other job, I go in prepared to walk from it if I feel that I am in a ethically untenable position. I never felt that. I felt frustrated that what I thought was pretty good political analysis was not being taken on board.

Somewhat later in the interview, Hutchings characterized the mind-set of the senior administration officials before the occupation. When I pushed him to be specific, he resisted.

ROBERT HUTCHINGS: There was a kind of a willful underestimation of the difficulties ahead. There was a fascination with what the military technology could do, and it was shock and awe. And that was such a spectacularly attractive option to the authors of the war that they failed to really think through just how difficult this occupation was going to be. ...

CHARLES FERGUSON: Okay. Did you ever say these things directly to senior policy officials?

ROBERT HUTCHINGS: Sure, I did. And wrote them as well. Maybe not quite as baldly as that.

CHARLES FERGUSON: Who did you say these things to?

ROBERT HUTCHINGS: Well, this came up in some meetings of the National Security Council. I don't want to get too specific about who said what to whom.

CHARLES FERGUSON: Why not?

ROBERT HUTCHINGS: I'm—

CHARLES FERGUSON: I'm serious—

ROBERT HUTCHINGS: It's just not my style. I mean, I don't want to start naming names. I'm perfectly willing to convey a general attitude on the part of senior policymakers, but to go beyond that, it's not my personal style. Sorry.

CHARLES FERGUSON: No, it's all right; you're drawing one line. But now I'll say, sorry, and I'm gonna push you on it. Why not? You say it's not your personal style, but I'm not asking you to make personal attacks on people; I'm not asking you to comment negatively on their ethics. I'm asking you what they said about the most critical policy decisions the United States has made in the last three decades. And you were there.

ROBERT HUTCHINGS: Yeah, yeah. We—either I or we, is the better sense—conveyed analysis to a lot of people, a lot of senior people. They had access to this analysis. So to try to pinpoint who failed to act where, it's really not only not my style, but probably not very pertinent, because the same analysis was provided to all the senior policy community. ...

CHARLES FERGUSON: You had a comment you wanted to make.

ROBERT HUTCHINGS: Well, I was just gonna say, again, without naming names, very early, in the weeks after the invasion and occupation, I was told by a very senior administration official that we were going to fix the Middle East the same way we fixed Europe after World War II. I remember the words verbatim 'cause I almost dropped off my chair.

So it was that kind of attitude that we were running up against, of sort of a supreme arrogance—and I would say also, quite a serious misreading of what happened in Europe after World War II—that tended to dismiss a lot of our analyses as just weak-kneed, weak-minded, pessimistic, nay-saying, hand-wringing. So it was hard to penetrate that hyperconfident mindset downtown.

CHARLES FERGUSON: Okay. So you said you were told this by a very senior administration official. Who?

ROBERT HUTCHINGS: I'm not gonna say who it was.

CHARLES FERGUSON: Okay. How come?

ROBERT HUTCHINGS: I don't believe it serves any purpose to name names this way. It was this mind-set. This might have been said by any of a number of people downtown.

CHARLES FERGUSON: Well, not by very many ... One of the most remarkable features of this war is that it was planned and conceived and all of its major policy decisions were made by a remarkably small number of people. Less than ten.

ROBERT HUTCHINGS: Yeah, and that comment could have [been] made by any of those ten.

CHARLES FERGUSON: Okay, all right, let's name the ten. Who would you—

ROBERT HUTCHINGS: I really don't want to go there. I mean, this is a comment that [I made], but I'm not gonna attribute it to anybody.

CHARLES FERGUSON: Okay. So if the way that you're gonna try and get out of this is by saying that it could have been made by any of a number of people ... let's hear your list. Who is in charge of this war? And who shared this view?

ROBERT HUTCHINGS: [sighs] I don't want to go through a list. I mean, it was the president, the vice president, secretary of defense, those around all those people.

CHARLES FERGUSON: Do you include the national security adviser?

ROBERT HUTCHINGS: Sure. They were all part of the inner team. Now, not everybody had the same ideological perspective. I mean, there were different shades of that. But that was the inner team that ... produced the thinking behind the war.

CHARLES FERGUSON: And none of whom criticized this thinking.

ROBERT HUTCHINGS: I don't know. Not in my presence ... but maybe I should just say, it's actually quite telling that I was not part of that inner circle and it was ... somewhat surprising to me, when I went to Washington, having served for the entire first George H. W. Bush administration, and having worked with most of these people, to see how different it was, and how closed this circle was. ... It was a very different decision-making process. The Bush 41 [George H. W. Bush] administration was pretty transparent in the way decisions were made: pretty open, pretty participatory. The decisions came from agencies; they were worked through the process; they got up to the president for his decision. The first President Bush believed in an orderly decision-making process, believed in cabinet government, didn't tolerate decisions coming to him for decision that didn't include the views of all the relevant people. That's the way he liked to operate, and ... to my mind, it's the way a good policy machine does operate. At the end of the day, the president [has] got the responsibility to make up his own mind and overrule the whole lot of them if he believes that's the case. But the system ought to be participatory, and ought to include people who are willing to say, "This makes no sense, Mr. President; this is a bad idea." And I don't think that kind of decision-making process existed in the Bush administration, or exists now in the Bush 43 administration. I certainly didn't feel myself participating in such a decision-making process.

CHARLES FERGUSON: Okay. How much do you think the president actually knew about all this?

ROBERT HUTCHINGS: About the decision-making process?

CHARLES FERGUSON: No, not about the process, but about the decisions that were being made with regard to Iraq, and the thinking behind them.

ROBERT HUTCHINGS: Well, my thought is he knew a great deal. It's not [as if] this is being made behind his back. So I have no reason to doubt that he was quite cognizant of all these decisions. ...

There's two analytic strands buried in there. One is the lack of attention to the postwar construction. I think—leave aside the time frame; that sounds right—that there was too little attention given to that. The other is the amount of time the president personally gave to individual areas under his control, and I didn't ... I don't see a President Bush that detached. I mean, every president, to some extent—with the possible exception of Bill

Clinton … and Jimmy Carter, maybe, as the two recent examples of highly detailed presidents—most presidents operate at a pretty high level of generality, which is not to say they're not engaged on the big decisions. So I don't know how much personal time the president gave to that kind of issues. But I would be confident that he was engaged in the broad decisions.

CHARLES FERGUSON: Okay. How much time did the national security adviser give?

ROBERT HUTCHINGS: You know, I don't know … I didn't spend that much time with her or with her deputy, Steve Hadley.

CHARLES FERGUSON: Did she know what she was talking about?

ROBERT HUTCHINGS: Sure.

CHARLES FERGUSON: She did.

ROBERT HUTCHINGS: I think so, yes.

CHARLES FERGUSON: She had command of the details?

ROBERT HUTCHINGS: I think pretty good command of the details—

CHARLES FERGUSON: She read your stuff.

ROBERT HUTCHINGS: Depends on how detailed we're getting here. She read some of it.

CHARLES FERGUSON: Well, the major things. So she knew about, and had some sense of, what the issues were with regard to the dissolution of the Iraqi Army?

ROBERT HUTCHINGS: I think so.

CHARLES FERGUSON: Hm. Okay. De-Baathification?

ROBERT HUTCHINGS: I certainly think she was aware of the arguments, pro and con, on these kinds of issues.

CHARLES FERGUSON: Okay. And who else was trying to make the same kind of points that you were making about Iraq policy?

ROBERT HUTCHINGS: I think these perspectives were pretty widely shared in the State Department.

CHARLES FERGUSON: Did people speak up?

ROBERT HUTCHINGS: They certainly did within the building. How much of that got into the NSC [National Security Council] system was a little different. How much the secretary [Colin Powell] chose to raise them in NSC meetings, I'm not entirely sure.

Everyone agreed with Hutchings that the ideological and social climate of the Bush administration discouraged honesty and direct dissent. Here are Feisal al-Istrabadi and Barbara Bodine:

FEISAL AL-ISTRABADI: And those of us who were saying things that were different, we were not allowed. There was a—I was going to say a glass barrier, but there was a concrete barrier. Our voices were silenced. Those who were not on board the ideological, you know, the sweets-and-flowers agenda, nobody wanted to hear from us.

BARBARA BODINE: The problem that I think that we brought to the administration is that because we had perspective, because we had history, because we had some understanding of the dynamics, we were raising warning flags, if not red flags, on why the assumptions that the administration was operating on were probably not valid. And when you have someone who is explaining that we're not gonna be accepted as liberators, we are going to be seen as occupiers, and one of the major ways of justifying the war is that we're going to be liberators, you don't want to hear from that person. And you will find a way to ignore them, denounce them, discredit them because we were bringing inconvenient facts to the table.

Part of the problem is that that's what we're supposed to do. I mean, that's what the job of a diplomat is—or the intelligence agent, or the scholar—is to explain why some of the assumptions that you have may not be accurate, why there are some facts that you need to put into your equation.

A friend of mine who is in the CIA and recently left said that he had spent his career bringing inconvenient facts to the attention of policymakers. And prior to this administration, they didn't always agree or, you know, change policy based on what he said, but they were always open to hear it. And he said, with this administration, the difference is they don't want to hear the inconvenient fact. And if removing you, excluding you, from the meeting or the process or the structure is the way not to have to deal with your inconvenience, then that's what they'll do. They prefer an echo chamber.

Better Next Time?

A. Heather Coyne commented on the lessons of the American occupation of Iraq.

A. HEATHER COYNE: A lot of people blame the whole failure on the lack of a plan—a good plan that would have taken us in and guided our actions throughout. I disagree with that because even if you have the perfect plan, you will still fail, because you need to have the capability to implement the plan. You need those people. You need organizations that work together, people who have shared concepts of the best practices and of the procedures that you need to make this happen, an entire organization that's steeped in the lessons learned from all the other operations that we've been through, all the other interventions that have taken those lessons learned and not only read them, but taught them within the organization. So that when you go, you all know what you're doing. And you can adjust and change. You're certainly not going to have everything planned out from the beginning, but you have a sense of what you're doing and how to do it right.

We didn't have that. We didn't have anything coming close to that. And the few occasions where we did something that worked made a huge difference. You could see the impact that doing it right could have. And that continued to fuel my belief that you can do this right. It's not impossible. It's not something that you should avoid in the future. But you should avoid it unless you have the ability to carry it through all the way to the end. I have a tirade that goes on for about an hour [*laughs*] about why our organizations aren't prepared to do it, and why they're not going to be. You can't change some of these organizations to make them better at doing this.

You have to accept that you need an organization dedicated to this mission and that trains, staffs, equips, and resources its people to do it right.

Finally, a detailed, telling excerpt from my first interview with Samantha Power, conducted in early 2006:

SAMANTHA POWER: One of the elements that kind of unites the U.S. relationship to Iraq across time is a disregard or just a nonconsideration of the welfare of the Iraqi people. So whether that is in the mid-1980s, seeing Iraq as a kind of billiard ball up against Iran and not opening it up and having much regard for how Saddam was treating his own people; or whether it was his use of chemical weapons and our decision to double our aid to his regime in terms of farm credits in the wake of chemical weapons use; or in 1991, when the decision was made to respond to his act of aggression against Kuwait, you still didn't see any debate in policy circles about the Iraqis, any opening up of the system and consideration of how this moment, this window of opportunity, might be used and the leverage [that] might be used to ameliorate the conditions in which Iraqis were living. In fact, as you know, the sanctions package was put in place, which in turn continued its neglect of how Iraqis were actually living. The peace settlement [of 1991] and the decision to allow Saddam Hussein to maintain his helicopter gunships, despite the fact that they had been used to dispense chemical weapons and to attack Kurds in Northern Iraq—I mean, all of these reflect a basic neglect of the welfare of those who lived within this society. Iraq had become a proper noun. It wasn't a country with people in it.

And so, flashing forward then twelve years, when you see the same architects of those policies on the one hand talking about getting right what they had gotten wrong back in 1991, you know, finishing the job, it was tempting to say, "Well, maybe they've learned. You know, maybe they realize that the way a regime treats its own people is in fact a very good indicator of the kind of long-term ally that that regime can be to the United States. Maybe they've come to understand the link between human rights and national security. Maybe they regret calling on Kurds and Shiites to rise up and then leaving them hanging in the lurch when Saddam Hussein cracked down against those rebellions. Maybe, maybe, maybe." But there wasn't much in the public debate, and certainly there has proven to be very little internally in 2002 and 2003 that reflected any greater regard for the Iraqis. In other words, the war in Iraq in 2003 was no more about advancing the welfare of the Iraqi people than the decision to remove Saddam Hussein from Kuwait was—or then the decision to double our aid to his regime after he used chemical weapons.

There were certain individuals within the Bush administration who I think were moved by Iraqi welfare. Like Paul Wolfowitz, of course, famously has said that he was involving weapons of mass destruction and the link with terrorism as kind of technicalities as a way of broadening the public appeal of this war, when in fact what he was very interested in is a kind of humanitarian intervention. This is what he has said. But almost no one else in President Bush's inner circle was motivated, primarily anyway, by the conditions which Iraqis were living under. ...

Some liberal hawks or humanitarian interventionist of the 1990s who were in favor of the war said, "You know, you can't make decisions about whether to go to war or whether to support a war on the basis of the company you keep." [I] heard this a lot from many of my colleagues and people I respect a great deal. I would say, "But wait a minute, isn't the company you keep kind of important, because the company you keep—namely, Don Rumsfeld and Dick Cheney and others—they're gonna be the ones who decide whether to park the tank in front of the hospital or the oil ministry? It is relevant who the company is that you're keeping."

The point of the humanitarian hawks who supported the war was, "Look, even if the Bush administration isn't motivated by humanitarian or human rights concerns, so what; you've got [to] break eggs to make an omelet. At least the effect of this war will be to liberate the Iraqi people, even if that's not the motivation for the war." But I was very worried about the predictive power, because we've seen it in other interventions, this other set of motives. In other words, if it were about weapons of mass destruction, if it were about oil, if it were about finishing what George Bush's father had started, if it were about Israel ... chances are the Iraqi people would yet again, for the umpteenth time, be last on the list of things to look out for in the planning and that that would be very detrimental to their long-term welfare.

CHARLES FERGUSON: And so, if this had been done differently by different people with different views, concerns, and ideals, would you have supported a war to depose Saddam Hussein?

SAMANTHA POWER: Well, because war is so dreadful—and having lived through a much tamer war, in fact, in Bosnia in the early '90s—I really do believe the propaganda on war that it should be a last resort. It seemed to me that there were two axes on which one would decide whether or not to go to war. One was the national security axis: Did Saddam pose a clear and present and imminent danger to U.S. citizens or to the U.S. welfare? And then, two, the human rights or humanitarian axis: Did he pose a clear and present and imminent danger to large numbers of Iraqis?

And certainly in 1987 or '88, he would have been in the red zone, sirens blaring on the humanitarian and the human rights axis. And I probably at least would have made some effort to draw attention to this and to urge some kind of international response and even potentially humanitarian intervention if he was committing genocide, as he was at that time.

The conditions, of course, in 2003 were very, very different. It was, in a sense, a postgenocidal state. ...

And so ironically, this war seemed to me the wrong war, because given how unliked we were before we went to war, it seemed to me we were going to generate many more enemies than we were going to neutralize. ...

Now, if a different cast of characters had been in place: characters who hadn't abrogated five international treaties in the eighteen months that preceded the war. A different cast of characters, who could have gone to the UN and been given a different hearing, I mean, had their arguments be taken seriously in the international arena, which I don't think they really were, not just because they proved to be bad arguments, but because the disposition was very much against the Bush administration in the run-up to the war ... Had you been able to get again the sort of wind in your sails, the world at your back, the sort of exploitation of past interventions—learning about nation-building that had gone awry in the 1990s, elaborate planning for the postconflict period—then maybe your odds of success would have been higher and you would have done far less damage to U.S. national security, to regional stability, and to international law.

ACKNOWLEDGMENTS

This book and the film on which it is based have constituted an extraordinary, intense journey, albeit far less so than the journeys taken involuntarily by the millions of Americans, Britons, and, above all, Iraqis who have been directly caught up in this war. My ability to embark on that journey, much less complete it, came from many sources.

In making the film on which this book is based, I benefited from the advice, support, and work of a very special group of people: Tom Luddy, who got me started; Alex Gibney, who agreed to look over my shoulder, occasionally to his horror, and give me advice; Maryse Alberti, who taught me a few lessons and introduced me to Tony Rossi, our cinematographer; David Hocs, sound engineer; Audrey Marrs, the film's principal producer (more about her later); Jennie Amias, the first producer to sign up; Jessie Vogelson, the postproduction supervisor; the stunningly kind and fun and talented Chad Beck and Cindy Lee, the film's editors; our assistant editors and producers, especially Mary Walsh and Emily Osborne; Christopher Murphy, for his thorough, fast, and always accurate research; Robin Cutter, our superb accountant; Alan Oxman and Will Cox, online people without peer; Pete Nashel, our great composer; Tracy McKnight, music supervisor; Jackie Eckhouse and Dan Steinman, legal eagles; John Sloss, unclassifiable engine of independent film deals; the people at the Sundance Film Festival, who gave us our first platform and then our first prize; Eamonn Bowles at Magnolia, who bought the film despite a rocky start caused by a complicated situation; Donna Daniels, Lauren Schwartz, Fredell Pogodin, and Bradley Jones, the opposite of the stereotype of publicists in their dedication and warmth; George Clooney, for his generous endorsement of a film made by someone he had never met; and the New America Foundation, the Center for American Progress, and Peggy Siegel, who so ably provided screenings. I would also like to thank the many reviewers and journalists who treated the film so generously.

Then there are the people who helped me with this book, whose construction was quite complex. Brandon Wolfe-Hunnicutt provided excellent and timely research; Emily Osborne temporarily switched from film to paper to help in many ways; Nir Rosen read the entire manuscript, sending comments from an army base outside Baghdad; Audrey Marrs (again, more on her below), who became in effect the producer of the book, selecting, checking, managing, and integrating photographs, fact-checking, biographical information, chronology, structure, style, and production processes with her usual finesse and accuracy. At PublicAffairs, Peter Osnos saw the virtue of doing this in the first place, and he and Susan Weinberg gave the project the resources it needed, and Christine Marra supervised production on an extraordinarily tight schedule with both humor and skill. Richard kept my computers working despite massive instability problems caused by Windows Vista and Word.

But in addition to those who helped make the film and the book in the technical sense, there are those who contributed to its substance and who kept me alive while we were interviewing and filming in Iraq. Dozens, in fact by now hundreds, of quite busy people in both the United States and Iraq allowed me to interview them, often for many hours, so that I might learn what they already knew. They are too numerous to list here, but a few deserve special mention: George Packer, James Fallows, General Jay Garner, Colonel Paul Hughes, Captain Seth Moulton, Colonel John Agoglia, Ambassador Barbara Bodine, Professor Larry Diamond, Deputy Minister Aida Ussayran, and a number of military and intelligence officers who cannot be named. For my work in Iraq, I am particularly indebted to Nir Rosen, who drove me crazy but also educated and helped me enormously; Warzer Jaff, who was just tense enough while navigating Baghdad and keeping me alive there; Dan, the head of my personal security detail, who was cool and smart and courageous without being stupid; and my Kurdish bodyguards, most of whose names I never knew, but who did their jobs very well. (When I filmed interviews on the street in Baghdad, Dan and the guards literally formed a human circle around me.) And huge thanks to John Anderson and Ellen Knickmeyer of the *Washington Post,* John for putting me in touch with Ellen, and Ellen for letting me stay at the *Post's* house in Baghdad.

Next, I thank my friends, especially those who put up with me while this was going on: Won Hee Chang, king of the universe, engaged in her own death march, writing philosophy papers while my deadline approached and then receded; Alex Schuessler, reliable source of very smart, very quick, very dark humor and excellent driving; Camille Leblanc, who made me several wonderful dinners at critical times; Rebecca (Slugger) Reid, who displayed patience even when it went against the grain; Nouriel Roubini, who actually cooked once; Tom Luddy, friend and example; and Paul Horwich, Charlie Morris, Ed Epstein, Maria Kukuruzinska, Carl Kaysen, Susannah Kaysen, Chitra Banu, Jessica Stern, Hilary Kivitz, Alessandra de Sousa, Alessandra Bastagli, Marianne Gimon, John Castro, Patricia Barbizet, Olivier Varenne, Camille Xin, Leena Nath, Kim Malone Scott, Teymour Farman-Farmaian and his wife Beth, Cyril Kormos, Suzanne Delbanco, Josh Cohen, Julia Marozzi, Michael Ratledge, Patrick Nee, Deborah Dyer, Heidi Bradner, Florian Idenberg, Ed Gargan, and my other wonderful friends in New York, California, and around the world who rarely or never saw me during the fall of 2007. Then there are a few critical institutions: Café Chez Panisse, Café Strada, and Café Milano in Berkeley, and The Mercer and its lobby staff in New York, perfect work environments all.

I would also like to thank my lovely cousin Cori, her husband Fred, and their many children, animals, and trees; and of course my biggest supporter, my mother, Charlotte Ferguson.

I also thank my ridiculously wonderful, meticulous, patient, good-humored, long-suffering, and generally great personal assistant, Anna Moot-Levin, for keeping my life sane, or as sane as it will ever be, while I was working on this book. She's fabulous. She is way too amazing to spend the rest of her life at her current job, but I'll take every minute I can get.

And finally, there is Audrey Marrs. I have had the absurd good fortune to work with Audrey for the last five years. Audrey was first my personal assistant; then she learned film production in the blink of an eye and, over time, became the indispensable principal producer of the film; then she took several months to manage the production of this book; and if I can persuade her, she will be the producer of as many films as I can make. Audrey has a zillion wonderful qualities—intelligence, wit, diligence, kindness, toughness, style, patience, impatience, intuition, integrity—but listing them doesn't do her justice. I have no idea where I'd be without her, but it wouldn't be here, or anywhere close.

So: thank you all. I'm very blessed. I hope that you feel that this book is worthy of you; certainly its defects are mine, not yours, while its qualities owe so much to all of you.

A BRIEF HISTORY OF IRAQ
BEFORE THE WAR

Located in the Middle East on the Persian Gulf, Iraq is a country roughly twice the size of the state of Idaho. It shares its eastern border with Iran, its northern border with Turkey, its western border with Syria and Jordan, and its southern border with Saudi Arabia and Kuwait. Iraq is the site of some of the oldest known human civilizations, including Sumer, Babylon, and Assyria, the earliest of which dates back to before 4000 BC. Iraq ranks as one of the three oil-richest nations in the world, and the oil industry provides the country's main source of income.

Iraq's history as one nation dates back to shortly after World War I. Up until that point, the geographical territory of present-day Iraq had been parts of various empires, most recently part of the Ottoman Empire for several centuries. But early in 1920, with the end of World War I and the dissolution of the Ottoman Empire, former Ottoman holdings in the Middle East were split between France and Great Britain. The borders of Iraq were drawn by Great Britain, which also received control over the state. By 1921, Iraq's first national government was formed, but the British, interested in the country's location on important trade routes and in its oil resources, remained the most influential power in Iraq. This situation held until the military coup and revolution of 1958. The Iraqi monarchy was overthrown, its leaders executed, and the military leaders of the coup declared the country to be a republic. A decade of instability followed. During that time, the Baath Party, a secular political group that believed all Arab states should join into one state, first gained power in 1963, thanks to the strength of its paramilitary forces. This would only hold for nine

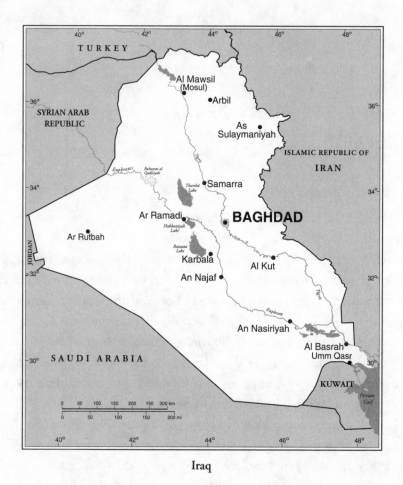

Iraq

months. But in 1968, the Baath Party regained power, this time for decades, under President Ahmed Hassan al-Bakr and his right-hand man, Saddam Hussein.

Also during the 1950s and 1960s, the United States first began to take a major role in the politics of the Middle East. During this time, in the aftermath of the World War II, the influence of the British Empire was waning and the United States was beginning to step in and fill the void. In 1953, the United States became involved with a coup against Iranian Prime Minister Mohammed Mossadegh after he nationalized the Anglo-Iranian Oil Company (now British Petroleum) in 1951. Two years later, in 1955, the United States inserted itself into Iraqi politics by becoming involved with, though not officially a signatory to, the Baghdad Pact. This diplomatic agreement established a regional security organization modeled after the North Atlantic Treaty Organization (NATO) and was called the Central Treaty Organization, or CENTO. The founding members were Iraq, Iran, Pakistan, Turkey, and the United Kingdom. But after the 1958 revolution, Iraq withdrew from the Baghdad Pact and aligned itself with the Soviet Union. From this point forward, the United States gradually displaced Britain and became the dominant Western power in the Middle East, while Iran replaced Iraq as the favored state of the region.

By the late 1960s, the Baath Party was firmly in control and Saddam Hussein began his long march to power. Once he became deputy chairman of Iraq's Revolutionary Command Council, Hussein began to remove anyone who posed a threat to him and his ambitions from positions of influence. By the middle of the 1970s, his path to leadership of Iraq was clear. Authority over many state and party functions had been concentrated in his hands, and he was the obvious successor to al-Bakr, whose health was failing. In 1979, al-Bakr resigned and was immediately succeeded by Hussein, who then carried out a series of purges and executions to eliminate from the government anyone who would question his authority.

The year 1979 also saw another event that would have an immediate and long-lasting impact on both the United States and Iraq. A revolution against the Shah of Iran led to the rise of an Islamic Republic led by Grand Ayatollah Ruhollah Khomeini. For Iraq, this meant its neighbor to the east was now an immediate threat. Iraq and Iran had repeatedly argued in the past over border issues. Now Iraq was suspicious that Iran's new Islamic government would urge Iraq's Shiite Muslim population, which formed a majority of the country but held almost no influence in the secular Sunni Muslim–dominated government, to carry out their own revolution. For the United States, the revolution meant the loss of one of its most loyal client states in the region and its replacement by one that was openly hostile to America and American interests. By late 1980, Iraq had invaded Iran, and the two countries were at war.

Although Iraq was initially successful, the war settled into a stalemate after the first few months. The United States was concerned that Iran's revolutionary, anti-American sentiment could spread throughout the Middle East and that the conflict was damaging oil shipping in the region. The

U.S. government began to throw its support behind Iraq, providing the country with military intelligence, economic aid, and weaponry. The administration of President Ronald Reagan at one point appointed Donald Rumsfeld as special envoy to the region, and in this capacity, Rumsfeld twice traveled to Baghdad to carry out negotiations with Saddam Hussein. Full diplomatic relations with Iraq, which had been severed since 1967, were reestablished in 1984. Even as reports began to surface that Iraq was using chemical weapons against Iranian troops, Iranian civilians, and even against its own civilians in its northern, Kurdish areas, U.S. support remained strongly behind Iraq and Saddam Hussein. The Iran-Iraq War ended in 1988 as the two sides finally agreed to a UN cease-fire. Neither gained any territory from the other, and casualty estimates for the war approach 900,000.

The aftermath of the war left Iraq and its leader in poor condition, politically and economically. Saddam Hussein had been unable to achieve his dream of becoming a glorified figure in the Arab world who had led his country to a great military victory and saved the rest of the Arab states by destroying the Iranian menace. On the contrary, Iraq owed large debts to several other Arab states from which it had borrowed to fund its military effort, and the country now faced the sudden unemployment of the large military it had built up during the war. One of the states Iraq owed money to was Kuwait, its small neighbor to the south. Kuwait also had a sizable coastline, at least in comparison to Iraq's. Saddam coveted the coastline for the military and trading opportunities it offered, and on Kuwait's and Iraq's common border, the two countries shared an oil field that they often quarreled over. In August 1990, in a move Saddam hoped would solve several of his problems at once, Iraq invaded Kuwait.

The international response was immediate. In less than a day, the UN Security Council called for the immediate withdrawal of Iraq's troops; the United States, United Kingdom, and France froze Iraq's assets. Within a week, the United States and the Soviet Union issued a joint declaration that suspended any arms deliveries to Iraq, and President George H. W. Bush ordered American troops to be airlifted into Saudi Arabia to defend against any further Iraqi military actions. A UN-backed coalition military force was formed, in which the United States held the major role. Key U.S.

military planners included then Secretary of Defense Dick Cheney and General Colin Powell, then chairman of the U.S. Joint Chiefs of Staff. When attempts at mediation failed, the Gulf War began with the coalition bombing campaign in January 1991. A decisive three-day-long ground campaign followed in February. The Iraqi Army was driven out of Kuwait, but the coalition stopped short of removing Saddam Hussein from power. In a 1994 interview with C-SPAN, Cheney was asked if he thought the decision to leave Saddam Hussein in power was a mistake. He said it was not, as a U.S. occupation of Baghdad would result in a "quagmire" and could destabilize the entire region.

It was expected that Saddam's failure would lead inevitably to his fall. Days after the cease-fire that ended the Gulf War, Iraq's Shiite population in the south and Kurdish population in the north rose up against the government of Saddam Hussein. The United States and its allies encouraged these uprisings, but provided no support and allowed Saddam to use his military freely against them. Faced with no opposition to its aerial superiority, Saddam's military brutally crushed the rebellions. Eventually, the United States provided humanitarian support to the Kurds in the North and established Northern and Southern "no-fly" zones from which Saddam's air force was prohibited. However, Saddam remained firmly in power.

This left the United States and the rest of the international community to deal with the question of what to do about Iraq. The United Nations had initially put sanctions in place against Iraq after the invasion, and those sanctions were clarified in April 1991. Iraq would not be permitted to import anything other than foodstuffs and materials essential to its civilian population. It would not be allowed to export oil. These sanctions would be lifted if Iraq met four demands: (1) if it identified and destroyed its weapons of mass destruction; (2) if it accepted Kuwaiti sovereignty and settled its borders with Kuwait; (3) if it released Kuwaiti prisoners as well as prisoners of other nationalities it still held after the war; and (4) if it established a Compensation Commission to pay for war damage via oil revenues. Saddam Hussein initially refused and eventually only backed down on the issue of Kuwaiti sovereignty. The sanctions remained in place, hitting the Iraqi civilian population the hardest.

With Iraq unwilling to reveal the details of its weapons of mass destruction programs, the United Nations forced Iraq to accept the presence of UNSCOM, the UN Special Commission established to inspect Iraq for evidence of nuclear, chemical, and biological weapons programs. From 1994 to 1998, UNSCOM inspectors worked in Iraq, but were often harassed and delayed by the Iraqi government. In December 1998, upset with Iraq's lack of cooperation, the United States and the United Kingdom launched a bombing campaign known as Operation Desert Fox. They targeted military-industrial facilities suspected of being used by Iraq to continue its weapons programs. The UN's weapons inspectors were evacuated prior to the bombing. They were not allowed back into the country until December 2002.

In the United States during the 1990s, various groups began to work toward the goal of seeking a change of regime in Iraq, possibly without the need for a full-scale U.S. military invasion. In 1995, the CIA funded an effort by the Iraqi National Congress (INC), an Iraqi opposition group operating in exile, to lead a resistance movement against Saddam Hussein. The INC, led by Ahmed Chalabi, set up a base of operations in the northern Kurdish region of Iraq, which enjoyed a degree of autonomy from the Iraqi government and was a UN-protected no-fly zone for the Iraqi air force. But political infighting led rival Kurdish factions to tip off Saddam's government to the group's presence. The INC was hopelessly outmatched, and hundreds were captured and executed. Those who escaped, including the INC's leader Ahmed Chalabi, returned to the United States and continued to lobby for action against Saddam.

The Project for the New American Century, a think tank of prominent conservatives in the United States, wrote an open letter to President Clinton in 1998, urging him to make the removal of Saddam Hussein from power one of the his top priorities. The writers of the letter argued that with his potential for developing weapons of mass destruction, Saddam could not be allowed to remain in power, and the full diplomatic, political, and military powers of the United States should be used to remove him. The signatories of the letter included several people who would later hold positions in the administration of President George W. Bush, including

Donald Rumsfeld, Paul Wolfowitz, Richard Armitage, John Bolton, and Zalmay Khalilzad.

Following Bush's election in 2000, Iraq became a more pressing issue in the eyes of those making U.S. foreign policy. And in the aftermath of the terrorist attacks of September 11, 2001, the possibility that Iraq could act as a source of weapons of mass destruction for terrorist groups seeking to use them against the United States created further cause for alarm. The success of the war in Afghanistan led the Bush Administration to believe that Americans could topple a hostile government and replace it with one that was more democratic and friendlier to the United States. Meanwhile, intelligence provided by sources in the Iraqi National Congress on Iraq's weapons programs seemed to support the Bush administration's worst fears about Saddam Hussein, although many in the intelligence community and the State Department suspected the information might not be accurate. And so, the United States, now without the support of the United Nations, but supported by the United Kingdom and a coalition of allied countries, invaded Iraq in March 2003.

TIMELINE OF THE WAR IN IRAQ

2000

George W. Bush is elected president, despite losing the popular vote by nearly half a million votes. His administration includes Dick Cheney as vice president, Donald Rumsfeld as secretary of defense, Paul Wolfowitz as deputy secretary of defense, Condoleezza Rice as national security adviser, Colin Powell as secretary of state, and Richard Armitage as deputy secretary of state.

2001

FEBRUARY 16: The United States and United Kingdom bomb Iraqi air defense systems throughout Iraq as part of ongoing efforts to enforce the "no-fly-zones" established after the 1991 Gulf War. The raids elicit strong condemnation from Russia and China, but the bombing continues throughout 2001 and 2002.

APRIL: Cheney Energy Task Force is convened. The activities of the task force remain classified, but according to documents acquired under the Freedom of Information Act, maps of all major oil fields in the Middle East, including Iraq, are prepared for the task force meetings.

MAY: The rail link with Turkey is reopened. Free-trade zone agreements are set up with neighboring countries. These developments indicate the extent to which the effort to isolate Iraq through UN sanctions is failing.

Saddam Hussein's son Uday Hussein assumes leadership of the Baath Party, indicating that he is being groomed as Saddam's successor, despite his record and reputation for psychotic violence, including multiple rapes and his beating to death one of his father's favorite servants in public at a dinner party.

MAY–JULY: The United States and United Kingdom try to persuade the UN to adopt "smart sanctions" in Iraq. Smart sanctions are designed to allow Iraq greater freedom to import civilian goods, while tightening up on the importation of military and "dual use" items. The efforts are blocked by Russia. These developments further indicate the extent to which the sanctions regime was failing.

AUGUST: The United States and United Kingdom bomb Iraqi air defense systems throughout Iraq.

SEPTEMBER 11: Terrorist attacks in the United States destroy the World Trade Center Towers and severely damage the Pentagon. According to Richard Clarke, an adviser on the staff of the National Security Council, Donald Rumsfeld expresses immediate interest in attacking Iraq, complaining that there "are no decent targets in Afghanistan." The next day, Undersecretary of Defense Douglas Feith raises the possibility of attacking Iraq with a senior military officer.

SEPTEMBER 20: United States identifies Osama bin Laden and al Qaeda as responsible for the 9/11 attacks.

OCTOBER 7: United States and NATO commence bombing of Afghanistan as part of "Operation Enduring Freedom."

OCTOBER: State Department begins planning the post–Saddam Hussein transition in Iraq. A group of more than two hundred Iraqis is assembled to address all aspects of the transition to democracy. A series of meetings is held, and the Future of Iraq Project is formed.

NOVEMBER: United Nations Security Council Resolution (UNSCR) 1382 renews oil-for-food program for six months. The oil-for-food program was designed to allow Iraq to export oil in exchange for essential food and medicine supplies. The resolution offers to lift sanctions in May 2002 in return for allowing UN weapons inspectors into the country. Saddam Hussein refuses.

NOVEMBER AND DECEMBER: A small group of senior U.S. military planners is instructed to begin planning for a possible invasion of Iraq.

2002

JANUARY 29: In his State of the Union address, President Bush declares that Iran, Iraq, and North Korea are part of an "axis of evil" and states that the United States "will not permit the world's most dangerous regimes to threaten us with the world's most destructive weapons."

MARCH: Arab League Summit in Beirut unanimously supports Middle East peace plan based on 1967 borders. Iraq supports the plan in an effort to win Arab support.

MARCH: Congress authorizes $5 million to the Future of Iraq Project.

JULY 23: According to the subsequently leaked "Downing Street memo," prepared by a senior British intelligence official, "Bush wanted to remove Saddam, through military action, justified by the conjunction of terrorism and WMD. But the intelligence and facts were being fixed around the policy." The memo was published by the *Sunday Times* of London in May 2005.

SEPTEMBER: The Department of Defense establishes the Office of Special Plans (OSP), as a counter to the CIA. The OSP is designed to produce intelligence on Iraqi weapons of mass destruction. The office is led by Paul Wolfowitz and Douglas Feith, and bypasses all normal intelligence analysis channels.

SEPTEMBER 8: National Security Adviser Condoleezza Rice describes the threat posed by Iraq: "The problem here is that there will always be some uncertainty about how quickly [Iraq] can acquire nuclear weapons. But we don't want the smoking gun to be a mushroom cloud."

OCTOBER 5: George Bush gives a speech in Cincinnati on the threat posed by Iraqi WMD. CIA Director George Tenet removes language suggesting that Iraq attempted to buy uranium from Niger.

NOVEMBER 8: After a U.S.-led diplomatic effort to secure UN approval for potential use of force against Iraq, UN Security Council Resolution 1441 declares Iraq in material breach of UNSCR 678, which called for Iraq to disarm.

NOVEMBER 27: UN weapons inspectors return to Iraq to look for banned weapons.

2003

JANUARY 20: President Bush signs National Security Presidential Directive Number (NSPD) 24, which gives control over postwar Iraq to the Pentagon. NSPD 24 establishes the Office of Reconstruction and Humanitarian Assistance (ORHA) as the organization to plan and manage the civilian occupation of Iraq. ORHA is to be run by the Department of Defense and will report directly to Secretary Rumsfeld.

JANUARY 28: President Bush, in his State of the Union address, declares that "the British government has learned that Saddam Hussein recently sought significant quantities of uranium from Africa."

FEBRUARY: General Eric Shinseki testifies before the Senate Armed Services Committee that "something in the order of several hundred thousand soldiers" would be required to stabilize Iraq after the fall of Saddam Hussein. Paul Wolfowitz publicly describes Shinseki's comments as "wildly off the mark," explaining that "the notion that it would take several hundred thousand American troops just seems outlandish."

FEBRUARY 6: Secretary of State Colin Powell addresses the UN Security Council to present America's case for war and to request a resolution authorizing the use of force. Pablo Picasso's *Guernica* painting is removed from the UN building for the occasion. The UNSC rejects issuing an explicit authorization for the use of force.

FEBRUARY 15–16: Major antiwar rallies, totaling several million demonstrators, are held in cities around the world.

SPRING: The United States offers Turkey substantial economic aid in return for allowing U.S. forces to enter Iraq from the north. Turkish parliament rejects the offer.

MARCH 16: When journalist Tim Russert asks Cheney if he thinks "the American people are prepared for a long, costly, and bloody battle with significant American casualties?" Cheney responds, "Well, I don't think it's likely to unfold that way, Tim, because I really do believe that we will be greeted as liberators."

MARCH 16: Retired Army General Jay Garner, the head of ORHA, and 168 other members of ORHA fly to Kuwait to await the U.S. occupation of Baghdad.

MARCH 18: UN weapons inspectors evacuate Iraq.

MARCH 19: Operation Iraqi Freedom commences with air strikes. Most Iraqi forces melt into the civilian population; the remaining Iraqi forces, including the elite Republican Guard, are quickly overwhelmed.

SPRING: Iran sends a letter to the United States offering a "grand bargain" that includes cooperation on Iranian nuclear issues, normalization of relations with the United States and Israel, and security assistance in Iraq. The United States does not respond.

MARCH 30: Journalist George Stephanopoulos questions Donald Rumsfeld about the failure to find WMD in Iraq during the first ten days of the war. Rumsfeld explains: "We know where they are. They're in the area around Tikrit and Baghdad and east, west, south, and north somewhat."

APRIL 9: U.S. Marines topple statue of Saddam Hussein in Firdos Square.

APRIL 10: Moqtada al-Sadr's militia assassinates a pro-American Shiite leader by hacking and stabbing him to death in public.

APRIL: Order in Iraq begins to break down amid widespread looting. The national archives and museum, and all government ministries, except the Ministry of Oil, are looted. Seventy-four American soldiers are killed in the month of April, indicating that an insurgency is already beginning to take shape. Rumsfeld explains in a press conference that "freedom is untidy."

APRIL 23: ORHA officials arrive in Baghdad.

MAY 6: The Bush administration publicly announces that L. Paul Bremer will succeed General Jay Garner as the supervisor of the civilian occupation of Iraq. Bremer begins work in the Pentagon.

MAY 2: Bush gives a speech aboard the USS *Lincoln,* declaring the "end of major combat operations," under a banner reading "Mission Accomplished."

MAY 9: Bremer, at the suggestion of Walt Slocombe, decides to disband the entire Iraqi military and Iraq's intelligence services. Douglas Feith gives Bremer the text of an order for the pervasive "de-Baathification" of Iraqi society.

MAY 10: L. Paul Bremer leaves the United States for Iraq, stopping in Qatar on May 11, where he is briefed by senior military officers. For the first time, Bremer reveals to military officers his and the Pentagon's plans for de-Baathification and the disbanding of the military. Military officers protest to Bremer and to the senior Pentagon civilian leadership.

MAY 12: L. Paul Bremer arrives in Baghdad as head of the Coalition Provisional Authority (CPA), which is to replace the ORHA.

MAY 16: Bremer issues CPA Order Number 1, which orders that 30,000 to 50,000 members of the Baath Party be banished for life from government employment.

MAY 23: Bremer issues CPA Order Number 2, which disbands the entire Iraqi military, including the Iraqi Army, Republican Guard, Special Republican Guard, as well as the secret police and intelligence services.

JULY 6: Former Ambassador Joe Wilson writes an op-ed in the *New York Times,* arguing that it would have been impossible for Saddam Hussein to acquire uranium from Niger.

JULY 13: ORHA efforts to form an interim government made up of Iraqi exiles are abandoned as Ambassador Bremer signs CPA Regulation 6, establishing a twenty-five-member Iraq Governing Council (IGC) that is selected by him and that reports directly to him. L. Paul Bremer has previously announced that instead of forming a provisional Iraqi government, the United States will institute a long-term occupation of Iraq, with no date set for restoring Iraqi sovereignty.

JULY 22: Saddam's sons Uday and Qusay are killed in a U.S. raid on a Mosul compound.

NOVEMBER 15: Under increasing pressure, the CPA lays out a plan for Iraq's transition to sovereignty. Ayad Allawi, a former CIA asset, is selected as the interim prime minister of Iraq.

AUGUST 19: UN Special Representative to Iraq Sergio Vieira de Mello and at least twenty-one others are killed in a bombing attack on the UN Headquarters in Baghdad. The bombing leads to the closing of the UN mission in Iraq.

DECEMBER 13: Saddam Hussein is captured in his hometown of Tikrit in Northern Iraq.

2004

MARCH 31: A convoy of Blackwater security personnel is attacked in Fallujah. The bodies of four private security contractors are dragged through the streets and hung from a bridge. The incident leads to the first siege of Fallujah, which has become the headquarters of the Sunni insurgency. The siege ends in a truce in May, but a second siege is conducted in November, when the city is attacked, largely destroyed, and occupied by U.S. forces.

APRIL 5: An arrest warrant is issued for radical Shiite cleric Moqtada al-Sadr for having ordered the April 2003 murder of rival cleric Imam Abdul Majid al-Khoei. The effort to arrest Sadr results in clashes between coalition forces and Sadr's militia, the Mahdi Army. After two months of clashes, a truce between Sadr and coalition forces is signed on June 5.

APRIL 30: Photos of prisoner abuse at Abu Ghraib are published.

MAY 8: Iraq's interim constitution, the Transitional Administrative Law (TAL), is ratified.

JUNE 28: CPA dissolves, and full governmental authority is transferred to the sovereign Iraqi Interim Government (IIG).

SEPTEMBER: U.S. war dead reach 1,000.

OCTOBER 29: The British medical journal *The Lancet* releases a study that estimates that 98,000 Iraqi civilians have died since April 2003.

2005

January 30: Iraqi national elections are held. Representative of the 275-member Iraq National Assembly are chosen. In part because Sunni political parties boycott the election, the United Iraqi Alliance, which is supported by Shia leader Grand Ayatollah Ali al-Sistani, emerges victorious, with 48 percent of the vote.

APRIL 3: Coalition forces attempt to arrest Sadr at his home in Najaf. The effort results in a ten-day battle in which the Mahdi Army suffers heavy casualties, but Sadr is allowed to escape after a new truce is signed on August 13.

APRIL 5: National Assembly appoints Ibrahim al-Jaafari as prime minister.

Aug 6: Hard-line Islamist mayor of Tehran, Mahmoud Ahmadinejad, is elected president of Iran. Many attribute the move to more hard-line leadership in Tehran to the war in Iraq.

OCTOBER: U.S. war dead reaches 2,000.

OCTOBER 15: Iraqi constitution is ratified by the National Assembly.

DECEMBER 15: General election for a permanent 275-member Iraqi National Assembly.

2006

JANUARY 7: Jill Carroll, an American journalist with the *Christian Science Monitor,* is kidnapped in Baghdad.

FEBRUARY 22: The Al-Askari Mosque in Samarra, one of the holiest sites in Shia Islam, is bombed. The bombing causes a dramatic escalation of violence, with Shiites for the first time engaging in large-scale sectarian killings of Sunnis.

MARCH 15: The Iraq Study Group (ISG) is formed to investigate deteriorating conditions in Iraq and analyze U.S. policy options.

MARCH 30: Jill Carroll is released after eighty-two days in captivity. Before she is released, she is forced to make a video criticizing American policy.

MAY 20: Nouri al-Maliki replaces al-Jaafari as prime minister of Iraq.

OCTOBER 11: The British medical journal *The Lancet* releases a study that estimates that 655,000 Iraqi civilians have died since 2003.

NOVEMBER 7: Republicans lose their majority in the U.S. House and Senate congressional elections. Donald Rumsfeld steps down as secretary of defense the following day and is replaced by Robert Gates, a moderate of the "realist" school who had been privately critical of the war.

NOVEMBER 15: Before Senate Armed Services Committee, CENTCOM Commander John Abizaid testifies that he opposes sending more American forces to Iraq.

DECEMBER 6: ISG issues its report, which concludes that "the situation in Iraq is grave and deteriorating" and "U.S. forces seem to be caught in a mission that has no foreseeable end." The report recommends opening diplomatic negotiations with Iran and Syria.

DECEMBER 29: Saddam hanged for his role in the deaths of 148 Shiites in 1982.

2007

JANUARY: U.S. war dead reach 3,000.

JANUARY 10: President Bush announces the deployment of additional forces to Iraq: the "surge."

JANUARY 26: General David Petraeus is nominated to implement the surge strategy.

JUNE: U.S. war dead reaches 3,500.

SEPTEMBER 10–11: General Petraeus and Ambassador Ryan Crocker testify before Congress regarding the success of the surge strategy in Iraq. The two men give a generally upbeat assessment of the situation in Iraq.

NOVEMBER 6: Six American soldiers are killed in Iraq, bringing the number of U.S. troop deaths to 852 for the year. This figure makes 2007 the deadliest year of the war for U.S. troops. Four days later, the U.S. military announces that 6 U.S. soldiers in Afghanistan are killed, bringing the number of American killed in Afghanistan in 2007 to 101. This figure makes 2007 the deadliest year of the war for U.S. troops in Afghanistan as well.

NOVEMBER AND DECEMBER: New statistics indicate a sharp decline in violence in Iraq, particularly in Baghdad, although analysts doubt that the decline is sustainable.

DECEMBER 3: The National Intelligence Council releases a National Intelligence Estimate that reverses earlier estimates and concludes that, in 2003, Iran abandoned its effort to develop nuclear warheads. The new estimate notes, however, that Iran continues to develop uranium enrichment capacity, a heavy-water reactor capable of producing plutonium, and ballistic missiles, suggesting that Iran is still trying to develop a nuclear weapons capability, if not a weapon itself.

CONTRIBUTORS AND KEY ACTORS

GHAITH ABDUL-AHAD

Ghaith Abdul-Ahad is an Iraqi journalist currently living in Beirut. Born and raised in Baghdad, he studied architecture. He was a practicing architect when, in 1998, he received notice that he would be drafted into the Iraqi military. To avoid military service, he went underground. In 2000, he began to teach himself English, and after the regime fell, he began working as a photographer and journalist. He has covered the Iraq occupation for the *Guardian,* the *Washington Post,* and other publications since 2003.

COLONEL JOHN AGOGLIA

Colonel Agoglia is the Director of the U.S. Army Peace Keeping and Stability Operations Institute (PKSOI) at the U.S. Army War College in Carlisle, Pennsylvania. The institute functions as the army's authority on strategic and operational peacekeeping and stability initiatives, focusing on issues concerning national decision-making and the deployment of force commanders and their staffs.

Prior to joining PKSOI, Agoglia served at the U.S. Central Command (CENTCOM), which he joined just four weeks before the September 11, 2001, attacks. During his three years with CENTCOM, Agoglia helped develop the organization's plans for Afghanistan and the Global War on Terror. He was also part of the initial planning group that initiated the campaign plan for Iraq beginning in late 2001. In May 2003, Agoglia served as CENTCOM liaison officer to L. Paul Bremer, U.S. Civil Ambassador in Iraq. In this capacity, Agoglia worked on priority matters, including the planning efforts between the Coalition Provisional Authority

(CPA) and the military, the transfer of police training from the CPA to the Coalition Joint Task Force 7, and the initial engagement strategy for senior military commanders with the newly appointed interim Iraqi government leaders (June 2004).

Colonel Agoglia is a 1980 graduate of the U.S. Military Academy. He earned a Masters in Military Arts and Sciences from the U.S. Army Command and General Staff College.

CHRIS ALLBRITTON

Beginning in the fall of 2002, American journalist Chris Allbritton began publishing and editing his own online publication, *Back to Iraq*, on the war with Iraq. He entered the country on the heels of the U.S. invasion in April 2003 and continued reporting from inside the country. In May 2004, *Time* magazine brought him on as its regional correspondent. He continued covering events on the ground in Iraq until he left for Beirut to cover the conflict between Lebanon and Israel in the summer of 2006. Allbritton has written for the Associated Press, the *New York Daily News*, the *Boston Globe*, *New York* magazine, and *Esquire*. He has a BA in journalism from the University of Arkansas at Little Rock and an MS from the Columbia University Graduate School of Journalism.

HADI AL-AMIRI

During the reign of Saddam Hussein, Hadi al-Amiri was commander of the Badr Corps, also known as the Badr Brigade and later the Badr Organization, the military wing of the Supreme Council for Islamic Revolution in Iraq (SCIRI). The SCIRI is a Shiite religious party formed in 1982 with close links to Iran and the Iranian Islamic Revolutionary Guards, which played a role in training the Badr Corps. In September 2003, the Badr Corps announced that the militia would become a civilian organization and renamed the Badr Organization for Reconstruction and Development, though it continued to call for its forces to play a role in policing and security matters in Shiite areas.

Al-Amiri is a member of the Iraqi parliament under the United Iraqi Alliance list, which mainly represents religious Shia parties, and was one of the first Shia politicians to call for regional federation in the south. In May

2007, the SCIRI was renamed the Supreme Iraqi Islamic Council (SIIC). The party and its militia continue to vie for control over southern cities such as Basra.

RICHARD ARMITAGE

From 2001 to 2005, Richard Armitage served as Deputy Secretary of State. Taking office in March 2001, Armitage was part of the George W. Bush administration's decision-making team during the September 11, 2001, terrorist attacks; "Operation Enduring Freedom" in Afghanistan; and the 2003 invasion of Iraq. During the 2000 presidential election, Armitage was a member of a group of foreign policy advisers to Bush known as the "Vulcans." The group would go on to hold government positions after Bush won the election, including current Secretary of State Condoleezza Rice, current National Security Adviser Stephen Hadley, and former Deputy Secretary of Defense Paul Wolfowitz.

Armitage graduated from the U.S. Naval Academy in 1967. After graduation, he served in Vietnam as an adviser to river forces, and was rumored to have relationships with the CIA. In 1973, he left active service and served with the U.S. Defense Attaché Office in Saigon until the city's fall, when he oversaw the removal of naval assets and personnel from the country. After Vietnam, Armitage served as a Pentagon consultant in Tehran, Iran, until 1976. Upon returning to the United States, he spent time in the private sector before serving on the staff of U.S. Senator Robert Dole and the Interim Foreign Policy Advisory Board of President-Elect Ronald Reagan. During Reagan's presidency, Armitage returned to the Pentagon, first as Deputy Assistant Secretary of Defense for East Asia and Pacific Affairs and then as Assistant Secretary of Defense for International Security Affairs. During his time in the second post, then National Security Advisor Colin Powell came under investigation for his knowledge of the Iran-Contra affair. The investigation concluded that Armitage, along with then Secretary of Defense Caspar Weinberger and Powell, had more detailed information about the affair than he had testified to.

During the presidency of George H. W. Bush, Armitage continued to hold positions in government, including Presidential Special Negotiator for the Philippines Military Base Agreement, Special Mediator for Water in the Middle East, and Coordinator for Emergency Humanitarian Assistance to the new independent states of the former Soviet Union. During the 1991 Gulf War with Iraq, Armitage was named Special Emissary to King Hussein of Jordan. From 1993 until he joined the George W. Bush campaign as an adviser in 1999, he was President of Armitage Associates L.C., a consulting firm. In November 2004, shortly after George W. Bush was reelected, Armitage announced his resignation as Deputy Secretary of State after the resignation of Secretary of State Colin Powell. Armitage departed upon the appointment of his successor in February 2005. He is currently President of the consulting firm Armitage International, L.C., and serves on the boards of directors of international petroleum company ConocoPhillips and government information technology supplier Man-Tech International Corporation.

James Bamford

James Bamford is an award-winning journalist and author of several books. In his most recent book, *A Pretext for War: 9/11, Iraq, and the Abuse of America's Intelligence Agencies*, he argues that the U.S. intelligence agencies had become too slow and institutionalized prior to the September 11, 2001, terrorist attacks and then too politicized leading up to the U.S. invasion of Iraq. Bamford is also the author of two investigations of the National Security Agency: *The Puzzle Palace* and *Body of Secrets*. He has written articles for several publications, including the *New York Times*, the *Washington Post*, the *Los Angeles Times*, *Rolling Stone*, and *The Atlantic Monthly*. He was a Washington investigative producer for ABC's *World News Tonight* from 1989 until 1998. Bamford graduated from Suffolk University, served in the navy during Vietnam, and then returned to attend Suffolk University Law School on the G.I. Bill.

Amazia Baram

Amazia Baram is a professor of Middle East history at the University of Haifa, Israel, specializing in the study of Iraq, and is well regarded for his knowledge, despite the fact that he has never visited the country. Prior to the 2003 invasion, he was an informal adviser to senior officials in the

Bush administration. He is the author of three books on Iraq's history: *Culture, History and Ideology in the Formation of Ba'athist Iraq: 1968–1989; Iraq's Road to War;* and *Building Toward Crisis: Saddam Husayn's Strategy for Survival.* Professor Baram is the Director of the Center for Persian Gulf Studies at the University of Haifa and has been a fellow of the Woodrow Wilson International Center for Scholars at the Smithsonian.

JAMAL BENOMAR

Jamal Benomar went to Iraq as principal political adviser to the UN Special Representative to Iraq, Sergio Vieira de Mello. Benomar was in New York on August 19, 2003, when Vieira de Mello and at least twenty-one others were killed in a bombing attack on the UN Headquarters in Baghdad. He remained involved in UN activities in Iraq until late 2004. Benomar is currently a diplomat with the United Nations, involved in peacebuilding and postconflict issues. He has served as Director of the Carter Center of Emory University and has a Ph.D. from the University of London and graduate degrees from the University of Rabat and the University of Paris.

LINDA BILMES

Linda Bilmes is a lecturer at the Kennedy School of Government at Harvard University, specializing in budgeting and public finance. With Joseph E. Stiglitz of Columbia University, she is the author of *The Three Trillion Dollar War,* which analyzes the economic effects of the Iraq war. Earlier, Bilmes and Stiglitz cowrote one of the first papers on the economic costs of the war, measuring both the immediate expenditures on the war and the long-term costs caused by increased oil prices, lost lives, medical treatment, losses to the workforce, and other factors. Bilmes served in the U.S. Department of Commerce from 1997 to 2001, holding the posts of Deputy Assistant Secretary of Commerce, Chief Financial Officer, and Assistant Secretary for Management and Budget. She has written for the *New York Times,* the *Financial Times,* the *Washington Post,* and *The Atlantic Monthly.* Bilmes has a BA in government from Harvard University and an MBA from the Harvard Business School.

BARBARA BODINE

Ambassador Barbara Bodine was placed in charge of the city of Baghdad by the Office for Reconstruction and Humanitarian Assistance (ORHA). She left the position shortly after the invasion on May 11, 2003, not long after L. Paul Bremer was brought in to replace Retired General Jay Garner as head of ORHA.

Bodine is a career member of the Senior Foreign Service. She served as U.S. Ambassador to Yemen at the time of the USS *Cole* bombing in 2000. While Deputy Chief of Mission to Kuwait, she volunteered to be held hostage in the U.S. Embassy during Iraq's invasion in 1990, and remained in the embassy for five months until the remaining U.S. citizens could be evacuated. In the course of her career, she has also served in Hong Kong, Bangkok, and several postings in Southwest Asia and the Arabian Peninsula. Bodine worked on the staffs of Secretaries of State Henry Kissinger and Cyrus Vance and Senator Robert Dole. She has a BA in political science and Asian studies from the University of California, Santa Barbara and an MA from the Fletcher School of Law and Diplomacy in Massachusetts.

L. PAUL BREMER

In May 2003, L. Paul Bremer flew to Iraq to act as head of the Coalition Provisional Authority (CPA), which replaced the Office of Reconstruction and Humanitarian Assistance (ORHA), a group led by Jay Garner. As administrator of the U.S. occupation of Iraq, Bremer authored a series of controversial decisions, including the decisions to disband the Iraqi military and intelligence services, to initiate a widespread de-Baathification program, and to institute a formal occupation of Iraq. Bremer left Iraq in June 2004, when the CPA formally transferred sovereignty to the Iraqi Interim Government. Bremer recorded his experiences in his book *My Year in Iraq: The Struggle to Build a Future of Hope* (2006), and defended his decision to disband the Iraqi Army in a September 2007 *New York Times* op-ed titled, "How I Didn't Dismantle Iraq's Army."

Before serving as the head of the CPA, Bremer was a career diplomat in the State Department. He served in Afghanistan, Malawi, Norway, and as a special adviser to Henry Kissinger. During the Reagan administration,

Bremer served as the Executive Secretary of the Department of State under Alexander Haig and as Ambassador-at-Large for Counterterrorism. Bremer retired from the Foreign Service in 1989 and became Managing Director at Kissinger and Associates, a worldwide consulting firm founded by Henry Kissinger.

GERALD BURKE

Gerald Burke worked for the Coalition Provisional Authority (CPA) as an adviser to Iraq's Ministry of the Interior, which supervises Iraq's national police. Burke was part of a team that conducted an initial assessment of the requirements for organizing and training a new Iraqi police force, established and managed the first postwar police training program, and then became senior adviser to the chief of police of Baghdad. He left Iraq in the spring of 2005. Before going to Iraq, Burke had served almost twenty-five years in the Massachusetts State Police, retiring with the rank of major. In 1994, he worked for the U.S. Department of Justice on an assignment in Haiti. For eight years, he was Director of the New England Institute of Law Enforcement Management at Babson College.

ASHTON CARTER

Ashton Carter is the Ford Foundation Professor of Science and International Affairs at the John F. Kennedy School of Government at Harvard University. Prior to the 2003 invasion of Iraq, he had argued in favor of the invasion on the grounds that Iraq possessed weapons of mass destruction (WMD). During the Clinton administration, he worked for the State Department as Senior Advisor to the North Korea Policy Review and for the Department of Defense as Assistant Secretary for International Security Policy. Carter is a coauthor of *Preventive Defense: A New Security Strategy for America,* and *Making the Nation Safer: The Role of Science and Technology in Countering Terrorism.* He has written op-eds on the proliferation of weapons of mass destruction and counterterrorism for the *Washington Post, New York Times, Wall Street Journal, Financial Times*, and *Boston Globe.* He has bachelor's degrees in medieval history and in physics from Yale University and a Ph.D. in theoretical physics from Oxford University, which he attended as a Rhodes scholar.

JUAN COLE

Juan Cole is Richard P. Mitchell Distinguished University Professor of History at the University of Michigan. He has written extensively about Egypt, Iran, Iraq, and South Asia. Cole is the current President of the Global Americana Institute and is a former President of the Middle East Studies Association. He maintains "Informed Comment," a widely read Web log of current events in Iraq and, more generally, the Middle East, and has a regular column at Salon.com. He is the author, or coauthor, of several books, including *Napoleon's Egypt: Invading the Middle East* (2007); *Sacred Space and Holy War: The Politics, Culture and History of Shi'ite Islam* (2002); and *Shi'ism and Social Protest* (1986).

Cole has lived in a number of places in the Muslim world, including Iraq and Lebanon, for extended periods and speaks Arabic, Persian, and Urdu. He holds a BA in history and literature of religions from Northwestern University, an MA in Arabic studies and history from the American University in Cairo, and a Ph.D. in Islamic studies from University of California, Los Angeles.

ANTHONY CORDESMAN

Anthony Cordesman holds the Arleigh A. Burke Chair in Strategy at the Center for Strategic and International Studies (CSIS), a bipartisan, nonprofit organization headquartered in Washington, D.C. He is also a national security analyst for ABC News. His analysis has been featured prominently during the Gulf War, Operation Desert Fox, the conflict in Kosovo, the fighting in Afghanistan, and the Iraq war. During his time at CSIS, he has directed the Gulf Net Assessment Project and the Gulf in Transition Study, and he has been the principal investigator for the CSIS Homeland Defense Project. He has led studies on national missile defense, asymmetric warfare and weapons of mass destruction, and critical infrastructure protection. He has visited and worked in Iraq for the U.S. government multiple times over the last several decades.

Cordesman is the author of more than fifty books, including a four-volume series on the lessons of modern war. He has been awarded the Department of Defense Distinguished Service medal. He is a former adjunct professor of national security studies at Georgetown University, and has twice been a fellow at the Woodrow Wilson International Center for Scholars in Washington, D.C.

A. HEATHER COYNE

A. Heather Coyne was recently the chief of party for U.S. Institute of Peace's (USIP) activities in Iraq. The USIP is an independent institution funded by the U.S. Congress with the mission of helping prevent and resolve violent international conflicts, encourage democratic transformations and stability in postwar nations, and increase the tools and information available to others working toward peace. Coyne previously served fifteen months in Iraq as a U.S. Army Reserve civil affairs officer, assigned to the Coalition Provisional Authority as the civil society officer for the Baghdad region. Her role was to promote the establishment and growth of indigenous Iraqi nongovernmental organizations, professional societies, and local citizens' committees to support the reestablishment of civil society. She is currently a senior program officer in the Center for Mediation and Conflict Resolution.

Before deploying, Coyne spent sixteen months studying Arabic at the Defense Language Institute in Monterey, California. She worked for four years at the White House Office of Management and Budget (OMB), in the National Security Division, where she managed OMB's review of federal programs to combat terrorism, defend against weapons of mass destruction, and protect critical infrastructure. In coordination with the National Security Council, she helped develop an interagency review process for these programs.

Coyne earned an MA in international relations and international economics from the School of Advanced International Studies at Johns Hopkins University.

OMAR AL-DAMLUJI

Omar al-Damluji earned his bachelor's, master's, and doctoral degrees in engineering from Baghdad University, where he eventually became a civil engineering professor. He also taught at the University of Technology's Civil Engineering Department and supervised about thirty graduate and doctorial students studying civil engineering in the Universities of Baghdad, Technology, Nahrain and Kufa. He wrote two books in soil mechanics and was a visiting professor to Hanover University and City University in London. In 2000, Professor al-Damluji became the head of the Civil Engineering Department at Baghdad University. He is a registered engineer in the Iraqi Engineers Society and American Engineers Society and is a member of UNESCO/Iraqi Higher Education Committee. In June 2004, al-Damluji was appointed Interim Minister of Housing and Reconstruction under the Iraqi interim government after the restoration of Iraqi sovereignty.

MARK DANNER

Mark Danner, longtime staff writer at *The New Yorker*, frequent contributor to *The New York Review of Books*, and professor at the University of California, Berkeley, and Bard College, writes about foreign affairs and American politics, including Latin America, Haiti, the Balkans and the Middle East. He speaks and debates widely about America's role in the world.

LARRY DIAMOND

Larry Diamond is a senior fellow at the Hoover Institution, Stanford University, and founding coeditor of the *Journal of Democracy*. He is also codirector of the International Forum for Democratic Studies of the National Endowment for Democracy. At Stanford University, he is professor by courtesy of political science and sociology and coordinates the democracy program of the new Center on Democracy, Development, and the Rule of Law. During 2002 and 2003, he served as a consultant to the U.S. Agency for International Development (USAID) and was a contributing author of its report, "Foreign Aid in the National Interest." Currently, he serves as a member of USAID's Advisory Committee on Voluntary Foreign Aid. He has also advised and lectured to the World Bank, the United Nations, the State Department, and other governmental and nongovernmental agencies dealing with governance and development.

During the first three months of 2004, Diamond served as a senior adviser on governance to the Coalition Provisional Authority in Baghdad. He is now lecturing and writing about the challenges of postconflict statebuilding in Iraq. His research and policy analysis are focused on the relationship between democracy, governance, and development in poor countries, particularly in Africa. He is the author of several books, including *Squandered Victory: The American Occupation and the Bungled Effort to Bring Democracy to Iraq.*

PAUL EATON

Major General Paul Eaton (Ret.) was placed in charge of rebuilding the Iraqi armed forces from 2003 to 2004. Eaton left his previous assignment as Commanding General of the U.S. Army Infantry School at Fort Benning, Georgia, to train and organize the New Iraqi Army and Iraqi security forces after the Coalition Provisional Authority disbanded the Iraqi Army.

Since leaving Iraq, Eaton retired from the armed forces and has been critical of Secretary of Defense Donald Rumsfeld's handling of the war in Iraq. In March 2006, he wrote an op-ed for the *New York Times.* There, he called on President Bush to replace Rumsfeld. Eaton is a 1972 graduate of the U.S. Military Academy at West Point.

ANNA EDWARD

Anna Edward is a member of both the Iraqi Women's Association and the Coordinating Committee for the Iraqi Women's Network, two Iraq-based nongovernmental organizations working to promote women's rights and civil society in Iraq. Edward graduated with law degree from Baghdad University in 1967. In the 1960s, she was a member of the Iraqi Communist Party, but was forced to leave Iraq after the Baath Party came to power. In 1972, she traveled to East Berlin to serve as the Secretariat of the Women's International Democratic Federation. She remained in East Berlin until 1982, at which point she moved to Damascus. In 1985, she joined the *Peshmerga* (Kurdish guerrilla army) in the mountains of Iraqi Kurdistan. After the 1988 cease-fire that ended the Iran-Iraq War, she returned to Damascus and then to Iraqi Kurdistan in 1996, where she continued to advocate for women's rights. After the fall of Saddam Hussein in 2003, Edward moved to Baghdad to continue her activism.

ALI FADHIL

Ali Fadhil was born in Baghdad and attended medical school in Iraq. He continued to practice medicine in Iraq after the war, until he began to work as a translator for reporters with the *Financial Times*. Fadhil was soon doing stories on his own for the *Guardian* and National Public Radio. He was chosen as the U.K. Foreign Press Association's Young Journalist of the Year in 2005 for work he did covering events in Fallujah. In January 2006, Ali Fadhil left Iraq to study journalism at New York University.

JAMES FALLOWS

Currently a national correspondent for the *Atlantic Monthly*, James Fallows has worked for the magazine for over twenty-five years. Fallows has written several books, his most recent being *Blind into Baghdad: America's War in Iraq*, a compilation of his National Magazine Award–winning articles on the Iraq war.

Fallows has also been editor of *U.S. News & World Report*, a software designer for Microsoft, and Chairman of the New America Foundation. He won an American Book Award for his book, *National Defense*. James Fallows holds an undergraduate degree in history and literature from Harvard University, was awarded a Rhodes scholarship, and holds a graduate degree in economics from Oxford University.

OMAR FEKEIKI

Omar Fekeiki was born in Baghdad in 1978. He was raised in Iraq, leaving the country only for a brief visit to Jordan in 1992. He attended a private university, earning a BA in English. In the days following the U.S. invasion in 2003, he began helping as a translator to reporters. Fekeiki was quickly hired as office manager of the Baghdad bureau of the *Washington Post*. He is completing an MA in journalism at the University of California, Berkeley.

SAM GARDINER

Sam Gardiner is a retired U.S. Air Force colonel who taught strategy and military operations at the National War College, the Air War College, and the Naval War College.

Before the 2003 invasion, Gardiner conducted war games to determine the effect of bombing on the civilian infrastructure in Iraq. He briefed the Joint Chiefs of Staff, the U.S. Agency for International Development, and the National Security Council on likely outcomes when the air war began. During the invasion, he worked as a military analyst for *The NewsHour with Jim Lehrer*, BBC radio and television, and National Public Radio. Since the war in 2003, Gardiner has written numerous articles arguing that the Bush administration used disinformation and psychological warfare against the American public in order to generate support for the war.

MARC GARLASCO

In 2003, Marc Garlasco served as a senior intelligence analyst at the Pentagon prior to the war in Iraq and as chief of high-value targeting during the war. Later in 2003, he left to become a senior military analyst for Human Rights Watch, where he is the resident expert on battle damage assessment, military operations, and interrogations. Garlasco led a Human Rights Watch mission in 2003 to assess the conduct of the war in Iraq. During his seven years at the Pentagon, Garlasco was on the Battle Damage Assessment team for Operation Desert Fox in Iraq in 1998 and led the Battle Damage Assessment team in Kosovo in 1999. He has a BA in government from St. John's University and an MA in International Relations from the Elliot School of International Affairs at George Washington University.

JAY GARNER

From January until May 2003, Jay Garner served as Director of the Organization of Reconstruction and Humanitarian Assistance (ORHA) for Iraq. He was replaced by L. Paul Bremer less than a month after arriving in Iraq.

Garner began his military career with the Florida Army National Guard. He enlisted in the U.S. Marines in 1962 and went on to serve two tours in Vietnam. After transferring to the army, Garner had a military career that lasted almost four decades and saw him serve as Commanding General of the U.S. Army Space and Strategic Defense Command, Assistant Deputy Chief of Staff for Force Development, Deputy Commanding General of V Corps in Frankfurt, Germany, and Deputy Commanding General of U.S. Army Air Defense School. In 1997, Garner retired with the rank of lieutenant general and became President of SY Coleman, Inc., a provider of space and missile defense technologies to the military. During the 1991

Gulf War, Garner was placed in charge of humanitarian efforts for the Kurdish zones of Northern Iraq.

ANN GILDROY

Captain Ann Gildroy joined the U.S. Marines in August 2001 and first arrived in Iraq in August 2004. She worked on a variety of missions, including training, equipping, and helping build up an infrastructure for the Iraqi Army. Before entering the military, Gildroy studied international security and diplomacy at the School of Foreign Service at Georgetown University.

HUGO GONZALES

Hugo Gonzales was a field artillery gunner with the U.S. Army. Gonzales first joined the Puerto Rico National Guard in 1995 and then switched to active duty in February 2003. He first arrived in Iraq in May 2004. While in Iraq, he participated in infantry raids, patrols, and convoy escorts. In June 2004, he was seriously injured when, while on a combat patrol, the vehicle he was riding in was hit by an improvised explosive device (IED). He spent two years in Walter Reed Army Medical Center before being discharged with a permanent disability pension.

Gonzales has a BA in advertising from Sacred Heart University in Puerto Rico.

JOOST HILTERMANN

Joost Hiltermann is the Middle East Project Director for the International Crisis Group, an independent, nonprofit, nongovernmental organization that produces reports and recommendations designed to prevent or reduce the escalation of violent conflict. Hiltermann leads a team based in Amman and Beirut that focuses on Iraq, Jordan, and the Israeli-Palestinian conflict, as well as larger Middle East issues. Before joining the International Crisis Group, he was Executive Director of the Arms Division of Human Rights Watch from 1994 to 2002 and the Director of Human Rights Watch's Iraq Documents Project from 1992 to 1994. He is the author of *A Poisonous Affair: America, Iraq and the Gassing of Halabja,* and has published articles in the *New York Times, Boston Globe,* and *Christian*

Science Monitor. He has a Ph.D. in sociology from the University of California, Santa Cruz, and is fluent in English, Arabic, and Dutch.

CHRISTOPHER HITCHENS

Christopher Hitchens writes for *Slate* and the *Daily Mirror* and is a contributing editor to *The Atlantic Monthly* and *Vanity Fair.* He is the author of many books on political and cultural subjects and contributes to numerous publications, including *Foreign Policy, The London Review of Books, Harper's,* the *Los Angeles Times Book Review, New Left Review, Newsweek International, The New York Review of Books, The New York Times Book Review,* the *Wall Street Journal,* the *Washington Post,* and the *Weekly Standard.*

Hitchens has been a visiting professor at the University of California, Berkeley, the University of Pittsburgh, and the New School for Social Research. He was born in Portsmouth, England, and was educated at the Leys School, Cambridge, and Balliol College, Oxford, where he studied philosophy, politics, and economics.

PAUL HUGHES

During the Iraq war, Colonel Paul Hughes was assigned to the Office of Reconstruction and Humanitarian Assistance (ORHA) and later the Coalition Provisional Authority (CPA) as Director of the Strategic Policy Office. In April and May 2003, Colonel Hughes was responsible for U.S. efforts to recall the Iraqi Army prior to the CPA's decision to disband it entirely.

Before going to Iraq, Hughes had been a senior military fellow at the Institute for National Strategic Studies at the National Defense University. His work there focused on weapons of mass destruction and peacekeeping operations. He is a graduate of the Army Command and General Staff College, the School of Advanced Military Studies, and the Army War College, with two master's degrees in military arts and sciences, concentrating in development and training in theater operations. He received his undergraduate degree in sociology from the University of Colorado. He led the Iraq Study Group's Military and Security Expert Working Group and is currently the Senior Program Officer, Center for Post-Conflict Peace and Stability Operations at the U.S. Institute of Peace.

Robert Hutchings

From 2003 to 2005, Robert Hutchings was Chairman of the National Intelligence Council (NIC), the U.S. intelligence community's center for middle-term and long-term strategic thinking. During Hutchings' time, the NIC was responsible for several intelligence estimates on the postwar situation in Iraq. Before becoming Chairman of the NIC, Hutchings had been Director of its Analytic Group and its Deputy National Intelligence Officer for Europe. During the presidency of George H. W. Bush, Hutchings was Director for European Affairs with the National Security Council and then Special Adviser to the Secretary of State. He has also held positions at Johns Hopkins University School of Advanced International Studies, Georgetown University's School of Foreign Service, and the Woodrow Wilson School of Public and International Affairs.

Hutchings graduated from the U.S. Naval Academy and received an MA from the College of William and Mary and a Ph.D. from the University of Virginia.

Feisel al-Istrabadi

Feisel al-Istrabadi was Iraq's Deputy Ambassador and then its Ambassador to the United Nations. He was born in the United States to Iraqi parents in exile, and then returned to Iraq during his childhood. After Baathists took power in 1968, his family fled again. He would spend the next thirty-three years in exile. During the 1990s, he became involved with the Iraqi opposition movement, writing articles for various publications in opposition to the Iraqi regime. He served as legal adviser to Adnan Pachachi during the meetings that followed the U.S. invasion of Iraq in March 2003. He began serving Iraq at the UN in August 2004 and resigned in 2007.

Warzer Jaff

Warzer Jaff is a journalist and photographer. He has reported for the *New York Times* from Iraqi Kurdistan on issues related to Kurdish autonomy and Iraq-Turkey relations. He is a former Kurdish intelligence officer who was arrested and tortured by Iraq's secret police under Saddam's regime. In March and April 2006, he served as Charles Ferguson's personal bodyguard and fixer in Iraq.

Ray Jennings

Ray Jennings is the Chief of Party in Iraq for the U.S. Institute of Peace, an independent institution funded by the U.S. Congress with the mission of helping prevent and resolve violent international conflicts, encourage democratic transformations and stability in postwar nations, and increase the tools and information available to others working toward peace.

Jennings has worked for the World Bank and the Cooperative Housing Foundation in Afghanistan. He has held positions with the U.S. Agency for International Development's Office of Transition Initiatives in Bosnia-Herzegovina, Serbia and Montenegro, Kosovo, Macedonia, Peru, and Sierra Leone. He has taught at Georgetown University's School of Foreign Service and at the Naval Post-Graduate School in Monterey, California, specializing in peace building.

He holds degrees from St. Michael's College and Idaho State University.

Bernard Kerik

Bernard Kerik served as Police Commissioner of New York City from 2000 to 2001 after having served as New York's Commissioner of Prisons. He rose to national prominence due to his role in responding to the September 11 attacks on the World Trade Center. In May 2003, he went to Iraq to serve as the Interim Minister of Interior and a senior policy adviser to Ambassador L. Paul Bremer. He left Iraq four months into his six-month term, returning to the United States to work as a security consultant. In December 2004, he was nominated for Secretary of Homeland Security, but withdrew his name a week later in the face of mounting charges of corruption and a variety of other charges of misconduct. He later pled guilty to two misdemeanors and, in late 2007, was indicted on multiple felony charges, including income tax evasion.

Kerik did not graduate from high school, but he received a General Equivalency Diploma while serving in the U.S. Army as military police officer and paratrooper between 1975 and 1978. While New York City Police Commissioner, he received a BS in public administration from Empire State College.

LAITH KUBBA

Laith Kubba is the Director for the Middle East and North Africa at the National Endowment of Democracy. Throughout 2005, he was a senior adviser to the Iraqi Prime Minister Ibrahim al-Jaafari and a spokesman for the Iraqi government. During the period 1993 to 1998, he was the Director of International Relations at the Al Khoei Foundation in London. Kubba has had extensive involvement in Iraqi politics. In 1992, he coordinated the Iraqi National Congress meeting in Vienna, was its spokesman, and served at its first executive committee. He also served on the boards of regional institutions, including the Iraq Foundation and the Arab Organization for Human Rights. He received a BA from the University of Baghdad, 1976, and a Ph.D. from the University of Wales in the United Kingdom.

ELLEN LAIPSON

Ellen Laipson is the President and CEO of the Henry L. Stimson Center, a nonprofit, nonpartisan institution devoted to enhancing international peace and security through analysis and outreach. Laipson joined the center in 2002 after nearly twenty-five years of government service. While in government, she focused on analysis and policymaking of Middle East and South Asian issues. Her key positions included Vice Chair of the National Intelligence Council (NIC) (1997–2002), Special Assistant to the U.S. Permanent Representative to the United Nations (1995–1997), Director for Near East and South Asian Affairs for the National Security Council (1993–1995), National Intelligence Officer for Near and South Asia (1990–1993), a member of the State Department's policy planning staff (1986–1987), and a specialist in Middle East Affairs for the Congressional Research Service.

At the center, Laipson directs the Southwest Asia project, which focuses on a range of security issues in the Gulf region. Laipson is a frequent speaker on Middle East issues and on U.S. foreign policy and global trends. She is a member of the Council on Foreign Relations, the International Institute of Strategic Studies, the Middle East Institute, and the Middle East Studies Association. In 2003, she joined the boards of the Asia Foundation and the Education and Employment Foundation. Laipson has an MA from the School of Advanced International Studies, Johns Hopkins University, and an AB from Cornell University.

Carl Levin

Carl Levin is a Democratic Senator from Michigan and the Chairman of the Senate Committee on Armed Services. He has been in the Senate since 1979. He graduated from Swarthmore College in 1956 and from Harvard Law School in 1959.

David McKiernan

Lieutenant General David McKiernan was the Commanding Officer of the Third U.S. Army. He led the ground forces that captured Baghdad in April 2003. Prior to the war, McKiernan favored a war plan that called for a larger number of ground troops and greater emphasis on combating irregular fighters. His views clashed with his superiors General Tommy Franks and Donald Rumsfeld. McKiernan was surprised when he and his staff were not given command for postwar operations in Iraq, which instead went to newly promoted Lieutenant General Ricardo Sanchez.

Before assuming command in Iraq, McKiernan served as the army's Deputy Chief of Staff for Operations in Washington, D.C. He also served in Korea, Germany, the 1991 Persian Gulf War, and Bosnia-Herzegovina. He graduated from the College of William and Mary in 1972.

Abbas Milani

Abbas Milani is Director of the Iranian Studies Program at Stanford University and a visiting professor in the Department of Political Science. In addition, Milani is a research fellow and codirector of the Iran Democracy Project at the Hoover Institution. His expertise is U.S.-Iran relations, Iranian cultural, political, and security issues. Milani is the author of several books, including *Lost Wisdom: Rethinking Persian Modernity in Iran* (2004); *The Persian Sphinx: Amir Abbas Hoveyda and the Riddle of the Iranian Revolution* (2000); *Modernity and Its Foes in Iran* (1998); and *Tales of Two Cities: A Persian Memoir* (1996). Milani has also translated numerous books and articles into Persian and English.

Milani was born in Iran in 1949, but was educated in the United States. He graduated from Oakland Technical High School in 1966. He earned a BA in political science and economics from University of California, Berkeley, and a Ph.D. in political science from the University of Hawaii. Upon completing his Ph.D., Milani returned to Iran, where he was an assistant professor of political science at the National University of Iran from 1975 to 1977, when he was jailed for a year as a political prisoner. After his release, he worked as a research fellow at the Iranian Center for Social Research, and an assistant professor of law and political science at the University of Tehran. He left Iran for the United States in 1987. He became a Hoover Institution research fellow in 2001.

MICHAEL MOSS

Michael Moss has been an investigative reporter with the *New York Times* since 2000. Before coming to the *Times*, Moss was a reporter for the *Wall Street Journal*, *New York Newsday*, *Atlanta Journal-Constitution*, *Grand Junction (Co.) Daily Sentinel*, and *Lander (Wyo.) High Country News*. He was a finalist for the Pulitzer Prize in 2006 for his reporting on the lack of protective armor for soldiers in Iraq, and in 1999 for a team effort on Wall Street's emerging influence in the nursing-home industry.

Moss is the author of *Palace Coup: The Inside Story of Harry and Leona Helmsley*. He has been an adjunct professor at the Columbia University Graduate School of Journalism. He has had fellowships with the German Marshall Fund and the Gannett Center for Media Studies, and in 1983 covered an expedition up the West Ridge of Mount Everest in Nepal.

Moss was born in Eureka, California, attended San Francisco State University, and dropped out without a degree.

SETH MOULTON

Captain Seth Moulton of the U.S. Marine Corps led an infantry platoon in Iraq. He has seen service across the country, including in the Sadr City area of Baghdad and in the city of Najaf, where in 2004 he led his platoon in combat with the Mahdi militia of Moqtada al-Sadr. He is currently serving as a special assistant to General Petraeus in Southern Iraq.

While in Iraq, Moulton and his translator, Mohammed Fawzi, produced a half-hour television program on the U.S. and Iraqi reconstruction efforts. Moulton holds a degree in physics from Harvard University.

JOSEPH S. NYE

Joseph S. Nye, Jr., University Distinguished Service Professor, is also the Sultan of Oman Professor of International Relations and former Dean of the Kennedy School at Harvard University. He received his BA summa cum laude from Princeton University, did postgraduate work at Oxford University on a Rhodes scholarship, and earned a Ph.D. in political science from Harvard. He has served as Assistant Secretary of Defense for International Security Affairs, Chair of the National Intelligence Council, and Deputy Undersecretary of State for Security Assistance, Science and Technology. He is the author of several books, including *Soft Power: The Means to Success in World Politics*; *Understanding International Conflict*; and *The Power Game: A Washington Novel*.

MAHMOUD OTHMAN

Active in the politics of Iraq's northern Kurdish region for decades, Mahmoud Othman is currently a member of the Iraqi National Assembly. After the U.S. invasion of Iraq, Othman was a member of the Iraqi Governing Council, the twenty-five-person committee appointed by the Coalition Provisional Authority (CPA) to advise it until the CPA handed sovereignty over to the Iraqi Interim Government in June 2004.

GEORGE PACKER

George Packer is a staff writer for *The New Yorker*. He is author of *The Assassins' Gate: America in Iraq*, which analyzes how decisions made by the Bush administration during the buildup to war in Iraq led to problems in the postwar period.

Packer has been published in *The New York Times Magazine*, *Mother Jones*, and *Harper's*. He is the author of several other books, including two novels, and has taught writing at Harvard University, Columbia University, Sarah Lawrence College, and Bennington College. He served in the Peace Corps in Togo. Packer is a graduate of Yale University.

ROBERT PERITO

Robert Perito is a former head of the U.S. Department of Justice's international police training program. He is currently a senior program officer in the Center for Post-Conflict Peace and Stability Operations at the U.S. Institute of Peace, a congressionally funded institution with the mission of helping prevent and resolve violent international conflicts, encourage democratic transformations and stability in postwar nations, and increase the tools and information available to others working toward peace. Before the Iraq war, Perito briefed U.S. Defense Department officials on what kind of peacekeeping operations they should expect in the postwar.

Perito was a career Foreign Service officer with the State Department before joining the Department of Justice. He held assignments in Europe, Africa, and China and served as Deputy Executive Secretary to the National Security Council. Perito worked in the Peace Corps in Nigeria and has taught at Princeton University, American University, and George Mason University. He has an MA in peace operations policy from George Mason University.

DAVID PHILLIPS

David L. Phillips is Executive Director of the Elie Wiesel Foundation for Humanity. Prior to that he was a senior fellow at the Council on Foreign Relations. He is a visiting scholar at Harvard's Center for Middle East Studies, a senior fellow at the Center for Strategic and International Studies, and an analyst for NBC News. He is the author of *Losing Iraq: Inside the Postwar Reconstruction Fiasco,* and has published opinion pieces in the *New York Times, Washington Post, Financial Times, Wall Street Journal,* and the *International Herald Tribune.*

PAUL PILLAR

From 2000 to 2005, Paul Pillar was National Intelligence Officer for the Near East and South Asia. After retiring from the Central Intelligence Agency, Pillar wrote an article in *Foreign Affairs* in which he criticized policymakers for ignoring U.S. intelligence analysis and attempting to exert political influence over U.S. intelligence analysis prior to the U.S. invasion of Iraq.

Pillar first joined the CIA in 1977 and has been chief of various units in charge of areas of the Persian Gulf, the Near East, and South Asia. Pillar has served as Executive Assistant to the CIA's Deputy Director for Intelligence, Executive Assistant to the Director of Central Intelligence, and Deputy Chief of the Director of Central Intelligence Counterterrorist Center. He is the author of two books, *Negotiating Peace* and *Terrorism and U.S. Foreign Policy*. He is also a retired U.S. Army Reserve officer who served a tour of duty in Vietnam. Professor Pillar has an AB from Dartmouth College, a BPhil from Oxford University, and an MA and a Ph.D. from Princeton University. He is currently a visiting professor at the Center for Peace and Security Studies at Georgetown University.

BARRY POSEN

Barry Posen is the Ford International Professor of Political Science at the Massachusetts Institute of Technology and Director of the MIT Security Studies Program. He is the author of two books, *Inadvertent Escalation: Conventional War and Nuclear Risks,* and *The Sources of Military Doctrine.* His areas of focus include strategic studies and international politics.

From 1998 to 2001, Posen was a member of the National Security Study Group at the Department of Defense. He has been a military consultant to Christian Science Monitor Television and a Consultant to the RAND Corporation. He has written op-eds on Iraq and on Iran for the *New York Times* and *Financial Times*. He received a BA from Occidental College and an MA and a Ph.D. from the University of California, Berkeley.

SAMANTHA POWER

Samantha Power is the Anna Lindh Professor of Practice of Global Leadership and Public Policy at Harvard's John F. Kennedy School of Government. She is the author of *"A Problem from Hell": America and the Age of Genocide*, which examines America's responses to the genocides of the twentieth century. The book won the 2003 Pulitzer Prize for general nonfiction, the 2003 National Book Critics Circle Award for general nonfiction, and the Council on Foreign Relations' Arthur Ross Prize for the best book on U.S. foreign policy. Power founded and served as the Executive Director of the Carr Center for Human Rights Policy at the John F.

Kennedy School of Government from 1998 to 2002. She covered the wars in the former Yugoslavia as a journalist for *U.S. News & World Report*, the *Boston Globe* and the *Economist*. Recently, she worked as a foreign policy fellow in the office of U.S. Senator Barack Obama of Illinois, and she has written a biography of the late UN envoy to Iraq, Sergio Vieira de Mello: *The Man for Dark Times: Sergio Vieira de Mello and the Fight to Save the World*. Power has an undergraduate degree from Yale University and a graduate degree from Harvard Law School.

NIR ROSEN

A freelance journalist, photographer, and filmmaker fluent in Arabic, Nir Rosen wrote *In the Belly of the Green Bird: The Triumph of the Martyrs in Iraq* after spending three years in Iraq. In the book, Rosen studies the rising sectarian tensions that followed the U.S. invasion of 2003. Rosen has published articles in several newspapers and magazines, including *The Atlantic Monthly*, the *Washington Post*, *The New York Times Magazine*, *The New Yorker*, *Harper's*, and *The New Republic*. He is a fellow at the New America Foundation, a nonprofit public policy institute.

DONALD RUMSFELD

Donald Rumsfeld served as Secretary of Defense between January 2001 and November 2006. As Secretary of Defense, Rumsfeld oversaw U.S. wars in Afghanistan and Iraq and was a leading proponent of what is known as "transformation" of the military establishment to meet the needs of the post–Cold War world. Transformation emphasizes a theory of warfare that envisions lighter, faster, more agile combat forces that rely on advanced-technology weapons systems rather than large troop contingents. This orientation led the United States to intervene in Afghanistan and Iraq with relatively small troop levels, which many critics believe is a leading cause of the continuing instability in those places.

Before becoming President Bush's Secretary of Defense, Rumsfeld was a highly successful business executive, serving in succession as the CEO of Searle, General Instrument, and Gilead Sciences. Earlier, he had been Chief of Staff, and then Secretary of Defense, in the administration of President Gerald Ford. During the Ronald Reagan administration, Rumsfeld was a special envoy to the Middle East. In that capacity, he twice traveled to Baghdad to meet with Saddam Hussein to discuss the normalization of U.S.-Iraq relations, despite Iraq's repeated use of chemical weapons in its eight-year war with Iran. Rumsfeld holds a B.A. from Princeton University and served as a navy pilot and trainer in the late 1950s.

Rumsfeld resigned as Secretary of Defense in November 2006 in the face of mounting criticism of his handling of the wars in Afghanistan and Iraq. In September 2006, he was appointed a visiting fellow at the Hoover Institution, Stanford University, where he serves on a task force of experts devoted to researching the "ideology of terrorism."

Brad Setser

Brad Setser is an economist specializing in emerging economies and international economics. He is the author of many articles and books, including *Oil and Global Adjustment,* Peterson Institute for International Economics (2007). He is a geoeconomics fellow at the Council on Foreign Relations.

Matt Sherman

Matt Sherman worked for the Coalition Provisional Authority (CPA) and later the State Department in Iraq, advising Iraqi and American personnel on issues relating to the creation of domestic security and the 2005 Iraqi elections. Before his work in Iraq, Sherman held positions with the State Department in Bosnia, Kosovo, Croatia, Montenegro, Ukraine, and Moldova. Sherman has worked for Colin Powell's nonprofit organization, America's Promise. He also worked for the Foreign Policy Advisory Board to George W. Bush's 2000 campaign for president, which was led by Condoleezza Rice. He is currently a senior adviser at the Scowcroft Group, an international business advisory firm managed by former National Security Adviser Brent Scowcroft. Sherman has a BA and JD from the University of North Carolina and an MPhil in international relations from Cambridge University.

Eric Shinseki

Eric Shinseki is a retired four-star general who served as the Chief of Staff of the U.S. Army between 1999 and 2003. On February 25, 2003, Shinseki told the U.S. Senate Armed Services Committee that he believed that "something on the order of several hundred thousand soldiers" would be required to bring stability to postwar Iraq. Two days later, Shinseki's comments were sharply rebuked by Donald Rumsfeld and Paul Wolfowitz, who, respectively, described his comments as "far off the mark" and "wildly off the mark." On August 1, 2003, Donald Rumsfeld appointed General Peter J. Schoomaker to replace General Shinseki as Army Chief of Staff.

Before serving as Army Chief of Staff, Shinseki received two Purple Hearts and four Bronze Star Medals for his service in Vietnam. He graduated from West Point with a BS and a commission as a second lieutenant. He earned an MA in English literature from Duke University.

WALTER SLOCOMBE

Walter Slocombe served as Senior Adviser for National Security and Defense to the Coalition Provisional Authority (CPA). During this time, he was responsible for recommending the disbanding of the entire Iraqi military as well as Iraq's intelligence services and secret police, and then overseeing the creation of the New Iraqi Army. After leaving the CPA, he served on the Commission on the Intelligence Capabilities of the United States Regarding Weapons of Mass Destruction, which reviewed the capability of the United States to deal with the proliferation of weapons of mass destruction.

Slocombe is a 1963 graduate of Princeton University, a Rhodes scholar, and a 1968 graduate of Harvard Law School. After graduation, he served as a clerk to Supreme Court Justice Abe Fortas, as a staffer in the Program Analysis Office of the National Security Council, and as a research associate at the International Institute for Strategic Studies in London before joining the law firm of Caplin & Drysdale in Washington, D.C., in 1971. He served as Principal Deputy Assistant Secretary for International Security Affairs and Deputy Undersecretary for Policy Planning during the Carter administration. During the Clinton administration, he was Under Secretary of Defense for Policy. Walter Slocombe is currently a member of the Washington, D.C., law firm of Caplin & Drysdale.

JESSICA STERN

Jessica Stern is a lecturer in Public Policy at Harvard's John F. Kennedy School of Government and is a faculty affiliate at the Belfer Center for Science and International Affairs. From 1994 to 1995, she served as Director for Russian, Ukrainian, and Eurasian Affairs at the National Security Council, where she was responsible for national security policy toward Russia and the former Soviet states and for policies to reduce the threat of nuclear smuggling and terrorism. Stern earlier worked at Lawrence Livermore National Laboratory. From 1998 to 1999, she was the Superterrorism Fellow at the Council on Foreign Relations, and from 1995 to 1996, she was a national fellow at the Hoover Institution at Stanford University. She is the author of *Terror in the Name of God* and *The Ultimate Terrorists*, as well as numerous articles on terrorism and weapons of mass destruction. She received a BS from Barnard College in chemistry, an MS from MIT, and a Ph.D. in public policy from Harvard.

JAMES TORGLER

James Torgler is a former lieutenant colonel in the U.S. Army Reserves and has worked as defense contractor on issues related to training and equipping the Afghan and Iraqi armies. In early 2003, he was working on efforts to train the Afghan National Army when Jay Garner recruited him to come to Iraq as part of the Organization for Reconstruction and Humanitarian Assistance. In May 2003, Torgler met with Walter Slocombe to warn him of the dangers of disbanding the Iraqi Army. Slocombe ignored Torgler's advice and announced the decision to disband the army, to Torgler's surprise, only a few days after their meeting.

YAROSLAV TROFIMOV

Yaroslav Trofimov is the author of *Faith at War,* which tells of his experiences traveling through over a dozen Islamic countries, including Iraq, in the hopes of better understanding the Muslim world in the aftermath of the events of September 11, 2001. He speaks both Hebrew and Arabic.

Trofimov has worked as a reporter in the United States, France, the former Soviet Union, the Middle East, and Italy. He currently writes for the

Wall Street Journal. Trofimov has a masters of arts degree from New York University.

AIDA USSAYRAN

Aida Ussayran is Iraq's Deputy Minister of Human Rights and a member of Iraq's parliament. As an activist for democracy and women's rights, she was arrested three times during the regime of Saddam Hussein. Sentenced to death, she fled the country, went into exile in England, and began working with Iraqi opposition groups, including the Iraqi National Congress. She returned to Iraq after the U.S. invasion of 2003. Ussayran holds an MA from the University of Hamburg.

SARAH LEAH WHITSON

Sarah Leah Whitson is Executive Director of the Middle East and North Africa Division of Human Rights Watch, an independent, nongovernmental organization that monitors human rights abuses around the world. Whitson graduated from Harvard Law School in 1991 and became involved in human rights activism related to the 1991 Persian Gulf War. She traveled to Iraq numerous times throughout the 1990s, working with a variety of different human rights organizations. Her grandparents are survivors of the 1915 Armenian Genocide. She speaks Armenian and Arabic.

LAWRENCE WILKERSON

Lawrence Wilkerson worked on the staff of Secretary of State Colin Powell, holding the position of Chief of Staff from August 2002 until Powell left office in 2005. Wilkerson was a longtime associate of Powell's, having first worked as his Deputy Executive Officer, U.S. Army's Forces Command in Atlanta in 1989. When Powell became Chairman of the U.S. Joint Chiefs of Staff, Wilkerson followed as his special assistant. When Powell retired in 1993, Wilkerson went on to become Deputy Director and Director of the U.S. Marine Corps War College at Quantico, Virginia. In 1997, Wilkerson retired from the military with the rank of colonel and began working for Powell as a consultant and adviser.

Since resigning as Powell's Chief of Staff, Wilkerson has frequently spoken critically of the Bush administration, notably of the influence of Vice

President Cheney and former Secretary of Defense Donald Rumsfeld on foreign policy decisions. Wilkerson is a Vietnam veteran who has been stationed and participated in combat exercises in Korea, Japan, and Hawaii. He has served on the faculty of the U.S. Naval War College and holds two advanced degrees in international relations and national security studies.

PAUL WOLFOWITZ

Paul Wolfowitz served as Deputy Secretary of Defense between 2001 and 2005. Wolfowitz, along with Secretary of Defense Rumsfeld, was a leading advocate of invading Iraq. He has been criticized for making overly optimistic statements about conditions in Iraq after the fall of Saddam Hussein. After stepping down from the Department of Defense, Wolfowitz went to work as the President of the World Bank, despite widespread opposition from European leaders. While at the World Bank, he led an anti-corruption campaign, but was forced to step down in May 2007 because of ethics violations involving a pay raise and promotion for his girlfriend, Shaha Riza. After stepping down from the World Bank, he joined the American Enterprise Institute to work on entrepreneurship and development issues, Africa, and public-private partnerships.

Before serving as Deputy Secretary of Defense for the George W. Bush administration, Wolfowitz was Director of Policy Planning for the State Department under Jimmy Carter, a military analyst under Ronald Reagan, and U.S. Ambassador to the Republic of Indonesia. Under President George H. W. Bush, Wolfowitz served as Undersecretary of Defense for Policy, and was heavily involved in planning the first Gulf War.

Wolfowitz graduated from Cornell University in 1965 with a BS in mathematics and chemistry. He received a Ph.D. in political science from the University of Chicago in 1972. While at Chicago, Wolfowitz studied under the legendary political philosopher Leo Strauss. Wolfowitz has taught at Yale University, Johns Hopkins University, and the National War College.

EDWARD WONG

Edward Wong is a foreign correspondent with the *New York Times*. He started out as an intern in 1998 and eventually worked at the Metro,

Sports, and Business desks. Since November 2003, Wong has been one of the *Times*'s primary foreign correspondents covering the Iraq war.

Wong graduated from the University of Virginia in 1994 with a BA in English. In 1999, he earned dual master's degrees in journalism and international studies from the University of California, Berkeley.

"OMAR X"

Omar X chose to remain anonymous for fear of his safety, the safety of his family, and his immigration status in the United States. He was born in Baghdad, graduated from the Baghdad Medical College, and worked as a physician in Baghdad until 2005. Omar then began to work as a journalist. As the security situation in Baghdad worsened in 2005, three of his brothers were kidnapped and his father was kidnapped and killed. In September 2006, Omar came to the United States on a three-year Fulbright scholarship. He is one of more than four million refugees from the Iraq war. Most of his family members have also fled Iraq, mostly to Jordan and Syria.

DAVID YANCEY

David Yancey was a military police specialist with the 155th Combat Team. He arrived in Iraq in January 2005 and acted primarily as a convoy escort. While on one such mission in March 2005, Yancey's Humvee was struck by an improvised explosive device, which nearly killed him. He has been discharged from the army with a disability pension.

STATISTICAL GRAPHS

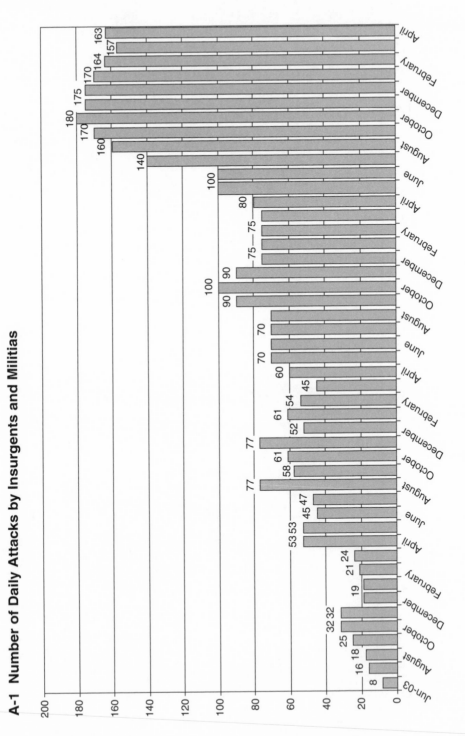

A-1 Number of Daily Attacks by Insurgents and Militias

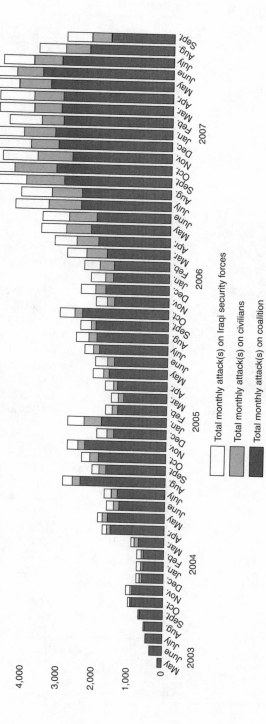

A-2 Enemy-Initiated Attacks against the Coalition, Iraqi Security Forces, and Civilians, May 2003 through September 2007[1]

Number of attacks

☐ Total monthly attack(s) on Iraqi security forces

▨ Total monthly attack(s) on civilians

■ Total monthly attack(s) on coalition

Source: GAO analysis of DIA-reported Multi-National Force-Iraq data, September 2007.

A-3 Iraqi Prison Population[2]

Peak prison population in 2003	10,000
June 2004	5,435
July	5,700
	(of which 90 are foreign nationals)
September	5,500
	(whereof 2 are women, 65–70 are juveniles and 130–140 are foreign nationals)
October	4,300
November	8,300
January 2005	7,837
June	10,783
July	15,000
August	14,000
September	14,000
October	13,000
November	13,000 held by American troops plus an additional 12,000 held by Iraqi authorities
December	~ 14,000 in US / Allied custody
January 2006	14,000 in US custody
February	14,767 in US / Allied custody
March	~ 15,000 in US / Allied custody
April	~ 15,000 in US / Allied custody
May	~14,000 in US / Allied custody
June	~14,500 in US custody, ~13,300 held by Iraqi authorities
September	~13,000 in US custody
October	~13,000 in US custody
November	~ 13,000 in US custody
December	~ 13,000 in US custody
January 2007	~ 14,000 in US custody
February	~ 15,000 in US custody
March	~ 17,000 in US custody ~20,000 in Iraqi custody
April	~ 18,000 in US custody
May	~ 19,500 in US custody
June	~ 21,000 in US custody
July	~ 21,000 in US custody
August	~ 23,000 in US custody ~ 37,000 in Iraqi custody
September	~ 25,000 in US custody
October	~ 26,000 in US custody
November	~ 25,800 in US custody

NOTE ON IRAQI PRISON POPULATION TABLE: MARCH 2007: 13,800 prisoners held in Camp Bucca in southern Iraq and 3,300 held in Camp Crocker outside of Baghdad. David Cloud also writes that 2,800 detainees have been released since August 2005. David Cloud, "Prisoner is Released Despite Evidence of Role in Bombing," New York Times, November 25, 2005. JULY 2007: U.S. and Iraqi government officials report that an estimated 44,000 of 65,000 suspected Iraqi insurgents or sectarian killers detained in Iraq have been released since March 2003. Cited reasons include prison overcrowding, global politics and corruption in the Iraqi justice system.

A-4 Estimated Strength of Insurgency Nationwide[3]

Month	Estimated strength of insurgency nationwide
November	5,000
December	5,000
January 2004	3, 000–5,000
February	N/A
March	N/A
April	5,000
May	15,000
June	15,000
July	20,000
August	20,000
September	20,000
October	20,000
November	20,000
December	"more than 20,000"
January 2005	18,000
February	18,000
March	16,000
April	16,000
May	16,000
June	15,000–20,000
July	"no more than 20,000"
August	N/A
September	"neither gaining strength nor weakening appreciably" (some estimates indicate higher numbers, please see footnote)
October	15,000 – 20,000
November	15,000 – 20,000
December	15,000 – 20,000
January 2006	15,000 – 20,000
February	15,000 – 20,000
March	15,000 – 20,000
April	20,000+
May	20,000+
June	20,000+
July	20,000+
August	20,000+
September	20,000+
October	20,000–30,000, including militias
March 2007	~70,000 (Sunni only), includes non-operational supporters

NOTE ON STRENGTH OF INSURGENCY TABLE: International Crisis Group estimates that there are approximately 5,000 to 15,000 insurgents in Iraq. *In Their Own Words: Reading the Iraqi Insurgency,* International Crisis Group, Middle East Report N. 50, February 15, 2006. The estimated strength of Al Qaida in Iraq is more than 1,000 nationwide, although the exact number is unknown. It is presumed this includes both Iraqis and foreign fighters. Country Reports on Terrorism, United States Department of State, Office for the Coordinator for Counterterrorism, April 2006. MARCH 2007: Estimate is of Sunni insurgents only. It comes from an analyst employed by the U.S. military and includes "hard-line operators" as well as "part-time supporters."

A-5 Economic and Quality of Life Indicators: Fuel[4]

	Fuel supplies available						
	Millions of barrels/day		Millions of liters/day			Tons/day	Overall fuel supplies as percentage of goal during that month
Time	Crude oil production	Crude oil export	Diesel (Prod. & Imp.)	Kerosene (Prod. & Imp.)	Gasoline/ Benzene (Prod. & Imp.)	Liquid Petroleum Gas (Prod. & Imp.)	
May 2003	0.3	0	N/A	N/A	N/A	N/A	10%
June	0.675	0.2	N/A	N/A	N/A	N/A	23%
July	0.925	0.322[i]	6.5	4.75	13.5	1,880	44%
August	1.445	0.646[ii]	10.25	6.2	14.0	2,530	57%
September	1.7225	0.983[iii]	14.25	6.9	17.3	3,030	70%
October	2.055	1.149[iv]	14.75	9.6	16.35	3,700	78%
November	2.1	1.524[v]	13.14	13.3	11.792	3,610	76%
December	2.30	1.541[vi]	12.29	9.4	12.9	3,460	72%
January 2004	2.440	1.537	13.91	11.3	13.32	3,445	78%
February	2.276	1.382[vii]	15.21	13.05	16.65	4,670	88%
March	2.435	1.825[viii]	15.03	17.28	17.19	5,010	92%
April	2.384	1.804[ix]	22.75	4.46	19.3	3,607	79%
May	1.887	1.380[x]	22.92	4.005	18.07	3,264	73%
June	2.295	1.148[xi]	16.47	4.9	22	3,086	75%
July	2.2	1.406[xii]	17.95	5.75	22.3	3,820	80%
August	2.112	1.114[xiii]	16	4.2	15.1	3,417	84%
September	2.514	1.703	16.35	6.35	14.6	2,707	72%
October	2.46	1.542	16.15	7.95	18.6	3,044	80%
November	1.95	1.320	16.5	7.7	17.9	3,324	77%
December	2.16	1.520	18.3	10.5	17.6	4,222	88%
January 2005	2.10	1.367	12.7	6.7	20.65	5,017	75%
February	2.10	1.431	15.9	8.55	21.2	5,003	84%
March	2.09	1.394	19.7	8.05	20.3	4,894	93%
April	2.14	1.398	18.3	7.6	23.7	5,219	97%
May	2.1	1.308	22.2	4.4	22.5	5,030	93%
June	2.17	1.377	18.9	6.25	18.3	5,137	97%
July	2.17	1.550	19.9	5.9	23.9	4,474	97%
August	2.16	1.504	19.3	5.2	23.8	5,072	96%
September[xiv]	2.11	1.60	17.3	4.4	20.9	4,888	87%
October	1.91	1.239	17.0	8.6	18.9	4,784	90%
November	1.98	1.168	17.3	8.2	19.9	5,526	88%
December	1.92	1.071	16.1	8.0	17.5	5,046	81%
January 2006	1.73	1.05	14.0	6.3	18.1	3,716	72%
February	1.83	1.47	10.1	5.0	12.2	2,263	55%
March	2.1	1.32	12.0	5.7	14.9	2,798	65%
April	2.14	1.60	13.5	4.5	16.9	2,855	67%
May	2.13	1.51	15.2	4.8	17.4	3,577	82%
June	2.30	1.67	15.7	4.3	16.1	3,217	80%
August	2.24	1.68	12.4	4.47	16.5	3,242	71%

(continues)

A-5 *(continued)*

Time	Millions of barrels/day		Millions of liters/day			Tons/day	Overall fuel supplies as percentage of goal during that month
	Crude oil production	Crude oil export	Diesel (Prod. & Imp.)	Kerosene (Prod. & Imp.)	Gasoline/ Benzene (Prod. & Imp.)	Liquid Petroleum Gas (Prod. & Imp.)	
September	2.34	1.65	13.4	6.0	18.3	3,270	77%
October	2.26	1.55	10.8	4.7	15.4	3,102	57%
November	2.10	1.44	11.1	6.4	13.9	2,747	54%
December[xv]	2.15	1.45	10.7	8.1	9.8	2,544	55%
January 2007	1.66	1.30	10.6	4.4	11.2	2,945	52%
February	2.08	1.50	11.3	5.7	13.0	3,101	61%
March	2.08	1.58	8.3	4.2	12.1	2,598	57%
April	2.14	1.50	12.8	5.3	13.8	2,841	66%
May	2.03	1.64	9.2	3.5	12.1	2,010	56%
June	2.00	1.47	9.7	3.7	11.0	2,282	57%
July	2.07	1.76	11.0	2.6	11.2	2,650	57%
August	1.91	1.69	8.9	3.4	9.6	1,918	47%
September	2.30	1.90	13.4	8.3	15.2	3,472	75%
October	2.34	1.85	12.4	8.5	14.4	3,724	69%
November	2.45	1.53	12.4	7.7	17.9	3,508	71%
Stated Interim Goal:	2.1 revised down from 2.5 in January 2007	N/A	24.5 revised up from 22.4 in August 2007	14.6 revised up from 13.4 in October 2007	26.8 revised up from 23.1 in October 2007	5,100 Revised down from 5,130 in May 2007	We assume that supplies for each category cannot exceed 100% of goal

Fuel supplies available

NOTE ON FUEL TABLE: Above data as of November 11, 2007. The ratio of Iraq price to international price is 4.0 for LPG, 3.0 for regular and 6.9 for premium gasoline, 0.7 for kerosene and 1.5 for diesel. Kerosene imports began 5 October, 2003. All previous months cover only production.

i   "Iraq Fact Sheet: Oil," *Joint Staff & CPA,* Unclassified. Provided to the author by CPA/DoD. As of December 11, 2003.
ii   Ibid.
iii   Ibid.
iv   Ibid.
v   "Iraq Fact Sheet: Oil, "*Joint Chiefs and CPA,* January 13, 2004. "Draft Working Papers: Iraq Status," Department of Defense, 20 January, 2004. Unclassified. Provided to the author by the CPA/DoD. Based on two week estimate.
vi   "Iraq Fact Sheet: Oil," *Joint Chiefs and CPA,* January 13, 2004.
vii   "Iraq Fact Sheet: Power "*Joint Staff and CPA,* March 15, 2004.
viii "Iraq Fact Sheet: Oil," *Joint Staff and CPA,* April 20, 2004.
ix   "Iraq Fact Sheet: Oil," *Joint Staff and CPA,* May 25, 2004.
x   Ibid.
xi   Draft Working Papers: Iraq Status," *Department of State,* October 6, 2004.
xii   Draft Working Papers: Iraq Status," *Department of State,* August 4, 2004.
xiii Draft Working Papers: Iraq Status," *Department of State,* October 6, 2004.
xiv   The statistics for September 2005 are based on incomplete data and represent averages for approximately half of the month.
xv   U.S. State Department's "Iraq Weekly Status Report" did not provide production amounts of diesel, kerosene, gasoline or LPG for the week of December 18-25 so averages for these categories are only for the 24 days in December for which exact figures are known. Country Report No. 05/294: Iraq: 2005 Article IV Consultation – Staff Report; Staff Supplement; Public Information Notice on the Executive Board Discussion; and Statement by the Executive Director for Iraq, International Monetary Fund, August 2005, p. 11.

A-6 Economic and Quality of Life Indicators:
Oil Revenue From Exports[5]

Time	Oil revenue ($ billions)	Time	Oil revenue ($ billions)
June 2003	0.2	November	1.67
July	0.36	December	1.60
August	0.44	January 2006	1.84
September	0.73	February	2.16
October	0.89	March	2.25
November	1.21	April	3.02
December	1.26	May	2.92
January 2004	1.26	June	3.03
February	1.10	July	3.41
March	1.61	August	3.44
April	1.50	September	2.73
May	1.36	October	2.45
June	1.28	November	2.19
July	1.40	December	2.46
August	1.24	January 2007	1.89
September	1.75	February	2.11
October	1.99	March	2.75
November	1.25	April	2.75
December	1.44	May	3.05
January 2005	1.49	June	2.87
February	1.34	July	3.39
March	1.99	August	3.49
April	1.83	September	3.79
May	1.57	October	4.44
June	2.03	November	1.19
July	2.47		
August	2.63	Total as of	
September	2.74	November 11, 2007	$109.9
October	1.90		

A-7 Economic and Quality of Life Indicators: Electricity[6]

Time	Average amount of electricity generated (megawatts)		Average hours of electricity per day		Average of megawatt hours (MWH)
	Nation-wide	Baghdad	Nationwide	Baghdad	
Estimated prewar level	3,958	2,500	4–8	16–24	95,000
May 2003	500	300	4–8	4–8	N/A
June	3,193	707	N/A	N/A	N/A
July	3,236	1,082	N/A	N/A	N/A
August	3,263	1,283	N/A	N/A	72,435
September	3,543	1,229	N/A	N/A	75,000
October	3,948	N/A	N/A	N/A	79,000
November	3,582	N/A	N/A	N/A	70,000
December	3,427	N/A	N/A	N/A	72,000
January 2004	3,758	N/A	N/A	N/A	79,000
February	4,125	1,307	13	13.4	90,000
March	4,040	1,192	16	16.4	86,000
April	3,823	1,021	15	14.8	78,000
May	3,902	1,053	11	12.2	80,000
June	4,293	1,198	10	11	93,500
July	4,584	N/A	10	12	100,300
August	4,707	1,440	13	15	109,900
September	4,467	1,485	13	14	107,200
October	4,074	1,280	13	16	99,306
November	3,199	845	13	N/A	76,550
December	3,380	N/A	N/A	N/A	81,114
January 2005	3,289	985	9	9.0	78,925
February	3,611	1,180	8.5	10.3	86,675
March	3,627	994	11.8	11.0	87,051
April	3,390	854	9	11.5	81,350
May	3,712	N/A	8.4	9.5	89,088
June	4,153	N/A	9.4	10.4	102,525
July	4,446	N/A	12.6	10.9	106,713
August	4,049	N/A	12.0	8.4	97,165
September	4,159	N/A	13.5	10.4	101,916
October	3,685	N/A	14.3	8.9	88,442
November*	3,742	N/A	13.3	8.8	89,800
December**	3,800	N/A	12.0	6.1	91,400
January 2006	3,640	N/A	9.8	4.0	87,400
February	3,700	N/A	10.3	5.9	88,600
March	4,000	N/A	13.1	7.8	96,300
April	3,700	N/A	10.9	4.5	88,500
May	3,900	N/A	9.9	3.9	92,700
June	4,400	N/A	11.9	8.0	106,100
July	4,400	N/A	11.4	7.0	106,700
August	4,430	N/A	10.9	6.2	106,400

(continues)

A-7 Economic and Quality of Life Indicators:
Electricity *(continued)*

Time	Average amount of electricity generated (megawatts)		Average hours of electricity per day		Average of megawatt hours (MWH)
	Nation-wide	Baghdad	Nationwide	Baghdad	
September	4,000	N/A	10.8	5.3	95,600
October	4,000	N/A	12.3	6.7	96,600
November	3,700	N/A	10.9	6.9	88,000
December	3,500	N/A	9.2	6.7	85,968
January 2007	3,590	N/A	8.0	4.4	86,100
February	3,600	N/A	9.3	6.0	86,500
March	3,600	N/A	10.9	6.0	86,400
April	3,830	N/A	11.7	5.8	91,930
May	3,720	N/A	10.1	5.6	89,245
June	4,200	N/A	10.6	5.9	100,728
July	4,220	N/A	10.4	5.9	101,270
August	4,380	N/A	10.2	6.3	105,050
September	4,860	N/A	11.8	7.4	116,560
October	4,725	N/A	12.9	9.0	113,390
November	4,000	N/A	12.9	9.4	95,740

NOTE ON ELECTRICITY TABLE: The demand for electricity ranges from 8,500 to 9,000 MW nationwide. Currently, at least 2,000 MW are provided off-grid by private owners of small generators.[xxii] From May 3 thru July 31, 2007, the U.S. State Department's *Iraq Weekly Status Report* discontinued its reporting of average hours of available electricity in Baghdad and nationwide. Beginning August 1, it was once again reported but stipulated that the figure given was "after meeting demand for essential services."
Above data as of November 13, 2007.

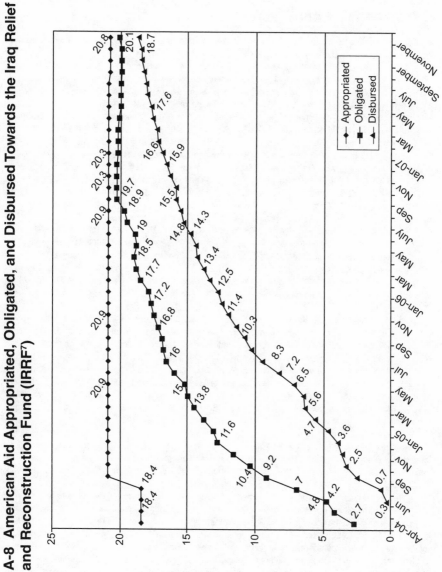

A-8 American Aid Appropriated, Obligated, and Disbursed Towards the Iraq Relief and Reconstruction Fund (IRRF⁷)

Notes to Graphs

1. GAO-08-231T, "Securing, Stabilizing and Rebuilding Iraq," statement of Joseph A. Christoff, General Accounting Office, October 30, 2007, page 5.

2. Doug Smith and Richard Boudreaux, "Bombs Kill at Least 15 in Baghdad," *Los Angeles Times,* January 20, 2006. Thom Shanker, "Abu Ghraib Called Incubator for Terrorists," *New York Times,* February 15, 2006. March and April 2006 numbers are author's estimates. Bushra Juhi, "Attack on Iraqi Interior Ministry Kills 2 Employees; Car Bomb in Hillah Kills at Least 5," *Associated Press Worldstream,* May 30, 2006. John F. Burns, "Iraq to Release Detainees in Bid to Ease Tensions," *New York Times,* June 7, 2006. Patrick Quinn, "US Wartime Prison Network Grows into Legal Vacuum for 14,000," *Associated Press,* September 18, 2006. William Mann, "Former US Attorney General Says Hanging Saddam Would Cause Bloodbath in Iraq," *Associated Press,* October 5, 2006. Thomas Wagner and Sinan Salaheddin, "US Choppers Back Iraqi Raid of Baghdad," *Associated Press Online,* December 1, 2006. Walter Pincus, "U.S. Expects Iraq Prison Growth; Crackdown Likely to Mean More Inmates at 2 Detention Centers," *Washington Post,* March 14, 2007. Gordon Lubold, "US Priority: Managing Captives in Iraq," *Christian Science Monitor,* April 6, 2007. Walter Pincus, "U.S. Holds 18,000 Detainees in Iraq," *Washington Post,* April 15, 2007 Joshua Partlow, "New Detainees Strain Iraq's Jails," *Washington Post,* May 15, 2007. Sinan Salaheddin, "Suicide bomber Kills 13 Iraqi Soldiers," *Associated Press Online,* June 9, 2007. Elaine M. Grossman, "U.S., Iraq Freed Roughly 44,000 Suspected Insurgents Since March 2003," *Inside the Pentagon,* July 12, 2007. Department of Defense conference call with Maj. Gen. Douglas Stone, Deputy Commanding General, Detainee Operations, MNF-I, August 7, 2007. Walter Pincus, "'Surge' has led to More Detainees," *Washington Post,* August 15, 2007. "U.S. detains nearly 25,000 in Iraq," *Agence France Presse,* October 10, 2007 Lauren Frayer, "US releases 500 Iraqi prisoners from camps overloaded with surge suspects," *Associated Press,* November 8, 2007.

3. Kirk Semple and John F. Burns, August 7, 2007. "All Day Suicide Bomb Blitz Claims 22 Lives in Baghdad," *New York Times,* July 16, 2005. John Diamond, "Intel Chief: Iraqis in Insurgency More Elusive," *USA Today,* September 13, 2005. Anthony Cordesman indicates the number could be as high as 30,000 in Dan Murphy, "Iraq's Foreign Fighters: Few But Deadly," *Christian Science Monitor,* September 27, 2005. Late 2005 and 2006 numbers are author's estimates. April 2006 number is from Country Reports on Terrorism, United States Department of State, Office for the Coordinator for Counterterrorism, April 2006. May–September 2006 numbers are author's estimates. Walter Pincus, "Violence in Iraq Called Increasingly Complex," *Washington Post,* November 17, 2006. Rowan Scarborough, "Sunni Insurgency Continues to Grow," *Washington Examiner,* March 21, 2007.

4. Iraq Weekly Status Report, *Department of State.* Accessed at: http://www.state.gov/p/nea/rls/rpt/iraqstatus/. The numbers for crude oil production, diesel, kerosene, gasoline/benzene, and liquid petroleum gas represent average data from the entire month, and are thus based on multiple Weekly Status Reports. The crude oil export reflects the total for the month. For all categories, data for a complete month is typically available in the Weekly Status Report for the first week of the next month.

5. Iraq Weekly Status Report, *Department of State.* Accessed at: http://www.state.gov/p/nea/rls/rpt/iraqstatus/. The number presented reflects the total oil revenue for the month. Data for a complete month is typically available in the Weekly Status Report for the first week of the next month.

6. Iraq Weekly Status Report, *Department of State.* Accessed at: http://www.state.gov/p/nea/rls/rpt/iraqstatus/. The average of megawatt hours and average hours of electricity per day reflect all the data available for the given month, and thus span multiple Weekly Status Reports. The average amount of electricity generated is derived from the average of megawatt hours. The statistics for September 2005 are based upon incomplete data and represent averages for approximately half of the month.

*The data for November for the average hours of electricity per day is updated in our source, representing the entire month. The numbers for average amount of electricity generated and average MW hours represents data through the 21st of November only. The data for December 2005 and thereafter for the average amount of electricity generated and average MW hours is estimated based on the graph relating to electricity in the Iraq Weekly Status Report, *Department of State.* National Target numbers are courtesy of the US Department of Defense, January 23, 2006.

7. "Iraq Weekly Status Report," *Department of Defense,* April-June, 2004. Available at http://www.defenselink.mil/news/. "Iraq Weekly Status Report," *Department of State,* August 2004-June 2006. Accessed at: http://www.state.gov/p/nea/rls/rpt/iraqstatus/.

NAME INDEX

Rumsfeld, Donald (*continued*)
  insurgency/violence and, 315, 316,
    333
  Iraqi police/security and, 118–119,
    124, 135, 137, 236, 250, 253
  occupation and, 120, 128, 141, 143,
    144, 145, 307, 308, 402–403, 610
  ORHA, 71, 72, 78, 79, 82–83
  preparation/invasion, ix-x, 17, 24, 25,
    26, 27, 28, 30, 31–32, 33–34, 35,
    36, 42, 57, 66, 67, 317, 579, 603
  reflections on, ix-x, 546–548, 563,
    595, 612–613
  resignation, 518, 544, 583, 609
  soldier confronting, 402–403
Russert, Tim, 579
Al-Ruweishid, Jordan refugee camp, **431**
Ruzicka, Marla, xvi

Saddam Hussein
  background/regime, 15, 16, 22, 47,
    55, 56, 60, 63, 68, 74, 133, 171,
    173–175, 182, 234, 296, 303, 326,
    333, 338, 342, 343, 355–356, 368,
    417, 442, 480, 501, 509, 523–525,
    533, 534, 568, 569, 570–571, 572,
    575, 576, 609
  reflections on removal of, 539–544,
    562–563, 564
  removal/effects, 3, 9, 19, 21, 34, 46,
    69, 100, 104, 132, 137, 321–322,
    371, 372, 381, 409, 443, 520,
    521–522, 524–525, 526–527, 534,
    577, 578, 581, 583
al-Sadr, Moqtada, xxi, 259, 260, 275,
    305, 312, 326, 327–328, **327, 328**,
    332–334, 411, 414, 415, 453,
    458–459, 464, 465, 494, 579, 581,
    582
  See also Mahdi Army
Sadr City, 328, 354, 364, 458

SAIC, 440
Salami, Hassan, 186
Salih, Barham, 22
Samarra mosque, 359, 582
Sanchez, Ricardo, 229, 294–295, 336,
    384, 603
Sawers, John, 112
Schoomaker, Peter J., 610
Schwarzkopf, Norman, 21, 541
SCIRI (Supreme Council for the Islamic
    Revolution in Iraq), 251, 256–258,
    333, 334, 339–341, 354, 362, 411,
    412, 419, 446–447, 453–454, 458,
    465, 476–477, 511, 534, 586–587
Scowcroft, Brent, 609
Secret Islamic Army, 259, 260, 326
Secret police/Mukhabarat, 61, 174, 242,
    474–475
Senor, Dan, 167, 191, 192, 289
Setser, Brad, 310, 609
Shadid, Anthony, xiii
Shah of Iran, 569
Sherman, Matt, 256–258, 261–262,
    265, 286–287, 362, 609
Shinseki, Eric, x, 30, 578, 609–610
al-Sistani, Grand Ayatollah Ali, 171,
    270, 272, 582
Slocombe, Walter
  background, 610
  disbanding Iraqi military and, xiv,
    167, 168, 169–170, 171, 173, 174,
    176, 177, 178–179, 180, 181, 182,
    183, 186–187, 190, 191, 192–193,
    194, 195, 196–197, 199–202, 204,
    205–211, 212, 212–216, 217–218,
    220–222, 224–225, 580, 611
  Iraqi police/security and, 240,
    241–242, 250
  occupation and, 124, 141, 156–158,
    206, 282
  ORHA, 75–76, 99, 101, 103

Charles Ferguson is director and producer of *No End in Sight,* which is his first film. Ferguson co-founded one of the earliest Internet software companies, Vermeer Technologies, which was sold to Microsoft. Ferguson has been a visiting scholar at MIT and UC Berkeley, and a Senior Fellow at the Brookings Institution. He is a life member of the Council on Foreign Relations, and a director of the French-American Foundation. He is the author of three books on information technology and its impact on society. He holds a BA in Mathematics from UC Berkeley and a Ph.D. in Political Science from MIT.

PublicAffairs is a publishing house founded in 1997. It is a tribute to the standards, values, and flair of three persons who have served as mentors to countless reporters, writers, editors, and book people of all kinds, including me.

I. F. Stone, proprietor of *I. F. Stone's Weekly*, combined a commitment to the First Amendment with entrepreneurial zeal and reporting skill and became one of the great independent journalists in American history. At the age of eighty, Izzy published *The Trial of Socrates*, which was a national bestseller. He wrote the book after he taught himself ancient Greek.

Benjamin C. Bradlee was for nearly thirty years the charismatic editorial leader of *The Washington Post*. It was Ben who gave the *Post* the range and courage to pursue such historic issues as Watergate. He supported his reporters with a tenacity that made them fearless, and it is no accident that so many became authors of influential, best-selling books.

Robert L. Bernstein, the chief executive of Random House for more than a quarter century, guided one of the nation's premier publishing houses. Bob was personally responsible for many books of political dissent and argument that challenged tyranny around the globe. He is also the founder and was the longtime chair of Human Rights Watch, one of the most respected human rights organizations in the world.

.   .   .

For fifty years, the banner of Public Affairs Press was carried by its owner Morris B. Schnapper, who published Gandhi, Nasser, Toynbee, Truman, and about 1,500 other authors. In 1983 Schnapper was described by *The Washington Post* as "a redoubtable gadfly." His legacy will endure in the books to come.

Peter Osnos, *Founder and Editor-at-Large*